Real-Time Volume Graphics

Real-Time Volume Graphics

Klaus Engel
Markus Hadwiger
Joe M. Kniss
Christof Rezk-Salama
Daniel Weiskopf

CRC Press
Taylor & Francis Group
Boca Raton London New York

CRC Press is an imprint of the
Taylor & Francis Group, an **informa** business

AN A K PETERS BOOK

CRC Press
Taylor & Francis Group
6000 Broken Sound Parkway NW, Suite 300
Boca Raton, FL 33487-2742

First issued in paperback 2020

© 2008 by Taylor & Francis Group, LLC
CRC Press is an imprint of Taylor & Francis Group, an Informa business

No claim to original U.S. Government works

ISBN-13: 978-1-56881-266-3 (hbk)
ISBN-13: 978-0-367-65942-4 (pbk)

Library of Congress Cataloging-in-Publication Data

Real-time volume graphics / Klaus Engel ... [et al.].
    p. cm.
    Includes bibliographical references and index.
    ISBN 13: 978-1-56881-266-3 (alk. paper)
    ISBN 10: 1-56881-266-3 (alk. paper)
    1. Computer graphics. 2. Three-dimensional display systems. I. Engel, Klaus, 1969-

T385.R43414 2006
006.6'93–dc22

                                                                2006041662

**Visit the Taylor & Francis Web site at
http://www.taylorandfrancis.com**

**and the CRC Press Web site at
http://www.crcpress.com**

Für Monika
—Klaus Engel

For Pilar
—Markus Hadwiger

To K. P.
—Joe M. Kniss

For Malak and Helene
—Christof Rezk-Salama

Für Bettina
—Daniel Weiskopf

Contents

Preface

I N TRADITIONAL COMPUTER GRAPHICS, 3D objects are created using high-level surface representations such as polygonal meshes, NURBS (nonuniform rational B-spline) patches, or subdivision surfaces. Using this modeling paradigm, visual properties of surfaces, such as color, roughness, and reflectance, are described by means of a shading algorithm, which might be as simple as the Lambertian diffuse reflection model or as complex as a fully-featured shift-variant anisotropic BRDF.[1] Because light transport is evaluated only at points on the surface, these methods usually lack the ability to account for light interaction that takes place in the atmosphere or in the interior of an object.

Compared with surface rendering, volume rendering describes a wide range of techniques for generating images from 3D scalar data. These techniques are originally motivated by scientific visualization, where volume data is acquired by measurement or generated by numerical simulation. Typical examples are medical data of the interior of the human body obtained by computerized tomography (CT) or magnetic resonance imaging (MRI). Other examples are data from computational fluid dynamics (CFD), geological and seismic data, and abstract mathematical data such as the 3D probability distribution of a random number, implicit surfaces, or any other 3D scalar function.

It did not take long for volume-rendering techniques to find their way into visual arts. Artists were impressed by the expressiveness and beauty of the resulting images. With the evolution of efficient rendering techniques, volume data is also becoming more and more important for applications in computer games. Volumetric models are ideal for describing fuzzy objects, such as fluids, gases, and natural phenomena like clouds, fog, and fire.

---

[1]BRDF = bidirectional reflection distribution function: a function used to describe complex optical material properties.

Many artists and researchers have generated volume data synthetically to supplement their traditional surface models. They have found that volume-rendering techniques are useful for producing a large variety of impressive visual effects.

Although, at first glance, volumetric data sets seem to be more difficult to visualize than surfaces, it is both worthwhile and rewarding to render them as truly 3D entities without falling back to 2D subsets. Efficient rendering techniques that generate high-quality images of volumetric objects including local and global illumination effects in real time, or at least at interactive frame rates, are the topic of this book.

Intended Audience

This book is intended for two groups of readers. The first group comprises members of the scientific community, such as computer scientists, engineers, physicists, and medical imaging professionals. The other group comprises game developers, visual artists and animators, technical directors, and all people that are concerned with the development of multimedia and visual-entertainment applications. For scientists, the clarity and the accuracy of the visual representation of their data is essential. The entertainment community will focus more on artistic merits and creative aspects such as aesthetics, expressiveness, and everything that helps them communicate with the audience and tell their story. Both groups will find that interactivity is essential.

Although most of the topics covered in this book deal with the programming of computer-graphics applications, the book is not solely intended for software developers or computer scientists. Content creators and visual artists, whose primary concern is usually not software development, will find out that volume graphics is not as difficult to realize as they might think. They will learn expressive and powerful techniques for creating visual effects that are hard to realize with traditional surface modeling. From our experience with various application areas, we know that there are also many people from scientific disciplines who need customized methods for visualizing their scientific data. They often find themselves writing programs to visually display their abstract data without really having a pool of working methods that they can build upon. For those people, this book will provide effective solutions, important concepts, and ideas for tailoring their applications to their specific needs.

How to Read This Book

From the didactic point of view, the best way to read this book is from cover to cover. Having said that, we encourage you to browse through the book and start reading wherever a passage or a figure catches your attention. As we know, many readers prefer to skip parts of the text and jump back and forth through the different chapters. In this section, we want to give you some hints about what you will find in which parts of the book and which chapters are built upon other chapters.

The first two chapters cover the basic prerequisites for the rest of the book. Chapter 1 explains the physical basics of light transport and lays the theoretical groundwork for later chapters. If you already feel familiar with optics and light transfer, or if you are more interested in practical implementation than theory, you can skip this chapter for now and return to it later. Chapter 2 gives an overview of programmable graphics hardware and its most important features. We assume that you are already familiar with graphics programming to a certain extent, and this chapter is only meant as a refresher.

The next few chapters are essential for all readers, regardless of whether you're interested in scientific visualization, visual arts, or games. Chapter 3 starts with a practical introduction to different approaches to texture-based volume rendering. After having worked through this chapter, you should be able to implement your first completely functional volume-rendering system. Some of the techniques described in this chapter do not even require programmable graphics hardware, but the algorithms are essential for the rest of the book. Chapter 4 introduces transfer functions, which are used to specify the optical properties based on your underlying volumetric data. You will learn different mechanisms to perform color mapping and understand their influence on image quality.

With the next two chapters, we increase the level of realism by integrating different aspects of light-matter interaction. Chapter 5 shows how to adapt popular local illumination techniques to volumetric data. This is important for applications both in science and entertainment. Chapter 6 introduces global illumination techniques such as shadows, scattering, and translucency. These advanced illumination effects are clearly motivated by visual arts, but scientific applications will also benefit from shadows and improved realism.

Although graphics hardware has been designed for object-order approaches, modern techniques also allow image-order approaches such as ray casting to be implemented. Chapter 7 explains GPU-based implementations of ray casting, including optimization techniques such as space leaping and early ray termination.

The next two chapters cover optimization strategies, which are important for all application areas. Chapter 8 analyzes rendering speed and covers effective techniques to get the maximum performance out of your graphics board. Chapter 9 provides methods to improve the visual quality of your images. Different types of visual artifacts and their real causes are analyzed, and efficient countermeasures are introduced. Chapter 10 revisits transfer functions and extends them to multiple dimensions and multivariate data. User interfaces for intuitive classification and guidance are demonstrated. These three chapters together are essential for implementing a state-of-the-art volume-rendering system.

Chapter 11 is a guide to volume-rendering techniques for game programmers. It discusses the value of volume-graphics techniques for games and compares them to traditional techniques. It explains how to seamlessly integrate volume graphics into a game engine. The next two chapters focus on visual arts. Chapter 12 covers practical techniques for generating volumetric models from scratch using polygonal surfaces and procedural techniques. Chapter 13 discusses techniques for volumetric deformation and animation. These techniques can be used to sculpt volumetric models or to deform measured data. Apart from visual arts, fast deformation techniques are important for scientific applications such as computer-assisted surgery.

Chapter 14 deals with illustrative volume-rendering techniques and non-photorealistic rendering. The goal of such approaches is to create contours and cutaways to convey the important information by *amplification through simplification*. The chapter covers approaches such as importance-driven visualization, focus-and-context techniques, and non-photorealistic shading, which are mainly important for scientific visualization. Chapter 15 explains a variety of interactive clipping techniques, which facilitate the exploration of volume data in scientific data analysis. Segmented volume data is often used in medical scenarios, where certain inner organs or anatomical structures are marked explicitly by different tags. Chapter 16 covers techniques for integrating segmentation data into our volume-rendering framework. Finally, with respect to the ongoing trend toward huge data sets, Chapter 17 introduces effective strategies to overcome memory and bandwidth limitations for rendering of large volume data.

Graphics Programming

Only a couple of years ago, real-time volume graphics was restricted to expensive graphics workstations and large rendering clusters. The past couple of years, however, have seen a breathtaking evolution of consumer graphics hardware from traditional *fixed-function* architectures (up to 1998) to *configurable* pipelines to *fully programmable* floating-point graphics processors with hundreds of millions of transistors. The first step toward a fully programmable GPU was the introduction of configurable rasterization and vertex processing in late 1999. Prominent examples are NVIDIA's *register combiners* and ATI's *fragment shader* OpenGL extensions. Unfortunately, at the time, it was not easy to access these vendor-specific features in a uniform way.

The major innovation provided by today's graphics processors is the introduction of true programmability. This means that user-specified microprograms can be uploaded to graphics memory and executed directly by the vertex processor (*vertex programs*) and the fragment processor (*fragment programs*).[2] Vertex and fragment programs consist of assembler-like instructions from the limited instruction set understood by the graphics processor (MOV, MAD, LERP, and so on). To spare the user the tedious task of writing assembler code, high-level shading languages for GPU programming have been introduced. They provide an additional layer of abstraction and allow access to the capabilities of different graphics chips in an almost uniform way. Popular examples of high-level shading languages are GLSL, the shading language introduced with the OpenGL 2.0 specification, and Cg, introduced by NVIDIA, which is derived from the *Stanford Shading Language*. HLSL, the high-level shading language introduced in Microsoft's DirectX 9.0 SDK, uses a syntax very similar to Cg.

We believe that code samples are essential for conveying algorithms. Throughout this book, we provide code samples that concretely illustrate our rendering algorithms. We have made an effort to keep the samples simple and easy to understand, and we have taken our choice of programming languages seriously. Unless stated otherwise, the samples in this book are written in C/C++ with OpenGL as the graphics API and Cg as the shading language.

C++ is the most popular programming-language choice of graphics programmers. There are many introductory textbooks on C++ programming, including [257]. The reason for choosing OpenGL as the graphics API is that it is consistently supported on the largest number of different platforms and operating systems. At this point, we assume that you already have a basic knowledge of graphics programming and OpenGL. If you are not familiar with OpenGL, we suggest studying the OpenGL Red Book [240] first. However, we do not expect that readers who are more familiar with the DirectX API will have major problems when adapting the code samples. The reason for choosing Cg as the high-level shading language rather than OpenGL's built-in shading language GLSL is that Cg can be used directly with both OpenGL and DirectX, and the current version of the Cg compiler is also able to generate GLSL code. The syntax of Cg should be intelligible to anyone familiar with C/C++, and even a less experienced programmer should not have major problems understanding the code and adapting the samples to any high-level shading language. Introductory material and sample code using Cg can be found on the NVIDIA developer site [34].

---

[2]The terms *vertex shader* and *vertex program* and also *fragment shader* and *fragment program* have the same meaning, respectively. We usually prefer the term *program* because a major part of the code is not related to shading at all.

Acknowledgments

This book has evolved as a result of several courses and tutorials held at ACM SIGGRAPH, IEEE Visualization, and Eurographics conferences in the past couple of years. We are indebted to many people who helped make it possible in one way or another.

Gordon Kindlmann and Aaron Lefohn have contributed significant parts to the text and to the original SIGGRAPH course notes. Gordon's work on curvature-based classification and Aaron's ideas on efficient data structures are essential parts of the book.

This book reflects the collective work of many researchers over several years and would not exist without the wealth of experience provided to us. Many of these researches have also supported the writing of this book by generously providing their material, especially images and data sets. We would like to thank (in alphabetical order): Dörte Apelt, Anna Vilanova í Bartroli, Christoph Berger, Stefan Bruckner, Katja Bühler, Min Chen, Roger Crawfis, Paul Debevec, Helmut Doleisch, Knut E. W. Eberhardt, David S. Ebert, Laura Fritz, Markus Gross, Stefan Guthe, Peter Hastreiter, Jiří Hladůvka, Shoukat Islam, Mark Kilgard, Andrea Kratz, Martin Kraus, Caroline Langer, Bob Laramee, Torsten Möller, Lukas Mroz, André Neubauer, Bernhard Preim, Werner Purgathofer, Stefan Röttger, Henning Scharsach, Christian Sigg, Wolfgang Straßer, Nikolai A. Svakhine, Thomas Theußl, Bernd F. Tomandl, Ivan Viola, Manfred Weiler, Rüdiger Westermann, and Xiaoru Yuan.

Volume data sets were generously provided by the Digital Morphology Project at the University of Texas at Austin, the Department of Neuroradiology at the University of Erlangen-Nuremberg, the University of Minnesota at Twin Cities, the University of North Carolina at Chapel Hill, Siemens Medical Solutions, Stanford University, the Universities of Tübingen and Stuttgart (Deutsche Forschungsgesellschaft, SFB 382), Tiani Medgraph, the United States National Library of Medicine, and the ETH Zürich.

Our deep respect is due to Tom Ertl, Günther Greiner, Meister Eduard Gröller, Charles Hanson, Helwig Hauser, Chris Johnson, and Rüdiger Westermann. They provided encouragement and valuable feedback throughout the years. It has been a pleasure working with you.

It is impossible to develop efficient graphics algorithms without the cooperative work of the hardware manufacturers. We wish to thank ATI and NVIDIA for their continuous support in knowledge and hardware, especially Mike Doggett and Mark Segal from ATI and Mark Kilgard, David Kirk, and Nick Triantos from NVIDIA.

Klaus Engel would like to thank everybody at Siemens Corporate Research for their input and support, particularly James Williams, Gianluca Paladini, Thomas Möller, Daphne Yu, John Collins, and Wei Li.

We are grateful to our students and all the attendees of our courses, who provided valuable feedback and suggestions to improve both the course and the book.

Kevin Jackson-Mead, Alice Peters, and all the staff at A K Peters have done a great job in making this book. We wish to thank you for your care and your patient attention.

Finally, and most of all, we wish to express our love and gratitude to our families for their support and for giving us the quiet time we needed to finish the book.

Additional Resources

Further information, sample programs, data sets, and links to other online resources can be found at http://www.real-time-volume-graphics.org.

1

Theoretical Background and Basic Approaches

THIS BOOK COVERS two seemingly very different applications of volume graphics: on the one hand, "special effects" and realistic rendering of clouds, smoke, fire, and similar effects for computer games, movie production, and so forth; on the other hand, the scientific visualization of volumetric data. How do these different fields fit together, and why are they covered in the same text?

The simple answer is that both fields rely on the same underlying physical models and therefore use identical, or at least very similar, rendering techniques. This chapter focuses on the physical model for volume rendering, discussing its fundamental mathematical description and its approximations typically used for real-time volume rendering. The basic idea is to model light transport in gaseous materials such as clouds or fog. Therefore, volume graphics targets the same goal as computer graphics in general: the simulation of light propagation in order to produce images as recorded by a virtual camera.

The specific challenge for volume graphics is the interaction between light and the participating media. Light may be absorbed, scattered, or emitted by the gaseous materials that virtually "participate" in light propagation. This interaction needs to be evaluated at all positions in the 3D volume filled by the gas, making volume rendering a computationally intensive task. Therefore, the techniques discussed throughout this book address the issue of efficient volume rendering. The remainder of this chapter focuses on the theoretical foundation for these rendering methods, and it provides a general overview of the volume-rendering process.

We have decided to lay out a theoretical background for volume rendering in the beginning of this book. Our motivation is to provide a sound foundation for the various algorithms that are presented in later chapters. However, for readers who would like to start with practical issues of volume rendering, we have included a brief summary of the most important equations of this chapter in the box in Figure 1.1. This book need not be read in sequential order; therefore, you are welcome to start with other chapters (such as the basic introduction to practical volume rendering in Chapter 3) if you prefer a hands-on approach. Nevertheless, we would like to encour-

---

Mathematics of Volume Rendering in a Nutshell

Radiance

Fundamental measure of radiative energy, defined as radiative energy Q per projected unit area $A_\perp$, per solid angle Ω, and per unit of time t:

$$I = \frac{dQ}{dA_\perp \, d\Omega \, dt}. \qquad (1.1)$$

Volume-Rendering Integral

The emission-absorption optical model leads to the volume-rendering integral:

$$I(D) = I_0 \, e^{-\int_{s_0}^{D} \kappa(t)\,dt} + \int_{s_0}^{D} q(s)\, e^{-\int_{s}^{D} \kappa(t)\,dt}\,ds\,, \qquad (1.7)$$

with optical properties κ (absorption coefficient) and q (source term describing emission) and integration from entry point into the volume, $s = s_0$, to the exit point toward the camera, $s = D$.

Compositing

Iterative computation of the discretized volume-rendering integral. Front-to-back compositing (from the camera into the volume):

$$
\begin{aligned}
C_{\text{dst}} &\leftarrow C_{\text{dst}} + (1 - \alpha_{\text{dst}})C_{\text{src}} \\
\alpha_{\text{dst}} &\leftarrow \alpha_{\text{dst}} + (1 - \alpha_{\text{dst}})\alpha_{\text{src}}\,.
\end{aligned} \qquad (1.14)
$$

Back-to-front compositing (toward the camera):

$$C_{\text{dst}} \leftarrow (1 - \alpha_{\text{src}})C_{\text{dst}} + C_{\text{src}}\,. \qquad (1.15)$$

Figure 1.1. Summary of mathematical equations for volume rendering.

age you to return to this theoretical chapter at a later time, especially once you plan to dive deeper into advanced topics of volume rendering.

1.1   Problem Setting

Volume graphics needs the participating medium to be modeled along with the actual light-transport mechanism. Although the realistic rendering of gaseous phenomena and the scientific visualization of volumetric data share the same mechanism of light propagation, they differ in the way that the participating medium is modeled.

Photorealistic volume rendering imitates the look of realistic gases and therefore requires a physically accurate description of the participating medium. Ideally, a physics-based simulation of the medium is employed to obtain such a description, e.g., by a reliable simulation of cloud behavior and fluid flow. This simulation heavily depends on the type of medium, and its detailed discussion would reach well beyond the scope of this book. However, rather simple procedural models of participating media may achieve convincing results without a physics simulation. The procedural approach is discussed in Chapter 12, followed by volume-animation techniques in Chapter 13.

Direct volume visualization has the goal of visually extracting information from a 3D scalar field, which can be written as a mapping

$$\phi: \ \mathbb{R}^3 \to \mathbb{R} \, ,$$

i.e., a function from 3D space to a single-component value (the scalar value). The 3D scalar field typically originates from simulations or measurements, defined on a discretized grid. Figure 1.2 illustrates a volume data set represented on a discrete grid. This discretization leads to the issue of reconstructing the function ϕ on all points in the 3D domain (see Section 1.5

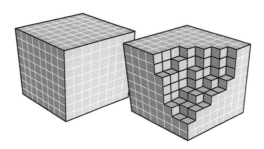

Figure 1.2. Volume data set given on a discrete uniform grid.

for details). For the time being, we assume that such a reconstruction is available and provides a function defined on the complete domain. Direct volume visualization maps the 3D scalar field to physical quantities that describe light interaction at the respective point in 3D space. This mapping mechanism is called classification and is usually based on the concept of a transfer function (see Chapter 4).

1.2 Physical Model of Light Transport

Both photorealistic volume rendering and direct volume visualization provide a volumetric description of the physical properties of a participating medium. These physical properties are then used to compute light transport for actual image synthesis. This section discusses both the fundamental equation of light transfer (Section 1.2.1) and different optical models based on this light transfer (Section 1.2.2). One version of the optical models leads to the so-called volume-rendering integral—the most frequently employed basis for volume rendering, which is discussed later in Section 1.3.

1.2.1 Equation of Light Transfer

The physical basis for volume rendering relies on geometric optics, in which light is assumed to propagate along straight lines unless interaction between light and participating medium takes place. Therefore, the interaction between light and matter is most interesting. The following types of interaction are typically taken into account.

Emission. The gaseous material actively emits light, increasing the radiative energy. In reality, for example, hot gas emits light by converting heat into radiative energy.[1]

Absorption. Material can absorb light by converting radiative energy into heat. In this way, light energy is reduced.

Scattering. Light can be scattered by participating media, essentially changing the direction of light propagation. If the wavelength (or the energy of photons) is not changed by scattering, the process is called *elastic scattering*. Conversely, *inelastic scattering* affects the wavelength. Unless otherwise noted, we only consider elastic scattering.

---

[1]We only consider spontaneous emission and neglect stimulated emission that plays an important role for lasers.

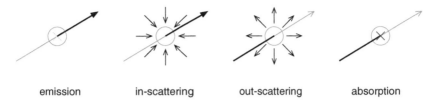

emission   in-scattering   out-scattering   absorption

Figure 1.3. Interactions between light and participating media that affect the radiance along a ray.

Absorption, emission, and scattering affect the amount of radiative energy along a light ray. The light energy can be described by its *radiance I*, which is defined as the radiative energy Q per unit area A, per solid angle Ω, and per unit of time t:

$$I = \frac{\mathrm{d}Q}{\mathrm{d}A_\perp \, \mathrm{d}\Omega \, \mathrm{d}t}. \tag{1.1}$$

The subscript $\perp$ indicates that the area is measured as projected along the direction of light: $A_\perp = A \cos\theta$, if θ is the angle between light direction and the normal vector on the surface A. Note that radiance is sometimes called specific intensity. However, we will use the term radiance throughout this book. In general, radiance is the fundamental quantity for computer graphics because it does not change along a light ray in vacuum. The two-volume book by Glassner [80] gives a comprehensive introduction to physical quantities for light measurements, including background information on the definition of radiance.

The presence of a participating medium affects the radiance along a light ray. Absorption reduces light energy, whereas emission adds light energy; see Figure 1.3. Scattering can both reduce and increase radiative energy along a light ray: through *in-scattering*, additional energy is redirected into the direction of the ray. Conversely, *out-scattering* removes energy from the current ray by scattering it into a different direction.

By combining the absorption, emission, and scattering effects, the following equation for the transfer for light is obtained:

$$\omega \cdot \nabla_\mathbf{x} I(\mathbf{x}, \omega) = -\chi I(\mathbf{x}, \omega) + \eta. \tag{1.2}$$

The term $\omega \cdot \nabla_\mathbf{x} I$ is the dot product between the light direction ω and the gradient of radiance I with respect to position $\mathbf{x}$ (the "nabla" operator $\nabla = (\partial/\partial x, \partial/\partial y, \partial/\partial z)$ is a short notation for the gradient operator). This dot product describes the directional derivative taken along the light direction. If a light ray is parameterized by arc length s, then $\omega \cdot \nabla_\mathbf{x} I$ can be written as the derivative $\mathrm{d}I/\mathrm{d}s$. The term χ is the total absorption coefficient and defines the rate that light is attenuated by the medium. The quantity η is the total emission and describes the extent to which radiative energy is increased through the participating medium. Here, we adopt the notation used by Hege et al. [103].

The total absorption coefficient consists of two parts: the true absorption coefficient κ (e.g., for the conversion of light energy into heat) and the scattering coefficient σ, which represents the energy loss from out-scattering. Therefore, the total absorption coefficient can be written as

$$\chi = \kappa + \sigma\,.$$

Analogously, the total emission coefficient can be split into a source term q, which represents emission (e.g., from thermal excitation), and a scattering term j:

$$\eta = q + j\,.$$

Please note that all quantities χ, η, κ, σ, q, and j may depend on position $\mathbf{x}$ and direction ω along a light ray. These parameters are typically left out for simplicity of writing the equations.

The terms κ, σ, and q are optical material properties that are directly assigned through a transfer function (see Chapter 4) or originate from a physical model of a gas (see Section 1.1). The scattering part j, however, needs to be indirectly computed from material properties. In fact, all possible contributions from all incoming light directions have to be considered, leading to

$$j(\mathbf{x}, \omega) = \frac{1}{4\pi} \int_{\text{sphere}} \sigma(\mathbf{x}, \omega')p(\mathbf{x}, \omega', \omega)I(\mathbf{x}, \omega')\,\mathrm{d}\Omega'\,. \tag{1.3}$$

Here, contributions from incident light $I(\mathbf{x}, \omega')$ are accumulated by integrating over all directions ω'. The contributions are weighted by the scattering coefficient σ and the *phase function* p, which describes the chance that light is scattered from the original direction ω' into the new direction ω. The phase function is responsible for representing the angle-dependency of scattering. Therefore, the phase function is an important optical property of a participating medium. Different materials may have different phase functions that can lead to very different "looks" of the volume—just like varying reflection properties of a surface-based object result in different looks of a surface-oriented scene. Chapter 6 discusses typical choices for phase functions in more detail.

We assume that the phase function is normalized according to

$$\frac{1}{4\pi} \int_{\text{sphere}} p(\mathbf{x}, \omega', \omega)\,\mathrm{d}\Omega' = 1\,.$$

The factor $1/4\pi$ is just used to cancel the factor 4π that is picked up by integrating a unit function over a whole sphere.

By combining emission, absorption, in-scattering, and out-scattering, the complete equation for the transfer for light is obtained:

$$\omega \cdot \nabla_{\mathbf{x}} I(\mathbf{x}, \omega) = -(\kappa(\mathbf{x}, \omega) + \sigma(\mathbf{x}, \omega)) I(\mathbf{x}, \omega) + q(\mathbf{x}, \omega)$$
$$+ \int_{\text{sphere}} \sigma(\mathbf{x}, \omega') p(\mathbf{x}, \omega', \omega) I(\mathbf{x}, \omega') \, d\Omega' . \quad (1.4)$$

This equation is a longer version of the original Equation 1.2. Large portions of this book deal with efficient methods to determine the radiance I from the above equation for the transfer for light. In particular, Chapter 6 on global illumination describes details of rendering methods and numerical approaches. Very often, only a subset of the full equation of transfer is solved in order to achieve less cost-intensive computations. The theoretical basis for choosing approximations or restricted models is discussed in the following sections.

So far, only grayscale images can be described by the radiance I. To facilitate color images, a wavelength-dependent behavior has to be taken into account, typically by computing the wavelength-dependent radiance $I_\lambda = dI/d\lambda$. Visible light roughly covers a range of wavelengths λ between 400 nanometers (nm), which is perceived as blue, to 800 nm, which is perceived as red. In most cases, no change of wavelength (i.e., no inelastic scattering) is considered, and then Equation 1.4 can be solved for each wavelength independently. The optical properties have to be specified in a wavelength-dependent way as well. With the assumption of elastic scattering, color images are commonly computed for a few wavelength bands only (for example, red, green, and blue).

1.2.2 Optical Models

Because the solution of the complete equation of transport for light is computationally intensive, simplified models are often used. The basic strategy is to remove or simplify one or more terms in Equation 1.4 in order to obtain an equation that is more tractable. The following models are commonly used.

Absorption Only. The volume is assumed to consist of cold, perfectly black material that may absorb incident light. No light is emitted or scattered.

Emission Only. The volume is assumed to consist of gas that only emits light but is completely transparent. Absorption and scattering are neglected.

Emission-Absorption Model. This optical model is most common in volume rendering. The gas can emit light and absorb incident light. However, scattering and indirect illumination are neglected.

Single Scattering and Shadowing. This model includes single scattering of light that comes from an external light source (i.e., not from within the volume). Shadows are modeled by taking into account the attenuation of light that is incident from an external light source.

Multiple Scattering. Here, the goal is to evaluate the complete illumination model for volumes, including emission, absorption, and scattering.

The emission-absorption model is the most widely used model for volume rendering because it provides a good compromise between generality and efficiency of computation. This model, of course, subsumes absorption only and emission only models as special cases. The emission-absorption model leads to the following equation,

$$\omega \cdot \nabla_{\mathbf{x}} I(\mathbf{x}, \omega) = -\kappa(\mathbf{x}, \omega) I(\mathbf{x}, \omega) + q(\mathbf{x}, \omega) \,, \qquad (1.5)$$

which is referred to as the *volume-rendering equation*. More precisely, this equation is the volume-rendering equation in its differential form because it describes light transport by differential changes in radiance. If only a single light ray is considered, Equation 1.5 can be rewritten as

$$\frac{\mathrm{d}I(s)}{\mathrm{d}s} = -\kappa(s) I(s) + q(s) \,, \qquad (1.6)$$

where positions are described by the length parameter s.

1.3 Volume-Rendering Integral

The volume-rendering equation in its differential form (Equation 1.6) can be solved for radiance by integrating along the direction of light flow from the starting point $s = s_0$ to the endpoint $s = D$, leading to the *volume-rendering integral*

$$I(D) = I_0 \, e^{-\int_{s_0}^{D} \kappa(t) \, \mathrm{d}t} + \int_{s_0}^{D} q(s) \, e^{-\int_{s}^{D} \kappa(t) \, \mathrm{d}t} \, \mathrm{d}s \,. \qquad (1.7)$$

The term I_0 represents the light entering the volume from the background at the position $s = s_0$; $I(D)$ is the radiance leaving the volume at $s = D$ and finally reaching the camera. The first term in Equation 1.7 describes the light from the background attenuated by the volume. The second term represents the integral contribution of the source terms attenuated by the participating medium along the remaining distances to the camera.

The term

$$\tau(s_1, s_2) = \int_{s_1}^{s_2} \kappa(t)\, \mathrm{d}t \tag{1.8}$$

is defined as the *optical depth* between positions s_1 and s_2. The optical depth has a physical interpretation in the form of a measure for how long light may travel before it is absorbed; i.e., optical depth indicates the typical length of light propagation before scattering occurs. Small values for the optical depth mean that the medium is rather transparent, and high values for the optical depth are associated with a more opaque material. The corresponding transparency (for a material between s_1 and s_2) is

$$T(s_1, s_2) = e^{-\tau(s_1, s_2)} = e^{-\int_{s_1}^{s_2} \kappa(t)\, \mathrm{d}t}. \tag{1.9}$$

With this definition of transparency, we obtain a slightly different version of the volume-rendering integral

$$I(D) = I_0\, T(s_0, D) + \int_{s_0}^{D} q(s) T(s, D)\, \mathrm{d}s.$$

The volume-rendering integral is the most common description of volume rendering. Large portions of this book are devoted to efficient algorithms for computing this integral.

1.3.1 Local Illumination for Volume Rendering

The volume-rendering integral in its classic form, Equation 1.7, accurately represents the emission-absorption model but no scattering effects. Single scattering of external light can be included to introduce greater realism into this optical model. In a simple volume-shading model, the external illumination is assumed to unimpededly reach a point in the volume from an outside light source, neglecting any absorption or scattering along its way.

Single scattering is often approximated by a local illumination model that imitates local surface rendering, such as the Phong or the Blinn-Phong illumination models. In volume shading, the gradient of the scalar field serves as the normal vector for these local illumination models because the gradient is identical to the normal vector on an isosurface through the respective point in space. In this way, volume shading produces an effect similar to an illuminated isosurface. Local illumination is included in the volume-rendering integral (see Equations 1.5 and 1.7) by extending the source term to

$$q_{\text{extended}}(\mathbf{x}, \omega) = q_{\text{emission}}(\mathbf{x}, \omega) + q_{\text{illum}}(\mathbf{x}, \omega).$$

The emissivity $q_{\text{emission}}(\mathbf{x}, \omega)$ is identical to the source term in the pure emission-absorption model. The additional scattering term $q_{\text{illum}}(\mathbf{x}, \omega)$ describes the additional light coming from local reflection (i.e., single scattering). We refer to Chapter 5 for a detailed discussion of local illumination in volume rendering. The advantage of local illumination is that it does not increase the complexity of the computations for the volume-rendering integral but improves the perception of volume models.

1.3.2   Density Model

Sometimes, optical properties are derived from a density model of the participating medium. In this description, ρ represents the density of the material, and all optical properties are weighted by this density. For example, the total absorption coefficient χ is replaced by χ' according to

$$\chi = \chi'\rho.$$

There are similar substitutions for the true absorption coefficient, $\kappa = \kappa'\rho$, the scattering coefficient, $\sigma = \sigma'\rho$, and the true emission term, $q = q'\rho$.

This density model builds upon a description of a density of particles that are responsible for emission, absorption, and scattering. Originally, such a particle model was proposed by Sabella [230] for his density-emitter model of volume rendering. Williams and Max [300] provide a detailed discussion of a volume-density model.

1.4   Discretization

The main goal of volume rendering is to compute the volume-rendering integral, Equation 1.7. Typically, the integral cannot be evaluated analytically. Instead, numerical methods are applied to find an approximation as close to the solution as possible.

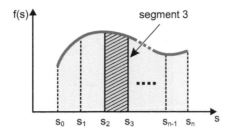

Figure 1.4. Partitioning of the integration domain into several intervals. The intervals are described by locations $s_0 < s_1 < \cdots < s_{n-1} < s_n$. The ith interval or segment is $[s_{i-1}, s_i]$. The hatched box indicates the integration result for the third segment.

1.4.1 Splitting into Several Integration Intervals

A common approach splits the integration domain into n subsequent intervals. The intervals are described by locations $s_0 < s_1 < \cdots < s_{n-1} < s_n$, where s_0 is the starting point of the integration domain and $s_n = D$ is the endpoint. Please note that the intervals do not necessarily have equal lengths. Figure 1.4 illustrates the partitioning of the integration domain into several intervals or segments.

Considering the light transport within the ith interval $[s_{i-1}, s_i]$ (with $0 < i \leq n$), we can obtain the radiance at location s_i according to

$$I(s_i) = I(s_{i-1})T(s_{i-1}, s_i) + \int_{s_{i-1}}^{s_i} q(s)T(s, s_i)\, ds\,.$$

We introduce a new notation for the transparency and color contribution (i.e., radiance contribution) of the ith interval:

$$T_i = T(s_{i-1}, s_i)\,, \quad c_i = \int_{s_{i-1}}^{s_i} q(s)T(s, s_i)\, ds\,. \tag{1.10}$$

The hatched box in Figure 1.4 illustrates the result of integration over one interval. The radiance at the exit point of the volume is then given by

$$I(D) = I(s_n) = I(s_{n-1})T_n + c_n = (I(s_{n-2})T_{n-1} + c_{n-1})\,T_n + c_n = \ldots\,,$$

which can be written as

$$I(D) = \sum_{i=0}^{n} c_i \prod_{j=i+1}^{n} T_j\,, \quad \text{with } c_0 = I(s_0)\,. \tag{1.11}$$

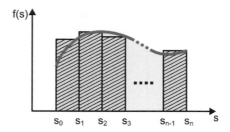

Figure 1.5. Approximation of an integral by a Riemann sum.

In general, the notation $\sum_{i=k}^{l} a_i$ means that all terms a_i (for $k \leq i \leq l$) are summed. Similarly, $\prod_{i=k}^{l} a_i$ is a notation for the multiplication of all terms a_i (for $k \leq i \leq l$). Often, transparency T_i is replaced by opacity $\alpha_i = 1 - T_i$.

At this point, we have halfway solved the problem of computing volume rendering: the integration domain is segmented into n discrete intervals, and the summations and multiplications in Equation 1.11 can be computed. The missing point is the evaluation of the transparency and color contributions of the intervals.

A most common approach approximates the volume-rendering integral by a Riemann sum over n equidistant segments of length $\Delta x = (D - s_0)/n$. Here, the function to be integrated is approximated by a piecewise-constant function, as illustrated in Figure 1.5. The integral over a single interval corresponds to the area of the rectangle defined by the function value at a sampling point and by the sampling width (see the hatched boxes in Figure 1.5).

In this approximation, the transparency of the ith segment is

$$T_i \approx e^{-\kappa(s_i)\Delta x} \tag{1.12}$$

and the color contribution for the ith segment is

$$c_i \approx q(s_i)\Delta x. \tag{1.13}$$

Many volume-rendering methods employ the above approximation with a piecewise-constant function over equidistant sampling points. A prominent example is the widely used approach with texture-based volume rendering, as explained in Chapter 3.

Despite the widespread use of a piecewise-constant approximation with equidistant sampling, other alternatives are sometimes employed to obtain a better solution for the segments' transparency and color contributions. One approach is to apply alternative quadrature rules (i.e., integration rules) for evaluating the volume-rendering integral, for example, the trapezoidal rule, Simpson's rule, or other higher-order rules according to Newton-Cotes formulas [217]. Unfortunately, the volume-rendering integral typically contains discontinuities, for example, at the boundary between different materials. Therefore, higher-order integration methods often do not provide appropriate accuracy. Instead, adaptive sampling is a much more common approach for improved volume rendering because it modifies the sampling rate based on the properties of the integrand (see Section 9.1 for details). Another alternative is a Monte Carlo approach that introduces a jittering in sampling positions to avoid artifacts from uniform sampling (also see Section 9.1 for details).

Finally, pre-integration partially computes the volume-rendering integral in a preprocessing step, which can be done with high accuracy. The essential idea is to pre-compute all possible results for the volume-rendering integral along a single segment, as described by Equation 1.10. During runtime, only the discrete summations and multiplications according to Equation 1.11 are evaluated. Therefore, pre-integration leads to high rendering quality at high speed, making it one of the most popular approaches for volume rendering. Details of pre-integration are given in Sections 4.5 and 9.3.

1.4.2   Compositing Schemes

Compositing is the basis for the iterative computation of the discretized volume-rendering integral (Equation 1.11). The idea is to split the summations and multiplications that are contained in Equation 1.11 into several, yet simpler operations that are executed sequentially. Two different basic compositing schemes are common: front-to-back compositing and back-to-front compositing.

The front-to-back compositing scheme is applied when the viewing rays are traversed from the eye point into the volume. Here, we use slightly different variable names: C represents a color, typically given as a three-channel RGB (red, green, blue) color value. Both the newly contributed radiance c and the accumulated radiance I from the previous sections are now associated with such a color description.

Then, the front-to-back iteration equations are

$$\hat{C}_i = \hat{C}_{i+1} + \hat{T}_{i+1} C_i\,,$$
$$\hat{T}_i = \hat{T}_{i+1}(1 - \alpha_i)\,,$$

with the initialization

$$\hat{C}_n = C_n\,,$$
$$\hat{T}_n = 1 - \alpha_n\,.$$

The results of the current iteration step are $\hat{C}_i$ and $\hat{T}_i$; $\hat{C}_{i+1}$ and $\hat{T}_{i+1}$ are the accumulated results of the previous computations. The source term C_i and the opacity α_i are given by the transfer function or they originate from a physical model of a gas (see Section 1.1). The iteration starts at the first sampling position $i = n$ (closest to the camera) and ends at $i = 0$ (at the backside of the volume).

By renaming the variables according to $C_{\text{dst}} = \hat{C}_j$ (with $j = i, i+1$), $C_{\text{src}} = C_i$, $\alpha_{\text{dst}} = 1 - \hat{T}_j$ (with $j = i, i+1$), and $\alpha_{\text{src}} = \alpha_i$, front-to-back compositing can be written in its most common way:

$$
\begin{aligned}
C_{\text{dst}} &\leftarrow C_{\text{dst}} + (1 - \alpha_{\text{dst}})C_{\text{src}}, \\
\alpha_{\text{dst}} &\leftarrow \alpha_{\text{dst}} + (1 - \alpha_{\text{dst}})\alpha_{\text{src}}.
\end{aligned}
\tag{1.14}
$$

This set of assignment equations explicitly shows the iterative nature of compositing. Variables with subscript $_{\text{src}}$ (as for "source") describe quantities introduced as inputs from the optical properties of the data set (e.g., through a transfer function or from a physical model of a gas), whereas variables with subscript $_{\text{dst}}$ (as for "destination") describe output quantities that hold accumulated colors and opacities. Equation 1.14 is repeatedly applied while marching along a ray, updating color C_{dst} and opacity α_{dst} along its way.

By reversing the traversal direction, we obtain the back-to-front compositing scheme:

$$
\begin{aligned}
\hat{C}_i &= \hat{C}_{i-1}(1 - \alpha_i) + C_i, \\
\hat{T}_i &= \hat{T}_{i-1}(1 - \alpha_i),
\end{aligned}
$$

with the initialization

$$
\begin{aligned}
\hat{C}_0 &= C_0, \\
\hat{T}_0 &= 1 - \alpha_0.
\end{aligned}
$$

The iteration starts at $i = 0$ and ends at $i = n$. Note that the accumulated transparency $\hat{T}_i$ is not needed to compute the color contribution $\hat{C}_i$ and can thus be omitted.

Analogously to the front-to-back scheme, we can also rewrite the back-to-front compositing in an explicitly iterative fashion:

$$
C_{\text{dst}} \leftarrow (1 - \alpha_{\text{src}})C_{\text{dst}} + C_{\text{src}}.
\tag{1.15}
$$

Note that there is no iterative update of opacity needed because accumulated opacity (or transparency) is not required to determine the color contribution.

In addition to the above compositing schemes, alternative approaches are sometimes used. For example, maximum intensity projection (MIP) and x-ray or weighted sum projections are often applied in medical imaging applications. MIP is computed according to the compositing equation

$$C_{\mathrm{dst}} \leftarrow \max(C_{\mathrm{dst}}, C_{\mathrm{src}}). \tag{1.16}$$

The final result is the maximum color contribution along a ray. This compositing scheme is independent of the traversal order; i.e., it may be applied in a back-to-front, a front-to-back, or any other order. The main application for MIP is virtual angiography—the display of vessel structures in medical scans (see the survey article [218]). More details on MIP and its implementation are provided in Section 3.2.3, along with an example image in Figure 3.4. X-ray or weighted sum projections result in a weighted sum of color contributions along a ray. All of these alternative schemes have an order-independent compositing process in common [187].

In the remainder of this book, unless otherwise noted, we use a compositing scheme that implements the emission-absorption model—either according to back-to-front or front-to-back traversal.

We would like to point out that colors C should be interpreted as radiances values (per wavelength band) in order to obtain a consistent and physically correct description of light transport. From the radiance that arrives at the virtual camera, the corresponding detector response on the image plane can be derived. For fixed camera parameters and a linear response of the camera, the strength of the recorded color values is proportional to the incident radiance. Therefore, the final radiance C can be interpreted as a measure for RGB colors. Moreover, it is common practice to already specify intermediate colors C as RGB values—and we often adopt this sloppy way of dealing with radiance throughout this book.

1.4.3 Opacity Correction

Volume rendering is typically described in terms of the discrete sum (Equation 1.11) or the corresponding compositing schemes. This discrete approach often assumes an equidistant sampling, for example, in conjunction with the approximation through a Riemann sum. A problem arises when the sampling rate needs to be changed: the discretized opacity and color contributions need to be modified accordingly because their values depend on the sampling distance (see Equations 1.10, 1.12, and 1.13). There are several reasons for changing the sampling rate, such as adaptive sampling for accelerated volume rendering and improved image quality (see Section 9.1) or purely geometric reasons in slice-based volume rendering (see the discussion of 2D texture slicing in Section 3.2).

According to Equations 1.9 and 1.10, the transparency of a segment of length Δx (ranging from position s_i to $s_i + \Delta x$) is

$$T = e^{-\int_{s_i}^{s_i + \Delta x} \kappa \, dt} = e^{-\kappa \Delta x},$$

if we assume a constant absorption coefficient κ within the segment. Analogously, a segment of different length $\Delta \tilde{x}$ has transparency $\tilde{T} = \exp(-\kappa \Delta \tilde{x})$. Therefore, the two transparency values are related to each other according to

$$\tilde{T} = T^{\left(\frac{\Delta \tilde{x}}{\Delta x}\right)}.$$

In terms of opacity, the two intervals of different lengths are related by

$$\tilde{\alpha} = 1 - (1 - \alpha)^{\left(\frac{\Delta \tilde{x}}{\Delta x}\right)}. \tag{1.17}$$

This equation describes *opacity correction* and allows for varying sample rates even if the optical properties are only given with respect to a discrete version of the volume-rendering integral, i.e., even if the optical properties are described by opacities and not by a continuous absorption coefficient $\kappa(s)$.

Analogously, the color contribution, which is approximately $c = q\Delta x$ for the original length of a segment, is transformed according to the color correction equation

$$\tilde{c} = c \left(\frac{\Delta \tilde{x}}{\Delta x}\right). \tag{1.18}$$

1.4.4 Associated Colors

So far, we have assumed *associated colors*, as introduced by Blinn [14]. Associated colors consist of color components that are already weighted by their corresponding opacity. An alternative description uses color components that have not been premultiplied with opacity. The previous equations have to be modified to allow for nonassociated colors: original color terms have to be replaced by color terms that are explicitly weighted by opacity.

For example, C_{src} needs to be substituted by $\alpha_{\text{src}} C_{\text{src}}$ in the iterative compositing equations. With nonassociated colors, the front-to-back compositing Equation 1.14 is replaced by

$$C_{\text{dst}} \leftarrow C_{\text{dst}} + (1 - \alpha_{\text{dst}}) \alpha_{\text{src}} C_{\text{src}}$$
$$\alpha_{\text{dst}} \leftarrow \alpha_{\text{dst}} + (1 - \alpha_{\text{dst}}) \alpha_{\text{src}}.$$

Similarly, the back-to-front compositing scheme is changed from Equation 1.15 to

$$C_{\mathrm{dst}} \leftarrow (1 - \alpha_{\mathrm{src}})C_{\mathrm{dst}} + \alpha_{\mathrm{src}}C_{\mathrm{src}} \,.$$

From a conceptual point of view, both associated and nonassociated colors are equivalent—except for a different interpretation of the color components. The only noticeable difference appears when these colors are computed by interpolation from a discrete set of color points. Color bleeding artifacts that may occur during interpolation are avoided by using associated colors [303]. The effects of color bleeding are discussed and explained in more detail in Section 3.2.3.

1.5   Volume Data and Reconstruction Filters

Volume rendering assumes a continuous 3D scalar field, which can be written as a mapping

$$\phi : \ \mathbb{R}^3 \to \mathbb{R} \,,$$

which is a function from 3D space to a single-component value.

In practice, however, a volumetric field is given on a discretized grid because it is the result of a simulation or a measurement. Figure 1.6 illustrates a volume data set represented on a discrete grid. A discrete representation leads to the following basic questions. First, how is the original data discretized? Second, how is the continuous function generated from a discrete set of samples? The first question leads to the issues of data storage (discussed in the following section) and of data acquisition (discussed in Section 1.5.2). The second question targets the issue of reconstructing a continuous function, which is addressed in Section 1.5.3.

1.5.1   Classification of Grids

A two-dimensional raster image serves as the role model for the discrete representation of a volume. An image consists of *pixels* (short for "picture elements") that are organized in a regular array. Pixels are the data elements of a 2D image, holding color values.

A discrete volume data set can be represented in a similar fashion by just "lifting" the description from two dimensions to three dimensions. Then, a 2D pixel is extended to a 3D *voxel* (short for "volume element"). Voxels are organized in a regular 3D array, covering the volume data set. Unfortunately, the term *voxel* has two slightly different interpretations in the literature. One interpretation is that a voxel is a small cube that fills

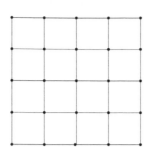 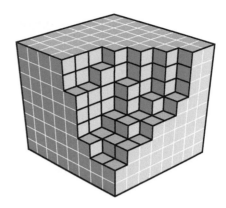

Figure 1.6. Examples of uniform grids: 2D uniform grid with quadratic cells (left) and 3D uniform grid with cuboid cells (right).

a small volumetric region with its associated data value. The other interpretation assumes that voxels are points in 3D space, along with an interpolation scheme that fills the in-between space. In this book, we adopt the second interpretation because it allows for a more flexible reconstruction of in-between data values (see Section 1.5.3).

Our definition of a voxel is compatible with a grid-based description of the volume data set: voxels serve as grid points of a *uniform* grid. The grid points are connected by edges, forming hexahedral (i.e., cube-like) cells. In fact, a 3D uniform grid can be defined as a collection of grid points that are connected to form rectangular, hexahedral cells of equal size. Figure 1.6 illustrates uniform grids in two and three dimensions.

A uniform n-dimensional grid has the advantage of being well-structured, which leads to a compact representation in computer memory (e.g., in the form of an n-dimensional array) and a fast access to selected data cells. Uniform grids, however, are not very flexible. Therefore, other grid structures may be used to represent discretized data. Higher flexibility can be achieved by permitting more flexible cell types or a more flexible combination of cells to a grid. For example, distorted hexahedra (i.e., with nonperpendicular cell axes) or completely different cell types (e.g., prisms) may be used. Moreover, different kinds of cells may be combined in a single grid.

A prominent example of a more flexible structure is a grid consisting of *simplices* (or *simplical cells*), as shown in Figure 1.7. A simplex (more specifically, an n-simplex) is defined as the convex hull of $(n + 1)$ affinely independent points in Euclidean space of a dimension equal to, or greater than, n. For example, a 0-simplex is a point, a 1-simplex is a line segment, a 2-simplex is a triangle, a 3-simplex is a tetrahedron, and so forth. Sim-

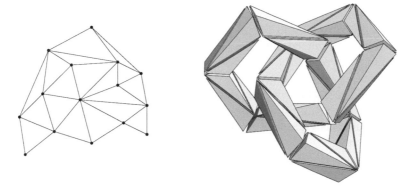

Figure 1.7. Examples of simplical grids: 2D triangular grid (left) and 3D tetrahedral grid (right). (Right image courtesy of M. Kraus and T. Ertl [134] (Figure 9), reprinted with kind permission of Springer Science and Business Media.)

plices can be used to build a triangulation of an n-dimensional domain. A triangulation partitions the domain without leaving any holes or introducing overlaps between simplices. Moreover, the boundaries (faces, edges, and points) of neighboring cells have to coincide. A triangulation can be used to approximately represent any kind of manifold. This advantage of a triangulation is widely used in surface-oriented computer graphics: triangle meshes are ubiquitously employed to model the surfaces of arbitrary objects. Similarly, a tetrahedral grid can be used to represent any kind of volume data set (at least approximately). For example, it is common practice to transform a grid with more complex cells (i.e., prisms, distorted hexahedra, etc.) into a tetrahedral grid by splitting these cells into several tetrahedra.

In the remainder of this book, we will exclusively discuss uniform or tetrahedral grids. We primarily focus on uniform grids because they offer great performance benefits and little memory consumption. Similarly, uniform grids are the most common data structure in practical applications. However, Section 7.5 covers a volume-rendering technique specifically designed for tetrahedral grids.

1.5.2 Data Sources and Volume Acquisition

Data for volume rendering can come from a variety of different areas of application. An important type of application is the scientific visualization of scalar data. More specifically, medical imaging was one of the early fields that adopted volume rendering. In medical imaging, 3D data is typically acquired by some kind of scanning device.

CT (computerized tomography) is a frequently used method for obtaining medical 3D data. The physical scanning process is based on x-rays. The x-rays are emitted onto the patient's body from one side and the radiation that traverses the body is recorded on the other side. Through the interaction between x-rays and the different materials that make up the patient's body, radiation is attenuated. The radiation emitter rotates around the patient to obtain attenuation data for different directions through the body. From this collection of detected radiation, a 3D image is finally reconstructed.

MRI (magnetic resonance imaging) relies on nuclear magnetic resonance to identify different materials in a 3D spatial context. An MRI scanner needs a strong magnetic field—often in the range of a few tesla—to align the spins of atomic nuclei. Through a separate, weaker magnetic field, MRI scanners can perturb the aligned spins of the nuclei by an excitation pulse. When the spin realigns with the outer magnetic field, radiation is emitted. This radiation is recorded by the scanner. Different types of nuclei (i.e., different types of atoms) have different radiation characteristics, which is used to identify materials. Moreover, the excitation field is modified by a magnetic gradient field in order to introduce a spatial dependency into the signals. In this way, materials can be located in 3D space.

Although MRI and CT are the most common methods for 3D medical imaging, other modalities are also used. For example, ultrasound or PET (positron emission tomography, which is based on the emission of positrons from a short-lived radioactive tracer isotope) can be applied for 3D reconstruction. All these medical imaging modalities have in common that a discretized volume data set is reconstructed from the detected feedback (mostly radiation). This means that some kind of transformation process takes place and that we typically do not use the original data for volume rendering. More examples for sources of volume data in medical imaging are described by Lichtenbelt et al. [165].

Simulation results are another class of data sources. Typical examples are CFD (computational fluid dynamics) simulations in engineering, computed electromagnetic fields in physical sciences, or simulations of fire and explosions for special effects. Here, the grid used for the simulation is often different from the grid used for visualization. The simulation grid might be designed for a well-behaved simulation and therefore adapted to the physical phenomenon (e.g., by using an adaptive, unstructured grid), whereas the visualization is often based on a uniform grid, which facilitates fast volume-rendering methods. As a consequence, even simulation data is often transformed before it is given to the volume renderer.

Another typical source of volume data is voxelization (see Section 12.2). Voxelization turns a surface representation of a 3D object (e.g., a triangle mesh representation) into a volumetric object description. Here, the accuracy of the representation can be controlled by choosing an appropriate resolution for the volumetric grid. A related data source is procedural modeling (see Section 12.3). Here, the volume is specified by algorithms or code segments that define rules to evaluate the scalar field at any given point in space. Therefore, procedural descriptions are not affected by accuracy problems.

In general, the type of data source has to be taken into account when the reliability and quality of volume rendering needs to be assessed. In particular, the errors introduced by measurements and the inaccuracies from data transformations should be considered. Whereas reliability might be less important for special effects rendering, it can be crucial in scientific and medical visualization.

1.5.3   Reconstruction

As discussed in Section 1.5.1, a volume data set is usually represented in discretized form—typically on a uniform or tetrahedral grid. This discretization leads to the issue of reconstructing a scalar function on all points in the 3D domain.

The problem of a faithful reconstruction is addressed intensively in the context of signal processing. In this book, we only briefly review a few, most relevant aspects of signal processing. More background information can be found in textbooks of the field, for example, by Oppenheim and Schafer [204].

We first consider the 1D case, and later extend the discussion to 3D reconstruction. An important question for an appropriate reconstruction is: is the number of samples sufficient to reconstruct the underlying continuous function? The answer to this question is given by the Nyquist-Shannon sampling theorem of information theory [201, 238]. This theorem states that the sampling frequency must be greater than twice the highest frequency of the input signal to be able to reconstruct the original signal from the sampled version. Otherwise the signal will be aliased; i.e., the continuous signal will be reconstructed incorrectly from the discrete signal.

In mathematical notation, appropriate sampling can be described as follows: for a continuous and periodic input signal represented by the function $f(t)$, we first determine its maximum frequency ν_f. Maximum frequency means that the Fourier transform of $f(t)$ is zero outside the frequency interval $[-\nu_f, \nu_f]$. Then the critical sampling frequency—the Nyquist frequency—is $\nu_N = 2\nu_f$. For an appropriate sampling, more than $2\nu_f$ samples have to be chosen per unit distance. For a uniform sampling at a frequency ν_s, the sample points can be described by $f_i = f(i/\nu_s)$, with integer numbers i.

Provided that the original signal is sampled at a frequency $\nu_s > \nu_N$, the signal can be recovered from the samples f_i according to

$$f(t) = \sum_i f_i \, \mathrm{sinc}(\pi(\nu_s t - i)) \,. \tag{1.19}$$

The sinc function (for *sinus cardinalis*) is defined

$$\mathrm{sinc}(t) = \begin{cases} \frac{\sin(t)}{t} & \text{if } t \neq 0 \\ 1 & \text{if } t = 0 \end{cases} \,.$$

A signal whose Fourier transform is zero outside the frequency interval $[-\nu_f, \nu_f]$ is called band-limited because its bandwidth (i.e., its frequency) is bounded. In practice, the frequency content of an input data set may be unknown. In these cases, a low-pass filter can be applied to restrict the maximum frequency to a controlled value.

Equation 1.19 is one example of a *convolution*. In general, the convolution of two discrete functions $f(i) = f_i$ and $h(i) = h_i$ is given by

$$g(m) = (f * h)(m) = \sum_i f(i)h(m - i) \,. \tag{1.20}$$

The summation index i is chosen in a way that $f(\cdot)$ and $h(\cdot)$ are evaluated at all positions within their respective supports (i.e., at all positions where $f(\cdot)$ and $h(\cdot)$ are nonzero). Therefore, the above sum is a finite sum if at least one of the functions $f(\cdot)$ and $h(\cdot)$ has finite support.

The analogue of the above equation for the continuous case leads to the *convolution integral*

$$g(t) = (f * h)(t) = \int_{-\infty}^{\infty} f(t')h(t - t') \, \mathrm{d}t' \,. \tag{1.21}$$

In general, convolution is a prominent approach to filtering. In this context, $f(\cdot)$ is the input signal, $h(\cdot)$ is the filter kernel, and $g(\cdot)$ is the filtered output. In this notation, Equation 1.19 describes the convolution of a sampled input signal f_i with a sinc filter kernel.

Unfortunately, the sinc filter has an unlimited extent; i.e., it oscillates around zero over its whole domain. As a consequence, the convolution has to be evaluated for all input samples f_i, which can be very time-consuming. Therefore, in practice, reconstruction filters with finite support are often applied. A typical example is the box filter, which leads to nearest-neighbor interpolation when the box width is identical to the sampling distance (i.e., the reconstructed function value is set to the value of the nearest sample point). Another example is the tent filter, which leads to piecewise linear

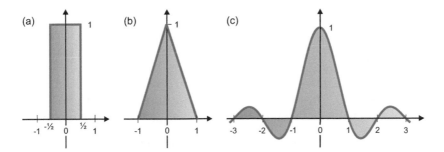

Figure 1.8. Three reconstruction filters: (a) box, (b) tent, and (c) sinc filters.

reconstruction when the width of one side of the tent is identical to the sampling distance. Figure 1.8 illustrates different reconstruction filters. Another approach to overcome the problem of the infinite support of the sinc filter is to compute the convolution in frequency space, where the sinc filter has finite support. For example, Artner et al. [3] adopt this approach in the context of volume rendering.

So far, we have discussed functions of only one variable. By applying a tensor-product approach, 1D reconstruction can be immediately extended to n dimensions and, in particular, to 3D volumes. The essential idea is to perform the reconstruction for each dimension in a combined way. For the 3D case, a tensor-product reconstruction filter is $h(x, y, z) = h_x(x)h_y(y)h_z(z)$, where $h_x(\cdot)$, $h_y(\cdot)$, $h_z(\cdot)$ are one-parameter filters along the x, y, and z directions. One important advantage of uniform grids (see Section 1.5.1) is their direct support for tensor-product reconstruction.

We discuss the example of tensor-product linear interpolations in more detail because they are widely used in volume rendering. As illustrated in Figure 1.9, the tensor-product approach separates the interpolations

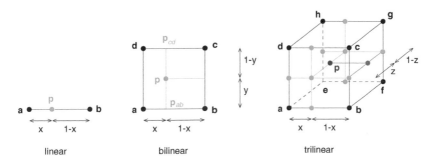

Figure 1.9. Tensor-product linear interpolations: linear, bilinear, and trilinear.

along the different dimensions and therefore allows us to compute the reconstructed value by a sequence of linear interpolations. To simplify the notation, the following discussion assumes normalized coordinate values x, y, and z that are in the interval $[0, 1]$ for points within the cell (i.e., line in 1D, rectangle in 2D, and cube in 3D). Normalized coordinates can be obtained from arbitrary coordinates by scaling and translation. Linear interpolation between two points $\mathbf{a}$ and $\mathbf{b}$ can then be computed by

$$f(\mathbf{p}) = (1 - x)f(\mathbf{a}) + xf(\mathbf{b}),$$

where $f(\mathbf{a})$ and $f(\mathbf{b})$ are the function values at the sample points $\mathbf{a}$ and $\mathbf{b}$, respectively. The result is the interpolated function value at point $\mathbf{p}$.

Tensor-product linear interpolation in two dimensions is called bilinear interpolation. Bilinear interpolation at point $\mathbf{p}$ can be computed by successive linear interpolations in the following way:

$$f(\mathbf{p}) = (1 - y)f(\mathbf{p}_{ab}) + yf(\mathbf{p}_{cd}),$$

with the intermediate results from linear interpolations along the x direction according to

$$f(\mathbf{p}_{ab}) = (1 - x)f(\mathbf{a}) + xf(\mathbf{b}),$$
$$f(\mathbf{p}_{cd}) = (1 - x)f(\mathbf{d}) + xf(\mathbf{c}).$$

By combining these expressions, we obtain a single expression for bilinear interpolation:

$$f(\mathbf{p}) = (1 - x)(1 - y)f(\mathbf{a}) + (1 - x)yf(\mathbf{d}) + x(1 - y)f(\mathbf{b}) + xyf(\mathbf{c}),$$

which explicitly shows that bilinear interpolation is not linear because it contains quadratic terms (terms of second order).

Similarly, trilinear interpolation in three dimensions can be computed by the linear interpolation between two intermediate results obtained from bilinear interpolation:

$$f(\mathbf{p}) = (1 - z)f(\mathbf{p}_{abcd}) + zf(\mathbf{p}_{efgh}).$$

The terms $f(\mathbf{p}_{abcd})$ and $f(\mathbf{p}_{efgh})$ are determined by bilinear interpolation within two faces of the cube. Trilinear interpolation contains terms up to cubic order; i.e., trilinear interpolation is not linear.

Tensor-product linear interpolations play a dominant role in volume rendering because they are fast to compute. In particular, graphics hardware provides direct support for this kind of interpolation within 1D, 2D, or 3D textures. Although tensor-product linear interpolations are often used,

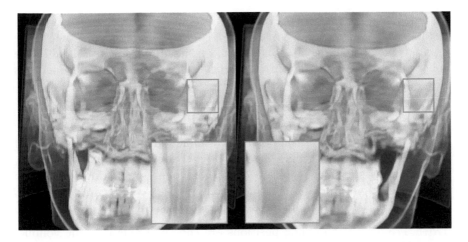

Figure 1.10. Comparison between trilinear filtering (left) and cubic B-spline filtering (right).

it should be noted that they might not result in appropriate rendering quality. As discussed in Chapter 9, especially in the context of volume filtering and reconstruction (Section 9.2), better filtering methods have been developed for real-time volume rendering. Figure 1.10 serves as an example image that motivates the use of more accurate reconstruction filters: trilinear interpolation (Figure 1.10 (left)) shows significant artifacts, whereas a higher-order filter (Figure 1.10 (right)) removes most of these artifacts.

Uniform grids are most often used in volume rendering and, thus, corresponding tensor-product reconstruction filters are frequently employed. For other grid structure, slightly different reconstruction methods may be applied. For example, barycentric interpolation is a common technique for tetrahedral cells. Barycentric interpolation provides a linear interpolant and it might be better known as the interpolation method for values within triangles. For example, graphics hardware interpolates in-between values of triangle meshes in this way.

1.6   Volume-Rendering Pipeline and Basic Approaches

In this section, we give a structural overview of volume-rendering algorithms. Volume-rendering techniques are typically used to compute the optical model from Section 1.2 by a discrete approximation (Section 1.4) of the volume-rendering integral (Section 1.3). Because of this common problem setting, the different volume-rendering techniques share most of their basic computational components. These components are briefly described in the following section, and the differences between volume-rendering methods are outlined in the subsequent section.

1.6.1   Components of the Volume-Rendering Pipeline

The evaluation of the optical model for volume rendering can be separated into several subsequent stages of a pipeline—the volume-rendering pipeline. The following stages are typically present in volume-rendering techniques: data traversal, interpolation, gradient computation, classification, shading, and compositing. The components are briefly described:

Data Traversal. Sampling positions are chosen throughout the volume. The samples serve as the basis for the discretization of the continuous volume rendering integral.

Interpolation. The sampling positions are usually different from grid points. Therefore, a continuous 3D field needs to be reconstructed from the discrete grid in order to obtain the data values at the sample points. Section 1.5.3 describes reconstruction methods. Trilinear interpolation is most common for uniform grids and is also used in most of the methods presented in this book.

Gradient Computation. The gradient of the scalar field is often used to compute local illumination (see the brief introduction in Section 1.3.1 and more details in Chapter 5). The gradient of a discretized volumetric data set is typically approximated by discrete gradient filters, such as central differences. Alternative methods for gradient computation are discussed in Section 5.3.1.

Classification. Classification maps properties of the data set to optical properties for the volume-rendering integral. Classification allows us to distinguish different areas or materials in a volume. It is usually based on transfer functions (see Chapter 4). The transfer function typically assigns the discretized optical properties in the form of color C and opacity α.

Shading and Illumination. Volume shading can be incorporated by adding an illumination term to the emissive source term that goes into the volume-rendering integral (see Section 1.3.1 and more details in Chapter 5).

Compositing. Compositing is the basis for the iterative computation of the discretized volume-rendering integral. The compositing equation depends on the traversal order. The front-to-back iteration equations are used when the viewing rays are traced from the eye point into the volume. The back-to-front compositing scheme is used when the data set is traversed from its backside.

The components interpolation, gradient computation, shading, and classification work on a local basis—they are performed in the neighborhood of, or directly at, a sample point. Therefore, these components are typically independent of the rendering method and can be reused within different methods. The rendering techniques can be primarily distinguished according to the way they traverse the data set. In addition, the order of traversal also affects the rendering scheme.

Volume-rendering techniques can be classified as either image-order or object-order methods. Image-order approaches work in 2D image space—the pixels on the image plane—as the starting point for volume traversal. Beginning at pixels, the data volume is traversed. On the other hand, object-order methods follow some organized scheme to scan the 3D volume in its object space. The traversed volume areas are then projected onto the image plane.

1.6.2 Overview of Rendering Methods

Ray casting. Ray casting is the most popular image-order method for volume rendering. The basic idea is to directly evaluate the volume-rendering integral along rays that are traversed from the camera. For each pixel in the image, a single ray is cast into the volume (neglecting possible supersampling on the image plane). Then the volume data is resampled at discrete positions along the ray. Figure 1.11 illustrates ray casting.

The natural traversal order is front-to-back because rays are conceptually started at the camera. Ray casting is the most important method

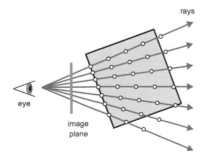

Figure 1.11. Ray-casting principle. For each pixel, one viewing ray is traced. The ray is sampled at discrete positions to evaluate the volume-rendering integral.

for CPU volume rendering; it has been used for quite some time (for some 20 years), and several acceleration methods have been developed. GPU ray casting is a rather new development (only in the past two or three years) because earlier GPUs did not support the functionality required for ray casting. GPU ray casting has the advantages that it can be easily extended to benefit from acceleration techniques (see Chapter 8) and that it supports both uniform grids and tetrahedral grids (see Chapter 7). Therefore, GPU ray casting has already become very popular in a short period of time—and it is safe to assume that ray casting will play an even more important role as GPUs further evolve.

Texture slicing. Today, texture slicing is the dominant method for GPU-based volume rendering. It is an object-order approach: 2D slices located in 3D object space are used to sample the volume. The slices are projected onto the image plane and combined according to the compositing scheme. Slices can be ordered either in a front-to-back or back-to-front fashion—and the compositing equation has to be chosen accordingly. Texture slicing is directly supported by graphics hardware because it just needs texture support and blending (for the compositing schemes). Therefore, texture slicing is widely available and very efficient. One drawback, however, is the restriction to uniform grids. This book primarily focuses on texture slicing. Chapter 3 presents the basic implementations of texture slicing.

Shear-warp volume rendering. Shear-warp volume rendering is strongly related to 2D texture–based slicing. In this object-order method, the volume is traversed in a slice-by-slice fashion. The basic idea of shear-warp is illustrated in Figure 1.12 for the case of orthogonal projection. The projection does not take place directly on the final image plane but on an intermediate image plane, called the base plane, which is aligned with the volume. The volume itself is sheared in order to turn the oblique projection direction into a direction that is perpendicular to the base plane, which allows for a fast implementation of this projection. In such a set-up,

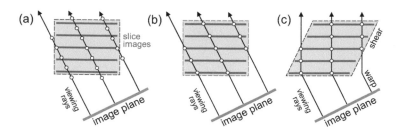

Figure 1.12. Shear-warp volume rendering.

an entire slice can be projected by 2D image resampling. Finally, the base plane image has to be warped to the final image plane. Note that this warp is only necessary once per generated image, not once per slice. Perspective projection can be accommodated by an additional scaling of the volume slices [235].

Two-dimensional texture slicing (Section 3.2) is directly related to shear-warp volume rendering. When 2D textures are used to store slices of the volume data, and a stack of such slices is texture-mapped and blended in graphics hardware, bilinear interpolation is also substituted for trilinear interpolation, similar to shear-warp. The difference between shear-warp rendering and 2D texture slicing is the order of performing the image warp and the compositing: texture slicing warps each slice and performs compositing on the final image, whereas shear-warp rendering only once warps the intermediate image.

A strength of the shear-warp algorithm is the possibility for several optimizations, which makes the shear-warp algorithm one of the fastest CPU methods for volume rendering. These optimizations require a nonuniform access to memory (for example, for run-length encoding), which are at the moment only feasible for CPU implementations. Therefore, we do not discuss shear-warp rendering any further in this book. For more details, we refer to the original paper by Lacroute and Levoy [149].

Splatting. The idea of splatting [299] is to project 3D reconstruction kernels onto the image plane. The 2D image of such a 3D kernel is called a footprint. Splatting is an object-order approach: it traverses the volume in object space and projects volume elements onto image space. In general, splatting allows for a quite flexible spatial order for traversing the volume. For example, it might be applied to traverse a uniform grid in a voxel-by-voxel fashion, or it might even be applied to scattered data (i.e., a cloud of arbitrarily distributed data points)—as long as some spatial sorting is provided to guarantee a correct result for back-to-front or front-to-back compositing. Image-aligned sheet-based splatting [188] chooses a specific order of traversal by sampling the volume along sheets (i.e., slicing slabs) that have the same orientation as the image plane. For more details on splatting, we refer to the survey chapter [36].

Cell projection. Cell projection is an object-order approach for the volume rendering of tetrahedral grids or even more complex unstructured meshes. The first cell projection algorithm that made efficient use of graphics hardware is the projected tetrahedra (PT) algorithm by Shirley and Tuchman [239]. The basic idea of the PT algorithm is to traverse the cells of the unstructured grid and project these cells onto the image plane. The projection itself leads to a collection of triangles that represent the image of the 3D cell on the image plane. The PT algorithm consists of the following steps.

1. Decomposition of the unstructured grid into tetrahedral cells.

2. Spatial sorting of the cells according to their distance from the camera.

3. Classification of each tetrahedron according to its projected profile, along with a decomposition of the projected tetrahedron into triangles (on the image plane).

4. Assignment of color and opacity values attached to the triangles.

5. Rendering and blending of triangles.

Unfortunately, cell projection with the emission-absorption model of volume rendering is connected to noncommutative blending (compositing). Therefore, it requires a view-dependent depth sorting of cells, which still has to be performed on the CPU. Whenever the camera or the volume is moved, new graphical primitives have to be generated by the CPU and transferred to the GPU. Therefore, cell projection benefits only in part from the performance increase of GPUs. Another problem of cell projection is that cyclic meshes require special treatment [132]. We do not cover cell projection further in this book and refer to the survey articles [121, 244] for more information.

1.7   Further Reading

Hege et al. [103] provide a comprehensive presentation of optical models, a derivation of the equation of transport of light, a connection to the rendering equation for surface-based graphics, and strategies for numerical solutions for volume rendering and light transport. Similarly, Max [181] gives a detailed presentation of optical models. We recommend these two papers for more background information on the mathematical and optical models of volume rendering.

Volume rendering is one example of the simulation of physical light transport. Therefore, the physics literature provides a wealth of information on this and related topics. For example, Chandrasekhar [23] describes radiative transfer in its breadth. Light transport can be considered a special case of a generic transport mechanism based on the Boltzmann equation. The mathematics of the Boltzmann equation is presented, for example, by Duderstadt and Martin [54] or Case and Zweifel [21]. In the context of volume visualization, Krueger describes the use of transport theory [137, 138].

Similarly, Arvo and Kirk [4] discuss a particle transport model for image synthesis in general. Good introductions to physically based light transport for computer graphics—in particular for surface-based graphics—are given in textbooks by Pharr and Humphries [211] and Dutré et al. [55].

Readers interested in the historic development of volume rendering are referred to some "classic" papers [13, 52, 118, 161, 230]. A modern description of volume rendering using graphics hardware is given in a book chapter by Pfister [208]. Finally, the book by Lichtenbelt et al. [165] gives a comprehensive overview of volume-rendering techniques, along with a description of practical OpenGL implementations on traditional (fixed-function) graphics hardware.

2

GPU Programming

T HE GRAPHICS BOARD of almost every modern PC is equipped with a specialized processor for hardware-accelerated 3D graphics. In general, such modern *graphics processing units* (GPUs) are highly optimized data-parallel streaming processors. The major innovation in recent years was the replacement of the traditional fixed-function pipeline by a programmable pipeline, which allows the programmer to upload user-written microprograms to be executed very fast and efficiently. Programming models for GPUs, however, differ significantly from those of traditional CPUs. Although GPU programs have a number of limitations, in the following chapters we will see that GPUs are superior to CPUs in many aspects. They turn out to be ideal for implementing object-order as well as image-order algorithms for direct volume rendering. If you want to leverage this computational power for real-time applications, it is important to know both the limitations and the strengths of the GPU programming model. This chapter gives an overview of the architecture of modern GPUs from the programmer's point of view. We also give a couple of examples on how to access the computational power using the programming language Cg.

2.1   The Graphics Pipeline

In order to prepare a virtual scene description for hardware-accelerated rendering, complex geometric descriptions (such as NURBS or subdivision surfaces) must first be decomposed into planar polygons. This process is called *tessellation*. The GPU is designed to generate raster images from tessellated scene descriptions very fast and efficiently. The process of converting a set of polygonal primitives into a raster image is called *display traversal.* Foley et al. [74] give several examples of display traversal for a variety of different rendering tasks. An excellent introduction to the rendering pipeline implemented by modern GPUs can be found in *The Cg Tutorial* [71] or in the second volume of *GPU Gems* [210].

All 3D graphics processors implement the display traversal as a pipeline consisting of a fixed sequence of processing stages. The ordering of operations in a modern graphics processor can be described by the graphics pipeline shown in Figure 2.1. The input of such a pipeline is an ordered stream of vertices. The result after display traversal is a raster image of the virtual scene in local video memory, which will finally be displayed on your video screen. At the topmost level of abstraction, the graphics pipeline can be divided into three basic stages.

Vertex Processing. Vertex processing, also termed *geometry processing*, computes linear transformations of the incoming vertices such as rotation, translation, and scaling in the 3D spatial domain. This step comprises the transformation of vertices from local model coordinates into world space (modeling matrix), subsequently into the camera space (viewing matrix), and finally into screen space (projection matrix). In the *primitive assembly*, groups of vertices from the incoming stream are joined together to form *geometric primitives* (points, lines, triangles). After clipping, culling, and viewport mapping, the primitives are handed over to the fragment processor.

Fragment Processing. The rasterization stage first decomposes each geometric primitive into a set of *fragments*. Every fragment corresponds to a single pixel in screen space. The attributes given at the vertices are interpolated in barycentric coordinates with perspective correction. The fragment processor is able to perform several *texture fetch* and *filtering* operations for each fragment. Eventually, the fragment program computes the final color of the fragment from the interpolated vertex attributes and the filtered texture samples.

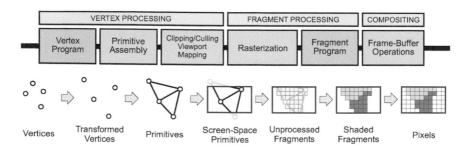

Figure 2.1. The programmable graphics pipeline.

Compositing. The compositing step is the final step before the fragments
are written into the frame buffer. Several tests are applied that finally
determine whether the incoming fragment must be discarded (e.g.,
due to occlusion) or displayed on the screen. Frame buffer operations
also decide how the color of the incoming fragment is combined with
the color value stored in the frame buffer at the corresponding raster
position.

In order to fully understand all the techniques explained in the following chapters, it is important to know the exact ordering of operations in
the graphics pipeline. Let us examine the different stages of the graphics
pipeline in a little more detail.

2.2   Vertex Processing

The vertex processor performs the so-called *per-vertex operations*. These
are operations that modify the incoming stream of vertices. It is important to note that the vertex processor can only modify existing vertices. It
can neither discard vertices nor insert additional vertices into the stream.
Every vertex that enters the pipeline has a set of attributes, such as its
position, the normal vector, and several texture coordinates and color values. The vertex processor usually computes linear transformations of the
position and the normal vector, such as translation, rotation, nonuniform
scaling, and projection. Position and normal vectors in general are represented by four-component vectors in homogeneous coordinates. The linear
transformations are carried out by multiplying the vertices with 4×4 ma-
trices, such as the well-known *modelview* matrix or the *projection* matrix.
Remember that, in order to maintain consistency, normal vectors must be
multiplied by the transposed inverse of the *modelview* matrix. This ensures
that they stay perpendicular to the surface elements.

In the traditional fixed-function pipeline, local illumination is calculated
for each vertex during geometry processing, and the illumination terms
have been interpolated for each fragment (*Gouraud* or *smooth* shading).
This is the reason why the vertex processor has formerly been referred
to as the *transform & light* unit (T&L). This term, however, is no longer
appropriate, because in the programmable pipeline, local illumination is
usually computed by the fragment processor (*Phong* shading).

2.2.1   Vertex Programs

Vertex programs are user-written microprograms that substitute major
parts of the traditional fixed-function computation of the geometry processing unit. They are used to customize the vertex transformations and

allow almost arbitrary modifications of the vertex attributes. A specified vertex program is executed *once per vertex*. Every time a vertex enters the pipeline, the vertex processor receives a set of vertex attributes, executes the vertex program, and finally emits the attributes for exactly one vertex.

The programmable vertex processor is outlined in Figure 2.2. The vertex program stored in the instruction memory of the vertex processor is executed for each vertex independently. At the beginning of the outer loop, an instruction is first fetched and decoded. The operands for the

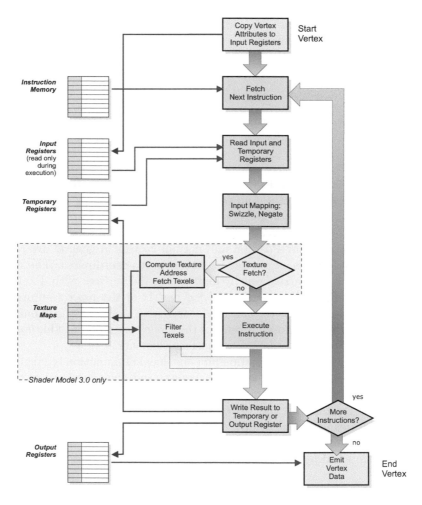

Figure 2.2. The programmable vertex processing unit executes a vertex program stored in local video memory. The vertex texture fetch is only available on graphics boards that support Shader Model 3.0. (Image inspired by Mark Kilgard's original diagram in *The Cg Tutorial* [71].)

instruction are then read from input registers, which contain the original vertex attributes, or from temporary registers, which store intermediate results. Constant parameters in the program are usually declared as uniform variables and are treated the same way as input parameters. Their values are specified by the programmer and cannot be changed during the execution. Most instructions are floating-point vector operations that are performed on xyzw components for homogeneous coordinates or the RGBA quadruplets for colors. Both notations are equivalent. Input mapping allows the programmer to specify, duplicate, and exchange the indices of the vector components (a process known as *swizzling*) and also to negate the respective values. After the operands are correctly mapped, the instruction is executed, and the result is eventually written to temporary or output registers. At the end of the loop, the vertex processor checks whether or not there are more instructions to be executed and decides to reenter the loop or terminate the program by emitting the output registers to the next stage in the pipeline. On modern GPUs that support loops and conditional branches in the vertex program, the next instruction to be executed does not have to be the next instruction in the command sequence.

A simple example of a vertex program in Cg is shown in Listing 2.1. The parameters declared in the main function specify the input and output parameters of the function as well as uniform parameters. The input and output parameters in this example are the same: a vertex consists of a po-

```
// A simple vertex program in Cg
void main( float4  Vertex    :  POSITION,
           half3   Color     :  COLOR,
           half3   TexCoord  :  TEXCOORD0,
 uniform float4x4  matModelViewProj,
       out float4  VertexOut    :  POSITION,
       out half3   ColorOut     :  COLOR,
       out half3   TexCoordOut  :  TEXCOORD0)
{
    // transform vertex into screen space
    VertexOut = mul(matModelViewProj, Vertex);

    // hand over color and texture coordinate
    ColorOut = Color;
    TexCoordOut = TexCoord;

    return;
}
```

Listing 2.1.   A simple example of a vertex program in Cg.

sition in 3D space, a color value, and a texture coordinate. The compound modeling, viewing, and projection matrix is specified as a uniform parameter in this program. The position of the incoming vertex is in local model coordinates and must be multiplied by this matrix to transform it into screen space. The color value and texture coordinates remain unchanged and are simply handed down the pipeline. This simple vertex program is all that we need for most of the rendering tasks described in this book. At the end of Chapter 3, we will see a couple of more sophisticated examples of vertex programs.

2.2.2 Vertex Textures

Until recently, only fragment programs were allowed to perform texture fetches. On graphics cards that support the Shader Model 3.0 specification, vertex programs can perform texture look-ups as well. In this case, there is a separate path in the vertex processing unit as shown in Figure 2.2. If the active instruction is a texture fetch operation, the vertex shader computes the memory address of the texel[1] from the given texture coordinates. It then fetches the texture samples that are required to compute the texel color. Depending on the underlying hardware, not all filtering methods available in the fragment processor may be supported by the vertex processor. Vertex texture fetches are often restricted to nearest-neighbor interpolation.

2.3 Fragment Processing

The fragment processing stage consists of the rasterization unit and the fragment program. Rasterization denotes the process of converting screen-space primitives into *fragments*. Each fragment corresponds to a single raster position in the resulting image, and many fragments may contribute to the final color of a pixel. The rasterization unit calculates a set of attributes for each fragment it generates by interpolating the vertex attributes given at the primitive's vertices. These primitive interpolants are the input of the fragment program. Based on this set of attributes, the fragment program computes the final color of the fragment.

2.3.1 Fragment Programs

Fragment programs are user-written microprograms that substitute major parts of the traditional fixed-function computation of the rasterization unit. They are used to compute the final color and optionally the depth value

---

[1]Texel: short for texture element.

of each fragment. The fragment program is executed *once per fragment*: Every time that primitive rasterization produces a fragment, the fragment processor receives a set of attributes, such as colors and texture coordinates, executes the fragment program once, and writes the final color and z-value of the fragment to the output registers.

The diagram for the programmable fragment processor is shown in Figure 2.3. The instruction cycle of the fragment processor is similar to the

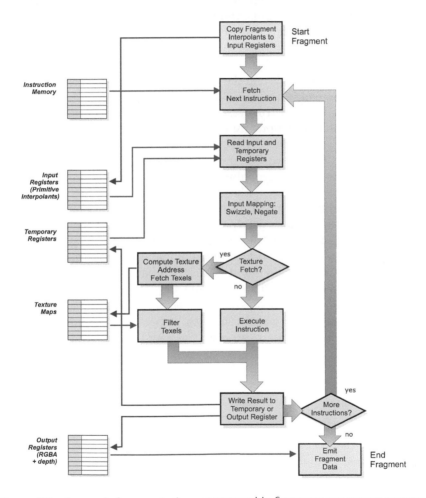

Figure 2.3. For each fragment, the programmable fragment processor executes a micro-program. In addition to reading the input and temporary registers, the fragment processor is able to generate filtered texture samples from the texture images stored in video memory. (Image inspired by Mark Kilgard's original diagram in *The Cg Tutorial* [71].)

vertex processor, with a separate path for texture fetch instructions. At first an instruction is fetched and decoded. The operands for the instruction are read from either the input registers, which contain the fragment's attributes, or from temporary registers, which are used to store intermediate results. The mapping step again computes the component swizzling and negation.

If the current instruction is a texture fetch instruction, the fragment processor computes the texture address with respect to texture coordinates and level of detail. Afterwards, the texture unit fetches all the texels that are required to interpolate a texture sample at the given coordinates. These texels are finally filtered to interpolate the texture color value.

If the current instruction is not a texture fetch instruction, it is executed with the specified operands and the result is written to the respective target registers. At the end of the loop, the fragment processor checks whether or not there are more instructions to be executed and decides to reenter the loop or terminate the program by emitting the output registers to the fragment processing stage.

Textures are (one-, two-, or three-dimensional) raster images that are mapped onto the polygon according to texture coordinates specified at the vertices. For each fragment, these texture coordinates are interpolated, and a texture look-up is performed at the resulting position. This process generates a texture sample, which refers to an interpolated color value sampled from the texture map. For maximum efficiency, it is also important to take into account that most hardware implementations maintain a texture cache. We will have a detailed look at texture caching and memory management strategies in Chapters 8 and 17.

In Cg, texture images are declared as uniform parameters of type `sampler1D`, `sampler2D`, or `sampler3D`, with respect to the dimension of the texture. The sampler types `samplerRECT` or `samplerCUBE` are used for recti-

```
// A simple fragment shader
float4 main ( half4 primary :   COLOR
              half2 uv       :   TEXCOORD0,
              uniform sampler2D texture) :   COLOR
{
    float4 texel = tex2D(texture,uv);
    return texel * primary;
}
```

Listing 2.2. A simple example of a fragment program in Cg. The final color is computed as the component-wise product of a texture sample and the primary color of the fragment.

linear textures and cube maps, respectively. The commands for sampling a given texture image are `tex1D`, `tex2D`, and so forth. As an example, a simple fragment program is shown in Listing 2.2. It performs a 2D texturing operation, which modulates the primary color with the texture color, equivalent to the fixed function pipeline in a standard OpenGL environment. We will see a variety of different fragment programs throughout this book.

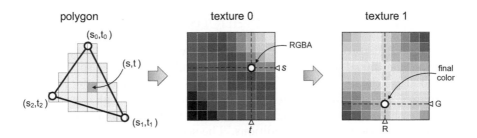

Figure 2.4. Dependent texture look-up: the texture coordinates (s, t) are interpolated as usual from the values given at the polygon vertices. An RGBA quadruplet is obtained from the first texture. The red (R) and the green (G) components of this quadruplet are used as texture coordinates for the second texture look-up. The resulting final texel value is used to color the fragment.

2.3.2 Texture Indirection

One important feature of the programmable fragment processor is its capability to perform *dependent* texture look-ups. This means that the texture coordinates used to access a texture image are not directly computed from the values given at the vertices. Instead, the texture coordinates are obtained by sampling another texture image. This concept is illustrated in Figure 2.4, and the corresponding fragment program is given in Listing 2.3.

```
// fragment program using texture indirection
half4 main( half2 texUV : TEXCOORD0,
            uniform sampler2D first_texture,
            uniform sampler2D second_texture) :  COLOR
{
    half4 texUV2 = tex2D(first_texture, texUV);
    half4 result = tex2D(second_texture, texUV2.xy);
    return result;
}
```

Listing 2.3. A simple Cg fragment program using texture indirection.

Dependent textures do not need to be interpreted as image data. In many real-time applications, dependent textures are used to implement abstract one-, two-, or three-dimensional functions as look-up tables. If you ever find that the analytical evaluation of a complex function is too expensive for real-time performance, it can probably be pre-computed as a large table and accessed via dependent texture look-up at runtime.

2.4   Frame-Buffer Operations

The fragments produced by rasterization are written into the *frame buffer*, a two-dimensional array of pixel attributes (color, alpha, depth) that corresponds to the final image. The color portion of the frame buffer is finally displayed on the video screen. When an incoming fragment is written, it modifies the values already contained in the frame buffer according to a number of parameters and conditions. The sequence of available tests and modifications is termed *frame-buffer operations* or *fragment operations* and comprise the following.

Alpha Test. The alpha test allows a fragment to be discarded conditional on the outcome of a comparison between the fragment's opacity α and a specified reference value. The alpha test can be useful in many ways, but the original idea was to discard fragments that are completely transparent. If the alpha test fails, the read and write operations from/to the frame buffer can be skipped.

Stencil Test. The stencil test allows a per-pixel mask to be applied to the visible frame buffer. The mask is contained in a separate portion of the frame buffer, called the *stencil buffer*, and is usually rendered in a pre-processing step. The stencil test conditionally drops a fragment if the stencil buffer is set for the corresponding pixel.

Depth Test. Because primitives are generated in arbitrary sequence, the depth test is needed to provide an effective mechanism for correct depth ordering of partially occluded objects. The depth value of a fragment is therefore stored in a so-called *depth buffer*. The depth test checks if an incoming fragment is occluded by a fragment that has been previously written. The occlusion test compares the incoming depth value to the value already stored in the depth buffer. This test allows occluded fragments to be discarded immediately. Because this decision is made according to the z-value of a fragment in screen space, the depth test is often referred to as *z-test* or *z-culling*.

Alpha Blending. To allow for semi-transparent objects, *alpha blending* combines the color of the incoming fragment with the color of the corresponding pixel currently stored in the frame buffer. We will see different blending set-ups in Chapter 3.

After the scene description has completely passed through the graphics pipeline, the resulting raster image contained in the frame buffer can be displayed on the screen or read back into main memory and saved to disk.

2.4.1 Early Z-Test

As mentioned above, the depth test discards all fragments that are occluded by previously drawn fragments according to a comparison of their z-values. The depth test is part of the frame buffer operations, which are performed after fragment processing. If the computation done in the fragment program, however, is rather expensive, it might be inefficient to perform fragment processing at all if we know in advance that the resulting fragment will be discarded afterwards.

In consequence, many modern GPUs allow the depth test to be performed before the fragment program execution. This concept is known as *early z-test*. The programmer, however, does not have explicit control over this feature. Instead, the graphics driver automatically decides whether an early z-test is feasible or not. The decision is made internally based on hardware-specific criteria. One basic condition for activating the early z-test is that the fragment program does not modify the z-value of the fragment. Some hardware architectures also decide to activate the early z-test only if some or all other fragment tests are disabled. For rendering scenes with a large overdraw due to a high depth complexity, the early z-test is an efficient means of increasing the rendering speed. For the early z-test to work most efficiently, however, it is mandatory to draw the objects in front-to-back order as possible.

2.4.2 Offscreen Buffers and Multiple Render Targets

For many advanced rendering algorithms, it is necessary to generate textures or intermediate images on-the-fly. These intermediate images are not directly displayed onscreen. Instead, they are used as texture images in successive rendering passes. Rendering intermediate results into a texture in OpenGL traditionally required copying the frame-buffer content to the texture using calls to `glCopyTexImage2D`. To circumvent resolution problems and performance penalties that arise from the copy operation, additional offscreen buffers in local video memory have been introduced. Such offscreen buffers can be used as alternative render targets to the visible frame buffer. Up until recently, the standard method for offscreen rendering was the pixel buffer, or *pbuffer*. In combination with the OpenGL extension WGL_ARB_render_texture (or similar extensions for Unix-style systems), which allows pbuffers to be bound directly as texture, this was an effective, yet heavyweight solution to generate texture images on-the-fly.

The main drawbacks of pbuffers are the inconvenient requirement of unique OpenGL contexts, expensive context switching, platform dependence, and limited flexibility. In response to these drawbacks, framebuffer objects (FBOs) have been introduced with the OpenGL extension GL_EXT_framebuffer_object. FBOs are a more flexible and lightweight solution to platform-independent, offscreen render targets, and they do not require separate OpenGL contexts. For volume graphics, FBOs are of great interest, because they allow us to directly render into z-slices of 3D textures. We will utilize this feature for creating 3D textures on-the-fly in Chapter 12. FBOs also provide an interface to *floating-point render targets*, which do not clamp pixel colors to unit range. Although floating-point rendering buffers cannot directly be displayed on the screen, they are important for implementing tone-mapping techniques for high dynamic range rendering as we will see in Chapter 5.

Another important feature of modern GPUs is the support for *multiple render targets* (MRTs). They allow fragment shaders to output multiple color values at one time and write them into separate offscreen render targets of the same resolution. MRTs are implemented as a separate OpenGL extension GL_ARB_draw_buffers, and FBOs provide a flexible interface to them. They can be used to efficiently generate multiple renditions in a single rendering pass.

2.4.3 Occlusion Queries

Another very useful and important feature of modern graphics hardware is the possibility to perform so-called *occlusion queries*. As we have seen in Section 2.4, not all of the fragments created during rasterization finally end up as pixels in the frame buffer. Depending on the configuration of the individual per-fragment tests, a significant number of fragments may be discarded. Occlusion queries allow an application to count the number of fragments that are actually passing all the tests.

The main purpose of this mechanism is to determine the visibility of a group of primitives. For example, an application might utilize an occlusion query to check whether or not the bounding box of a complex geometry is visible. If the rasterization of the bounding box returns an insignificant number of fragments, the application might decide to completely skip the rendering of the complex geometry.

Occlusion queries are implemented by the OpenGL extension GL_ARB_occlusion_query. A code example is given in Section 8.5 in the context of occlusion culling.

2.5 Further Reading

There are many excellent introductory texts on graphics and shader programming. If you are looking for a general source of information on real-time graphics, we recommend the book *Real-Time Rendering* by Akenine-Möller and Haines [2], which provides a practical overview on the current state of the art. For readers focusing more on game development, the first volume of *3D Games* by Watt and Policarpo [283] might also be an alternative.

The *OpenGL Programming Guide* [240], commonly known as the Red Book, is a must-have for everybody concerned with graphics programming in OpenGL. Make sure you have an up-to-date edition on your shelf for reference. Another very recommendable book is *Advanced Graphics Programming in OpenGL* by McReynolds and Blythe [184]. They provide deep insights into OpenGL that go far beyond the programming manual.

The developer's toolkit for the high-level shading language Cg is freely available for Windows and Linux at NVIDIA's developer website [33]. As a developer's guide to Cg, we recommend *The Cg Tutorial* book by Fernando and Kilgard [71]. This is an excellent book for learning Cg in addition to the *Cg User Manual* included in the Cg Toolkit.

The Internet is a huge source of information on graphics and shader development in general. The official OpenGL website, http://www.opengl.org, is always a good starting point. Additionally, all major manufacturers of graphics boards maintain a developer website with software development kits, white papers, code samples, and demos. Everybody involved in GPU programming is well advised to regularly visit the developer sites at http://www.ati.com and http://www.nvidia.com to look for new hardware features and other improvements.

3

Basic GPU–Based
Volume Rendering

A FTER HAVING WORKED THROUGH the important prerequisites, we are now ready to start with a first GPU-based implementation. We will first identify the individual components that a volume renderer is built upon. Afterwards, we examine different implementations and analyze their strengths and weaknesses both in terms of image quality and rendering performance.

We assume that the scalar volume is sampled on an equidistant rectangular 3D grid. This is the most common discrete representation of volume data in practice. All the techniques described in this chapter are object-order approaches. The graphics hardware is used in the way it was designed for in the first place. We decompose the object into geometric primitives and then render these primitives using the GPU. Image-order techniques and the GPU-based ray-casting approach will be discussed in Chapter 7.

3.1   Software Components

If you have read the introduction to graphics hardware in the previous chapter, you might have noticed that the graphics pipeline only supports polygonal rendering primitives. We cannot directly use *volumetric* primitives, such as solid tetrahedra or hexahedra. Instead, we are forced to decompose our volumetric object into primitives supported by the graphics pipeline.

To understand how object-order techniques work, it is helpful to recognize how we usually visualize 2D scalar fields. A simple photograph can be viewed as a 2D scalar field (if we neglect color information for now). Such a 2D image can directly be displayed on our video screen. If we utilize 3D graphics hardware, we can easily use such a photograph as a 2D texture image and map it onto a planar quadrangle in 3D. We can then decide that some pixels in the texture image should be transparent, and the observer will be able to see through parts of the quadrangle.

In object-order volume rendering, we make use of the fact that a discrete 3D scalar field can be represented as a stack of 2D slices. Hence, we can visualize a 3D data set by displaying a high number of semi-transparent 2D slices extracted from it. The polygons that correspond to the slices are the geometric primitives used for rendering. It is important to notice that these geometric primitives only represent a *proxy geometry*. They only describe the *shape of the data domain*, usually the bounding box, not the shape of the object contained in the data. We will examine different texture-based approaches that mainly differ in the way these slice images are extracted.

The data itself is stored as one or more texture images—2D or 3D textures depending on the specific implementation. As we have seen in Chapter 1, optical properties such as emission and absorption coefficients are required to generate an image. Let us assume for now that we are directly given such optical properties instead of scalar values. We store these coefficients in the texture images. When we introduce transfer functions in Chapter 4, we will examine effective ways of deriving optical properties from the scalar data at runtime.

The two most important operations related to volume rendering are *interpolation* and *compositing*. Both types of operation can efficiently be performed on modern graphics hardware. Texture mapping operations basically interpolate or *filter* a texture image to obtain color samples at locations that do not coincide with the original grid. Texture mapping hardware is thus an ideal candidate for performing repetitive resampling tasks. Compositing individual samples can easily be done by exploiting fragment operations in hardware. We can now identify the basic components an object-order GPU-based volume renderer is built upon.

Geometry Set-Up. This component performs the decomposition of the volume data set into polygonal slices. It calculates the position and texture coordinates of the vertices that need to be rendered.

Texture Mapping. This component determines how the volume data is stored in memory and how the data is used during fragment processing. For our first implementation, we keep this module very simple. In the forthcoming chapters dealing with classification and illumination, more sophisticated techniques will be implemented in this module.

Compositing Set-Up. This component defines how the color values of the textured polygons that we draw are successively combined to create the final rendition. This module determines whether we calculate a physically-based solution or use an empirical model, such as maximum intensity projection.

You might have noticed that there is no strict one-to-one correspondence between the described software components and the volume-rendering pipeline outlined in Section 1.6.1. Geometry set-up mainly corresponds to the data-traversal step, which determines the sampling positions. Another important aspect of data traversal, however, is memory management, which involves the texture-mapping step as well. We will examine memory-management techniques later in Chapter 8. Interpolation is completely handled by the fragment programs in the texture-mapping component. In subsequent chapters, we will see that classification and shading are also implemented by this component. The gradient computation mentioned in Section 1.6.1 is explained in Chapter 5. It is also part of the texture-mapping component, either performed as a pre-processing step before texture set-up or implemented by a fragment program. The compositing stage of the volume-rendering pipeline directly corresponds to the compositing set-up in the software components.

3.2   2D Texture–Based Volume Rendering

The first implementation we are going to examine manages with 2D textures and bilinear interpolation only. If we want to exploit 2D texture mapping capabilities, the volumetric data must be stored in several texture images. An implication of using 2D textures is that the hardware is only able to sample 2D subsets of the original 3D data.

The proxy geometry in this case is a stack of *object-aligned* slices, as displayed in Figure 3.1. In the literature, object-aligned slices are some-

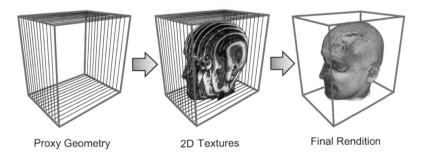

Proxy Geometry   2D Textures   Final Rendition

Figure 3.1. Object-aligned slices used as proxy geometry with 2D texture mapping.

times referred to as *axis-aligned* slices. We prefer the term object-aligned, to emphasize the fact that the slices are defined with respect to the object's local coordinate system.

All polygons are required to be aligned with one of the major axes in object space (either the x, y, or z axis). The reason for this requirement is that 2D texture coordinates are used to access the texture data. The third coordinate in space must therefore be constant. For every point in 3D object space, one coordinate determines the texture image to be used from the stack of slices. The remaining two vector components become the actual 2D texture coordinates. The polygons are mapped with the respective 2D texture, which, in turn, is resampled by the hardware-native bilinear filtering.

3.2.1 Texture Set-Up

To allow an interactive rotation of the data set, the slicing direction must be chosen with respect to the current viewing direction. The major axis must be selected in a way that minimizes the angle between the slice normal and an assumed viewing ray. This will effectively circumvent the problem of viewing rays passing between two slices without intersecting one of them. As a consequence, three stacks of texture images are stored, one stack of slices for each major axis. This is necessary to enable switching between different stacks at runtime. Figure 3.2 illustrates this idea in 2D by showing an incremental rotation of a volume object. With an angle between viewing direction and slice normal of 45° (in Figure 3.2 (d)), the slicing direction becomes ambiguous and can be chosen arbitrarily. With an angle larger than 45°, the stacks must be switched.

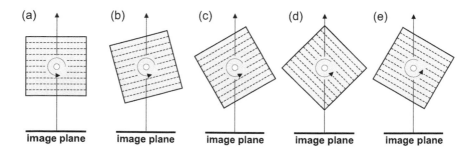

Figure 3.2. Switching the slice stack according to the viewing direction illustrated in 2D. The slice stack used for rendering must be switched between frames (c) and (e) in order to minimize the angle between the slice normal and the viewing direction. In frame (d) the slicing direction is ambiguous, as both alternatives result in the same angle.

```
// simple 2D texture sampling
float4 main (half2 texUV : TEXCOORD0,
             uniform sampler2D slice) :   COLOR
{
    float4 result = tex2D(slice, texUV);
    return result;
}
```

Listing 3.1. A simple fragment program in Cg that samples the given 2D texture image.

During texture set-up, we must prepare the texture images for the three stacks of slices and upload it to local graphics memory. During rendering, the geometry set-up will take care that the correct textures are bound for each polygon. OpenGL automatically performs a least-recently-used (LRU) texture management strategy. If storage space is needed to roll in additional textures, those texture images with the oldest time stamp are swapped out. This is appropriate as long as we have enough local graphics memory to store all textures required during one frame. In some cases the LRU strategy is inefficient. In fact, a most-recently-used (MRU) strategy is advantageous, if the texture data required to render one frame does not fit into local graphics memory all at once. In this case, texture priorities must be used to control the memory management.

As mentioned above, we assume for now that we are directly given emission and absorption values for each voxel instead of the scalar value. The information stored in each texel is an RGBA quadruplet. The RGB part defines intensity and color of the emitted light. The A component specifies opacity, i.e., the amount of light absorbed by the voxel. For now, we create a number of texture objects with an internal texture format of RGBA. We will change the internal format later, when we assign the optical properties using transfer functions (see Chapter 4).

For shading the fragments, we use the simple fragment program displayed in Listing 3.1. The final color of the fragment is replaced by the sample from the active 2D texture. More elaborate fragment programs will be introduced in later chapters, when we look at transfer functions and illumination techniques.

3.2.2 Geometry Set-Up

A code fragment implementing the view-dependent geometry set-up in OpenGL is given in Listing 3.2. To compute the viewing direction rela-

```
GLfloat pModelViewMatrix[16];
GLfloat pModelViewMatrixInv[16];

// get the current modelview matrix
glGetFloatv(GL_MODELVIEW_MATRIX, pModelViewMatrix);

// invert the modelview matrix
InvertMatrix(pModelViewMatrix,pModelViewMatrixInv);

// rotate the initial viewing direction
GLfloat pViewVector[4] = {0.0f, 0.0f, -1.0f, 0.0f};
MatVecMultiply(pModelViewMatrixInv, pViewVector);

// find the maximal vector component
int nMax = FindAbsMaximum(pViewVector);

switch (nMax) {
case X:
   if(pViewVector[X] > 0.0f) {
      DrawSliceStack_PositiveX();
   } else {
      DrawSliceStack_NegativeX();
   }
   break;
case Y:
   if(pViewVector[Y] > 0.0f) {
      DrawSliceStack_PositiveY();
   } else {
      DrawSliceStack_NegativeY();
   }
   break;
case Z:
   if(pViewVector[Z] > 0.0f) {
      DrawSliceStack_PositiveZ();
   } else {
      DrawSliceStack_NegativeZ();
   }
   break;
}
```

Listing 3.2. OpenGL code for selecting the slice direction. An example implementation for the drawing functions can be found in Listing 3.3.

tive to the volume object, the modelview matrix must be obtained from the current OpenGL state. This matrix represents the transformation from the local coordinate system of the volume into camera space. The viewing direction in camera space (the negative z-axis in OpenGL) must be transformed by the inverse of this matrix. According to the maximum component of the transformed viewing vector, the appropriate stack of slices is chosen. This code sample assumes that all object and camera transformations are stored in the modelview matrix stack. You should not misuse the projection matrix for storing them. Note that the multiplication of the negative z-axis with the viewing matrix in this example can further be simplified by directly extracting and negating the third column vector from the 4×4 matrix.

The selected stack of object-aligned polygons is displayed by drawing it in back-to-front order. During rasterization, each polygon is textured

```
// draw slices perpendicular to x-axis
// in back-to-front order
void DrawSliceStack_NegativeX() {

    double dXPos = -1.0;
    double dXStep = 2.0/double(XDIM);

    for(int slice = 0; slice < XDIM; ++slice) {
        // select the texture image corresponding to the slice
        glBindTexture(GL_TEXTURE_2D, textureNamesStackX[slice]);

        // draw the slice polygon
        glBegin(GL_QUADS);
            glTexCoord2d(0.0, 0.0); glVertex3d(dXPos,-1.0,-1.0);
            glTexCoord2d(0.0, 1.0); glVertex3d(dXPos,-1.0, 1.0);
            glTexCoord2d(1.0, 1.0); glVertex3d(dXPos, 1.0, 1.0);
            glTexCoord2d(1.0, 0.0); glVertex3d(dXPos, 1.0,-1.0);
        glEnd();

        dXPos += dXStep;
    }
}
```

Listing 3.3. OpenGL code for drawing a stack of object-aligned textured polygons in back-to-front order along the negative x-axis. The volume is assumed to lie within the unit cube and has a resolution of XDIM×YDIM×ZDIM voxels. In a practical implementation, a display list should be used and the geometry should be written into vertex buffers in order to minimize the number of function calls.

with the image information directly obtained from its corresponding 2D texture map. Bilinear interpolation within the texture image is accelerated by the texturing subsystem. Note that the third interpolation step for a full trilinear interpolation is completely omitted in this approach.

Let us assume that our volume is defined within the unit cube $(x, y, z \in [-1, 1])$ and has a resolution of XDIM×YDIM×ZDIM voxels. Listing 3.3 shows the code for drawing a slice stack along the negative x-axis. The drawing function for the positive x-axis is simply obtained by reversing the `for` loop in Listing 3.3. This means that `dXPos` is initialized with a value of 1.0 and decremented with each pass. In this case, the texture names must be bound in reverse order, the index into the array must be XDIM-slice-1 instead of `slice`.

Drawing functions for the remaining viewing directions are simply obtained by permutation of the vector components and by using the array of texture names that corresponds to the selected major axis. For most efficient rendering, the geometry should also be stored in a vertex array or a vertex buffer, if available. This will reduce the number of function calls and the amount of data transferred to the GPU. The entire `for` loop including the texture binding operations can be compiled into a display list.

3.2.3 Compositing

According to the physical model described in Section 1.4, the equation of radiative transfer can be iteratively solved by discretization along the viewing ray. As described above, the internal format for our 2D textures is RGBA, which means that each texel allocates four fixed-point values, one value for the red (R), green (G), and blue (B) components, respectively, plus one for the opacity (A) value. For each voxel, the color value (RGB) is the source term c_i from Equation 1.13. The opacity value A is the inverted transparency $(1 - T_i)$ from Equation 1.12. Using this configuration, the radiance I resulting from an integration along a viewing ray can be approximated by the use of alpha blending.

The blending equation specifies a component-wise linear combination of the RGBA quadruplet of an incoming fragment *(source)* with the values already contained in the frame buffer *(destination)*. If blending is disabled, the destination value is replaced by the source value. With blending enabled, the source and the destination RGBA quadruplets are combined by a weighted sum forming a new destination value. In order to compute the iterative solution according to Equation 1.11, opacity $(1 - T_i)$ stored in the A component of the texture map must be used as blending factor. To implement the back-to-front compositing scheme from Equation 1.15, a color

```
// alpha blending for colors pre-multiplied with opacity
glEnable(GL_BLEND);
glAlphaFunc(GL_ONE, GL_ONE_MINUS_SRC_ALPHA);
```

```
// standard alpha blending setup
glEnable(GL_BLEND);
glAlphaFunc(GL_SRC_ALPHA, GL_ONE_MINUS_SRC_ALPHA);
```

Listing 3.4. Compositing: OpenGL code for back-to-front alpha blending. The upper listing assumes that the color values are pre-multiplied with opacity in order to avoid color bleeding during interpolation. The lower listing is the standard set-up for alpha blending in OpenGL

component $C \in \{R, G, B\}$ is computed by a blending equation as follows:

$$C'_{\text{dest}} = C_{\text{src}} + C_{\text{dest}} (1 - A_{\text{src}}). \qquad (3.1)$$

This blending scheme corresponds to the OpenGL alpha blending set-up displayed in the upper part of Listing 3.4. It is important to note that this blending set-up uses *associated* colors as explained in Section 1.4.4. Associated colors consist of RGB components that are already weighted by their corresponding opacity A.

The described blending set-up is different from the standard way of alpha blending you might be familiar with. OpenGL applications often use

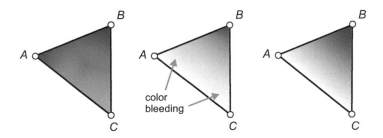

Figure 3.3. Example of color bleeding during interpolation: a triangle is drawn with different colors specified at the vertices. Color values are interpolated in the interior of the triangle. In the middle image, the red and green vertices have been set to completely transparent, but their colors are still "bleeding" into the interior of the triangle due to linear interpolation. In the right image, color bleeding was suppressed by pre-multiplying the vertex colors by their opacity value before interpolation.

a different equation for back-to-front blending, denoted

$$C'_{\text{dest}} \;=\; C_{\text{src}} \cdot A_{\text{src}} \;+\; C_{\text{dest}} \left(1 - A_{\text{src}}\right). \qquad (3.2)$$

This equation is equivalent to the blending set-up displayed in the lower part of Listing 3.4. It assumes that the RGB components of the incoming fragment are not pre-multiplied with opacity A. The color values are thus weighted by the opacity at the blending stage, before they are written into the frame buffer. Although at first glance both set-ups seem to be equivalent, they are actually not. The benefit of associated colors is the fact that color-bleeding artifacts that may occur during interpolation are avoided.

To understand the principle of color bleeding, let us examine the simple case outlined in Figure 3.3. A triangle is drawn with different color values at the vertices. If we enable smooth shading, the color values for fragments in the interior of the triangle are interpolated from the values given at the vertices. If we set the opacity value A for some of the vertices to 0 (full transparency), the color value of the vertex should not have any influence on the rendering at all. However, as can be seen in the middle image in Figure 3.3, this is not the case if standard interpolation and blending is used. The color of the red and green vertices are still visible, due to component-wise linear interpolation of the RGBA quadruplets across the triangle. Examine a fragment that lies halfway between the fully transparent red vertex (RGBA $= [1, 0, 0, 0]$) and the fully opaque blue vertex (RGBA $= [0, 0, 1, 1]$). It will receive an RGBA value of $[\frac{1}{2}, 0, \frac{1}{2}, \frac{1}{2}]$. The red component is not equal to 0, although the red vertex should be invisible.

Contrary to the example illustrated in Figure 3.3, in our volume-rendering approach, color-bleeding effects occur during texture filtering instead of fragment color interpolation, but the effect is the same. Both effects can easily be suppressed by using associated colors. To avoid color bleeding, it is only necessary to pre-multiply the RGB vertex colors by their corresponding opacity value A prior to interpolation. In this case, a completely transparent vertex would receive an RGBA value of (RGBA $= [0, 0, 0, 0]$) regardless of its original color. As can be seen in the right image of Figure 3.3, the color-bleeding artifacts have been successfully removed. The blending weight for the source color is here set to *one* (see Listing 3.4, top), because we already have multiplied it with the source opacity value before the interpolation. As we see, such a blending set-up allows color-bleeding effects to be removed at no additional cost.

As an alternative, the back-to-front scheme may be substituted by front-to-back compositing (see Section 1.4.2). Only a few modifications to the code are necessary: the slices must now be drawn in reverse order. This can easily be achieved by exchanging the drawing functions for the positive and the negative case in Listing 3.3. In the upper part of Listing 3.4, the blending weights must be replaced by GL_ONE_MINUS_DST_ALPHA and GL_ONE for associated colors. The result is a blending equation according to

$$C'_{\text{dest}} = C_{\text{src}} \left(1 - A_{\text{dest}}\right) + C_{\text{dest}}. \tag{3.3}$$

For nonassociated colors, the RGB value of each fragment must be multiplied by its alpha component in the fragment program. The drawback of front-to-back compositing is that an alpha buffer is required for storing the accumulated opacity. The back-to-front compositing scheme manages without the alpha buffer because the alpha value of the incoming fragment is used as the blending weight. Front-to-back compositing, however, is required to implement early ray termination and occlusion-culling techniques, as we will see in Chapter 8.

Maximum intensity projection. As an alternative to solving the equation of radiative transfer, *maximum intensity projection* (MIP) is a common technique that does not require numerical integration at all. Instead, the color of a pixel in the final image is determined as the maximum of all the intensity values sampled along the ray, according to

$$I = \max_{k=0..N}\left(s_k\right), \tag{3.4}$$

with s_k denoting the original scalar value sampled along the ray.

Unfortunately, the maximum operation in the blending stage is not part of the standard OpenGL fragment operations. Implementing MIP is a simple example for the use of the widely supported OpenGL extension EXT_blend_minmax. This extension introduces a new OpenGL function glBlendEquationEXT, which enables both maximum and minimum computation between source and destination RGBA quadruplets. The respective blending set-up is displayed in Listing 3.5.

```
#ifdef GL_EXT_blend_minmax
    // enable alpha blending
    glEnable(GL_BLEND);

    // enable maximum selection
    glBlendEquationEXT(GL_MAX_EXT);

    // setup arguments for the blending equation
    glBlendFunc(GL_SRC_COLOR, GL_DST_COLOR);
#endif
```

Listing 3.5. OpenGL compositing set-up for maximum intensity projection in the per-fragment operations using the widely supported extension EXT_blend_minmax.

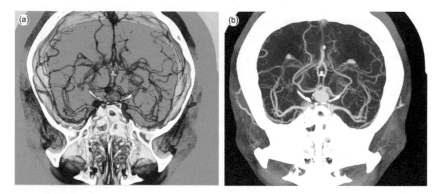

Figure 3.4. CT angiography: a comparison between the *emission-absorption model* (a) and *maximum intensity projection* (b). Note that the depth relations in image (b) are unclear because only the largest value along the ray is displayed regardless of occlusion.

Maximum intensity projection is frequently used in medical applications. It is applicable to tomographic data recorded after injecting contrast dye of high signal, such as *angiography* data. A visual comparison of MIP and ray integration is exemplified in Figure 3.4 by means of CTA[1] data of blood vessels inside the human head. Whereas for the emission-absorption model (Figure 3.4 (a)) a transfer function table must be assigned to extract the vessels (see Chapter 4), the same vascular structures are immediately displayed in the MIP image (Figure 3.4 (b)). Note that in comparison to ray integration, the surface structure of the bone is not visible in the MIP image. Bone structures have the highest signal intensity in CT data. Hence, all rays that hit a bone voxel somewhere inside the data set are set to bright white. In consequence, a major drawback of MIP is the fact that depth information is completely lost in the output images. This comes with a certain risk of misinterpreting the spatial relationships of different structures.

3.2.4   Discussion

The main benefits of our first solution based on 2D texture mapping are its simplicity and its performance. The high rendering speed is achieved by utilizing bilinear interpolation performed by the graphics hardware. Because only 2D texturing capabilities are used, fast implementations can be achieved on almost every OpenGL compliant hardware. We will see, however, that this first solution comes with several severe drawbacks if we analyze the quality of the generated images.

---

[1] CTA: computerized tomography angiography.

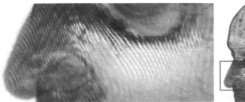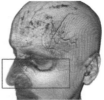

Figure 3.5. Aliasing artifacts become visible at the edges of the slice polygons.

The image quality is equivalent to a CPU implementation using a shear-warp factorization [149], because the same computational mechanisms are applied. Magnification of the images often results in typical aliasing artifacts, as displayed in Figure 3.5. Such artifacts become visible at the edges of the slice polygons and are caused by an insufficient sampling rate.

The sampling rate in our implementation cannot be changed. It is determined by the distance between two slice images. This distance is fixed and restricted by the number of texture images we have created. We will see in Chapter 4 that a fixed sampling rate is impractical, especially if used in conjunction with transfer functions that contain sharp boundaries. The sampling rate must be increased significantly to accommodate to additional high frequencies introduced into the data.

The strong aliasing artifacts in Figure 3.5 originate from an inaccuracy during ray integration. We could easily remove such artifacts by pre-computing and inserting multiple intermediate slices. This would be equivalent to increasing the sampling rate. Interpolating additional slices from the original discrete volume data and uploading them as texture images, however, would mean that we waste graphics memory by storing redundant information on the GPU. Obviously, the sampling rate we use is too low and bilinear interpolation is not accurate enough. In Chapter 4, we will examine the sampling rate problem in more detail. It becomes evident that we need a mechanism for increasing the sampling rate at runtime without increasing the resolution of the volume in memory.

Before we proceed, let us have a look at other inaccuracies introduced by the algorithm. In order to analyze image quality, it is important to examine how numerical integration is performed in this implementation. Let us reconsider the physical model described in Chapter 1. Both the discretized transparency T_i and the source term c_i are built upon the notion of a constant length Δx of ray segments. This segment length is the distance between subsequent sampling points along the viewing ray, and it is determined by the spacing between two adjacent slice planes with respect to the viewing direction. The distance between two slices of course is fixed. The source terms and opacity coefficients stored in the 2D textures

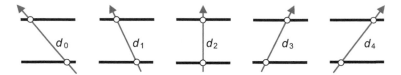

Figure 3.6. The distance between adjacent sampling points depends on the viewing angle.

are only valid if we assume a fixed distance between the sampling points along a ray. This, however, is not true for the described algorithm, because the distance between adjacent sampling points depends on the angle at which the assumed viewing ray intersects the slices (see Figure 3.6). In consequence, the result of the numerical integration will only be accurate for one particular viewing direction in case of orthographic projection. For perspective projection, the angle between the viewing ray and a slice polygon is not even constant within one image. Throughout our experiments, however, we have observed that this lack of accuracy is hardly visible as long as the field of view is not extremely large.

In addition to the sampling artifacts, a flickering may be visible when the algorithm switches between different stacks of polygon slices. The reason for such effects is an abrupt shift of the sampling positions. Figure 3.7 illustrates this problem. Figures 3.7 (a) and (b) show the viewing direction at which the slicing direction is ambiguous. If we examine the location of the sampling points by superimposing both configurations (Figure 3.7 (c)), it becomes clear that the actual position of the sampling points changes abruptly, although the sampling rate remains the same. According to the sampling theorem, the exact position of the sampling points should not have any influence on the reconstructed signal. However, this assumes an ideal reconstruction filter and not a tent filter. The magnitude of the numerical error introduced by linear approximation has an upper limit that

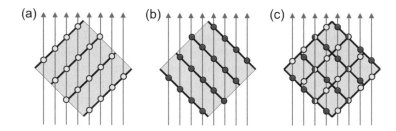

Figure 3.7. Flickering is caused by changing between different slice stacks (a) and (b). The superposition (c) shows that the location of the sampling points abruptly changes, which results in visible switching effects.

is determined by the sampling rate. Within its bounds, however, the numerical error can change abruptly from frame to frame and this causes the flickering effects. Again, if we find a way of increasing the sample rate, we could alleviate this effect by lowering the error bounds. We will completely circumvent this effect in the following section by the use of viewport-aligned slices and 3D textures.

Due to the inability to increase the sampling rate, the value of the 2D texture–based implementation so far is very limited in practice, unless you have a very outdated graphics system that does not support multitextures or 3D textures. However, the algorithm is easy to understand and serves as a basis for implementing a more sophisticated multitexture-based algorithm, as we will see in Section 3.4. Before we turn to multitextures, however, let us have a look at another quite intuitive implementation using 3D texture mapping.

3.3   3D Texture–Based Approach

Several problems of the 2D texture–based approach are caused by the fixed number of slices and their static alignment within the object's coordinate system. The reason why we had to put up with these restrictions was that 2D textures did not provide the trilinear interpolation capabilities required. If we use 3D textures instead of 2D textures, this situation changes.

Those who have not used 3D textures before should be aware of the fact that 3D textures do not represent volumetric rendering primitives. They are nothing more than volumetric texture objects, which means that the image information used to texture-map a planar polygon can be "cut out" of a solid 3D texture block.

In consequence, using 3D textures does save us from the necessity of decomposing the volume object into planar polygons. Compared with our first approach, we now have greater flexibility on how to compute this decomposition.

As we have already seen, one drawback of using object-aligned slices is the inconsistent sampling rate that results from the static proxy geometry. Because 3D textures allow the slice polygons to be positioned arbitrarily in the 3D space, a more consistent sampling rate for different viewing directions could be achieved by adapting the distance of the object-aligned slices to the current viewing angle. This is actually done in the 2D multitexture–based approach described later in this chapter. Adjusting the slice distance, however, does not remove the flickering artifacts that occur when the algorithm switches between different slice stacks.

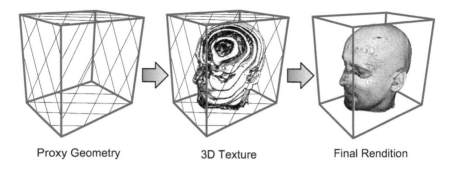

Proxy Geometry   3D Texture   Final Rendition

Figure 3.8. Decomposition of the volume object into viewport-aligned polygon slices.

Both problems are efficiently solved by the use of viewport-aligned slices as displayed in Figure 3.8. This means that the volumeric object is cut into slices parallel to the image plane. The proxy geometry, however, must be recomputed whenever the viewing direction changes. In case of parallel projection, the decomposition into viewport-aligned slices ensures a consistent sampling rate for all viewing rays as illustrated in Figure 3.9 (a). In the perspective case, the sampling rate is still not consistent for all rays (Figure 3.9 (b)). The distance of sampling points varies with the angle between the slice polygon and the viewing ray. Such effects, however, are only noticeable if the field of view is extremely large.

The compositing process in case of 3D texture–based volume rendering is exactly the same as for the 2D texture–based algorithm described in Section 3.2.3. The intersection calculation for viewport-aligned slices algorithm, however, requires a more detailed description.

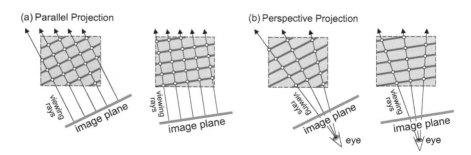

Figure 3.9. Sampling illustrated for viewport-aligned slices in the case of parallel (a) and perspective projection (b).

3.3.1 Geometry Set-Up

Compared with object-aligned slicing, the procedure of intersection calculation between the bounding box and a stack of viewport-aligned slices is computationally more complex. To make matters worse, these slice polygons must be recomputed whenever the viewing direction changes. Because the whole computation must be performed several times per second to achieve an interactive frame rate, an efficient algorithm is required. One way of computing the plane-box–intersection can be formulated as a sequence of three steps.

1. Compute the intersection points between the slicing plane and the straight lines that represent the edges of the bounding box.

2. Eliminate duplicate and invalid intersection points. Invalid points may occur if the plane intersects the straight line but the intersection point does not lie on the edge.

3. Sort the remaining intersection points to form a closed polygon.

The intersection between a plane and a straight line in step 1 can easily be solved analytically. To determine whether an intersection point actually lies on an edge of the bounding box, a bounding-sphere test can be applied in step 2. Points that are located outside the bounding sphere do not lie on an edge and are thus discarded from the list of valid intersection points. Additionally, duplicate points that coincide with a corner vertex of the bounding box are merged together.

In order to facilitate the sorting of the remaining edge intersection points in step 3, a set of six flags is stored for each edge, one flag for each of the six faces of the bounding box. As outlined in Figure 3.10, a

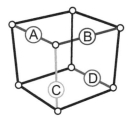
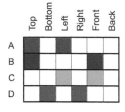

Figure 3.10. Sorting of edge intersection points to form a valid polygon: Each edge holds a set of six flags (left), one flag for each face of the bounding box. A flag is set if the edge belongs to the corresponding face and cleared otherwise. Edges that share a common face are easily determined by OR-ing the edge flags. If the result is nonzero, a common face exists. Four examples for edge flags are displayed (A–D).

flag is set if the edge belongs to the corresponding face and cleared otherwise. The sequence of intersection points that form a valid polygon is found when the flags of two adjacent edge intersection points have one flag in common. This property can be easily verified by computing a bitwise OR operation of the edge flags. If the result is nonzero for every pair of adjacent points, the sequence is valid and the resulting polygon is exactly the cross section between the plane and the bounding box. A valid ordering of intersection points can be obtained by the use of a greedy algorithm starting with an arbitrary point. Further optimization of the slicing algorithm can be achieved by computing the intersection points for the subsequent slice plane incrementally.

The geometry set-up described in this chapter assumes that the intersection calculation is performed on the CPU and the resulting vertices are uploaded to the graphics processor for each frame. You will probably end up with a well-balanced process that efficiently exploits all the available resources in parallel: the computational power of the CPU and the GPU, as well as the storage capacity and the memory bandwidth. The only part of the pipeline that currently is somewhat underemployed is the vertex processor. In Section 3.5, we will see that the cube-plane intersection can be efficiently performed by a customized vertex program.

3.3.2 Texture Set-Up

Listing 3.6 shows the sequence of commands necessary to upload a single 3D texture into local graphics memory. The internal format is set to

```
// bind 3D texture target
glBindTexture( GL_TEXTURE_3D, volume_texture_name );

// set texture parameters such as wrap mode and filtering
glTexParameteri(GL_TEXTURE_3D, GL_TEXTURE_WRAP_S, GL_CLAMP);
glTexParameteri(GL_TEXTURE_3D, GL_TEXTURE_WRAP_T, GL_CLAMP);
glTexParameteri(GL_TEXTURE_3D, GL_TEXTURE_WRAP_R, GL_CLAMP);
glTexParameteri(GL_TEXTURE_3D, GL_TEXTURE_MAG_FILTER, GL_LINEAR);
glTexParameteri(GL_TEXTURE_3D, GL_TEXTURE_MIN_FILTER, GL_LINEAR);

// upload the 3D volume texture to local graphics memory
glTexImage3D(GL_TEXTURE_3D, 0, GL_RGBA,
             size_x, size_y, size_z,
             GL_RGBA, GL_UNSIGNED_BYTE, volume_data_rgba );
```

Listing 3.6. OpenGL set-up for a 3D texture.

GL_RGBA, which means that the emission/absorption values are stored as an RGBA quadruplet for each texel. Note that the code is not much different from a 2D texture set-up, except for the third dimension parameter in glTexImage3D and the additional wrap mode setting.

Compared with the previous approach using 2D textures, memory management for 3D textures, however, is a little bit more difficult. Because the whole volume data set is defined as a single 3D texture, it must entirely fit into the texture memory at one time. With the increasing size of volume data sets, the available texture memory becomes the limiting factor. Now two questions arise immediately:

1. How do we determine whether or not a texture fits onto the graphics boards?

2. What can we do if the texture does not entirely fit into graphics memory?

The answer to the first question is simple. OpenGL provides a mechanism called *proxy texture*, which allows us to test in advance whether or not a desired texture resolution will work. For more details on proxy textures, please refer to the OpenGL Red Book.

The answer to the second question is called *bricking*. Bricking tackles the memory problem by subdividing a large data set into smaller chunks (usually called *bricks*) that entirely fit into local graphics memory, one at a time.

The naive approach of simply splitting the data set into bricks and rendering each brick separately introduces additional artifacts at the brick boundaries. To explain these artifacts, we have to look at how texture

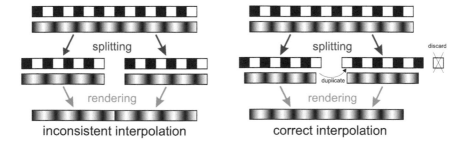

inconsistent interpolation   correct interpolation

Figure 3.11. Bricking illustrated for the 1D case. Simply splitting the texture leads to inconsistent interpolation at the transition (left). Duplicating a voxel at the boundary between bricks (a plane of voxels in 3D) leads to correct interpolation results (right). The discarded white voxel must be accommodated by the adjacent brick, together with a duplicate of the leftmost black voxel.

interpolation is performed at the transition between neighboring bricks. Figure 3.11 (left) illustrates this problem. At the boundary between texture tiles, the interpolation is incorrect, as the texture unit does not have enough information to consistently interpolate across texture boundaries. The solution to this problem is to duplicate a plane of voxels at each brick boundary. If two neighboring bricks share a common plane of voxels, the texture units can be set up to deliver the correct interpolation results, as displayed in Figure 3.11 (right). More details on bricking and memory-management techniques will be discussed in Chapter 17.

3.3.3 Discussion

In comparison with the 2D texture–based solution, the 3D texture–based approach has proved superior in terms of image quality, removing some of the significant drawbacks while preserving almost all the benefits. The 2D texture–based approach requires three copies of the data set to be stored in local memory. With 3D textures, this is no longer necessary because trilinear interpolation allows the extraction of slices with arbitrary orientation. In this context, viewport-aligned slices guarantee a sampling distance that is consistent among adjacent frames for parallel projection. The problem of variable sample rate for perspective projection, however, still remains. As long as the virtual camera views the volume object from an exterior position, the effect of the inconsistent sampling rate is hardly visible.

As we have already noted in our first 2D texture–based implementation, adjusting the sampling rate is essential to remove sampling artifacts. Hardware support for trilinear interpolation provides us now with a natural means of increasing the sampling rate. This is important to accurately account for a transfer function of high frequency as we will see later in Chapter 4.

For large volume data sets, however, the bricking strategy turns out to be inefficient. In this case, the rendering process is limited by the memory bandwidth between the GPU and the host memory, while the GPU is stalled until the required texture data is fetched from host memory. To make matters worse, bricking increases the overall memory for storing the volume data set. As explained, correct interpolation across brick boundaries requires one plane of voxels to be duplicated at the boundary between any two bricks.

The size of the bricks has significant influence on the overall performance. In order to optimize cache coherency, the bricks should be kept small enough to fit into the texture cache. On the other side, however, the bricks should not be too small, otherwise the duplicated voxels at the brick boundaries would significantly increase the memory required for storing the volume. Additionally, a large number of bricks results in a higher number of intersection calculations for the CPU. In consequence, a higher number of vertices must be transferred to the GPU for each frame, and we will end up with a worsening of the bandwidth problem. As a result, the frame rate for large data will be significantly lower compared with 2D textures. Note that this is true even though the 2D texture–based approach requires the storing of three copies of the volume data.

Memory management is a crucial point in the 3D texture–based implementation. We will examine this aspect in detail in Chapter 8. The efficiency of 3D texture look-ups greatly depends on the individual graphics processor, the amount of graphics memory available, and on driver optimization. Unfortunately, there is no general rule to determine the optimal level of subdivision. Experimenting with different brick sizes is thus essential in order to optimize the performance for different graphics systems. GPU manufacturers might decide to store 3D textures as a linear array of samples in local video memory. This might lead to texture caching being effective only if texture coordinates are shifted in u or v direction. Cache misses are likely to happen when texture coordinates are shifted in w direction. Other implementations might decide to rearrange the data in order to optimize 3D texture cache coherency. This, however, may come at the cost that 3D textures cannot be transferred asynchronously from host to video memory anymore, because the CPU is required to rearrange the data. More details on improving texture-cache coherence are given in Chapter 8.

At the bottom line, 3D textures are usually not as efficient as 2D textures with respect to memory management and texture cache coherency. Because the texture map for a single polygon slice is cut out of a volumetric texture block, it is obvious that there must be redundant data in texture memory. In our first implementation based on 2D textures, there was a strict one-to-one correspondence between slices and textures. In this case, we knew exactly which portion of the texture data was required to texture the polygon beforehand. The main drawback using 2D textures was the lack of trilinear filtering. In the next section, we will switch back to the 2D texture–based approach and examine a way to implement trilinear interpolation using 2D multitextures instead of 3D textures.

3.4 2D Multitexture–Based Approach

The 2D texture–based method is capable of rendering a volume data set at high frame rate. The mathematical accuracy, the subjective image quality, and the memory requirements, however, are far from being optimal. In the previous section, we saw that the 3D texture–based approach removes some of these limitations at the cost of a less efficient memory management. At this point, let us make a list of the main advantages of 3D texture–based volume rendering over our first implementation.

- Trilinear instead of bilinear interpolation.

- A more consistent sampling rate between adjacent frames.

- Lower memory requirements.

We will now examine a third alternative approach, which supplements the original 2D texture–based implementation by removing at least two of the above-mentioned limitations and preserving the benefit of more efficient memory management.

The advantage of 3D textures over 2D textures is that trilinear interpolation is directly supported by the graphics hardware. In our multitexture-based implementation, we take advantage of the fact that a trilinear interpolation operation can be decomposed into two bilinear interpolation operations followed by one linear interpolation. Bilinear interpolation is efficiently performed by the 2D texture unit. The idea to accomplish trilinear interpolation with 2D multitextures is to use a fragment program that samples two adjacent 2D textures and performs the missing linear interpolation step afterwards. In comparison with our first 2D texture–based implementation, such a fragment program will allow intermediate slices to be interpolated on the fly, without the need to pre-compute the corresponding texture map. More generally, this approach allows us to draw correct object-aligned slices at an arbitrary position along the chosen major axis.

```
// fragment program for trilinear interpolation
// using 2D multi-textures
float4 main (half3 texUV : TEXCOORD0,
             uniform sampler2D texture0,
             uniform sampler2D texture1 ) :   COLOR
{
    // two bilinear texture fetches
    float4 tex0 = tex2D(texture0, texUV.xy);
    float4 tex1 = tex2D(texture1, texUV.xy);

    // additional linear interpolation
    float4 result = lerp(tex0,tex1,texUV.z);

    return result;
}
```

Listing 3.7. Cg fragment program for trilinear interpolation of 2D multitextures.

The fragment program that computes the trilinear interpolation is displayed in Listing 3.7. For a slice image at an arbitrary position along a chosen major axis, the two adjacent 2D textures are bound as multitextures. The fragment program samples both textures at the same texture coordinate. Bilinear filtering is performed automatically by the texture

```
// draw slices perpendicular to x-axis
// in back-to-front order
void DrawSliceStack_NegativeX(int nNumSlices)
{
   double dXPos = -1.0;
   double dXStep = 2.0/double(nNumSlices);

   for(int slice = 0; slice < nNumSlices; ++slice) {
      // select the texture images corresponding
      // to the two adjacent slices
      double dXPosTex = (XDIM * (dXPos + 1.0)/2.0);
      int nTexIdx = int(dXPosTex);
      double dAlpha = dXPosTex - double(nTexIdx);

      glActiveTexture(GL_TEXTURE0);
      glBindTexture(GL_TEXTURE_2D, texNamesStackX[nTexIdx]);
      glActiveTexture(GL_TEXTURE1);
      glBindTexture(GL_TEXTURE_2D, texNamesStackX[nTexIdx+1]);

      // draw the slice polygon
      glBegin(GL_QUADS);
         glTexCoord3d(0.0, 0.0, dAlpha);
         glVertex3d(dXPos,-1.0,-1.0);
         glTexCoord3d(0.0, 1.0, dAlpha);
         glVertex3d(dXPos,-1.0, 1.0);
         glTexCoord3d(1.0, 1.0, dAlpha);
         glVertex3d(dXPos, 1.0, 1.0);
         glTexCoord3d(1.0, 0.0, dAlpha);
         glVertex3d(dXPos, 1.0,-1.0);
      glEnd();

      dXPos += dXStep;
   }
}
```

Listing 3.8. OpenGL code for drawing a stack of object-aligned multitextured polygons in back-to-front order along the negative x-axis.

unit. The remaining linear interpolation step between these two samples is performed by the `lerp` operation afterwards.

3.4.1 Geometry Set-Up

An example implementation for the geometry set-up is displayed in Listing 3.8. It is essentially the same as in our first implementation (see Listing 3.3) with only a few modifications. The number of slices to be drawn does not have to be equal to the dimension of the volume in the respective direction. It is now specified as an argument to the function and can be chosen arbitrarily. In our example, the spatial position `dXPos` within the unit cube is transformed into texture space (`dXPosTex`). The integer part of this position is used to select the two neighboring texture images.

Texture coordinates are now 3-component vectors according to the fragment program in Listing 3.7. The third component is used as the interpolation weight `dAlpha` for the third interpolation step. This weight is obtained by taking the fractional part of the position in texture space `dXPosTex`. Drawing functions for the other slicing direction are again obtained by permutation of the vertex coordinates and by reversing the polygon order as explained in Section 3.2.2.

3.4.2 Discussion

The 2D multitexture–based approach fills the gap between the traditional 2D and 3D texture–based methods. With the possibility to trilinearly interpolate intermediate slices within the graphics hardware, two drawbacks of the traditional 2D texture–based approach have been removed as promised.

- Trilinear interpolation can be performed by multitexture blending. This allows the rendering of axis-aligned slices at arbitrary positions.

- Consistent sampling rate in parallel projection can be achieved by adjusting the distance between the slice images to the viewing angle.

The third critical point is the high storage requirements that come with the necessity of keeping three copies of the data set in memory. Besides the memory requirement, there are some considerable differences between the 3D texture and the 2D multitexture–based approaches. The switching artifacts that can be observed when the 2D texture–based algorithm switches between orthogonal slice stacks are still evident in the 2D multitexture–based method. However, due to the ability to adapt the slice distance arbitrarily, the effect appears less disturbing.

The multitexture-based interpolation allocates two texturing units to interpolate one slice. These texturing units cannot be used for classification and illumination calculations, as we will see in the following chapters. The main advantage of the 2D multitexture approach over 3D textures is the more efficient memory management. The bricking mechanism that must be applied for volumes that do not fit entirely into texture memory is rather inefficient, as a huge part of the graphics memory must be swapped at a time. Using 2D textures to represent the volume is advantageous, as the graphics memory is partitioned into small portions, which can be replaced more efficiently.

There is also a possibility to completely get rid of the additional two stacks of slices. The idea is to store only one stack and reconstruct the missing stacks on-the-fly using offscreen rendering targets. In order to reconstruct a slice image for a missing slice direction, we can render one line from each of the original 2D textures into an offscreen render target. This offscreen rendering target is then bound as a textures image to render the proxy geometry.

Such an approach, however, is only feasible if enough local video memory is available to store one stack of textures, but not enough to store all three stacks. It is obvious that if all three stacks fit into video memory, storing them would be more efficient because offscreen rendering could be omitted. If not even one stack of textures fits entirely into memory, the on-the-fly reconstruction would be very inefficient because all textures must be swapped in from host memory to reconstruct one slice. Because only one line from each texture is used in the reconstruction, this will result in much redundant data traveling over the bus again and again during one frame. Such problems can only be solved by very complex paging strategies, similar to the texture management strategies proposed by Lefebvre et al. [157].

Another reason one might not want to deal with three sets of slices is if the volume data is dynamically created either by the CPU or the GPU. We will see examples of on-the-fly computation in Chapter 12. In the case where the data is coming from the CPU, it must be transferred over the graphics port. Using a single set of slices decreases bus bandwidth by a factor of three. In the case where the GPU is creating the volume data set, copy operations in video memory can be completely avoided. In this case, efficiency will greatly depend on the ratio between rendering and computation time. If the volume is not updated very frequently, it might be worth it to cache three sets of slices. If rendering and computation processes are balanced, creating three stacks in memory will most likely not be worthwhile.

3.5 Vertex Programs

The performance limit for all GPU-based approaches we have seen so far is either the pixel fill-rate or the memory bandwidth. The major workload is handled by the fragment processor, and only a negligible computational load is assigned to the vertex processor. In the remainder of this chapter,

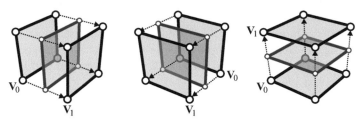

Figure 3.12. Extracting an object-aligned slice can be formulated as a vertex blending operation between the first slice and the last slice along a fixed major axis.

```
// vertex program for computing object aligned slices
void main( float4 Vertex0   :   POSITION,
           float4 Vertex1   :   TEXCOORD0,
           half2  TexCoord0  :   TEXCOORD1,

           uniform float     slicePos,
           uniform float4x4 matModelViewProj,

           out float4 VertexOut    :   POSITION,
           out half3  TexCoordOut  :   TEXCOORD0)
{
    // interpolate between the two positions
    float4 Vertex = lerp(Vertex0, Vertex1, slicePos);

    // transform vertex into screen space
    VertexOut = mul(matModelViewProj, Vertex);

    // compute the correct 3D texture coordinate
    TexCoordOut = half3(TexCoord.xy, slicePos);

    return;
}
```

Listing 3.9. Cg vertex program for calculating intermediate slices.

we will examine ways of incorporating the programmable vertex processor into the algorithms.

3.5.1   Object-Aligned Slices

Let us first examine the approaches that draw object-aligned slices. As we have noted in Section 3.2.2, for maximum performance the vertex data should not be transferred over the memory bus for each frame. To reduce the bus-load, it is advantageous to pre-compute the vertices, transfer them once, and store them as a vertex buffer in local graphics memory. A large number of slices, however, will result in a considerable amount of memory allocated for the geometry.

The geometry set-up, however, is rather simple in the case of object-aligned slices. It can easily be encoded into a vertex program that reduces the size of the vertex buffer to a minimum. An arbitrary object-aligned slice can be described by blending vertices from the front face and the back face with respect to a fixed major axis. This idea is illustrated in Figure 3.12. For drawing slices along one fixed major axis, all we need to store in the vertex buffer are the eight corner vertices of the bounding box. An arbitrary slice image can then be rendered using the vertex program displayed in Listing 3.9.

An input vertex structure is here carrying a pair of position vectors `Vertex0` and `Vertex1` as well as a 2D texture coordinate `TexCoord`. The position of the slice inside the cube is specified by a uniform parameter `slicePos`, which is updated for each slice to be rendered. This value is used as an interpolation weight for blending the two corresponding vertices of the front and the back polygon. Additionally, the value of `slicePos` can be used directly as a third texture coordinate, using the fragment shader for 2D multitexture interpolation (Listing 3.7).

3.5.2   Viewport-Aligned Slices

Calculating the intersection between a cube and an arbitrarily oriented plane is a more complicated task, as we have seen in Section 3.3.1. However, there also exist vertex programs that are capable of performing the intersection calculation in this case.

In Chapters 8 and 17, we will examine memory management strategies and empty-space skipping techniques. Efficient vertex programs can minimize the amount of data that must be transferred from host memory to the GPU. This allows us to render significantly smaller bricks, resulting in a much higher flexibility for memory management.

The intersection between a box and a plane results in a polygon with three to six vertices (assuming that the plane actually intersects the box). The different cases are illustrated in Figure 3.13. Our vertex program must

Figure 3.13. Intersecting a box with a plane. The resulting polygon has between three and six vertices. Symmetric cases are omitted.

compute the correct sequence of vertices for such intersection polygons directly. The vertex processor, however, can neither insert new vertices nor remove vertices from the stream. As a consequence, we will design a vertex program that always receives six vertices and outputs six vertices. If the intersection polygon consists of less than six vertices, the vertex program will generate one or more duplicate vertices (i.e, two identical vertices with an edge of length zero in between). Such duplicate vertices will result in degenerated triangles that do not produce any fragments in the rasterization step.

Intersecting an edge of the box with the slice plane is easy if the plane is given in Hessian normal form,

$$\mathbf{n}_P \cdot \mathbf{x} = d, \qquad (3.5)$$

with $\mathbf{n}_P$ denoting the normal vector of the plane and d the distance to the origin. For viewport-aligned slicing, the normal vector $\mathbf{n}_P$ is the viewing direction. An edge between two vertices $\mathbf{v}_i$ and $\mathbf{v}_j$ of the bounding box can be described as

$$E_{i\rightarrow j}: \qquad \mathbf{x} \;=\; \mathbf{v}_i + \lambda\left(\mathbf{v}_j - \mathbf{v}_i\right) \qquad (3.6)$$
$$=\; \mathbf{v}_i + \lambda\,\mathbf{e}_{i\rightarrow j} \qquad \text{with } \lambda \in [0,1].$$

Note that the vector $\mathbf{e}_{i\rightarrow j}$ does not have unit length in general. The intersection between the plane and the straight line spanned by $E_{i\rightarrow j}$ is calculated by

$$\lambda = \frac{d - \langle \mathbf{n}_P \circ \mathbf{v}_i \rangle}{\langle \mathbf{n}_P \circ \mathbf{e}_{i\rightarrow j} \rangle}. \qquad (3.7)$$

The denominator becomes zero only if the edge is coplanar with the plane. In this case, we simply ignore the intersection. We have found a valid intersection only if λ is in the range $[0,1]$, otherwise the plane does not intersect the edge.

The main difficulty in performing the intersection calculation in the vertex processor is to maintain a valid ordering of the intersection points. The result must form a valid polygon. To understand the slicing algorithm, let us assume for now that we have one vertex $\mathbf{v}_0$ that is closer to the camera than all other vertices, as displayed in Figure 3.14 (left). Vertex

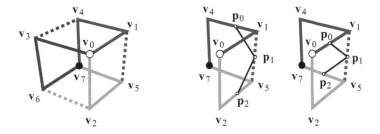

Figure 3.14. Left: the vertices are numbered sequentially. There always exist three independent paths from the front vertex $\mathbf{v}_0$ to the back vertex $\mathbf{v}_7$ as marked by the solid lines. Right: the intersection point of the dotted line must be inserted between the intersection points from the solid lines.

$\mathbf{v}_7$ is then identified as the vertex lying on the opposite corner across the cube's diagonal. In the following, we will refer to the vertex indices given in Figure 3.14 (left).

If $\mathbf{v}_0$ is the front vertex and $\mathbf{v}_7$ is the back vertex, there are exactly three independent paths from $\mathbf{v}_0$ to $\mathbf{v}_7$ as marked in Figure 3.14 (left) by the solid lines in red, green, and blue. In this context, *independent* means that these paths do not share any vertices other than the start and the end vertex. Each path consists of a sequence of three edges $\{E_1, E_2, E_3\}$, e.g., $E_1 = E_{0 \to 1}$, $E_2 = E_{1 \to 4}$, and $E_3 = E_{4 \to 7}$ for the red path. For a given front vertex, we can construct these three paths uniquely by forcing that the vectors corresponding to E_1, E_2, and E_3 for each path form a right-handed system.

Now imagine we are sweeping a viewport-parallel plane from front to back through the box in Figure 3.14 (left). The first vertex that the plane touches is $\mathbf{v}_0$. Before this happens, we do not have any valid intersection with the box. The last vertex that the plane touches, if we proceed from front to back, is vertex $\mathbf{v}_7$. After that, we will not have any valid intersection anymore. As a consequence, any viewport-aligned plane that intersects the box will have exactly one unique intersection point along each of the three paths, respectively. In the case that our intersection polygon has only three vertices, they will be exactly those intersection points with the three paths. As a result, we can compute three of the possible six intersection points $\mathbf{p}_i$ by checking intersections with sequences of edges, respectively:

$$\mathbf{p}_0 = \text{Intersection with } E_{0 \to 1} \text{ or } E_{1 \to 4} \text{ or } E_{4 \to 7},$$
$$\mathbf{p}_2 = \text{Intersection with } E_{0 \to 2} \text{ or } E_{2 \to 5} \text{ or } E_{5 \to 7},$$
$$\mathbf{p}_4 = \text{Intersection with } E_{0 \to 3} \text{ or } E_{3 \to 6} \text{ or } E_{6 \to 7}.$$

Now, let us consider where the remaining intersection points must lie if our polygon has more than three vertices. We will first examine the red

```
void main( int2 Vin :  POSITION,

    uniform float3   vecTranslate,      // updated per cube
    uniform float    dPlaneStart,

    uniform int      frontIdx,          // updated per frame
    uniform float3   vecView,
    uniform float4x4 matModelViewProj,

    uniform float    dPlaneIncr,        // never updated
    uniform int      nSequence[64],
    uniform float3   vecVertices[8],
    uniform int      v1[24],
    uniform int      v2[24],

    out float4 VertexOut :  POSITION,
    out half3 TexCoordOut :  TEXCOORD0)
{
    float dPlane = dPlaneStart + Vin.y * dPlaneIncr;
    float3 Position;

    for(int e = 0; e < 4; ++e) {
        int vidx1 = nSequence[int(frontIdx *8 +v1[Vin.x *4 +e])];
        int vidx2 = nSequence[int(frontIdx *8 +v2[Vin.x *4 +e])];
        float3 vecV1 = vecVertices[vidx1];
        float3 vecV2 = vecVertices[vidx2];
        float3 vecStart = vecV1+vecTranslate;
        float3 vecDir = vecV2-vecV1;
        float denom = dot(vecDir,vecView);
        float lambda = (denom!=0.0) ?
            (dPlane-dot(vecStart,vecView))/denom :  -1.0;
        if((lambda >= 0.0) && (lambda <= 1.0)) {
            Position = vecStart + lambda * vecDir;
            break;
        } // if(...
    } // for(...

    VertexOut = mul(matModelViewProj,float4(Position,1.0));
    TexCoordOut = 0.5 * (Position) + 0.5;
    return;
}
```

Listing 3.10.   Cg vertex program for box-plane intersection.

dotted edge $E_{1 \to 5}$ in Figure 3.14. If there exists a valid intersection with this edge, then it must be inserted between the intersection points with the red path and the green path as can be easily seen in Figure 3.14 (right). If an intersection with the dotted edge does not exist, we simply set the point equal to $\mathbf{p}_0$, which is the intersection point with the red path. The other dotted edges can be treated analogously, resulting in the remaining three intersection points:

$$\mathbf{p}_1 = \text{Intersection with } E_{1 \to 5}, \text{ otherwise } \mathbf{p}_0 \,,$$

$$\mathbf{p}_3 = \text{Intersection with } E_{2 \to 6}, \text{ otherwise } \mathbf{p}_2 \,,$$

$$\mathbf{p}_5 = \text{Intersection with } E_{3 \to 4}, \text{ otherwise } \mathbf{p}_4 \,.$$

We have now determined all six intersection points of the plane with the box in a sequence that forms a valid polygon. It is easy to check that the same sequence works fine if the front edge or the front face of the box is coplanar with the viewing plane. We simply select one of the front vertices as $\mathbf{v}_0$ and set $\mathbf{v}_7$ to the opposite corner. Remember that we ignore any intersections with an edge that is coplanar with the plane.

3.5.3 Implementation

The algorithm for computing the correct sequence of intersection points as described in the previous section can be implemented as a vertex program in Listing 3.10. The program has been designed for slicing a high number of equally-sized and equally-oriented boxes with a stack of equidistant planes. Care has been taken to minimize the number of state changes and the amount of data transferred to the graphics board for each frame.

The input stream of vertices for one intersection polygon is specified in Listing 3.11. The x-coordinate of the vertex is an index that speci-

```
glBegin(GL_POLYGON);
    glVertex2i(0, nPlaneIndex);
    glVertex2i(1, nPlaneIndex);
    glVertex2i(2, nPlaneIndex);
    glVertex2i(3, nPlaneIndex);
    glVertex2i(4, nPlaneIndex);
    glVertex2i(5, nPlaneIndex);
glEnd();
```

Listing 3.11. OpenGL example vertex stream for calculating one intersection polygon: stores the indexes of the intersection point to be calculated and of the plane. The vertex stream is stored in a vertex buffer for maximum efficiency.

fies which of the six possible intersection points should be computed. The y-coordinate of the vertex is the index of the plane that is used for intersection. As the plane index is constant for one polygon, it could alternatively be specified as a separate parameter in the vertex stream (e.g., as texture coordinate). However, current hardware implementations do not support vertices that have only one coordinate, so we incorporate the plane index into the y-coordinate of the vertex.

In this implementation, we assume that all the boxes have the same size and orientation, although simple modifications to the program will allow arbitrary size and orientation at the cost of a slightly larger number of state changes. In our case, each box consists of the same set of vertices and a translation vector `vecTranslate`. The translation vector is specified once for each box to be rendered. The vertices of one box are kept in a constant uniform vector array `vecVertices[8]` and will not be changed at all.

Besides the usual modelview projection matrix, we specify for each frame the index of the front vertex with respect to the viewing direction in the uniform parameter `frontIndex`. Because all our boxes are equally oriented, the front index will not change during one frame. Additionally, we set the uniform parameters `vecView` to the normal vector $\mathbf{n}_P$ of the plane and `dPlaneIncr` to the distance between two adjacent planes. The correct distance d for the plane equation is computed as the variable `dPlaneDist`.

The constant uniform index array `nSequence` stores the permutation of vertex indices with respect to the given index of the front vertex `frontIndex`. As described in the previous section, several edges must be checked for intersection in sequence, according to the index of the intersection point.

In order to calculate the intersection points $\mathbf{p}_1$, $\mathbf{p}_3$, and $\mathbf{p}_5$, we must first check for an intersection with the dotted edge, and if this intersection does not exist we must check for intersection with the corresponding path (solid line, Figure 3.14). Hence, the maximum number of edges that must be tested for intersection is four. This is done within the `for` loop. For the intersection points $\mathbf{p}_0$, $\mathbf{p}_2$, or $\mathbf{p}_4$, we have to check only three edges. In this case, the program breaks out of the `for` loop when the intersection point is found after a maximum of three iterations.

The two constant index arrays `v1` and `v2` store the indices of start and end vertices of the edges that must be tested successively for intersection. They are indexed by the intersection index `Vin.x` from the vertex stream in combination with the current iteration count `e`.

At first, the program computes the correct vertex indices of the edge that must be tested for intersection. The vertices are fetched from the constant uniform array `vecVertices`. Subsequently, we compute the correct start point and the edge vector for the current edge, taking into account the local translation of the box. The denominator `denom` from Equation 3.6 is computed. If the denominator is unequal zero (which means that the edge is not coplanar with the plane), the `lambda` value for the edge is computed as in Equation 3.6. Finally, we test if we have a valid intersection. If this is true, the program breaks out of the `for` loop. The resulting intersection point is transformed into screen space, and texture coordinates for the vertex are calculated. The texture coordinates in this example are obtained by scaling and biasing the vertex position to the range $[0, 1]$. Alternatively, texture coordinates could be specified by another uniform parameter similar to `vecVertices`.

This admittedly intricate implementation allows one box to be intersected with several parallel planes using one single function call that feeds a predefined vertex buffer into the graphics pipeline.

3.6   Further Reading

The types of proxy geometry used in this chapter are all based on planar slices. This implies that the sampling rate in perspective projection will inevitably increase toward the edges of the image. This might result in noticeable artifacts if the field-of-view angle is relatively large. Constant sampling rate for perspective projection can only be achieved by the use of spherical rendering primitives instead of slices as proposed by LaMar et al. [152]. Rendering spherical shells is only applicable in combination with 3D texture mapping. In most practical cases, however, the improvement of the image quality does not outweigh the computational cost for the tessellation of spherical primitives.

Large field-of-view angles are usually applied in virtual fly-through applications. An interesting algorithm especially designed for navigation within the volume has been proposed by Brady et al. [17]. It is based on CPU ray casting accelerated by 2D texture mapping.

Besides the presented vertex program for cube-plane intersection, there also exist efficient programs for slicing other types of cells. Lensch et al. [160] describe a slicing procedure for triangular prisms. Reck et al. [219] demonstrate how tetrahedra can be sliced in a vertex program.

4

Transfer Functions

F OR SOLVING THE LIGHT-TRANSFER EQUATIONS from Chapter 1, we need to know the optical properties, such as the emission and absorption coefficients, at each point inside the volume. In the previous chapter, we assumed that we are given these coefficients directly, and we examined different implementations that compute the volume-rendering integral.

In scientific visualization, however, we are given a volumetric data set that contains abstract scalar data values that represent some spatially varying physical property. In general, there is no natural way to obtain emission and absorption coefficients from such data. Instead, the user must decide how the different structures in the data should look by assigning optical properties to the data values using arbitrary mappings. This mapping is called a *transfer function*. This process of finding an appropriate transfer function is often referred to as *classification*.[1]

4.1 Classification

In the context of volume visualization, classification is defined as *the process of identifying features of interest based on abstract data values*. Classification is essentially a pattern-recognition problem. Different patterns found in raw data are assigned to specific categories, or *classes*. An overview of

---

[1] The use of the term *classification* in the literature might be confusing. Sometimes, classification is used as a synonym for applying a transfer function. Other places in the literature use the term classification to refer to a pattern-recognition process, such as segmentation. Even though we want to differentiate between the process of identifying different regions in the data and the process of specifying optical properties to those regions, for brevity the terms *pre-classification* and *post-classification* will be used to refer to pre-interpolative and post-interpolative transfer functions, respectively.

general theory and popular methods can be found in the classic text by
Duda, Hart, and Stork [53].

Traditionally, the transfer function is not thought of as a feature classi-
fier at all. Often, it is simply viewed as a function that takes the domain of
the input data and transforms it to the range of red, green, blue, and alpha.
With the evolution of volume visualization, however, transfer function design is going far beyond a simple color-table set-up. Transfer functions are
used to identify specific patterns and assign them to ranges of values in the
source data that correspond to features of interest.

In addition to the emission and absorption coefficients, we will see a
variety of other optical properties, such as reflectivity or translucency coefficients, in the forthcoming chapters. All of them can be derived from the
original scalar data using transfer functions. Although a few approaches
exist to automatically generate transfer functions by some image- or data-
driven mechanisms [123], the design of a transfer function in general is a
manual, tedious, and time-consuming procedure, which requires detailed
knowledge of the spatial structures that are represented by the data set.
In order to facilitate this assignment process, it is crucial for the user to
be provided with direct visual feedback of his action. In consequence, implementations must allow the transfer function to be modified in real time
while continuously rendering the volume.

In the previous chapters, we stored the optical properties directly in
the volume. There are at least two reasons why this is not advisable in
practice. First, it is inefficient to update the entire volume each time the
transfer function changes. Second, evaluating the transfer function (assigning optical properties) at each sample point prior to data interpolation
(i.e., texture filtering) might violate the sampling theorem and cause strong
visual artifacts. Both problems are addressed in this chapter.

4.1.1 Principles

Although analytic descriptions of continuous functions are applicable in
theory, almost all practical volume graphics applications use a discretized
version of the transfer function, implemented as a look-up table of fixed size.
The emitted radiance c_i (Equation 1.13) is represented as an RGB value to
allow for the emission of colored light. The opacity $(1 - T_i)$ (Equation 1.12)
is represented by a scalar value between 0 and 1. We have already seen in
Chapter 3 that both coefficients can be combined into one RGBA quadruplet.

Discrete volume data is usually represented by a 3D array of sample
points. According to sampling theory, a continuous signal can be reconstructed from these sampling points by convolution with an appropriate
reconstruction filter kernel. Sampling theory thus allows us to reconstruct
as much of the original continuous data as necessary to create images in

a desired screen-space resolution. The transfer function can either be applied directly to the discrete sampling points before the reconstruction (pre-interpolative) or alternatively to the signal reconstructed in screen-space resolution (post-interpolative). Both methods lead to different visual results. Accordingly, there are two possible ways to perform the assignment in hardware, which differ in the positioning of the table look-up with respect to the graphics pipeline. Implementations of color-table look-ups strongly depend on the underlying hardware architecture. Multiple different hardware implementations are described later in this chapter.

4.1.2 Pre-Interpolative Transfer Functions

Pre-interpolative mapping denotes the application of a transfer function to the discrete sample points before the data interpolation. The reconstruction of the signal in screen-space resolution is performed subsequently based on the emission and absorption values. Figure 4.1 (left) outlines this concept. The transfer function is here represented as the graph of a 1D function. In practice, several of these curves would be used to describe individual transfer functions for each of the RGBA components separately. The original sampling values on the x-axis are mapped to emission and absorption values on the y-axis. As displayed in the diagram, the emission and absorption coefficients for a sample point that does not lie on an exact grid position is determined by interpolating between the emission and absorption coefficients given at the neighboring grid points.

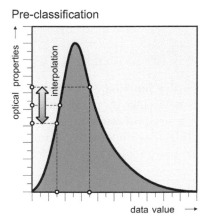 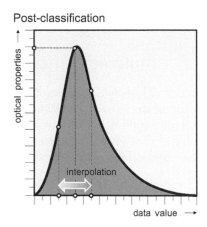

Figure 4.1. Transfer functions are used to map data values to physical quantities, which describe the emission and absorption of light. This mapping can be applied either before the interpolation (pre-classification) or after the interpolation of data values (post-classification), leading to different visual results.

With respect to the graphics pipeline, pre-interpolative mapping means that the color-table look-up is performed before or during the rasterization step, however in any case before the texture filtering step. The transfer function is applied to every texel before interpolation. The advantage of this concept is that an implementation of a pre-classification table is possible on almost every graphics hardware. Before we examine and evaluate different implementations, we will have a look at the alternative concept of post-classification.

4.1.3   Post-Interpolative Transfer Functions

Post-classification reverses the order of operations. Transfer function application is performed after the reconstruction in screen space. The classification function is thus applied to the continuous signal instead of its discrete sampling points. This idea is illustrated in Figure 4.1 (right). For a sample point that does not lie on an exact grid position, the data value itself is interpolated. Subsequently, the emission and absorption values are determined by using the interpolated data value as index into the color look-up table. It is easy to see in Figure 4.1 that pre- and post-classification lead to different results. Both alternatives will be evaluated and discussed in Section 4.4.

In the following sections, we will examine several ways of implementing transfer functions that work together with all the texture-based approaches described in Chapter 3. Both pre- and post-interpolative transfer functions are discussed. Our main objective is to implement a fast color-table update, allowing the transfer function to be modified in real time.

4.2   Implementation of Pre-Classification

As defined above, a pre-interpolative transfer function is applied a priori to the texture images. Although there is no technical restriction that forbids the application of a color table as a pre-processing step, it is very unlikely that such an implementation will achieve interactive frame rates while updating the transfer function. The reason for this is twofold:

- A modification of the transfer function would require a reconstruction of the whole volume in main memory and a reload of the texture image into the local video memory of the graphics board. This will inevitably result in a memory bandwidth bottleneck, which significantly degrades performance.

- For storing the emission (color) and absorption (opacity) values directly in the texture, an internal RGBA format is required that allocates four bytes per texel. An index into a color table, however, would only require one or two bytes per texel. As a result, using color indices significantly reduces both the memory footprint and the bandwidth problem.

4.2.1 Pixel Transfer

The standard OpenGL specification provides a way to apply a color map during the pixel transfer from main memory to the graphics board. This is exactly what is done when a texture image is defined and transferred to the graphics board. Because changing the color table requires uploading the texture again, this is of course not a very fast way to apply the transfer function. However, for graphics hardware that does not support some of the OpenGL extensions described in the following chapters, it represents the only way to achieve the color mapping. The OpenGL code for setting up the pixel transfer is displayed in Listing 4.1.

Besides the poor performance, the main drawback of this approach is again the amount of data that must be allocated in local video memory. Although only the scalar data values are stored in main memory, the pixel transfer converts every scalar value into an RGBA quadruplet when writing it into the portion of video memory that is allocated for the texture image. As a result, the size of the data that must be stored increases by a factor of four in the worst case. To work around this problem, some hardware manufacturers have decided to implement a mechanism that allows for the storage of color indices in the texture image together with a separate color table. This concept is known as *paletted textures.*

```
// enable and set up pixel transfer
glPixelTransferi(GL_MAP_COLOR, GL_TRUE);
glPixelMapfv(GL_PIXEL_MAP_I_TO_R, m_nTableSize, m_pColorMapR);
glPixelMapfv(GL_PIXEL_MAP_I_TO_G, m_nTableSize, m_pColorMapG);
glPixelMapfv(GL_PIXEL_MAP_I_TO_B, m_nTableSize, m_pColorMapB);
glPixelMapfv(GL_PIXEL_MAP_I_TO_A, m_nTableSize, m_pColorMapA);

// (re-)create texture image
glTexImage3D(...);

// disable pixel transfer
glPixelTransferi(GL_MAP_COLOR, GL_FALSE);
```

Listing 4.1. OpenGL set-up for color mapping during the pixel transfer from main memory to the local texture memory.

4.2.2   Paletted Textures

Similar to many 2D image file formats that include a color table, texture palettes can significantly reduce the memory that must be allocated for storing the texture on the graphics board. Additionally, this feature can be used to implement coloring effects by modifying the color palette without the necessity of modifying the texture object itself. Instead of storing the RGBA values for each texel, an index into a color look-up table of fixed size is used. This color table is stored together with the index texture in local video memory. During the texture-generation step, the indices are replaced by the respective color values stored in the texture palette. It is important to notice that the color-table look-up is located before the usual texture generation. The interpolation is performed after the look-up using the color values obtained from the look-up table, resulting in a pre-interpolative transfer function. The amount of local video memory that must be allocated for storing an RGBA texture is significantly reduced, as only a single index value must be stored for each texel, instead of four values for the four color components. Taking into account the memory that is allocated for the texture palette itself, the required texture memory is thus reduced almost by a factor of four.

The access to texture palettes is controlled by two separate OpenGL extensions. The first extension EXT_paletted_texture enables the use of texture palettes in general. A paletted texture is created in the same way as a conventional RGBA texture. The only difference is that, during texture specification, the internal format of RGBA (GL_RGBA) must be substituted by an indexed format, such as GL_COLOR_INDEX8_EXT, GL_COLOR_INDEX12_EXT, or GL_COLOR_INDEX16_EXT according to the intended size of the color table

```
#if defined GL_EXT_shared_texture_palette

  glEnable(GL_SHARED_TEXTURE_PALETTE_EXT);
  glColorTableEXT(
    GL_SHARED_TEXTURE_PALETTE_EXT, // GLenum target
    GL_RGBA,                       // GLenum internal format
    m_nColorTableSize,             // GLsizei size of the table
    GL_RGBA,                       // GLenum external format
    GL_UNSIGNED_BYTE,              // GLenum data type
    m_pColorTable);                // const GLvoid *table

#endif // GL_EXT_shared_texture_palette
```

Listing 4.2.   OpenGL set-up for the paletted texture extension.

(see [35] for details). Although the specification of this extension defines texture palettes with a resolution of 1, 2, 4, 8, 12, or 16 bits, resolutions larger than 8 bits are rarely supported by existing hardware. In this case, a unique texture palette must be maintained for each texture separately. A second OpenGL extension named GL_EXT_shared_texture_palette additionally allows a texture palette to be shared by multiple texture objects. This further reduces the memory footprint for a volume data set, if 2D textures or 2D multitextures are used or if a 3D texture is split up into several bricks. The OpenGL code for creating and updating a shared texture palette is displayed in Listing 4.2.

Compared with the pixel-transfer method described in the previous section, the main advantage of the shared texture palettes is the ability to change the texture palette—and thus the transfer function—without having to reload the texture itself. In addition, the palette sizes of 12 or 16 bits enable high-precision transfer functions for tomographic data. As a result, the most efficient way of implementing pre-interpolative transfer functions is to use paletted textures. Unfortunately, at the time of the writing of this book, an up-to-date consumer-level graphics board that supports paletted textures does not exist. The described OpenGL extension was supported by older NVIDIA GPUs (up to GeForce 3), but it is not available on the new architectures.

4.3 Implementation of Post-Classification

Implementing a post-interpolative transfer function requires a mechanism to realize a color-table look-up after the texture sample is interpolated in screen space. Using the programmable fragment processor, implementing such a color-table look-up at fragment level is straightforward.

4.3.1 Dependent Textures

The dependent texture mechanism outlined in Section 2.3.1 can efficiently be used to implement a color-table look-up at fragment level. To achieve this, the color indices of the voxels are stored as luminance values in the first multitexture (which can be a 2D or 3D texture). The second multitexture is defined as a 1D texture, which has the same resolution as the color table. During rasterization, the color index obtained from the first texture is used as texture coordinate for the second texture, which stores the color table. The resulting RGBA quadruplet now represents a color value obtained via post-interpolative index look-up. A code example is given in Listing 4.3.

```
// fragment program for post-classification
// using 3D textures
half4 main (half3 texUV : TEXCOORD0,
            uniform sampler3D volume_texture,
            uniform sampler1D transfer_function) :  COLOR
{
    half index = tex3D(volume_texture, texUV);
    half4 result = tex1D(transfer_function, index);
    return result;
}
```

```
// fragment program for post-classification
// using 2D multitextures
half4 main (half3 texUV : TEXCOORD0,
            uniform sampler2D slice_texture0,
            uniform sampler2D slice_texture1,
            uniform sampler1D transfer_function) :  COLOR
{
    half index0 = tex2D(slice_texture0, texUV.xy);
    half index1 = tex2D(slice_texture1, texUV.xy);
    half index  = lerp(index0, index1, texUV.z);
    half4 result = tex1D(transfer_function, index);
    return result;
}
```

Listing 4.3.   Fragment programs for post-classifications via dependent texture look-up in Cg. The upper listing uses 3D textures. The lower listing uses 2D multi-texture interpolation.

The major benefit of dependent textures compared with all the other implementations is that also higher-dimensional transfer functions can be realized with this concept. We will focus our interest on multidimensional transfer functions in Section 10.2.

4.3.2   Texture Color Tables

There exists an older OpenGL extension named SGI_texture_color_table, which goes back to the era before graphics hardware became fully programmable. This rarely supported extension has been designed specifically for post-interpolative texture look-up. The mechanism to set up the tex-

```
#if defined GL_SGI_texture_color_table

    glEnable(GL_TEXTURE_COLOR_TABLE_SGI);
    glColorTableSGI(
        GL_TEXTURE_COLOR_TABLE_SGI,   // GLenum target
        GL_RGBA,                      // GLenum internal format
        m_nColorTableSize,            // GLsizei size of the table
        GL_RGBA,                      // GLenum external format
        GL_UNSIGNED_BYTE,             // GLenum data type
        m_pColorTable);               // const GLvoid *table

#endif // GL_SGI_texture_color_table
```

Listing 4.4. OpenGL set-up for the texture color-table extension. Although this code fragment is very similar to the paletted-texture set-up in Listing 4.2, in this case the color-table look-up is performed after the interpolation of texture samples.

ture look-up table is similar to paletted textures. The extension must be enabled, and a color table must be set up as described in Listing 4.4. Although this code looks very similar to the code presented in Listing 4.2, here the color-table look-up is performed after the texture interpolation. The texture color table, which is enabled by this extension, is not restricted to a specific texture object, so it can be efficiently shared among multiple texture images.

4.4 Pre- versus Post-Interpolative Transfer Functions

A transfer function usually tries to separate different objects inside the volume data set according to their scalar value. Due to the band limitation of the voxel data set, however, sharp boundaries between different objects do not exist in the data. Thus, trying to display objects as isosurfaces with a sharp peak of infinite frequency in the transfer function is not appropriate to represent the fuzzy boundary. The transfer function of course should account for this fuzziness and simultaneously be able to separate tiny detail structures. A good transfer function will be a compromise between a sharp edge and a smooth transition between different objects.

We have seen two different ways of applying a transfer function for direct volume rendering. Pre-classification applies the transfer function for each sample point on the data grid before interpolation. Contrary, post-classification evaluates the transfer function for each sample point in screen space after the filtering step. The question of which is the *correct* way of applying a transfer function caused much discussion a couple of years ago.

If we compare the visual quality of pre- and post-classification, the answer is simple. The two images in Figure 4.2 have been created with exactly the same sampling rate and the same transfer function. The left image uses pre-classification, while the right image uses post-classification. The left image is cluttered with lots of blocky artifacts, which seem to arise from the underlying data grid. In order to explain these disturbing visual artifacts, we have to look again at sampling theory.

In all our volume-rendering approaches, we assume that the discrete samples of a voxel data set represent a continuous 3D scalar field. We also assume that the sampling theory has guided the discretization of the data set, which means that the grid size has been chosen according to the maximal frequency component inherent in the data. Without loss of generality, let us restrict our considerations to a continuous 1D signal that is obtained by casting a ray through the volume. According to sampling theory, a continuous signal $f(x)$ can be exactly reconstructed from discrete values $f(k \cdot \tau)$ sampled at a step size τ, according to

$$f(x) = \sum_k f(k \cdot \tau) \cdot \mathrm{sinc}\left(\frac{1}{\tau}(x - k\tau)\right), \qquad k \in \mathbb{N} \qquad (4.1)$$

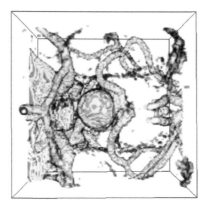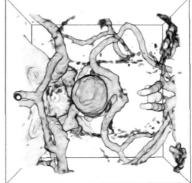

Figure 4.2. Comparison of pre- (left) and post-classification (right) of a CTA data set using a transfer function of high frequency. Both images were generated with exactly the same transfer function and with exactly the same number of slice images. The pre-classified image is rather disturbing due to its blocky artifacts. The volumetric shapes are much better represented by the high frequency of the transfer function applied as post-classification.

Obviously, the application of a transfer function T to the discrete sampling points instead of the continuous signal yield different results:

$$T\big(f(x)\big) \;\neq\; \sum_k T\big(f(k\cdot\tau)\big)\cdot\mathrm{sinc}\Big(\frac{1}{\tau}(x-k\tau)\Big). \qquad (4.2)$$

Figure 4.3 illustrates the difference between pre- and post-classification with respect to sampling and reconstruction. The left column shows an example of an original continuous signal and a box transfer function applied to it, resulting in the modified signal shown at the bottom. The original signal, however, must be discretized to be processed in digital computing devices. Digitization leads to the discretized signal shown in the top row. If we reconstruct this signal with linear interpolation (tent filter), we will

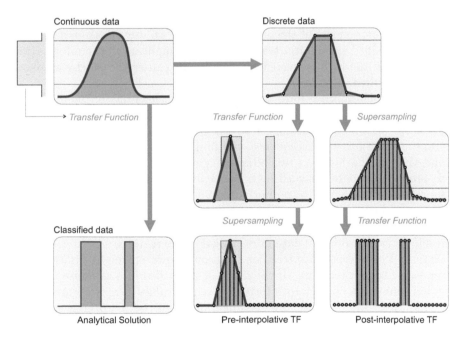

Figure 4.3.   Comparison of pre- (left) and post-interpolative transfer functions (right) with respect to sampling and reconstruction using a box transfer function, which contains infinite frequencies. The original continuous data is first discretized. Pre-interpolative look-up applies the transfer function first and reconstructs the signal in screen space afterwards. It cannot account for the additional high frequencies introduced by the transfer function. Post-interpolative look-up first reconstructs the signal in screen space and applies the transfer function afterwards. The result is much closer to the analytical solution, because it much better represents the high frequencies of the transfer function.

obtain a piecewise linear approximation of the original signal. Here we see the difference between pre- and post-classification. Pre-classification (as shown in the middle column) first applies the transfer function on the discrete samples, replacing every sample point by its classified value. Afterwards, the signal is reconstructed in screen space by supersampling with linear interpolation. If we compare the result to the analytic continuous solution, we see that the shape of the signal is poorly approximated. Note that the second narrow peak in the analytical solution is completely missing in the pre-classified signal. Post-classification first reconstructs the original signal in screen resolution by supersampling and linear interpolation. The transfer function is then applied for every sample in screen space and the resulting signal is much closer to the analytic solution. The reason for this is that the transfer function introduces additional high-frequency components into the result signals, such as the sharp edges in the example. The data grid used during discretization, however, only accounts for the frequency components of the original signal. If we use the same data grid for the classified signal after transfer function application, the information contained in the high frequencies is lost. This causes the blocky artifacts seen in Figure 4.2.

As a conclusion, we have seen that the transfer function modifies the frequency spectrum of the original scalar field. The original data grid does not account for the high-frequency components introduced by the transfer function. In consequence, the number of slices must be increased and the spacing between two adjacent slices must be decreased in order to properly account for such high frequencies. Post-interpolative transfer functions must be used to properly evaluate the classified signal in screen-space resolution. Pre-interpolative transfer functions are not capable of removing aliasing artifacts because the classified signal is evaluated in the resolution of the original data grid instead of the required screen-space resolution. Pre-interpolative transfer functions, however, might be useful for rendering segmented data. If the data set is divided into separate regions, it is usually not correct to interpolate scalar values across segmentation boundaries. In this case, pre-classification might be a working solution. Rendering techniques for segmented data are discussed in Chapter 16.

4.5   Pre-Integrated Transfer Functions

As we have seen before, the transfer function introduces additional high-frequency components into the signal that can cause aliasing artifacts during ray integration. A high frequency in the transfer function is easily introduced by using a simple step-transfer function with steep slope. Such transfer functions are very common in many application domains. To capture these high frequencies, oversampling (i.e., additional slice polygons or sampling points) must be added. In turn, they directly decrease performance.

Classification employs transfer functions for color densities $q(s)$ and extinction densities $\kappa(s)$, which map scalar values $s = s(\mathbf{x})$ to colors and extinction coefficients. In order to overcome the limitations discussed above, the approximation of the volume-rendering integral has to be improved. In fact, many improvements have been proposed, e.g., higher-order integration schemes [199, 39], adaptive sampling (see Section 9.1.2), etc. However, these methods do not explicitly address the problem of high Nyquist frequencies (see Section 9.1.1) of the color after the classification $q\big(s(\mathbf{x})\big)$ and an extinction coefficient after the classification $\kappa\big(s(\mathbf{x})\big)$ resulting from nonlinear transfer functions. On the other hand, the goal of *pre-integrated classification* [226, 64] is to split the numerical integration into two integrations: one for the continuous scalar field $s(\mathbf{x})$ and one for each of the transfer functions $q(s)$ and $\kappa(s)$ in order to avoid the problematic product of Nyquist frequencies [135].

The first step is the sampling of the continuous scalar field $s(\mathbf{x})$ along a viewing ray. Note that the Nyquist frequency for this sampling is not affected by the transfer functions. For the purpose of pre-integrated classification, the sampled values define a 1D, piecewise linear scalar field. The volume-rendering integral for this piecewise linear scalar field is efficiently computed by one table look-up for each linear segment. The three arguments of the table look-up are the scalar value at the start (front) of the segment $s_f := s\big(\mathbf{x}(id)\big)$, the scalar value at the end (back) of the segment $s_b := s\big(\mathbf{x}((i+1)d)\big)$, and the length of the segment d (see Figure 4.4). More

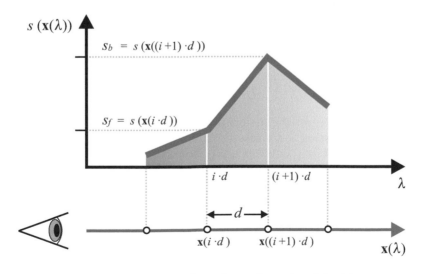

Figure 4.4. Scheme for determining the color and opacity of the ith ray segment.

precisely spoken, the opacity α_i of the ith segment is approximated by

$$
\begin{aligned}
\alpha_i &= 1 - \exp\left(-\int_{i\,d}^{(i+1)d} \kappa\Big(s\big(\mathbf{x}(\lambda)\big)\Big)d\lambda\right) \\
&\approx 1 - \exp\left(-\int_0^1 \kappa\big((1-w)s_f + ws_b\big)d\,dw\right).
\end{aligned}
\tag{4.3}
$$

Thus, α_i is a function of s_f, s_b, and d (or of s_f and s_b, if the length of a segment is constant). The (associated) colors c_i are approximated correspondingly:

$$
\begin{aligned}
c_i &\approx \int_0^1 q\big((1-w)s_f + ws_b\big) \\
&\quad \times \exp\left(-\int_0^w \kappa\big((1-w')s_f + w's_b\big)d\,dw'\right)d\,dw.
\end{aligned}
\tag{4.4}
$$

Analogous to α_i, c_i is a function of s_f, s_b, and d. Thus, pre-integrated classification calculates the volume-rendering integral by evaluating the equation

$$
I \approx \sum_{i=0}^{n} c_i \prod_{j=0}^{i-1}(1 - \alpha_j)
$$

with colors c_i pre-computed according to Equation 4.4 and opacities α_i pre-computed according to Equation 4.3. For a nonassociated color-transfer function $\tilde{q}(s)$, i.e., when substituting $q(s)$ by $\tau(s)\tilde{q}(s)$, we will also employ Equation 4.3 for the approximation of α_i and the following approximation of the associated color $c_i^{(\kappa)}$:

$$
\begin{aligned}
c_i^{(\kappa)} &\approx \int_0^1 \kappa\big((1-w)s_f + ws_b\big)\tilde{q}\big((1-w)s_f + ws_b\big) \\
&\quad \times \exp\left(-\int_0^w \kappa\big((1-w')s_f + w's_b\big)d\,dw'\right)d\,dw.
\end{aligned}
\tag{4.5}
$$

Note that pre-integrated classification always computes associated colors, regardless of whether a transfer function for associated colors $q(s)$ or for nonassociated colors $\tilde{q}(s)$ is employed.

In either case, pre-integrated classification allows us to sample a continuous scalar field $s(\mathbf{x})$ without increasing the sampling rate for any nonlinear transfer function. Therefore, pre-integrated classification has the potential to improve the accuracy (less undersampling) and the performance (fewer samples) of a volume renderer at the same time.

One of the major disadvantages of the pre-integrated classification is the need to integrate a large number of ray segments for each new transfer function dependent on the front and back scalar value and the ray-segment length. Consequently, an interactive modification of the transfer function is not possible in all cases. Therefore, several modifications to the computation of the ray segments were proposed [64] that lead to an enormous speed-up of the integration calculations by employing integral functions.

Integral functions are used to facilitate the calculation of the integrals in Equations 4.3, 4.4, and 4.5 for all combinations of scalar values s_f and s_b. The integral of a function $f(x)$,

$$F(x) = \int_a^b f(x)\, \mathrm{d}x\,, \qquad (4.6)$$

for arbitrary values of a and b can be calculated using integral functions $K(s)$,

$$G(s) = \int_0^s f(x)\, \mathrm{d}x\,, \qquad (4.7)$$

according to

$$F(x) = G(b) - G(a)\,. \qquad (4.8)$$

To our pre-integration method, this means that we only have to evaluate an integral function $G(s)$ for all scalar values. The integrals for all combinations of scalar values s_f and s_b can then be obtained by computing differences according to Equation 4.8. Equation 4.3 can be rewritten as

$$
\begin{aligned}
\alpha_i &\approx 1 - \exp\left(-\int_0^1 \kappa\big((1-w)s_f + w s_b\big)d\, \mathrm{d}w\right). \\
&= 1 - \exp\left(-\frac{d}{s_b - s_f}\int_{s_f}^{s_b}\kappa(s)\mathrm{d}s\right) \qquad (4.9) \\
&= 1 - \exp\left(-\frac{d}{s_b - s_f}\big(T(s_b) - T(s_f)\big)\right). \qquad (4.10)
\end{aligned}
$$

using the integral function

$$T(s) = \int_0^s \kappa(s')\, \mathrm{d}s'\,. \qquad (4.11)$$

Using integral functions to calculate Equation 4.4 requires neglecting the self-attenuation within a ray segment, i.e, the exponential term. Yet, it is a common approximation for post-classification and well justified for small products $\kappa(s)\,d$. Equation 4.4 can thus be approximated by

$$c_i \;\approx\; \int_0^1 q\big((1-\omega)s_f + \omega s_b\big)d\;\mathrm{d}\omega. \tag{4.12}$$

$$= \;\frac{d}{s_b - s_f} \int_{s_f}^{s_b} q(s)\mathrm{d}s \tag{4.13}$$

$$= \;\frac{d}{s_b - s_f}\big(K(s_b) - K(s_f)\big). \tag{4.14}$$

with an integral function

$$K(s) = \int_0^s q(s')\,\mathrm{d}s'. \tag{4.15}$$

An approximation for Equation 4.5 using integral functions can be found in the thesis by Martin Kraus [135].

The dimensionality of the look-up table can easily be reduced by assuming constant ray segment lengths d. This assumption is correct for orthogonal projections and view-aligned proxy geometry. It is a good approximation for perspective projections and view-aligned proxy geometry, as long as extreme perspectives are avoided. The assumption is correct for perspective projections and shell-based proxy geometry.

4.6   Implementation of Pre-Integrated Transfer Functions

In the following GPU implementation, 2D look-up tables for the pre-integrated ray segments are employed. As we assume a constant ray segment length, those look-up tables are only dependent on s_f and s_b. First we compute a look-up texture that stores pre-integrated ray segments for all possible combinations of s_f and s_b. The C code in Listing 4.5 computes a 256×256 pre-integration look-up texture from an 8-bit RGBA transfer function using integral functions.

Note that, for transfer functions with higher precision, the pre-integration texture becomes quite large. For example, a 12-bit transfer function results in a 4096×4096 texture, which consumes 64 MB of memory. To prevent having to compute and store such large look-up textures, it is possible to shift the integral functions–based integral computation into the fragment processing stage on the GPU. For this, the integral functions are stored in a single 1D RGBA texture. During rendering, we perform two look-ups with s_f and s_b as texture coordinates into this integral function

```c
void createPreintegrationTable(GLubyte* Table) {
  double r=0.,g=0.,b=0.,a=0.;  int rcol, gcol, bcol, acol;
  double rInt[256],gInt[256],bInt[256],aInt[256];
  GLubyte lookupImg[256*256*4];  int smin,smax,preintName;
  double factor;  int lookupindex = 0;
  rInt[0] = 0.;gInt[0] = 0.;bInt[0] = 0.;aInt[0] = 0.;
  // compute integral functions
  for (int i=1;i<256;i++) {
      tauc =  (Table[(i-1)*4+3]+Table[i*4+3])/2.;
      r = r + (Table[(i-1)*4+0]+Table[i*4+0])/2.*tauc/255.;
      g = g + (Table[(i-1)*4+1]+Table[i*4+1])/2.*tauc/255.;
      b = b + (Table[(i-1)*4+2]+Table[i*4+2])/2.*tauc/255.;
      a = a + tauc;
      rInt[i] = r;gInt[i] = g;bInt[i] = b;aInt[i] = a; }
  // compute look-up table from integral functions
  for (int sb=0;sb<256;sb++)
      for (int sf=0;sf<256;sf++) {
          if (sb < sf) { smin = sb;smax = sf; }
          else { smin = sf;smax = sb; }
          if (smax != smin) {
              factor = 1.  / (double)(smax - smin);
              rcol = (rInt[smax] - rInt[smin]) * factor;
              gcol = (gInt[smax] - gInt[smin]) * factor;
              bcol = (bInt[smax] - bInt[smin]) * factor;
              acol = 256.*
              (1.-exp(-(aInt[smax]-aInt[smin])*factor/255.));
          } else {
              factor = 1.  / 255.;
              rcol = Table[smin*4+0]*Table[smin*4+3]*factor;
              gcol = Table[smin*4+1]*Table[smin*4+3]*factor;
              bcol = Table[smin*4+2]*Table[smin*4+3]*factor;
              acol = (1.-exp(-Table[smin*4+3]*1./255.))*256.; }
          lookupImg[lookupindex++] = clamp(rcol,0,255);
          lookupImg[lookupindex++] = clamp(gcol,0,255);
          lookupImg[lookupindex++] = clamp(bcol,0,255);
          lookupImg[lookupindex++] = clamp(acol,0,255); }
  // create texture
  glGenTextures(1,&preintName);
  glBindTexture(GL_TEXTURE_2D,preintName);
  glTexImage2D(GL_TEXTURE_2D, 0, GL_RGBA, 256, 256, 0,
               GL_RGBA, GL_UNSIGNED_BYTE, &lookupImg);
  glTexParameteri(GL_TEXTURE_2D, GL_TEXTURE_WRAP_S, GL_CLAMP_TO_EDGE);
  glTexParameteri(GL_TEXTURE_2D, GL_TEXTURE_WRAP_T, GL_CLAMP_TO_EDGE);
  glTexParameteri(GL_TEXTURE_2D, GL_TEXTURE_MIN_FILTER, GL_LINEAR);
  glTexParameteri(GL_TEXTURE_2D, GL_TEXTURE_MAG_FILTER, GL_LINEAR);
}
```

Listing 4.5. C code for computing a 256×256 pre-integration look-up texture from an 8-bit transfer function using integral functions.

```
// Pre-integration vertex program in Cg
struct appin {
    float4 Position :  POSITION;
    float4 TCoords0 :  TEXCOORD0;
};
struct v2f {
    float4 HPosition :  POSITION;
    float4 TCoords0 :  TEXCOORD0;
    float4 TCoords1 :  TEXCOORD1;
};
v2f main(
    appin IN,
    uniform float4x4 ModelViewProj,
    uniform float4x4 ModelView,
    uniform float4x4 ModelViewI,
    uniform float4x4 TexMatrix,
    uniform float SliceDistance)
{
    v2f OUT;
    // compute texture coordinate for sF
    OUT.TCoords0 = mul(TexMatrix, IN.TCoords0);

    // transform view pos and view dir to obj space
    float4 vPosition = float4(0,0,0,1);
    vPosition = mul(ModelViewI, vPosition);
    float4 vDir = float4(0.f,0.f,-1.f,1.f);
    vDir = normalize(mul(ModelViewI, vDir));

    // compute position of sB
    float4 eyeToVert = normalize(IN.Position - vPosition);
    float4 sB = IN.Position
      - eyeToVert * (SliceDistance / dot(vDir, eyeToVert));

    // compute texture coordinate for sB
    OUT.TCoords1 = mul(TexMatrix, sB);

    // transform vertex position into homogeneous clip space
    OUT.HPosition = mul(ModelViewProj, IN.Position);
    return OUT;
}
```

Listing 4.6. A vertex program for pre-integration in Cg that computes the texture coordinate for s_b from the given texture coordinate for s_f.

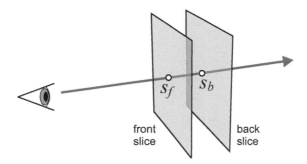

Figure 4.5. A slab of the volume between two slices. The scalar value on the front (back) slice for a particular viewing ray is called s_f (s_b).

texture and compute the integral on-the-fly. Consequently, large look-up tables are not required; however, a higher fragment-processing load is produced.

For a GPU implementation of pre-integrated volume rendering, texture coordinates for two subsequent sampling points s_f and s_b along rays through the volume must be computed. The two sampling points define a ray segment through a view-orthogonal volume slab between two adjacent slice polygons with a thickness equivalent to the sampling distance (see Figure 4.5). The Cg vertex program in Listing 4.6 computes the second texture coordinates for s_b from the standard primary 3D texture coordinates given for s_f.

The distance between s_f and s_b is determined using the input parameter SliceDistance. In the fragment stage, the texture coordinates for s_f and s_b allow two subsequent samples along a ray to be looked up. These two samples are then used as texture coordinates for a dependent texture lookup into a 2D texture containing the pre-integrated ray segments (see Cg fragment shader code in Listing 4.7). The result obtained from the pre-integration table is then blended into the frame buffer.

Slicing-based volume rendering is equivalent to ray casting where all rays are traced in parallel into the volume. Unfortunately, there is no efficient means to cache the previous sample along each ray from one slice polygon to the next slice polygon. Consequently, slicing-based pre-integration requires two samples to be taken for each integration step; i.e., twice the amount of samples must be taken in comparison with post-interpolative classification. Note that additional samples considerably reduce rendering performance, as memory access is generally "expensive."

To overcome the problem of the additional sample that has to be considered, we need a means of caching the sample from the previous sampling position. The problem can thus be reduced by computing multiple integra-

```
// Pre-integration fragment program in Cg
struct v2f {
    float4 TexCoord0 :   TEXCOORD0;
    float4 TexCoord1 :   TEXCOORD1;
};
float4 main(
    v2f IN,
    uniform sampler3D Volume,
    uniform sampler2D PreIntegrationTable) :   COLOR
{

    float4 lookup;
    // sample front scalar
    lookup.x = tex3D(Volume, IN.TexCoord0.xyz).x;
    // sample back scalar
    lookup.y = tex3D(Volume, IN.TexCoord1.xyz).x;
    // lookup and return pre-integrated value
    return tex2D(PreIntegrationTable, lookup.xy);
}
```

Listing 4.7. A pre-integration fragment program in Cg for a slicing-based volume renderer. Note that two samples have to be fetched from the volume for a single integration step.

tion steps at once; e.g. if we compute five integrations at once, we need six samples from the volume instead of ten compared with single integration steps [227]. Current graphics hardware allows us to perform the complete integration along the rays in a single pass. In this case, pre-integration does not introduce any significant performance loss compared with the standard integration using post-interpolative classification.

4.7   Discussion

A comparison of the results of pre-interpolative classification, post-interpolative classification, and pre-integrated classification is shown in Figure 4.6. Obviously, pre-integration produces the visually most pleasant results. However, for slicing this comes at the cost of looking up an additional filtered sample from the volume for each sampling position. This considerably reduces performance due to the fact that memory access is always expensive. Additionally, texture-cache misses are more likely to happen if the transfer function is stored in a 2D texture than if it is stored in a 1D texture. However, using pre-integration, a substantially smaller sampling rate is required when rendering volume with high-frequency transfer func-

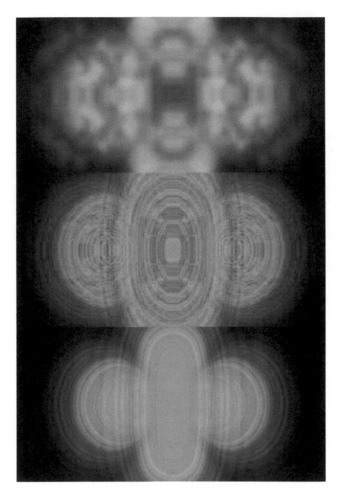

Figure 4.6. Comparison of the results of pre-, post-, and pre-integrated classification for a random transfer function. Pre-interpolative classification (top) does not reproduce high frequencies of the transfer function. Post-interpolative classification reproduces the high frequencies on the slice polygons (middle). Pre-integrated classification (bottom) produces the best visual result due to the integration of high frequencies from the transfer function in the pre-processing step. (Image from [63], © Eurographics Association 2002.)

tions. Another advantage is that the computation of the pre-integration table is performed as a pre-processing step with the full precision of the CPU. Consequently, pre-integrated transfer functions reduce quantization artifacts from blending, even when using low-precision frame buffers (see Section 9.5).

Pre-integrated transfer functions allow us to use much lower sampling rates than post-interpolative transfer functions when using transfer functions that contain high frequencies. In that sense, pre-integration can also be seen as a performance optimization for rendering volume data. However, it should be noted that pre-integrated transfer functions still require the volume to be sampled at the Nyquist frequency of the volume data itself (see Section 9.1.1).

Another important fact that should be stressed is that pre-integrated transfer functions assume a linear progression of the scalar values between two subsequent sampling points inside the volume. In fact, the progression of the scalar value in the volume is dependent on the employed filtering scheme. As we usually employ a trilinear filter for the volume, the assumption of a linear progression of the scalar value is not correct. However, post-interpolative classification assumes that there is an abrupt change of the scalar value from one to the next sampling point along a ray, i.e., no change of the scalar value happens in between two subsequent sampling points inside the volume. In that sense, though pre-integration is still not fully correct, the assumptions made for pre-integrated transfer functions are still far superior than the assumptions for post-interpolative transfer functions.

4.8   Further Reading

Up until now, we have determined color and opacity values for a voxel simply as function of its scalar value. Although this is the most common method of deriving the physical quantities required for ray integration, it is not the only possibly way. In addition to the traditional one-dimensional transfer function of the scalar intensity, the transfer function domain can be expanded by taking other local features of the data set into account. Such *multidimensional* transfer functions will be discussed in detail in Chapter 10.

Pre-integrated volume rendering has additional nice properties, such as the ability to render arbitrary numbers of isosurfaces without a performance penalty compared with rendering a single isosurface [226, 64].

5

Local Volume Illumination

IN THE SOLUTIONS TO DIRECT VOLUME RENDERING we have seen so far, radiant energy has only been emitted by the voxels themselves. The emission-absorption model we used is based on the assumption of a dense cloud of particles where each particle simultaneously emits and absorbs light. We did not account for illumination effects caused by external light sources. There was no interaction between light coming in from outside the volume and the volume itself. The only exception was the intensity of the background light, which is absorbed to some degree and thus attenuated by the volume before it reaches the eye. Light energy also traveled along linear rays only. We did not allow for reflection, refraction, and scattering of light. Such illumination effects, however, add a great deal of realism to the resulting images. Surfaces properties, such as roughness, are very hard to recognize without external lighting. Illumination effects provide additional depth cues and greatly enhance the perception of small-scale spatial structures, which is of great importance for scientific visualization.

The major optical effect that is missing in the emission-absorption model is *scattering* of light. Loosely speaking, we are using the term scattering as the volumetric equivalent to reflection and refraction of light at material boundaries. In volume rendering, light is scattered by particles in 3D space instead of surfaces. For surfaces, the local reflection of light is fully described using the *bidirectional reflectance distribution function* (BRDF), which determines the intensity of reflected light for given directions. Similar concepts exist for transmission and refraction. With volumetric light scattering, the directions and intensities of light particle interaction are described by a *phase function* (see Equation 1.3 in Chapter 1). For realistic visual effects, it is important to properly account for indirect illumination caused by scattering. Light that enters the volume or is emitted inside in a direction that does not reach the eye directly can be scattered toward the eye when it interacts with particles in the volume. This way, light becomes visible although the direct path to the eye is occluded.

Local vs. Global Volume Illumination

A single light-matter interaction that changes both direction and intensity of emitted light before it reaches the eye is called *single scattering*. Single-scattering effects are modeled using traditional *local illumination* models. The most simple volumetric illumination model accounts for such local effects only. For simplicity, external light is assumed to reach any point within the volume directly and unimpededly, without absorption or scattering. A single reflection calculation is performed inside the volume, and the light intensity scattered towards the eye is added to the radiant energy emitted at that point (see Figure 5.1 (left)). Despite the doubtfulness of the physical plausibility, single-scattering approaches and local illumination models allow fast and easy implementations and usually result in meaningful images. Although multiple scattering effects, attenuation, and shadows can also be implemented efficiently for real-time volume rendering, the most prevalent models are still based on local illumination.

Traditional local illumination models for surface lighting can be easily adapted to volumetric representations. Local illumination models use the notion of a normal vector, which describes the local orientation of a surface. Such an illumination model calculates the reflection of light as a function of this normal, the viewing direction, the angle of incidence, and a couple of material properties. As we will see in Section 5.3, almost any surface illumination model can be used in volume rendering by substituting the surface normal by the normalized gradient vector of the volume. It is worth noting that, in homogeneous media such as fog of constant density, it is possible to evaluate such effects analytically [259]. More details about this can be found in Chapter 11.

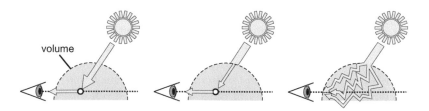

Figure 5.1. Different types of volumetric illumination models. Left: single scattering. Light reaches any point inside the volume unimpededly. Middle: single scattering with attenuation. Light intensity is reduced due to absorption inside the volume. Right: multiple scattering. Light is scattered several times before it reaches the eye.

The next step in volume illumination is to consider the spatial distance between the light source and the point where it is scattered toward the eye. This will account for the *visibility* of the light source and thus the incorporation of *shadows*. In the volumetric case, shadowing is caused by the absorption of light between the light source and a point inside the volume (see Figure 5.1 (middle)). Going further, the scattering of light on the way to a given point and further scattering on its way toward the eye can also be considered (see Figure 5.1 (right)). Taking such *multiple scattering* interactions into account leads to full *indirect* or *global illumination* of the volume. Volumetric shadows and approximations to global volume illumination are the topic of Chapter 6.

5.1   Terminology

Before we begin, let us review some of the terms that are important for all physically based lighting computations. This is only intended as a refresher and an introduction to the terminology we are using. More detailed descriptions can be found in standard texts on the topic [80, 211].

5.1.1   Radiant Flux

The radiative power emitted by a light source is defined by its *radiant flux* Φ, measured in watts (W). In general, radiant flux specifies the amount of energy Q that passes through a surface, such as a sphere surrounding the light source, per unit of time. In computer graphics, the time dependency is usually omitted, as we are only interested in the equilibrium state.

5.1.2   Irradiance

Irradiance E is defined as the area density of radiant flux, i.e., the radiative power per unit area,

$$E = \frac{\mathrm{d}\Phi}{\mathrm{d}A},\tag{5.1}$$

measured in watts per square meter (W/m^2). Pharr and Humphries [211] explain irradiance in an illustrative way by considering two concentric spheres, with different radii, that surround a light source. The radiant flux measured on both spheres will be equal, but the area density, the irradiance E, will be less on the larger sphere since it has a larger area. This also explains why perceived illumination falls off with the squared distance from a light source.

5.1.3   Radiance

As defined in Section 1.2.1, *radiance* is the most important quantity in computer graphics. The radiance I is a measure of the radiant flux at a point in space per projected unit area, per solid angle:

$$I = \frac{d\Phi}{d\Omega\, dA_\perp}\,. \tag{5.2}$$

Radiance values are the ones that we finally store as pixels. In this chapter, we will often refer to radiance simply as *illumination*.

Surface-rendering techniques often require the calculation of the radiance reflected in a certain direction at an intersection point between a ray and a surface. For points on a nonemissive surface, this outgoing radiance is a function of the outgoing direction, the incoming radiance from all directions on the hemisphere around the point, and the reflective properties of the surface material (the BRDF). In volume rendering, the outgoing radiance at a point in a given direction is a function of the incoming radiance from *all* directions and the reflective properties of the participating medium specified by the phase function (see Equations 1.2 and 1.3 in Section 1.2.1).

5.1.4   Radiance and Irradiance Distribution Function

The incoming radiance at a point can be described as a function of the incoming direction. Such a function is called the *incident radiance distribution function*. Likewise, the irradiance E for all points on the unit sphere centered around a given point can be described by the *irradiance distribution function*. A practical way of storing such functions is to use *environment maps*. An environment map is created using a discretized 2D parameterization of all spatial directions. Environment maps storing the incident radiance and the irradiance are called *reflection maps* and *irradiance maps*, respectively. We will examine environment maps in detail in Section 5.7.

5.2   Types of Light Sources

There is a variety of different types of light sources in computer graphics. Each type creates a unique visual effect and adds a specific amount of computational complexity to the scene. Some types of light sources, such as point lights, are cheap to compute. Other types, such as area lights, cause a significant computational load. In consequence, each light source in visual arts or visualization should have a designated purpose and the type of light source should be carefully chosen.

- *Point light sources*, or *omnidirectional light sources*, emit light at a single point in space equally in all directions. A fall-off function specifies the reduction of intensity with respect to distance from the light source.

- *Spotlights* are point light sources that emit light only in certain directions, which are usually specified as a cone with its apex at the position of the light source. In addition to fall-off due to distance, a radial fall-off function is commonly used, e.g., with respect to the angle between the major axis of the cone and the light direction.

- *Directional light sources* are point light sources at infinity. They are solely described by their light direction, and all emitted light rays are parallel to each other. In computer graphics, the sun is often assumed to be sufficiently for away to be treated as a directional light source.

- *Environment maps* can fundamentally be considered as a collection of an infinite number of directional light sources that completely surround the space of interest. An environment map stores the incoming illumination for all directions over an entire sphere. Different representations for environment maps that are used in practice are discussed in Section 5.7.

- *Area light sources* emit light over an entire specified area such as a triangle or other geometry. For illumination computations, they are often sampled as multiple point light sources. Due to their computational complexity, they are not commonly used to illuminate volumes, except when they can be approximated as an environment map.

- *Volume light sources* represent the light emitted by a volume, e.g., in the most general case computed by full volume rendering. Using the idea of environment maps in an inverse manner, the light emitted by a volume light source can be stored in or rendered into an environment map.

Another important property of light source types is whether they give rise to hard-edged or soft-edged shadows. Soft shadows consist of two different regions: an umbra and a penumbra. Umbral regions are parts of the geometry that do not receive light due to complete occlusion. Penumbral regions occur when an area light source is only partially occluded. Hard shadows consist of an umbral region only. Point lights, spotlights, and directional lights produce hard shadows, whereas environment maps, area light sources, and volume light sources generally lead to soft shadows. The latter are inherently hard to compute, although powerful and robust real-time methods have been developed in recent years. Shadow-computation techniques for volume graphics are discussed in Chapter 6.

5.3   Gradient-Based Illumination

Traditional local illumination models are built upon the notion of the normal vector, which describes the local orientation of a surface patch. In order to adapt such local illumination models to volume graphics, we assume that external light is reflected at *isosurfaces* inside the volume data. If we consider a point $\mathbf{p}$ inside a volume with an associated scalar value $f(\mathbf{p})$, we can imagine the isosurface $I(\mathbf{p})$ passing through that point as the union of all points that share the same scalar value,

$$I(\mathbf{p}) = \{\, \mathbf{x} \mid f(\mathbf{x}) = f(\mathbf{p}) \,\}. \tag{5.3}$$

As we see, this structure is a subset of the original volume in general. Except for singular points and homogeneous regions of the volume, however, it turns out to be a surface. The normal vector we use for shading a point is thus the unit vector perpendicular to the isosurface through that point. The gradient vector of the scalar field $f(\mathbf{x})$,

$$\nabla f(\mathbf{x}) = \begin{pmatrix} \frac{\partial f(\mathbf{x})}{\partial x} \\ \frac{\partial f(\mathbf{x})}{\partial y} \\ \frac{\partial f(\mathbf{x})}{\partial z} \end{pmatrix}, \tag{5.4}$$

points into the direction of steepest ascent, which is always perpendicular to the isosurface. Specifically, if we move away from $\mathbf{p}$ by a very small vector $\mathbf{v}$, the change in scalar value $\Delta f(\mathbf{x}, \mathbf{v})$ can be approximated by the directional derivative, which is defined as dot product $\nabla f(\mathbf{p}) \cdot \mathbf{v}$. We will get the most significant change by moving in the direction of the gradient and zero change if we move perpendicular to it, because the dot product of two perpendicular vectors is zero. No change in scalar value, however, means staying on the isosurface. The tangent plane to the isosurface at $\mathbf{p}$ is thus perpendicular to the gradient $\nabla f(\mathbf{p})$.

The normal vector used in local illumination models must always have unit length. Because this is not true for the gradient vector in general, it must be normalized to meet this requirement:

$$\mathbf{n}(\mathbf{x}) = \frac{\nabla f(\mathbf{x})}{\|\nabla f(\mathbf{x})\|}, \qquad \text{if } \|\nabla f(\mathbf{x})\| \neq 0. \tag{5.5}$$

If the gradient vector becomes zero, the scalar field is either homogeneous or it has a local extremum. In both cases, we set the normal vector to zero, which implies that also the illumination term becomes zero. This corresponds to the idea that light is reflected at boundaries between different optical media only and passes though homogeneous regions unaffectedly.

As we see, determining the normal vector for local illumination boils down to estimating the gradient vector at **p**. Before we examine different local illumination models, we will have a closer look at how to estimate gradients in practice.

5.3.1 Gradient Estimation

There is a variety of techniques for estimating the gradient from discrete volume data. In GPU-based volume rendering, gradient estimation is usually performed in one of two major ways. Either the gradient vector will be pre-computed and stored in an additional volume texture that is sampled at runtime, or gradient estimation is implemented on-the-fly, which means that directional derivatives must be estimated in real time at any point in the volume. The major difference between the two approaches is that pre-computed gradients are commonly calculated at the integer positions of the original grid and interpolated trilinearly, whereas on-the-fly gradients are computed on a per-pixel basis in the fragment shader. There are different methods for estimating gradient vectors, which differ in the computational complexity and the accuracy of the resulting gradients.

Finite differences. Finite differencing schemes are fast and efficient methods for estimating partial derivatives and gradients on discrete data. All finite differencing schemes are based on a Taylor expansion of the function to be differentiated. The Taylor series of a 1D scalar function $f(x)$ in the

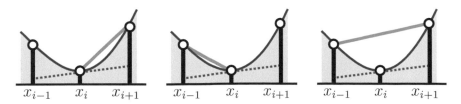

Figure 5.2. Finite differencing schemes approximate the derivative of a curve (blue) by substituting the slope of the tangent (dotted red) by the slope of the secant (green). Forward differences (left) construct the secant from the current sample to the next, backward differences (middle) from the current sample and the previous one. Central differences construct the secant from the previous sample to the next.

neighborhood of a point x_0 is defined as the infinite sum,

$$
\begin{aligned}
f(x_0 + h) &= f(x_0) + \frac{f'(x_0)}{1!} h + \frac{f''(x_0)}{2!} h^2 + \dots \\
&= \sum_{n=0}^{\infty} \frac{f^{(n)}(x_0)}{n!} h^n .
\end{aligned}
\tag{5.6}
$$

If we stop the Taylor expansion after the second term,

$$
f(x_0 + h) = f(x_0) + \frac{f'(x_0)}{1!} h + o(h^2),
\tag{5.7}
$$

and solve for the first-order derivative, we obtain a first approximation,

$$
f(x_0)' = \frac{f(x_0 + h) - f(x_0)}{h} + o(h),
\tag{5.8}
$$

This approximation is called a *forward difference*. As we see, the approximation error is of the same order as the step size h. The same approach can be used with a backward Taylor expansion,

$$
f(x_0 - h) = f(x_0) - \frac{f'(x_0)}{1!} h + o(h^2),
\tag{5.9}
$$

and results in another approximation for the first-order derivative called *backward difference*:

$$
f(x_0)' = \frac{f(x_0) - f(x_0 - h)}{h} + o(h).
\tag{5.10}
$$

The approximation error of the backward differencing scheme has the same order as the forward differences. To obtain a finite differencing scheme with a higher-order approximation error, we write down one forward and one backward Taylor expansion up to the third term,

$$
f(x_0 + h) = f(x_0) + \frac{f'(x_0)}{1!} h + \frac{f''(x_0)}{2!} h^2 + o(h^3)
\tag{5.11}
$$

$$
f(x_0 - h) = f(x_0) - \frac{f'(x_0)}{1!} h + \frac{f''(x_0)}{2!} h^2 + o(h^3),
\tag{5.12}
$$

subtract the second equation from the first one,

$$
f(x_0 + h) - f(x_0 - h) = 2 f'(x_0) h + o(h^3),
\tag{5.13}
$$

and solve for the first-order derivative,

$$
f'(x_0) = \frac{f(x_0 + h) - f(x_0 - h)}{2h} + o(h^2).
\tag{5.14}
$$

The result is a finite differencing scheme called *central differences* with an approximation error within the order of magnitude $o(h^2)$. The approximation error for central differences thus is of higher order compared with forward or backward differences.

Central differences are the most common approach for gradient estimation in volume graphics. Each of the three components of the gradient vector $\nabla f(\mathbf{x}) = \nabla f(x, y, z)$ is estimated by a central difference, resulting in

$$\nabla f(x, y, z) \approx \frac{1}{2h} \begin{pmatrix} f(x + h, y, z) - f(x - h, y, z) \\ f(x, y + h, z) - f(x, y - h, z) \\ f(x, y, z + h) - f(x, y, z - h) \end{pmatrix}. \tag{5.15}$$

As we see, six additional neighbor samples are taken with a distance h around the position where the gradient is estimated. For pre-computing gradient vectors, the step size h can simply be set to the grid size in order to avoid unnecessary interpolation operations. For computing gradients on the fly, the step size h is set to a constant value that is small with respect to the grid size.

One important property of central differences in this regard is that the order of applying linear, bilinear, or trilinear interpolation and central differencing does not matter, as the result will be exactly the same. This can be easily verified:

$$\alpha \left(\frac{f(x + 2) - f(x)}{2} \right) + (1 - \alpha) \left(\frac{f(x + 1) - f(x - 1)}{2} \right)$$
$$= \frac{1}{2} \Big(\alpha f(x + 2) + (1 - \alpha) f(x + 1) \Big) - \frac{1}{2} \Big(\alpha f(x) + (1 - \alpha) f(x - 1) \Big).$$

As an implication, central difference gradients stored in an RGB texture that is sampled using linear, bilinear, or trilinear interpolation are equivalent to performing the six neighbor look-ups of Equation 5.15 with linear, bilinear, or trilinear interpolation on-the-fly, respectively. In practice, however, care has to be taken with regard to the texture filtering precision of the GPU. We will address this issue in Chapter 9.

Convolution filtering for gradient estimation. Although finite differences often yield gradients of sufficient quality, more general approaches based on larger filter kernels might achieve considerably better results, yet at a higher computational cost.

The standard approach for filtering a signal or function is to perform a mathematical operation called a *convolution* of the function with a *filter kernel*, which is covered in more detail in Sections 1.5.3 and 9.2. The described gradient-estimation techniques based on finite differences are, in fact, special cases of convolution filtering. An important property of convolution is that differentiation and convolution with a linear filter obeys the associative law. Instead of computing the derivative of a function and filtering it afterwards, the function can as well be convolved with the derivative of a filter kernel, yielding the same result.

However, such a linear filter can compute a partial derivative in one direction only. Three different filter kernels are necessary for estimating the full gradient vector. Each filter calculates the directional derivative along one of the major axes. The results yield the x-, y-, and z-components of the gradient. Each of these 3D filter kernels is computed by performing the tensor product of a 1D derivative filter for one axis with a 1D function reconstruction filter for each of the other two axes, e.g., $h'_x(x, y, z) = h'(x)h(y)h(z)$ for the directional derivative along the x axis, where $h(x)$ is the function reconstruction filter and $h'(x)$ is the first-order derivative of the reconstruction filter. For example, Figures 9.8 and 9.14 in Section 9.2 show the cubic B-spline for function reconstruction and its first derivative for derivative reconstruction, respectively.

Discrete filter kernels. When the derivative is only needed at the grid points, it is sufficient to represent the filter kernel as a collection of discrete filter weights, which are the values of the filter kernel where it intersects the grid. This approach is very common in *image processing*. Because a discrete filter has a single value at its center, the width of such a filter is usually odd, e.g., $3 \times 3 \times 3$ or $5 \times 5 \times 5$ in 3D.

A common discrete filter kernel for gradient estimation is the *Sobel operator*, which is also often used for edge detection. The standard 3D Sobel kernel has size 3^3 and can be computed from a triangle filter for function reconstruction with smoothing ($h(-1) = 1$, $h(0) = 2$, $h(1) = 1$; with normalization factor $1/4$) and central differences ($h'(-1) = -1$, $h'(0) = 0$, $h'(1) = 1$; with normalization factor $1/2$) for derivative reconstruction. The 3D kernel for derivation in x is then $h'_x(x, y, z) = h'(x)h(y)h(z)$ with $x, y, z \in \{-1, 0, 1\}$:

$$
\begin{array}{llll}
 & z = -1 & z = 0 & z = 1 \\
h'_x(\ -1, \quad 1, \quad z\ ) = & -1 & -2 & -1 \\
h'_x(\ -1, \quad 0, \quad z\ ) = & -2 & -4 & -2 \\
h'_x(\ -1, \ -1, \quad z\ ) = & -1 & -2 & -1 \\
h'_x(\ \ 0, \quad y, \quad z\ ) = & 0 & 0 & 0 \quad \forall y \\
h'_x(\ \ 1, \quad 1, \quad z\ ) = & 1 & 2 & 1 \\
h'_x(\ \ 1, \quad 0, \quad z\ ) = & 2 & 4 & 2 \\
h'_x(\ \ 1, \ -1, \quad z\ ) = & 1 & 2 & 1
\end{array}
\tag{5.16}
$$

In order to estimate the correct gradient magnitude, these weights have to be normalized by a factor of $1/32$. The other two kernels $h'_y(x, y, z)$ and $h'_z(x, y, z)$ can be obtained by computing the respective tensor product or by simply rotating the axes of $h'_x(x, y, z)$. There are several variants of the Sobel kernel that use slightly different weights, e.g., using $h(-1) = 3$, $h(0) = 10$, and $h(1) = 3$ with a normalization factor of $1/16$.

Although it produces gradients of better quality than the simple central differences scheme, an obvious disadvantage of a full $3 \times 3 \times 3$ filter kernel such as the Sobel is its computational complexity. The Sobel kernel shown above requires 54 neighbor sample look-ups (18 for each of the three gradient components) and the corresponding multiplications and additions for evaluating the convolution. Therefore, filter kernels of this size are usually only used for pre-computing gradients that are then stored in a texture for easy and fast retrieval in the fragment shader.

Other examples of filter kernels for gradient reconstruction would be the Prewitt edge detection filter that uses a box filter where the Sobel filter uses a triangle filter, and a Gaussian and its derivative, which, however, is usually only used with size $5 \times 5 \times 5$ and above.

Continuous filter kernels. When the function or derivative is needed between grid points and the discrete filters described above are used, they have to be applied at all neighboring grid points, e.g., at the eight corners of a cube, and then interpolated, e.g., using trilinear interpolation. However, a much more natural choice is to use continuous filter kernels instead of discrete filters in order to reconstruct the function and its derivatives at arbitrary points in the volume directly from the original grid of function samples.

Fast filtering with a continuous cubic B-spline and its derivatives is described in detail in Section 9.2. On-the-fly gradient reconstruction with the cubic B-spline is possible in real time on current GPUs for rendering isosurfaces. This is especially easy when deferred shading is used, a general image-space method that is described in Section 8.7. The cubic B-spline can also be used as a basis for real-time computation of implicit isosurface curvature, which is described in Section 14.4.

5.3.2   Problems with Gradient-Based Volume Illumination

In practice, several problems can occur when gradient information is used for volume illumination. First, gradients can easily be of zero length. There is no data variation in homogeneous areas, and thus the gradients in such areas will be $(0, 0, 0)$. Zero-length gradients make it impossible to compute a well-defined gradient direction. This also corresponds to the fact that the normalized gradient can be interpreted as normal vector to the isosurface passing through a given point, as described in Section 5.3. If this point is within a homogeneous area, there exists no well-defined surface passing through it.

Even when an area is not entirely homogeneous, the gradient directions of very small gradients will be very unreliable due to numerical inaccuracies. In this case, neighboring gradient directions may vary wildly, which usually results in noticeable noise when these directions are used for shading computations. In general, the larger the gradient magnitude is, the more reliable the corresponding gradient direction will be. Numerical problems also depend significantly on the gradient estimation scheme in use; filters with larger kernels take more neighbor samples into account and thus in general produce more reliable results than central differences, for example. Moreover, in contrast to CPU implementations, GPU volume renderers very often do not check for division by zero or by very small values, resulting in *NaN* (*not a number*) results that will propagate into all following calculations.

Because the gradient magnitude is more reliable than gradient direction, the major approach for coping with the associated numerical problems is to modulate computations that depend on gradient direction with the gradient magnitude. This degree of "surface-ness" of a given point is sometimes called the *surface scalar*. As an alternative, a heuristic shading technique that manages completely without gradient estimation has been recently proposed by Desgranges, Engel, and Paladini [46].

5.4   Local Illumination Models

Local illumination models only consider light that comes directly from the light sources to the point being shaded. Every point is basically considered independently from all other points. To incorporate volume illumination into the emission-absorption model, we modify the emission by adding a contribution from external illumination. The amount of reflected light can be computed using any local surface illumination model.

The light source is assumed to be either a point light or directional light. Spotlights are seldom used in volume graphics but could be easily implemented, analogously to surface lighting, and we refer the reader to the lighting chapters in *The Cg Tutorial* [71]. Area and volume lights for local illumination are usually approximated using clusters of point light sources.

5.4.1   Blinn-Phong Illumination

The local illumination model most frequently used in computer graphics is the Blinn-Phong model. Although it does not fulfill the physical requirements of energy conservation or Helmholtz reciprocity, it is definitely the most popular phenomenological illumination model in practice.[1]

---

[1] There is also a less popular version of the original Phong model, called the *modified Phong model*, which is physically plausible. See [202] for details.

Like many popular illumination models, the Blinn-Phong model computes the light reflected by an object as a combination of three different terms, an *ambient*, a *diffuse*, and a *specular* term:

$$\mathbf{I}_{\text{Phong}} = \mathbf{I}_{\text{ambient}} + \mathbf{I}_{\text{diffuse}} + \mathbf{I}_{\text{specular}}. \qquad (5.17)$$

Note that illumination terms are denoted as RGB triplets. The frequency dependency of the illumination equations are omitted by considering color components separately. The product between two RGB triplets, such as the multiplication of an illumination term by a material color, is always performed component-wise.

The *ambient* term $\mathbf{I}_{\text{ambient}}$ is modeled as a constant global light multiplied by the ambient color and the ambient coefficient of the material:

$$\mathbf{I}_{\text{ambient}} = k_a \, \mathbf{M}_a \, \mathbf{I}_a. \qquad (5.18)$$

The color and intensity of the global ambient light is specified by the RGB triplet $\mathbf{I}_a$. It is multiplied component-wise by the ambient material color $\mathbf{M}_a$. The scalar ambient coefficient k_a is a constant between 0 and 1 that controls how much of the ambient light that arrives at the surface is actually reflected by it. Often the ambient coefficient k_a and the ambient material color $\mathbf{M}_a$ are combined into a single RGB triplet. Ambient light is the easiest way to compensate for missing indirect illumination and to lighten up shadow regions. In the real world, such illumination effects are caused by light that arrives indirectly at the surface via multiple scattering.

Without ambient lighting, every surface not directly facing a light source would be completely black, which is often found unrealistic. Ambient light will alleviate this by adding constant light. The ambient term, however, has only been introduced for practical reasons. It does not have any physically based justification. It is important to understand that ambient light will always reduce the contrast and the dynamic range of the

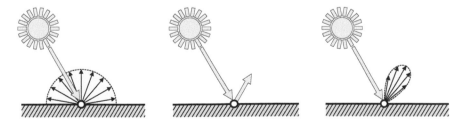

Figure 5.3. Different types of reflections. Left: *Lambertian* surfaces reflect light equally in all directions. Middle: *perfect mirrors* reflect incident light in exactly one direction. Right: shiny surfaces reflect light in a *specular lobe* around the direction of perfect reflection (*specular reflection*).

image. For good reasons, many artists prefer setting the ambient light to zero and using additional light sources called *fill lights* to lighten up dark regions.

The diffuse and specular parts of the Blinn-Phong model are illustrated in Figure 5.3. The diffuse term (Figure 5.3 (left)) models the view-independent part of reflected light. A perfect mirror (Figure 5.3 (middle)) reflects incident light in exactly one direction. The specular term (Figure 5.3 (right)) is a generalization of a mirror, where light is scattered around the direction of perfect reflection. The shape of the specular term in Figure 5.3 is called *specular lobe* and depends on the material coefficients.

The *diffuse* term $\mathbf{I}_{\text{diffuse}}$ corresponds to *Lambertian* reflection, which means that light is reflected equally in all directions. Diffuse reflection is exhibited by a dull, matte surface. Its brightness is independent of the viewing angle and depends only on the *angle of incidence* φ between the direction l of the incoming light and the surface normal n (see Figure 5.4 (left)). All vectors used in local illumination computations are assumed to have unit length, so that the cosine of the angle between two vectors can be computed by the dot product. Diffuse illumination term can be written as:

$$\mathbf{I}_{\text{diffuse}} = k_d \, \mathbf{M}_d \, \mathbf{I}_d \cos\varphi \qquad \text{if } \varphi \leq \frac{\pi}{2} \qquad (5.19)$$

$$= k_d \, \mathbf{M}_d \, \mathbf{I}_d \max((\mathbf{r} \cdot \mathbf{v}), 0). \qquad (5.20)$$

The diffuse material color $\mathbf{M}_d$ is multiplied component-wise by the color $\mathbf{I}_d$ emitted by the light source. The scalar diffuse coefficient k_d is a constant between 0 and 1 that specifies the amount of diffuse reflection of the material. Again, the diffuse coefficient k_d and the diffuse material color $\mathbf{M}_d$ can

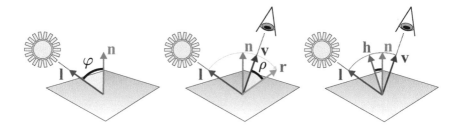

Figure 5.4. Left: the diffuse illumination term depends on the angle of incidence φ between the normal n and the light direction l. Middle: in the original Phong model, the specular term is based on the angle ρ between the reflected light vector r and the viewing direction v. Right: the specular term depends on the angle between the normal and a vector h, which is halfway between the viewing and the light direction.

be combined into a single RGB triplet. In order to avoid surfaces being lit from behind, $\mathbf{I}_{\text{diffuse}}$ should be zero when the angle φ becomes larger than $\pi/2$, which is ensured by the maximum operator. In order to simplify the notation, we are going to omit these maximum operators in the following equations.

The *specular* lighting term $\mathbf{I}_{\text{specular}}$ models the reflection behavior of shiny surfaces, which cause so-called specular highlights. It depends on the viewing vector $\mathbf{v}$, which points from the surface point to be shaded to the eye position. The specular term of the original Phong model (see Figure 5.4 (middle)) uses the direction of perfect reflection $\mathbf{r}$, which is calculated by mirroring the light vector $\mathbf{l}$ about the surface normal $\mathbf{n}$. The amount of specular reflection is determined by the cosine of the angle ρ between $\mathbf{r}$ and the viewing vector $\mathbf{v}$,

$$\cos\rho = (\mathbf{r}\cdot\mathbf{v}), \qquad \text{with} \tag{5.21}$$

$$\mathbf{r} = 2(\mathbf{l}\cdot\mathbf{n})\mathbf{n} - \mathbf{l}, \tag{5.22}$$

resulting in a specular term according to

$$\mathbf{I}_{\text{specular}} = k_s\,\mathbf{M}_s\,\mathbf{I}_s\cos^n\rho, \qquad \text{if } \rho \le \frac{\pi}{2} \tag{5.23}$$

$$= k_s\,\mathbf{M}_s\,\mathbf{I}_s\,(\mathbf{r}\cdot\mathbf{v})^n. \tag{5.24}$$

In the Blinn-Phong model, the specular term is computed more efficiently by introducing the vector $\mathbf{h}$, which is halfway between $\mathbf{v}$ and $\mathbf{l}$,

$$\mathbf{I}_{\text{specular}} \approx k_s\,\mathbf{M}_s\,\mathbf{I}_s\,(\mathbf{h}\cdot\mathbf{n})^n, \qquad \text{with} \tag{5.25}$$

$$\mathbf{h} = \frac{\mathbf{v}+\mathbf{l}}{\|\mathbf{v}+\mathbf{l}\|}. \tag{5.26}$$

The dot product $(\mathbf{h}\cdot\mathbf{n})$ is also clamped to a positive range to account for angles $\rho \le \frac{\pi}{2}$ only. The specular material color $\mathbf{M}_s$ is multiplied component-wise by the radiance $\mathbf{I}_s$ of the light source. The scalar specular coefficient k_s determines the amount of specular reflection of the material. The specular exponent n is called the *shininess* of the surface and is used to control the width of the specular lobe and thus the size of the resulting highlights.

Both the original Phong model and Blinn-Phong model are *phenomenological* illumination models. This means that they might produce believable illumination effects, although certain aspects are not physically plausible. The degree of realism greatly depends on the choice of the material coefficients. The law of energy conservation requires that the amount of reflected light never exceeds the incident radiant energy. As a rule of thumb, the sum of the scalar coefficients k_a, k_d, and k_s should not exceed 1 in practice and the ambient coefficient k_a should be as small as possible. Straightforward implementations of the Blinn-Phong model for per-fragment surface shading with different types of light sources can be found in *The Cg Tutorial* [71].

In order to use a local illumination model in volume graphics, we utilize the fact that light is additive. In fact, we can render a scene several times, each time with a different light source and add up all the resulting images afterwards to obtain a final image that will correctly contain the contribution of all the light sources. For incorporating local illumination into the emission-absorption model, we can simply add the scattered light to the volume emission term $\mathbf{I}_{\text{emission}}$ at each sample.

$$
\begin{aligned}
\mathbf{I}_{\text{volume}} &= \mathbf{I}_{\text{emission}} + \mathbf{I}_{\text{BlinnPhong}} \qquad\qquad\qquad\qquad (5.27) \\
&= \mathbf{I}_{\text{emission}} + \mathbf{I}_{\text{ambient}} + \mathbf{I}_{\text{diffuse}} + \mathbf{I}_{\text{specular}} \\
&= k_e\,\mathbf{I}_e + k_a\,\mathbf{M}_a\,\mathbf{I}_a + k_d\,\mathbf{M}_d\,\mathbf{I}_d\langle \mathbf{l} \circ \mathbf{n}\rangle + k_s\,\mathbf{M}_s\,\mathbf{I}_s\langle \mathbf{h} \circ \mathbf{n}\rangle^n\,.
\end{aligned}
$$

The maximum operators are again omitted in the equation. For volume illumination in practice, there are different possibilities for specifying the material coefficients. The scalar coefficients k_e, k_a, k_d, and k_s are usually specified as global constants. Note that in order to avoid clamping of illumination values when their sum exceeds 1, floating-point render targets and high dynamic range rendering must be used. In this case, k_e can be allowed to be arbitrarily big, e.g., $k_e > 1$. Section 5.8 contains more information on high dynamic range volume rendering.

The emitted radiance $\mathbf{I}_e$ is defined as a function of the underlying scalar field $s(\mathbf{x})$. It is specified by a transfer function,

$$
\mathbf{I}_e(\mathbf{x}) = \mathbf{T}_{\mathbf{I}_e}(s(\mathbf{x}))\,. \qquad\qquad (5.28)
$$

The material colors $\mathbf{M}_a, \mathbf{M}_d, \mathbf{M}_s$, the shininess n, and the emitted radiance can either be defined as a global parameter or as a function of the scalar field. The ambient term is often omitted. The diffuse material coefficient $\mathbf{M}_d$ is usually set to the same color as the emitted light $\mathbf{I}_e$. The coefficients of the specular term $\mathbf{M}_s$ and n are often specified as global parameters.

In general, however, nothing prevents us from specifying all material coefficients as function of the scalar field. A separate transfer function can be used for each optical property. In practice, there are two factors that limit this approach. The first factor is a technical limit. Every transfer function must be implemented as a dependent texture look-up in the fragment program, as explained in Chapter 4. There might be an upper limit for the possible number of texture look-ups, and every texture look-up will also decrease the rendering performance noticeably. The second factor is the practical aspect. Setting up a transfer function is often a tedious and time-consuming task of manual parameter tweaking. If every parameter is specified separately, the expenditure for user interaction will significantly

```
// Blinn-Phong illumination
half4 shading(float3 N, float3 V, float3 L) {

    // material properties
    float3 Ka = float3(0.1, 0.1, 0.1); // ambient
    float3 Kd = float3(0.6, 0.6, 0.6); // diffuse
    float3 Ks = float3(0.2, 0.2, 0.2); // specular
    float  n = 100.0; // shininess

    // light properties
    float3 lightColor = float3(1.0, 1.0, 1.0);
    float3 ambientLight = float3(0.3, 0.3, 0.3);

    // Calculate halfway vector
    float3 H = normalize(L + V);

    // Compute ambient term
    float3 ambient = Ka * ambientLight;

    // Compute the diffuse term
    float diffuseLight = max(dot(L, N), 0);
    float3 diffuse = Kd * lightColor * diffuseLight;

    // Compute the specular term
    float specularLight = pow(max(dot(H, N), 0), shininess);
    if (diffuseLight <= 0) specularLight = 0;
    float3 specular = Ks * lightColor * specularLight;

    return ambient + diffuse + specular;
}
```

Listing 5.1.   Cg function implementing the Blinn-Phong local illumination model.

increase. With these two aspects in mind, however, we encourage the reader to experiment with whatever concept for parameter specification will turn out to be appropriate for your application.

A sample implementation of the Blinn-Phong illumination model can be found in Listing 5.1. The model is implemented as a separate function, which will be called from different main programs later in this chapter. The material coefficients k and $\mathbf{M}$ have again been combined into one coefficient $\mathbf{K}$ for the diffuse and the specular term, respectively. To keep the code as simple as possible, the light and material properties have been hard-coded. In practical applications, these parameters will be passed as uniform

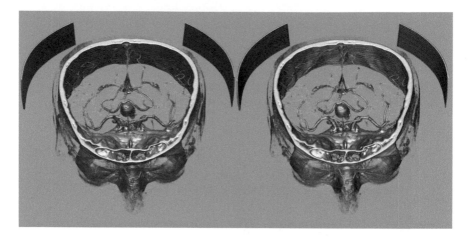

Figure 5.5. Examples of gradient-based volume illumination using the local illumination models by Blinn-Phong (left) and Cook-Torrance (right)

variables to the main function and handed over to the shading function as additional arguments. An example rendition demonstrating gradient-based volume illumination using the Blinn-Phong model is displayed in Figure 5.5 (left).

5.4.2 Other Shading Models

Apart from the Phong and the Blinn-Phong model, a variety of other shading models can be found in [202], such as Lafortune's model, Banks' anisotropic model, and the physically based model of Ashikhmin. A popular physically based illumination model is the microfacet model introduced by Cook and Torrance [74]. The microscopic structure of a surface is here modeled as a distribution of randomly oriented perfect mirrors. Like most illumination models, the Cook-Torrance model consists of a diffuse and a specular term. The diffuse term is defined similarly to the Phong model:

$$\mathbf{I}_{\text{diffuse}} \;=\; k_d \, \mathbf{M}_d \, \mathbf{I}_d \, (\mathbf{l} \cdot \mathbf{n}) \,. \tag{5.29}$$

The maximum operator on the dot product has again been omitted. The specular part of the model,

$$\mathbf{I}_{\text{specular}} \;=\; k_s \, \mathbf{M}_s \, \mathbf{I}_s \, \frac{F \cdot D \cdot G}{(\mathbf{n} \cdot \mathbf{v})} \,, \tag{5.30}$$

consists of a Fresnel term F, a statistical distribution D that describes the orientation of the microfacets, and a geometric self-shadowing term G:

$$F \approx (1 + (\mathbf{v} \cdot \mathbf{h}))^4 \; ; \tag{5.31}$$

$$D \approx C \cdot \exp\left(\frac{(\mathbf{h} \cdot \mathbf{n})^2 - 1}{m}\right) \; ; \tag{5.32}$$

$$G = \min\left(1, \frac{2\,(\mathbf{n} \cdot \mathbf{h})\,(\mathbf{n} \cdot \mathbf{v})}{(\mathbf{h} \cdot \mathbf{v})}, \frac{2\,(\mathbf{n} \cdot \mathbf{h})\,(\mathbf{n} \cdot \mathbf{l})}{(\mathbf{h} \cdot \mathbf{v})}\right) . \tag{5.33}$$

```
// Cook-Torrance local illumination
half3 shading(float3 N, float3 V, float3 L) {

    // material properties
    float3 Kd = float3(0.6, 0.6, 0.6); // diffuse
    float3 Ks = float3(0.2, 0.2, 0.2); // specular
    float mean  = 0.7; // mean value of microfacet distribution
    float scale = 0.2; // constant factor C
    // light properties
    float3 lightIntensity = float3(1.0, 1.0, 1.0);

    float3 H = normalize(L + V);
    float n_h = dot(N,H);
    float n_v = dot(N,V);
    float v_h = dot(V,H);
    float n_l = dot(N,L);

    half3 diffuse = Kd * max(n_l,0);
    // approximate Fresnel term
    half fresnel = pow(1.0 + v_h,4);
    // approximate microfacet distribution
    half delta = acos(n_h).x;
    half exponent = -pow((delta/mean),2);
    half microfacets = scale * exp(exponent);
    // calculate self-shadowing term
    half term1 = 2 * n_h * n_v/v_h;
    half term2 = 2 * n_h * n_l/v_h;
    half selfshadow = min(1,min(term1,term2));
    // calculate Cook-Torrance model
    half3 specular = Ks *fresnel *microfacets *selfshadow / n_v;

    return lightColor * (diffuse + specular);
}
```

Listing 5.2. Cg function implementing the physically based microfacet illumination model introduced by Cook-Torrance.

The parameter m describes the mean value of the statistical distribution of microfacets. The constant C is chosen to normalize the model. Further details on the Cook-Torrance model and the specific terms can be found in [74, 202]. To be physically correct, the light colors must be equal for the diffuse and the specular term, and the intensity $\hat{\mathbf{I}}$ of the point light source must be weighted by the inverse square of its distance r:

$$\mathbf{I}_s = \mathbf{I}_d = \frac{\hat{\mathbf{I}}}{\pi r^2} . \tag{5.34}$$

A sample implementation for a single point light source can be found in Listing 5.2. The material coefficients k and $\mathbf{M}$ have again been combined into one coefficient $\mathbf{K}$ for the diffuse and the specular term, respectively. Material and light properties have again been hard-coded in the shading function to keep the notation simple. An example rendition demonstrating the Cook-Torrance model is displayed in Figure 5.5 (right).

5.5   Pre-Computed Gradients

A couple of years ago, the only practical way of gradient-based shading in volume rendering was to pre-compute all gradient vectors. The idea of gradient pre-computation is to perform the entire gradient estimation step in a pre-processing phase. For each sample point of the original scalar data set, a gradient vector is calculated with one of the gradient estimation schemes discussed in Section 5.3.1. The pre-computed gradients are stored as additional 2D or 3D textures and uploaded to GPU memory. This way, a gradient vector of relatively high quality can be obtained at runtime with a single texture fetch operation and native texture filtering.

There are several different approaches to storing the gradient information in textures. The most straightforward way uses the same internal format as a standard normal map. The x-, y-, and z-components of the normalized gradient $\hat{\nabla} f(\mathbf{x})$ are directly stored as an RGB triplet in an RGB texture:

$$\hat{\nabla} f(\mathbf{x}) = \begin{pmatrix} g_x \\ g_y \\ g_z \end{pmatrix} \begin{array}{l} \longrightarrow \\ \longrightarrow \\ \longrightarrow \end{array} \begin{array}{l} \mathtt{R} = \frac{(g_x + 1)}{2} \\ \mathtt{G} = \frac{(g_y + 1)}{2} \\ \mathtt{B} = \frac{(g_z + 1)}{2} \end{array} .$$

Floating-point texture formats are not required if the components are scaled and biased to fit into the unsigned color range $[0, 1]$. The values are expanded again to the original signed range $[-1, 1]$ in the fragment shader. The RGB format is appropriate if only the gradient direction is needed, and the gradient magnitude is not used.

If the gradient magnitude is also required, e.g., for weighting the opacity or for multidimensional transfer functions (see Chapter 10), an internal texture format of RGBA can be used instead of RGB. The magnitude of the gradient is then stored in the additional A component of the texture:

$$\hat{\nabla} f(\mathbf{x}) = \begin{pmatrix} g_x \\ g_y \\ g_z \end{pmatrix} \begin{array}{l} \longrightarrow \\ \longrightarrow \\ \longrightarrow \end{array} \begin{array}{l} \mathtt{R} = \frac{(g_x + 1)}{2} \\ \mathtt{G} = \frac{(g_y + 1)}{2} \\ \mathtt{B} = \frac{(g_z + 1)}{2} \end{array}$$
$$\|\nabla f(\mathbf{x})\| \qquad \longrightarrow \quad \mathtt{A} = \|\nabla f(\mathbf{x})\| \quad \text{(scaled to } [0,1])$$

Note that the range of gradient magnitude must also be scaled to the unit range $[0, 1]$ and expanded afterwards in the fragment program.

One of the most popular texture formats is a structure that combines the original scalar field with the normalized gradients into a single RGBA texture. The normalized gradient is scaled, biased, and stored in RGB components as described above. The A component stores the values of the scalar field itself and is used as an index into a post-interpolative transfer function table:

$$\hat{\nabla} f(\mathbf{x}) = \begin{pmatrix} g_x \\ g_y \\ g_z \end{pmatrix} \begin{array}{l} \longrightarrow \\ \longrightarrow \\ \longrightarrow \end{array} \begin{array}{l} \mathtt{R} = \frac{(g_x + 1)}{2} \\ \mathtt{G} = \frac{(g_y + 1)}{2} \\ \mathtt{B} = \frac{(g_z + 1)}{2} \end{array}$$
$$f(\mathbf{x}) \qquad \longrightarrow \quad \mathtt{A} = f$$

A fragment shader that implements this idea using 3D textures is displayed in Listing 5.3. The fragment program first obtains an RGBA value by sampling the 3D texture. The RGB portion contains the x-, y-, and z-components of the normalized gradient scaled to the unit interval $[0, 1]$. The RGB portion is thus expanded to its original signed range $[-1, 1]$ and then normalized again to eliminate interpolation artifacts. The normal vector is used for local illumination. The shading function has been omitted in this example. Possible implementations of the shading function have been discussed in Section 5.4. The A portion of the texture sample is used as index into a dependent texture that stores the post-interpolative transfer function as explained in Chapter 4. The same techniques can also be used with 2D multitextures instead of 3D textures as displayed in Listing 5.4. The 3D texture look-up is here substituted by two samples from 2D textures and a subsequent interpolation operation.

The same texture format can efficiently be used without the dependent texture look-up for rendering shaded isosurfaces. A single texture fetch yields all information needed for determining whether the isosurface has been intersected. The OpenGL alpha test can efficiently be used to discard all fragments that do not belong to the isosurface. The modified fragment

```
//fragment program for local illumination and
//post-interpolative transfer function using 3D textures
half4 main (half3 texUV     : TEXCOORD0,
            float3 position :  TEXCOORD1,

            uniform float3 lightPosition,
            uniform float3 eyePosition,
            uniform sampler3D volume_texture,
            uniform sampler1D transfer_function) :   COLOR
{
    float4 sample = tex3D(volume_texture, texUV);

    // expand and normalize the normal vector
    float3 N = normalize(2.0*sample.xyz - 1..xxx);
    // calculate light and viewing directions
    float3 L = normalize(lightPosition - position);
    float3 V = normalize(eyePosition - position);

    // emission and absorption from transfer function
    half4   result  = tex1D(transfer_function, sample.w);

    // add local illumination
    result.rgb += shading(N,V,L);

    return result;
}
```

Listing 5.3. Cg fragment program for local illumination with 3D textures. Possible implementations of the shading function can be found in Listings 5.1 and 5.2

shader and the C++ code for setting up the alpha test are displayed in Listing 5.5. Strictly speaking, the code does not really produce an isosurface but a filled region bounded by an isosurface. A real isosurface could be generated by setting the alpha function to GL_EQUAL, but this would require an enormous number of slices to be rendered to capture the infinitesimally thin surface. The code sample, however, represents a working solution for isosurface display. Because this approach allows isosurfaces to be rendered without extracting an explicit polygonal representation (like in the marching cubes algorithm [168]), this approach is often referred to as *nonpolygonal isosurfaces*. Example images are displayed in Figure 5.6.

The texture formats described above directly store the x-, y-, and z-components of the gradient vector and thus require three 8-bit values per voxel in GPU memory. A unit vector, however, is fully described by

```
// fragment program for local illumination and
// post-interpolative transfer function using 2D multi-textures
half4 main (half3  texUV     : TEXCOORD0,
            float3 position :  TEXCOORD1,

            uniform float3 lightPosition,
            uniform float3 eyePosition,
            uniform sampler2D slice_texture0,
            uniform sampler2D slice_texture1,
            uniform sampler1D transfer_function) :   COLOR
{
    // sample the texture
    float4 sample0 = tex2D(slice_texture0, texUV.xy);
    float4 sample1 = tex2D(slice_texture1, texUV.xy);
    float4 sample  = lerp(sample0, sample1, texUV.z);

    // expand and normalize the normal vector
    float3 N = normalize(2.0*sample.xyz - 1..xxx);
    // calculate light- and viewing direction
    float3 L = normalize(lightPosition - position);
    float3 V = normalize(eyePosition - position);

    // add local illumination
    result.rgb += shading(N,V,L);

    // emission and absorption from transfer function
    half4  result  = tex1D(transfer_function, sample.w);

    return result;
}
```

Listing 5.4. Cg fragment program for local illumination with 2D multitextures.
Possible implementation of the shading function can be found in Listings 5.1 and 5.2.

specifying a point on the unit sphere, which again can be described by an azimuth and an elevation angle. Converting the normalized gradient vector into spherical coordinates,

$$
\begin{aligned}
\varphi &= \arctan(\tfrac{c_y}{c_x}), & \varphi &\in \ [\,0, 2\pi\,] \\
\vartheta &= \arccos(c_z), & \vartheta &\in \ [-\tfrac{\pi}{2}, \tfrac{\pi}{2}] \ ,
\end{aligned}
\tag{5.38}
$$

allows us to store a normalized gradient as two angles instead of three Cartesian coordinates. These two angles can efficiently be stored in a two-

```
// disable alpha blending
glDisable(GL_BLEND);

// enable alpha test for isosurface
glEnable(GL_ALPHA_TEST);
glAlphaFunc(GL_LESS, fIsoValue); // or GL_GREATER
```

```
//fragment program for non-polygonal isosurfaces
// with local illumination using 3D textures
half4 main (half3 texUV    : TEXCOORD0,
            float3 position :  TEXCOORD1,

            uniform sampler3D volume_texture) :  COLOR
{
    float4 sample = tex3D(volume_texture, texUV);

    // expand and normalize the normal vector
    float3 N = normalize(2.0*sample.xyz - 1..xxx);
    // calculate light- and viewing direction
    float3 L = normalize(lightPosition - position);
    float3 V = normalize(eyePosition - position);

    half4  result;
    result.rgb = shading(N,V,L);
    result.a = sample.a;

    return result;
}
```

Listing 5.5. OpenGL compositing set-up for the alpha test (top) and Cg fragment program for rendering shaded isosurfaces using 3D textures. The same approach can be used with 2D multitextures as in Listing 5.4.

component texture format such as luminance-alpha, which effectively saves texture memory. The two angles can be converted back to Cartesian coordinates:

$$c_x = \cos\varphi \sin\vartheta; \tag{5.39}$$
$$c_y = \sin\varphi \sin\vartheta; \tag{5.40}$$
$$c_z = \cos\vartheta. \tag{5.41}$$

This conversion can either be directly implemented in a fragment shader using the **sincos** function to simultaneously compute sine and cosine func-

Figure 5.6. Examples of nonpolygonal isosurfaces using the set-up in Listing 5.5 and the Blinn-Phong model for different isovalues.

tions, or the two angles can be used as texture coordinates to look-up the Cartesian coordinates in a pre-computed 2D texture.

The main drawback of pre-computed gradients is the amount of memory that is consumed by the additional gradient data, which is usually three times as much memory as is needed for the basic volume data. Also, the time it takes to perform gradient pre-computation is often perceived as a disadvantage. If data sets do not change, pre-computed gradient volumes can be cached on disk but still need to be loaded and consume a significant amount of both CPU memory and GPU texture memory.

5.6 On-the-Fly Gradients

Many current state-of-the-art volume renderers do not use pre-computed gradients anymore. The advent of powerful GPU fragment shader hardware now allows us to compute gradients on-the-fly during rendering, wherever they are needed. That is, gradients are computed for every sample of the volume where shading with gradient directions is performed or where the gradient magnitude is needed by the transfer function. This is still slower than using pre-computed gradients, but volume sizes are getting bigger and bigger and the considerable amount of memory consumed by gradient data makes computing them on-the-fly very attractive. For the visualization of really large data sets as described in Chapter 17, computing gradients on-the-fly is mandatory. For a detailed discussion of the benefits of on-the-fly gradient estimation for improving image quality, we refer the reader to Chapter 9.

On-the-fly gradient computation usually approximates gradient vectors using the central differences scheme. A Cg fragment program for on-the-fly gradient estimation is displayed in Listing 5.6. This simple scheme requires six additional neighbor samples for each gradient. Note that it

```
// fragment program for on-the-fly gradient estimation
#define DELTA (0.01)
#define THRESHOLD (0.1)

half4 main (half3  uvw       :  TEXCOORD0,
            float3 position :  TEXCOORD1,

            uniform sampler3D texture,
            uniform sampler1D transfer_function) :  COLOR
{
    // one texture sample for the scalar value
    half  sample = tex3D(texture,uvw).x;
    // emission and absorption from transfer function
    half4 result = tex1D(transfer_function, sample);

    if (result.a > THRESHOLD) {
        float3 sample1, sample2;
        // six texture samples for the gradient
        sample1.x = tex3D(texture,uvw-half3(DELTA,0.0,0.0)).x;
        sample2.x = tex3D(texture,uvw+half3(DELTA,0.0,0.0)).x;
        sample1.y = tex3D(texture,uvw-half3(0.0,DELTA,0.0)).x;
        sample2.y = tex3D(texture,uvw+half3(0.0,DELTA,0.0)).x;
        sample1.z = tex3D(texture,uvw-half3(0.0,0.0,DELTA)).x;
        sample2.z = tex3D(texture,uvw+half3(0.0,0.0,DELTA)).x;

        // central difference and normalization
        float3 N = normalize(sample2-sample1);

        // calculate light- and viewing direction
        float3 L = normalize(lightPosition - position);
        float3 V = normalize(eyePosition - position);

        // add local illumination
        result.rgb += shading(N,V,L);
    }
    return result;
}
```

Listing 5.6.   Cg fragment program for local volume illumination and on-the-fly gradient estimation. Possible implementation of the shading function can be found in Listings 5.1 and 5.2.

```
// fragment program for on-the-fly gradient estimation
#define DELTA (0.01)
#define THRESHOLD (0.1)

half4 main (half3  uvw      :  TEXCOORD0,
            float3 position :  TEXCOORD1,

            uniform float3 lightPosition,
            uniform float3 eyePosition,
            uniform sampler3D texture,
            uniform sampler1D transfer_function) :  COLOR
{
    // one texture sample for the scalar value
    half  sample  = tex3D(texture,uvw).x;
    // emission and absorption from transfer function
    half4 result  = tex1D(transfer_function, sample);

    if (result.a > THRESHOLD) {
      float3 sample1, sample2, alpha1, alpha2;
      // six texture samples for the gradient
      sample1.x = tex3D(texture,uvw-half3(DELTA,0.0,0.0)).x;
      sample2.x = tex3D(texture,uvw+half3(DELTA,0.0,0.0)).x;
      sample1.y = tex3D(texture,uvw-half3(0.0,DELTA,0.0)).x;
      sample2.y = tex3D(texture,uvw+half3(0.0,DELTA,0.0)).x;
      sample1.z = tex3D(texture,uvw-half3(0.0,0.0,DELTA)).x;
      sample2.z = tex3D(texture,uvw+half3(0.0,0.0,DELTA)).x;
      // six texture samples for the transfer function
      alpha1.x = tex1D(transfer_function,sample1.x).a;
      alpha2.x = tex1D(transfer_function,sample2.x).a;
      alpha1.y = tex1D(transfer_function,sample1.y).a;
      alpha2.y = tex1D(transfer_function,sample2.y).a;
      alpha1.z = tex1D(transfer_function,sample1.z).a;
      alpha2.z = tex1D(transfer_function,sample2.z).a;
      // central difference and normalization
      float3 N = normalize(alpha2-alpha1);
      // calculate light- and viewing direction
      float3 L = normalize(lightPosition - position);
      float3 V = normalize(eyePosition - position);
      // add local illumination
      result.rgb += shading(N,V,L);
    }
    return result;
}
```

Listing 5.7. Cg fragment program for local volume illumination and on-the-fly gradient estimation on the classified data. Possible implementation of the shading function can be found in Listings 5.1 and 5.2.

would be more efficient to calculate the texture coordinates for these additional lookups in the vertex program. In the sample code, we have chosen to do this in the fragment program to keep the code understandable and modular. Although this approach provides good image quality, sampling the texture six times is quite costly with respect to performance. On GPUs that support true conditional branches, the `if` clause in Listing 5.6 will skip the gradient computation if the opacity of the sample is below a specified threshold. Gradient estimation and shading is only performed when the alpha value of a sample is high. Samples with high transparency are used without shading. For older hardware that does not support conditional branches, the `if` clause can just as well be omitted.

If rendering performance is more important than image quality, the central differences can be substituted by either forward or backward differences. They only require three additional texture samples instead of six for estimating a full gradient vector, however at the expense of a significantly reduced numerical accuracy. Also, if 2D multitextures are used instead of 3D textures, central differences are rather intricate to implement and require an even greater number of texture samples. In this case, forward or backward differences might be a working alternative.

More expensive gradient estimation schemes such as a $3 \times 3 \times 3$ or even larger filter kernels are currently too expensive to be calculated on-the-fly in such a naive way as described. In Section 8.7, however, we will examine deferred-shading techniques. Such approaches allow more expensive gradient-estimation techniques to be applied in real time.

One popular objection to pre-computed gradients is the fact that gradient estimation is performed on the original, unclassified data. The transfer function, however, might map two different data values to the same optical properties. It is obvious that this will change the direction of a gradient vector if it is based on the actual opacity instead of the original data values. Such a gradient pre-computation can only account for a static transfer function and would become incorrect if the transfer function changes at runtime. When gradient estimation is performed on-the-fly, however, the transfer function can be considered during gradient estimation, which results in an estimation scheme that computes gradient vectors on the classified data, however at the cost of a greater number of dependent texture look-ups. An example implementation of this idea is given in Listing 5.7. In practice, such an expensive implementation will hardly be necessary, and the improvement in terms of image quality is usually negligible.

5.6.1 Approximating Directional Derivatives

Sampling a texture several times for full on-the-fly gradient estimation often implies a significant performance penalty. If the gradient vector is

```
// fragment program for on-the-fly Lambertian illumination
#define DELTA (0.01)
#define THRESHOLD (0.1)

half4 main (half3  uvw       :  TEXCOORD0,
            float3 position  :  TEXCOORD1,

            uniform float3 lightPosition,
            uniform half3 lightColor,
            uniform half3 Kd, // diffuse coefficient k_d * M_d
            uniform sampler3D volume_texture,
            uniform sampler1D transfer_function) :  COLOR
{
   // one texture sample for the scalar value
   half sample   = tex3D(volume_texture,uvw).x;
   // emission and absorption from transfer function
   half4 result  = tex1D(transfer_function, sample.x);

   if (result.a > THRESHOLD) {
     // calculate light direction
     float3 L = normalize(lightPosition - position);

     // approximate the directional derivative by a
     // forward difference in direction of the light
     half sampleL  = tex3D(volume_texture,uvw+ DELTA*L).x;
     half n_l = (sampleL - sample);

     // Lambertian term
     half3 diffuse = Kd * lightColor * n_l;

     // add local illumination
     result.rgb += diffuse;
   }

   return result;
}
```

Listing 5.8. Cg fragment program for Lambertian illumination with directional derivatives to directly approximate $(\mathbf{n} \cdot \mathbf{l})$ instead of using a full gradient estimation.

used solely for illumination terms, a full estimation of the gradient vector might not be necessary. Illumination calculations usually compute the dot product between the normal $\mathbf{n} = \hat{\nabla} f$ and another vector. The Lambertian term $\langle \mathbf{n} \circ \mathbf{l} \rangle$ is a simple example for this. If we neglect the normalization of the gradient, we can interpret such a dot product as the directional derivative of the scalar field f in direction of the vector $\mathbf{l}$. In fact, the directional derivative is defined exactly that way,

$$\frac{\partial f(\mathbf{x})}{\partial \mathbf{l}} \;=\; \langle \nabla f(\mathbf{x}) \circ \mathbf{l} \rangle . \tag{5.42}$$

A numerical approximation of such a directional derivative can be obtained directly by a forward difference,

$$\langle \nabla f(\mathbf{x}) \circ \mathbf{l} \rangle \;\approx\; \frac{f(\mathbf{x} + h\mathbf{l}) - f(\mathbf{x})}{h} \;+\; o(h) , \tag{5.43}$$

a backward difference,

$$\langle \nabla f(\mathbf{x}) \circ \mathbf{l} \rangle \;\approx\; \frac{f(\mathbf{x}) - f(\mathbf{x} - h\mathbf{l})}{h} + o(h) , \tag{5.44}$$

or a central difference,

$$\langle \nabla f(\mathbf{x}) \circ \mathbf{l} \rangle \;\approx\; \frac{f(\mathbf{x} + h\mathbf{l}) - f(\mathbf{x} - h\mathbf{l})}{2h} + o(h^2) . \tag{5.45}$$

As an example, we can approximate Lambertian illumination directly by a forward difference in a fragment program that only requires one additional texture fetch. The code for such an implementation is displayed in Listing 5.8. Note that the dot product with the halfway vector $\mathbf{h}$ in Equation 5.25 can as well be approximated by a finite difference. The only drawback of this approximation is the missing gradient normalization. The resulting dot product can easily become larger than one, and it might be difficult to find a global scaling factor to compensate for this.

5.7   Environment Mapping

The idea of environment mapping is to either capture or pre-compute complex illumination scenarios. The usefulness of this approach derives from its ability to approximate local illumination with an infinite number of lights and arbitrary types of light sources in real time. Environment mapping [87] in general is a two-stage process that involves the construction of a reflection map and/or an irradiance map as a pre-computation step.

Figure 5.7.   Examples of a reflection map (left) and a corresponding irradiance map (right). (Eucalyptus Grove Light Probe Image © 1998 Paul Debevec, www.debevec.org.)

Environment maps store the light intensity emitted into, or arriving from, all spherical directions around a point in 3D space. Storing an environment map thus requires a 2D parameterization of a spherical surface. In practice, different representations of environment maps exist.

- *Spherical maps* store the entire incoming illumination in a single circular image. An example is displayed in Figure 5.7. The basic idea is that when a perfectly mirroring sphere is rendered (or, as an approximation, photographed) with an orthographic projection, the resulting image contains the reflection of almost all spherical directions around a point. In the limit, where the sphere is infinitely small, a spherical map actually captures *all* spherical directions. However, with this approach distortions for directions behind the view direction are very severe, and thus a spherical map can only be used for the view direction for which it has been generated or for very similar directions.

- *Dual paraboloid maps* reduce the distortions of spherical maps by mapping all spherical directions to two circular images. The parameterization corresponds to the orthogonal projection of a paraboloid for each of these two images.

- *Cube maps* store all spherical directions in the six faces of a cube. For each of these faces, standard rendering and projection of the environment with a field of view of 90 degrees can be used, and thus cube maps are extremely easy to generate on-the-fly on GPUs. Because of this property, cube maps are currently the most versatile representation for real-time rendering. They can be easily updated every frame. For example, in order to capture the volumetric illumination of a volume light source, the volume simply has to be rendered from six sides.

- *Spherical harmonics* are a frequency-based approach for representing spherical functions. Spherical harmonic coefficients correspond to frequencies and also have the same property that low-frequency signals

```
// irradiance and reflection mapping with
// post-classification using 3D textures
half4 main (half3 texUV     : TEXCOORD0,
            float3 position :  TEXCOORD1,

            uniform float3 Kd, // diffuse,
            uniform float3 Ks, // specular
            uniform float3 eyePosition,
            uniform sampler3D volume_texture,
            uniform sampler1D transfer_function,
            uniform samplerCUBE irradiance_map,
            uniform samplerCUBE reflection_map) :  COLOR
{
    float4 sample = tex3D(volume_texture, texUV);

    // expand and normalize the normal vector
    float3 N = normalize(2.0*sample.xyz - 1..xxx);
    // calculate viewing and reflection vectors
    float3 V = normalize(eyePosition - position);
    float3 R = reflect(V,N);
    // sample irradiance map (normal direction)
    float3 diffuse = Kd * texCUBE(irradiance_map,N);
    // sample reflection map (mirrored viewing direction)
    float3 specular = Ks * texCUBE(reflection_map,R);

    // emission and absorption from transfer function
    half4  result  = tex1D(transfer_function, sample.w);
    // add illumination
    result.rgb += diffuse + specular;

    return result;
}
```

Listing 5.9. Cg fragment program for local volume illumination with environment mapping. The specular term is looked up in a reflection cube map, and the diffuse term is obtained from a pre-computed irradiance cube map.

can be represented quite accurately by storing only a few coefficients and setting high frequencies to zero. Thus, spherical harmonics are especially powerful in the case of low-frequency lighting or diffuse lighting. For example, an environment map that will be used only in conjunction with diffuse reflection can be represented with a very small number of spherical harmonic coefficients without almost any noticeable error.

Environment maps can be used to efficiently implement different illumination effects. In general, they cache the incident illumination from all directions at a single point in space. The light reflected into our eye by a perfect mirror comes from exactly one spatial direction. For a perfect mirror, the incident illumination can thus directly be looked up in an environment map using the reflection direction $\mathbf{r}$ as in Equation 5.22.

Lambertian reflection requires integration of the incident illumination over the hemisphere centered about the normal vector. Such an integration can again be pre-computed as a so-called *irradiance map*, which stores the value of the integral over the hemisphere as function of the normal direction. An example of such an irradiance map is displayed in Figure 5.7 (right).

Nonperfect specular reflection can be implemented by pre-filtering environment maps for isotropic BRDFs and a rotational symmetric specular lobe. Just as in standard polygon-based rendering, environment maps can also be used in volume rendering to capture the entire external illumination surrounding a volume. Theory and practice of diffuse and glossy pre-filtering of environment maps can be found in [202]. An example implementation of local volume illumination using an irradiance map for the diffuse term and a reflection map for the specular term is given in Listing 5.9. In a reversed sense, environment maps can also be used to capture the entire illumination emitted by a volume into the surrounding space.

5.8   High Dynamic Range Illumination and Volume Rendering

The dynamic range of an image is defined as the ratio between the brightest and the dimmest measurable light intensity. In traditional real-time graphics applications, the color and light intensities are represented as 24-bit RGB triplets with 8-bit fixed point precision for each primary color component. This color representation is mainly motivated by the dynamic range and the color gamut of commercial CRT[2] display monitors. The limited 8-bit precision, however, turns out to be inadequate to describe light intensities

---

[2]CRT: cathode ray tube.

in the real world. This can be easily verified if you use a digital camera with variable exposure time. If you are taking several images of a real scene with varying exposure, you will most likely notice that every image contains illumination details that cannot be found in the other images.

The goal of high dynamic range imaging (HDRI) [282] is to capture as much of the original light intensities of a scene as possible and store the result at floating-point precision. In practice, HDR images are either synthesized by physically based rendering algorithms or obtained by HDR photography [40], which is based on multiexposure image-capture techniques as mentioned above. But why should we capture more information that we are able to display on our monitor? The answer to this question is twofold. The first reason is that we want to mimic the capabilities of the human eye to adapt itself to different brightness levels by contracting and dilating the pupil. The second reason comes from physically based rendering and image-based lighting. The appearance of realistic materials with different reflective behavior is dominated by different portions of the dynamic range of light. Fully realistic lighting can only be achieved if all the subtleties caused by the entire dynamic range are considered.

One of the most popular applications of HDR images is image-based lighting as introduced by Paul Debevec [41]. A virtual scene is illuminated by images from the real world. The basic idea is essentially the same as reflection mapping described above, except for the high dynamic range. The incident light from a real environment is captured by taking omnidirectional multiexposure photographs and reconstructing the incident light intensities (environment maps). Similar techniques can be used to derive HDR irradiance maps.

Tone-mapping techniques are used to map the high dynamic range back to the low dynamic range of conventional display monitors. Many tone-mapping techniques have been proposed in recent years [47]. Basically, they can be divided into global and local approaches. Global tone mapping approaches calculate a spatially uniform scaling function to map the high dynamic range to 8-bit RGB. These approaches are based on the total brightness of an image. Local tone mapping operators only consider the light intensities in a limited neighborhood of each pixel. The scaling function is spatially varying and parts of the image with different brightness levels are handled separately.

In recent years, many rendering methods have incorporated formats of a higher dynamic range for representing illumination or colors. High dynamic range techniques require all rendering operations to be performed at floating-point precision. In response to this requirement, current GPU architectures support texture formats and render targets with 16-bit and 32-bit floating-point precision for each primary color component.

Apart from external illumination with HDR environment, the idea of treating volumes as light-emitting entities makes a high dynamic range

Figure 5.8. Examples of a high dynamic range volume-rendering system. Turbulent mixing of air and sulfur hexafluoride (SF$_6$). The small images are generated at different exposure levels. (Images courtesy of Xiaoru Yuan, Minh X. Nguyen, Baoquan Chen, and David Porter, University of Minnesota at Twin Cities. Data provided by David Porter and Paul Woodward, Lab of Computer Science and Computer Engineering (LCSE), University of Minnesota at Twin Cities (© 2005 IEEE).)

approach very attractive. High dynamic range volume rendering requires floating-point render targets as well as alpha blending and transfer functions in floating-point precision. High-precision alpha blending with floating-point render targets is discussed in Section 9.5. Appropriate transfer functions are implemented using floating-point texture formats for the dependent texture look-ups. Finally, tone mapping operators must be applied to map the pixel values from the floating-point render target to the visible frame buffer with the usual 24-bit RGBA format. Yuan et al. demonstrate a working implementation of a HDR volume rendering system [307]. They propose effective methods and user interfaces for specifying HDR transfer functions. An adaptive logarithmic mapping function is used for tone reproduction. Example images produced by their implementation are displayed in Figure 5.8. Another volume-rendering framework that supports high dynamic range rendering was presented by Vollrath et al. [275].

5.9   Further Reading

Although most of the local illumination techniques described in this chapter violate the laws of physics in one way or the other, they significantly contribute to the comprehensibility and the visual quality of the image results. Global illumination techniques will be discussed in the next chapter. Optimization strategies such as deferred shading is explained in Chapter 8. Non-photorealistic approaches to volume illumination are discussed in Chapter 14.

For further reference on accurate illumination, Glassner has written a very detailed and comprehensive book on the theory of physically based illumination in two volumes [80]. A more practical text on illumination and rendering techniques is *Physically Based Rendering* by Pharr and Humphries [211]. The book *Real-Time Shading* by Olano et al. is an excellent introduction to physically accurate illumination and programmable shading for real-time applications.

For more information on high dynamic range imaging and image-based lighting, we refer to the comprehensive guide by Reinhard et al. [221]. There also exist several SIGGRAPH course notes on image-based lighting that can be used as reference [281].

6

Global Volume Illumination

CHAPTER 5 COVERS VARIOUS techniques for rendering semitransparent volume surfaces using an approximation to the Blinn-Phong local surface shading model. Although this model is adequate for shading surfaces, it does not provide sufficient lighting characteristics for translucent materials or materials where scattering dominates the visual appearance. Furthermore, the normal required for the Blinn-Phong shading model is derived from the normalized gradient of the scalar field. Although this normal is well defined for regions in the volume that have high gradient

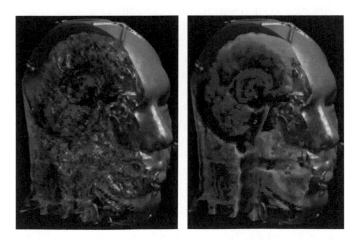

Figure 6.1. Surface-based shading versus volume shading. Surface shading cannot adequately shade homogeneous regions such as the soft tissue in a CT scan (left). A more general volume-shading model is needed to render the classified regions (right). (Images reprinted from [129], © 2003 IEEE.)

magnitudes, this normal is undefined in homogeneous regions, i.e., where the gradient is the zero vector, as seen in Figure 6.1 (left). The use of the normalized gradient is also troublesome in regions with low gradient magnitudes, where noise can significantly degrade the gradient computation. In Chapter 10, we discuss volume rendering and transfer function techniques that can be used to directly visualize multivariate data sets. Although a type of derivative measure can be computed for these data sets, it is not suitable for deriving a normal for surface shading.

Several studies have shown that the appearance of many common objects is dominated by scattering effects [16, 113]. This is especially true for natural phenomena such as smoke and clouds but it is also true for wax, skin, and other translucent materials.

Although the effects of multiple scattering are important, the physically accurate computation of these effects is not necessarily required to create meaningful images. In fact, most interactive graphics applications already employ non–physically based or heuristic methods (e.g., ambient light, OpenGL style fog, even the Blinn-Phong surface shading model), which are substantially less computationally expensive than their physically based analogues. Interactivity for visualization is important because it aids in the rapid and accurate setting of transfer functions, as well as provides important visual cues about spatial relationships in the data. Although it is possible to pre-compute multiple scattering effects, such methods are inevitably dependent on the viewpoint, light position, transfer function, and other rendering parameters, which limits interactivity.

The following section describes an approximation of the transport equation (discussed in Chapter 1), which is designed to provide interactive or near-interactive frame rates for volume rendering when the transfer function, light direction, or volume data are not static. This requires the light intensity at each sample to be recomputed every frame. The method for computing light transport is done in image-space resolutions, allowing the computational complexity to match the level of detail. Because the computation of light transport is decoupled from the resolution of the volume data, we can also accurately compute lighting for volumes with high frequency displacement effects, like those described in Chapter 12.

6.1   Volumetric Shadows

The design of a general, interactive volume-shading model can best be understood if we first examine the implementation of direct lighting. A brute force implementation of direct lighting, or volumetric shadows, can be accomplished by sending a shadow ray toward the light for each sample along the viewing ray to estimate the amount of extinction caused by the portion of the volume between that sample and the light. This algorithm would have the computational complexity of $O(nm) \equiv O(n^2)$ where n is the total number of samples taken along each viewing ray, and m is the number of samples taken along each shadow ray. In general, the algorithm would be far too slow for interactive visualization. It is also very redundant because many of these shadow rays overlap. One possible solution would be to pre-compute lighting, by iteratively sampling the volume from the light's point of view, and storing the light intensities at each spatial position in a so-called shadow volume. Although this approach reduces the computational complexity to $O(n + m) \equiv O(n)$, it has a few obvious disadvantages. First, this method can require a significant amount of additional memory for storing the shadow volume. When memory consumption and access times are a limiting factor, one must trade the resolution of the shadow volume, and thus the resolution of direct lighting computations, for reduced memory footprint and improved access times. Another disadvantage of shadow-volume techniques is known as "attenuation leakage," caused by the interpolation kernel used when accessing the illumination in the shadow volume.

If direct lighting could be computed in lock step with the accumulation of light for the eye, the integrals for both (the eye and light) could be computed iteratively in image space using 2D buffers; one for accumulating the rendered image from the eye's point of view and another for accumulating attenuation from the light source point of view. This can be accomplished using the method of *half-angle slicing*, where the slice axis is halfway between the light and view directions or halfway between the light and inverted view directions depending on the sign of the dot product. If the sign of the dot product between the view and light directions is positive, the slicing and rendering proceeds in front-to-back order with respect to the eye. If the dot product is negative, rendering proceeds in back-to-front order with respect to the eye. Rendering from the light's point of view is always front to back. This is illustrated in Figure 6.2.

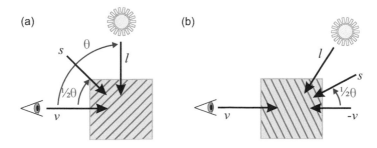

Figure 6.2. Half-angle slice axis for light transport.

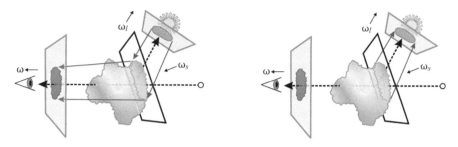

Figure 6.3. Two-pass shadows using half-angle slicing. For each slice, first render into the eye's buffer, sampling the positions that the slice projects to in the light buffer (left). Next render the slice into the light buffer, updating the light attenuation for the next slice. ω_s indicates the slice axis (right).

```
Generate volume slices using half-angle.
Initialize light buffer to 1,1,1,1.
For each slice:
   Render slice into eye buffer.
      Bind eye buffer as render target.
      Bind light buffer as texture.
      Compute light buffer texture coordinates.
      For each sample (fragment program):
         Evaluate sample color.
         Read light intensity from light buffer.
         Multiply color by light intensity.
      End for
   Render slice into light buffer.
      Bind light buffer as render target.
      Set blend to "over".
      For each sample (fragment program):
         Evaluate sample opacity (a).
         Output color {0,0,0,a}.
      End for
End for
```

Listing 6.1.   Pseudocode for volume shadows.

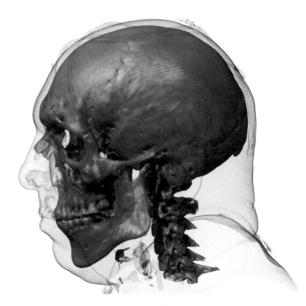

Figure 6.4. An example of a volume rendering with direct lighting.

The modification of the slicing axis provides the ability to render each slice from the point of view of both the observer and the light, thereby achieving the effect of a high-resolution shadow volume without the requirement of pre-computation and storage.

Volumetric shadows can be implemented very efficiently on graphics hardware using multipass, slice-based volume-rendering techniques. The approach requires an additional pass for each slice, updating the light intensities for the next slice. Each slice is first rendered from the eye's point of view, where the light intensity at each sample on the slice is acquired by sampling the position it would project to in the light's buffer. This light intensity is multiplied by the color of the sample, which is then blended into the eye's buffer. This step is illustrated in Figure 6.3 (left). Next the slice is rendered into the light buffer, attenuating the light by the opacity at each sample in the slice. This step is illustrated in Figure 6.3 (right). Listing 6.1 shows the algorithm in pseudo code. An example of direct lighting in volume-rendering applications can be seen in Figure 6.4.

6.2   Phase Functions

The role of the phase function in volume light transport is similar to that of the bidirectional reflectance distribution function (BRDF) in surface-based

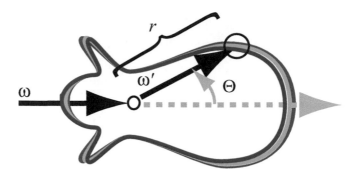

Figure 6.5. An example of a symmetric phase function plotted in polar coordinates. The incoming direction ω is fixed, whereas outgoing direction ω' varies over all directions.

light transport problems. It describes the distribution of light after a scattering event for each outgoing direction ω' given an incoming light direction ω. Whereas the BRDF is only defined over a hemisphere of directions relative to the surface normal, the phase function describes the distribution of light over the entire sphere of directions. Phase functions are generally only dependent on the cosine of the angle between the incoming and outgoing directions ω and ω': $\cos\theta = \omega\cdot\omega'$. Although true phase functions are normalized, $\int_{4\pi} P(\omega,\omega')d\omega' = 1$, this is not required (or even useful) for interactive graphics applications. We will discuss this issue further in the next section (6.2.1). Figure 6.5 shows a plot of a simplified phase function in polar coordinates. The radius r is essentially the weighting for a particular direction. Notice that the phase function is wavelength dependent, indicated by the colored contours. This class of phase functions is referred to as symmetric phase functions because the distribution of scattered energy is rotationally symmetric about the incoming direction. Symmetric phase functions are valid for spherical or randomly oriented particles. For most applications, this class of phase functions is quite adequate.

Symmetrical phase functions can be implemented in conjunction with direct lighting by computing the dot product of the unit vector from the sample to the eye with the unit vector from the light to the sample, and then using this scalar value as an index into a 1D look-up table, i.e., this dot product is used as texture coordinate for reading from a 1D texture that stores the phase function term. The light and view directions can be computed for each vertex that defines the corners of the current slice being rendered and assigned to texture coordinates for each vertex. These coordinates are interpolated over the slice during rasterization. In the fragment program, we need to renormalize these vectors and compute the dot product between them. Because the range of values resulting from the

Figure 6.6. Phase-function effects on a spherical cloud. The images use the Henyey-Greenstein phase function with $g = 1 - \alpha$, i.e., the phase-function anisotropy is proportional to the transparency at each sample. Notice that the back-lit cloud (upper-left) has very bright fringes, whereas the front-lit cloud (upper-right) has dark fringes. This is because these regions have a highly forward peaked phase function. The center of the cloud has an isotropic phase function, which makes it brighter in the front-lit clouds. The lower-left image shows the spherical cloud lit at a 45° angle to the viewer. The lower-right image was rendered using the Henyey-Greenstein phase function plus a Mie phase function generated using MiePlot; it is the Mie phase function that creates the subtle glory effect.

dot product are $[-1..1]$, we first scale and bias the values $(x' = (x+1)/2)$, so that they are in the range $[0..1]$, and then read from the 1D phase function texture. The result is then multiplied with the direct lighting and reflective color. Figure 6.6 shows some effects of phase functions.

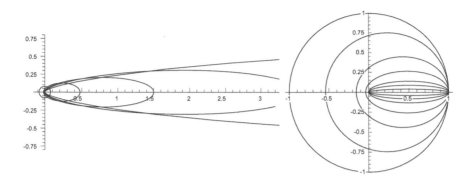

Figure 6.7. Henyey-Greenstein phase functions. Each graph plots multiple phase functions with g varying from 0 to .9. The plot on the left shows phase functions that integrate to 1 over the sphere (normalized). The plot on the right shows phase functions that have been "renormalized" into the range [0..1] for use in interactive graphics with generic lighting.

6.2.1   Henyey-Greenstein Phase Function

For most purposes, wavelength dependence is not an important character-istic of the phase function. In general, we need the phase function only to describe the degree to which the scattering of light prefers forward (or backward) scattering. In this case, the Henyey-Greenstein phase function is an excellent choice:

$$G(\theta, g) = \frac{1 - g^2}{4\pi(1 + g^2 - 2g\cos\theta)^{1.5}}, \tag{6.1}$$

where g is the *anisotropy* of the phase function. When $g = 0$, the scattering of light is equal in all directions, positive values of g in the range [0..1] indi-cate forward scattering. Figure 6.7 plots two phase functions using different g values. Note that this phase function is normalized, $\int_{4\pi} P(\omega, \omega')d\omega' = 1$. The units of this *probability density function* are 1/steradian or sr^{-1} (stera-dians are the units associated with solid angles, a sphere has 4π steradians). This is not exactly a quantity we are accustomed to dealing with in inter-active graphics. A normalized phase function is really only meaningful if the light intensity is expressed in terms of radiometric irradiance, which has the units of watts per square meter. When the phase function and ir-radiance are multiplied together we get the radiance for a scattering event, which has the units of watts per steradian per meter squared. The prob-lem is twofold: (1) in interactive graphics applications, we are generally using some generic light intensity, restricted to the range [0..1] for each RGB color component, with no real associated units, and(2) the shading models we use, e.g., Blinn-Phong, do not conserve energy. These issues becomes clear when we attempt to use a normalized phase function in this "generic light" setting. If we take a white light ($I = \{1, 1, 1\}$) and use the isotropic phase function $G(0, 0)$ to compute light scattered in the forward direction ($I_{\text{forward}} = IG(0, 0))$), we get the value $I_{\text{forward}} = \{0.079, 0.079, 0.079\}$, which is nearly black when displayed as a color. In contrast, if we compute the forward scattered light using a forward peaked phase function, $G(0, .8)$, we get the value $I_{\text{forward}} = \{3.58, 3.58, 3.58\}$, which is not even a displayable color besides the fact that this implies we are scattering three times as much light in the forward direction than we had to begin with. Even though the Blinn-Phong shading model does not (necessarily) conserve energy, it does not reflect more light than it began with. How can we take advantage of these phase functions in interactive rendering that does not deal directly with radiance and irradiance? Obviously, the phase function should be limited to the range [0..1] for any given phase angle, and we do not require it to integrate to unity over the sphere of directions. We could *renormalize* for our generic light environment by dividing the phase function by its maximum value. Because we know that the Henyey-Greenstein phase function will always have a maxima at the 0 phase angle for positive values of g, the renormalized phase function is

$$G'(\theta, g) = \frac{G(\theta, g)}{G(0, g)}, \tag{6.2}$$

where negative values of g (back-scattering) would have a maxima at $180°$ and therefore require $G(180, g)$ in the denominator. Here's the rub: renormalizing the phase function in this way will eliminate the essential intensity differences between isotropic scattering and forward scattering at the 0 phase angle. That is, $G'(0, g) = 1$ for all g greater than or equal to 0, which means that there will be no difference in the scattered intensity for different phase functions when the phase angle is 0. However, this is probably not an issue, as this situation requires the material to be back-lit and even then, only a single pixel in the image plane will have a zero phase angle. This is not unlike the specular highlight in the Blinn-Phong shading model; regardless of what specular power is specified, the specular weight in the direction of the reflection vector will always be 1.

In practice, it is useful to cache a range of these phase functions in a 2D texture, where the first index is based on the phase angle θ (scaled and biased to the [0..1] range) and the second texture coordinate is the g value. When we are rendering a volume using phase functions, the g term can be specified as an additional optical property in the transfer function along with color and opacity. This is useful when rendering clouds, since the less dense outer fringes will have a highly forward peaked phase function, while the dense interior will have an isotropic phase function. In this case, one could set the g value to $1 - \alpha$ and achieve excellent results, as seen in

Figure 6.6. Notice that when the light is coming from behind the viewer, the outer fringes of the cloud are darker than the interior, while a back-lit cloud has very bright fringes.

6.2.2   Mie Scattering Phase Functions

Wavelength-dependent phase functions come into play when we are seeking the more exotic scattering effects like rainbows and glories. The reason that these phenomena are so exotic or rare is that they require very specific physical conditions, i.e., raindrops of a relatively uniform size or a very fine mist of relatively uniform water particles suspended in air. The phase functions themselves require very sophisticated physically based simulation over hundreds of individual wavelengths to compute. Fortunately, a tool exists for computing, visualizing, and analyzing these complicated effects. MiePlot by Philip Laven is an excellent tool for generating these special-purpose phase functions. Keep in mind that, while this tool can generate scattering functions for specific wavelengths, a three-wavelength phase function (one for each of red, green, and blue) will not produce very good results for rendering. The reason for this is that the RGB channels that we use for display are meant to cover three wavelength *intervals*, not three individual wavelengths. Also, this tool is designed to simulate scattering effects for water particles of very specific sizes, and changing the size of particles can result in very different phase functions. This tool allows one to simulate scattering for a distribution of particle sizes; when this is done, we can observe that increasingly heterogeneous particle sizes result in phase functions that have little or no wavelength dependence.

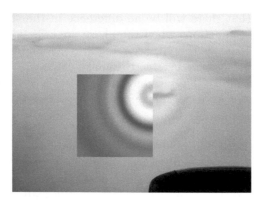

Figure 6.8. A glory effect computed using MiePlot (inset) overlaid with a real photograph of the phenomena. The phase function required a simulation involving 200 individual wavelengths of light and a uniform water particle size of 4.8 microns.

This is why clouds, which (generally) have a wide distribution of water particle sizes, do not necessarily require this kind of sophisticated phase function simulation, thus motivating the use of simple Henyey-Greenstein phase functions for general applications. Figure 6.8 shows a glory simulation generated using MiePlot, and Figure 6.6 (lower-right) shows the effect rendered using a modified version of this phase function combined with a variable Henyey-Greenstein phase function. Because the phase function values that represent the glory phenomena are 1/1000th of those in the forward direction, we only used the Mie phase function for angles from 90° to 180° and renormalized based on the max of these values.

Note that MiePlot will display a color map of the phase function above the plots of "intensity vs. scattering angle"; you can quickly generate phase function look-up tables by doing a screen grab of the tool and extracting this row of pixels, which will already be "renormalized" for generic lighting as discussed in the previous section. MiePlot can also save the floating point values into a file; it only takes a little extra work to extract the RGB components. Remember that the best results will involve a simulation over a wide range of wavelengths. MiePlot will do the integration of these wavelengths for the RGB intervals we need for rendering, but you will need to do the renormalization.

6.3   Translucent Volume Lighting

Once direct lighting has been implemented, computing the higher-order scattering terms becomes a simple extension of this algorithm. As light is propagated from slice to slice, some scattering is allowed. This scattering is forward-only due to the incremental nature of the propagation algorithm. Thus, this method is only an approximation of the general volume light transport problem, in much the same way that the Blinn-Phong model is an approximation of physically based surface lighting.

One major difference between this translucent volume shading model and the volume-rendering approaches discussed in the previous chapters is the additional optical properties required for rendering to simulate higher-order scattering. The key to understand this treatment of optical properties comes from recognizing the difference between absorption and extinction. The attenuation of light for direct lighting is proportional to extinction, which is the sum of absorption and out-scattering. The goal of this method is to account for the portion of light that was scattered and not absorbed.

The traditional volume-rendering pipeline only requires two optical properties for each material: extinction and material color. However, rather than specifying the extinction coefficient τ, which is a value in the range zero to infinity (see Chapter 1 for more details), the more intuitive opacity,

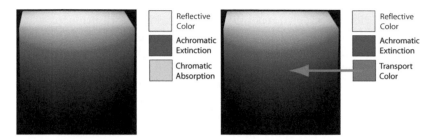

Figure 6.9. To attenuate scattered light, a chromatic indirect alpha, or absorption, term is required (left). However, this tends to be difficult for a user to specify. The complement of this color (right), which is the color that light will become as it is attenuated, is a more intuitive way to understand and specify this term. (Images reprinted from [129], © 2003 IEEE.)

or alpha, term is used:

$$\alpha = 1 - e^{-\tau(\mathbf{x})} . \tag{6.3}$$

For the remainder of this section, this opacity will be referred to as the direct opacity or attenuation $\alpha_\mathbf{d}$. In addition to color and opacity, this model adds an indirect attenuation term to the transfer function. This term is chromatic, meaning that it describes the indirect attenuation of light for each of the R, G, and B color components. Similar to direct attenuation, the indirect attenuation can be specified in terms of an indirect alpha:

$$\alpha_\mathbf{i} = 1 - e^{-\tau_\mathbf{i}(\mathbf{x})} . \tag{6.4}$$

Although this is useful for describing indirect attenuation mathematically, it is not very intuitive for user specification. We prefer to specify a *transport color* that is $1 - \alpha_\mathbf{i}$, because this is the color the indirect light will become as it is attenuated by the material. Figure 6.9 illustrates the difference between the absorption, or indirect alpha, and the transport color.

The indirect opacity $\alpha_\mathbf{i}$ can be treated as a means for capturing the attenuation of light due to absorption only, i.e., the light absorbed by the participating medium, whereas the direct opacity $\alpha_\mathbf{d}$ is meant to capture the *total extinction*, i.e, the light lost due to both absorption and out-scattering. Therefore, it is easy to see that *if* the indirect opacity is absorption-only, then it should always be less than or equal to the direct opacity:

$$\|\alpha_\mathbf{i}\| \leq \alpha_\mathbf{d} . \tag{6.5}$$

The decision to leave the direct opacity achromatic, as it is in the traditional volume-rendering pipeline, was purely for practical reasons. First, it is convenient to keep track of only four attenuation terms (three for indirect light, and one for direct light), because 4-vectors are a natural data

Figure 6.10. An opalescent material lit from above. The complex scattering effects needed to create the characteristic hue shift from blue to red are *approximated* using an empirical translucent volume-shading model. The reflective color is a de-saturated blue and the transport color is a desaturated red.

quantum in graphics hardware. Second, it can be very difficult for a user to understand and specify chromatic (direct) attenuation, as this could affect how overlapping materials blend with each other from the viewer's perspective, leading to very unintuitive results. This need for intuitive, user-specified parameters is the reason we prefer the transport color for indirect opacity specification, it is easy to grasp the idea that this is the color light will become as it penetrates deeper into the material. Finally, although the characteristic hue-shift in translucent materials can be due to scattering as well as absorption, these effects can be still be captured by appropriately adjusting the material color (sometimes referred to as the *reflective color* in this section) and the chromatic indirect attenuation. For instance, materials with an "opalescent" quality (like the daytime sky) exhibit the hue-shift effect (from bluish to red) almost entirely due to wave-length dependent scattering. In this case, shorter (bluer) light wavelengths are scattered more than the longer (redder) wavelengths, with little or no loss due to absorption. The net effect, however, is the loss of blue wave-lengths as light penetrates deeper into the material. We can achieve this effect by making the reflective material color a desaturated blue, as the reflection of light is a scattering phenomena and we know that this ma-terial preferentially scatters blue, and making the transport color slightly red, as we know that red wavelengths exhibit less out-scattering attenua-tion. In this case, we are using the indirect attenuation term to capture the gradual, wavelength-dependent loss of light due to scattering rather than absorption. Figure 6.10 shows an example rendering using this approach. Naturally, this description is purely empirical but nonetheless based on and motivated by physical principles.

6.3.1   Algorithm Overview

This volume-rendering pipeline computes the transport of light through the volume in lock step with the accumulation of light for the eye. Just as we

updated the direct lighting (shadows) incrementally, the indirect lighting
contributions are computed in the same way. To account for scattering, we
must integrate the incoming light over a range of incoming directions; thus
we need to sample the light buffer in multiple locations within a disk to
accomplish the blurring of light as it propagates.

The algorithm utilizes three buffers; one buffer for the eye, which ac-
cumulates the image that the viewer will see, and two buffers for the light
view, which accumulate the attenuation and scattering of light. Both light
buffers are initialized to 1 for all (RGBA) components. Whereas the shadow
method only required a single buffer for light attenuation, this method requires two in order to accommodate a custom blending operation. Unlike
the volume shadow method described earlier, instead of a single (achromatic) attenuation of light intensity, the light buffer will be storing four
different attenuation terms; independent red, green, and blue indirect-light
(stored in the RGB components) plus the (achromatic) direct light (stored
in the alpha component). In the light update step, the direct light will
be attenuated in the usual fashion; the opacity of the incoming sample is
used to attenuate the light previously available at that position in the light
buffer. The update (blend) function for direct light $L_{\mathbf{d}}$ attenuation is

$$L'_{\mathbf{d}} = (1 - \alpha_{\mathbf{d}})L_{\mathbf{d}} , \qquad (6.6)$$

where $\alpha_{\mathbf{d}}$ is the achromatic direct light opacity for a sample. This is identical to the blend function used for volume shadows. The indirect attenuation, however, is updated by examining N locations in a neighborhood
around the samples location in the light buffer, computing the amount of
light in-scattered based on this neighborhood, and attenuating this light
per wavelength. The general expression for updating the value stored in
the light buffer for indirect light is

$$L'_{\mathbf{i}} = (1 - \alpha_{\mathbf{i}}) \sum_{i}^{N} (w_{\mathbf{d},i}L_{\mathbf{d},i} + w_{\mathbf{i},i}L_{\mathbf{i},i}) , \qquad (6.7)$$

where $\alpha_{\mathbf{i}}$ is the chromatic indirect light opacity for the sample being rendered, $w_{*,i}$ are blur weights for the direct and indirect light scattering with
$\sum w_{*,i} = 1$, and $L_{*,i}$ is the direct and indirect light (respectively) currently
in the light buffer for each of the N neighborhood samples. The indirect
light weights $(w_{\mathbf{i},i})$ can be set to $1/N$, resulting in a simple average over the
neighborhood. The direct light weights $(w_{\mathbf{d},i})$ could be based on the phase
function (P) times the difference between indirect and direct opacity, for
instance

$$w_i = \frac{P(\theta_i)(\alpha_{\mathbf{d}} - \alpha_{\mathbf{i}})}{N} , \qquad (6.8)$$

where θ_i is the angle between the light direction and the vector from the
neighbor sample to the current sample. Of course if no phase function has

been specified, we can set $P(\theta_i) = 1$. There are several issues to consider here. (1) A weighting function like Equation 6.8 can end up being quite expensive and therefore cut into our rendering performance. (2) Because this is effectively a blur, an inaccurate w_i weight will not affect the results dramatically. (3) Using the difference between direct opacity and indirect opacity assumes that the indirect opacity is being used to represent absorption only. As noted earlier, this term could also be used to account for attenuation due to scattering. In this case, the difference of direct and indirect opacity isn't really meaningful. Arguably, the most important thing about the direct light weights is that they account for the presence (or lack thereof) of material at the neighbor sample, because when no material is present, we should not expect any in-scattering from that location. One could also argue that the same is true for the indirect light weights, and indeed it makes sense to only scatter indirect light when there is something there to scatter it. However, we can also think of the indirect light as *diffuse*, i.e., light that does not really have a preferred direction. In this case, we are thinking of the indirect light at a neighbor sample simply as the amount of diffuse light that has not been attenuated by the participating media. Notice that we initialized the indirect light in the light buffers to 1; this diffuse treatment of indirect light is the reason. The main point of this discussion is the ideal weights used to integrate light in-scatter will depend on the application, though the qualitative difference in the images for different weighting schemes can be subtle at best. After all, it is really just a fancy blur operation.

Because we need to sample the light buffer in multiple locations, we cannot use the native OpenGL frame buffer blending operations. This is why two buffers are required; we cannot read-from and write-to the same buffer simultaneously. The reason we cannot do this is complicated, and OpenGL does not explicitly forbid it, but doing so can generate inconsistent results. In the following algorithm explanation, one light buffer will be referred to as the *next* light buffer; it is the buffer that will be rendered to (bound as the render target) in the light update step. The other is referred to as the *current* light buffer, it is bound as a texture and read from in both the eye update step and light update step. After each slice has been rendered (both passes completed), the light buffers are swapped, i.e., *next→current* and *current→next*.

6.3.2   Algorithm Details

Set-up. When slicing the volume, you will need to add additional texture coordinates for each vertex. In all, you will need three or four sets: (1) 3D texture coordinates for the volume data, as with any texture-based volume rendering application, (2) 2D texture coordinates for the position that the vertex projects to in the light buffer, much like geometric shadow mapping algorithms, (3) 3D texture coordinates for representing the view direction from the eye to the vertex, and if the light is not infinitely far from the volume, (4) texture coordinates representing the light direction from the light to the vertex. Texture coordinates 3 and 4, the light and view directions, are needed to evaluate the phase function.

Pass 1: Observer update. In the first pass, a slice is rendered from the observer's point of view. The eye buffer is the render target, and the *current* light buffer is bound as a texture. In the fragment program, the transfer function is evaluated and the material color is multiplied by the sum of the indirect and direct light previously computed at that slice position in the *current* light buffer. Remember that the direct light component is achromatic, i.e., it is a scalar value. The total light intensity is expressed as

$$I' = (L_\mathbf{i} + L_\mathbf{d})\, I_0 \,, \tag{6.9}$$

where I' is the total (RGB) light intensity available at the current sample, $L_\mathbf{i}$ is the indirect (RGB) light color from the *current* light buffer, $L_\mathbf{d}$ is the direct (achromatic/scalar) light intensity from the *current* light buffer, and I_0 is the original light color. If phase functions or surface lighting is used, this term should only be applied to the direct lighting component, since we are assuming that the scattered, indirect light is diffuse,

$$I' = (L_\mathbf{i} + L_\mathbf{d}S())\, I_0 \,, \tag{6.10}$$

where $S()$ is a surface shading or phase function. This color is then blended into the observer buffer using the alpha value from the transfer function in the usual fashion.

Pass 2: Light update. In the second pass, the same slice is rendered into the *next* light buffer from the light's point of view to update the lighting for the next iteration. The *current* light buffer is bound as a texture. In the fragment program for this pass, the texture coordinates for the neighborhood samples can be computed by adding a random 2D vector to the current sample location's texture coordinate. This random vector is stored in a noise texture, similar to those used for volume perturbation discussed in Chapter 12. Four neighborhood samples are usually enough to produce good results. Randomizing the neighborhood sample offsets in this way can mask some artifacts caused by a coarse, regular sampling. The amount of this offset is scaled by either a user-defined blur angle (θ) or an angle based on the anisotropy of the phase function, times the slice-plane spacing (d):

$$\text{offset} \leq d \tan\left(\frac{\theta}{2}\right) \,. \tag{6.11}$$

The *current* light buffer is then read using the new texture coordinates. These values are weighted and summed to compute the blurred inward flux (scattered light) at the sample. The transfer function is evaluated for the current sample based on the volume data to obtain the indirect attenuation (α_i) and direct attenuation (α_d) values for the current slice. The blurred inward flux is attenuated as described before (Equation 6.7) and written to the RGB components of the *next* light buffer. The direct light intensity, i.e., the alpha component from the *current* light buffer read using the unmodified texture coordinates, is attenuated by α_d (Equation 6.6) and written out to the alpha component of the *next* light buffer.

After this pass has been completed, the light buffers are swapped, so that the **next** buffer becomes the **current** and *vice versa*. That is, the last light buffer rendered-to will be read-from when the next slice is rendered. This approach is called *ping pong blending* and is discussed further in Section 9.5.

6.3.3 Analysis

This empirical volume shading model adds a blurred indirect light contribution at each sample:

$$I(\mathbf{x}_1, \omega) = T(0, l)I(\mathbf{x}_0, \omega) + \int_0^l T(0, s)C(s)I_l(s)ds, \qquad (6.12)$$

where $\tau_i(s)$ is the indirect light attenuation term, $C(s)$ is the reflective color at the sample s, $S(s)$ is a surface shading parameter, and I_l is the sum of the direct light and the indirect light contributions. These terms are defined as follows:

$$C(s) = E(s)\left((1 - S(s)) + f_s(s)S(s)\right); \qquad (6.13)$$

$$I_l(s) = I_l * \exp\left(-\int_s^{lt} \tau(x)dx\right)P(\theta) +$$

$$I_l \exp\left(-\int_s^{lt} \tau_i(x)dx\right)\mathbf{Blur}(\theta), \qquad (6.14)$$

where I_l is the intensity of the light as before, $I_l(s)$ is the light intensity at a location on the ray as it gets attenuated, and $P(\theta)$ is the phase function. Note that the final model in Equation 6.12 includes direct and indirect components as well as the phase function that modulates the direct contribution. Spatially varying indirect contribution (scattering) and phase function were not included in the classical volume-rendering model discussed in previous chapters.

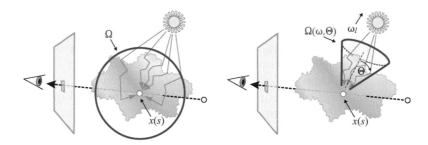

Figure 6.11. Left: general light transport scenario, where at any sample $x(s)$ we must consider incoming light scattered from all directions over the unit sphere Ω. Right: the approximation, which only considers light scattered in the forward direction within the cone of directions, the light direction ω_l with apex angle θ.

It is interesting to compare the nature of this approximation to the physically based light transport equation. One way to think of it is as a forward diffusion process. This is different from traditional diffusion approximations [247, 280, 70] because it cannot backpropagate light. A perhaps more intuitive way to think of the approximation is in terms of what light propagation paths are possible. This is shown in Figure 6.11. The missing paths involve lateral movements outside the cone or any backscattering. This can give some intuition for what effects this model does not approximate, such as a reverse bleeding under a barrier. This, however, is less of a problem in volume rendering than it is with surface-based translucency techniques, as materials below the surface *are* being rendered and will contribute to light paths toward the eye.

Because the effect of indirect lighting in dense media is effectively a diffusion of light through the volume, light travels farther in the volume than it would if only direct attenuation is taken into account. Translucency implies blurring of the light as it travels through the medium due to scattering effects. This effect is approximated by simply blurring the light in some neighborhood and allowing it to attenuate less in the light direction. Figure 6.12 shows how the important phenomenological effect of translucency is captured by this model. The upper-left image, a photo of a wax candle, is an example of a common translucent object. The upper-right image is a volume rendering using this model. Notice that the light penetrates much deeper into the material than it does with direct attenuation alone (volumetric shadows), seen in the lower-right image. Also notice the pronounced hue shift from white to orange to black due to an indirect attenuation term that attenuates blue slightly more than red or green. The lower-left image shows the effect of changing just the reflective (material) color to a pale blue.

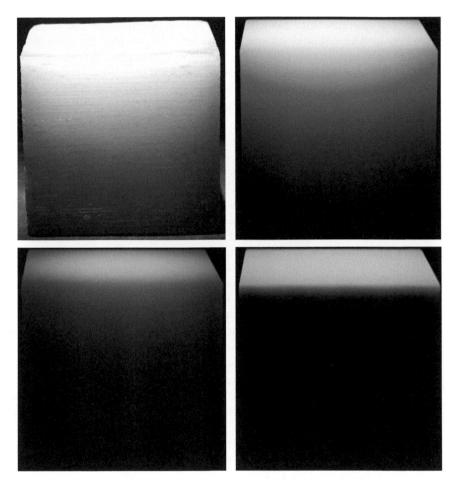

Figure 6.12.   Translucent volume-shading comparison. The upper-left image is a photograph of a wax block illuminated from above with a focused flashlight. The upper-right image is a volume rendering with a white reflective color and a desaturated orange transport color (1 − *indirect attenuation*). The lower-left image has a bright blue reflective color and the same transport color as the upper-right image. The lower-right image shows the effect of light transport that only takes into account direct attenuation. (Images reprinted from [129], © 2003 IEEE.)

Surface shading can also be added for use with scalar data sets. For this we recommend the use of a surface-shading parameter, the so-called surface scalar. This is a scalar value between one and zero that describes the degree to which a sample should be surface shaded. It is used to interpolate between surface shading and no surface shading. This value can be added to the transfer function, allowing the user to specify whether or not a classified material should be surface shaded. It can also be determined automatically using the gradient magnitude at the sample. In this case, we assume that classified regions will be surface-like if the gradient magnitude is high and therefore should be shaded as such. In contrast, homogeneous regions, which have low gradient magnitudes, should only be shaded using light attenuation.

6.4   Shading Strategies

The translucent shading model discussed earlier is not meant to replace surface shading in volumes. If the volumetric objects we are rendering are best represented as surfaces, they should be shaded as such. The translucent shading model can be used as a replacement for the diffuse component of the Blinn-Phong shading model. In fact, this diffuse, or Lambertian, shading *is* an approximation of subsurface shading, a special case of light transport in participating media. It was shown as early as 1914 that there is no opaque surface configuration that can produce equal reflection in all directions. Surfaces that exhibit true Lambertian reflectance are always composed of highly translucent materials, i.e., their appearance is dominated by scattering in a participating media. Examples include the outer gas-giant planets, Jupiter, Saturn, Neptune, and Uranus. Uranus is a particularly good example; due to its uniform cloud layer, visible light images of this planet tend to look like a perfectly diffuse shaded sphere (Figure 6.13).

When we combine surface shading and translucent volume shading, specular highlights are essential, as the translucent model essentially provides the diffuse component. Figure 6.14 compares different combinations of lighting models. All of the renderings use the same color map and alpha values. The image on the upper left is a typical volume rendering with surface shading using the Blinn-Phong shading model. The image on the upper right shows the same volume with only direct lighting, providing volumetric shadows. The image on the lower right uses both direct and indirect lighting. Notice how indirect lighting brightens up the image. The image on the lower left uses direct and indirect lighting combined with specular surface shading where surface shading is only applied to the leaves where there is a distinct material boundary.

The model/framework described in this chapter should not be thought of as a physically based *simulation* of light transport. Although this model is inspired by physically based solutions and has much in common with its physically based brethren, it was really designed to capture the qualitative effects that physically based solutions simulate. For example, the

Figure 6.13. An image of the planet Uranus taken during the Voyager flyby. Notice how this gas giant appears to be a perfectly diffuse shaded ball. Image courtesy of NASA.

Figure 6.14. A comparison of shading techniques. Upper-left: surface shading only. Upper-right: direct lighting only (shadows). Lower-right: direct and indirect lighting. Lower-left: direct and indirect lighting with surface shading only on leaves. (Images reprinted from [129], © 2003 IEEE.)

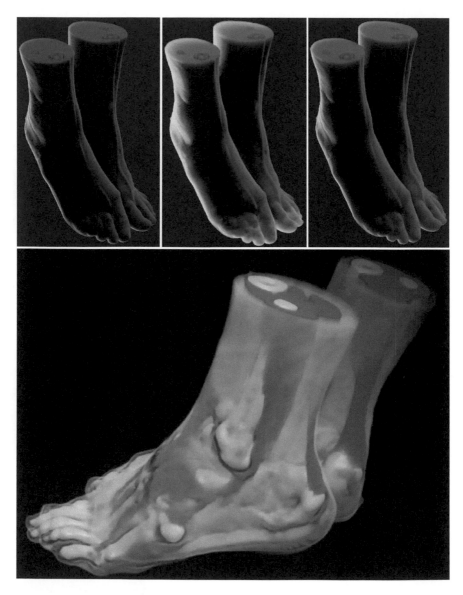

Figure 6.15. The feet of the Visible Female CT. The top-left image shows a rendering with direct lighting only, the top-center image shows a rendering with achromatic indirect lighting, and the top-right image shows a rendering with chromatic indirect lighting. (Images reprinted from [129], © 2003 IEEE.)

opalescent material shown in Figure 6.10 would require a physically based path-tracer to simulate hundreds of ray paths per pixel, each one simulating potentially hundreds of scattering events, to recreate this effect. Perhaps the fact that the model is not restricted to rigorous physical constraints is advantageous. Accurate physically based simulations of light transport require material optical properties to be specified in terms of scattering and absorption coefficients. Unfortunately, these values are difficult to acquire. There does not yet exist a comprehensive database of common material optical properties. Even if a user has access to a large collection of optical properties, it may not be clear how to customize them for a specific look. Interactivity combined with a higher-level description of optical properties (e.g., diffuse reflectivity, indirect attenuation, and alpha) will allow you the freedom to explore and create images that achieve a desired effect, in much the same way one would "tune" the parameters of a surface shading model to recreate the visual appearance of a material.

Figure 6.15 (top) demonstrates the familiar appearance of skin and tissue. The optical properties for these illustrations were specified quickly (in several minutes) without using measured optical properties. Figure 6.15 (bottom) demonstrates the effectiveness of this lighting model in the context of scientific visualization.

6.5 Further Reading

The optical effects caused by participating media are diverse and fascinating. The book *Clouds in a Glass of Beer* by Craig F. Bohren provides a gentle and entertaining introduction to physical principles behind atmospheric lighting phenomena. *Absorption and Scattering of Light by Small Particles* by Craig F. Bohren and Donald R. Huffman is a very in-depth treatment of the physics and mathematics of light-particle interactions.

For those interested in understanding physically based approximations for volume light transport in realistic computer graphics, *Physically Based Rendering* by Pharr and Humphries [211] provides a superb coverage of this topic in addition to a comprehensive treatment of surface-based methods and integration techniques.

GPU-Based Ray Casting

S O FAR, THIS BOOK HAS MAINLY DISCUSSED a traditional and widely used approach to GPU-based volume rendering that uses a 2D proxy geometry to sample the underlying 3D data set (see, in particular, Chapter 3 on basic GPU-based volume rendering for details on this approach). The predominant proxy geometries are either view-aligned slices (through a 3D texture) or axis-aligned slices (oriented along a stack of 2D textures). Slice-based volume rendering owes its success and popularity to a number of important reasons:

- a high bandwidth between texture memory and rasterization unit,

- built-in interpolation methods for a fast resampling (bilinear for stacks of 2D textures or trilinear in 3D textures), and

- a high rasterization performance.

Moreover, the core rendering routines are quite simple to implement.

Despite these advantages, slice-based volume rendering has a number of significant disadvantages—especially for large data sets. As the number and the position of the slices are directly determined by the volume data set, this object-space approach is strongly influenced by the complexity of the data set. Output sensitivity, however, should be the ultimate goal of any computer graphics algorithm. An image-space approach that takes into account the complexity of the generated image may come closer to this goal. In volume rendering, the overhead for a naive object-space technique can be quite large because a significant number of fragments does not contribute to the final image. Typically, only 0.2% to 4% of all fragments are visible [139]. Most volume-rendering applications focus on visualizing boundaries of objects or selected material regions. Therefore, large parts of a volume data set are set completely transparent and are not visible. In addition,

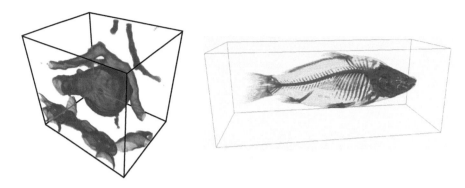

Figure 7.1. Volume rendering of an aneurysm data set (left) and a CT scan of a carp (right). In these two images, only a small portion of all voxels contributes to the final image, which is a common observation for most volume-rendered pictures.

many of the remaining fragments are invisible due to occlusion effects. Figure 7.1 shows two typical examples of volume visualization that contain only a small fraction of visible fragments.

Generalizing the possible problems of slice-based volume rendering: it is rasterization-limited, it has difficulties in incorporating acceleration methods and improved rendering algorithms, and it is rather inflexible. In contrast, ray casting is an appropriate approach to address these issues. The basic idea of ray casting is to trace rays from the camera into the volume, computing the volume-rendering integral along these rays. The main advantage is that these rays are handled independently from each other. This flexibility allows for several optimization strategies, such as early-ray termination, adaptive sampling, and empty space leaping. These approaches are discussed in detail in Chapter 8. Another advantage of ray casting is its straightforward generalization from uniform grids to tetrahedral grids, as described later in this chapter in Section 7.5.

Ray casting is a well-known method for CPU-based volume rendering that has been used early on, dating back to the 1980s (see, e.g., the discussion by Levoy [161]). On the other hand, GPU ray casting is a rather new development, with its first implementations [227, 139] published in 2003. The reason for the late development of GPU ray casting is the demand for advanced fragment shader functionality that was not available earlier. GPU ray casting often builds upon previous CPU methods, essentially adopting these for graphics hardware. The main goal of this chapter is to describe how ray casting can be realized on GPU architectures.

Section 7.1 discusses ray casting on a generic level, laying out the basic ideas and algorithmic structure. The subsequent sections cover GPU aspects of ray casting. Section 7.2 focuses on ray casting for uniform grids that can be accomplished by single-pass rendering. The following Section 7.3 describes acceleration methods that are tightly connected to ray casting, and Section 7.4 shows how ray casting can be implemented by multipass rendering. Finally, Section 7.5 describes ray casting for tetrahedral grids.

7.1 Basic Structure of Ray Casting

The ray-casting idea is to directly evaluate the volume-rendering integral (see Chapter 1 for a discussion of the volume-rendering integral) along rays that are traversed from the camera. For each pixel in the image, a single ray is cast into the volume (neglecting possible supersampling on the image plane). Then the volume data is resampled at discrete positions along the ray. Figure 7.2 illustrates ray casting. By means of the transfer function, the scalar data values are mapped to optical properties that are the basis for accumulating light information along the ray. Typically, compositing can be performed in the same order as the ray traversal. Therefore, front-to-back compositing (see Equation 1.14) is applied:

$$C_{dst} = C_{dst} + (1 - \alpha_{dst})C_{src}$$
$$\alpha_{dst} = \alpha_{dst} + (1 - \alpha_{dst})\alpha_{src} . \tag{7.1}$$

The ray-casting algorithm can be described by the pseudocode from Listing 7.1. Accordingly, ray casting can be split into the following major components.

Ray Set-up. First, a viewing ray needs to be set up according to given camera parameters and the respective pixel position. This component

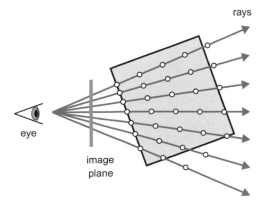

Figure 7.2. Ray-casting principle. For each pixel, one viewing ray is traced. The ray is sampled at discrete positions to evaluate the volume-rendering integral.

```
Determine volume entry position
Compute ray direction
While (ray position in volume)
   Access data value at current position
   Compositing of color and opacity
   Advance position along ray
End while
```

Listing 7.1. Pseudocode for ray casting.

computes the volume entry position—the coordinates of the first intersection between ray and the bounding geometry of the volume data set. This component also determines the direction of the ray.

Traversal Loop. This main component traverses along the ray, evaluating the volume-rendering integral. The ray is sampled at discrete positions, and the traversal loop scans the rays along these positions. Each iteration of the loop consists of the following subcomponents.

   Data Access. The data set is accessed at the current ray position, which might involve a reconstruction filter (i.e., interpolation). The corresponding color and opacity are computed by applying the transfer function. Either point-wise classification or pre-integrated classification are possible.

   Compositing. The previously accumulated color and opacity are updated according to the front-to-back compositing equation (Equation 7.1).

   Advance Ray Position. The current ray position is advanced to the next sampling location along the ray.

   Ray Termination. The traversal loop ends when the ray leaves the data set volume. This subcomponent checks whether the current ray position is inside the volume and it only enters the next iteration of the loop when the ray is still inside.

The ray-casting algorithm and its components are well known and have been frequently used in CPU-based implementations. The following sections describe how ray casting can be mapped to GPU architectures.

   Ray casting exhibits an intrinsic parallelism in the form of completely independent light rays. This parallelism is compatible with hardware parallelism in GPUs: for example, by associating the operations for a single ray with a single pixel, the built-in parallelism for GPU fragment processing (multiple pixel pipelines) is used to achieve efficient ray casting. In addition, volume data and other information can be stored in textures and thus accessed with the high internal bandwidth of a GPU.

7.2 Single-Pass GPU Ray Casting for Uniform Grids

Uniform grids have a simple geometric and topological structure (see Section 1.5.1). In particular, a 3D uniform grid can be identified with a 3D texture—in the same way as for 3D texture slicing. Therefore, uniform grids are widely used for GPU ray casting. The actual rendering algorithm (see pseudocode in Listing 7.1) can be almost directly mapped to a fragment program. Here, a fragment or a pixel on the image plane is identified with its corresponding ray.

Listing 7.2 shows the Cg fragment shader for single-pass ray casting. It facilitates all components mentioned in the previous section: ray set-up (computing entry position and ray direction), ray traversal, data access, compositing, and ray termination. The entry points are attached as texture coordinates `TexCoord0`. All positions and direction vectors are described with respect to the local coordinate system of the volume data set. The bounding box of the volume can be assumed to be oriented along the main coordinate axes in the local reference frame. Therefore, the bounding box can be described by two 3D points `volExtentMin` and `volExtentMax`, which provide the minimal and maximal coordinates of the bounding box, respectively. The position of the `camera` and the `stepsize` are also given with respect to the local coordinate system of the volume. The ray `direction` is computed as the normalized difference between entry position and camera position.

Ray traversal is implemented by a shader loop. Here, the volume data set, stored in the 3D texture `SamplerDataVolume`, is accessed. Trilinear interpolation is a built-in feature of graphics hardware and automatically provides a reconstruction filter when the current ray position is different from a grid point. Corresponding `RGBA` values are computed by applying the transfer function, which is held in the 1D texture `SamplerTransferFunction`. Then, front-to-back compositing is performed and the ray position is advanced. A fixed step size is used in this example. The last part of the shader implements ray termination. The ray traversal is only continued when all three coordinates x, y, and z of the current ray `position` are greater than the respective coordinates of `volExtentMin` and smaller than the respective coordinates of `volExtentMax`. Only in this case the dot product yields a value of 3 for `inside`.

Fragments for single-pass ray casting are generated by rendering the front faces of the bounding box of the volume. The entry points (with

```
// Cg fragment shader code for single-pass ray casting
float4 main(float4 TexCoord0 :  TEXCOORD0,
            uniform sampler3D SamplerDataVolume,
            uniform sampler1D SamplerTransferFunction,
            uniform float3 camera,
            uniform float stepsize,
            uniform float3 volExtentMin,
            uniform float3 volExtentMax
            ) :  COLOR
{
    float4 value;
    float scalar;
    // Initialize accumulated color and opacity
    float4 dst =  float4(0,0,0,0);
    // Determine volume entry position
    float3 position = TexCoord0.xyz;
    // Compute ray direction
    float3 direction = TexCoord0.xyz - camera;
    direction = normalize(direction);
    // Loop for ray traversal
    for (int i = 0; i < 200; i++)  // Some large number
    {
        // Data access to scalar value in 3D volume texture
        value = tex3D(SamplerDataVolume, position);
        scalar = value.a;
        // Apply transfer function
        float4 src = tex1D(SamplerTransferFunction, scalar);
        // Front-to-back compositing
        dst = (1.0-dst.a) * src + dst;
        // Advance ray position along ray direction
        position = position + direction * stepsize;
        // Ray termination:  Test if outside volume ...
        float3 temp1 = sign(position - volExtentMin);
        float3 temp2 = sign(volExtentMax - position);
        float inside = dot(temp1, temp2);
        // ... and exit loop
        if (inside < 3.0)
            break;
    }
    return dst;
}
```

Listing 7.2.   Cg fragment shader for single-pass ray casting.

```
// Cg fragment shader code for single-pass ray casting
// Add-ons for pre-integration
...

float4 main(float4 TexCoord0 :   TEXCOORD0,
            uniform sampler3D SamplerDataVolume,
            uniform sampler2D SamplerPreintegrationTable,
...
{
...
    float2 scalar = float2(0,0);
...
    for (int i = 0; i < 200; i++)  // Some large number
    {
        // Data access to scalar value in 3D volume texture
        value = tex3D(SamplerDataVolume, position);
        scalar.y = value.a;
        // Lookup in pre-integration table
        float4 src = tex2D(SamplerPreintegrationTable,
                           scalar.xy);
...
        position = position + direction * stepsize;
        // Save previous scalar value
        scalar.x = scalar.y;
...
}
```

Listing 7.3. Cg fragment shader for single-pass ray casting with pre-integration. Only the changes with respect to the original shader (Listing 7.2) are included.

respect to the local coordinate system of the volume) are attached as texture coordinates to the vertices of the bounding box. Scanline conversion automatically fills in-between values via interpolation. In this way, exactly one ray is traversed through each pixel that is covered by the volume.

The code in Listing 7.2 implements a most basic volume renderer, just with point-sampling of the volume-rendering integral and without illumination. However, a more sophisticated assignment of optical properties can be easily included. For example, local illumination (see Chapter 5) can be directly incorporated by slightly extending the computation of colors and opacities (in src).

Another direct extension leads to pre-integrated classification (see Section 4.5). Here, color and opacity are assigned according to the scalar values at the beginning and the end of a ray segment. Listing 7.3 shows the (slight) changes required for pre-integration. First, the look-up in the transfer function is replaced by a look-up in the pre-integration table, based on the two scalar values. Second, the scalar value from the current ray position is saved for the pre-integration look-up in the following iteration of the ray traversal loop. In this way, only one scalar value has to be accessed for each iteration. In contrast, pre-integrated texture slicing requires two look-ups in the data set for each fragment.

Additional technical background on single-pass ray casting can be found in a paper by Stegmaier et al. [251], who describe a flexible framework for ray casting along with an implementation via assembler-level fragment programs. They provide the source code of their implementation. Another demo code for ray casting is available from NVIDIA [200].

7.3   Performance Aspects and Acceleration Methods

Ray casting can easily incorporate a number of acceleration techniques to overcome the aforementioned problems of slice-based volume rendering. This section discusses acceleration techniques that are immediately related to ray casting: early ray termination, adaptive sampling, and empty-space skipping.

7.3.1   Cost of Ray Termination

The previously described implementation of single-pass ray casting (Listing 7.2) is a direct mapping of the conceptual ray-casting process to a GPU. It should be pointed out, however, that the ray termination part of the pipeline can consume a large portion of the overall render costs. First, the evaluation of the termination criterion (here, the check for positions within the bounding box of the volume) needs a couple of shader instructions. Second, dynamic branching—the conditional break out of the traversal loop—may be associated with performance costs (which is true for current Shader Model 3.0 GPUs). Therefore, alternative implementations may be useful to increase the rendering performance.

One approach is based on overshooting. Essentially, overshooting completely removes the ray termination part. Instead, a constant and conservative number of ray traversal steps is taken so that it is guaranteed that at least the whole volume is traversed. Normally, rays are traversed beyond the back face of the volume. A texture border of zero opacity and color needs to be set in order to avoid incorrect contributions to the volume-rendering integral from behind the volume.

A compromise can be found between mere overshooting and the exact ray termination in Listing 7.2: ray termination is computed and performed

```
    . . .
        // Additional termination condition for
        // early ray termination
        if (dst.a > 0.95)
            break;
    . . .
```

Listing 7.4.   Cg fragment shader part for early ray termination.

only every nth traversal step. The cost of ray termination can be weighed against its benefit in the form of a reduced number of ray-traversal steps, optimizing for a good value of n. This hybrid method can be implemented by a nested loop. Ray termination is only included in the outer loop, the inner loop iterates over a fixed number of steps, n. It should be noted that nested loops might be necessary anyway for large volumes because the maximum number of iterations is often restricted by GPUs.

Another method makes use of early fragment tests (e.g., early z-test or early stencil test) to avoid costly dynamic branching during fragment processing. Technical details and alternative ways of implementing ray termination are described in Section 8.6.2.

7.3.2   Early Ray Termination

Early ray termination allows us to truncate light rays as soon as we know that volume elements further away from the camera are occluded. Ray traversal can be stopped when the accumulated opacity α_{dst} reaches a certain user-specified limit (which is typically very close to 1).

The stopping criterion is added to the ray termination criteria that might already be part of ray casting, for example, the test for leaving the bounding box of the volume. Listing 7.4 shows the part of the fragment shader that implements early ray termination by dynamic branching that leaves the traversal loop. Here, the limit value is chosen $\alpha_{threshold} = 0.95$.

Section 8.6.2 discusses an alternative implementation of this termination by means of the early z-test.

7.3.3   Adaptive Sampling

Another advantage of ray casting is that the step sizes for one ray can be chosen independently from other rays, e.g., empty regions can be completely skipped or uniform regions can be quickly traversed by using large step sizes.

A typical volume data set has different regions with different characteristics. On the one hand, there can be largely uniform, or even completely

(a)   (b)   (c)

Figure 7.3. Comparison of the number of rendering steps for different transfer functions. Image (a) shows the original volume visualization, image (b) the corresponding number of sampling steps (black corresponds to 512 samples). Image (c) visualizes the number of sampling steps for a more opaque transfer function; this illustrates the effect of early ray termination. (Images courtesy of Röttger et al. [227], © The Eurographics Association, 2003.)

empty, regions in which a fine sampling of the ray integral is not necessary. On the other hand, details at boundaries between different regions should be represented by an accurate sampling of the ray. Adaptive sampling along rays can be used to address this issue [227].

Adaptive sampling relies on an additional data structure that controls the space-variant sampling rate. This *importance volume* describes the minimum isotropic sampling distance and is computed from a user-specified error tolerance and the local variations of the scalar data set. The importance volume is stored in a 3D texture whose resolution can be chosen independently from the resolution of the scalar data set. During ray traversal, an additional 3D texture look-up in the importance volume (at the current position) yields the step size for the following iteration. This space-variant step size is now used to compute the next sampling point—instead of a fixed step distance.

This approach relies on pre-integration (see Section 4.5) to determine a segment's contribution to the volume-rendering integral. A key feature of pre-integration is its separation of the sampling criteria for the data set and the transfer function [135]. Without pre-integration, the rate for an accurate sampling of the volume-rendering integral has to be based on the variations of the RGBA values that result from a mapping of scalar values via the transfer function. If, for example, the scalar values vary only very smoothly and slowly, but the transfer function contains very high frequencies, a high overall sampling rate will have to be chosen for the volume-rendering integral. In other words, the sampling rate has to take into account the frequencies of the data set and the transfer function.

In contrast, pre-integration "absorbs" the effect of the transfer function by means of a pre-computed look-up table. Accordingly, only the spatial variations of the data set have to be taken into account for an accurate sampling. Therefore, the construction of the importance volume makes use of the structure of the data set only and does not consider the transfer function. A benefit of this approach is that the importance volume is fixed for a stationary data set, i.e., it is computed only once (by the CPU) and downloaded to the GPU. Note that adaptive sampling requires us to modify the opacity value and color contribution for each discrete ray segment. This can be achieved by using a 3D pre-integration table that depends on the segment length as well as the two scalar values at the entry and exit points of the segment. Alternatively, an approximation according to the equation for opacity correction (see Section 1.4.3) can be used in combination with a 2D pre-integration table.

Figure 7.3 shows an example image generated by ray casting with adaptive sampling. Figure 7.3 (a) depicts the original volume visualization. Figure 7.3 (b) visualizes the corresponding number of sampling steps. Due to adaptive sampling, only few steps are needed for the uniform, empty space around the bonsai. Early ray termination reduces the number of samples in the region of the opaque trunk. In the region of the leaves, the importance volume indicates that a fine sampling is required (due to strongly varying scalar data values). Therefore, many sampling steps are used for this part of the image. Figure 7.3 (c) visualizes the number of sampling steps if a more opaque transfer function is applied to the same data set and under the same viewing conditions. The reduced number of samples for the leaves is striking. This effect is caused by early ray termination: after the first hit on an opaque leaf, a ray is ended.

Section 9.1 discusses adaptive sampling in the context of rendering quality.

7.3.4   Empty-Space Skipping

Empty-space skipping is useful when a volume visualization contains large portions of completely transparent space. Transparency is determined after the transfer function is applied to the data set. An additional data structure is used to identify empty regions. For example, an octree hierarchy can be employed to store the minimum and maximum scalar data values within a node. In combination with the transfer function, these min/max values allow us to determine completely transparent nodes.

Krüger and Westermann [139] reduce the octree to just a single level of resolution—in their implementation to $(1/8)^3$ of the size of the scalar data set. This reduced "octree" can be represented by a 3D texture, with the R and G components holding the minimum and maximum values for each node. Empty regions can only be identified by applying the transfer function to the original data and, afterwards, checking whether the data is rendered visible. We need a mapping from the min/max values to a Boolean value that classifies the node as empty or not. This two-parameter function is realized by a 2D texture that indicates for each min/max pair whether there is at least one non-zero component in the transfer function in the range between minimum and maximum scalar value. This 2D empty-space table depends on the transfer function and has to be updated whenever the transfer function is changed. The empty-space table is computed on the CPU and then uploaded to the GPU. Note that the "octree" 3D texture depends on the data only and has to be generated just once for a stationary data set.

The fragment program for ray termination is extended to take into account empty-space skipping. The front faces of the volume are rendered in the same way as before, while the step size is increased according to the size of the "octree" structure. Due to the larger step size, the number of traversal iterations is decreased. The min/max values are sampled from the "octree" and serve as parameters for a dependent texture look-up in the empty-space table. Empty space is skipped by setting the z-value of the depth buffer to the maximum; the code for the fine-grained sampling of the scalar data set is skipped by the early z-test. Conversely, a nonempty node leads to a z-value of zero and a subsequent integration of the ray segment. The z-value is reset to zero as soon as a nonempty node is found (and if the opacity is still below the threshold for early ray termination).

We refer to Section 8.4 for more information on empty-space leaping.

7.4 Multipass GPU Ray Casting for Uniform Grids

This section describes GPU ray casting implemented by multipass rendering. Historically, multipass ray casting was developed before single-pass ray casting because GPUs did not facilitate the functionality needed for single-pass ray casting at the time of the first GPU ray-casting methods. The following key features were missing. First, loops were not supported in fragment programs. Therefore, the traversal of a ray needed to be initiated by a CPU-based program. Second, it was hard to implement conditional breaks, which are required to stop ray traversal.

The multipass approach is included in the book because it allows us to implement ray casting on all GPUs that support Pixel Shader 2.0 functionality (e.g., ATI Radeon 9700 or higher, NVIDIA GeForce FX or higher). Therefore, multipass ray casting is recommended if availability of the latest graphics hardware cannot be assumed. This section is based on the two original papers on GPU ray casting [227, 139].

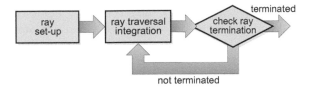

Figure 7.4. Principal structure of multipass rendering for GPU ray casting.

We discuss the two main ingredients of GPU-based ray casting: (a) data storage and (b) fragment processing. In graphics hardware, data can be stored in, and efficiently accessed from, textures. The data set (its scalar values and, possibly, its gradients) are held in a 3D texture in the same way as for single-pass ray casting. In addition, ray casting needs intermediate data that is "attached" to light rays. Due to the direct correspondence between ray and pixel, intermediate data is organized in 2D textures with a one-to-one mapping between texels and pixels on the image plane.

Accumulated colors and opacities are held in such 2D textures to implement the front-to-back compositing equation (Equation 7.1). In addition, the current sampling position along a ray can be stored in an intermediate texture. Typically, just the 1D ray parameter is held, i.e., the length between entry point into the volume and current position [227]. The mentioned intermediate values are continuously updated during ray traversal. Because OpenGL (as well as DirectX) has no specification for a simultaneous read and write access to textures, a ping-pong scheme makes such an update possible. Two copies of a texture are used; one texture holds the data from the previous sample position and allows for a read access while the other texture is updated by a write access. The roles of the two textures are exchanged after each iteration. Textures can be efficiently modified via render-to-texture functionality (e.g., by means of a frame-buffer object).

Some intermediate parameters can either be stored in 2D textures or, alternatively, computed on-the-fly within a fragment program. For example, the ray direction can be computed once and then stored in a texture (as in [139]) or computed on-the-fly (as in [227]). As in single-pass ray casting, the ray direction can be determined by taking the normalized difference vector between exit point and entry point or the normalized difference between entry point and camera position.

Other important aspects deal with the implementation of the fragment programs. Different programs are used in different parts of a multipass rendering approach. Figure 7.4 shows the principal structure of multipass rendering for GPU ray casting.

Ray set-up for multipass rendering is analogous to ray set-up for single-pass ray casting. The ray set-up is performed once per frame to compute the initial parameters for the rays, i.e., the entry points into the cube-shaped volume and the direction of the rays (in [139]) or the initial ray parameter (in [227]). The entry points are determined by rendering the front faces of the volume and attaching the positions to the vertices.

Ray traversal is performed via multiple render passes. Fragments are generated by rendering the front faces of the volume bounding box. The new position is computed by shifting the previous position along the ray direction according to the integration step size. The contribution of this ray segment (between previous and subsequent position) is accumulated according to front-to-back compositing (Equation 7.1). The source color C_{src} and source opacity α_{src} can be obtained by evaluating the transfer function at the sample points [139]. Alternatively, the pre-integrated contribution of the ray segment between the two points can be taken into account [227]. Regardless whether pre-integration or point sampling are used, a ping-pong scheme is employed to iteratively update the colors and opacities along the rays.

Another important aspect is the implementation of the stopping criterion. In particular, ray traversal has to end when the ray is leaving the volume. In addition, early ray termination leads to cancellation of ray traversal as soon as a certain opacity level is reached. This ray termination cannot be included in the above fragment program for ray traversal and integration because we cannot assume that the GPU provides the functionality for a conditional break of the loop. Therefore, ray termination is implemented in another fragment program that is executed after the shader for traversal and integration (see Figure 7.4). Actual ray termination is implemented by using a depth test and setting the z-buffer accordingly, i.e., the z-value is specified in a way to reject fragments that correspond to terminated rays. In addition to the termination of single rays on a pixel-by-pixel basis, the whole iteration process (the outer loop in multi-pass rendering) has to stop when all rays are terminated. An asynchronous occlusion query (see Section 2.4.3) allows us to check how many fragments are actually drawn in a render process; multipass rendering is stopped when the occlusion query reports no drawn fragments [227]. An alternative solution is based on the early z-test (as used in [139]). The maximum number of render passes has to be known beforehand, e.g., by computing the worst-case number of sampling steps. Here, all sampling steps are always initiated by multipass rendering. Fragments that correspond to terminated rays, however, are rejected by the efficient early z-test. In this way, the time-consuming fragment programs are skipped for terminated rays.

In the remainder of this section, the two implementations [139, 227] are described separately. The approach by Röttger et al. [227] is realized as follows. Three floating-point textures, with two components each, are used for intermediate values: the first texture for accumulated RG values, the second texture for accumulated BA values, and the third texture for the single-component ray parameter (i.e., the other component is not used). In all rendering passes, fragments are generated by rendering the front faces of the volume box. Ray set-up and the first integration step are combined in a single render pass (and therefore in a combined fragment program). The implementation uses multiple render targets to update the three aforementioned 2D textures.

A second fragment program realizes a single ray traversal and integration step. Nonnormalized ray directions are attached as texture coordinates to the vertices of the volume's bounding box and interpolated during scanline conversion. Actual direction vectors are determined within the fragment program by normalizing to unit length. The current sampling position is computed from the direction vector and the ray parameter (as fetched from the intermediate texture). The subsequent position is obtained by adding the fixed traversal step size. A 3D texture look-up in the data set provides the scalar values at the two endpoints of the current ray segment. These two scalar values serve as parameters for a dependent look-up in the pre-integration table. If (optional) volume illumination is switched on, the gradients included in the 3D data texture are used to evaluate the local illumination model (typically Phong or Blinn-Phong). Finally, all contributions are added and combined with the previously accumulated RGBA values according to the compositing equation (Equation 7.1).

A third fragment program is responsible for ray termination. It is executed after each traversal step. The ray termination program checks whether the ray has left the volume or the accumulated opacity has reached its limit. When a ray is terminated, the z-buffer is set so that the corresponding pixel is no longer processed (in any future rendering pass for ray traversal).

An asynchronous occlusion query is applied to detect when all rays are terminated. A total number of $2n+1$ render passes is required if n describes the maximum number of samples along a single ray.

Krüger and Westermann [139] use a similar algorithmic structure but include some differences in their implementation. Their ray set-up is distributed over two different rendering passes. The first pass determines the entry points into the volume. The front faces of the volume box are rendered, with the 3D positions attached to the vertices. In-between positions are obtained via interpolation during rasterization. The 3D positions are written to a 2D render texture that we denote POS. The second pass computes the ray direction by taking the normalized difference between exit and entry points (at the boundaries of the volume). Only in this second pass are fragments generated by rendering the back faces of the volume box. The 3D positions of the exit points are attached to the vertices and interpolated during scanline conversion. The entry points are read from the texture POS. In addition to the ray direction, the length of each ray is computed and stored in a 2D render texture denoted DIR.

The main loop iterates over two different fragment programs. In these rendering passes, fragments are generated by drawing the front faces of the volume. The first program implements ray traversal and integration. Each render pass samples m steps along the ray by partially rolling out the traversal loop within the fragment program. This avoids some data transfer between fragment program and textures (for the accumulated RGBA values) and therefore increases the rendering performance. In addition, the traversal shader checks whether the ray has left the volume, based on the length of a ray that is read from the texture DIR. If a ray has left the volume, opacity is set to a value of one. The second shader program implements ray termination. Here, opacity is checked against a given threshold. If the ray is ended (due to early ray termination or because it has left the volume), the z-buffer is set so that the corresponding pixel is no longer processed.

Krüger and Westermann [139] use a fixed number of rendering passes and do not employ an occlusion query. The number of passes depends on the maximum length of a ray, the traversal step size, and the number of intermediate steps m. Due to the efficiency of the early z-test, the overhead for possibly unnecessary render passes is small.

7.5   Ray Casting in Tetrahedral Grids

Unstructured grids are widely used in numerical simulations to discretize the computational domain. Their resolution can be locally adapted to achieve a required numerical accuracy while minimizing the total number of grid cells. For example, unstructured grids are popular in applications like computational fluid dynamics (CFD). Although unstructured grids may contain a variety of different cell types (such as tetrahedra, hexahedra, or prisms), these grids can always be decomposed into a collection of tetrahedra. Therefore, tetrahedral meshes are the most important type of unstructured grids. Section 1.5.1 provides more information on tetrahedral grids.

Volume rendering of tetrahedral meshes is traditionally implemented on graphics hardware by means of cell projection, e.g., according to Shirley and Tuchman [239]. Unfortunately, cell projection with noncommutative blending requires a view-dependent depth sorting of cells, which still has to be performed on the CPU. Whenever the camera or the volume is moved, new graphical primitives have to be generated by the CPU and transferred to the GPU. Therefore, cell projection benefits only in parts from the performance increase of GPUs. Another problem of cell projection is that cyclic meshes require special treatment [132]. With the R-buffer architecture [305, 125] order-independent cell projection could be achieved; however, the R-buffer has not been realized yet.

Fortunately, ray casting for tetrahedral meshes can overcome these problems. This chapter describes a ray-casting approach that can be completely mapped to the GPU. This approach was proposed by Weiler et al. [289], who provide details of their implementation and additional background information. Similar to ray casting in uniform grids (see previous sections), the algorithm can be readily parallelized because the operations for each ray are independent. A ray is once again identified with its corresponding pixel on the image plane. Therefore, rays can be processed in parallel on the GPU by mapping the ray-casting operations to fragment programs. The rendering performance can additionally be increased by early ray termination.

7.5.1 Basic Structure of the Algorithm

GPU ray casting is based on a ray-propagation approach similar to the CPU approach by Garrity [77]. Figure 7.5 illustrates how each viewing ray is propagated in a front-to-back fashion from cell to cell until the whole grid has been traversed. The traversal follows the links between neighboring cells. A ray begins at its first intersection with the mesh, which is determined during an initialization phase.

In the implementation of Weiler et al. [289], the traversal is performed in multiple render passes. In each pass, the color and opacity contribution of a pixel's current cell is computed analogously to the GPU-based view-independent cell projection by Weiler et al. [290]. Pre-integrated volume rendering is used to determine the contribution of a ray segment within a tetrahedron [226]. Finally, these contributions are accumulated according to the front-to-back compositing equation (Equation 7.1). The convexifi-

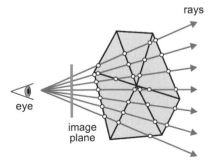

Figure 7.5. Ray traversal in a tetrahedral grid. For each pixel, one viewing ray is traced. The ray is sampled at all intersected cell faces (white dots).

```
Ray setup (initialization)
While (within the mesh)
   Compute exit point for current cell
   Determine scalar value at exit point
   Compute ray integral within current cell
      via pre-integration
   Accumulate colors and opacities by blending
   Proceed to adjacent cell through exit point
End while
```

Listing 7.5.   Pseudocode for ray casting in a tetrahedral grid.

cation approach by Williams [302] is used to allow for reentries of viewing
rays in nonconvex meshes. Convexification converts nonconvex meshes
into convex meshes by filling the empty space between the boundary of the
mesh and a convex hull of the mesh with imaginary cells. An alternative
approach [291] applies a technique similar to depth peeling [67] to handle
nonconvex meshes. Here, the basic idea is to perform ray casting for several depth layers of the boundary of the tetrahedral mesh. Each of these
depth layers can be processed by the above ray-casting method, which is
only designed for convex grids.

Although ray casting for uniform grids and tetrahedral grids are
strongly related to each other, some important differences have to be taken
into account to process tetrahedral meshes. First, the topological information about the connectivity of neighboring cells has to be stored, i.e., more
complex data structures have to be handled. Second, ray traversal samples
the volume at entry and exit points of cells, i.e., intersections between ray
and cells need to be computed.

Fragment programs are used to perform all computations for the ray
propagation. Fragments are generated by rendering screen-filling rectan-
gles. Each rendering pass executes one propagation step for each viewing
ray. The whole mesh is processed by stepping through the volume in multiple passes. The pseudocode of the algorithm is given in Listing 7.5.

The algorithm starts by initializing the first intersection of the viewing
ray, i.e., an intersection with one of the boundary faces of the mesh. This
can be implemented using a rasterization of the visible boundary faces,
similar to ray casting in uniform grids. However, it may also be performed
on the CPU as there are usually far less boundary faces than cells in a
mesh, and thus, this step is not time critical.

The remaining steps can be divided into the handling of ray integration
and ray traversal. These steps have to transfer intermediate information
between successive rendering passes. This information is represented by

several 2D RGBA textures that have a one-to-one mapping between texels and pixels on the image plane. The textures contain the current intersection point of the ray with the face of a cell, the index of the cell the ray is about to enter through this face (including the index of the entry face), and the accumulated RGBA values.

The intermediate textures are read and updated during each rendering pass. Because OpenGL (as well as DirectX) has no specification for a simultaneous read and write access to textures, a ping-pong scheme makes such an update possible. Two copies of a texture are used; one texture holds the data from the previous sample position and allows for a read access while the other texture is updated by a write access. The roles of the two textures are exchanged after each iteration. Textures can be efficiently modified via render-to-texture functionality (e.g., by means of a frame-buffer object; see Section 2.4.2).

7.5.2   Mesh Representation

Before we discuss ray integration and ray traversal in more detail, we would like to show how the rather complex mesh data can be represented on the GPU. A tetrahedral mesh contains information on topology (neighboring cells), geometry (position of vertices, normal vectors), and scalar data values. Figure 7.6 illustrates how this information is attached to a mesh for the example of a 2D mesh. Cells are labeled by an integer index t that ranges from 0 to $n - 1$, where n is the number of cells in the mesh. Each tetrahedron t has four faces. The normal vectors on the faces are labeled $\mathbf{n}_{t,i}$, where $i \in \{0, 1, 2, 3\}$ specifies the face. Normal vectors are assumed to point outwards. The four vertices of a tetrahedron t are denoted $\mathbf{v}_{t,i}$; vertex $\mathbf{v}_{t,i}$ is opposite to the ith face. The neighbor of a tetrahedron t that

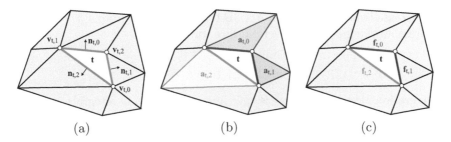

Figure 7.6. Terminology for the tetrahedral mesh representation. (a) The vertex $\mathbf{v}_{t,i}$ is opposite to the ith face of cell t; the normal $\mathbf{n}_{t,i}$ is perpendicular to the ith face. (b) The neighboring cell $a_{t,i}$ shares the ith face. (c) The ith face of t corresponds to the $f_{t,i}$th face of t's neighbor $a_{t,i}$. (Figures adapted from Weiler et al. [289].)

Data in	Tex coords			Texture data			
texture	u	v	w	r	g	b	α
Vertices	t		i	$\mathbf{v}_{t,i}$			—
Face normals	t		i	$\mathbf{n}_{t,i}$			$f_{t,i}$
Neighbor data	t		i	$a_{t,i}$		—	—
Scalar data	t		—	$\mathbf{g}_t$			$\hat{g}_t$

Table 7.1. Mesh data represented by textures (adopted from Weiler et al. [289]).

is adjacent to the ith face is labeled $a_{t,i}$. The index of the face of $a_{t,i}$ that corresponds to the ith face of t is called $f_{t,i}$.

In addition to the structure of the mesh, the data values play an important role. The scalar field value $s(\mathbf{x})$ at a point $\mathbf{x}$ can be computed by

$$s(\mathbf{x}) = \mathbf{g}_t \cdot (\mathbf{x} - \mathbf{x}_0) + s(\mathbf{x}_0) = \mathbf{g}_t \cdot \mathbf{x} + (-\mathbf{g}_t \cdot \mathbf{x}_0 + s(\mathbf{x}_0)) \ . \qquad (7.2)$$

The gradient of the scalar field, $\mathbf{g}_t$, is constant within a cell because a linear (barycentric) interpolation is assumed. The advantage of this representation is that the scalar values inside a cell can be efficiently reconstructed by computing one dot product and one scalar addition, while we still need to store only one vector $\mathbf{g}_t$ and one scalar $\hat{g}_t = -\mathbf{g}_t \cdot \mathbf{x}_0 + s(\mathbf{x}_0)$ for each cell ($\mathbf{x}_0$ is the position of an arbitrary vertex of the cell).

The mesh data is stored in 2D and 3D RGBA textures at floating-point resolution. Because the mesh data is constant for a stationary data set, these textures are generated in a pre-processing step on the CPU. Table 7.1 gives an overview of this texture representation. Cell indices are encoded in two texture coordinates because their values can exceed the range of a single texture coordinate. 3D textures are used for vertices, face normals, and neighbor data; a 2D texture is used for the scalar data. The textures are accessed via the cell index. For 3D textures, the additional w coordinate represents the index of the vertex, face, or neighbor.

7.5.3   Ray Integration and Cell Traversal

Integration along a whole ray is split into a collection of integrations within single cells. The evaluation of the volume-rendering integral within a cell can be efficiently and accurately handled by pre-integration (see Section 4.5). Röttger et al. [226] describe pre-integration in the specific context of tetrahedral cells.

For the following discussion, we assume that we have a 3D pre-integration table that provides the color C_{src} and opacity α_{src} of a ray segment. The parameters for the look-up table are the scalar values at the entry point and exit point of the segment, as well as the length of the segment.

The entry point and its scalar value are communicated via the intermediate 2D textures. In addition, the index of the current cell is given in these textures. The exit point is computed by determining the intersection points between the ray and the cell's faces and taking the intersection point that is closest to the eye (but not on a visible face). We denote the index for the entry face by j, the position of the eye by $\mathbf{e}$, and the normalized direction of the viewing ray by $\mathbf{r}$. Then the three intersection points with the faces of cell t are $\mathbf{e} + \lambda_i \mathbf{r}$, where $0 \leq i < 4 \wedge i \neq j$ and

$$\lambda_i = \frac{(\mathbf{v} - \mathbf{e}) \cdot \mathbf{n}_{t,i}}{\mathbf{r} \cdot \mathbf{n}_{t,i}}, \quad \text{with} \quad \mathbf{v} = \mathbf{v}_{t,3-i}.$$

Note that no intersection is checked for the entry face j because this intersection point is already known. A face is visible and its corresponding intersection point should be discarded when the denominator in the above equation is negative. The minimum of the values λ_i is computed in the fragment program to determine the exit point.

The exit point is used to calculate the corresponding scalar value according to Equation 7.2. Also, the distance between exit and entry point is determined. With the length of the ray segment and the two scalar values at the endpoints of the segment, a look-up in the 3D pre-integration table yields the color C_{src} and opacity α_{src} of this segment. Finally, this RGBA contribution is accumulated according to the compositing equation (Equation 7.1).

The traversal of the whole mesh is guided by the current cell index stored in the intermediate textures. The fragment program takes the current index and updates each texel of the texture with the index of the cell adjacent to the face through which the viewing ray leaves the current cell. This index is given by $a_{t,i}$ for the current cell t, where i is the index that corresponds to the exit face. Boundary cells are represented by an index -1, which allows us to determine whether a viewing ray has left the mesh. The current cell index is also used to implement early ray termination: the index is set to -1 when the accumulated opacity has reached the user-specified threshold.

This approach is only valid for convex meshes, where no "reentries" into the mesh are possible. Therefore, nonconvex meshes are converted into convex meshes by filling the empty space between the boundary of the mesh and a convex hull of the mesh with imaginary cells during a preprocessing step [302]. An alternative approach [291] applies a technique similar to depth peeling [67] to handle nonconvex meshes.

Another aspect is the implementation of ray termination. Two issues have to be taken into account. First, for each fragment we have to detect

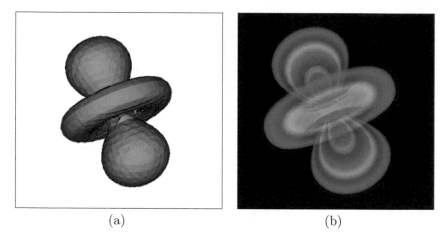

(a)   (b)

Figure 7.7.   GPU-based ray casting in a tetrahedral grid. Image (a) shows the isosurface of an orbital data set, image (b) a semi-transparent volume rendering. (Images courtesy of M. Weiler.)

whether the corresponding ray is terminated (due to early ray termination or because the ray has left the volume). Second, the whole render loop has to be stopped when all rays are terminated (see the discussion in Section 7.4). Ray termination is realized by using a depth test and setting the z-buffer accordingly, i.e., the z-value is specified in a way to reject fragments that correspond to terminated rays. Actual ray termination is implemented in another fragment program that is executed after the shader for traversal and integration. The ray termination shader checks whether the current index is -1. In this case, the z-value is set to a value that prevents further updates of the corresponding pixel, i.e., subsequent executions of the shader for ray integration and cell traversal are blocked by the efficient early z-test. An asynchronous occlusion query is employed to determine when all rays have been terminated. The asynchronous delivery of the occlusion query result leads to some additional rendering passes.

Figure 7.7 shows example images generated by GPU-based ray casting in a tetrahedral grid. Figure 7.7 (a) depicts the isosurface of an orbital data set, Figure 7.7 (b) a semitransparent volume rendering.

7.6   Further Reading

GPU ray casting was introduced by Röttger et al. [227], followed by an alternative implementation by Krüger and Westermann [139]. These two approaches rely on multipass rendering. Single-pass ray casting is described by Stegmaier et al. [251]. They provide the source code of their implementation, which is based on assembler-level fragment shaders. Klein et al. [127] describe empty-space leaping in order to accelerate GPU ray casting.

The aforementioned papers discuss ray casting for uniform grids. The first GPU ray-casting approach for tetrahedral meshes was proposed by Weiler et al. [289]. In a follow-up paper, Weiler et al. [291] include the compression of tetrahedral strips to accommodate larger data sets within GPU memory in order to achieve a fast rendering of these large meshes. An overview of GPU methods for tetrahedral meshes, including ray casting, is given by Silva et al. [244].

8

Improving Performance

THE PERFORMANCE OF GPU-BASED volume-rendering algorithms is usually bounded by the fragment processor. With larger data sets, higher sampling rate and image resolution, more fragments are processed to accurately represent the data. With a larger number of fragments, memory bandwidth and latency become increasingly critical, because multiple data values from the volume are read for each fragment. Because memory bandwidth and latency strongly depend on the employed memory access patterns, we have to find ways to access the volume data during rendering in an optimized way.

In addition to memory access bottlenecks, complex fragment program computations with a lot of ALU[1] instructions can also be a major bottleneck. Therefore, the number of fragments for which complex shaders are executed must be reduced. One way to achieve this is by performing "expensive" computations and accessing memory only selectively. Furthermore, methods like leaping over empty space, skipping occluded parts, and termination of rays that have accumulated sufficient opacity help to accomplish this goal.

8.1 Improving Memory Access

Even though today's GPUs provide an enormous peak memory bandwidth of more than 30 GB per second, the visualization of large-volume data requires optimization techniques to achieve satisfying frame rates.

Consider a 1-GB volume: in theory a memory bandwidth of 30 GB per second should provide us with sufficient bandwidth to access the complete volume data 30 times per second; thus, neglecting rendering times, this

---

[1]ALU: arithmetic logic unit.

should yield 30 frames per second frame rate. In practice however, there are several reasons why this calculation is totally academic.

- For a single trilinear interpolation, eight data values from the volume must be read. Many of those data values will be read multiple times, because neighboring fragments might require the same data values to compute a trilinear interpolation. GPU-internal texture-caches try to address this problem by providing fast access to data values that were read by a previous texture fetch, however they cannot completely prevent multiple access to volume data values.

- Some algorithms require multiple interpolated data values for computing a per-fragment result. For instance, for high-quality filtering the contribution of many voxels is required. In addition, on-the-fly shading requires fetching neighboring voxels for computing the local gradient.

- The theoretical GPU memory bandwidth can only be achieved if memory is solely accessed in a texture-cache friendly manner. This is not typical in many cases, especially when using 3D textures or when the results of previous texture fetches is used as the texture-coordinate for a subsequent texture fetch (dependent texture fetch). Thus, the actual sustained bandwidth is usually much lower than we would expect.

In addition to memory bandwidth limitations, the role of memory latency is often underestimated. For read access to memory, the term *memory latency* refers to the time between a request and the delivery of the data value. Because GPUs are designed as streaming processors with an optimized memory controller, memory latency can be hidden quite efficiently if data is read or written sequentially. Pairing memory access with math instructions is another efficient method to hide memory latency. This optimization is usually carried out automatically by the shading language compiler or the GPU driver.

Despite all of these optimizations, image-order algorithms such as ray casting produce noncoherent memory access patterns that significantly reduce the performance of the memory subsystem. Even object-order rendering algorithms can show strange dependencies of the frame rate on the current viewing direction. For 3D texture–based slicing on some graphics hardware, the performance when looking mainly along the z-direction is much faster compared with other viewing directions. This is due to inconsistent texture-cache efficiency. Let us assume that we have implemented an object-order volume-rendering algorithm that accesses the volume data

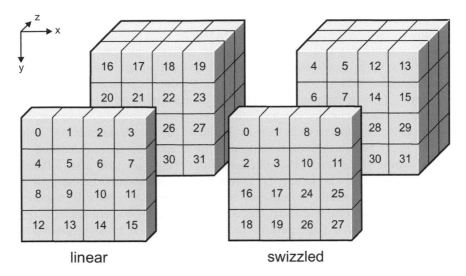

linear   **swizzled**

Figure 8.1. In a linear memory layout (left), the distance between neighboring voxels differs depending on the major axis, whereas in a swizzled memory layout, neighboring voxels have a more consistent distance (block-based).

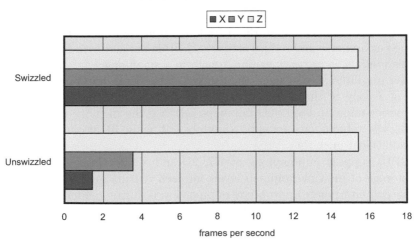

Figure 8.2. Comparison of the rendering performance along the three main axes for an on-the-fly gradient shader using swizzled and unswizzled 3D textures. Measurements were done with an NVIDIA GeForce 6800 GT PCIe x16 graphics card. Note that, in contrast with the unswizzled 3D texture, the swizzled 3D texture provides a consistent frame rate along the viewing directions.

in Figure 8.1 (left) in the x-direction first, followed by the y-direction and finally the z-direction. Because the data will be read in a linear fashion, the memory controller and texture caches are utilized very efficiently. Please recall that each time memory is read, a certain number of sequential data values are loaded into a cache-line. If a data value with an address close to a previously read data value is read, the probability that the data value is already in the cache-line is very high. In slice-based volume rendering, the memory access patterns will be very similar to the scenario described above if the proxy geometry is oriented mainly orthogonal to the z-direction.

However, if we access the volume data in the z-direction first, followed by the y-direction and finally the x-direction, we will access the data values in a nonlinear fashion, actually we will jump forth and back in memory. This access pattern is disadvantageous for memory controllers and texture caches, reducing the performance significantly. If proxy geometry in slice-based volume rendering is oriented mainly orthogonal to the x- or y-direction, memory access patterns will be very similar to this scenario. Due to the inconsistent utilization of the memory controller and texture caches, we will obtain very different rendering performance depending on the viewing direction (see Figure 8.2).

8.1.1   Mipmapping

For minification of volume data, i.e., if the projected voxel size on the output image is smaller than the pixel size, mipmapping can improve rendering performance and reduce artifacts. MIP is the acronym for the Latin phrase *multum in parvo*, meaning "much in a small space." Mipmaps are smaller pre-filtered versions of the original data. Each mipmap level consists of a copy of the pixel or voxel data with half the resolution of the next lower mipmap level. 2D mipmaps increase the memory required for storing the volume data by approximately 1/3, while 3D mipmaps require 1/7 additional memory.

GPUs support mipmapping of 1D, 2D and 3D textures. They allow the storage of multiple mipmap levels for each texture and automatically choose and interpolate appropriate mipmap levels during rendering depending on the zoom factor. Due to the smaller size of mipmaps and the closer proximity of neighboring voxels in lower-resolution mipmap levels, texture caches in graphics hardware can be utilized much more efficiently. Thus, mipmapping improves the rendering performance for minified volume data significantly. Minification is typical for computer games, where volumetric effects like clouds, fire, or explosions are often far away from the camera (see Chapter 11).

Since users exploring scientific volume data are often interested in small details hidden in the data, volume data in scientific applications is usually magnified. Consequently, the full resolution version of the volume data must be used during rendering and mipmapping will therefore not improve the rendering performance.

8.1.2 Block-Based Swizzling

To circumvent this problem, one option is to store the volume data in a block-based fashion as shown in Figure 8.1 (right). This kind of rearrangement of the voxels is often referred to as *swizzling*. A block-based swizzling approach is conceptually equivalent to bricking as described in Section 17.2, but now in the context of optimized memory access instead of the context of limited texture memory. Note that the block size of 2^3 in Figure 8.1 is used for clarification only. Large block/brick sizes such as 32^3 might be more efficient. In this context, you should also keep in mind that we need at least one voxel overlap between neighboring blocks to ensure continuous interpolation (see Sections 3.3.1 and 17.2). The smaller the block size, the greater the induced memory overhead due to the overlap.

With a block-based approach, it is already possible to increase the locality of most neighboring voxels significantly. If we access neighboring data values inside a block, the addresses of the data values will most of the time be closer than in an unswizzled memory layout. Once again, please keep in mind that local memory access increases the cache hit probability. However, there is still a big distance between two neighboring voxels belonging to different blocks. Anyhow, the blocks/bricks are sorted and rendered one-by-one as described in Section 17.2. Consequently, no data values from neighboring blocks will be required, because memory access across block-boundaries is handled by the overlap.

8.1.3 Multioriented Swizzling

In order to further improve the average frame rate for different viewing directions, we can alternate the orientation of neighboring blocks [294]; that is, the fastest, the medium, and slowest axis for storage of data inside a block are alternated. The following storage pattern ensures a balanced memory access performance (fastest, medium, slowest):

(x,y,z), (y,z,x), (z,x,y),
(x,y,z), (y,z,x), (z,x,y),
(x,y,z), (y,z,x), etc.

Consequently, the varying performance for different viewing directions is averaged out within a single image.

A swizzled volume data memory layout can provide a more consistent rendering performance for all viewing directions. Note that some GPUs already provide consistent 3D texture performance if all texture dimensions are a power of two (all NVIDIA GPUs), while other GPUs require additional effort such as described in this section to achieve view-independent frame rates (most ATI GPUs).

8.2   Asynchronous Data Upload

Asynchronous data transfer allows components inside a PC to exchange data without involvement of the CPU; i.e., the CPU can continue working on other tasks while the data is transferred. While the CPU initiates the transfer, the transfer itself is performed by the DMA[2] controller.

If the volume data is too large to be stored entirely in GPU memory, data blocks must be reloaded into GPU memory during rendering (see Section 17.2). To achieve the best performance during the upload, the blocks of data should already be prepared in main memory in such a way that they can be sent to the GPU as a contiguous block of data; that is, the data should be stored in a contiguous block of main memory including the overlap to neighboring blocks.

When sending texture data to the GPU using the `glTexSubImage3D` or `glTexSubImage2D` OpenGL commands, the CPU usually copies the data into AGP[3] memory and blocks until all the data has been sent to the GPU. Consequently, all subsequent OpenGL commands are stalled until the data transfer has been completed. The pixel buffer object (PBO) OpenGL extension (see `ARB_pixel_buffer_object` extension) allows for the uploading of texture data to the GPU asynchronously using DMA; i.e., the CPU does not block if this extension is used for data transfer. However, the data has to be available in AGP memory already in the GPU internal format.

As discussed in the previous section, some graphics cards use a rearranged format for 3D texture data in GPU memory to increase the locality of neighboring data values. This has the consequence that the CPU will be rearranging the data in main memory before uploading the brick to GPU memory. One possible solution to prevent involving the CPU for uploading texture data to the GPU is to store the bricks in main memory in the same format that the GPU uses internally and tell the driver that the data is already prepared. Currently however, there is no official OpenGL mechanism available to achieve this.

Non–power-of-two (NPOT, see `ARB_texture_non_power_of_two` OpenGL extension) textures, however, are not rearranged and copied by the driver before they are uploaded into GPU memory. Consequently, NPOT textures can be uploaded asynchronously with an upload bandwidth that is usually much closer to the theoretical limit.

---

[2] DMA: direct memory access.
[3] AGP: accelerated graphics port.

```
void *pboMemory, *texData;

// create and bind texture image buffer object
glGenBuffers(1, &texBuffer);
glBindBuffer(GL_PIXEL_UNPACK_BUFFER_EXT, texBuffer);
glBufferData(GL_PIXEL_UNPACK_BUFFER_EXT, texSize, NULL,
GL_STREAM_DRAW);
// get first brick
texData = getNextBrick();

while (texData) {
    // map the texture image buffer
    pboMemory = glMapBuffer(GL_PIXEL_UNPACK_BUFFER_EXT,
                            GL_WRITE_ONLY);
    // modify (sub-)buffer data
    memcpy(pboMemory, texData, texsize);
    // unmap the texture image buffer
    if (!glUnmapBuffer(GL_PIXEL_UNPACK_BUFFER_EXT)) {
        // Handle error case
    }
    // update sub-volume from texture image buffer
    glTexSubImage3D(GL_TEXTURE_3D, 0, 0, 0, 0,
                    brickWidth, brickHeight, brickDepth,
                    GL_LUMINANCE8, GL_UNSIGNED_SHORT,
                    BUFFER_OFFSET(0));
    // draw the brick
    glBegin(GL_QUADS);
        ...
    glEnd();

    texData = getNextBrick();
}

glBindBuffer(GL_PIXEL_UNPACK_BUFFER_EXT, 0);
```

Listing 8.1. Fast transfer of 3D texture data from main memory to GPU memory using the pixel buffer object OpenGL extension.

It should be noted that such NPOT textures should be kept small to prevent view-dependent rendering performance due to cache-inefficient memory access patterns (see Section 8.1). An additional option already discussed in the previous section is to store blocks oriented differently along the main axes [294]. We recommend using NPOT textures with a resolution close to $64 \times 64 \times 64$ voxels, for example $64 \times 64 \times 63$.

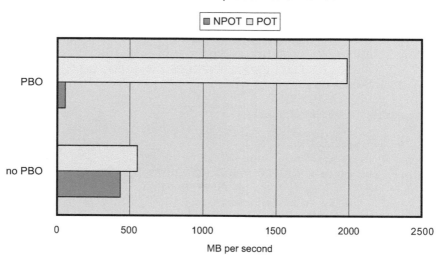

Figure 8.3. Comparison of the upload bandwidth on an NVIDIA GeForce 6800 GT PCIe x16 with power-of-two (POT) 3D textures and non–power-of-two (NPOT) 3D textures with and without pixel buffer objects (PBO).

To achieve the best upload performance, the texture data should be streamed asynchronously to the GPU using the ARB_pixel_buffer_object OpenGL extension. The example C code in Listing 8.1 uses PBOs to upload data from AGP memory asynchronously to GPU memory using the DMA controller.

Our own measurements on an NVIDIA GeForce 6800 GT PCIe x16 show that uploading NPOT 3D textures with PBO yields approximately four times the transfer rate compared with uploading POT 3D textures without PBO (see Figure 8.3). Note that the bandwidth in the optimal case is still far away from the maximum theoretical bandwidth of 4 GB/sec on PCIe x16. This might be due to the AGP/PCIe bridge on the used NVIDIA board. The poor performance of the PBO/POT combination probably indicates a driver problem (driver version 78.01).

8.3   Bilinear Filtering

Each time we sample a 3D texture in a fragment program, the graphics hardware has to request 8 data values from the memory to perform a tri-linear interpolation. Hence it is no surprise that texture fetches from 3D

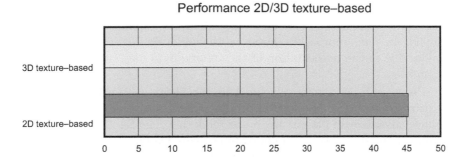

Figure 8.4. Performance comparison of 2D and 3D texture–based pre-integrated volume rendering with an NVIDIA GeForce 6800 GT PCIe x16 graphics card.

textures are "expensive" operations. One naive idea to overcome these expensive operations to achieve a performance improvement would be to replace linear filtering for 3D textures by nearest-neighbor filtering. Unfortunately, because most modern GPUs do not implement an optimized path in the graphics hardware for different filtering modes, a performance benefit cannot be achieved for nearest-neighbor filtering.

In contrast with 3D textures, a 2D texture fetch however only requires 4 data values from memory to perform a bilinear interpolation. Consequently, linearly interpolated samples from 2D textures only require half the memory bandwidth as filtered 3D textures fetches. Due to their smaller size, 2D textures have the additional advantage that they are much simpler to handle for GPU-internal texture caches. Furthermore, because GPUs are mainly designed to render computer games, which mostly employ 2D textures, GPUs are more optimized to handle them.

As discussed in Section 3.2, we can employ 2D textures to render volume data. In our experience, the frame rate of 2D texture–based volume rendering is approximately 50% faster compared with its 3D texture–based counterpart (see Figure 8.4). However, to have one stack of slices for each of the main axes, the data has to be tripled. Quite often, tripling the volume might not be a feasible solution, especially in the case of large-volume data. But on the other hand, volume-rendering engines often use a subsampled copy of the volume data for interactive frames. For such a subsampled version of the volume data, we usually have sufficient GPU memory to store three copies of the data. Another example is very large data that needs bricking to fit into GPU memory (see Chapter 17). Here, no drawback of the 2D textures occurs because data needs to be downloaded for each frame anyway.

A possible solution that avoids storing three copies of the data in GPU memory is to reorient the volume data along the dominant main axis on-the-fly. In such approaches, however, the small delays at certain viewing angles due to the reorientation of the volume data may be noticeable and disturbing.

Please note that reintroducing trilinear filtering by utilizing a multi-texture approach as described in Section 3.4 will nearly absorb the performance advantage of 2D texture–based rendering. Hence, 2D texture–based volume rendering with only bilinear interpolated volume samples should be used for best performance. The reduced image quality is a trade-off that is acceptable, especially in many application areas where interactivity is more important than image quality.

8.4   Empty-Space Leaping

Volumetric data sets contain many features that are not required for the final rendering. Typically, they are removed by setting zero alpha values in the transfer function. In order to not waste time on features that have been removed by the transfer function, empty-space leaping can be employed to reduce memory access and save computation power (see also Section 7.3.4).

For that purpose, the volume is subdivided into smaller blocks. In order to detect empty space, all blocks of the volume are classified in a

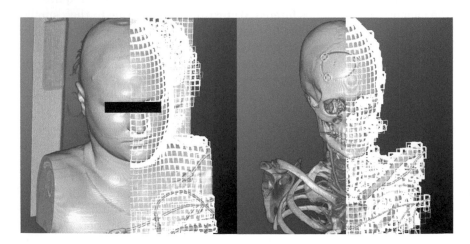

Figure 8.5. Nonempty blocks of a CT volume for two different transfer functions. Roughly 40% of the fragments are skipped with the left transfer function, whereas 80% of the fragments are skipped with the right transfer function.

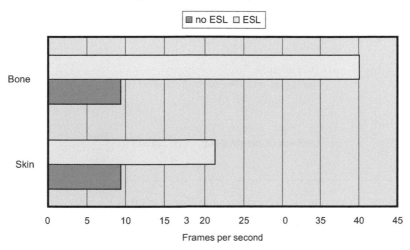

Figure 8.6. Performance improvement due to empty-space leaping (ESL) for renderings showing bone and skin of the CT data set from Figure 8.5. Note that the performance improvement is bigger with the bone transfer function, because more empty space can be skipped.

pre-processing step. For each block, the minimum and maximum scalar values are stored. Based on the transfer function and the minimum and maximum density values, the visibility of each block can quickly be determined after each change of the transfer function [164]. This allows slicing to be restricted to visible blocks only (see Figure 8.5), thus increasing the number of vertices but reducing the number of fragments.

Because the vertex processor is usually idle during volume rendering in most of the cases anyway (the number of slice polygons is rather small), this technique provides significant performance improvements for many transfer functions and balances out the rendering pipeline more evenly. See Figure 8.6 for a comparison of rendering with and without empty-space block-based leaping for different transfer functions. The performance numbers were measured with an NVIDIA GeForce 6800 GT PCIe x16 graphics card.

8.5 Occlusion Culling

A block-based rendering technique as used for empty space skipping is also usable to prevent the rendering of blocks that are completely occluded by objects in front of them.

```
struct v2f_simple {
    float2 Position :  WPOS;
};


float4 main(v2f_simple IN,
            uniform samplerRect FrameBuffer
           ) :  COLOR
{
    // sample frame buffer
    return texRect(FrameBuffer, Position);
}
```

Listing 8.2. Cg code for filtering frame-buffer pixels that have accumulated sufficient opacity.

To exploit occlusion for higher performance, blocks have to be sorted and rendered in a front-to-back manner. Before slicing or ray casting each block, we first render the front faces of the bounding box of each block with the current contents of the frame buffer applied as a texture; i.e., each fragment covered by the bounding box of a block outputs the RGBA values of the frame buffer at this position (see Listing 8.2). Fragments are filtered out that have an alpha value larger than the occlusion threshold. Using an alpha test we prevent those fragments from being rendered; i.e., we use glAlphaFunc(GL_LESS, threshold). Again we prefer using the alpha test to a fragment discard operation, because the latter operations implicitly disable early fragment tests on most graphics hardware.

The ARB_occlusion_query OpenGL extension is then employed to count the pixels that pass this so-called occlusion pass. This extension allows us to create a query that counts the number of fragments written into the frame buffer for all rendering commands between the start and the end of the query. Due to the filtering for the pixels covering the current block, only fragments are counted that have low opacity (see Listing 8.3). If the number of pixels counted is 0, all pixels that are covered by the bounding box of the block whose occlusion we want to find out already have accumulated sufficient opacity; that is, the block is completely occluded and thus does not need to be rendered. In the other case, we render the block in the main volume-rendering pass using any volume-rendering technique.

Because the contents of the frame buffer cannot be accessed in a fragment program with current graphics hardware, we have to render to a texture in the volume-rendering pass (see WGL_ARB_render_texture and GL_EXT_framebuffer_objects OpenGL extensions). This texture is used as

```
GLuint query;
GLuint sampleCount;
GLint available;

glGenQueriesARB(1, &query);
...

// for all blocks sorted front-to-back
for (i = 0; i < N; i++) {
    // save frame buffer bandwidth
    glColorMask(GL_FALSE, GL_FALSE, GL_FALSE, GL_FALSE);
    glDepthMask(GL_FALSE);

    glBeginQueryARB(GL_SAMPLES_PASSED_ARB, query);
    cgGLEnableProfile(pixelFilteringProfile);
    // only render fragments with small alpha
    glAlphaFunc(GL_LESS, threshold);
    glEnable(GL_ALPHA_TEST);
    // render with frame buffer as input texture
    renderBoundingBox(i);
    glFlush();
    glEndQueryARB(GL_SAMPLES_PASSED_ARB);
    glDisable(GL_ALPHA_TEST);

    // wait for result of query
    do {
        glGetQueryObjectivARB(query,
                              GL_QUERY_RESULT_AVAILABLE_ARB,
                              &available);
    } while (!available);
    glGetQueryObjectuivARB(query, GL_QUERY_RESULT_ARB,
                           &sampleCount);
    // if some pixels do not have enough opacity
    if (sampleCount > 0) {
        // write to frame buffer
        glColorMask(GL_TRUE, GL_TRUE, GL_TRUE, GL_TRUE);
        glDepthMask(GL_TRUE);
        cgGLEnableProfile(volumeRenderingProfile);
        // reenable other state, such as 3D texturing
        renderBlock(i);
    }
}
```

Listing 8.3. C code for block-based rendering of a volume with occlusion culling.

an input texture in the occlusion pass to read the alpha values from the frame buffer for pixels covering the current block. Because nothing is actually rendered in the occlusion pass (see the color and depth mask in Listing 8.3), we can utilize the frame-buffer texture as the rendering target and the input texture at the same time. It is usually advised not to do so; however, read-write race-conditions, which are the main reason for such advice, cannot occur in our case. If you feel uncomfortable with this solution, you may alternatively use a ping-pong technique such as described in Section 9.5. As usual, it should be understood that context switches with heavyweight rendering targets such as pbuffers are quite "expensive"; thus, frame-buffer objects are preferable.

The speed-up sustained by occlusion culling is dependent on the block size and the transfer function. It can provide a significant speed-up for isosurface like transfer functions and small block sizes.

8.6   Early Ray Termination

Finer occlusion test granularity than block-based occlusion culling is provided by early ray termination, another important optimization technique known from ray casting (see Chapter 7). When tracing rays through a volume in a front-to-back fashion, many rays quickly accumulate full opacity. This means that features in the data set in the back are occluded and need not be considered for rendering the image. Thus the ray can be terminated.

8.6.1   Dynamic Branching

As the primary design principle behind a GPU is basically that of a streaming processor, dynamic branching, i.e., branching based on data values produced during processing, was not supported on older GPUs. Early branching support was based on conditional writing; i.e., the GPU had to execute both sides of the branch before the result of one branch was written into some output register. Consequently, branching on older GPUs did not provide any performance benefit. Newer generation GPUs with support for Shader Model 3.0 (e.g., NVIDIA GeForce7 series and ATI 1xxx series) support dynamic branching and provide a performance benefit under certain conditions.

Early ray termination can be easily implemented in a simple ray caster using dynamic branching. As demonstrated in the Cg fragment program in Listing 8.4, we branch out of the ray marching loop as soon as the accumulated opacity has reached a given threshold. This requires front-to-back compositing along the rays.

```
// a simple fragment program for raycasting
// with early ray termination
struct v2f_simple {
    float4 TexCoord0 :  TEXCOORD0;
    float4 TexCoord1 :  TEXCOORD1;
};

fragout main(v2f_simple IN,
    .           uniform sampler3D Volume :  TEXUNIT0,
                uniform sampler1D TransferFunction :  TEXUNIT1,
                uniform float3 rayDir
                ) :  COLOR
{
    fragout OUT;
    // set ray start position
    float3 samplePos = IN.TexCoord0.xyz;
    OUT.col = float4(0,0,0,0);
    float sample;
    // integrate along the ray
    for (int i=0;i<200;i++)
    {
        // sample the volume
        sample = tex3D(Volume, samplePos).x;
        // classification
        float4 color = tex1D(TransferFunction, sample);
        // blend
        OUT.col = (1-OUT.col.a) * color + OUT.col;

        // early-ray termination
        if (OUT.col.a > .95)
            break;

        // march
        samplePos = samplePos + rayDir;
    }
    return OUT;
}
```

Listing 8.4. A ray-casting Cg fragment program that uses a dynamic branch for early ray termination.

Unfortunately, dynamic branches often introduce a significant overhead on current GPUs and provide a speed-up only in the case that many neighboring fragments take the same branch. This is due to the fact that graphics hardware works in parallel on neighboring pixels and cannot finish processing a pixel before all pixels that are processed at the same time are finished. Additionally, the branching statement, which is a very "expensive" operation for current graphics hardware, has to be executed for every single fragment.

8.6.2   Early Fragment Tests

Because of this problem, other technique employ early z- or early-stencil operations to "simulate" dynamic branching [140, 227]. In the standard OpenGL rendering pipeline, the z- and stencil tests are performed after the fragment-program stage. Consequently, z- or stencil tests would not provide any speed-up when using expensive fragment programs. Newer graphics hardware, however, perform a stencil test and a z-test before the fragment processing stage to prevent unnecessary computations and memory reads in the fragment stage. These early tests can be employed as a more efficient dynamic branching mechanism for early ray termination. However, to achieve a speed-up for direct volume rendering, at least ATI 9500 and NVIDIA GeForce6 class hardware is required.

There exists no explicit API to program early z- and early stencil tests. Instead, early tests are performed automatically by the graphics hardware. The hardware may automatically disable early tests without any notification. For instance, the early z-test is usually disabled if the fragment program changes the depth of the incoming fragment. Note that hardware limitations, other OpenGL states, and driver settings might also implicitly disable early z- and stencil tests. In general it can be said that speed-ups using early tests are much trickier to achieve on NVIDIA than on ATI graphics hardware. You should always refer to the GPU programming guide from the particular GPU vendor to find out about limitations that might prohibit performance improvements with early tests (see the developer websites of GPU vendors for those guides).

In order to mask pixels corresponding to rays in the z-buffer that should not be processed any further, an intermediate pass is performed, in which the alpha channel of the frame buffer is checked for high alpha values (see Listing 8.5). Because this intermediate pass is relatively "expensive," it turned out to be better to perform this test only every n integration steps along each ray. For slice-based volume rendering, for example, the intermediate ray-termination test pass is only performed every n rendered slices, where $n = 10$ is usually a good choice. For ray casting, the rendering

```
for (int j=1;j<=numSlices;j++)
{
    // check if ert-test should be performed
    if (j % checkEveryN) == 0))
        earlyRayTermination(ertThreshold);

    // compute a slice through the volume
    computeSlice(j);

    // render slice
    renderSlice(j);
}
```

Listing 8.5. C code that checks the frame buffers every n passes for early ray termination.

of the volume is split into multiple alternating ray-integration and ray-termination passes. Only few integration steps are performed for each ray per ray-integration pass; i.e., the ray front is only advanced slightly. After each integration pass, the rays are checked for possible termination in a ray-termination pass.

Because only properties of the current fragment, program arguments, and texture can be read in a fragment program on current hardware, we render to a texture and bind this texture as an input texture in the ray-termination pass. Hence the frame-buffer contents can be read for the ray-termination check.

Before rendering the volume, the depth buffer is cleared with the (default) maximum depth value. In the main volume-rendering pass, depth writes are disabled and the depth test is set to GL_LESS. In the ray-termination pass, the front faces of the bounding box of the volume are rendered, textured with the frame buffer, to check all pixels covered by the volume. Alternatively and slightly less efficiently, we can use a screen-filled quad with depth 0 to cover all pixels of the screen.

Only for pixels in the frame buffer with an alpha value above a certain threshold (e.g., 0.95) is a depth value written. Obviously, the alpha test can be used to perform this threshold test. Each fragment passing the alpha test will write a depth value into the frame buffer, preventing later fragments at this position from passing the GL_LESS depth test.

Note that ping-pong rendering with two frame buffers as in Chapter 9.5 should be employed to prevent race conditions when reading from and writing to the same frame buffer. Our tests showed that this technique

```
void earlyRayTermination(float ertThreshold)
{
    // write depth
    glDepthMask(GL_TRUE);
    // don't write colors
    glColorMask(GL_FALSE,GL_FALSE,GL_FALSE,GL_FALSE);

    // test alpha channel of the framebuffer
    glAlphaFunc(GL_GEQUAL, ertThreshold);
    glEnable(GL_ALPHA_TEST);

    glEnable(GL_DEPTH_TEST);
    glDepthFunc(GL_LESS);

    // disable volume rendering fragment program
    cgGLDisableProfile(volumeRenderingProfile);
    // bind the framebuffer as input texture
    bindFramebufferTexture();
    // render all pixels covered by the volume
    renderFramebufferToScreen();

    // enable volume rendering fragment program
    cgGLEnableProfile(volumeRenderingProfile);
    // disable alpha test
    glDisable(GL_ALPHA_TEST);
    // continue integration
    glColorMask(GL_TRUE,GL_TRUE,GL_TRUE,GL_TRUE);

    // stop writing depth values
    glDepthMask(GL_FALSE);
    // test rays for early ray termination
    glEnable(GL_DEPTH_TEST);
    glDepthFunc(GL_LESS);
}
```

Listing 8.6.   C code of the intermediate rendering pass that masks pixels with depth values, preventing further processing of rays through pixels that have accumulated sufficient opacity.

even works without ping-pong rendering on current graphics hardware. The code for the intermediate pass is outlined in Listing 8.6.

For many transfer functions with high opacity values, early ray termination provides a significant speed-up. See Figure 8.7 for a comparison of the performance with and without early ray termination of a 2D texture–based

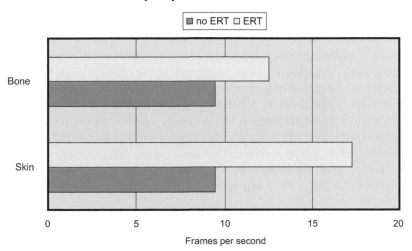

Figure 8.7. Performance improvement due to early ray termination (ERT) when rendering bone and skin of the CT data set from Figure 8.5. Note that the performance improvement is bigger with the skin transfer function, as rays can be terminated earlier once they hit the skin surface.

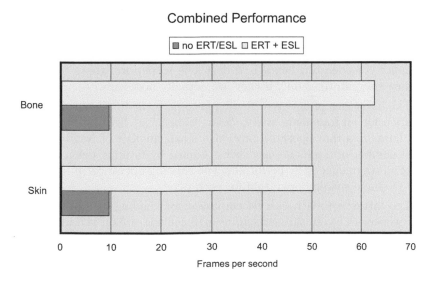

Figure 8.8. Combined performance improvement of empty-space leaping (ESL) and early ray termination (ERT) when rendering bone and skin of the CT data set from Figure 8.5. Note that because the methods are complementary, the performance is improved significantly for both skin and bone renderings.

volume renderer with on-the-fly gradient-based shading on an NVIDIA
GeForce 6800 GT PCIe x16 graphics card. Early ray-termination tests
were performed every 15 integration steps and early z-tests were employed
to obtain the results.

In fact, early ray termination and occlusion culling are complementary
acceleration techniques to empty-space skipping. See Figure 8.8 for the
combined performance improvement obtain with empty-space leaping and
early ray termination on an NVIDIA GeForce 6800 GT PCIe x16 graphics
card. If the volume contains a lot of empty space, empty-space skipping
performs quite well while early ray termination and occlusion culling do
not. Vice versa, if the volume does not contain much empty space and
the transfer function is not too transparent, early ray termination and
occlusion culling provide a big speed-up while empty-space skipping does
not perform well.

8.7   Deferred Shading

For shading large volumetric data, it is impractical to store pre-computed
gradients in texture maps. Hence, gradients are often computed on-the-
fly (see Sections 9.4 and 5.6). The resulting gradients have a very high
quality and do not produce any memory overhead; however, many texture
fetches are required for the per-fragment gradient calculation (for example,
six for central differences). A large number of texture fetches decrease performance considerably, hence it is desirable to perform those "expensive"
shading computations only if they are actually necessary.

The basic idea of deferred shading is to perform an "inexpensive" computation for all fragments and to defer "expensive" lighting computations
to a later pass that operates only on a small number of fragments. This
small number of fragments is either obtained by filtering out a small subset of all fragments or by performing the shading operation in image-space
only (a single shading operation for each pixel).

The latter approach can be employed for shading opaque isosurfaces
(see Section 14.5). In this section, we will concentrate on volumetric shading by deferring shading operations to fragments with alpha values from
classification greater than a given threshold, as shading effects are only apparent if the transparency of a fragment is not too small. We first perform
post-interpolative classification for all fragments. If the alpha value from
classification is below the shading threshold, we blend the result into the
frame buffer. The "expensive" on-the-fly gradient shading computation is
only performed for the remaining fragments.

The simplest method to implement this is to perform post-interpolative classification and then use a dynamic branch in a fragment program that is performing shading only for high opacity fragments. Because the dynamic branching capabilities on most GPUs only provide a measurable speed-up when most of the fragments in a particular area of the frame buffer take the same branch, we will instead once again employ early z-tests for dynamic branching (see Section 8.6.2). Especially in the case of a quite complex and expensive fragment program, a two-pass approach with an early z-test that defers the complex computation to a second pass can provide a huge performance benefit.

In the first pass, the slice polygon is rendered with a post-classification fragment program. An alpha test that only allows fragments to pass with an opacity below the shading threshold ensures that only low-alpha fragments are blended into the frame buffer. By enabling depth writes in this pass, we also write a depth value for those fragments.

In the second pass, we render the same slice polygon again. Because we enable the OpenGL depth test with the GL_NOTEQUAL comparison function,

```
struct v2f_simple {
    float3 TexCoord0 :   TEXCOORD0;
};

half4 main(v2f_simple IN,
           uniform sampler3D Volume,
           uniform sampler1D TransferFunction,
           uniform float magnitudeThreshold
           ) : COLOR
{
    // fetch volume scalar and gradient magnitude
    // from 2 channel texture
    half2 sample = tex3D(Volume, IN.TexCoord0).xy;
    // check if gradient magnitude is small
    if (sample.y < magnitudeThreshold)
        // render unshaded
        return tex1D(TransferFunction, sample.x);
    else
        // render nothing (shade in 2nd pass)
        return half4(0,0,0,0);
}
```

Listing 8.7. Cg fragment program that performs post-interpolative classification for small gradient magnitudes. All other fragments are shaded in the second pass.

now only the fragments that were removed in the first pass are processed by the complex fragment program. Because the depth test is performed after the fragment stage in the traditional OpenGL rendering pipeline, this requires an early z-test (see Section 8.6.2). Such a test is performed by the graphics hardware before the actual fragment program is run for a certain fragment, thus providing a performance benefit if a large number of fragments have an opacity below our shading threshold after classification.

In addition to the selective computation of gradients based on the alpha values from classification, gradient computation can also be deferred to regions of the volume that provide "good" gradients. "Bad" gradients come from homogeneous regions of volume data sets, where the gradient magnitude is low and gradients have arbitrary orientation, resulting in very noisy shading results. To remove those noisy regions, a common technique is to check the gradient magnitude before the computation of the shading coefficients. If the magnitude of the gradient is below a certain threshold, the fragment is rendered with the color obtained directly from classification. However, this does not provide any significant speed-up, because the expensive gradient computation has to be performed before the gradient magnitude can be derived. Thus it is necessary to pre-compute the gradient magnitude for each voxel of the volume data and store this information together with the volume data, for example in a two-channel texture.

As before, we render each slice polygon twice. In the first pass, we fetch the gradient magnitude and scalar data from a two-channel texture (see Listing 8.7). If the magnitude is below a certain threshold, we classify and render the unshaded result into the frame buffer. If the magnitude is above the threshold, we set the alpha value to zero. Using the alpha test, we make sure that only fragments with alpha greater than zero are rendered; i.e., we use `glAlphaFunc(GL_GREATER, 0.0)`. We enable depth writes to allow z-values to be written for fragments that are not shaded. We prefer using the alpha test for selective writing of z-values to a fragment program `discard` operation, as such operations implicitly disable early z-tests on most graphics hardware.

In the second pass, a standard fragment program with gradient and shading computation is used (see Listing 5.6 in Chapter 5). This expensive second pass is only performed for a relatively small fraction of the total fragments rendered, as we enable the depth test to prevent pixels from being processed that were rendered in the first pass again. The depth test is set to `GL_LESS` for back-to-front and `GL_GREATER` for front-to-back rendering. If the volume data consists of many homogeneous regions, the depth test will make sure that most of the fragments will be processed in the first pass only.

If completely transparent fragments are already culled by empty-space leaping (see Section 8.4), deferred shading based on low opacity only provides a measurable speed-up when using transfer functions with many small alpha values. As a matter of course, it is possible to defer expensive shading operations based on other volume properties, such as material properties from segmentation information. Such properties can be pre-computed, stored into texture maps, and used during the first pass for computational masking.

8.8 Image Downscaling

As mentioned before, the performance of direct volume rendering is usually bounded by fragment processing. This is due to the fact that either a very large number of fragments is produced in slicing-based algorithms or very long and thus "expensive" fragment programs are executed in ray casting–based algorithms. Reducing the number of fragments by culling fragments in object-space as described earlier is only one option.

In addition, we can also reduce the number of fragments by rendering the image into an offscreen render target with lower resolution (for example, with half the resolution in x and y) and zoom up the image when displaying it on the screen. Rendering to a texture (see `WGL_ARB_render_texture` OpenGL extension) or frame-buffer object (see `EXT_framebuffer_object` OpenGL extension) are ideal for this purpose, because the volume-rendering result can be rendered directly to the screen and scaled up to the desired resolution at the same time. For that purpose, a single screen-filled quad polygon textured with the low-resolution rendering result is rendered to the onscreen frame buffer. Built-in texture filters or handcrafted filters can be applied during this process to make the reduced image resolution less apparent to the user (see Listing 8.8).

The performance improvement is usually linear with the number of pixels rendered, i.e., when rendering with half the resolution in x and y we obtain nearly four times the performance, as the rendering and scaling of the resulting low-resolution image to the frame buffer does not introduce significant overhead (see Figure 8.9).

An adaptive image resolution dependent on the homogeneity of the image area could also be a feasible solution. This technique is similar to adaptive sampling as discussed in Section 9.1.2, but now in image-space as opposed to object-space. It is known from CPU ray casting where additional rays are often shot in areas with high variance. To our knowledge, this method has not yet been applied to GPU-based volume rendering.

```
// disable depth test and blending
glDisable(GL_DEPTH_TEST);
glDisable(GL_BLEND);

glMatrixMode(GL_PROJECTION);
// save projection matrix & load identity
glPushMatrix(); glLoadIdentity();
glMatrixMode(GL_MODELVIEW);
// save modelview matrix & load identity
glPushMatrix(); glLoadIdentity();

// disable fragment and vertex program
cgGLDisableProfile(fProfile);
cgGLDisableProfile(vProfile);
// bind offscreen buffer texture
glActiveTextureARB(GL_TEXTURE0_ARB);
glBindTexture(GL_TEXTURE_2D, offscreenResult);
glEnable(GL_TEXTURE_2D);

// use bilinear filtering
glTexParameteri(GL_TEXTURE_2D, GL_TEXTURE_MIN_FILTER,
                GL_LINEAR);
glTexParameteri(GL_TEXTURE_2D, GL_TEXTURE_MAG_FILTER,
                GL_LINEAR);

// render screen-filled quad
glBegin(GL_QUADS);
glTexCoord2f(0, 0); glVertex2i(-1,-1);
glTexCoord2f(1, 0); glVertex2i( 1,-1);
glTexCoord2f(1, 1); glVertex2i( 1, 1);
glTexCoord2f(0, 1); glVertex2i(-1, 1);
glEnd();

// restore projection matrix
glMatrixMode(GL_PROJECTION);
glPopMatrix();

// restore modelview matrix
glMatrixMode(GL_MODELVIEW);
glPopMatrix();
```

Listing 8.8. C code for upscaling an offscreen rendering result to the screen with bilinear interpolation.

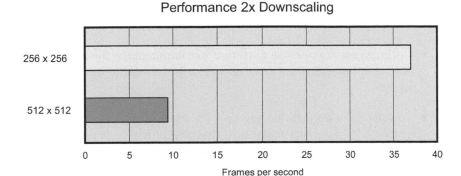

Figure 8.9. Performance comparison between rendering with half the viewport resolution (256 × 256 pixels) and rendering at the full viewport resolution (512 × 512 pixels). The performance of the reduced resolution rendering includes the final blow-up to the full viewport size.

8.9   Discussion

The mastery of GPU-based volume rendering is to prevent idle times by delivering volume data values efficiently to the computational units in the fragment-processing pipelines. This still remains a challenge, as limited bandwidths and high latencies of the involved memory subsystems prevent a constant delivery of data values to the fragment pipelines. Even though modern GPUs implement several methods to hide memory latency, idle times often cannot be circumvented. Hence, the number of fragments that are processed must be reduced to prevent these data delivery delays. In this chapter, we discussed several methods to offload the fragment-processing stage by removing fragments early in the rendering pipeline of graphics hardware. Despite the fact that modern GPUs provide plenty of computational horsepower, reducing the number of fragments also helps to reduce the load in the fragment-processing stage.

The following are general guidelines for high-performance volume rendering.

- Find the optimal distribution of the processing subtasks to all pipeline stages to utilize the processing power of graphics hardware to its maximum. Algorithms that are fragment processing bound should offload some of the tasks to the vertex pipelines, while vertex processing bound algorithms should offload tasks to the fragment stage.

- Keep volume data as close to the GPU as possible. GPU memory provides very high bandwidth and low latency. Employing other types of

memory will result in copying, rearrangement, and transfer of volume
data, which can significantly reduce performance.

- Optimize memory-access patterns: use mipmapping for minification,
  swizzle volume data for magnification, and avoid dependent texture
  fetches.

- Transfer data asynchronously to GPU memory. If the data does not
  fit into GPU memory, make sure that you provide a constant stream
  of data to the GPU. Asynchronous transfer of data over AGP or PCIe
  allows you to bring in new data while other data is rendered. Data
  must be stored in main memory in the native GPU data format to
  prevent "expensive" data conversion.

- Cull data that does not contribute to the final image early in the
  volume-rendering pipeline. Empty-space leaping, early ray termination, and occlusion culling are effective methods to achieve this goal.
  Early fragment tests such as early z- and early stencil culls often
  provide higher speed-ups than dynamic branching.

- Perform "expensive" per-fragment operations selectively. Deferring
  such operations to image-space or to only a small subset of the fragments can provide a huge performance benefit.

- Optimize your fragment programs. Complex fragment programs introduce a high-performance penalty for fragment-bound algorithms
  such as volume rendering. Constant parameters should be pre-
  computed and passed into the fragment program as parameters. Parameters that change linearly over the proxy geometry should be
  computed in the vertex stage.

- Employ multiple levels of resolution to access fewer data values in
  regions which are homogeneous or far away from the camera (also see
  Section 17.3).

- Use adaptive sampling to reduce the number of trilinear interpolations and memory read operations from the volume.

- Scale down the image size during interaction to reduce the number
  of fragments that need to be computed. A reduced image resolution
  during interaction is often acceptable for the user.

- Avoid OpenGL context switches by employing lightweight rendering
  targets such as frame-buffer objects.

GPU manufacturers provide several performance optimization tools that allow one to find bottlenecks in rendering algorithms. NVIDIA offers NVShaderPerf to report shader performance metrics, an instrumentation driver (NVPerfKit) to monitor low-level performance counters inside the driver, and NVPerfHUD for displaying real-time statistics on top of running applications (see NVIDIA developer website at http://developer.nvidia.com). ATI offers a plugin for Microsoft's PIX (Performance Investigator for DirectX) tool. PIX is a performance-analysis tool that Microsoft has introduced with the DirectX 9 SDK (see ATI developer website at http://www.ati.com/developer).

9

Improving Image Quality

R EAL-TIME EXPLORATION OF VOLUMETRIC DATA is an important tool that allows finding details hidden within the data that would usually be overlooked, thus providing additional insight compared with static visualizations. Hence, one of the most important goals of volume rendering is to generate results under a given time constraint to provide a high frame rate and thus interactivity to the user. Time constraints, however, quite often require trade-offs between quality and performance, which can be made at different stages of the volume-rendering pipeline. Depending on the trade-offs made, more or less apparent artifacts are visible in the resulting images. In this chapter, we will therefore first identify possible sources of artifacts during the volume-rendering process. After this improved understanding of the sources of artifacts, we can then find methods to produce high-quality volume visualizations even under given time constraints.

Artifacts are introduced in the various stages of the volume-rendering pipeline. Generally speaking, the volume-rendering pipeline consists of five stages (see Figure 9.1). First, a sampling stage, which accesses the volume data to obtain the value of voxels along straight rays through the volume.

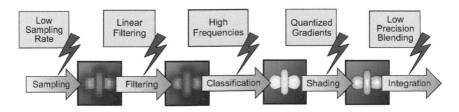

Figure 9.1. The volume-rendering pipeline. Each step in this pipeline is a potential source of artifacts.

Second, a filtering stage, which interpolates the voxel values. Third, a classification step, which maps interpolated values from the volume to emission and absorption coefficients. An optional fourth stage is required if external light sources are taken into account to compute the shading of the volume data. Finally, the integration of the volume data is performed. This is achieved in graphics hardware by blending emission colors with their associated alpha values into the frame buffer. This pipeline is repeated until all samples along the rays through the volume have been processed. Each stage of the pipeline is a potential source of artifacts.

Note that sampling and filtering are actually performed in the same stage in graphics hardware; i.e., during slice-based volume rendering, we define sample positions using texture coordinates of slice polygons. In image-order–based approaches, sample positions are explicitly computed in the fragment program. The hardware automatically performs filtering once the volume is accessed with a texture fetch operation. The position and weighting factors for the interpolation of data values is identified using the corresponding texture coordinate, interpolated inside the proxy geometry, or computed along the ray. The type of filtering performed by the graphics hardware is specified by setting the appropriate OpenGL state of the volume texture. Current graphics hardware only supports nearest-neighbor and linear filtering, i.e., linear, bilinear, and trilinear filtering. However, due to the programmability of graphics hardware, additional filtering methods such as cubic filters can be added. Consequently, we will treat sampling and filtering as two steps, as they become two separate operations once we implement our own filtering method.

The goal of this chapter is to remove or at least suppress artifacts that occur during volume rendering while maintaining real-time performance. For this purpose, all proposed optimizations will be performed directly on the GPU in order to avoid expensive readback of data from the GPU memory. We will review the stages of the volume-rendering pipeline step-by-step, identify possible sources of error introduced in the corresponding stage, and explain techniques to remove or suppress those errors while ensuring interactive frame rates.

9.1 Sampling Artifacts

The first stage in the process of volume rendering consists of sampling the discrete voxel data. Current GPU-based techniques employ explicit proxy geometry to trace a large number of rays in parallel through the volume (slice-based volume rendering) or directly sample the volume along rays (ray casting). The distance of those sampling points influences how accurately we represent the data. A large distance between sampling points,

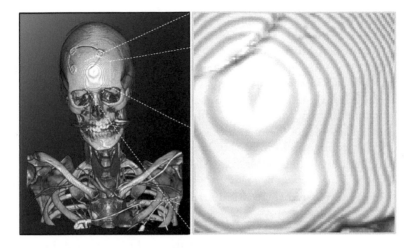

Figure 9.2. Wood-grain artifacts caused by a low sampling rate.

i.e., a low sampling rate, will result in severe artifacts (see Figure 9.2). This effect is often referred to as undersampling and the associated artifacts are often referred to as wood-grain artifacts.

The critical question: how many samples do we have to obtain along rays in the volume to accurately represent the volume data? The answer to this question lies in the so-called Nyquist-Shannon sampling theorem of information theory.

9.1.1   Sampling Theorem

The theorem is one of the most important rules of sampling [201, 238]. It states that, when converting analog signals to digital, the sampling frequency must be greater than twice the highest frequency of the input signal to be able to later reconstruct the original signal from the sampled version perfectly. Otherwise the signal will be aliased; i.e., high frequencies will be reconstructed incorrectly from the discrete signal. An analog signal can contain arbitrary high frequencies, therefore an analog low-pass filter is often applied before sampling the signal to ensure that the input signal does not have those high frequencies. Such a signal is called band-limited.

For example, for an audio signal the sampling theorem has the consequence that, if we want to sample the audio signal with 22 kHz as the highest frequency, we must at least sample the signal with twice the sampling rates; i.e., with at least 44 kHz. As already stated, this rule applies if we want to discretize contiguous signals. But what does this rule mean for sampling an already discretized signal? Well, in volume rendering we assume that the data represents samples taken from a contiguous band-limited volumetric field. During sampling, we might already have lost some information due to a too-low acquisition sampling rate. This is certainly something we cannot fix during rendering. However, the highest frequency in a discrete signal that is assumed to be contiguous is an abrupt change in the data from one sampling position to an adjacent one. This means that the highest frequency is one divided by the smallest distance between adjacent voxels of the volume data. Thus, in order to accurately reconstruct the original signal from the discrete data, we need to take at least two samples per smallest inter-voxel distance.

There is actually no easy way to get around this theorem. We have to take two samples per voxel to avoid artifacts. However, taking a lot of samples along rays inside the volume has a direct impact on the performance. We achieve this high sampling rate by either increasing the number of slice polygons or by reducing the sampling distance during ray casting. Taking twice the number of samples inside the volume will typically reduce the frame rate by a factor of two. However, volumetric data often does not only consist of regions with high variations in the data values. In fact, volume data can be very homogeneous in certain regions while other regions contain a lot of detail and thus high frequencies. We can exploit this fact by using a technique called adaptive sampling.

9.1.2   Adaptive Sampling

Adaptive sampling techniques cause more samples to be taken in inhomogeneous than in homogeneous regions of the volume. In order to distinguish homogeneous and inhomogeneous parts of the volume during integration along our rays through the volume, a 3D texture containing the sampling rate for each region can be employed. This texture, the so-called importance volume, can be computed in a pre-processing step and may have smaller spatial dimensions than our volume data. For volume ray casting on the GPU, it is easy to adapt the sampling rate to the sampling rate obtained from this texture because sampling positions are generated in the fragment stage. Slice-based volume rendering, however, is more complicated because the sampling rate is directly set by the number of slice polygons. In other words, the sampling rate is set in the vertex stage, while the sampling rate from our importance volume is obtained in the fragment stage.

However, the texture coordinates for sampling the volume interpolated on the slice polygons can be considered as samples for a base sampling rate. We can then take additional samples along the ray direction at those sampling positions in a fragment program, thus sampling higher in regions where the data set is inhomogeneous. In order to obtain a performance improvement by a only locally high sampling rate, such an implementation requires dynamic branching in a fragment program to adapt the number of volume samples in the fragment program to the desired sampling rate at this position. Such dynamic branching is available on Pixel Shader 3.0 compliant hardware. Alternatively, computational masking using early z- or stencil-culls can be employed to accelerate the rendering for regions with lower sampling rate. The slice polygon is rendered multiple times with different fragment programs for the different sampling rates, and rays (pixels) are selected for the different passes by masking the corresponding pixels using the stencil- or z-buffer. For a more detailed description on the implementation of dynamic branching using early tests, please see Section 8.6.2.

9.1.3 Opacity Correction

Changing the sampling rate globally or locally requires correction of the opacity of fragments being blended into the frame buffer. This prevents regions from getting brighter in sparsely sampled regions and darker in highly sampled regions. This can be implemented globally by changing the alpha values in the transfer function or locally by adapting the alpha values before blending in a fragment program. The corrected opacity is a function of the stored opacity α_{stored} for the base sample distance and the actual sample distance with the sample spacing ratio $\Delta x / \Delta x_0$:

$$\alpha_{corrected} = 1 - [1 - \alpha_{stored}]^{\Delta x / \Delta x_0} .$$

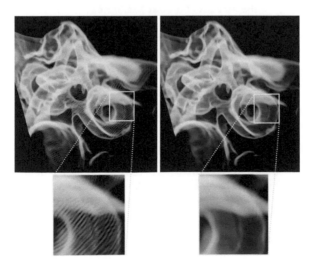

Figure 9.3. Comparison of a visualization of the inner ear with low (left) and high (right) sampling rate.

Rendering a volumetric data set with globally or locally high sampling rates allows us to remove wood-grain artifacts (see Figure 9.3). However, such high sampling rates can significantly reduce performance. To make things even worse, in most volumetric renderings complex transfer functions are used in the classification stage. Those can introduce high frequencies into the sampled data, thus increasing the required sampling rate well beyond the Nyquist frequency of the volume data itself. We will discuss this effect in detail in Section 9.3 and provide a solution to the problems by using a technique that separates those high classification frequencies from high frequencies in the scalar field in a pre-processing step.

9.1.4 Stochastic Jittering

As an alternative to removing wood-grain artifacts, we can try to hide them. Wood-grain artifacts are due to a sudden change in the depth between neighboring opaque fragments belonging to the same surface. The alternative to high sampling rates for artifact removal is called *stochastic jittering*. This technique hides wood-grain artifacts by adding small offsets to the sampling positions of rays in the viewing direction. The sampling

```
int size = 32;
unsigned char* buffer = new unsigned char[size*size];
srand( (unsigned)time( NULL ) );
for (int i=0;i<(size*size);i++)
    buffer[i] = 255.*rand()/(float)RAND_MAX;
glGenTextures(1,&noiseTex);
glActiveTextureARB(GL_TEXTURE3_ARB);
glBindTexture(GL_TEXTURE_2D,noiseTex);
glTexImage2D(
    GL_TEXTURE_2D,      // target
    0,                  // level
    GL_LUMINANCE8,      // internal
    size,               // width
    size,               // height
    0, GL_LUMINANCE, GL_UNSIGNED_BYTE, buffer);
glTexParameteri(GL_TEXTURE_2D, GL_TEXTURE_WRAP_S, GL_REPEAT);
glTexParameteri(GL_TEXTURE_2D, GL_TEXTURE_WRAP_T, GL_REPEAT);
glTexParameteri(GL_TEXTURE_2D, GL_TEXTURE_MIN_FILTER, GL_NEAREST);
glTexParameteri(GL_TEXTURE_2D, GL_TEXTURE_MAG_FILTER, GL_NEAREST);
delete buffer;
```

Listing 9.1. C code creating a texture containing random numbers, used to offset ray sampling positions.

positions along each ray through a pixel are offset by a different random factor. Consequently, coherence between pixels that becomes manifest in artifacts is suppressed by noise.

For the implementation, we create a single-channel GL_LUMINANCE 2D texture containing random numbers. A small 2D texture with 32×32 random numbers, tiled over the output image usually provides sufficient randomization. During rendering, we acquire different random numbers from this 2D texture for each pixel to offset the sampling positions for the ray through the corresponding pixel. Listing 9.1 creates such a 2D texture. Note that the GL_REPEAT texture environment allows us to tile the texture over the output image:

Due to the implicit computation of the sampling positions in slicing-based volume rendering using proxy geometry, the same offset must be added to every sampling position along the rays.

To fetch a different random number for each pixel, we divide the window position WPOS by the size of the random number texture. This results in texture coordinates for the look-up into the 2D texture containing our random numbers; i.e., the texture is tiled over the output image. We pass the ray direction vector with a length equal to the sampling distance and the dimensions of the random number texture as uniform variables to the fragment shader (see Listing 9.2). By multiplying the random number for

```
struct v2f_simple {
    float3 TexCoord0 :   TEXCOORD0;
    float3 Position  :   WPOS;
};

half4 main(v2f_simple IN,
              uniform sampler3D Volume            :   TEXUNIT0,
              uniform sampler1D TransferFunction :   TEXUNIT1,
              uniform sampler2D Random            :   TEXUNIT3,
              half3 rayDir, half2 tileSize) :  COLOR {
    // offset sampling position
    IN.TexCoord0 = IN.TexCoord0 + rayDir
        * tex2D(Random, IN.Position.xy / tileSize.xy).x;
    // sample
    half4 sample = tex3D(Volume, IN.TexCoord0);
    // classify and return
    return tex1D(TransferFunction, sample.r);
}
```

Listing 9.2. Cg fragment shader for jittering the sampling position in a slicing-based volume renderer along the viewing direction.

```
struct v2f_simple {
    float3 TexCoord0 :  TEXCOORD0;
    float3 Position  :  WPOS; };

float4 main(v2f_simple IN,
    uniform sampler3D Volume              :  TEXUNIT0,
    uniform sampler1D TransferFunction :  TEXUNIT1,
    uniform sampler2D Random             :  TEXUNIT3,
    half3 rayDir, half2 tileSize) :  COLOR {
    float4 OUT;
    // jitter ray start position along ray direction
    float3 samplePos = IN.TexCoord0.xyz + rayDir *
        tex2D(Random, IN.Position.xy / tileSize.xy).x;
    col = float4(0,0,0,0);
    float2 sample = float2(0,0);
    // integrate along the ray
    for (int i=0;i<200;i++) {
        // sample the volume
        sample.x = tex3D(Volume, samplePos).x;
        // classification
        float4 color = tex1D(TransferFunction , sample.x);
        // blend
        col = (1-col.a) * color + col;
        samplePos = samplePos + rayDir;
    }
    return OUT;
}
```

Listing 9.3. Cg fragment shader for jittering the sampling position in a ray casting–based volume renderer along the viewing direction.

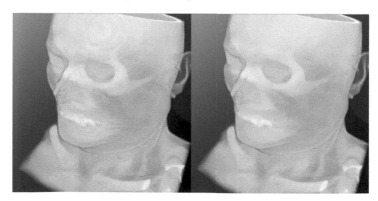

Figure 9.4. Volume rendering without (left) and with (right) stochastic jittering of the sampling positions.

each pixel (in the range $[0, 1]$) with the ray direction vector and adding the resulting vector to the sampling position, we obtain differently offset sampling positions for each ray; i.e., a different sampling pattern with a maximum offset equal to the sampling distance is created for each pixel.

Though stochastic jittering in slicing only requires a look-up into a very small noise texture and a few additional arithmetic instructions, the jitter offset has to be fetched and added for each integration step. This results in reduced rendering performance compared with standard slice-based volume rendering. For short fragment programs, such as a simple post-interpolative classification fragment program, the overhead is significant. For complex fragment programs, such as an on-the-fly gradient computation fragment program (see Section 5.3.1), the overhead is only small. In contrast, for ray casting the offset can be added only once in the ray–set-up phase as demonstrated by the Cg fragment program in Listing 9.3; i.e., in contrast with slicing, the jittering is done only once for a complete ray. Thus the overhead is negligible. As before, we provide the ray direction vector with a length equal to the sampling distance and the size of the random number texture as input variables to the fragment shader.

This method is quite effective for hiding wood-grain artifacts without requiring high sampling rates. The resulting images contain more noise, but noise is often less annoying than regular patterns. Even for very low sampling rates, volume rendering with stochastic jittering can produce acceptable results. Figure 9.4 shows a comparison of standard volume rendering and volume rendering with stochastic jittering of the sampling position.

9.2   Filtering Artifacts

The next possible source for artifacts in volumetric computer graphics is introduced during the filtering of the volume data. Basically, this phase converts the discrete volume data back to a continuous signal. To reconstruct the original continuous signal from the voxels, a reconstruction filter is applied that calculates a scalar value for the continuous 3D domain (R^3) by performing a convolution of the discrete function with a filter kernel. It has been proved that the perfect, or ideal, reconstruction kernel is provided by the sinc filter [204].

Unfortunately, the sinc filter has an unlimited extent; i.e., it oscillates around zero over its whole output domain. Therefore, in practice simpler reconstruction filters like tent or box filters are used (see Figure 9.5). Current graphics hardware supports pre-filtering mechanisms like mipmapping and anisotropic filtering for minification. For magnification, linear, bilinear, and trilinear filters are provided. The internal precision of the filtering on current graphics hardware is dependent on the precision of the input texture; i.e., 8-bit textures will internally only be filtered with 8-bit preci-

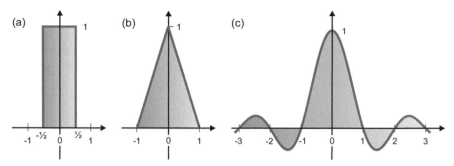

Figure 9.5. Three reconstruction filters: (a) box, (b) tent, and (c) sinc filters.

sion. To achieve higher quality filtering results with the built-in filtering techniques of GPUs, we must use a higher-precision internal texture format when defining textures (i.e., the LUMINANCE16 and HILO texture formats). Note that floating-point texture formats often do not support filtering.

However, the use of higher internal precision for filtering cannot on its own provide satisfactory results with built-in linear reconstruction filters (see Figure 9.6 (left)). Quite efficient techniques that use multitextures and programmable rasterization hardware have been developed to evaluate arbitrary filter kernels during rendering [91].

High-quality filters implemented in fragment programs can considerably improve image quality. However, it must be noted that performing higher-quality filtering in fragment programs on current graphics hardware is expensive; i.e., frame rates drop considerably. We recommend higher-quality filters only for final image quality renderings. During interaction

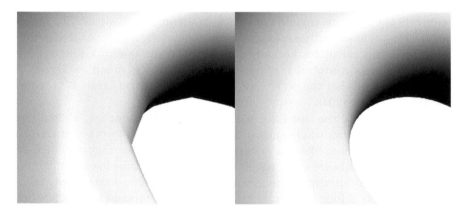

Figure 9.6. Comparison between trilinear filtering and cubic B-spline filtering.

with volume data or during animations, it is probably better to use built-in reconstruction filters, as artifacts will not be too apparent in motion. To prevent unnecessary calculations in transparent or occluded regions of the volume, the optimization techniques presented in Chapter 8 should be used.

9.2.1 Convolution Filtering

A linear filtering operation is usually described via an operation called the *convolution* of a filter kernel function $h(\cdot)$ with a signal function $s(\cdot)$. Note that, although this is a linear operation, the filter kernel function is usually not a linear function. Linear in this case means that the filter kernel $h(\cdot)$ does not depend on the signal $s(\cdot)$. In the general continuous case, convolution is described by the *convolution integral* over an infinite extent:

$$g(x) = (s * h)(x) = \int_{-\infty}^{\infty} h(x')s(x - x')dx' . \qquad (9.1)$$

However, we are interested in filtering sampled signal functions, i.e., texture maps, which we denote as a series of samples f_i at locations $x = i$. We consider only finite filter kernels $h(\cdot)$, where the convolution need only be evaluated over a certain range, i.e., the width of the filter. The convolution integral then simplifies to the finite *convolution sum*:

$$g(x) = (f * h)(x) = \sum_{i=-m+1}^{m} h(u - i)f_i \quad \text{with} \quad u = x - \lfloor x \rfloor . \quad (9.2)$$

Here, $g(x)$ is the filtered output at a given fractional resampling position x. The f_i are the samples of the discrete input texture given at the integers of x. The continuous filter kernel is denoted by $h(\cdot)$, and m is half the filter width, e.g., for cubic filters $m = 2$. Figure 9.7 illustrates the convolution sum with a cubic B-spline filter.

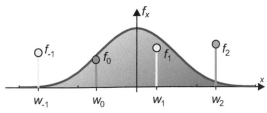

Figure 9.7. Convolution with a cubic B-spline filter. Because this filter has width four, it subtends four input samples f_i that are multiplied by four corresponding filter weights $w_i(u) = h(u - i)$ with $i \in \{-1, 0, 1, 2\}$. See Equations 9.2 and 9.3.

Instead of using a single function $h(\cdot)$ to describe the filter kernel, we can use multiple weight functions $w_i(u)$ that are each defined over the interval $u \in [0, 1]$, where $u = x - \lfloor x \rfloor$, defining $w_i(u) := h(u - i)$:

$$g(x) = \sum_{i=-m+1}^{m} w_i(u)f_i \quad \text{with} \quad u = x - \lfloor x \rfloor. \tag{9.3}$$

Note that, in order to simplify the equations and the discussion below, we always assume a relative numbering of input samples, that is, f_0 to the left of the current position x, and f_1 to the right of x. If the input samples are given a constant global numbering, each f_i in the equations would become an f_j with $j = \lfloor x \rfloor + i$.

9.2.2   Evaluating the Convolution Sum

There are several ways in which evaluation of the convolution sum for filtering can be approached on graphics hardware. These approaches differ with regard to performance, the types of filter kernels for which they work well, their simplicity of implementation, and the fragment shader hardware features they require.

The two fundamental parts of this computation are (1) computing filter weights $w_i(u)$ and (2) fetching the required input samples f_i. In general, the convolution sum is often stated with infinite extent, but in practice of course only a relatively low number of filter weights will be nonzero. If the filter kernel is polynomial, its degree determines the number of input samples and corresponding weights that are required. In particular, certain kinds of filters such as cubic filters provide a very good trade-off between quality and speed. For this reason, many implementations are optimized for special cases. However, it is possible to evaluate all kinds of finite convolution filters in graphics hardware with a simple general multipass approach that has minimal requirements on fragment shader resources and features.

9.2.3   Convolution in 2D and 3D

In the following, we illustrate all the different approaches using 1D convolution. However, they can all be extended to 2D and 3D. The most common approach for extending 1D filter kernels to 2D or 3D is to use the *tensor product*. The weights for all dimensions are computed by fetching weights from 1D filter functions for each of the axes and multiplying, i.e., $w_{ij}(u, v) = w_i(u)w_j(v)$ and $w_{ijk}(u, v, w) = w_i(u)w_j(v)w_k(w)$. Another approach is to use *radially symmetric* filters, e.g., $h(x, y) = h(\sqrt{x^2 + y^2})$. The general texture-based approach described in Section 9.2.5 is able to use arbitrary 2D and 3D extensions of 1D filters by simply using 2D or 3D filter weight textures.

9.2.4   Procedural Convolution

The most straightforward approach for evaluating the convolution sum is to compute all weights procedurally in the fragment shader. As long as the function that describes the filter kernel can be evaluated in the fragment shader at arbitrary positions x, all required weights $w_i(u)$ can be computed easily. All input samples f_i are fetched from the input texture with nearest-neighbor interpolation. The convolution sum is then evaluated directly as given in Equation 9.3.

Example: Cubic B-spline. The cubic B-spline is part of the family of the BC-splines [185] ($B = 1, C = 0$). It is depicted in Figure 9.8. Like all cubic filters, it has width four and thus requires four weights and subtends four input samples. The weights are defined as

$$w_0(u) \;=\; \frac{1}{6}(-u^3 + 3u^2 - 3u + 1), \tag{9.4}$$

$$w_1(u) \;=\; \frac{1}{6}(3u^3 - 6u^2 + 4), \tag{9.5}$$

$$w_2(u) \;=\; \frac{1}{6}(-3u^3 + 3u^2 + 3u + 1), \tag{9.6}$$

$$w_3(u) \;=\; \frac{1}{6}u^3. \tag{9.7}$$

The parameter u is the fractional position in $[0, 1]$ between two neighboring samples, i.e., $u = x - \lfloor x \rfloor$. Note that for every u, $\sum_i w_i(u) = 1$, which is called the *partition of unity* property. The fact that the cubic B-spline is $2/3$ in its center (see Figure 9.8) implies that this filter is *approximating* or *smoothing*, instead of *interpolating*. That is, it modifies the values at

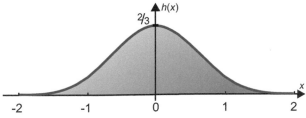

Figure 9.8.   The cubic B-spline. The filter kernel $h(x)$ is defined over the interval $[-2, 2]$ and never negative, and it is $2/3$ in the center. Thus, it is an *approximating* or *smoothing* filter. However, it is the only cubic BC-spline with a continuous second derivative (see Figure 9.14) which is important for derivative measurements.

the original sample positions. It is also nonzero at other integers of x (at both $x = -1$ and $x = 1$, it has a value of $1/6$), which is also a property of smoothing filters. In contrast, interpolating filters are one at the center and zero at all other integers, such as the Catmull-Rom spline described below. Smoothing is often a desired filter property, especially in combination with derivative filtering, but some applications demand that the original samples are not modified, e.g., in medical imaging.

For procedural evaluation of filter weights in the fragment shader, it is useful to first compute u, u^2, and u^3. The coefficients in the formulas for the weights can be stored in one 4-vector (i.e., a single fragment shader parameter) per weight, which for the cubic B-spline yields

$$
\begin{aligned}
vec_{w_0} &= \left(-\tfrac{1}{6}, \quad \tfrac{1}{2}, \quad -\tfrac{1}{2}, \quad \tfrac{1}{6} \right), \\
vec_{w_1} &= \left(\tfrac{1}{2}, \quad -1, \quad 0, \quad \tfrac{2}{3} \right), \\
vec_{w_2} &= \left(-\tfrac{1}{2}, \quad \tfrac{1}{2}, \quad \tfrac{1}{2}, \quad \tfrac{1}{6} \right), \\
vec_{w_3} &= \left(\tfrac{1}{6}, \quad 0, \quad 0, \quad 0 \right).
\end{aligned}
$$

Each weight can then be computed for a given u by taking the dot product of the weight vector with the vector containing the exponentiated u values:

$$
w_i(u) = vec_{w_i} \cdot (u^3, u^2, u, 1).
$$

This scheme can be used for any polynomial filter. Thus, a single fragment shader can be used for polynomial filtering of a certain order, e.g., for order three as used here. The actual filter shape can then be determined by simply supplying different fragment shader constants.

Example: Catmull-Rom spline. The Catmull-Rom spline is another cubic spline in the family of the BC-splines [185] ($B = 0, C = 0.5$). It is shown in Figure 9.9. However, in contrast with the cubic B-spline, it is an *interpolating* filter. It is the only cubic BC-spline that has this property. Using the vector notation given above, the weights of the Catmull-Rom spline are defined as

$$
\begin{aligned}
vec_{w_0} &= \left(-0.5, \quad 1, \quad -0.5, \quad 0 \right), \\
vec_{w_1} &= \left(1.5, \quad -2.5, \quad 0, \quad 1 \right), \\
vec_{w_2} &= \left(-1.5, \quad 2, \quad 0.5, \quad 0 \right), \\
vec_{w_3} &= \left(0.5, \quad -0.5, \quad 0, \quad 0 \right).
\end{aligned}
$$

Because it is interpolating, the Catmull-Rom spline is one at the center and zero at all other integers of x. The interpolation property is important in applications where no smoothing is desired, which for example is often the case in medical imaging.

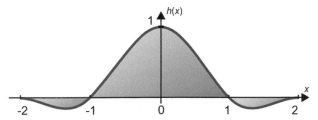

Figure 9.9. The cubic Catmull-Rom spline. The filter kernel $h(x)$ is defined over the interval $[-2, 2]$ and has zero-crossings at the integers except at zero where it is one. Thus, it is an *interpolating* filter that leaves the original samples intact.

However, in contrast with the cubic B-spline, the cubic Catmull-Rom spline does not have a continuous second derivative. In spline terminology, the cubic Catmull-Rom spline is only C^1 continuous, whereas the cubic B-spline is C^2 continuous. These continuity considerations have many implications. An example is the curvature measurements with convolution filters described in Chapter 14. There, curvature is computed from second derivatives, and the resulting curvature information is only continuous if the second derivatives also are, which is determined by the continuity property of the filter that is used.

9.2.5 Texture-Based Convolution

Many GPU algorithms pre-compute complicated functions and store the resulting look-up tables in texture maps in order to reduce arithmetic complexity to simple texture fetches. This approach is especially common in the evaluation of complex shading equations, e.g., lighting models based on the BRDF of a surface [182, 156]. The same principle can be applied to computation of filter kernel weights, by pre-evaluating the function that describes the filter and storing it in one or multiple textures. Pre-computing filter kernel weights is only the first step, however, as a major part of evaluating the convolution sum is also to multiply input samples f_i with the exactly corresponding weights $w_i(u)$ that depend on the current resampling position x, which in this case can also be done without any fragment shader computations.

The most important advantage of texture-based convolution is that it allows one to make the fragment shader completely independent from the size and the shape of the filter kernel. The filter is determined by the contents of texture maps, and an arbitrary finite filter size can be evaluated by simply using multiple rendering passes with the same exact fragment shader. Another advantage is that the computation of texture coordinates

Figure 9.10. A 1D cubic filter kernel (here, cubic B-spline) is sampled and stored in the four channels of a single **RGBA** texture map. The four channels correspond to the four $w_i(u)$ functions given in Section 9.2.4.

for either the input samples or the filter weights need not be performed on a per-fragment basis, as all coordinates needed for texture look-ups can be linearly interpolated from the vertices. This property allows evaluation of arbitrary convolution filters on graphics hardware without dependent texture look-ups and even on current GPUs saves fragment shader computation time by moving most operations to the vertex shader.

Before we describe the completely general approach, however, we illustrate texture-based filtering for the cubic case.

Simple texture-based cubic filtering. We have seen above that a 1D cubic filter kernel can be described by four weight functions $w_i(u)$ that are defined over $u \in [0, 1]$. These four functions can be sampled over this $[0, 1]$ domain and stored in the four channels of an **RGBA** texture map (see Figure 9.10). During rendering, this filter texture is replicated over the input texture such that the entire filter texture corresponds to a single texel of the input texture. Replication is performed by setting the filter texture wrap mode to **GL_REPEAT**. The texture coordinate u for indexing the filter texture is determined as $u(x) = x \cdot T_{size} - 0.5$, where x is the resampling coordinate of the source texture and T_{size} is the size of the source texture in texels. This is illustrated in Figure 9.11, where the vertical black lines are the locations

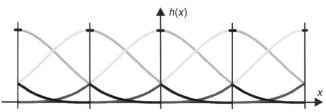

Figure 9.11. Replicating an interleaved **RGBA** filter texture over the output sample grid yields a distribution of basis functions familiar from spline curves. All four weights needed for convolution at any given re-sampling location are available via a single texture fetch.

```
// vector program for texture-based cubic filtering
void main_vp (float input_coord :  TEXCOORD0,
                uniform float t_size,
                out float4 neighbor_coords :  TEXCOORD0,
                out float filter_coord_u :  TEXCOORD1)
{
    neighbor_coords.x = input_coord - 1 / t_size;
    neighbor_coords.y = input_coord;
    neighbor_coords.z = input_coord + 1 / t_size;
    neighbor_coords.w = input_coord + 2 / t_size;
    filter_coord_u = input_coord * t_size - 0.5;
    // do standard stuff (transformation, ...)
}
// fragment program for texture-based cubic filtering
float4 main_fp (float4 neighbor_coords :  TEXCOORD0,
                float filter_coord_u :  TEXCOORD1,
                uniform sampler1D input_tex,
                uniform sampler1D filter_tex ) :  COLOR
{
    float4 neighbors;
    neighbors.x = tex1D(input_tex, neighbor_coords.x);
    neighbors.y = tex1D(input_tex, neighbor_coords.y);
    neighbors.z = tex1D(input_tex, neighbor_coords.z);
    neighbors.w = tex1D(input_tex, neighbor_coords.w);
    float4 filter = tex1D(filter_tex, filter_coord_u);
    float4 result = dot(neighbors, filter);
    return result;
}
```

Listing 9.4.   Cg program for texture-based cubic filtering of a monochrome 1D texture.

of the input texture samples. The input texture is simply used with nearest-neighbor interpolation, and the offset of -0.5 in the computation of $u(x)$ compensates for the fact the OpenGL centers texels at 0.5. The steps just outlined ensure a correct match of input samples with filter weights.

Listing 9.4 shows Cg code for this approach. The convolution sum becomes a single dot product of one 4-vector containing the input samples and one 4-vector containing the corresponding filter weights. In practice, the resolution of the filter texture need not be very high in order to achieve high-quality results. Usually a resolution of 64 or 128 texels is sufficient.

General texture-based filtering.   The simple texture-based approach for cubic filtering just outlined can be extended to filters of arbitrary width and thus arbitrary order. This also includes non-polynomial filter kernels such as windowed sinc filters. Fundamentally, the convolution sum consists of a series of terms where each is a multiplication of one input sample f_i by one corresponding filter weight $w_i(u)$, followed by the summation of all of these terms. We can formulate a very simple but general multipass filtering algorithm that evaluates exactly one of these terms for all output pixels in one rendering pass. Summing the results of these individual passes together yields the result of the convolution sum.

This idea is illustrated in Figure 9.12 with the simplest example: a tent filter that results in linear interpolation. However, the same exact approach works for filters of arbitrary shape and width, which is also true for 2D and 3D filter kernels. Each weight function $w_i(u)$ is sampled into a texture and used in a single rendering pass that samples the replicated filter weight texture. The input texture is sampled with a given texture coordinate offset. For each pixel, these two values are multiplied and stored in the output buffer. In the next pass, another filter weight texture is used, and the input texture is used with a different offset. What this amounts to is that instead of *gathering* the contribution of all relevant input pixels in the convolution sum to a single output pixel, such as in procedural convolution as shown above, the contribution of input pixels is *distributed* to all relevant output pixels.

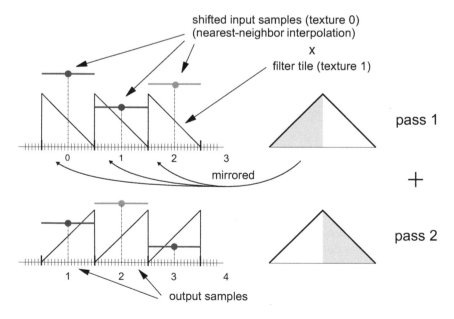

Figure 9.12. Tent filter (width two) used for reconstruction of a 1D function in two passes. Imagine the values of the output samples added together from top to bottom.

Of course, it is once again possible to combine four weight textures $w_i(u)$ into a single RGBA texture as in the previous section. Also, this multi-pass approach can be executed in its entirety in a single actual rendering pass when the hardware fragment shader allows the necessary number of texture fetches and instructions.

9.2.6 Recursive Convolution

For certain types of splines, there are algorithms for computing filter weights from repeated linear interpolations in a recursive fashion. For example, the standard recursive approach for evaluating B-splines is the *de Boor* scheme. A major property of this algorithm is that the function describing the filter kernel need not be known at all, as the weights $w_i(u)$ are never computed explicitly. The *de Boor* scheme also works for all orders of B-splines, e.g., if it is applied for order one, it simply results in linear interpolation. In the cubic case, one output sample can be calculated hierarchically from six linear interpolations with interpolation weights $\alpha_i^l(u)$, where l is the level of recursion and i is the weight number in a given level. This is illustrated in Figure 9.13 (a). The parameter u once again is the fractional position in $[0, 1]$ between two neighboring samples, i.e.,

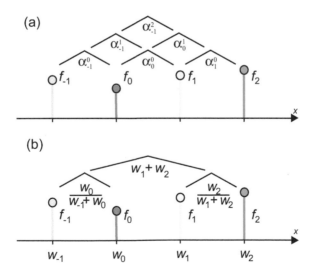

Figure 9.13. Comparing the *de Boor* scheme in the cubic case (a) with a recursive scheme tuned for the characteristics of graphics hardware and a minimum number of linear interpolations (b). The scheme in (a) needs no knowledge of the weights, but they can easily be pre-computed and stored in a 1D texture, which we will use for (b).

$u = x - \lfloor x \rfloor$. Thus, the same u is used for all interpolation weights $\alpha_i^l(u)$. Each interpolation step is $(1 - \alpha_i^l)f_i^l + \alpha_i^l f_{i+1}^l$ with $f_i^0 = f_i$. The weights can be computed as

$$\alpha_i^l(u) = \frac{u - i - l + 1}{3 - l}, \quad \text{with} \quad i \in [-1, 1 - l]; \ l \in \{0, 1, 2\}; \ u \in [0, 1].$$

Thus, they are

$$\alpha_{-1}^2(u) = u,$$
$$\alpha_{-1}^1(u) = \frac{u + 1}{2}, \qquad \alpha_0^1(u) = \frac{u}{2},$$
$$\alpha_{-1}^0(u) = \frac{u + 2}{3}, \qquad \alpha_0^0(u) = \frac{u + 1}{3}, \qquad \alpha_1^0(u) = \frac{u}{3}.$$

For an arbitrary order n instead of the cubic case $n = 3$ that is illustrated here, adapting these formulas is straightforward.

The complexity of the *de Boor* scheme for filtering can be stated as $\sum_{i=1}^n i^d$ *d-linear* interpolations, where n is the order and d is the dimension, i.e., 36 trilinear interpolations for tricubic filtering ($n = 3, d = 3$). The lowest level of the linear interpolation pyramid ($l = 0$) can be evaluated by native texturing hardware using linear texture filtering. Still, the number of interpolation operations is quite significant, and many weights have to be computed, especially in 2D and 3D filtering.

GPU-optimized recursive cubic convolution. If we employ the idea of texture-based convolution that stores filter weights in textures instead of computing them, we can use a simpler and much faster approach with fewer linear interpolations [241]. In order to achieve independent weights w_i and w_{i+1} in a general linear combination $w_i f_i + w_{i+1} f_{i+1}$, we rewrite it as

$$(w_i + w_{i+1}) \left(\frac{w_i}{w_i + w_{i+1}} f_i + \frac{w_{i+1}}{w_i + w_{i+1}} f_{i+1} \right) = w \cdot lerp(\alpha, f_i, f_{i+1}) \quad (9.8)$$

$$\text{with} \quad w := w_i + w_{i+1} \quad \text{and} \quad \alpha := w_{i+1}/(w_i + w_{i+1}).$$

For brevity, we are now denoting linear interpolations as

$$lerp(\alpha, u, v) := (1 - \alpha)u + \alpha v, \quad \text{with} \quad 0 \leq \alpha \leq 1.$$

In order to enforce a convex combination where $0 \leq \alpha \leq 1$, w_i and w_{i+1} must satisfy

$$0 \leq \frac{w_{i+1}}{w_i + w_{i+1}} \leq 1, \quad (9.9)$$

which is exactly the case when w_i and w_{i+1} have the same sign and are not both zero, a requirement fulfilled by the B-spline. Additionally, B-spline and most other filters used for function reconstruction purposes fulfill the partition of unity: $\sum_i w_i = 1$. The cubic convolution sum can then be written as three linear interpolations, illustrated here for $x \in [0,1]$ without losing generality as

$$g(x) = lerp\left(w_1 + w_2, lerp(\frac{w_0}{w_{-1} + w_0}, f_{-1}, f_0), lerp(\frac{w_2}{w_1 + w_2}, f_1, f_2)\right),$$
(9.10)

yielding the pyramidal scheme shown in Figure 9.13 (b). The bottom row of the pyramid is computed automatically via texture filtering, and the top row in the fragment shader. The case where the filter weights do not sum up to one, e.g., in derivative filters, can also be handled easily, as will be shown below.

After considering how a single output sample can be computed in principle, the scheme is extended to all output samples simultaneously when a texture is rendered. The blending weights in Equation 9.2.6 that determine the linear interpolations depend directly on the filter kernel weights $w_i(u)$, and thus the sampling location x. However, like the $w_i(u)$ they are defined entirely on the interval $u \in [0,1]$, due to the truncation $x - \lfloor x \rfloor$ that is always part of the argument to $h(\cdot)$ in Equation 9.2. Thus, instead of calculating weights in the fragment shader, they can be pre-computed over the range $[0,1]$ and stored in a texture map. Fetching weights from a texture is both faster and simpler than calculating them in the fragment shader. Moreover, filtering with different kernels can be done using the same fragment program with different weight textures. We store all three weights in the three channels of an RGB texture map $F(u)$:

$$F_r(u) \quad = \quad \frac{h(u)}{h(u+1) + h(u)} - u - 1, \tag{9.11}$$

$$F_g(u) \quad = \quad \frac{h(u-2)}{h(u-1) + h(u-2)} - u + 1, \tag{9.12}$$

$$F_b(u) \quad = \quad h(u-1) + h(u-2), \tag{9.13}$$

where $u \in [0,1]$ is the 1D weight texture coordinate, and $h(\cdot)$ is the filter kernel function defined over $[-2,2]$. We can state $h(\cdot)$ by concatenating the weight functions of the cubic B-spline filter given in Equations 9.4–9.7:

$$h(x) = [-2,-1]w_3(x+2) + [-1,0]w_2(x+1) + [0,1]w_1(x) + [1,2]w_0(x-1),$$

where the notation is such that $[a,b]$ is one when $x \in [a,b)$ and zero otherwise. $F_r(u)$ and $F_g(u)$ contain additive factors of $-u \pm 1$, which yield the correct sampling offset with respect to texture coordinates linearly interpolated automatically by the graphics hardware, i.e., $-u$ compensates for the linear ramp in the source texture coordinates, and ± 1 offsets the coordinate for the left and right pair of input samples, respectively. Cubic filtering of a source texture $T(x)$ can then be implemented as

$$T_{cubic}(x) = lerp\left(F_b(u), \quad T\left(x + F_r(u)/T_{size} \right), \quad T\left(x + F_g(u)/T_{size} \right) \right),$$

where u is the weight texture coordinate, which is directly determined by the source texture coordinate as $u = x \cdot T_{size} - 0.5$, where T_{size} is the size of the source texture in texels. The clamp mode of the weight texture is set to GL_REPEAT, which ensures that $F(u) = F(u - \lfloor u \rfloor)$. Evaluating the bottom row of the pyramid in Figure 9.13 (b) is achieved by setting the filter mode of the source texture $T(x)$ to GL_LINEAR. Note that in higher dimensions all blending weights along an axis $i \in \{0, 1, 2\}$ can still be retrieved from a single 1D texture, which is simply indexed with each sampling coordinate x_i.

Recursive derivative filters. It is easily possible to extend the recursive scheme described above to derivative filters, which have very interesting applications. Filtering with the derivatives of the cubic B-spline is, for example, employed in Chapter 14 for computing implicit isosurface curvature and non-photorealistic volume rendering. When a derivative filter is applied to a texture, the result is not a reconstruction of the original function but of its derivative. In order to reconstruct first and second derivatives, for example, the original scalar volume is convolved with the first and second derivative of the cubic B-spline kernel, respectively. These filter kernels are depicted in Figure 9.14.

With respect to the restriction stated in Equation 9.9, the first derivative of the cubic B-spline fortunately still has the property that both pairs of w_i have the same sign. In this case, $h'(x) \geq 0 \, \forall x \leq 0$, and $h'(x) \leq 0 \, \forall x \geq 0$

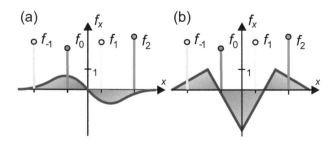

Figure 9.14. The first and second derivatives of the cubic B-spline for derivative filtering. Note that the second derivative is still continuous, a property that is unique to the B-spline among polynomial filters of order three. This implies that the resulting reconstructed derivative of the filtered function will also be continuous.

(see Figure 9.14 (a)). The only difference to the case of reconstructing the original function is that now for the first derivative $\sum_i w_i = 0$. Consequently, the top of the pyramid in Figure 9.13 (b) is not a linear interpolation anymore. Thus, the cubic first derivative filter becomes

$$T'_{cubic}(x) = -F_b(u)T\left(x + F_r(u)/T_{size}\right) + F_b(u)T\left(x + F_g(u)/T_{size}\right).$$

The second derivative of the cubic B-spline must be evaluated differently. It consists of four piecewise linear functions, where $h''(x) \leq 0 \ \forall x \in [-1, 1]$, and $h''(x) \geq 0$ everywhere else (see Figure 9.14 (b)). The latter property and the simple shape of $h''(x)$ allow us to evaluate the convolution sum for the second derivative as

$$T''_{cubic}(x) = T(x - 1/T_{size}) - 2T(x) + T(x + 1/T_{size}).$$

In the 2D and 3D cases, a derivative filter simply consists of a derived filter kernel along the axis of derivation, and the standard B-spline kernel for all other axes.

9.3   Classification Artifacts

Classification (see Chapter 4) is a crucial phase in the volume-rendering pipeline and yet another possible source of artifacts. Classification employs transfer functions for color densities and extinction densities, which map scalar values to colors and extinction coefficients. The order of classification and filtering strongly influences the resulting images, as demonstrated in Figure 9.15. The image shows the results of pre-interpolative and post-interpolative classification for a small 16^3 voxel hydrogen orbital volume and a high-frequency transfer function for the green color channel.

Notice that pre-interpolative classification, i.e., classification before filtering, does not reproduce high frequencies in the transfer function. In contrast with this, post-interpolative classification, i.e., classification after filtering, reproduces high frequencies in the transfer function. However, high frequencies (e.g., isosurface spikes) may not be reproduced in between two subsequent sampling points along a ray through the volume. To capture those details, oversampling (i.e., additional slice polygons or sampling points) must be added. It should be noted that a high-frequency transfer function is not only introduced by a random transfer function, such as used for Figure 9.15. Random transfer functions were merely used to demonstrate the differences between the classification methods. A high frequency in the transfer function is also introduced by using a simple step transfer

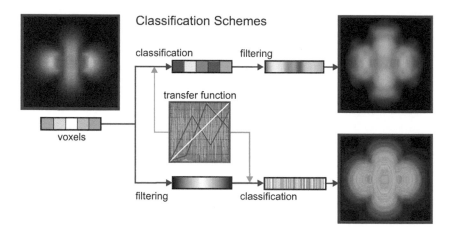

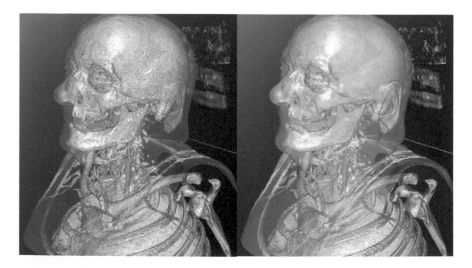

Figure 9.15. Comparison of pre-interpolative and post-interpolative classification. Alternate orders of classification and interpolation lead to completely different results. For clarification, a random transfer function is used for the green color channel. Piecewise linear transfer functions are employed for the other color channels. Note that, in contrast with pre-interpolative classification, post-interpolative classification reproduces the high frequencies contained within the transfer function.

Figure 9.16. Quality comparison of post-classification (left) and pre-integrated classification (right) for a CT data set. The transfer function used for these images contains a very thin spike for the semi-transparent skin isosurface and a few trapezoids with steep slopes for bone and vessels. In contrast with post-interpolative classification, pre-integrated classification does not show holes in the isosurface and significantly reduces slicing artifacts.

function with steep slope. Such transfer function are very common in many application domains.

The basic idea of pre-integrated classification (see Section 4.5) is to capture high frequencies in the transfer function in a pre-processing step. The numerical integration is split into a pre-integration of the transfer functions and an integration of the continuous scalar field. Consequently, it is not necessary to increase the sampling rate once high frequencies are added to the transfer function. In pre-integrated volume rendering, a sampling rate that is independent of the transfer function and close to the Nyquist frequency of the data is sufficient to capture all high frequencies.

See Figure 9.16 for a comparison of a post-classification and pre-integrated classification rendering result. Obviously, pre-integrated classification produces a visually much more pleasant result. Spikes in the transfer function that correspond to isosurfaces in the resulting images do not contain any holes when using pre-integration. In addition, even though the same sampling rate was used for rendering, slicing artifacts are less apparent in the pre-integrated result.

9.4   Shading Artifacts

The most common shading model for volumetric data interprets a volume as a self-illuminated gas that absorbs light emitted by itself. In this case, the shading is implicitly done during blending colors from the transfer function into the frame buffer. However, if external light sources are taken into account, a shading stage has to be added to the volume-rendering pipeline (see Chapter 5).

Shading can greatly enhance depth perception and manifest small features in the data; however, it is another common source of artifacts (see Figure 9.17 (left)). Shading requires a per-voxel gradient to be computed that is determined directly from the volume data by investigating the neighborhood of the voxel. Although the newest generation of graphics hardware permits calculating of the gradient at each sampling position (see also Section 5.3.1), in the majority of the cases the voxel gradient is precomputed in a pre-processing step. This is due to the limited number of texture fetches and arithmetic instructions of older graphics hardware in the fragment-processing phase of the OpenGL graphics pipeline, as well as to improve rendering performance. For scalar volume data, the gradient vector is defined by the first-order derivative of the scalar field $I(x, y, z)$, which is constructed using the partial derivatives of I in the x-, y-, and z-direction:

$$\nabla I = (I_x, I_y, I_z) = \left(\frac{\partial}{\partial x} I, \frac{\partial}{\partial y} I, \frac{\partial}{\partial z} I \right). \quad (9.14)$$

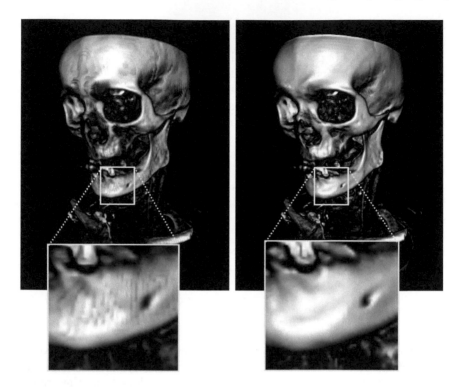

Figure 9.l7. Comparison between pre-computed, quantized gradients (left) and on-the-fly gradient computation (right).

The length of this vector defines the local variation of the scalar field and is computed using the following equation:

$$\|\nabla I\| = \sqrt{I_x^2 + I_y^2 + I_z^2}. \qquad (9.15)$$

Gradients are often computed in a pre-processing step. To access those pre-computed gradient during rendering, gradients are usually normalized, quantized to 8 bits, and stored in the RGB channels of a separate volume texture. For performance reasons, the volume data is often stored together with the gradients in the alpha channel of that same texture so that a single texture look-up provides the volume data and gradients at the same time.

Aside from the higher memory requirements for storing pre-computed gradients and the pre-processing time, quantizing gradients to 8-bit precision can cause artifacts in the resulting images, especially if the original volume data is available at a higher precision. Even worse, gradients are interpolated in the filtering step of the volume-rendering pipeline. Note that, when interpolating two normalized gradients, an unnormalized normal may be generated. Previous graphics hardware did not allow renormalization of gradients in the fragment stage. Such unnormalized and quantized gradients cause dark striped artifacts, which are visible in Figure 9.17 (left).

One possible solution to this problem is to store the pre-computed gradients at higher precision in a 16-bit fixed-point or 32-bit floating-point 3D texture and apply normalization in the fragment processing stage on interpolated gradients. Those high-precision texture formats are available on newer graphics hardware; however, the increased amount of texture memory required to store such high-precision gradients does not permit this solution for high-resolution volumetric data.

A significantly better solution is to compute high-precision gradients on-the-fly. For a central-differences gradient, six additional neighboring voxels need to be fetched. For this purpose, it is advantageous to provide six additional texture coordinates to the fragment program computed in the vertex stage, each shifted by one voxel distance to the right, left, top, bottom, back, or front. Using this information, a central differences gradient can be computed per fragment. The resulting gradient is normalized and used for shading computations. The Cg fragment program Listing 5.6 in Chapter 5 demonstrates the computation of gradients for shading during rendering. For simplicity, this code computes the offset texture coordinates for the look-up of the neighbors in the fragment stage. However, we recommend computing the offset texture coordinates for all neighbors in the vertex stage for optimal performance.

The resulting quality of on-the-fly gradient computation is shown in Figure 9.17 (right). The enhanced quality compared with pre-computed gradients is due to the fact that we used filtered scalar values to compute the gradients compared with filtered gradients. This provide much nicer and smoother surface shading, which even allows reflective surfaces to look smooth (see Figure 9.18). Besides this advantage, no additional memory is wasted to store pre-computed gradients. This is especially important for high-resolution volume data that already consumes a huge amount of texture memory or must be bricked to be rendered (see Chapter 17). This approach facilitates even higher-quality gradients, for example, Sobel gradients with 26 texture fetches.

However, the improved quality comes at the cost of additional texture memory fetches, which considerably decrease performance. Even though graphics hardware memory provides a very high memory bandwidth compared with other types of memory, the memory latency and bandwidth is most likely to become the limiting factor in this case. It is thus important that expensive gradient computations are only performed when necessary. Several techniques, like empty-space leaping, occlusion culling, early ray

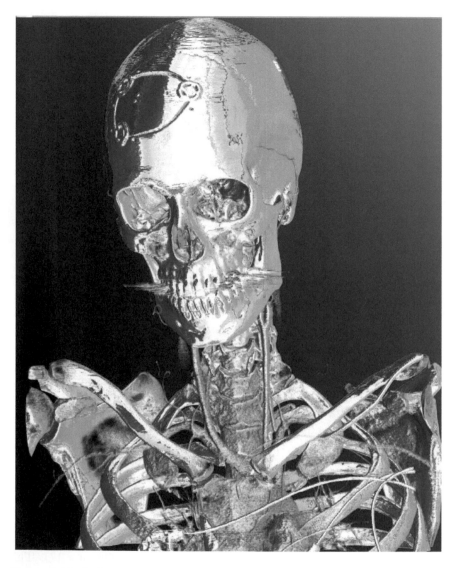

Figure 9.18. Reflective environment mapping computed with on-the-fly gradient computation. Note the smoothness of the surface.

termination, and deferred shading (which are discussed in Chapter 8), are effective in achieving real-time performance, even when computing gradients on-the-fly.

9.5   Blending Artifacts

The final step of the rendering pipeline involves combining color values generated by previous stages of the pipeline with colors written into the frame buffer during integration. As discussed in previous chapters, this is achieved by blending RGB colors with their alpha values into the frame buffer. A large number of samples along the rays through the volume are blended into the frame buffer. Usually, color values in this stage are quantized to 8-bit precision. Therefore, quantization errors are accumulated very quickly when blending a large number of quantized colors into the frame buffer, especially when low alpha values are used. This is due to the fact that the relative error for small 8-bit fixed point quantization is much greater than for larger numbers. Figure 9.19 demonstrates blending artifacts for a radial distance volume renderer with low alpha values. In contrast with fixed point formats, the relative error remains constant for small and large numbers using a floating-point representation.

Whereas graphics hardware performed all vertex processing with floating-point precision from the start, older GPUs computed per-fragment operations with only 8 to 10 bits of precision. Just recently, floating-point precision was also brought into the pixel processing part of graphics hardware. However, the first generation of graphics hardware with floating-point precision throughout the graphics pipeline still had a number of restrictions. For example, such hardware did not support blending when using higher-precision formats. Such restrictions are slowly falling, however even some of the newest generation of graphics hardware is still limited to 16-bit floating-point precision for built-in blending.

As an alternative to built-in functionality, blending can also be implemented manually in a fragment shader. Because the onscreen frame

Figure 9.19. Comparison between 8-bit (left), 16-bit (middle), and 32-bit blending (right).

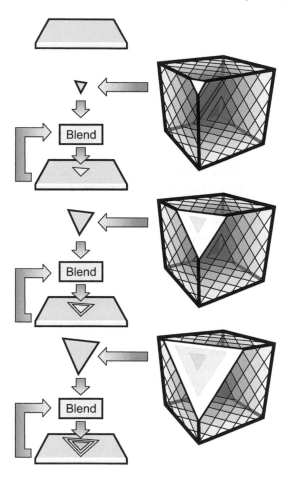

Figure 9.20. Programmable blending with a pbuffer as input texture and render target at the same time.

buffer only supports 8-bit precision, offscreen pbuffers (WGL_ARB_pbuffer extension) are required for blending with higher precision. The fragment shader is programmed to read the current contents of the floating-point pbuffer, blend the incoming color with the frame-buffer content, and write the result back into the pbuffer. To bind a pbuffer as an input image to a fragment program, the pbuffer is defined as a so-called render texture (see WGL_ARB_render_texture); i.e., a texture that can be rendered to. To read the current contents of the pbuffer at the current rasterization position, the window position (WPOS), which is available in fragment programs, can directly be used as a texture coordinate for a rectangle texture fetch.

```
// Volume rendering with floating-point blending
struct v2f {
    float3 TexCoord0 :  TEXCOORD0;
    float2 Position :  WPOS;
};
float4 main(v2f IN,
    uniform sampler3D Volume,
    uniform sampler1D TransferFunction,
    uniform samplerRECT RenderTex,
    ) :  COLOR {
    // get volume sample
    float4 sample = tex3D(Volume, IN.TexCoord0);
    // perform classification to get source color
    float4 src = tex1D(TransferFunction, sample.r);
    // get destination color
    float4 dest = texRECT(RenderTex, IN.Position);
    // blend
    return (src.rgba * src.aaaa) +
        (float4(1.0, 1.0, 1.0, 1.0) - src.aaaa) * dest.rgba;
}
```

Listing 9.5. A Cg fragment program that implements back-to-front floating-point blending.

Figure 9.20 illustrates the approach while the Cg source code in Listing 9.5 demonstrates the approach with a simple post-interpolative classification fragment program with over-operator compositing.

It should be noted that the specification of the render texture extension explicitly states that the result is undefined when rendering to a texture and reading from the texture at the same time. However, current graphics hardware allows this operation and produces correct results when reading from the same position that the new color value is written to. If you feel uncomfortable with this solution, you can employ ping-pong blending as an alternative (see Figure 9.21). Ping-pong blending alternates two rendering targets between subsequent blending operations to prevent read-write race conditions. The first rendering target is used as an input texture while the result is written into the second rendering target. For every blending operation, the input and output rendering targets are swapped.

Note that pbuffers are heavyweight; i.e., each pbuffer comes with its own full-blown OpenGL context. It should be emphasized that switching between two heavyweight contexts introduces a significant overhead, because it requires to flush the entire OpenGL rendering pipeline and to exchange the complete OpenGL state. To avoid context-switching overhead

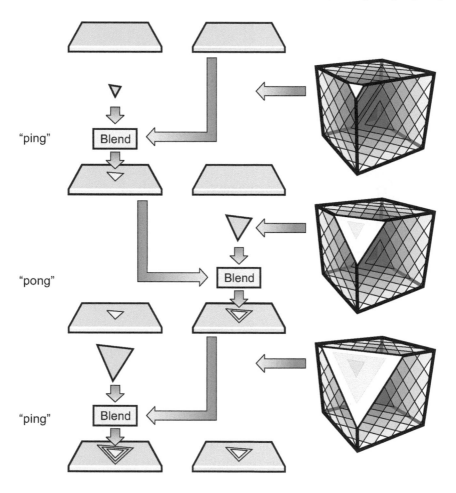

Figure 9.21. Programmable ping-pong blending with two pbuffers.

when changing rendering targets, one option is to employ a double-buffered pbuffer, i.e., a single pbuffer whose back and front buffer are then used for ping-pong blending. Another option is to employ lightweight rendering targets, such as provided by the **EXT_framebuffer_object** extension.

As you can see in Figure 9.19 (middle), even 16-bit floating-point precision might not be sufficient to accurately integrate colors with low alpha values into the frame buffer. However, as memory access does not come for free, performance decreases as a function of precision. Therefore, it is necessary to find a good balance between quality and performance. For most applications and transfer functions, 16-bit floating-point blending should produce acceptable results. Pre-integration (see Section 9.3) and performing the blending of complete rays in the pixels shader, such as in pure ray-casting approaches, also help to prevent blending artifacts.

9.6 Discussion

As we have seen, artifacts are introduced in various stages of the volume-rendering process. Fortunately, high-precision texture formats and floating-point computations in combination with the advanced programmability of today's GPUs allow for suppression of artifacts or even the complete removal of such artifacts. All of the techniques presented in this chapter can be implemented quite efficiently using programmable graphics hardware and thus lead to real-time performance. However, those optimization do not come for free—to maximize performance, trade-offs between quality and performance are often necessary.

Perceptual considerations such as the fact that the human visual system is less sensitive to artifacts in moving pictures than static images should also be taken into account. Therefore, for some applications it is acceptable to trade off quality for performance while the volumetric object is moving and use higher quality when the object becomes stationary.

10

Transfer Functions Reloaded

CHAPTER 4 INTRODUCES THE CONCEPTS OF transfer-function design and implementation. Recall that the transfer function is the mechanism used in volume rendering to transform raw data values into the optical properties needed to make a picture. Although the transfer function essentially plays the role of a simple color map, it is one of the most important stages of the volume-rendering pipeline, especially when we are using volume rendering to visualize medical or scientific data. Because the transfer function is responsible for making features of interest in the data visible as well as hiding unimportant regions, the quality of transfer-function specification will have a dramatic impact on the quality of the visualization.

This chapter explores techniques for generalizing transfer-function design. In Chapter 4, the transfer function was defined as a mapping from a single *scalar* data value to color and opacity. In contrast, this chapter discusses the utility and design of *multidimensional transfer functions*. By multidimensional, we mean that the *input* to the transfer function consists of multiple data values, or a vector of values, which are used to determine the optical properties for rendering.

10.1 Image Data versus Scalar Field

In the vast majority of cases that use volume rendering to visualize 3D data, the data is a single, spatially varying value. For instance, in a medical application we may be interested in visualizing a CT (computerized tomography) scan of a human tooth, in which the data is represented as a 3D grid of radio-opacity measurements. If we know the range of data values for dentin (the soft "body" of the tooth), we can create a 1D transfer

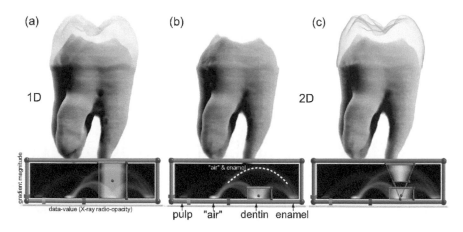

Figure 10.1. 1D versus 2D transfer functions using the human tooth CT. (a) The result of a 1D transfer function (data value only) that attempts to assign opacity to the range of values that represent the dentin. Unfortunately, it also assigns opacity to "air"-enamel boundary. These boundary values overlap with the values for dentin. Because boundaries will have high gradient magnitudes, we can fix this by restricting the opacity assignment to dentin values *and* low gradient magnitudes (b). (c) The "air"–enamel boundary is added back in with a different color.

function that assigns this range of values for color and opacity, as seen in Figure 10.1 (a). However, when we use this transfer function, we see that opacity is also given to a very thin region around the enamel (the hard "business end" of the tooth). Why does this happen? It is clearly not the intended result.

Two reasons that the transfer function unintentionally assigns opacity to boundaries between distinct features are: (1) we are (artificially) treating the image data as a smooth scalar field, and (2) we are simply unable to capture boundary discontinuities using discrete sampling. We learned in Chapter 4 that it is important to interpolate data values first and then apply the transfer-function color map. As a result, data values will *smoothly* transition from one spatial position to the next. In the tooth example, notice that the enamel has high values and the background has low values. When these materials are next to each other, the interpolated data values near this boundary must transition through the range of values that represent dentin, which is more dense than the background and less dense than enamel. Even if we were able to come up with an interpolation scheme that did not let the values at the boundary between enamel and background cross the values for dentin, we would still see this artifact. The reason for this is expressed by the sampling theorem, which relates the maximum reproducible frequency in the reconstructed signal to the sample spacing. The boundary between enamel and air (the background) is in reality distinct, but such a distinct boundary would result in an infinitely high frequency with respect to the signal captured by the imaging system and thus require infinitesimally small sample spacing. Distinct boundaries are effectively blurred, resulting in artificially smooth transitions in data values near these boundaries. Alternatively, you can think of the sampled data value as the *average* data value over some small region around its spatial location in the real world. In fact, image data is "blurry" for both of these reasons, limited frequency and spatial averaging (a.k.a. partial voluming). To make matters worse, due to thermal variation and electromagnetic interference, images also have noise, introducing an element of random variation.

There are plenty of instances where it is perfectly acceptable to assume that data values *should* make smooth transitions from one spatial position to the next, for instance when the physical interpretation of the data value is temperature or electric charge in a homogeneous medium. In this case, the interpretation of the data as a smooth scalar field agrees with reality. It is safe to assume that temperature will not suddenly change from one spatial location to the next. The tooth rendering is in fact a correct rendering of the scalar field. The artifact is really conceptual; we would like to impose a model or interpretation of data behavior (i.e., distinct materials and boundaries) that cannot be supported by a smooth scalar field.

10.2 Multidimensional Transfer Functions: Introduction

One way to address the disconnect between our conceptual model of features in image data (i.e., an aggregate of distinct objects) and the mathematical model of the data (i.e., smooth scalar field) is to use additional information that will allow us to disambiguate data values representing materials as opposed to those representing "fuzzy" boundaries. The inspiration for this comes from edge detection methods used in image processing and computer vision. The key idea is to measure how "fast" data value changes from one sample to the next; data values near boundaries should be changing faster than those inside a homogeneous material. If we assume that the data is a scalar field, then the gradient of the field (a vector valued quantity) gives the direction and magnitude of greatest change. Recall from Chapter 5 that the normalized gradient is often used as the normal for surface-based shading, and Section 5.3.1 provides details on measuring the gradient. When the gradient magnitude at some location in the data is large, we can say that we are near a boundary. Furthermore, when the gradient magnitude is at a maxima (with respect to spatial position) we can say that we are at the center of the boundary. A maximum gradient magnitude can be detected using the *second directional derivative*. Further details of these measurements will be discussed later. For now let's examine how this works in our tooth example, Figure 10.1.

Recall that we wanted to assign opacity to data values representing the dentin, but inadvertently assigned opacity to the enamel–air boundary. We now know that this problem is due to the fact that the data values must transition smoothly from the low-intensity air to the high-intensity enamel, causing us to assign opacity to these transitional values just because they happen to be the same intensity as dentin. We can exclude these transitional value opacity assignments by only assigning opacity to values that are both within the data value range for dentin *and* within the gradient magnitude range for a homogeneous material, Figure 10.1 (b). Ideally, a homogeneous material would have a gradient magnitude of 0, i.e., the value is not changing spatially. But, in reality there is almost always some variation in the intensity for a material as well as noise. As such, a homogeneous material will tend to have small gradient magnitudes, usually much smaller than gradient magnitudes near boundaries.

A transfer function that uses both data value and gradient magnitude can be built using a 2D look-up table. The data value for a sample gives us the x index and the gradient magnitude gives us the y index. We can now assign opacity for each unique combination of data value and gradient magnitude. The simplest way to implement this is to first compute the gradient magnitude for each sample in the data set, storing this quantity as an additional 3D texture. When we are rendering the volume, we now

```
// fragment program for 2D transfer functions
// using data value and gradient magnitude
half4 main (half3 texUVW : TEXCOORD0,
            uniform sampler3D data_texture,
            uniform sampler3D gradient_magnitude_texture,
            uniform sampler2D transfer_function_2D) : COLOR {
    half2 index;
    index.x = tex3D(data_texture, texUVW);
    index.y = tex3D(gradient_magnitude_texture, texUVW);
    half4 result = tex2D(transfer_function_2D, index);
    return result;
}
```

Listing 10.1. A fragment program for evaluating a 2D transfer function using data value and gradient magnitude.

read from both the data texture and the gradient texture. These values can then be used as the coordinates into the 2D transfer-function texture, which returns the color and opacity values. Listing 10.1 shows an example Cg program for evaluating a 2D transfer function using data value and gradient magnitude.

10.3 Data Value and Derivatives

Let's take a closer look at the relationship between derivative measures and boundary behavior in image data. This relationship requires some minimal assumptions:

- Distinct materials have roughly constant data value.

- Data values transition smoothly from one material to the next.

The second assumption is grounded in the fact that any physical measurement process (such as CT or MRI scanning) is necessarily band-limited, because infinitely high frequencies cannot be measured, ensuring that measured material boundaries are smooth. Figure 10.2 first shows an idealized material boundary, along which data value $f(x)$ and its first and second derivatives, $f'(x)$ and $f''(x)$, are plotted along a path through the boundary, parameterized by x. Second, parametric plots of $f'(x)$ versus $f(x)$ and $f''(x)$ versus $f(x)$ are drawn from the same boundary.

Most important for the task of transfer-function specification is how the parametric plots of first and second derivatives form characteristic curves, in particular the arch formed by the relationship between $f(x)$ and $f'(x)$. The strategy, common in computer vision, of locating a material edge or surface at the maximum of the first derivative, or the zero crossing in the

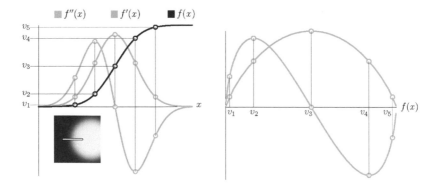

Figure 10.2. Relationships between f, f', f'' in an ideal boundary.

second derivative, applies to both Figure 10.2 (left) and (right). Transfer functions are often designed to emphasize the surfaces of materials, implying opacity should be assigned to those data values associated with a maximum in the first derivative, namely, at the middle of the $f'(x)$ arch. Opacity assignment can be successfully guided by inspecting scatter plots (joint histograms) of data value and gradient magnitude as they appear throughout the data, in order to detect the arches signifying material boundaries.

During volume processing or volume rendering, the derivatives playing the role of $f'(x)$ and $f''(x)$ above are directional derivatives of f along the gradient of f, $\mathbf{g} = \nabla f = [\partial f/\partial x \; \partial f/\partial y \; \partial f/\partial z]^{\mathrm{T}}$. Considering the directional derivatives along the normalized gradient $\hat{\mathbf{g}} = \mathbf{g}/\|\mathbf{g}\|$, we know from vector calculus that the first directional derivative of f along $\mathbf{v}$ is

$$\mathbf{D_v}f = \nabla f \cdot \mathbf{v} \Rightarrow \mathbf{D_{\hat{g}}}f = \nabla f \cdot \hat{\mathbf{g}} = \mathbf{g} \cdot \hat{\mathbf{g}} = \|\mathbf{g}\|\,.$$

The second directional derivative of f along the normalized gradient direction may be found by Taylor expansion:

$$\mathbf{D_{\hat{g}}^2}f = \frac{1}{\|\mathbf{g}\|^2}\mathbf{g}^{\mathrm{T}}\,\mathbf{H}\,\mathbf{g}\,,$$

where $\mathbf{H}$ is the Hessian of f, the 3×3 matrix of second partial derivatives of f. Using a combination of first and second central differences to measure the coefficients in the gradient $\mathbf{g}$ and the Hessian $\mathbf{H}$ provides a simple way of evaluating $\mathbf{D_v}f$ and $\mathbf{D_{\hat{g}}^2}f$ at the data sample points in a regular volume.

Figure 10.3 illustrates how one can "read" histogram information to infer where features of interest are located in the transfer-function domain. The top-left image shows a (1D) histogram of data values in the Chapel Hill CT head. Notice that it is very difficult to see where one might set

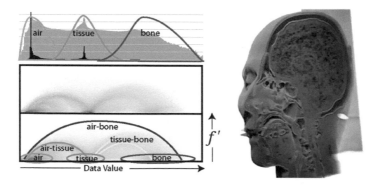

Figure 10.3. Gradient magnitude as an axis of a 2D transfer function. (Images reprinted from [128], © 2001 IEEE.)

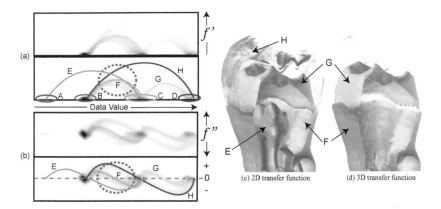

Figure 10.4. The second directional derivative as an axis of a 3D transfer function. The labeled materials are (A) pulp, (B) air or background, (C) dentin, and (D) enamel. The labeled boundaries are (E) pulp–dentin, (F) air–dentin, (G) dentin–enamel, and (H) air–enamel. (Images reprinted from [128], © 2001 IEEE.)

opacity to visualize the annotated features. The bottom-left image shows a joint histogram of data value versus gradient magnitude, with key features annotated. Now, it is clear where homogenous features are located (blobs at the bottom) as well as boundaries (arches connecting the blobs). The image on the right shows a volume rendering with each of the key features of interest using a 2D transfer function.

Figure 10.4 shows how the second directional derivative (f'') can help disambiguate multiple boundaries that share values, in much the same way that gradient magnitude helped disambiguate boundaries and materials. Figure 10.4 (a) shows joint histograms of data value versus gradient magnitude. Notice that the arches for boundaries E (pulp–dentin), F (air–dentin), and H (air–enamel) all collide in the circled region. Figure 10.4 (b) shows a joint histogram of data value versus second derivative; notice that now the boundaries in the circled region no longer overlap. Figure 10.4 (c) and (d) compare volume renderings that attempt to visualize the air–dentin boundary (yellow) and the dentin–enamel boundary (blue) using 2D (Figure 10.4 (c)) versus 3D (Figure 10.4 (d)) transfer functions.

10.4 General Multidimensional Transfer Functions

The previous sections demonstrated the utility of extending the domain (input) of the transfer function to include derivative information. How-

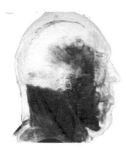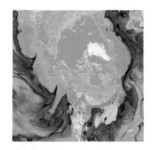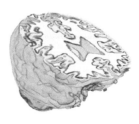

Figure 10.5. Examples of multivariate data sets rendered using multidimensional transfer functions. Left: the NIH-NLM Visible Human Color Cryosection data set has three values at each sample (RGB). Center: a numerical weather simulation from the Canadian Meteorological Center requires multiple physical quantities (temperature, humidity, etc.) to identify air masses and fronts. Right: MRI scanners can measure multiple chemical characteristics for identifying different tissue types in a human brain.

ever, the addition of derivative information is not the only way we can leverage the enhanced specificity of multidimensional transfer functions. What if the data isn't scalar to begin with? Imagine that instead of a single value at each sample, we had several values. This is analogous to the difference between a grayscale image (one value per pixel) and a color image (3 values per pixel). For instance, the National Institute of Health's *Visible Human Project* provides 3D color data for an entire human body. In this case, we could utilize a multidimensional transfer function to make optical property assignments based on unique color values; i.e., the transfer function would be a 3D table indexed by the individual red, green, and blue values. Figure 10.5 shows a volume rendering of this data using 3D transfer functions.

When there are multiple values that represent features in the data set in different ways, we can use the unique combinations of these values to identify features far better than we could with any single value by itself. In the previous section, gradient magnitude by itself would only allow us to discriminate between edge and non-edge characteristics; it is the combination of data value and gradient magnitude *together* that allows us to discriminate individual materials and the pair-wise boundaries between them. In the color data set example, no single color channel can adequately differentiate each of the tissue types. Another example is MRI data. Unlike CT data, MRI can measure a number of different quantities related to the chemical makeup of tissues in the body. However, for any single MRI scanning modality, multiple tissue types tend to share the same measured intensities. By combining multiple scanning modalities, we can differentiate tissue types that may share intensities in one modality but not in another.

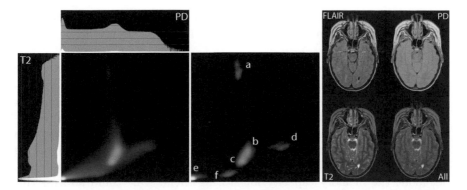

Figure 10.6. Combining multiple MRI scanning modalities to better separate different materials in the transfer function domain. Left: a 2D log-scale joint histogram of proton density (PD) and T2 MRI scans with the corresponding 1D histograms. Center: a joint histogram with high gradient magnitude values excluded. The labeled materials are (a) cerebro-spinal fluid, (b) gray matter, (c) white matter, (d) fat, (e) background, and (f) blood. Right: slices from three scans.

Figure 10.6 illustrates how combining proton density and T2-weighted MRI modalities helps us to better distinguish key issues.

Depending on the task, multiple values can be essential in identifying features of interest. A good example of this is the identification of weather phenomena based on principal physical quantities like temperature, pressure, and humidity. Features such as weather fronts are defined based on the relationships between these physical quantities.

10.5   Engineering Multidimensional Transfer Functions

If two data values are better than one, and three are better than two, why not assign optical properties based on as many different data characteristics as possible? While this would be ideal for identifying features in our data, there are a number of engineering issues that can make this approach quite impractical. Each new channel of data increases the size of the data set. With limited memory resources and bandwidth, data size and interactivity become trade-offs. For instance, we would expect a data set using four channels of data to take roughly twice as long to render as a data set consisting of only two channels. It is important to consider *how* each channel of data contributes to our ability to differentiate features. At some point we face the issue of "diminishing returns." That is, eventually adding additional channels of data will only improve our ability to differentiate features marginally, while its negative impact on rendering performance continues to increase linearly.

The issue of data set size versus rendering speed is considerably easier to understand and manage than the issue of generating arbitrarily high-dimensional transfer functions. Whereas it is a simple matter to represent a 2D transfer function using a 2D texture, a 3D transfer function represented as a 3D texture could easily take up more memory than the data set itself. Furthermore, we have no built-in mechanism for representing higher-dimensional look-up tables (four or more dimensions) in hardware, let alone the memory capacity for storing them. One could address this problem by creating transfer functions for each individual axis (or pairs of axes) of the transfer-function domain, and combine them in some way. For instance, you could assign opacity based on one set of values and assign color based on another. Or, you could create multiple transfer functions for different axes of the transfer-function domain and combine them by multiplying the optical properties from each transfer function. We call this kind of transfer function *separable* because we treat the axes of the transfer function as separate or independent entities and combine them with a simple operator. This approach solves the problem of increased memory requirements, four 1D look-up tables require substantially less memory than one 4D look-up table. Unfortunately, this approach also dramatically limits our ability to identify features and assign optical properties based on unique combinations of data values. Figure 10.7 illustrates this issue. In general, it is not possible to localize our optical property assignments using separable transfer functions.

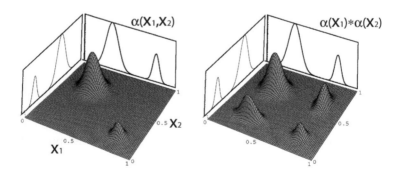

Figure 10.7. A comparison of general and separable 2D transfer functions. Left: a general 2D transfer function transforms unique combinations of x_1 and x_2 data values into opacity (vertical axis). Right: a separable 2D transfer function, composed of two 1D transfer functions multiplied together, will generate opacity where it many not have been intended.

The first and most important strategy for addressing the issues described above is to choose the axes of the transfer function wisely. The more you understand about how the different data values relate to the features you are interested in visualizing, the better you will be at selecting the minimal set of values needed to accurately visualize the features.

10.5.1 Factor Analysis

One approach for addressing the engineering constraints of multidimensional transfer functions involves reducing the dimensionality of the transfer-function space in an intelligent way. For instance, if we are given a data set with N data values at each sample, we could identify a 2D subspace of the N-dimensional transfer-function domain that best captures the important characteristics of the data's behavior. This approach is commonly used in statistics and falls in to the broad category of *factor analysis* methods. Two commonly used techniques are principal component analysis (PCA) and independent component analysis (ICA). Both of these methods develop a linear transformation of the data space (i.e., the transfer-function domain) in such a way that the axes of the new space best represent the behavior of the data. In particular, both of these methods rank these axes based on their "importance." For PCA, importance is based on how much the data samples vary along that axis; axes with large variation will be ranked higher than axes with very little variation. For ICA, importance is based on how well an axis separates values that are far apart in the original ND data space; that is, axes with less projected overlap of dissimilar data values are ranked higher. The transformation provided by PCA or ICA may make it easier to localize features in the transfer-function domain. However, the transformation may remove the user's intuitive understanding of what the original axes represented. For example, if we are visualizing meteorological simulation data using physical quantities (pressure, temperature, humidity, and wind speed), these values are meaningful to the user. When we perform ICA or PCA and end up with a new set of axes, these axes are made up of arbitrary linear combinations (mixtures) of the original physical quantities, which may not be intuitively understandable for the user. Furthermore, factor-analysis techniques reduce the dimensionality of the data space by discarding the "unimportant" axes. This means that (1) differing data values in the original space may project to the same value in the new space, and (2) we cannot easily detect when this overlap is causing incorrect results. These disadvantages should not deter you from making the best of this approach. In many cases, the original axes aren't necessarily meaningful to a user. Consider how unintuitive the RGB color space is; what combination of RGB values result in a "burnt sienna" color? MRI data is another example; the actual measured intensities can vary widely from scanner to scanner and are dependent on a number of variables. What really matters for MRI data is *contrast*, i.e., the difference between the measured values representing dissimilar tissue types, a data characteristic that factor analysis methods strive to preserve.

10.5.2   Procedural Transfer Functions

The practical limitations of look-up table–based transfer-function implementations can also be addressed in a more direct fashion. Perhaps a single look-up table is not the best way to represent transfer functions. Per-fragment programming capabilities allow us to represent the transfer function as an explicit mathematical formula. If we can identify mathematical primitives that are simultaneously efficient to evaluate and useful for accurately assigning optical properties for features of interest, we can avoid the pitfalls of look-up tables and design transfer functions of virtually any dimension. One function that is well suited to this task is the Gaussian:

$$g(\mathbf{x}, h, \mathbf{c}, \mathbf{K}) = h e^{-\|\mathbf{K}(\mathbf{x}-\mathbf{c})\|^2} . \qquad (10.1)$$

This function describes a "blob"-like primitive, where $\mathbf{x}$ is a vector of data values for a sample being rendered, h is the height of the blob, $\mathbf{c}$ is its center, and $\mathbf{K}$ is a linear transform that has the role of scaling and orienting the blob. Figure 10.8 shows a 2D example of a Gaussian. This function can be used to generate useful optical property assignments, where opacity $= g(\mathbf{x}, h, \mathbf{c}, \mathbf{K})$ and color is constant. In this case h controls the maximum opacity assigned to data values covered by the blob. This canonical form is a useful opacity function because materials tend to be represented as a localized distribution in the data space. In fact, it is often a default assumption, due to noise and other factors, that a homogeneous material will have measured values that follow a Gaussian distribution.

However, just because our features have a Gaussian distribution, this does not necessarily mean that a Gaussian is an ideal opacity function. The problem is that we would like to have more control over how the opacity ramps from high to low. There is a key insight here; the Gaussian

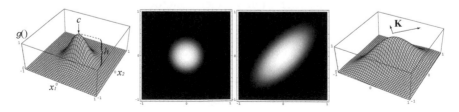

Figure 10.8. A 2D Gaussian.

is effectively a function of the squared distance from a point ($\mathbf{c}$). A more general definition of a blob primitive might be

$$\text{blob}(\mathbf{x}, \mathbf{c}, \mathbf{K}, \alpha_{max}) = \alpha_{max} f(\|\mathbf{K}(\mathbf{x} - \mathbf{c})\|^2), \qquad (10.2)$$

where α_{max} is the maximum opacity generated by the *blob* function, $f(x)$ is any function with the domain $x \in [0..\inf]$, and range $f(x) \in [0, 1]$. Notice that the input to $f(x)$ is the squared distance to $\mathbf{c}$ under the transform $\mathbf{K}$. Using the squared distance is an important optimization that allows us to avoid costly square root operations in the fragment program. Here, we are also leveraging the fact that the squared length of a vector is the dot product of the vector with itself, i.e., $\|\mathbf{x}\|^2 = \mathbf{x} \cdot \mathbf{x}$. Using this blob definition, a Gaussian blob would have

$$f(x) = e^{-x*9}, \qquad (10.3)$$

where the factor of 9 is used to scale the width of the Gaussian to fit nicely in the range $x \in [0..1]$, i.e., the value of this function is "effectively" 0 outsize of this range. The nice thing about this kind of transfer-function primitive representation is that $f(x)$, which determines the *shape* or profile of the opacity function, is a simple 1D scalar function that can have predefined domain bounds. That is, we can limit the domain of this function to something like $x \in [0..1]$, where $f(x > 1) = 0$, i.e., $f(x)$ is clamped to zero outside the chosen range. This allows us to store $f(x)$ in a 1D texture, or a family of $f(x)$s with varying profiles in a 2D texture. Figure 10.9 shows two different $f(x)$ profiles.

A complete transfer function is built by combining multiple primitives. The opacity for multiple primitives can be summed, and color can be determined using a weighted average based on opacity (see Figure 10.10):

$$C_{\text{final}} = \frac{\sum_i C_i \alpha_i}{\sum_i \alpha_i}. \qquad (10.4)$$

Listing 10.2 is a Cg program that shows how this approach works for a volume with four values at each sample, thus requiring a 4D transfer function. In this example, the arrays `alpha[]`, `C[]`, and `K[]` are user-defined constants. Because we know ahead of time how many primitives we have (`num_tf_primitives`), this term is also constant and allows Cg to unroll the loop in `eval_tf()`. This detail is important, as an unrolled loop will be far more efficient and more easily optimized by the compiler than a general loop. Notice that the $f(x)$ function is stored in a 1D texture (`fx_tex`), indicating that we are using a single profile for all of the blob primitives. The $f(x)$ texture could also be a 2D texture, where the second texture coordinate indexes a different profile. This "profile index" would be another user-defined per-primitive constant array. Also, notice that the last

Figure 10.9. Two transfer-function primitive profiles. Because x is the *squared* distance, the plots are also shown with the x axis varying as the square root of x, so that you can see how the profile would look in a linear space.

line of code in the function `eval_tf()` in Listing 10.2 is a texture read using the texture named `alpha_scale_tex`. This texture read is another function stored in a texture, much like the $f(x)$ texture used in the `blob()` function. This function is absolutely essential for maintaining the appearance of the visualization when the sample rate changes. The function stored in this texture is

$$\texttt{alpha\_scale}(\alpha) = 1 - (1-\alpha)^{\frac{1}{s}}\,, \qquad\qquad (10.5)$$

where s is the current sample spacing. This function effectively lowers the opacity for each sample as the sample spacing decreases, thus ensuring that the overall opacity in the final visualization remains the same. The derivation of this alpha scale function can be found in Chapter 1. When we are using a single texture for the entire transfer function, as is often the case with simple 1D or 2D transfer functions, this scaling of opacity is usually taken into account when the entries of the look-up table are filled.

This approach of procedurally evaluating the transfer function as the composition of multiple mathematical primitives is advantageous for a number of reasons. First, simple mathematical primitives can be designed in any dimension, like the blob example above, which allows us to avoid building troublesome N-dimensional look-up tables. Even though we are using a look-up table for $f(x)$ in the blob example, $f(x)$ is only a 1D function in a "normalized" space and is only used to control how opacity falls-off as

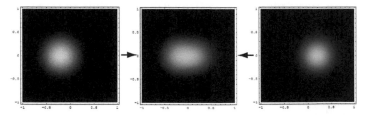

Figure 10.10. Combining two transfer-function primitives using a weighted average based on opacity.

```
// fragment program for procedural 4D transfer function
// blob function
half blob (half4 value,
           uniform half4 center,
           uniform half4x4 K,
           uniform sampler1D fx_tex)
{
   half4 vmc= K*(value-center);
   half dsq= dot(vmc,vmc);
   return tex1D(fx_tex, dsq);
}
// function that evaluates transfer function, returns color
// and opacity
half4 eval_tf (half4 value, uniform sampler1D fx_tex,
               uniform sampler1D alpha_scale_tex) {
   half4 ret_color = half4(0,0,0,0);
   for(half i= 0; i<num_tf_primitives; ++i){
       half b= alpha[i] * blob(value,C[i],K[i],tf_tex);
       ret_color+= half4(color[i]*b, b);
   }
   ret_color.rgb /= ret_color.a;
   ret_color.a = tex1D(alpha_scale_tex, ret_color.a);
   return ret_color;
}
// main
half4 main (half3 texUVW : TEXCOORD0,
            uniform sampler3D volume_texture,
            uniform sampler1D fx_tex,
            uniform sampler1D alpha_scale_tex) :  COLOR
{
   half4 index = tex3D(volume_texture, texUVW);
   half4 result = eval_tf(index, fx_tex, alpha_scale_tex);
   return result;
}
```

Listing 10.2. An example fragment program for evaluating a 4D transfer function using multiple "blob" primitives. The arrays alpha[], C[], and K[] are the per-primitive constants for alpha, primitive center, and blob transforms, respectively.

a function of distance. Second, mathematical primitives allow us to easily generate transfer functions for high-precision data formats, e.g., 16-bit and floating-point. For instance, the blob function can assign opacity to an arbitrarily narrow range of data values by increasing the scale term associated with the **K** transform. In contrast, look-up tables need to have as many entries as there are distinct data values, meaning that 8-bit data requires 256 look-up–table entries and 16-bit data requires 65536 entries (which is currently larger than the maximum allowed OpenGL texture size). It may not be clear how many look-up–table entries would be required for floating point data. The problem becomes even more pronounced when we attempt to build look-up tables for multidimensional transfer functions; for instance, a 2D look-up table for 16-bit data would require $65536^2 > 4 \times 10^9$ entries. One disadvantage of procedural transfer functions is the cost of evaluating the primitives. Because the transfer function must be evaluated for each primitive and each rendered sample, the performance penalty when we are using a large number of primitives can be significant. This emphasizes the importance of choosing simple primitives and using them wisely. Look-up tables, on the other hand, only require a single texture read. In practice, however, four or five well-placed primitives are enough for both a high-quality visualization and interactive performance.

There are several transfer-function primitives that we have found useful; the "sharp blob" (s-blob), the gradient magnitude triangle blob (t-blob), and line blob (l-blob).

The sharp blob is just like the blob primitive discussed earlier, with the addition of a sharpness term (s) that controls the steepness of the profile's fall-off:

$$\texttt{s\_blob}(\mathbf{x}, \mathbf{c}, \mathbf{K}, \alpha_{\max}, s) = \alpha_{\max}\texttt{gain}\left(f(\|\mathbf{K}(\mathbf{x} - \mathbf{c})\|^2), s/2 + .5\right), \quad (10.6)$$

where s varies from $[0..1]$ with $s = 1$ being the sharpest setting (a step function). Gain is a function that smoothly transitions from a linear ramp to a step function,

$$\texttt{gain}(x, g) = \begin{cases} x < .5 & \left((2x)^{\log(1-g)/\log(.5)}\right)/2 \\ x \geq .5 & 1 - \left((2 - 2x)^{\log(1-g)/\log(.5)}\right)/2, \end{cases} \quad (10.7)$$

where g varies from $(0..1)$ and $g = .5$ leaves the value of x unchanged, i.e., $\texttt{gain}(x, .5) = x$. In Equation 10.6 we are only using the range of g from $(0.5..1]$. Figure 10.11 shows how $\texttt{gain}(x, g)$ changes a Gaussian profile

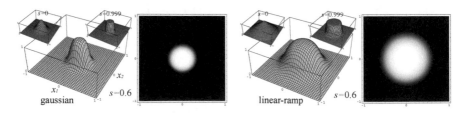

Figure 10.11. The sharp blob, using two different profiles.

as well as the function $f(x) = \max(1 - \sqrt{x}, 0)$, which is a simple linear ramp. When we are using an s-blob, we can take any $f(x)$ and generate a 2D texture, where the first dimension indexes the x value and the second dimension indexes the sharpness term (s).

When gradient magnitude is used as an axis of the transfer function, we can visualize material boundaries by assigning opacity to high gradient magnitudes. It has been observed that, by increasing the width of the opacity profile as a function of gradient magnitude, we can create visualizations of surfaces that appear to have constant thickness. This effect can be achieved by scaling the input to the $f(x)$ profile function as the squared reciprocal of gradient magnitude:

$$\texttt{t\_blob}(\mathbf{x}, \mathbf{c}, \mathbf{K}, \alpha_{\max}, g) = \alpha_{\max} f\left(\|\mathbf{K}(\mathbf{x} - \mathbf{c})\|^2 \frac{g_{\max}^2}{g^2 + \epsilon}\right), \qquad (10.8)$$

where g is the gradient magnitude (or a multigradient magnitude), $g_{\max}$ is the largest significant gradient magnitude, and ϵ is a small positive number (e.g., 0.0001) needed to ensure that we never divide by 0. Figure 10.12 shows how this scale term affects the width of the blob as a function of gradient magnitude. Just as in the s-blob example, we can cache the evaluation of the profile in a 2D texture indexed by x and g/g_{max} (i.e., gradient magnitude normalized into the range $[0..1]$).

The final primitive is the line blob, or l-blob. This function effectively elongates the blob in a particular direction in the transfer-function domain. It is useful for a number of reasons. First, when the values that represent a feature of interest do not follow a localized distribution (like a Gaussian), a blob-based primitive may not be the best way to generate an opacity function. For instance, when we have a boundary between two materials, the values that represent this boundary are composed of linear combinations

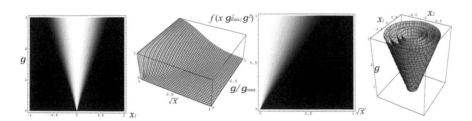

Figure 10.12. The triangle blob. Left: a 2D t-blob for value (x_1) and gradient magnitude (g). Center: the t-blob profile, indexed by the squared distance x and gradient magnitude normalized by the maximum gradient magnitude $g/g_{\max}$. Right: several isocontours of a 3D t-blob for two measured values $(x_1$ and $x_2)$ and a (multi)gradient magnitude (g).

of the values for each material, and therefore follow a fuzzy line segment connecting the two material distributions. Second, the **K** transform used in all of the previous blob functions is an $N \times N$ matrix, where N is the dimension of the transfer-function domain. This transform requires N dot products per-primitive, which can be a very expensive operation. It is often the case that we only need to elongate a blob primitive in one direction, thus it would seem that N dot products is overkill. The line blob can be defined as

$$\texttt{l\_blob}(\mathbf{x}, \mathbf{c}, \mathbf{l}, w_l, w_p, d_l, \alpha_{\max}) =$$

$$\alpha_{\max} f\left(\left(\|\mathbf{x} - \mathbf{c}\|^2 - ((\mathbf{x} - \mathbf{c}) \cdot \mathbf{l})^2 \right) \frac{1}{w_p^2} + \max\left(((|(\mathbf{x} - \mathbf{c}) \cdot \mathbf{l}| - d), 0)^2 \frac{1}{w_l^2} \right), \right.$$

$$(10.9)$$

where $\mathbf{l}$ is a unit vector in the direction of the line segment centered on $\mathbf{c}$, w_l is the width of the profile in the direction of the line, w_p is the width of the profile perpendicular to the line, and d_l is $1/2$ of the line segment's length. Although this function seems complicated, it is actually quite simple and lends itself well to efficient implementations. The derivation of this function utilizes the Pythagorean theorem $(h^2 = a^2 + b^2)$ to get the squared distance perpendicular to the line (the first half inside $f(x)$) and the distance in the direction of the line (the second half inside $f(x)$). We know that $\|\mathbf{x} - \mathbf{c}\|^2 = (\mathbf{x} - \mathbf{c}) \cdot (\mathbf{x} - \mathbf{c})$ is by definition the squared distance from $\mathbf{x}$ to $\mathbf{c}$ (h^2). Because $\mathbf{l}$ is a unit vector, $((\mathbf{x} - \mathbf{c}) \cdot \mathbf{l})^2$ is the squared distance from $\mathbf{x}$ to $\mathbf{c}$ in the $\mathbf{l}$ direction (a^2). Therefore, the squared distance from $\mathbf{x}$ to $\mathbf{c}$ perpendicular to $\mathbf{l}$ is simply $b^2 = h^2 - a^2$. The second term in $f(x)$, $\max((|(\mathbf{x} - \mathbf{c}) \cdot \mathbf{l}| - d), 0)^2$, is designed to force the distance computation in the $\mathbf{l}$ direction to be measured from the endpoints of the line segment. This primitive is typically used in one of two ways. The first way uses the same profile widths (i.e., $w_l = w_p$) and a nonzero segment length d_l, which is a line-like blob; useful for the material boundary problem discussed earlier. The second way sets the segment length $d_l = 0$ and uses different values for w_l and w_p, which generates elongated blobs. In this case $\max((|(\mathbf{x} - \mathbf{c}) \cdot \mathbf{l}| - d)^2, 0)$ becomes simply $|(\mathbf{x} - \mathbf{c}) \cdot \mathbf{l}|^2$. Figure 10.13 illustrates this profile in a 2D transfer-function domain.

The goal when using the aforementioned primitives or developing your own is to eliminate or simplify any unnecessary operations without sacrificing the quality of the opacity function. As noted earlier, the **K** transform can be an expensive operation, but it is only necessary when you need an oriented (rotated) primitive with different widths along each of the axes. If you do not need rotation, the **K** transform will only have nonzero entries along the diagonal and can be replaced with a component-wise vector multiplication. If you do not need different widths along the axes of the transfer-

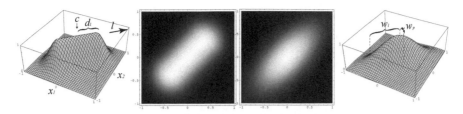

Figure 10.13. The line blob. Left: a fuzzy line segment blob, created using a nonzero d_l. Right: an elongated blob, created by setting $d_l = 0$ with $w_l > w_p$.

function domain, $\mathbf{K}$ can be replaced with a single scalar width term. On the other hand, if all primitives require roughly the same orientation, consider transforming the data space instead, using PCA for instance (without discarding axes). Another big optimization is the use of a texture for the opacity profiles $f(x)$, which evaluates the function based on the knowledge that the x variable has been squared. Because many useful profiles are defined by relatively complex expressions, replacing these operations with a single texture read is a big win. To some degree, we can rely on the Cg and graphics-card–driver compilers to optimize our code for us, especially when we make judicious use of constant variables. However, it is always a good idea to understand and leverage the underlying basic machine operations. For instance, a 4-vector dot product is a single instruction, as is a 4-vector "multiply-add" (multiply two vectors and add a third). However, square root is only a scalar operation and actually requires two hardware instructions, a reciprocal square root followed by a reciprocal: two very expensive operations. This is why we pass the squared distance to $f(x)$. Another example optimization is the elimination of the max() operation in the l-blob function (Equation 10.9). The max() function requires two hardware operations: a subtraction and a compare. The compare operation is currently the most expensive (slowest) hardware instruction on the NVIDIA GeForce FX 7800. The idea is to use a 2D texture for the $f(x)$ profile indexed by

$$s = \left(\|\mathbf{x} - \mathbf{c}\|^2 - ((\mathbf{x} - \mathbf{c}) \cdot \mathbf{l})^2 \right) \frac{1}{w_p^2}, \tag{10.10}$$

$$t = \left(|(\mathbf{x} - \mathbf{c}) \cdot \mathbf{l}| - d \right) \frac{1}{w_l}, \tag{10.11}$$

where $f'(s,t) = f(s + \max(t,0)^2)$. Notice that the max() is now pre-computed in the texture, and we were also able to remove a scalar multiply. However, we now have the possibility of indexing the texture $f'(s,t)$ using negative values of t. The key here is to use the GL_CLAMP_TO_EDGE as the texture wrap mode for the t coordinate of the texture. This mode ensures that texture coordinate values of t less than 0 are clamped to 0, implementing exactly the $\max(t, 0)$ that we want. In fact, the $\max()$ operation in the definition of $f'(s, t)$ is completely superfluous, since the texture will only contain positive t values.

Another final issue that must be addressed when using procedural transfer functions is the fact that the fragment program, or at least the function that evaluates the transfer function (`eval_tf`), must be dynamically generated. One way to address this is to write code that generates the transfer-function program on the fly, so-called metaprogramming. That is, the application executable assembles the Cg code for this function based on the current primitives being used. This problem of having to dynamically generate variations of a fragment program or function is quite common in real-world interactive graphics applications. As such, there are a number of frameworks available for handling exactly this situation. CgFx is a framework and API, which is built on Cg and designed to help manage complex and dynamic fragment programs. It allows one to not only handle variations of a function or sequence of functions, but also handle specific instances of these functions that are optimized for a particular hardware platform.

10.6   Transfer-Function User Interfaces

The design of user interfaces for specifying transfer functions is an active research topic unto itself. Although techniques exist for (semi-)automatically generating transfer functions, at some point the user must be able to decide what they want to see and how it should look. The majority of volume-rendering applications today only utilize 1D transfer functions. One-dimensional transfer-function interfaces are substantially easier to design than an interface for general multidimensional transfer functions. The simplest 1D transfer-function interface would have the user "hand-draw" the opacity and color function, as seen in Figure 10.14. There are two major issues with this approach. First it is extremely difficult to generate a desired color by manipulating the red, green, and blue components directly. Second, this user interface does not provide a mechanism for easily manipulating the optical properties associated with a particular feature of interest. For instance, how would one change the color of bone when visualizing CT data? The problem is that this method does not provide the user with any notion of object locations in the transfer-function domain. This problem is made worse by the fact that the behavior of data in the transfer-function domain can be difficult to understand, especially for a naive user. Furthermore, "hand-drawing" opacity and color functions as

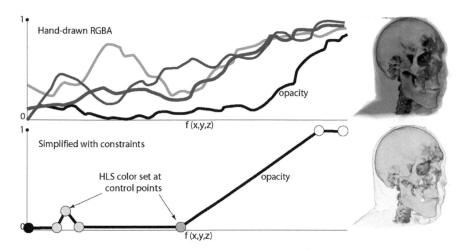

Figure 10.14. 1D transfer-function user interfaces. Top, a "hand-drawn" transfer function makes it difficult for the user to produce a clear and meaningful visualization. Bottom, a constrained user interface can make the task of transfer-function specification more manageable.

a user interface paradigm simply does not extend to higher-dimensional transfer functions.

Ideally, a user interface would have the user select which objects they would like to see, and how they should look; leaving the details of generating opacity functions and other optical properties to more principled automatic algorithms. Unfortunately, fully automatic transfer-function design is not practical because the definition of an object or feature of interest depends on the task and the kind of data being visualized. An acceptable compromise would have the user interface:

1. constrain user interaction with the transfer-function domain in a meaningful way,

2. provide the user with a semantic notion of features of interest, and

3. guide the user toward "good" transfer functions based on application-specific information.

The design of transfer-function interfaces implicitly involves the fundamental question: What kinds of tools benefit the different kinds of visualization needs? More specifically, how much knowledge (on the part of the user) can be assumed when creating interfaces for handling complicated parameter settings? When is it better to simply create guidance through a parameter space versus enforce constraint to some heuristically determined subset of the parameter space? What is the appropriate amount of automation? What is the best context to present new information extracted from a given data set, beyond what is used in any particular parameter setting task?

There is a wide range of reported techniques for transfer-function user interfaces and specification. We will refer the reader to Section 10.7 for a short survey of these methods. The remainder of this section will focus on a user-interface framework that has been useful for a wide range of users and applications. This approach centers on the idea that the user will have an intuitive understanding of the objects they wish to visualize when they are presented in the spatial domain. That is, the user can generally identify their features of interest when they view the data as slices or a volume rendering. This interface allows the user to point at features on slice images or "probe" the volume and have the transfer function set automatically based on the data values at these user specified locations. This process, involving interactions in the spatial domain that in tern affect the transfer-function domain, has been dubbed *dual-domain interaction*. Dual-domain interaction is effectively a reversal of the traditional approach to transfer-function specification, where the user makes changes directly to the transfer function and observes their affect on the visualization. The traditional approach can be a tedious and time-consuming process of trial and error, which becomes increasingly problematic as the dimension of the transfer function increases. Figure 10.15 (a) illustrates this process: a clipping plane is placed in conjunction with the volume rendering and mapped with the corresponding data slice, the user then clicks on the slice (green crosshair), the data values at this location are read from the volume data, a small region of opacity is then set in the transfer-function domain

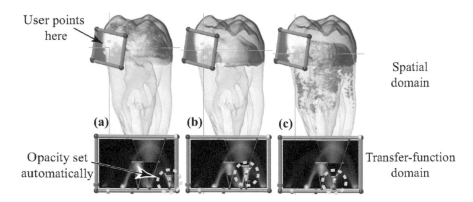

Figure 10.15. Dual-domain interaction as a user interface paradigm. The user points at features in the spatial domain, and opacity is automatically set in the transfer-function domain. (Images reprinted from [128], © 2001 IEEE.)

centered on these data values, and the visualization is updated to reflect this change to the transfer function. Figure 10.15 (b) and (c) shows the transfer function and visualization updating dynamically as the user moves the query location from one material to another.

This volume probing or point-and-click data query method can be used in a variety of ways. In the previous example, the opacity function (in the transfer-function domain) followed the values pointed to by the user (in the spatial domain). If we are using the primitive opacity functions described in Section 10.5.2, the value or vector of values at the queried position can be used to specify the center ($\mathbf{c}$) of a primitive opacity (blob) function. For this method to work, however, the $\mathbf{K}$ transform (width and orientation of the primitive) must also be specified. One could choose a reasonable constant width (w) to begin with, i.e., $\mathbf{K} = (1/w^2)\mathbf{I}$. Or, in addition to the value(s) at the query location, we could sample values in a region around the queried position in the volume data, analyze the variation in these values, and tailor the width of the primitive based on this variation. For instance we could set the $\mathbf{K}$ transform equal to the inverse covariance matrix derived from neighborhood samples. In practice, it is important to ensure that we maintain some minimum width, so that truly homogeneous regions of the data do not generate transfer-function primitives with zero width. Once the user has identified a feature of interest, they should be able to save the current primitive and continue probing. After the user has identified the important objects in the data, they can then improve, update, and modify the parameters of the transfer-function primitives. This can be accomplished by providing tools that allow the user to modify the parameters for the primitives in the transfer-function domain. Figure 10.16 shows an example interface for manipulating primitives in two dimensions. When the transfer function has more than two dimensions, the parameters can be manipulated using multiple 2D "views" of the transfer-function do-

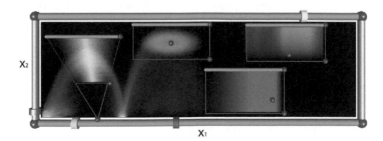

Figure 10.16. Tools for manipulating a transfer function. The transfer-function domain "lives" within the outer frame. Transfer function primitive parameters are modified by moving control-points.

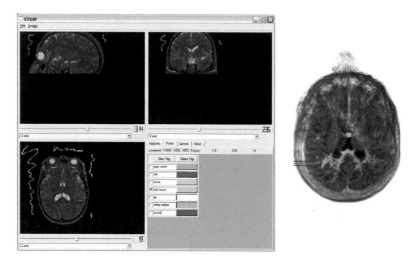

Figure 10.17. A user interface for "probing" the data to automatically set/specify transfer-function primitives. Left: a slice-based interface allows the user to "see" the data, and mark locations where their features of interest are located. The user can select these features by name (lower-right box in slice interface) and set their optical properties.

main. Alternatively, the user could continue working the spatial domain by selecting a previously defined primitive (from a list) and updating its parameter settings by identifying additional locations where the object is present. In this case, we could assign the center of the primitive ($\mathbf{c}$) as the average of the values associated with the probed locations; similarly, the $\mathbf{K}$ transform would be the inverse covariance matrix associated with the set of queried values. Figure 10.17 shows an example user interface that allows the user to revisit and refine transfer-function primitives by identifying object locations in the slice data. As a user-interface developer, the key thing to keep in mind when building this kind of interface is that the data behavior of materials may not always follow a Gaussian distribution (an implicit assumption when using the mean and covariance). For instance, if the user probes the boundaries between materials, the distribution for this feature of interest, with respect to nonderivative values, will follow a line-like distribution like the l-blob primitive discussed in Section 10.5.2. With respect to the gradient magnitude, material boundaries follow a parabolic arch as discussed in Section 10.3. It is a relatively simple matter to detect whether or not a sampled value is likely to be a boundary value and adjust the primitive type accordingly. However, a more semantic approach might allow the user to specify whether the feature they are updating is a material or a boundary.

10.7   Further Reading

For a concise survey of classic transfer-function specification research, we refer the reader to a white paper by Gordon Kindlmann, "Transfer Functions in Direct Volume Rendering: Design, Interface, Interaction." This paper covers many notable methods developed before 2002. Often, the goal of transfer-function specification is, in essence, the same goal as pattern recognition and classification in image processing and computer vision. *Pattern Classification* by Richard Duda, Peter Hart, and David Stork is an excellent handbook on classification and data analysis methods. Unfortunately, few of the methods are specific to 2D or 3D *image data* classification. A recent book by Scott Umbaugh, *Computer Imaging: Digital Image Analysis and Processing*, provides a nice introduction to the fundamentals of image processing and feature classification. The research paper "An Intelligent System Approach to Higher-Dimensional Classification of Volume Data" by Fan-Yin Tzeng, Eric Lum, and Kwan-Liu Ma describes a system that directly combines advanced ideas from the pattern recognition field with an extreme form of dual-domain interaction (i.e, no transfer-function domain interaction whatsoever). This is an excellent example of the current direction being taken with volume-rendering and transfer-function research: utilizing high-quality classification and segmentation methods when the more traditional transfer-function methods fail.

11

Game Developer's Guide to Volume Graphics

T HE POWER OF CURRENT CONSUMER GRAPHICS HARDWARE increasingly allows the integration of truly volumetric graphics into applications with very high real-time demands. Computer and video games are certainly the prime example. In many traditional volume-rendering applications, such as medical volume rendering, frame rates between 10 and 20 frames per second are usually considered to be sufficient. In games, however, the overall frame rate needs to be much higher than that, including all the simulation and rendering for the entire scene, of which volumetric effects are but a small part.

This chapter describes approaches for integrating volume graphics into game engines and provides an overview of recent developments in simulating and rendering volumetric effects with very high frame rates. It is also intended as a guide to the other chapters of this book from a game developer's perspective.

11.1 Volume Graphics in Games

Traditionally, many volumetric effects in games have been rendered with approximations such as *animated billboards* and *particle systems*. Because these terms are sometimes used interchangeably and terminology can be confusing, we clarify the terminology we are using in this chapter below in Section 11.1.1. Common examples for volumetric effects in games are explosions, fire, or smoke. The influence of participating media such as fog or the earth's atmosphere is also a very important part of realistic rendering that has traditionally been approximated using very limited methods such as OpenGL's fog color blending.

Although we believe that particle systems per se will continue to play a very important role in games in the future, we argue that on current and

275

future GPUs the use of simple animated billboards can often be replaced by truly volumetric effects for much better results. The effect of participating media can also be simulated with increasing accuracy, moving away from earlier extremely simplified real-time models. Recently, the interest in incorporating true volume rendering into games has been increasing [86]. GPU performance has reached a level where convincing truly volumetric effects are possible in real time. Moreover, with recent GPU features such as data-dependent looping and branching, volumes have also become much easier to render and integrate with game engines. General references on game programming can be found in Section 11.9.

11.1.1 Billboards, Sprites, Impostors, Particle Systems, and Terminology

Generally speaking, *billboards* or *sprites* are textured 2D geometry that represents objects that are too complex to render in real time. However, there is no really consistent terminology and there are various techniques that make use of this basic idea in one way or another [2]. The most basic billboard is simply a quad with a single texture on it that in each frame is automatically rotated such that it is perpendicular to the view direction. This kind of billboard is often called a *sprite*, which was the common term in early arcade, computer, and video games. In these early examples, sprite textures were usually hand-drawn, whereas later on they were pre-rendered using offline 3D rendering software.

Billboards can also be used to represent complex geometric objects, such as in billboard clouds [44], where their position and orientation, and texture images, are automatically optimized for good results with a minimum number of billboards in a pre-process. A common application for this kind of object representation is rendering trees and foliage [9]. In games, such billboards have traditionally been generated manually or semi-manually by artists.

A related technique that uses billboards as basic drawing primitives are *impostors* [2, 233, 237]. However, impostor billboards act as image caches and are usually dynamically updated by rendering into offscreen buffers. They "stand in" for actual geometry or volumes for several frames; that is, impostor images are usually not updated every frame, e.g., by performing an update only when a certain maximum approximation error is exceeded. These kinds of billboards often are not aligned with the view but with scene geometry, which is illustrated in Figure 11.1. Expensive volumetric effects such as clouds are a natural candidate for impostor rendering [94].

In the current generation of games, many effects are rendered with billboards that have a static geometric position but are rendered with animated textures, i.e., *animated billboards*. Examples are a log fire or flames

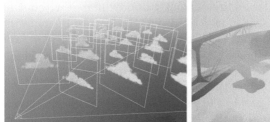

Figure 11.1. A powerful combination of volume and billboard rendering is to use billboards as impostors [2], e.g., for cloud rendering (left). The cached impostor images are updated only when the error with respect to the real view becomes too large [94, 233, 237]. A major problem of using billboards or impostors are potential clipping artifacts where they intersect scene geometry (center). (Images courtesy of Mark Harris [97].)

on candles or torches that are rendered as an arrangement of intersecting semitransparent billboards with texture animations. These animations are either pre-computed or computed procedurally on-the-fly, depending on the performance cost and required quality.

Individual particles of a particle system are commonly also rendered as billboards. The textures used on particle billboards are often animated; i.e., multiple texture frames are played back in order to change the *appearance* of the particles in addition to animating their *position* in 3D space. Common examples in games are rendering fire, smoke, or clouds of dust. Sometimes, the terms *particle systems* and *billboards* are used to describe the same kind of effect. In this chapter, however, when we use the term *particle systems*, we are most of all concerned with the *dynamic behavior* of these systems, i.e., the animation of particle positions. In this context, the term *billboard* refers to the *animated appearance* of texture sprites. This distinction is only important insofar as we argue below that volume rendering can increasingly replace animated billboards, and particle systems are a complementary technique. For games, we can say that some effects traditionally based on particle systems and billboard rendering can be substituted entirely by real-time volume rendering, whereas sparse widely distributed effects, such as water splashing from a fountain, or effects with small particles, such as sparks, are most likely still best rendered with particle systems.

11.1.2   Where Volumes Are Present in Games

In the following, we give an overview of the main areas where volumetric structures and effects are present in games, focusing on rendering aspects.

Most of these effects and volumes are currently approximated without an underlying volumetric representation. However, the nature of many effects in games is volumetric, and with the rapid move toward more and more realistic graphics and increasing GPU power, they will increasingly be computed based on actual volumetric representations.

Volumetric effects. A major problem of using billboards for effects such as fire, smoke, and explosions is that the geometry of the billboards is often clearly visible. The worst case of this happens when billboards clip into scene geometry. The resulting intersection lines can clearly be seen and the illusion of a volumetric effect breaks down completely. This problem is illustrated in the center image of Figure 11.1. Effects based on billboards usually also have the problem that the 2D nature of the underlying geometry, i.e., the underlying image or stack of images, becomes visible when the view is rotated. When billboard geometry is aligned with the viewer, billboards are often perceived as rotating by themselves. If they are static with respect to the world, their planar geometry often becomes clearly discernible when they are viewed close to edge-on.

Even for real-time rendering, billboard effects can increasingly be replaced by truly volumetric effects, which provides a consistent model for rendering and the basis for also simulating these effects in real time. Procedural effects can be computed on GPUs in real time and rendered directly as volumes. Clipping artifacts can, in principle, be removed entirely. Even if the sampling rate during rendering is rather low, scene intersections are much less visible in volume rendering than with billboard rendering. Section 11.6 covers rendering volumetric effects, and Section 11.7 takes this a step further toward real-time simulation of the underlying data.

Figure 11.2. The standard OpenGL fog model using simple distance-based blending with a constant fog color (left). A recent, more accurate real-time single scattering model [259] (right). Note that, in the right image, even the reflectance behavior of surfaces is modified due to scattering between the surface and the viewer (insets). (The images are included courtesy of Bo Sun et al. [259], © 2005 ACM, Inc. Reprinted by permission.)

Participating media. Most rendering deals with light interaction only at a small part of the entire 3D space, i.e., commonly at points on surfaces that are part of the scene geometry. In this case, the media, such as air or water, that fills up the space between these surfaces is not participating in lighting computations. However, effects such as light scattering in the earth's atmosphere or in fog are a very important part of the realism of the resulting rendered images. An example in indoor scenes is light that is scattered by dust particles in the air, e.g., resulting in "light shafts" emanating from windows. All these scattering interactions are often subsumed as taking the effect of participating media into account.

One example is a recent method that allows OpenGL fog blending to be replaced with a more accurate method that takes single scattering into account [259] (Figure 11.2). Other approaches avoid the approximation of "light shafts" with simple semitransparent polygonal geometry by using more accurate models [51, 186].

Semitransparent and flexible objects. In a completely different vein from volumetric effects and participating media, volumes can also be used as highly flexible object representations. Volumes naturally allow the interior of objects to be taken into account. Semitransparent objects can thus be rendered in their entirety. As described in Chapter 13, such volumes can be animated and deformed in real time.

Even surface-based models can be converted into a volumetric representation, for example by converting an object into a *distance field* [205]. In this representation, operations such as constructive solid geometry (CSG) or morphing are very easy and fast to compute. Complex deformations with complicated changes of surface shape and even topology can be computed on volumes using level set methods [205].

Particle effects. For completeness, we also include in Section 11.6.2 a brief discussion of recent advances in rendering particle systems composed of millions of independent particles on current GPUs. Rendering particle systems is usually not considered a volume-rendering method, although it shares basic properties with *splatting*, which is described in Section 1.6.2. However, the basic goal is to render effects composed of a complex structure that is distributed throughout a volume.

In general, particle systems are a very powerful method that is complementary to using volume rendering for visual effects. They are especially useful when accurate volume rendering is still too expensive, e.g., when the volume encompassing the effect is big but very sparsely populated, such as in water splashing from a fountain. However, certain kinds of effects that in real-time rendering have traditionally been rendered using particle systems, such as explosions, can now be rendered in higher quality with

Figure 11.3. Pre-computed radiance transfer for volume illumination [245]. Global lighting is represented by a low-frequency environment map that can be rotated arbitrarily with real-time updates of volume lighting. (Images courtesy of Peter-Pike Sloan, Jan Kautz, and Jon Snyder, © 2002 ACM, Inc. Reprinted by permission.)

volume rendering. A fully volumetric representation also allows for GPU-based simulation, which is described in Section 11.7.

Irradiance volumes. Irradiance volumes [88] are the 3D analog of 2D light maps. Their use is becoming common in GPU-based real-time rendering [262]. However, irradiance volumes are used like solid textures [58]. That is, although they are a volumetric representation, they are not rendered as volumes but usually sampled on geometrically represented surfaces.

Pre-computed radiance transfer. Pre-computed radiance transfer (PRT) [245] is traditionally computed for surfaces but can also be used to capture the illumination in a volume as illustrated in Figure 11.3. In this case, radiance transfer is stored at the grid points of the volume. For surface rendering, radiance transfer information is stored at the vertices of a mesh or in surface textures. However, a special variant called *neighborhood transfer* caches radiance transfer data in a solid, i.e., volumetric, texture. This texture can then be used to compute radiance transfer effects such as soft shadowing in the corresponding subvolume of 3D space surrounding an object.

Subsurface scattering. Subsurface scattering approaches [279] consider the volume below an object's surface to a certain depth in order to capture the translucent and smooth appearance of surfaces such as skin. However, rendering is performed using customized algorithms for computing light transfer due to scattering and not general volume rendering.

Displacement mapping and relief mapping. Displacement mapping and relief mapping [203, 213] are usually not considered to be volume-rendering approaches, although they capture the volume above a base surface. However, common implementations use ray casting in fragment programs and thus have close similarities to the volume ray-casting approaches presented in this book.

Hair and fur rendering. Common approaches for rendering fur employ 3D representations [119] or use volume slabs above surfaces [159]. High-quality shadowing when rendering hair can be computed using a fundamentally volumetric representation such as *deep shadow maps* [167]. Although deep shadow maps are not a real-time method, they are described in Section 11.8.4 as they facilitate a comprehensive understanding of volumetric shadowing and the combination of geometry and volumes, which is crucial for volume rendering in games.

11.1.3   Simulation and GPGPU

The recently emerging field of *general purpose computations on GPUs* (GPGPU [85]) allows one to move the simulation of effects from the CPU to the GPU. This very often has significant performance advantages. For visual effects, it also has the property of moving the simulation of effects much closer to where the resulting data are actually needed for rendering. As GPUs become more powerful, the simulation and simultaneous visualization of volumetric effects is rapidly becoming a reality. Section 11.7 gives an overview of simulating volumetric effects in real time.

11.2   Differences from "Standalone" Volume Rendering

Most research publications, and indeed also most of this book, deal with volume rendering as an isolated problem. Usually, a single volume is viewed from the outside without intervening geometry, and the external lighting environment is relatively simple, e.g., consisting of only one or two directional or point light sources, or a single environment map. However, in the context of a game engine, volumes have to be integrated in a consistent manner with the rest of the engine. They have to fit in with the projection that is used, clip correctly with surrounding geometry, and use the same lighting environment that is used for all other parts of the scene. In the most general case, they also have to interact with each other. This section summarizes the major differences between volume rendering as part of a bigger system and volume rendering as a "standalone" application.

11.2.1   Integration with Scene Geometry

The first major issue when integrating volume graphics into games is to ensure proper interaction with the majority of the scene, which is represented by geometry. This geometry must be allowed to intersect volumes. In doing so, opaque and semitransparent scene geometry must be handled differently. Due to its importance, Section 11.4 is devoted entirely to the topic of integrating volumes with scene geometry.

Interaction with semitransparent geometry. Semitransparent geometry is a special case in virtually all rendering engines. In contrast with opaque geometry, triangles that are not fully opaque have to be rendered in correct visibility order. Fundamentally, semitransparent volumes in a scene are very similar to regular semitransparent geometry. Like their geometric counterparts, they also have to be rendered after all opaque parts of the scene. The visibility order of volumes and transparent geometry is an inherently hard problem and is discussed in Section 11.4.

11.2.2   Handling Multiple Volumes

Games naturally require a multitude of different effects to be visible at the same time, so when they are rendered as volumes, multiple volumes must be handled seamlessly. Traversal of these volumes has to be performed in correct visibility order. In the most general case, a correct visibility ordering must be established even when volumes are interpenetrating.

11.2.3   Integration with Occlusion Culling

As all other objects and effects, volumes have to be integrated with the occlusion culling system. In general, this is easily accomplished using the existing occlusion culling solution by considering a volume's bounding box or bounding geometry (e.g., a room filled entirely with volumetric fog), which is discussed in Section 11.4.5.

11.2.4   Integration with Scene Lighting

Game engines are moving toward more and more realistic lighting, increasingly allowing all light sources to change dynamically. Where for many years different kinds of lights and light-surface interactions have been treated as individual special cases, now all these different cases are becoming unified in order to provide completely consistent lighting. Therefore, when volume rendering is incorporated into a game engine, it also has to be integrated with its existing scene lighting in a consistent manner.

That is, volumes have to be integrated with how lighting and especially shadows are computed in the scene. The illumination that is external to the volume is determined by global scene lighting. Unfortunately, the feasibility of completely consistent volume lighting is very dependent on whether shadows are computed using *shadow volumes* [37] or *shadow maps* [301]. Going a step further, the light emitted and scattered by a volume can be used in order to provide illumination for the rest of the scene. With respect to shadowing, semitransparent volumes give rise to soft shadows due to absorption of light.

11.2.5   Integration with High Dynamic Range Rendering

If the game engine uses high dynamic range (HDR) lighting and rendering, the embedded volumes also have to interact correctly with it. Basically, this just means that all lighting computations in the volume have to be performed with the same dynamic range that is used for all other lighting. This also allows one to use high dynamic range volume rendering, where the transfer function maps interpolated values from the volume to emission values with high dynamic range and high-precision alpha. Section 5.8 contains more information on high dynamic range volume rendering.

11.3   Guide to Other Chapters

This section provides pointers to the most important chapters in this book with respect to their relevance to volume rendering in games. We start out with the most basic ingredient, which is traversing the volume and sampling it for rendering.

11.3.1   Slicing

The traditional way for GPU-based volume rendering is to resample the volume using slicing planes. These planes act as *proxy geometry* that generates the fragments that allow the volume to be resampled in a fragment program. The slicing planes are parallel to each other, spaced with a distance that is inversely proportional to the sampling rate, and composited in either back-to-front or front-to-back order.

Chapter 3 describes this basic approach to volume rendering in detail. Although slicing is very common, we recommend using GPU ray casting for volume rendering in games instead. With slicing, it can be quite tedious to set up all the geometry of the slicing planes, especially when multiple volumes are rendered in a single frame and scene geometry might be intersected. Planar resampling also does not easily allow for correct compositing when perspective projection is used, which is the kind of projection used in games.

11.3.2 Ray Casting

We propose to use single-pass GPU ray casting as the main approach for volume rendering in games. Single-pass ray casting is much easier to implement and integrate with game engines than slicing approaches. All computations can be performed in a fragment program with trivial geometry set-up. No special vertex program computations are necessary. Traversal of the volume is done entirely in the fragment program using data-dependent loop instructions, and no special blending set-up is required.

Section 11.5 describes a really simple GPU ray caster that already supports most of what is needed for simple volume rendering in games. Chapter 7 covers GPU ray casting in detail. For volume rendering in games, only the sections on ray casting in regular grids are relevant. Ray casting in irregular grids is more geared toward scientific visualization and is also much more computationally involved.

11.3.3 Local and Global Illumination

In the context of games, many volumetric effects can be treated as purely emitting and absorbing light, that is, volume rendering with the basic emission-absorption model and no external illumination or scattering. However, volumes without external illumination appear to be separate from their environment because they are completely independent of it. A big advantage of volume rendering compared with rendering billboards or particle systems is that illumination can be computed consistently with the environment. Note, however, that some special effects such as fire are dominated by the light they emit, and the impact of external illumination is negligible.

Chapters 5 and 6 cover both local and global volume illumination in detail. Although still very expensive, approximations of multiple scattering are able to produce extremely convincing results and will probably also become a part of games in the future.

11.3.4 Pre-Integration

The concept of pre-integration is one of the major approaches to achieving high quality with low sampling rates. It is thus ideal for volume rendering in games where the sampling rate should be as low as possible as long as convincing overall quality can be retained. Section 4.5 covers pre-integrated volume rendering in detail. Pre-integration for ray casting is discussed in Section 7.2.

11.3.5 Volume Modeling and Animation

Chapter 12 describes how volumes can be created for artistic purposes. Approaches include conversion from originally polygonal models with various post-processing stages and procedural modeling. A very powerful example of procedural modeling is to use a hierarchy of volume resolutions for modeling high-quality clouds. A low-resolution volume is perturbed with multiple octaves of high-resolution noise to obtain a cloud of convincing quality. In order to save texture space, high-resolution noise can also be added on-the-fly during rendering. Motion and dynamics are important for increasing immersion and a sense of reality. Chapter 13 discusses real-time volume animation techniques including real-time deformation and sculpting of volumetric models.

11.3.6   Performance Optimizations

Since games are very time-critical applications and volume rendering is very demanding with respect to performance, optimization is naturally a crucial issue. Chapter 8 contains a detailed discussion of performance optimization in volume rendering. An issue that is especially important when volume rendering is used in games is mipmapping. In most "traditional" volume-rendering applications, volumes are always magnified; i.e., the pixel-to-voxel ratio is greater than one. However, when volumes are used for special effects, a pixel-to-voxel ratio of less than one is common, i.e., the volume is minified. In this case, using mipmapped volume textures is very important for performance. Also, when 3D textures are used, the memory overhead of mipmapping is reduced to just 1/7 of the volume size, which is a very good trade-off with respect to improving performance. Of course, when a volume is minified, using mipmapping also improves visual quality, which is the standard motivation for using mipmapping. Chapter 8 discusses the performance implications of using mipmapped textures.

11.4   Integrating Volumes with Scene Geometry

The most important task when integrating volume rendering in a game engine is the proper interaction with scene geometry and lighting. Integration with scene geometry is foremost a task of proper clipping and visibility order. In this chapter, we focus on integrating volume rendering using ray casting. We believe that it is the most flexible and easiest way to integrate volume rendering with game engines on GPUs that support data-dependent looping in fragment programs, i.e., Shader Model 3.0 or higher.

In the following sections, we cover all the different combinations of scene/volume intersections. First, we start with the case where opaque scene geometry intersects the volume. We continue by describing what happens when the near clipping plane intersects the volume, i.e., when the viewpoint is moved inside the volume.

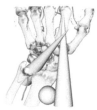

Figure 11.4. Geometry intersection using the depth image of the geometric part of the scene (right). During ray casting, rays are stopped at the depth of the corresponding scene intersection (center), which can be done entirely in image space. Blending the volume image on top of the scene geometry yields the final image (left).

11.4.1 Opaque Scene Geometry Intersection with a Ray-Cast Volume

When opaque scene geometry intersects a volume, the resulting effect is that some rays may not be allowed to be started at all, and some rays are not cast until they exit the volume, but only until they hit some scene geometry. These decisions can be made based solely on the view depth of scene geometry and the depth positions of samples on rays cast into the volume.

Thus, the easiest way to combine scene geometry with volume ray casting is to build on a completed depth image of the scene. All opaque scene geometry is rendered first, initializing the depth buffer. The depth buffer then has to be bound as a texture that is used by the ray-casting fragment program in order to terminate rays when they hit scene geometry. Rays are terminated depending on depth comparisons of ray sample depths with the scene's depth at the corresponding location in the depth buffer. The basic steps for proper intersection of a ray-cast volume with opaque scene geometry are, in order:

- Render all opaque parts of the scene to initialize the depth buffer. Note that in current game engines, the first rendering pass is usually a depth-only pass for visibility determination without shading, and shading is performed in subsequent passes. This is done in order to exploit early z-test functionality (Section 8.6.2). The completed depth buffer must subsequently be available as a depth texture.

- In order to start rays, rasterize the bounding box of the volume by rendering its six faces with back face culling and the depth test enabled. This ensures that start positions that are already behind visible scene geometry will not generate fragments and thus the corresponding rays will never be started.

- Each fragment that has not been discarded by the depth test starts to cast a ray into the volume. For each new sample along a ray, the depth in the scene's depth range is updated along with the current position in the volume. A depth comparison with the depth buffer value at the fragment's pixel position determines whether the ray has intersected scene geometry and thus needs to be terminated. Of course, a ray is also terminated when it exits the volume.

- Optionally, when a ray intersects scene geometry, one last sample is taken at the exact intersection position in volume coordinates. This helps to hide the position of intersection when the sampling rate is very low and thus removes the clipping artifacts known from billboard rendering, especially when pre-integration is used. Opacity correction must be performed in order to compensate for the reduced sampling distance and obtain the correct volume-rendering integral (see Section 1.4.3).

```
float4 main(float2 window_position:  TEXCOORD0,
            uniform sampler2D depth_texture,
            uniform float4x4 ModelViewProjInverse) :  COLOR
{
    // compute the homogeneous view-space position
    // window_position is in [0,1]^2 and depth in [0,1]
    float4 hviewpos;
    hviewpos.xy = window_position;
    hviewpos.z  = tex2D(depth_texture, window_position);
    hviewpos.w  = 1.0;
    // we need this to be in [-1,1]^3 clip space
    hviewpos = hviewpos * 2.0 - 1.0;

    // back-project to homogeneous volume space
    float4 hvolpos = mul(ModelViewProjInverse, hviewpos);

    // return normalized volume-space position
    return (hvolpos / hvolpos.w);
}
```

Listing 11.1. Cg function that back-projects a depth image of the geometric part of the scene into volume space. The depth range is assumed to be [0, 1].

The simple addition of the scene's depth buffer to the ray-casting fragment program allows scene/volume intersection to be performed on a per-pixel basis with the same precision that is used by the depth buffer itself and thus for geometry/geometry intersections. The only problem is the transformation between depth buffer values and volume coordinates. Listing 11.1 illustrates Cg code that performs the necessary back-projection given a depth texture as input.

When the ray-casting fragment program is started, the target color buffer can either be an entirely separate buffer or the color buffer that already contains the final shaded view of the opaque scene. In order to obtain a correct visibility ordering, the entire contribution of the ray-casting pass must be blended on top of the entire scene's color buffer. The ray caster can either use a separate buffer and store the overall alpha of each ray in the alpha buffer, which allows correct blending with scene geometry at any later time. Alternatively, the result of the ray-casting pass can be blended directly into the color buffer of the scene, given that it has been rendered in its entirety before.

11.4.2   Moving the Viewpoint into a Volume

A problem that is often ignored in games is what happens when the viewpoint is moved inside an object. This issue is often neglected for simplicity reasons, and also because it is hard to define the interior of polygonal objects if they are not texture-mapped with a solid texture, for example. Also, due to collision detection, the viewpoint in a game is rarely inside an object. If it is nevertheless the case, the player can usually see the geometry being clipped by the near clip plane, and it becomes clear that the object consists only of its surface and there is nothing inside.

Although ignoring this problem for surface-based objects might be a good trade-off, handling this issue correctly for volumes is much more important. Moving the viewpoint into a volume in a game is a common case. The obvious example is volume rendering of participating media, where the whole point might be to move the viewpoint inside the volume. Another example is special effects such as fireballs that frequently hit the player, and the volume thus encompasses the viewpoint for a few animation frames. For a convincing result, it is important that the inside of the volume never disappears. And, maybe even more importantly, the inside of a volume is well-defined and thus can be rendered correctly, whereas for polygonal game models this is usually not the case.

What changes for volume ray casting, when the viewpoint enters the volume, is that not all rays are started at the bounding box of the volume anymore. Some of them have to be started at the near clipping plane instead. This is illustrated in Figure 11.5. When the entire near clipping

Figure 11.5. When the near clipping plane intersects the volume, some rays must be started at the near clipping plane (left) in order to avoid wrong ray starting positions (center). Near clipping and termination of rays at scene geometry intersections must be combined correctly (right). The volume is shown subdivided into small bricks for efficient empty-space skipping. (Images reprinted from [232], © Eurographics Association 2006.

plane is inside the volume, *all* rays are started at the volume coordinates corresponding to the near clipping plane. An easy way for deciding where rays need to be started is to use depth values once again, similar to clipping with scene geometry as described in the previous section. In the ray-casting fragment program, before a ray is started, the depth value of the near plane must be compared with the depth value where a ray would enter the volume's bounding box. If the depth on a front face of the bounding box is farther away, ray casting starts as usual. If it is closer and thus the near plane already clips the volume for that ray, the near plane depth at that position must be transformed into volume coordinates and ray casting has to start there instead. Listing 11.1 shows how depth values can be back-projected into volume coordinates. A simple very effective approach for handling all different combinations has been described in detail in the context of ray casting for virtual endoscopy [232].

11.4.3   Semitransparent Scene Geometry and Volumes

Determining the visibility order for semitransparent geometry is an inherently hard problem. In contrast with opaque geometry, where in principle an arbitrary rendering order can be used when depth buffering is employed, semitransparent geometry must be blended in either back-to-front or front-to-back order. Note that in practice some kind of ordering is usually also used for opaque geometry. Performance increases when as much geometry as possible is discarded during early depth testing. However, in this case no exact ordering is necessary, and there is a huge difference between slightly reduced performance and an incorrectly rendered image. In general, obtaining an exact visibility order is very expensive, and even splitting of geometry is often necessary.

Game engines use a variety of different approaches in order to determine a visibility order, many of which only approximate an exact order, accepting errors to a certain degree. The basis for integrating volume rendering into such a scheme is to treat a volume as a solid semitransparent block corresponding to its bounding box.

Visibility ordering using BSP trees. The most well-known approach for determining an exact visibility order in game engines is to use *BSP trees* [2]. A BSP tree employs recursively repeated *binary space partitions* in order to subdivide the entire 3D space into convex polytopes for which an exact visibility order is easy to determine using the structure of the tree. The tree itself represents a hierarchy of convex polytopes, and its leaves constitute a subdivision of the entire space without overlap. When it is used for visibility determination, BSP tree traversal fundamentally represents a sorting algorithm for all scene geometry with linear time complexity. Fortunately, for sorting semitransparent geometry, all opaque parts of the scene can be neglected, and common scenes in games contain only very few nonopaque parts.

If an exact visibility order is desired and a BSP tree is available for all semitransparent parts of the scene, a volume's bounding box can be clipped into the tree as a "solid" object. This effectively splits it up into smaller convex parts that are each assigned to one leaf of the BSP tree, respectively. Volume rendering then has to be performed for these parts individually, in the visibility order determined by BSP tree traversal.

Visibility ordering using depth peeling. Depth peeling is a depth buffer-based approach that ensures a correct visibility order without requiring sorting [67, 193]. For geometry, it is easy to implement, and because it does not require any sorting, it also does not require any of the related data structures, such as BSP trees, or associated sorting time. Depth peeling generates a drawing order by successively generating layers of a given depth complexity. Each rendering pass uses the depth image of the previous pass in order to discard everything that is nearer (or farther) than the previous depth layer. The algorithm terminates when the number of layers corresponds to the depth complexity of the scene. A more detailed discussion of depth peeling in the context of clipping can be found in Section 15.3.3. The major drawback of depth peeling, however, is that it is very rasterization-intensive and can only deal with a small number of depth or visibility layers in real time. In practice, depth peeling is usually not a feasible option for rendering all semitransparent scene geometry. It is also hard to extend efficiently to yield a mixed visibility order of volumes and geometry. However, when a very limited amount of semitransparent

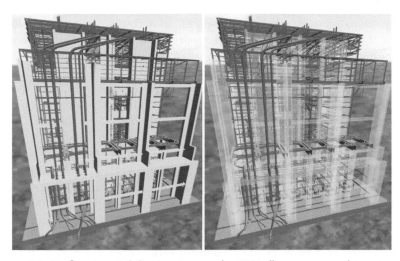

Figure 11.6. Performing visibility sorting on the GPU allows one to achieve interactive frame rates for very complex models [84]. This model has 820K triangles, 91K of which are semitransparent in the right image. A full sorting can be done with between 7 and 10 frames per second on a GeForce 6800. (Images are courtesy of Naga Govindaraju et al. [84], © 2005 ACM, Inc. Reprinted by permission.)

geometry *intersects* a volume and an exact ordering is desired, it might be a feasible alternative.

GPU-based visibility ordering. Instead of sorting geometric primitives on the CPU in order to bring them into visibility order, this sorting can also be done on the GPU [84], as illustrated in Figure 11.6. An object-level visibility order among geometric primitives is computed by leveraging hardware occlusion queries and temporal coherence. A basic assumption is that there are no visibility cycles, i.e., no geometry needs to be split in order to determine a visibility ordering. However, this algorithm could be extended to yield a mixed visibility order of volumes and geometry.

Approximate visibility ordering. In practice, an exact visibility ordering for integrating volumes with semitransparent scene geometry is only feasible when a game engine supports exact visibility ordering for already existing geometry. For many volumetric effects, it is probably sufficient to determine the order of rendering semitransparent geometry and volumes in an approximate manner.

The most common approach for obtaining an approximate visibility ordering is to simply sort the centroids of primitives or objects according to distance. In the case of rendering relatively small volumes, the centroid of the volume's bounding box can be used. Moreover, the six faces of a bounding box give rise to six separating planes that separate space into two half-spaces each. Any point outside the volume lies at least in one of the half-spaces that are on the opposite side of the volume. When semitransparent geometry is tested against all six faces for inclusion in one of these half-spaces, the resulting information can be used to obtain a visibility ordering. When the entire geometry is contained in the respective half-space, this ordering will be exact. If it straddles the separating plane, it will only be approximate but is often still a good approximation.

Semitransparent geometry that intersects a volume. Although resolving this issue in a correct way is probably not very attractive for the majority of volumetric effects, it becomes important when volumes have a large extent in a scene, especially with regard to rendering participating media. It is indeed possible to correctly resolve the problem of semitransparent geometry that intersects or is actually inside a volume, although this is a potentially expensive process when an exact order is desired. First, all geometry outside the volume has to be clipped and treated in the same way as all non–volume-intersecting semitransparent geometry. Then, we are only dealing with geometry that is entirely contained inside the volume.

One possibility is to create a BSP tree of all semitransparent geometry that intersects the volume and to render the volume in the order determined by BSP leaves as they are encountered during tree traversal. This approach is only feasible if the relationship between the volume and intersecting primitives is static. In that case, the BSP tree inside the volume can be pre-computed.

If the relationship between the geometry and the volume is dynamic, and the amount of semitransparent geometry inside the volume is very limited, depth peeling [67, 193] can be an attractive alternative. The approach described above in Section 11.4.1 for intersecting opaque geometry with a volume rendered with ray casting can be modified in such a way that every depth layer obtained via depth peeling is treated as being opaque and ray casting stops at the respective intersection positions. The number of ray-casting passes is determined by the number of depth layers, plus one additional pass for the foremost layer of the volume. All passes after the first pass start rays at the locations of the previous depth layer and terminate at the intersection with the current depth layer or because they exit the volume.

11.4.4   Visibility Ordering for Multiple Volumes

When multiple volumes are visible at the same time, a visibility ordering has to be determined. Given that no volumes are interpenetrating, this amounts to the problem of determining a visibility order of the volumes' bounding boxes.

Interpenetrating volumes (volumes inside volumes). The case when volumes interpenetrate is relevant when there are small volumes for volumetric effects and very large space-filling volumes, e.g., in the case of participating media. There are two basic approaches for coping with this problem.

The simplest approach is to consider both (or all) potentially intersecting volumes in the same ray-casting fragment program over the extent of both volumes. All that is needed then is a transformation that maps volume coordinates from one volume to the other volume. Note that care must be taken that resampling one volume outside of its bounding box does not introduce artifacts. Although this allows both volumes to be resampled at the same time and handle simultaneous emission of both in the same region of space correctly, it introduces a lot of overhead when the amount of overlap is small. All regions that are not actually overlapping still have to sample either both volumes in any case, or perform expensive checking on a per-sample basis whether there is an overlap at that sample position or not.

Another approach is to determine the intersection of both volumes before ray casting and use a fragment program that considers both volumes only in this intersection region. All regions that contain only a single volume can then be rendered with a regular ray-casting fragment program that considers only a single volume.

11.4.5 Occlusion Culling

Since the advent of hardware-accelerated depth buffering, occlusion culling systems in games as well as in most other applications are usually *conservative*. That is, geometry that is not occluded in its entirety is never reported as being invisible. However, geometry that is indeed completely occluded might still be reported as being visible or partially visible. This case, however, will only reduce performance and not produce artifacts when depth buffering is used for visibility determination at the pixel level. Occlusion culling thus is not for exact visibility determination but a performance improvement. It discards large chunks of geometry that are known to be invisible in any case before they are submitted to later pipeline stages of the rendering pipeline, e.g., polygon rasterization.

As such, integrating volumes with an existing occlusion culling system of a game engine is straightforward. The simple approach of using the volume's bounding box for all occlusion computation purposes is sufficient in many cases. Likewise, if the volume is "room-filling," such as fog, occlusion culling can be handled by using the enclosing structure. If a volume is very large, and thus more fine-grained performance optimization is desired, it can be subdivided and occlusion culling can be performed for individual parts, e.g., smaller bounding boxes, of this subdivision. Chapter 17 covers different approaches for subdividing large volumes in order to handle them in smaller chunks.

11.5 A Simple Volume Ray Caster for Games

In this section, we describe a simple ray caster for volume rendering in games. We build on the single-pass ray casting described in Chapter 7 (Listing 7.2) and extend it to work with geometry intersection. The two major modifications are as follows.

- Stop rays when they intersect opaque scene geometry before they leave the volume's bounding box (see Section 11.4.1). This is done in the fragment program (Listing 11.2) by back-projecting the scene geometry's depth image into volume space and stopping rays at these locations.

- Make sure all rays are started even when the near clipping plane intersects the bounding box of the volume (see Section 11.4.2). This modification is not done by changing the fragment program but the geometry set-up instead.

The first step is to render and shade all opaque scene geometry and obtain the corresponding depth image. After that, volumes can be blended on top. In order to render a volume, we must first determine whether the near clipping plane intersects the volume's bounding box. If this is not the case, the volume can be rendered by simply rasterizing its front faces, e.g., by rendering all six faces and using an OpenGL culling mode of GL_BACK. If the near clipping plane is intersected, we need the geometry of the intersection of the bounding box and the near plane. This geometry is a polygon that *caps* the bounding box where it is cut open by the near clipping plane. The simplest way to do this is to generate a quad for the near clipping plane and clip it against all six planes of the volume bounding box on the CPU, which yields a polygon for the near plane cap. For rendering the volume, both the front faces of the volume bounding box and the near plane cap must be rasterized. Note that the near plane cap has to be rendered with a small depth offset in front of the clipping plane in order to avoid it being clipped by the near clipping plane.

It is important that during rasterization of the front faces (and the near plane cap) the OpenGL depth test is enabled and compares depth values of the volume's bounding geometry with the depth buffer of the scene. The early z-test makes sure that rays that are entirely behind opaque scene geometry will never be started.

```
float4 main(float4 TexCoord0 :  TEXCOORD0,
            float4 windowPosition :  WPOS,
            uniform float2 windowSizeInv,
            uniform sampler3D SamplerDataVolume,
            uniform sampler1D SamplerTransferFunction,
            uniform float3 camera,
            uniform float stepsize,
            uniform float3 volExtentMin,
            uniform float3 volExtentMax ) :  COLOR {
    // Initialize accumulated color and opacity
    float4 dst = float4(0,0,0,0);
    // Determine volume entry position
    float3 startPos = TexCoord0.xyz;
    // Compute ray direction
    float3 direction = TexCoord0.xyz - camera;
    direction = normalize(direction);
    // Compute position of geometry in volume coordinates
    float2 windowPos01 = windowPosition.xy * windowSizeInv;
    float3 geometryIntersect = BackProjectDepth(windowPos01);
    // Compute ray length until geometry intersection
    float stopLength = distance(startpos, geometryIntersect);
    // Loop for ray traversal
    float curLength = 0.0;
    for (int i = 0; i < 255; i++) {
        // Data access to scalar value in 3D volume texture
        float3 position = startPos + direction * curLength;
        float4 value = tex3D(SamplerDataVolume, position);
        float4 src = tex1D(SamplerTransferFunction, value.a);
        dst = (1.0 - dst.a) * src + dst;
        // Advance ray position along ray direction
        curLength += stepsize;
        // Ray termination:  Test if at geometry intersection
        if (curLength >= stopLength)
            break;
        // Ray termination:  Test if outside volume
        float3 temp1 = sign(position - volExtentMin);
        float3 temp2 = sign(volExtentMax - position);
        float inside = dot(temp1, temp2);
        if (inside < 3.0)
            break;
    }
    return dst;
}
```

Listing 11.2. Cg function for single-pass ray casting with geometry intersection.
BackProjectDepth() is essentially the function in Listing 11.1. Note that, to improve performance, the two loop-termination criteria could be combined.

During rasterization, the fragment program shown in Listing 11.2 performs ray casting that is almost identical to Listing 7.2 in Chapter 7. In addition to that, it back-projects the scene's depth image into volume coordinates and determines the distance between the point where a ray enters the volume and where it intersects scene geometry and must be terminated. For the corresponding comparison of ray lengths, it is not necessary to determine whether the distance to the scene geometry is positive or negative, because the OpenGL depth test makes sure that rays are only started when they are in front of scene geometry.

The function `BackProjectDepth()` is essentially the code shown in Listing 11.1. The only conversion that has to be performed is converting window positions (obtained via the `WPOS` binding) from the `[width, height]` coordinate system of the window to `[0, 1]`. In order to be able to do this, the fragment program needs to know the size of the window in pixels, the reciprocal values of which are supplied in the uniform parameter `windowSizeInv`.

11.6 Volumetric Effects

One of the main application areas of volume rendering in games are volumetric effects, such as fire, fireballs, and explosions. As an example, Section 11.6.1 describes a procedural fireball effect. Section 11.6.2 describes the complementary technique of using particle systems. Procedural models are covered in detail in Section 12.3.

11.6.1 Procedural Effects Animation

In order to capture the characteristics of many volumetric objects such as clouds, fire, smoke, trees, hair, and fur, Ebert [58] uses a coarse technique for modeling the macrostructure and uses procedural noise-based simulations for the microstructure. Perlin noise [207, 98] is a noise function that is ideal to model such effects because it is band limited, changes smoothly, and is defined everywhere.

Figure 11.7 shows a fireball that is rendered with a small modification of the pre-integrated volume-rendering approach from Section 4.5. A single RGB 3D texture is employed that contains the volume scalars from a radial distance function in the red channel, a low-frequency noise texture in the green channel, and a high-frequency noise texture in the blue channel. Using a single texture fetch, we can obtain the scalar value and two noise values with different scales. The three components can be mixed by performing a dot product of the RGB vector from the texture fetch with a constant passed into the fragment program. This constant determines the contribution of the macrostructure and the two noise functions to the resulting scalar value. For example, a weighting constant of $(1.0, 0.0, 0.0)$ will result in the radial distance value only, whereas a constant of $(0.33, 0.33, 0.33)$ will weight all channels equally. Pre-integrated volume rendering requires two such weighted scalar values along a ray for a look-up into a pre-integrated high-frequency transfer function (see Listing 11.3).

It is very easy to animate the fireball by varying the weights passed into the fragment program smoothly. An outwards movement of the flames is simply produced by color cycling in the transfer function. The combination of both effects will create the impression that the fireball actually burns.

Because the procedural effect is produced with a single texture fetch and a single dot product operation (2 fetches and 2 dot products for pre-

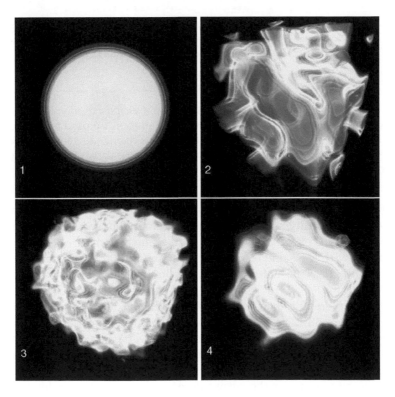

Figure 11.7. Pre-integrated volume rendering of a fireball. The fireball effect is created by mixing different channels of a 3D texture using a dot-product during rendering. (1) Radial distance channel with high frequency fire transfer function. (2) Perlin noise channel with fire-transfer function. (3) Weighted combination of the distance volume and two Perlin noise channels. (4) Like (3) but with higher weights for the Perlin noise channels. (Image from [63]. © Eurographics Association 2002.)

```
// Pre-integration fragment program in Cg
struct v2f {
    float3 TexCoord0 :  TEXCOORD0;
    float3 TexCoord1 :  TEXCOORD1;
};
float4 main(
    v2f IN,
    uniform sampler3D Volume,
    uniform sampler2D PreIntegrationTable,
    uniform float3 weights ) :  COLOR
{

    float2 lutPos;
    // sample front scalar
    lutPos.x = dot(tex3D(Volume, IN.TexCoord0).rgb, weights);
    // sample back scalar
    lutPos.y = dot(tex3D(Volume, IN.TexCoord1).rgb, weights);
    // look up and return pre-integrated value
    return tex2D(PreIntegrationTable, lutPos);
}
```

Listing 11.3. Fireball fragment program in Cg for a slicing-based volume renderer. Two scalars, resulting from weighting two RGB samples, are used for the look-up into the pre-integration table. Note that the texture coordinates for the look-up of subsequent samples along a ray are computed with the vertex program discussed in Section 4.5.

integrated slicing), procedural effects based on this algorithm perform very well. The disadvantage is that we cannot have arbitrarily high frequencies in the resulting effect because the coarse macrostructure and the noise are stored with the same resolution in the individual color channels of the RGB texture; i.e., the noise frequency is limited by the resolution of the macrostructure.

On newer graphics hardware, it is no problem to compute the radial distance function on-the-fly in a fragment program. Because graphics hardware does not have built-in noise functions yet, the computation of the noise functions on-the-fly is usually too expensive. Consequently, only the noise functions are stored in a texture. Higher frequencies can then tile a small noise texture over the output domain. It is simple to achieve this on graphics hardware by using a GL_REPEAT texture environment for the noise texture and applying large texture coordinates. The noise texture is tiled n times over the output domain by applying texture coordinates in the range $[0, n]$. To obtain noise functions at different scales, it might be necessary to employ multiple texture fetches into a single noise texture with differently scaled texture coordinates.

11.6.2   Particle Systems

Particle systems are ideal for modeling realistic visual effects, such as smoke, fire, water splashes, and all objects whose geometry is hard to capture and dynamically changing. In this section, we give a short overview of existing techniques. Particle systems describe complex visual effects as a set of particles. The appearance and the motion of each individual particle is computed using procedural animation or physically-based simulation, usually based on Newton's laws of motion.

The simulation of particles can be independent of each other, or particles can be coupled statically or dynamically. We focus on uncoupled particles, which means that there is no interaction between individual particles in the system. Such particle simulations are most frequently used in computer games. Static coupling is important for cloth simulation as in [270], where forces are introduced between pairs of particles such as stretching or bending springs. The term static means that the set of forces associated with an individual particle does not change over time. Dynamic particle coupling on the other hand is used in applications like swarm simulation, where forces are created dynamically between different individuals to avoid collision or keep them moving in the same direction. The *boids* simulation created by Reynolds [222] is a popular example of a dynamically coupled particle simulation. Uncoupled particle systems for visual effects were originally introduced by Reeves [220] for the *Genesis effect* in the second *Star Trek* movie. The basic data structure and the laws he used to describe particle motion are still present in most particle systems today.

In real-time applications, the performance of simulating and rendering large particle systems is usually bounded either by the fill-rate or by the bus bandwidth, if the particle simulation is done on the CPU. The fill-rate limit is taking effect if the depth complexity of the particle system is high

Figure 11.8. Examples of dynamic visual effects implemented by particle systems with collision detection running entirely on the GPU.

and there is a large overdraw due to relatively large particles in screen space. For a large number of small particles, the available bus bandwidth becomes the bottleneck. In a typical real-time application that performs the particle simulation on the CPU, the bandwidth limitation usually prohibits particle systems larger than 10,000 particles per frame. The bandwidth limit, however, can be overcome if the particle simulation is done on the GPU, instead of the CPU. There are two different approaches.

In *stateless particle systems*, the position and appearance of an individual particle is calculated as a function of its initial state only. The initial state comprises a set of static attributes such as the position from which the particle was emanated, its time of birth, the initial velocity and acceleration. These attributes are stored in a vertex buffer, and the vertex program calculates the current position as a closed-form function of the initial state and the current time. The path of a particle in such a stateless simulation is always deterministic in the sense that a particle cannot react to object collisions or other forces imposed by a dynamically changing environment. An example implementation of a stateless particle system can be found in Chapter 6 of the Cg Tutorial book [71].

State-preserving particle systems can utilize numerical, iterative integration schemes to compute the motion of each individual particle and allow them to react to collision and to external forces. State-preserving simulations running entirely on the GPU introduce the problem that the vertex buffer that stores the state for each individual particle must be updated at runtime. A state-of-the-art solution to this problem is a two-pass approach. The particle data is stored in a large 2D texture, where each texel represents an individual particle. In the first pass, the particle simulation is computed by rendering a textured quad with the same resolution as the data texture. A fragment program updates the particle data for the current time step and renders the result back into a 2D texture. In the second pass, the resulting 2D texture is re-interpreted as a vertex buffer and used to render the particle system as point sprites into the final image. An example implementation of such a state-preserving particle system is part of the NVIDIA SDK [34] and supports collision detection with height fields.

More elaborate implementations of state-preserving particle systems also allow the depth-sorting of particles for correct back-to-front compositing to be performed entirely on the GPU. The implementation by Kipfer et al. [126] supports both interparticle collision and depth sorting. The implementation proposed by Kolb et al. [130] enables efficient detection and handling of collisions with arbitrary objects. For efficiency, they propose to distribute the depth-sorting procedure over multiple frames, which results in convincing visual effects, although at no point in time is a fully sorted list of particles available.

11.7   Simulation

One step further in rendering volumetric effects in games is performing the actual underlying simulation in real time as well. This section gives a brief overview of simulating volumetric effects on GPUs. Traditionally, effects simulation has been performed on the CPU. For real-time rendering, the results are then transferred to the GPU. In general, the field of simulating volumetric effects such as 3D flow, e.g., for fire, water, or smoke, is huge. Most of the simulation methods in the computer graphics literature are heavily optimized for performance but have nevertheless been developed for offline rendering. However, recent advances in *general purpose computations on GPUs* (GPGPU) have introduced a subset of this field to real-time rendering. For an in-depth treatment of the simulation aspect of volumetric effects, we refer to the literature [96, 206, 85].

11.7.1   Computing Simulations on GPUs

The basis for computing numerical simulations on GPUs are the solvers for the underlying systems of equations, e.g., for computational fluid dynamics (CFD). Physical phenomena such as fluid flow [249] are described by partial differential equations. These PDEs are then discretized and transform the problem into the solution of large sparsely populated systems of linear equations. In recent years, powerful GPU solvers for large linear systems have been proposed [142, 141].

11.7.2   Simulating Flow, Clouds, and Other Gaseous Phenomena

A very powerful basic method for a variety of gaseous and flow-like phenomena is the simulation of fluid flow using the incompressible Navier-Stokes

Figure 11.9.   Cloud dynamics computation on GPUs. (Images courtesy of Mark Harris [95].)

equations. Stable solvers for these equations have been proposed [249]. One example application is the simultaneous simulation and rendering of clouds [95, 94], which is illustrated in Figure 11.9. Other gaseous phenomena such as smoke can also be computed in real time, e.g., using the lattice Boltzmann model [287].

11.7.3   A Practical System for Volumetric Effects Simulation in Games

Krüger and Westermann have presented a practical system for both simulating and rendering convincing volumetric effects in real time [143]. Their system integrates two different approaches. The first performs the simulation on a regular 2D grid and extends this grid on-the-fly to 3D during regular volume rendering. This extension can be done very effectively by rotating the 2D grid about the "main axis" of the effect and perturbing the result using 3D noise. Examples of explosions generated in real time using this approach are shown in Figure 11.10.

The second approach uses particle systems. The simulation of flow, e.g., for smoke propagation, is computed for all particles in a fragment program that reads the previous simulation state from a texture and writes the updated state to another texture. The resulting texture data are then used as a vertex array for particle rendering [145]. An example is illustrated in Figure 11.11 (left).

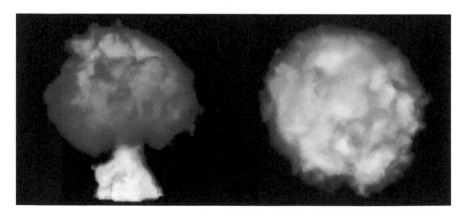

Figure 11.10.   Complex volumetric explosions can be simulated and rendered in real time by performing simulation on a 2D grid and transforming this grid into 3D space during rendering. (Images courtesy of Jens Krüger and Rüdiger Westermann [143], © Eurographics Association 2005.)

Figure 11.11. Depending on the nature of a volumetric effect, it is either rendered using particle systems, such as the smoke shown in the left image, or full volume rendering, such as the log fire in the right image. (Images courtesy of Jens Krüger and Rüdiger Westermann [143], © Eurographics Association 2005.)

11.8 Integrating Volumes with Scene Shadowing and Lighting

In order to truly integrate volumes into a surrounding scene, it is important that the lighting environment for the volume is determined by the scene that surrounds it. That is, the volume has to be lit with the same light sources as the scene and integrate well with how shadows are computed in the geometric part of the scene. This is crucial for volumes that represent objects or purely absorbing media such as fog. In contrast, the appearance of special effects such as fire is dominated by their own emission of light, and thus the occlusion from external light sources is a negligible factor. This leads to the second important problem of scene integration: shadows cast by volumes onto geometry.

As general global illumination is still not possible in real time, current game engines employ many simplifications, assumptions, and approximations. The main choice with respect to scene lighting is whether to use consistent and fully dynamic *direct* illumination or combine dynamic direct illumination with static *indirect* illumination that has been pre-computed. The standard approach for pre-computing static global illumination in games is to use *light maps* [2]. However, when the scene lighting changes and these changes are only applied using direct illumination, the inconsistency between dynamic direct lighting and static indirect lighting becomes very visible.

One traditional approach for coping with this problem that has been common in film rendering for many years is to use only direct illumination and place additional light sources that compensate for the problem of too little illumination in a scene due to the lack of indirect illumination. However, computing shadows for a large number of direct light sources is very expensive. Another approach is to improve the realism of global ambient lighting by using a position-dependent variant called *ambient occlusion* [212]. In this case, global ambient lighting is modulated locally at each point by how much of the hemisphere above it is occluded.

In general, there is a lot of current real-time rendering research that focuses on bridging the gap between direct illumination and fully global illumination. One recent example uses pre-computed local radiance transfer that allows one to adapt indirect scene illumination to a new lighting situation [136].

Integration with lighting. In our discussion, we are focusing on integrating volumes with fully dynamic direct lighting. First of all, this means illuminating the volume with the same light sources that are used for scene illumination. Different kinds of light sources and how they can be used for lighting volumes are discussed in Chapters 5 and 6. Lighting in this case means computing the amount of illumination that potentially arrives at a certain point in space, e.g., inside the volume, if it is not occluded from the light source. Naturally, the second step is then to determine this occlusion, which is the computation of shadows. Integrating volume rendering with shadows is the focus of the remainder of this section.

Integration with shadows. The major factor in computing direct illumination, given that the light emitted by the light source has already been determined, is the computation of *shadows*, which is the occlusion of the light source as seen from a given point in the scene.

Section 11.8.1 starts out by discussing the relation between objects that cast shadows and those that are receivers. The two major approaches for computing shadows in real time are based on *shadow volumes* [37, 104], and *shadow maps* [301]. Sections 11.8.2 and 11.8.3 cover how *hard shadows* can be computed using either one of these two methods, respectively. In principle, hard shadows result from a single point or directional light source and are computed from a binary light source visible/not visible decision. Hard shadows from multiple light sources can be computed by superimposing separate lighting and shadowing for individual light sources.

In Section 11.8.4, we consider a larger view of the concept of shadow maps including *soft shadows* due to volumes that are absorbing light. Section 11.8.5 extends the previous discussion of hard shadows from geometry to soft shadows from geometry, which result from area or volumetric light sources.

11.8.1 Shadow Casters and Shadow Receivers

In shadow computations, we can distinguish between two major types of objects with respect to their interaction. Objects that cast shadows, i.e., objects that occlude some parts of the scene as "seen" by a light source, are called *shadow casters*. Objects that can potentially be occluded from a light source, i.e., some or all parts of them do not receive direct lighting from that light source, are called *shadow receivers*.

Shadow algorithms very often make assumptions with respect to the properties and relations of these two types of objects in a scene. This is especially true when volumetric objects and geometric objects are mixed. A general method that handles all different cases seamlessly are *deep shadow maps*, which are described below in Section 11.8.4 and can be used for building up an intuition of all the different cases. The different cases of casting and receiving shadows in our context are as follows.

1. Shadows cast by geometry onto geometry.

2. Shadows cast by geometry onto a volume.

3. Shadows cast by a volume onto geometry.

4. Shadows cast by a volume onto a volume.

5. Shadows within a volume.

The first case is the standard case for shadow computations that can either be handled by using shadow volumes or shadow maps. In the following sections, we focus on the relation to volume rendering. More detailed discussions that focus on geometric scenes not including volumes can be found in standard textbooks on the topic [2].

The second case can be computed by using the same set-up as in the first case with regard to shadow casters and using it in an appropriate way to modify the incoming illumination when a volume is rendered. As we will see below, shadow volumes cannot easily be used for this purpose in real-time rendering, whereas shadow maps are easy to integrate. Sections 11.8.2 and 11.8.3 focus on this case.

The third case is considerably more expensive than the two previous cases. It can be handled by using full volume rendering from the point of view of the light source in order to generate a special shadow map that stores accumulated absorption instead of depth. There is no universal term for such a map. We will refer to it as an *attenuation map*, because this term is more common than calling it an absorption map, for example. An attenuation map can be stored in an alpha-only texture map that is accessed just as with shadow mapping, but instead of a depth value for a binary decision, it yields an alpha value that modulates the light source intensity depending on how much absorption occurs between it and the receiving point.

If the volume not only absorbs but also emits light, this emission could be included here as well. The whole process then turns into a full volume rendering from the point of view of the light source, resulting in a map containing both color and alpha channels. Note that Chapter 5 suggests representing a volumetric light source with an environment map, which is a very similar idea. The only difference is the addition of an absorption term if the volume also casts shadows.

Shadows that are cast by a volume onto receiving geometry or a volume are related to soft shadows that are due to area light sources in many respects. The latter kind of soft shadows are discussed in Section 11.8.5.

The fourth case is a mixture between the third case, for the shadow casting part, and the second case, for the shadow receiving part, and can also be implemented that way. Fortunately, the overall contribution of this case is often much less important than the three previous cases. Therefore, in real-time rendering this case is likely to be neglected. However, this naturally depends a lot on the structure of the scene. An example where this case can indeed be a very important part would be a dense field of clouds.

The last case is definitely the most expensive to compute in general. Unfortunately, shadows within a volume due to absorption by the volume itself are often a very important part of a realistic overall appearance. Apart from the unified discussion in Section 11.8.4, we do not handle this case in this chapter. This general case of shadows in volumes is discussed in detail in Chapter 6.

11.8.2 Volume Rendering and Shadow Volumes

The basic shadow-volume approach allows one to compute high-quality shadows with exact hard edges [37]. In contrast with shadow mapping (Section 11.8.3), it does not introduce sampling artifacts inherent to the shadows themselves because the resolution of shadow computation depends directly on the resolution of the output image. The key is to consider the volume spanned by a point or directional light source and shadow-casting geometry. This volume is represented by its bounding polygons, which are composed of extruded geometry edges. This extrusion happens in the plane that is spanned by an edge and the light-source position.

The standard approach for using the resulting shadow volume geometry in real-time rendering is to employ the hardware stencil buffer [104]. This real-time variant of the shadow volumes algorithm is usually called *stencil shadow volumes*, or simply *stencil shadows*. All opaque scene geometry is rasterized into the depth buffer first, as seen from the viewpoint. Then, the bounding geometry of shadow volumes is rasterized into the stencil buffer in such a way that front-facing polygons increase the stencil value and back-facing polygons decrease it. The depth test is enabled during this rasterization, which effectively intersects scene geometry with shadow volume geometry on a per-pixel basis. After all shadow volume geometry has been rasterized, the stencil buffer identifies which pixels of the scene geometry are in shadow and which are not, depending on the corresponding stencil value.

Implementing robust stencil shadow volumes is not straightforward due to several special cases, e.g., when the viewpoint itself is inside a shadow volume [2]. The standard approach is now often called *z-pass stencil shadows*, because it renders shadow volumes where the depth test passes. However, a more robust approach is to use *z-fail stencil shadows* instead, which is the inverse approach [66]. There are also several combinations and alternatives, e.g., [107, 150].

Unfortunately, using stencil shadow volumes for computing the effect of scene shadows on true volume rendering is very complicated and not possible with a direct approach. The major problem is that stencil shadows essentially store the state of inside/outside shadow for each pixel only for one 3D position per pixel. This position corresponds to the visible opaque scene geometry for that pixel, which is determined using depth buffering and is only a single location in three-space. In order to integrate this with volume rendering, however, the decision whether a point in three-space is in shadow or not has to be made for many points along a ray shot through a single pixel. One possibility to do this with shadow volumes would be to track all intersections of viewing rays with shadow volume bounding polygons and store all intersections for a single ray as a linked list associated with each pixel. Then, during shadow determination at any point in the volume, this linked list can be queried for which segment contains the point in question and what the count of shadow volume entries and exits is at that point. This would essentially be a stencil buffer with an arbitrary number of entries per pixel instead of just one. Naturally, such an approach is not feasible for real-time rendering. It is in fact very similar to the idea of *deep shadow maps*, which are discussed in Section 11.8.4 below.

Another possibility would be to clip a volume's bounding box against the planes constituting a shadow volume and rendering the resulting subvolumes separately. In this case, each subvolume can be rendered with a constant lighting value with respect to a shadow-casting light source.

However, a practical implementation of this approach would be extremely complicated if not impossible, most of all due to overlapping shadow volumes.

Fortunately, instead of shadow volumes, it is much easier to integrate the alternative approach of *shadow mapping* with volume rendering. This is described in the next section.

11.8.3   Volume Rendering and Shadow Maps

Shadow mapping uses the idea of determining visibility via depth buffering, but with respect to the light source instead of the viewpoint. This can be used for computing shadows because the concepts of being in shadow or not and the visibility of the light source from a point in the scene are equivalent.

In order to generate a *shadow map*, the opaque scene geometry is rasterized using depth buffering as seen from the light source. The resulting depth map then is the shadow map. The major operation apart from the creation of the shadow map is mapping coordinates from view space into the space of the light source that has been used for generating the shadow map. When the distance of a point on scene geometry to the light source is known, a simple comparison with the depth, i.e., also a distance, stored in the shadow map at the corresponding location suffices. It determines whether the point in question is in shadow or not.

Fortunately, in contrast to shadow volumes, shadow mapping is easy to integrate with volume rendering. The major difference is that a shadow map allows one to query visibility with respect to the light source for any point in three-space at any time with a single shadow-map look-up and without requiring additional storage. So for every point in the volume where illumination is to be computed, e.g., using one of the methods described in Chapter 5, an additional shadow-map look-up is performed. The light source is enabled or disabled at that point depending on the result of the depth comparison of the shadow-map value with the distance to the external light source at that point.

11.8.4   Deep Shadow Maps

Shadow mapping with *deep shadow maps* [167] currently is not a real-time rendering method. However, they provide a very powerful unified description of shadows from and inside of volumes, semitransparent geometry, and opaque geometry. All the different combinations are handled seamlessly without assigning special cases of shadow casters and shadow receivers. We describe deep shadow maps in this section in order to give a better understanding of volumetric shadowing that is due to absorption, as well as its interaction with the scene's geometry.

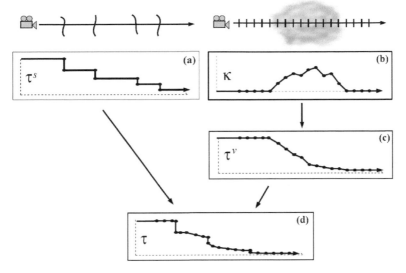

Figure 11.12. Deep shadow maps unify absorption events along rays: (a) shows the reduction of transmittance at discrete locations in space where semitransparent geometry is intersected; (b) shows local extinction of light due to intersection of a volume, which is integrated to yield transmittance in (c); (d) a deep shadow map stores the combined visibility (transmittance) function along viewing rays. (Illustration courtesy of Tom Lokovic and Eric Veach [167]. Used by permission. © 2000, ACM, Inc.)

Deep shadow maps extend the idea of shadow mapping where instead of a single depth per pixel the entire *visibility function* along the ray corresponding to that pixel is stored. The visibility function can be stored in terms of attenuation of light or light transmittance, its inverse. The latter is used in the original work on deep shadow maps [167], where the contribution for each pixel is also pre-filtered in order to obtain high-quality results. Figure 11.12 illustrates different visibility functions using transmittance. Naturally, when such visibility functions are available, the absorption of light at a certain position in front of the deep shadow map can be obtained by querying it at that position. In order to make storing visibility functions practical, they are stored in a compressed format that both reduces storage and makes querying them faster. In general, a query operation of a visibility function in a deep shadow map requires a search until the entry corresponding to the position in question has been found.

Deep shadow maps naturally integrate all possibilities of light being occluded or partially absorbed along rays. Opaque geometry basically sets transmittance to zero at the corresponding position (or to a value that is

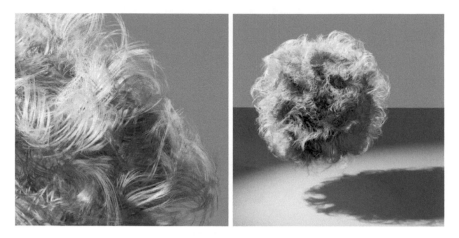

Figure 11.13. A major application of deep shadow maps is the computation of shadows in highly complex semitransparent geometry such as a collection of hair fibers. (Images courtesy of Tom Lokovic and Eric Veach [167]. Used by permission. © 2000, ACM, Inc.)

Figure 11.14. Deep shadow maps allow one to correctly combine geometry and volume rendering without taking care of special cases. (Images courtesy of Tom Lokovic and Eric Veach [167]. Used by permission. © 2000, ACM, Inc.)

not completely zero if pixel filtering is employed for antialiasing). Semi-transparent geometry basically reduces the transmittance by a constant amount at the corresponding location, resulting in a step function in the visibility. General volumes influence the visibility function in accordance with their absorption of light.

11.8.5 Volume Rendering and Soft Shadows

A topic that is related to shadows cast by volumes is rendering soft shadows. However, when shadows are cast by opaque geometry, soft shadows result when area light sources are used instead of point light sources. Naturally, as soon as a light source is not a single point, a varying amount of some geometry can be occluded depending on its relative position to the light and occluding geometry. This results in *umbra* and *penumbra* regions. Umbra regions are completely occluded from the entire light source and thus in shadow. Penumbra regions are only partially occluded from the light source and thus receive less light but are not completely in shadow.

Recently, the topic of computing approximate or exact soft shadows with modified shadow-volume approaches has made significant advances [6, 7, 22]. The capability to cast soft shadows from video textures as light sources [6] could be used to render shadows cast by a volume onto geometry. Instead of a video texture, an attenuation map that also records volume emission would be used.

11.9 Further Reading

There exists a wealth of introductory and advanced material on game programming. The books by Watt and Policarpo [283, 284] provide a very good overview, as well as more details on using programmable graphics hardware in game graphics [285]. Another very good introductory text for game-engine design is the book by Eberly [56]. For game graphics, *Real-Time Rendering* by Akenine-Möller and Haines [2] is a very good resource. The Game Programming Gems series [59] also offers many good articles on game-related topics, including special-effects rendering in games. The *GPU Gems* books [72, 210] are a very good resource for shader programming and GPU-tailored graphics algorithms. Another collection of articles that focuses exclusively on shader programming is contained in the ShaderX books [60].

Rendering isosurfaces or level sets of volumes is a topic that is very relevant to rendering special effects such as physically based fire [196] and water [65]. In general, level set methods are a powerful approach to deforming or editing surfaces [192] and morphing shapes [267]. Although these methods are not yet intended for real-time use, they are already common in the special-effects industry. The book by Osher and Fedkiw [205] is a very good introduction to the area of level set methods. Level set computations can be performed on GPUs [158, 96, 206], and a fast volume renderer for isosurfaces enables viewing the results in real time, e.g., using ray casting [93].

Natural phenomena such as fog can also be simulated and rendered on unstructured grids [250]. As described in Chapter 7, ray casting can be used to efficiently render such unstructured volumes.

12

Volume Modeling

IN SCIENTIFIC SCENARIOS, VOLUMETRIC DATA is frequently obtained by 3D measurement, such as computerized tomography (CT) or magnetic resonance imaging (MRI). The volumetric objects used for visual arts and animation usually do not exist in the real world. They cannot be simply obtained by scanning an existing object. This chapter deals with modeling techniques that support the artist in creating volumetric models from scratch. Voxelization techniques allow volumetric representations to be created from polygonal surface descriptions by spatial discretization. Procedural modeling techniques are used to describe internal structures. Similar to photographed texture images for polygonal models, real 3D image data acquired by tomographic measurement can be used to supplement volumetric models.

As an example, Figure 12.1 illustrates the creation of a volumetric model for a three-legged creature. The outer shell of the creature as well as the inner organs, such as bones and muscles, are created using traditional surface modeling techniques. For internal structures, both procedural volumes and measured data has been used. 3D image processing operations, such as blurring and edge enhancement, are used on the voxelized polygonal models. All individual textures are finally combined using 3D compositing techniques. Finally, transfer functions are applied to define the optical properties inside the volume, and the model is rendered using a specified shading model.

Another possibility of creating or modifying volumetric models is to deform or sculpt them directly in 3D. Approaches to volume deformation will be addressed in Chapter 13. There, we will also see how the described tripod creature can be animated using procedural techniques.

Although the process of creating volumetric models is usually performed offline, the artist wants to see the effect of his modeling operation on the

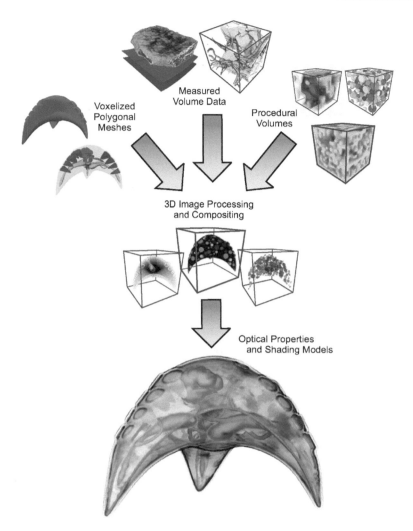

Figure 12.1. An example of volume modeling: volume data can be created by voxelization of polygonal surfaces, by measurement, or by a procedural model. Different source volumes are composited together using arithmetic operations and 3D image processing algorithms.

final model immediately on the screen. This is important to seamlessly integrate volumetric models into a production pipeline for visual arts. The voxelization, filtering, and compositing steps described above can of course be easily implemented in software. The resulting volume must be recomputed and uploaded to the graphics board whenever the artist applies some changes. Such a procedure will hardly result in direct visual feedback dur-

ing interaction. For this reason, it is important to perform as much of the
described operations as possible directly on the graphics board, efficiently
avoiding unnecessary bus transfers.

12.1   Rendering into a 3D Texture

One of the basic operations that frequently recur during volume modeling
is the creation of a 3D texture in real time. Such a texture can store
a voxelized volume object, a sampled version of a procedural texture, or
the result of compositing multiple volumetric objects into a 3D texture.
In order to speed up the volume modeling and compositing pipeline, 3D
textures can be used to cache intermediate results whenever it is necessary.

As mentioned in Section 2.4.2, frame-buffer objects allow a graphics
application to directly render into slices of a 3D texture. Depending on the
underlying graphics processor, directly rendering to a 3D texture might be

```
#ifdef GL_EXT_framebuffer_object
  GLuint framebufferObject;
  // create a frame-buffer object
  glGenFramebuffersEXT(1, &framebufferObject);
  // create a 3D texture object
  GLuint textureName;
  glGenTextures(1, &textureName);
  glBindTexture(GL_TEXTURE_3D, textureName);
  glTexImage3D(GL_TEXTURE_3D, 0, GL_RGBA8,
    size_x, size_y, size_z, GL_RGBA, GL_UNSIGNED_BYTE, NULL);
  glBindFramebufferEXT(  // bind the frame-buffer object
    GL_FRAMEBUFFER_EXT, framebufferObject);
  for(int z = 0; z < size_z; ++z) {
    // attach a z-slice to color target
    glFramebufferTexture3DEXT(
      GL_FRAMEBUFFER_EXT,         // bind target
      GL_COLOR_ATTACHMENT0_EXT,   // attachment point
      GL_TEXTURE_3D,              // texture target
      textureName,                // texture object
      0,                          // render target id
      z);                         // 3D texture slice
    renderIntoSlice(z); // now render into the z-slice
  } // for(..
  // unbind the frame-buffer object
  glBindFramebufferEXT(GL_FRAMEBUFFER_EXT, 0);
#endif // defined GL_EXT_framebuffer_object
```

Listing 12.1.   OpenGL code for rendering into a 3D texture using frame-buffer
objects.

```
#ifdef GL_EXT_framebuffer_object
// Create depth buffer
GLuint depthBuffer;
glGenRenderbuffersEXT(1, &depthBuffer);
glBindRenderbufferEXT(GL_RENDERBUFFER_EXT, depthBuffer);
glRenderbufferStorageEXT(GL_RENDERBUFFER_EXT,
    GL_DEPTH_COMPONENT16, width, height);
// attach the depth buffer to the currently bound FBO
glFramebufferRenderbufferEXT(
    GL_FRAMEBUFFER_EXT, GL_DEPTH_ATTACHMENT_EXT,
    GL_RENDERBUFFER_EXT, depthBuffer);
#endif // defined GL_EXT_framebuffer_object
```

Listing 12.2. OpenGL code for creating and attaching a depth buffer to an existing frame-buffer object.

fast or slow. Performance will depend on the storage scheme that is used to lay out the voxel data in memory. If the 3D texture data is not stored as planes of voxels, the graphics driver will possibly have to copy the texture data after the rendering. With frame-buffer objects, however, such a copy operation is completely hidden from the user.

An OpenGL code sample for direct rendering into slices of 3D textures is given in Listing 12.1 using the frame-buffer object extension. If necessary, multiple render targets can be used, to simultaneously render into more than one slice at a time. For more details on frame-buffer objects, please refer to the original specification document available at the OpenGL extension registry [243]. On systems that do not support frame-buffer objects, the contents of the frame buffer must be copied into the 3D texture for each slice using the OpenGL command glCopyTexSubImage. This approach will most likely result in reduced performance compared with frame-buffer objects. One important advantage of frame-buffer objects is the flexibility to only create those buffers that are actually needed for rendering. This means that the set-up described in Listing 12.1 does not initially provide a depth buffer to handle occlusion. If a depth buffer is required, it must be created separately and attached to the render target as displayed in Listing 12.2

12.2   Voxelization

Voxelization refers to the conversion of a polygonal surface into a volume data set and represents the conversion of a *parametric* into an *implicit* sur-

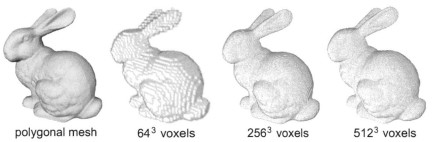

polygonal mesh 64^3 voxels 256^3 voxels 512^3 voxels

Figure 12.2. Results of the voxelization of a polygonal mesh into volume data of 64^3, 256^3, and 512^3 resolution.

face description. Apart from volume graphics, such a conversion is often required in multiscale surface analysis or constructive solid geometry. Figure 12.2 displays the result of the voxelization of a polygonal mesh into volume data sets of different resolution.

In this section, we will examine a simple voxelization approach, which is efficient for polygonal meshes of arbitrary shape and will run on almost any graphics hardware. Voxelization is closely related to clipping. With slight modifications, the surface-based clipping techniques described in Chapter 15 can as well be used for voxelization. In some cases, clipping might even be more efficient than the described voxelization algorithm, depending on the underlying hardware and the depth complexity of the clipping object.

On-the-fly voxelization requires the calculation of the intersection of a polygonal model with each slice plane of the volume. Such a plane intersection can be easily implemented in hardware using a multipass technique that renders the intersection polygons directly into a 2D or 3D texture. Only a few simple requirements for the polygonal surface must be met.

1. The surface must be a closed polygonal mesh without boundaries. Of course, this property is always necessary for the definition of an inner and an outer region of the object for voxelization.

2. The surface must consist of planar polygons. It is easy to meet this requirement by tessellating arbitrary polygons into triangles. Such a tessellation is performed by the graphics hardware anyway, but the OpenGL specification does not guarantee the internal tessellation to be consistent over several frames.

3. The vertex ordering and orientation of the normal vectors must be consistent. This is the most important requirement. It means that the normal vectors should not flip direction for adjacent faces, which

is ensured by using either clockwise or counterclockwise orientation of the vertices for each face. Consistent vertex ordering is crucial to identify front and back facing polygons at run-time.

The following algorithm works for multiple closed polygonal surfaces of arbitrary shape at the same time. It requires a depth buffer, however, which must be cleared once for every slice to be computed. Two colors (or scalar values) must be specified, one for the interior and one for the exterior of the object. In the following, we refer to these colors as *foreground* and *background* colors. We assume that the color rendering target is cleared with the background color and that the depth buffer is cleared with its default value of 1.0. The projection matrix must be set to orthogonal projection, and the viewing volume must contain the entire polygonal mesh. The bounding box of the polygonal mesh can be used as viewing volume.

The multipass rendering technique is outlined in Figure 12.3. The viewing direction for the orthogonal projection is indicated by the arrows. The procedure of calculating the intersection between a polygonal object and a plane (Figure 12.3 (a)) is divided into four steps:

1. A clipping plane is set up with the same position and orientation as the current slice plane (Figure 12.3 (b)). This clipping plane removes the portion of geometry that faces the camera, so that the interior of the polygonal object becomes visible.

2. Front-face culling is enabled (Figure 12.3 (c)). Only the back faces of the polygonal object are rendered using the foreground color and the depth buffer is updated simultaneously. The cross section drawn into the color buffer is indicated by the red circle. The result, however, is not yet correct because some back faces might be occluded by front faces with respect to the camera position.

3. In a second rendering pass, the erroneous portions from Step 2 are removed by drawing the front faces again in background color (Figure 12.3 (d)). The depth test is required here in order to ensure that only those parts of the back faces are overdrawn that are actually occluded by front faces.

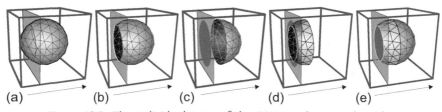

(a)   (b)   (c)   (d)   (e)

Figure 12.3. The individual steps of the GPU voxelization algorithm.

4. The color buffer now contains the correct cross section of the polygonal clipping object (Figure 12.3 (e)). The next slice of the volume can now be created by shifting the clipping plane to the next raster position and starting again with Step 2. This loop is repeated until the whole volume is created.

An example implementation in OpenGL is displayed in Listing 12.3. The performance depends both on the size of the volume and on the size of the polygonal mesh. For each slice, the whole polygonal mesh must be traversed twice. The original idea for this algorithm was introduced by Westermann and Ertl [296] in the context of volume clipping.

```
void renderIntoSlice(z) {

  GLclampf pForeColor[3] = {1.0,1.0,1.0};
  GLclampf pBackColor[3] = {0.0,0.0,0.0};

  // clear the color and depth buffer
  glClearColor(
    pBackColor[0], pBackColor[1], pBackColor[2],1.0);
  glClear(GL_COLOR_BUFFER_BIT |GL_DEPTH_BUFFER_BIT);
  glEnable(GL_DEPTH_TEST); // activate the depth test

  // STEP 1:  Setup a clipping plane
  glEnable(GL_CLIP_PLANE0);
  glClipPlane(GL_CLIP_PLANE0, /* ... */);

  // STEP 2:  First rendering pass
  glColor3fv(pForeColor); // draw in foreground color
  glEnable(GL_CULL_FACE); // enable front face culling
  glCullFace(GL_FRONT);
  drawPolyMesh();  // draw the polygonal object

  // STEP 3:  Second rendering pass
  glColor3fv(pBackColor); // draw in background color
  glCullFace(GL_BACK); // enable back face culling
  drawPolyMesh(); // draw the polygonal object

  glDisable(GL_CULL_FACE);

}
```

Listing 12.3. OpenGL code sample for on-the-fly voxelization using multipass rendering. The procedure can be used in Listing 12.1 to directly render into a 3D texture.

Although the algorithm is outlined for a spherical object in Figure 12.3, it is not restricted to convex shapes. Indeed, for the special case of convex shapes, the algorithm will perform well even without the depth buffer, but the clipping approach for convex surfaces described in Chapter 15 will be much more efficient in this case. As we will see later, the benefit of this algorithm over the surface-based clipping approaches is that it is independent of the depth complexity of the polygonal mesh.

12.3   Procedural Modeling

In contrast with the voxelization, procedural modeling techniques do not define the volume explicitly as a set of discrete samples. Instead, the volume is specified by algorithms or code segments, which define rules to evaluate the scalar field at any given point in space. Procedural modeling approaches comprise powerful techniques for simultaneously creating shape and appearance with both macro- and microstructures that are tedious or even impossible to model by hand. They are useful for creating apparently infinite irregular patterns, such as the structure of wood, marble, stone, and many other natural materials. They also allow the creation of complex shapes such as smoke and fire.

The main advantages of procedural models are their flexibility, their low memory requirements, and their resolution-independence. As drawbacks, procedural models are usually difficult to create and to debug, and the results of complex procedures are often hardly predictable. A major problem with procedural textures are aliasing effects, which are caused by inadequate discretization of the result. Possible methods to alleviate such aliasing effects are to integrate anti-aliasing techniques into the procedure or use stochastic multisampling techniques as outlined in Section 9.1.

When creating a 3D texture with procedural models, you can follow many different strategies. You can easily create hand-crafted procedures from simple building blocks, such as ramps, step functions, or conditionals. Alternatively, you can use spectral synthesis with sine waves, other periodic signals, or band-limited noise functions. There are also very effective random placement strategies that allow simple items to be inserted at irregular patterns into your 3D texture. All of these techniques can of course be combined to create complex procedural textures. A detailed discussion of the wide variety of procedural modeling techniques is far beyond the scope of this book. As an introduction and reference for procedural approaches to texturing and modeling, we point the reader to the excellent book by Ebert et al. [58].

Procedural 3D textures can be evaluated at run time using elaborately designed fragment programs instead of texture fetches. Depending on the computational complexity, the time it takes to evaluate a procedural model, however, might slow down the overall rendering speed. For real-time applications, it is sometimes useful to pre-cache complex procedural textures or intermediate results at a certain resolution. This is easily achieved by rendering the procedural model directly into a 3D texture image.

As an example, a simple procedural 3D texture is displayed in Listing 12.4. The procedure uses spectral synthesis to create the smoke-like structures displayed in Figure 12.4. Note that there is no texture fetch instruction in the fragment shader, because the entire texture is defined as a closed-form function. In spectral synthesis, the value is calculated as a weighted sum of periodic functions, such as sinusoids

$$v(x) = \sum_{i=0}^{N} A_i \sin(f_i\, x + \varphi_i)\,, \tag{12.1}$$

with different frequencies f_i, phases φ_i and amplitudes A_i. The 3D version of this function is obtained as the product of different sine waves in x-, y-, and z-directions as outlined in Listing 12.4. The smoke-like structure is modeled by a fractal power spectrum, which means that the amplitude A_i is proportional to $1/f_i$. For each loop iteration in the code sample, the amplitude is halved and the frequency is doubled. The phase shifts φ_i are defined as uniform parameters for each direction separately.

On modern GPUs, the evaluation of a sinusoid is as efficient as a single multiplication. If the computation gets too complex, however, we can simply render the procedural texture into slices of a 3D texture as explained in Section 12.1. In order to capture the complex shape of many volumetric objects such as clouds, smoke, or fur, high-frequency details are essential. We have already seen an example of a procedural fireball effect in Section 11.6.1. This was very similar to Ebert's approach to cloud modeling [58]. A coarse geometry is used to describe the macrostructure and procedural noise is added for the microstructure. With atmospheric lighting added, such an approach can efficiently be used to model clouds as

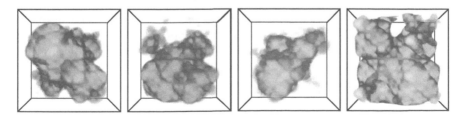

Figure 12.4. Procedural 3D textures obtained by spectral synthesis. The images have been created by the fragment program in Listing 12.4 with different settings for the uniform parameters.

```
half4 main(half3  uvw  :  TEXCOORD0,
           uniform half3 phases[5],
           uniform half  startStep,
           uniform half  endStep) :  COLOR
{
    float value = 0.0;
    float frequency = 3.0;
    float amplitude = 0.5;

    for (int i = 0; i < 5; ++i) {
        half3 phase = phases[i];

        value += amplitude *
            sin(frequency*uvw.x + phase.x) *
            sin(frequency*uvw.y + phase.y) *
            sin(frequency*uvw.z + phase.z);

        amplitude /= 2.0;
        frequency *= 2.0;
    }

    value = abs(value);
    float alpha = smoothstep(startStep,endStep,value);

    return half4(value.rrr, alpha*alpha);
}
```

Listing 12.4. Cg fragment program for a procedural 3D texture using spectral synthesis. The texture is created by adding up multiple sine waves with different amplitude, frequency, and phase. Resulting images are displayed in Figure 12.4

shown in Figure 12.5. The idea is to randomly perturb the texture coordinates with a turbulence function. This turbulence function is essentially the same as the fractal sum from Equation 12.1, except that a 3D noise texture is used instead of the sinusoids. Perlin noise [207, 98] is ideal in this case because it is band-limited and reproducible. Similar approaches can be used to model fur and hair as shown in Figure 12.6.

The volume-perturbation approach employs a small 3D perturbation texture, not larger than 32^3 voxels. Each texel is initialized with three random 8-bit numbers, stored as RGB components, and then blurred slightly to hide the artifacts caused by trilinear interpolation. The wrap mode for the texture coordinates of the noise texture is set to repeat. This allows us to create noise fields of different frequency simply by scaling the

Figure 12.5. Procedural clouds. The image on the top shows the underlying data, 64^3. The center image shows the perturbed volume. The bottom image shows the perturbed volume lit from behind with low-frequency noise added to the indirect attenuation to achieve subtle iridescence effects.

Figure 12.6.   Procedural fur generated by texture-coordinate perturbation. The left figure shows the original data set of the veiled chameleon. In the right figure, fur was added by perturbing texture coordinates using a procedural turbulence function. The amplitude of the perturbation is modulated as a function of the original scalar value. (The data set of the veiled chameleon is courtesy of the UTCT data archive (http://utct.tacc.utexas.edu/).)

```
half4 main(half3  uvw  :  TEXCOORD0,
           uniform half      amplitude
           uniform sampler3D noiseTex,
           uniform sampler3D dataTex) :  COLOR
{
    // calculate the turbulence field
    half3 perturb = 0.0;
    perturb += 1.0   * tex3D(noiseTex, 2.0*uvw) - 0.5;
    perturb += 0.5   * tex3D(noiseTex, 4.0*uvw) - 0.25;
    perturb += 0.25  * tex3D(noiseTex, 8.0*uvw) - 0.125;
    perturb += 0.125 * tex3D(noiseTex,16.0*uvw) - 0.0625;

    uvw += amplitude * perturb;

    return tex3D(dataTexture,uvw);
}
```

Listing 12.5.   Cg fragment program for texture coordinate perturbation using a turbulence function. The perturbation field is created by spectral synthesis with predefined noise textures.

Figure 12.7.   Volumetric model of the Stanford bunny with procedural fur and translucent shading. The hollow model is rendered as a highly scattering material with low absorption (high albedo). See Chapter 6 for the shading techniques.

texture coordinates. A fragment shader for texture coordinate perturbation is displayed in Listing 12.5. The turbulence function is calculated by adding multiple copies of the noise texture at different scales:

$$\text{turbulence}(\mathbf{x}) = \sum_{i=0}^{N} A_i \cdot \text{noise}(f_i \mathbf{x}) \,. \qquad (12.2)$$

The result is used to perturb the texture coordinates for the 3D texture that contains the macrostructures. The amplitude A_i of the noise field should again be inversely proportional to its frequency f_i. To animate the perturbation, variable offsets can be added to each noise texture coordinate and updated with each frame. Procedural techniques can be applied to most volumetric natural phenomena. As we have seen, high-frequency details can be added to a coarse macrostructure volume by the use of small noise textures, and there is no need to deal with large volumetric data. The modeling techniques described in this chapter can of course be combined with translucency and global illumination effects, as described in Chapter 6. An example of a translucent volumetric model with procedurally defined fur is displayed in Figure 12.7.

12.4   Compositing and Image Processing

Sophisticated volumetric models can be created by combining voxelized polygonal surfaces with procedural models and acquired 3D image data.

The source volumes are modified using image processing operations, such as linear and nonlinear filters. There exist a vast number of image processing operations that can be used to emphasize certain features of the volume. Compositing operations are used to combine multiple source volumes. For an overview of image-processing operations, we refer the reader to *The Image Processing Handbook* [229] or any other introductory text on image processing.

Low-pass filtering with 3D box filters or Gaussian filter kernels should be applied to slightly blur the boundaries of voxelized surfaces. This will effectively remove wood-grain artifacts in the final image. Gradient estimators, such as the ones described in Section 5.3.1 or other high-pass filters, can be used to emphasize skin-like structures. If the voxelized surface should appear more like a membrane than like a solid object, the gradient magnitude can be computed for a slightly blurred voxelized surface and added to the final volume. Nonlinear range filters can be applied, such as morphological operations (erosion, dilation, etc.) to enhance selected features inside the volume data. Median filters and anisotropic diffusion filters are helpful in removing noise from measured 3D data without blurring the original boundaries too much. Both linear and non-linear filters can be easily implemented as fragment programs that sample a source texture multiple times, do the convolution, and render the result back into a 3D texture. As an alternative, many GPUs support linear filter convolution directly in hardware. In OpenGL, applying a linear filter simply requires a copy operation in GPU memory. For more information on hardware convolution, see the OpenGL programming guide [240].

12.5   Further Reading

Besides the described GPU-based voxelization method, there exist many other approaches to voxelization. Fundamental techniques of voxelization are described in a paper by Cohen-Or and Kaufman [30]. Šrámek and Kaufman [246] propose a method for voxelizing analytically defined objects by the use of linear filters. Fang and Liao [68] demonstrate a GPU-based voxelization algorithm for constructive solid geometry applications. The ideas described in this paper can easily be adapted to modern graphics hardware. A voxelization technique that incorporates antialiasing techniques has been proposed by Wang and Kaufman [277].

Texture-synthesis techniques are used to generate infinite, nonrepeating textures from a set of small example images. The goal and the challenge here is to create an output image that is perceptually similar to the input texture. Perceptual similarity is often modeled by Markov random fields as demonstrated in a variety of publications [42, 62, 286, 61]. The perceptual quality of the input texture is preserved by forcing that pixels from similar neighborhoods in the input image are chosen as neighbors in the synthesized texture.

The first approaches to texture synthesis tried to derive a parametric model of the input images, which is used to synthesize new textures [214]. Other techniques perform texture synthesis by transferring pixels from the input image to the output image [42, 62, 286]. More recent approaches copy whole patches from the input image and calculate the *seam* between neighboring patches [61, 148] afterwards. Similar approaches utilize Wang tiles for nonperiodic tiling of repetitive patterns [248, 29]. Although these techniques are used to synthesize 2D textures, most of them are well applicable to 3D textures and can be used to create interesting structures from scanned 3D data.

In the context of biomedical imaging, the term *fusion* refers to the combination of complementary information obtained from multiple data sets into a final image. Similar to compositing in digital arts, multiple data sets are merged together in an intelligent way that generates a new data set that contains the joint information. Fusion techniques for multimodal images in medicine, machine vision, and remote sensing applications [1, 28, 175] are still topics of active research. Li et al. [163] have suggested a fusion algorithm that performs a sequence of forward and backward wavelet transformations. Matsopoulos et al. [179] perform hierarchical fusion based on feature extraction from morphological pyramids. Other approaches utilize pixel classification approaches [15] such as the Bayesian probabilistic method [109] or entropy-based fusion [189]. Mukhopadhyay and Chanda [190] introduced an image fusion method based on multiscale morphology. Most of these approaches are based on information theory, and their application as compositing operators for visual arts is questionable. The computational complexity of many of these techniques will probably prohibit a fast evaluation at interactive frame rates.

13

Volume Deformation and Animation

UP UNTIL NOW, WE HAVE CONSIDERED our volumetric object to be static. In medicine, engineering, and many other scientific disciplines, volumetric objects undergo dynamic nonlinear deformations. A prominent example arises in computer-assisted surgery, where tomography data from therapy planning must be deformed to match nonrigid patient motion during the intervention.

Volumetric deformation is also important as a supplement to traditional surface models in visual arts. As with almost all models in computer graphics, motion and dynamics are important means of conveying the artist's intention. In this chapter, we are going to investigate possibilities of changing the shape of volumetric objects dynamically and interactively. Before we start looking at volumetric deformation techniques, however, we will first reconsider how deformation is performed with traditional surface descriptions.

13.1 Modeling Paradigms

One of the most common modeling paradigms is the separation of *shape* from *appearance*. In traditional modeling, the shape of an object is described by means of an *explicit* geometric surface representation. Its appearance is defined by material properties and texture maps, which together form a complex *shading model*. Sophisticated modeling techniques, such as bump mapping or displacement mapping, may blur and shift the stripline between shape and appearance in one direction or the other, but the separation is always evident in computer graphics.

In character animation, for example, models usually have a skeleton and a skin, and their motion is calculated using forward and inverse kine-

329

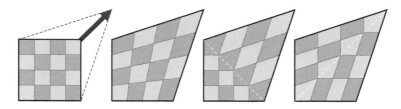

Figure 13.1. Far left: a texture-mapped quadrangle is deformed by displacing one vertex. Middle left: bilinear interpolation of texture coordinates within the quadrangle would result in an evenly mapped texture. Middle right and far right: splitting the quadrangle into two triangles with barycentric interpolation results in different distortions depending on the actual tessellation (white dotted line).

matics. The shape of a model's skin is deformed based on the motion of the joints and the corresponding skin weights, but the appearance of the skin is usually not modified. Of course, there are sophisticated virtual characters who have bump maps that are controlled by the skeleton in order to create wrinkles, but let us neglect such specific cases for now. This means that most of the time we are displacing vertices (or control points) while maintaining the original texture coordinate binding. As an example, if we displace one vertex of a triangle by modifying its position without changing the texture coordinate, the assigned texture map will stretch to fit onto the modified area of the triangle.

It is important to notice that the *texture coordinate* for a fragment is always interpolated in *barycentric* coordinates within triangles (including perspective correction). The *texture color* for a fragment, however, is obtained with *bilinear* interpolation from a 2D texture map (or trilinear interpolation in case of 3D textures). As shown in Figure 13.1, a rectangular texture image does not map evenly onto a deformed quadrangle. The reason for this is the fact that the GPU always tessellates quadrangles into triangles before rasterization. For polygonal surfaces, this is an imperfection that we can either simply neglect or alleviate by inserting additional vertices or by adjusting the texture coordinates for different animation poses.

If we want to adapt existing surface deformation tools to volumetric objects, the first thing we notice is that a strict separation of shape from appearance does not exist here. The drawn proxy geometry is usually not related to the shape of the object contained in the volume data. Both shape and appearance are defined by the 3D texture map in combination with an appropriate transfer function. The shape of the volumetric object can then be thought of as a collection of implicit surfaces or isosurfaces.

As a result, there are two ways of deforming volumetric objects in general: modifying either the proxy geometry in model coordinates (the shape in traditional modeling) or distorting the mapping of the 3D texture in texture space (the appearance). Visually, both methods will result in a deformation of the shape of the volumetric object. We will examine them in the following sections.

13.2   Deformation in Model Space

As we have seen in the previous chapters, texture-based approaches decompose the volume data set into a proxy geometry by slicing the bounding box into a stack of planar polygons. Unfortunately, applying a deformation by simply displacing the vertices of the volume bounding box before the slice decomposition does not work properly. The first problem we notice is the slice decomposition itself. If we allow the vertices of a hexahedron to be moved freely in 3D space, its quadrangular faces will soon become non-planar. Intersection calculation with nonplanar quadrangles is extremely difficult to perform and will result in curved line segments instead of proper polygon edges. Even if we ensure that the faces of the hexahedra remain planar, the deformation will inevitably lead to inconsistent visual results after the slice decomposition. This is due to the same interpolation problems as outlined in Figure 13.1.

In order to achieve a consistent mapping of a 3D texture image to a deformed hexahedron, the hexahedron must be tessellated into several tetrahedra before computing the proxy geometry. Subdivision into tetrahedra also ensures consistent results for slice intersection if the faces of the hexahedron become nonplanar due to the deformation.

The easiest way of subdividing a hexahedron is to split it into five tetrahedra as outlined in Figure 13.2. The first tetrahedron is created by

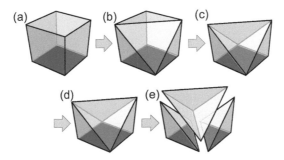

Figure 13.2. A hexahedron (a) is split into five tetrahedra. The first two tetrahedra are created by cutting away the foremost (b) and the rearmost vertex (c) of the top face. The remaining trunk (d) is divided into three tetrahedra (e) by splitting the bottom face along its diagonal.

removing the foremost vertex of the top face and the three edges connected
to it (Figure 13.2 (b)). The second tetrahedron is calculated the same way
for the rearmost vertex (Figure 13.2 (c)) on the top face. The remaining
simplex (Figure 13.2 (d)) can then be divided similarly into three tetrahedra
by cutting away the leftmost and the rightmost vertex of the bottom face
(Figure 13.2 (e)).

The deformation of a single tetrahedron can be described as an affine
transformation,

$$\Phi(\mathbf{x}) = \mathbf{A}\mathbf{x}, \tag{13.1}$$

in homogeneous coordinates. The 4×4 deformation matrix $\mathbf{A}$ is fully
determined by specifying four translation vectors at the tetrahedron's vertices. The deformation of the entire volumetric object is then composed
from piecewise linear transformation. The deformed tetrahedra are finally
decomposed into view-aligned slices and rendered back-to-front via alpha
blending.

13.2.1   Depth Sorting

Back-to-front compositing of tetrahedral data usually requires depth-
sorting to obtain the correct visibility ordering of the cells. Cell sorting of
tetrahedra data in general is not a trivial task, especially not for nonconvex
data or meshes that contain visibility cycles [135] for certain viewpoints.
Possible solutions can be found in [27, 120, 180, 304]. Most of the complex
sorting algorithms can be avoided if the tetrahedral cells are generated
by splitting hexahedra as outlined above. In this case only the hexahedra must be depth sorted using the distance from the eye point. For each
hexahedron, the respective tetrahedra are finally sorted separately. This
however only works properly if the common faces of adjacent hexahedra
are kept planar and if the cells do not intersect each other (a condition
that is required by most sorting algorithms).

13.3   Deformation in Texture Space

The other alternative for volumetric deformation is keeping the vertices of
the geometry static and modifying only the texture coordinates. Because
the shape of the object is defined as an implicit surface in the 3D texture,
distorting the texture space results in a deformation of the object.

To achieve higher flexibility for the deformation, we first subdivide the
original cuboid into a fixed set of subcubes by inserting additional vertices
(Figure 13.3 (left)). A deformation is specified in this refined model by
displacing only the texture coordinates for each vertex. The displacement
of the texture coordinate $\mathbf{u}$ for a point $\mathbf{x}$ in the interior of a patch is

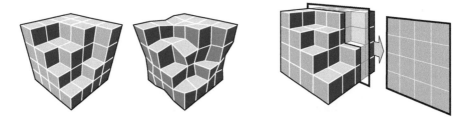

Figure 13.3. Model space (left): the volume is subdivided into a fixed set of sub-cubes. The geometry remains undeformed. Texture space (middle): the deformation is modeled by displacing texture coordinates. Right: such a deformation model allows the extraction of object aligned slices at low computational cost.

determined by trilinear interpolation of the translation vectors $\mathbf{t}_{ijk}$ given at the vertices. The result is a trilinear mapping

$$\Phi(\mathbf{u}) = \mathbf{u} + \sum_{i,j,k \in \{0,1\}} a_{ijk}(\mathbf{x})\mathbf{t}_{ijk}, \qquad (13.2)$$

with the interpolation weights $a_{ijk}(\mathbf{x})$ determined by the position $\mathbf{x}$ in (undeformed) model space.

If we now set up the proxy geometry, we want to preserve the benefit of our model being based on a static geometry, because the intersection calculation for all the small subcubes contributes a considerable computational load. We use object-aligned slices (see Figure 13.3 (right)), which keeps us from having to recompute all the cross sections for each frame. Object-aligned slices can also be easily computed in a vertex shader.

Again, the straightforward approach of slicing each subcube and assigning texture coordinates at the resulting polygon vertices will not lead to a correct trilinear mapping as specified in Equation 13.2. There are consistency problems similar to the ones described in Section 13.1. In Figure 13.4,

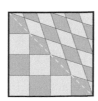

Figure 13.4. The trilinear deformation in texture space (far left) is poorly approximated if the graphics API internally tessellates the textured quad into two triangles with barycentric interpolation (middle left and middle right). Inserting an additional vertex (far right) usually approximates the trilinear interpolation sufficiently close.

the texture coordinate of the upper-right vertex of the quad is displaced. The correct trilinear mapping (Figure 13.4 (far left)) is poorly approximated by the internal triangulation of the graphics API (Figure 13.4 (middle left) and (middle right)). As a solution to this problem, inserting one additional vertex in the middle of the polygon usually results in a sufficiently close approximation to the original trilinear deformation with respect to screen resolution. If higher accuracy is required, additional vertices can be inserted. Such a manual tessellation also provides a consistent triangulation of the *nonplanar* texture map, which is the result of an arbitrary deformation of 3D texture space.

13.3.1 Practical Aspects

In an intuitive modeling application, the artist most likely does not want to specify texture coordinate deformation manually. Instead, the user should be provided with a mechanism that allows him to pick and drag a vertex to an arbitrary position. Such a manipulation, however, requires the inverse transformation Φ^{-1} of our trilinear mapping. The caveat here is that the inverse of a trilinear mapping in general is not again a trilinear mapping, but a function of higher complexity.

For the purpose of modeling, however, the exact inverse transformation is not necessarily required. In the usual case, an intuitive modeling mechanism similar to placing control points of a NURBS patch should suffice. An approximate inverse Φ^{-1} that allows intuitive dragging of vertices can be calculated by negating the original translation vectors at the vertices:

$$\widetilde{\Phi}^{-1}(\mathbf{u}) = \mathbf{u} + \sum_{i,j,k \in \{0,1\}} a_{ijk}(\mathbf{x}) \cdot (-\mathbf{t}_{ijk}). \qquad (13.3)$$

This simple approximation is easy to implement and turns out to be accurate enough for intuitive modeling.

13.3.2 Nonuniform Subdivision

Using a deformation model like this as a basis, it is easy to increase flexibility adaptively by further subdividing single patches as required. This results in a hierarchical octree structure as illustrated in Figure 13.5 (left). In order to maintain a consistent texture map at the boundary between patches with different subdivision levels, additional constraints are required. Such constraints must be set up for all vertices that are located on edges or faces shared by patches of different levels. Without these constraints, undesired gaps and discontinuities would emerge in texture space. In 3D, we must further differentiate between face and edge constraints.

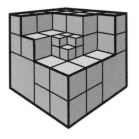
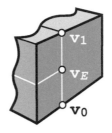
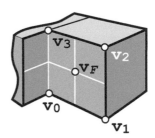

Figure 13.5. Left: nonuniform subdivision is used to increase flexibility for the deformation. Edge constraints (middle) and face constraints (right) are necessary to prevent gaps in texture space.

Edge Constraints. At common edges between patches with different subdivision levels, a constraint is necessary to ensure that the two half-edges of the higher level stay collinear. The inner vertex[1] in Figure 13.5 (middle), which was inserted by the higher subdivision level, must stay at its fixed position relative to the two neighboring vertices. Note that this vertex is not even allowed to move in direction along the edge, as this would also result in discontinuities in texture space:

$$\mathbf{v}_E = \frac{(\mathbf{v}_0 + \mathbf{v}_1)}{2}. \tag{13.4}$$

Face Constraints. At faces shared by different subdivision levels, another type of constraint is required to ensure coplanarity. The middle vertex in Figure 13.5 (right) must stay at a fixed position relative to the four vertices that form the original face:

$$\mathbf{v}_F = \frac{1}{4} \sum_{i=0}^{3} \mathbf{v}_i. \tag{13.5}$$

To circumvent recursive constraints, we additionally follow a general rule, known from surface modeling, that says that two neighboring patches must not differ by more than one subdivision level. This means that any patch can only be further subdivided if all neighboring patches have at least the same subdivision level.

13.3.3 Deformation via Fragment Shaders

The texture-space deformation model can be efficiently implemented using *dependent textures* or *offset textures*. The basic idea of an offset texture is to

---

[1]Note that the constraints are set up in texture space only. When we refer to vertices, we actually mean texture coordinates (= vertices in texture space).

```
// Cg fragment shader for
// texture-space volume deformation
half4 main (float3 uvw :  TEXCOORD0,
            uniform sampler3D offsetTexture,
            uniform sampler3D volumeTexture) :  COLOR0
{
    // obtain the deformation vector from the first texture
    float3 offset = tex3D(offsetTexture, uvw);
    uvw = uvw + offset;

    // sample the volume at the displaced coordinates
    half4 result = tex3D(volumeTexture, uvw);
    return result;
}
```

Listing 13.1.   Cg fragment program for volumetric deformation using 3D offset textures.

```
// Cg fragment shader for texture-space volume
// deformation with blending of two keyframes
half4 main (float3  uvw :  TEXCOORD0,
            uniform sampler3D offsetTexture1,
            uniform sampler3D offsetTexture2,
            uniform sampler3D volumeTexture,
            uniform float time) :  COLOR
{
    // obtain the deformation vectors for two keyframes
    float3 offset1 = tex3D(offsetTexture1, uvw);
    float3 offset2 = tex3D(offsetTexture2, uvw);
    // interpolate between the two keyframes
    uvw += lerp(offset1, offset2, time);
    // sample the the texture at the displaced coordinates
    half4 result = tex3D(volumeTexture, uvw);
    return result;
}
```

Listing 13.2.   Cg fragment program for volumetric deformation using linear keyframe interpolation between 3D offset textures.

use the RGB triplet obtained from one texture as a texture-coordinate offset for a second texture. On a graphics board with support for 3D dependent textures, the computation of the texture-space deformation model can be performed completely within the graphics hardware. The corresponding fragment program is shown in Listing 13.1.

The idea here is to store the deformation vectors in the RGB channels of a 3D offset texture and to use the dependent texture look-up to obtain the deformed volumetric information from a second 3D texture map, which stores the undeformed volume. Note that there is no need for the first texture to have size equal to the original volume, so it should be possible to keep it small enough to allow an interactive update of the deformation field. This technique also allows the rendering of view-aligned slices instead of object-aligned slices, as a uniform trilinear mapping of voxels to transformation vectors is guaranteed by the first 3D texture.

Such a fragment shader can also be easily modified to handle linear keyframe interpolation. The fragment shader in Listing 13.2 takes two offset textures as input and interpolates the offset vectors using the lerp command.

13.4 Deformation and Illumination

Local illumination techniques as described in Chapter 5 cannot directly be used with the described deformation models. Due to the deformation, pre-calculated gradient vectors become invalid. In this section, we want to examine possibilities to adapt pre-calculated vectors to the applied deformation.

For the deformation in model space described in Section 13.2 such an adaptation is easy because we know the exact affine deformation matrix for each tetrahedron. We also know that, if an object is transformed with a linear matrix $\mathbf{M}$, its normal vectors must be transformed with the transposed inverse matrix $(\mathbf{M}^{-1})^T$. All we have to do is multiply the pre-calculated normal vectors with the transposed inverse of matrix $\mathbf{A}$ from Equation 13.1, which is constant for each tetrahedron. The local illumination term can then be computed as usual.

The texture-space deformation model, however, is based on a trilinear mapping (Equation 13.2), whose inverse is a rather complex function. Calculating the exact deformation of the normal vectors becomes expensive. One working alternative is to use on-the-fly gradient estimation as described in Section 5.6.

Another alternative is to approximate the inverse of the trilinear function using a linear transformation. The idea is to find an affine mapping, which approximates the original trilinear mapping $\Phi(\mathbf{x})$ and then use the transposed inverse matrix to transform the pre-computed normal vectors. The affine transformation is a 4×4 matrix in homogeneous coordinates, denoted

$$\overline{\Phi}(\mathbf{x}) = \overline{\mathbf{H}}\mathbf{x}, \qquad \text{with} \quad \overline{\mathbf{H}} = \left(\begin{array}{c|c} \mathbf{H} & \mathbf{b} \\ \hline 0\,0\,0 & 1 \end{array} \right) \in \mathbb{R}^{4 \times 4}. \qquad (13.6)$$

The optimal approximation $\overline{\Phi}$ is determined by minimizing the quadratic difference between the transformation of the eight static corner vertices $\overline{\Phi}(\mathbf{x}_i)$ and their real transformed positions $\mathbf{y}_i = \Phi(\mathbf{x}_i)$, according to

$$\frac{\partial}{\partial \mathbf{H}} \sum_{i=1}^{8} \|\overline{\Phi}(\mathbf{x}_i) - \mathbf{y}_i\|^2 = 0, \qquad (13.7)$$

which leads to

$$\sum_{i=1}^{8} (\mathbf{x}_i \mathbf{x}_i^T \mathbf{H}^T - \mathbf{x}_i \mathbf{y}_i^T) = 0. \qquad (13.8)$$

Solving this equation for $\mathbf{H}^T$, results in

$$\mathbf{H}^T = \mathbf{M}^{-1} \sum_{i=1}^{8} \mathbf{x}_i \mathbf{y}_i^T, \qquad \text{with} \quad \mathbf{M} = \sum_{i=1}^{8} \mathbf{x}_i \mathbf{x}_i^T \in \mathbb{R}^{4 \times 4}. \qquad (13.9)$$

It is easy to verify that the inverse of matrix $\mathbf{M}$ always exists. One important fact is that matrix $\mathbf{M}$ is constant for each patch because the undeformed corner vertices $\mathbf{x}_i$ are static in this model. Matrix $\mathbf{M}$ can thus be pre-computed for efficiency. Taking also into consideration that the corner vertices are located on an axis-aligned grid, the computation can be further simplified, such that calculating each entry h_{ij} of the matrix $\mathbf{H}$ will require only eight multiplications.

The performance benefit of this approximation should become clear, if we consider the dot product that is required to calculate the Lambertian illumination term

$$\mathbf{I}_{\text{diffuse}} = k_d \, \mathbf{M}_d \, \mathbf{I}_d (\mathbf{n} \cdot \mathbf{l}). \qquad (13.10)$$

In this context, $\mathbf{n}$ is the surface normal, which coincides with the voxel gradient in our model. $\mathbf{I}_{\text{diffuse}}$ denotes the color of the light source, weighted by a material-dependent diffuse reflection coefficient. As we have seen in Chapter 5, the per-pixel dot product computation can be efficiently performed in hardware using fragment shaders.

For the undeformed volume, the gradient vectors are pre-calculated and stored within a 3D normal map. In order to achieve realistic illumination results for deformable volumetric data, we have to adapt the gradient vectors to the actual deformation. According to our linear approximation, the new diffuse term after the transformation is determined by

$$\widetilde{\mathbf{I}}_{\text{diffuse}} = k_d \, \mathbf{M}_d \, \mathbf{I}_d(((\mathbf{H}^{-1})^T \mathbf{n}) \cdot \mathbf{l}) \,. \tag{13.11}$$

Note that, because the gradients $\mathbf{n}$ are obtained from a texture, this calculation requires a per-pixel matrix multiplication, which can be computed using fragment shaders. If we further assume directional light, the light vector $\mathbf{l}$ is constant for the whole scene and there is an easy way to handle illumination, which avoids these per-pixel matrix multiplication. Consider that the dot product in Equation 13.11 can also be written as

$$((\mathbf{A}^{-1})^T \, \mathbf{n}) \cdot \mathbf{l}) = (\mathbf{n} \cdot (\mathbf{H}^{-1}\mathbf{l})) \,. \tag{13.12}$$

In relation to our method, this means that all the pre-computed normal vectors can be left untouched. The only thing we have to do is to transform the light vector for each patch to obtain an equivalent visual result.

Regardless of whether the normal deformation is exact or approximative, using a light vector constant within each patch, but different for neighboring patches, will inevitably result in visible discontinuities as depicted in Figure 13.6 (center). To tackle this problem, there should be smooth transitions for the diffuse illumination term of neighboring patches. This can be achieved by assigning light vectors to the vertices instead of the patches. To each vertex a light vector is assigned, which is averaged from the light vectors of all the patches, which share this vertex. Analogously to the translation vectors, the light vectors given at the vertices are interpolated within each patch. To achieve this during rasterization, the light vectors must be assigned as color values to the vertices of each rendered polygon, thus allowing the interpolation to be performed by hardware Gouraud shading. As displayed in Figure 13.7, this method will lead to approximate illumination without any discontinuities.

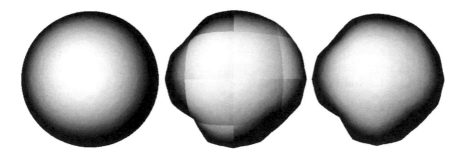

Figure 13.6. Diffuse illumination of an undeformed sphere (left). Extremely deformed sphere with discontinuities at the patch boundaries (center). Correct illumination by smoothing the deformed light vectors (right) at the vertices.

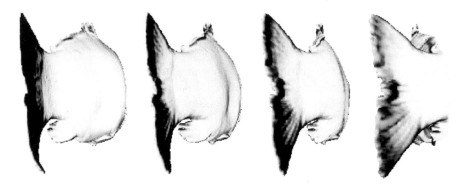

Figure 13.7. Animated tail fin of a carp demonstrates realistic illumination effects during real-time deformation.

13.5   Animation Techniques

The deformation approaches we have seen so far were grid-based approaches. As in a polygonal model, the overall deformation of the object was achieved by specifying deformation vectors at designated vertices or control points. Grid-based deformation is not a very popular technique. In practice, motion is controlled using higher-level animation techniques that can as well be adapted to volumetric deformation. The most popular deformation techniques for surface models are *blend shapes* and *skeletal animation*.

The different approaches to volumetric deformation we have seen so far can be adapted to higher-level animation techniques. The model-space approach is used for large-scale deformation; its effective use, however, raises the problem of efficient depth-sorting of tetrahedral cells. Skeletal animation, blend shapes, and any other animation technique based on vertex transformation can be used with the model-space deformation approach without modification.

In principle, the same is true for the texture-space approach. The possible range of motion, however, is limited by the static proxy geometry. It is thus better suited for interpolative animation such as blend shapes.

13.5.1   Blend Shapes

In computer animation, *blend shapes* are used to model a wide range of small but complex movements, such as muscle movements or facial expressions. A typical set of blend shapes consists of several concurring extreme shapes that are blended together to form subtle but complex movements.

```
// A vertex program for implementing blend shapes
// with piecewise linear patches
void main( float4 Vertex    :  POSITION,
           half3  TexCoord0  :  TEXCOORD0, // blend shape 0
           half3  TexCoord1  :  TEXCOORD1, // blend shape 1
           half3  TexCoord2  :  TEXCOORD2, // blend shape 2
           half3  TexCoord3  :  TEXCOORD3, // blend shape 3
           uniform float4   weights, // blend shape weights
           uniform float4x4 matModelViewProj,
           out float4 VertexOut    :  POSITION,
           out half3  TexCoordOut  :  TEXCOORD0) {
    // transform vertex into screen space
    VertexOut = mul(matModelViewProj, Vertex);

    //hand over color and texture coordinate
    TexCoordOut  = weights.x * TexCoord0;
    TexCoordOut += weights.y * TexCoord1;
    TexCoordOut += weights.z * TexCoord2;
    TexCoordOut += weights.w * TexCoord3;

    return;
}
```

Listing 13.3. Cg vertex program for texture-space deformation using pre-defined blend shapes and piecewise linear patches.

The final pose $\mathbf{p}$ is defined as a weighted sum of all pre-deformed instances $\mathbf{p}_i$:

$$\mathbf{p} = \sum_{i=0}^{N} w_i\,\mathbf{p}_i, \qquad \text{with } \sum_{i=0}^{N} w_i = 1. \tag{13.13}$$

N is the number of pre-defined blend shapes, and the weights w_i are used to control the animation. The vector of weights

$$\mathbf{w} = (w_0, w_1, \ldots, w_N)^T \tag{13.14}$$

thus defines the possible range of motion. Although blend shapes in general do not impose an upper limit on range of motion, in practice they are used to model small and subtle deformations such as facial expressions.

The texture-space approach to volumetric deformation is ideal for movements that are relatively small with respect to the size of the volume object itself. As described in Section 13.3, the deformation in texture space is modeled by shifting texture coordinates. As we have seen, this displacement can be modeled intuitively by negating the displacement vectors to

```
half4 main (float3 texcoords :  TEXCOORD0,
    // blend shapes (offset textures)
    uniform sampler3D offsetTexture0, // blend shape 0
    uniform sampler3D offsetTexture1, // blend shape 1
    uniform sampler3D offsetTexture2, // blend shape 2
    uniform sampler3D offsetTexture3, // blend shape 3
    // volume texture
    uniform sampler3D volumeTexture,
    // blend-shape weights
    uniform float3 weights) :  COLOR
{
    float3 offset = 0..xxx;
    if (weights.x != 0.0) {
        float3 offset0 = tex3D(offsetTexture0, uvw);
        offset += weights.x * offset0;
    }
    if (weights.y != 0.0) {
        float3 offset1 = tex3D(offsetTexture1, uvw);
        offset += weights.y * offset1;
    }
    if (weights.z != 0.0) {
        float3 offset2 = tex3D(offsetTexture2, uvw);
        offset += weights.z * offset2;
    }
    if (weights.w != 0.0) {
        float3 offset3 = tex3D(offsetTexture3, uvw);
        offset += weights.w * offset3;
    }
    texcoords += offset;
    // sample the the texture at the displaced coordinates
    half4 result = tex3D(volumeTexture, texcoords);
    return result;
}
```

Listing 13.4. Cg fragment program for texture-space deformation using pre-defined blend shapes and offset textures.

approximate the inverse transformation. Blend shapes can thus be easily integrated into the texture-space deformation model based on piecewise linear patches (Section 13.3).

With piecewise linear patches, blend shapes are designed by specifying more than one set of texture coordinates for each vertex. During vertex processing the final texture coordinate is interpolated as a weighted sum of all defined sets according to Equation 13.13. A simple implementation of this idea with four different blend shapes is given in Listing 13.3. The four weights w_i are specified as vector components of the uniform parameter `weights` in the vertex program. The implementation can easily be extended to more than four blend shapes, only limited by the number of available texture coordinate sets.

The deformation technique based on offset textures (Section 13.3.3) can as well be used to implement blend shapes. A straightforward implementation defines each blend shape as a separate 3D offset texture. The weighted sum from Equation 13.13 is then calculated for each fragment in the fragment program. A sample implementation is given in Listing 13.4. Note that piecewise linear patches in this case are more efficient because the weighting is done for each vertex instead of each fragment. As an alternative to the straightforward implementation described above, it might be advantageous to calculate the weighted sum in a separate rendering pass in advance. As mentioned in Section 2.4.2, frame-buffer objects can be used to render into slices of 3D textures. The final offset texture for one animation frame is created in a pre-processing step by rendering slices of all offset textures into the 3D texture, multiplied by their respective weight and summed up by additive blending.

13.5.2 Skeletal Animation

Skeletal animation techniques define a character's possible range of motion by means of a hierarchical chain of articulated joints and bones. High-level control of the skeleton's pose is implemented by forward and inverse kinematics solvers. Forward kinematics (FK) refers to the direct specification of angles between joints. Inverse kinematics (IK) allow the endpoint of a joint chain, such as the position to the hand, to be specified. The position of the remaining joints in an IK chain are then automatically calculated by an IK solver. A typical skeleton consists of a combination of both forward and inverse kinematics. As examples, arms and legs are frequently controlled by inverse kinematics, whereas the animation of the spine is often performed with forward kinematics. In a typical model, skeletal animation is often combined with blend shapes to implement realistic motion. As an example, the movement of an elbow is controlled by an IK chain, while the rising of the biceps is modeled by a blend shape.

The process of binding a given model to an articulated skeleton is called *skinning*. For *rigid skinning*, each vertex of the model is attached to exactly one bone of the skeleton. If this bone undergoes a certain transformation, the same motion is simultaneously applied to all vertices attached to that bone.

For *smooth skinning*, the transformation of one vertex is controlled by several bones at the same time. Each vertex is associated with several bones. The transformation of a vertex is then calculated as a weighted sum of the transformation of all associated bones. As the weights that control the influence of specific bones are specified for each vertex, the resulting deformation will be smooth and flexible.

The model-space deformation approach for volumetric objects is well suited for large-scale motions usually modeled by skeleton animation. After subdivision of the hexahedra into tetrahedra for deformation, the free vertices can be attached to existing skeletons using smooth or rigid binding.

The texture-space approach based on piecewise linear patches can as well be easily adapted to skeletal animation. However, care must be taken that the deformed model stays within the boundary of the static geometry of subcubes, otherwise parts of the volume might be cut off.

13.5.3   Procedural Animation

The animation techniques described above create a significant amount of data, such as geometry with multiple weights and large sets of offset textures. The considerable memory requirements imposed by such models can be reduced by substituting predefined deformation fields by procedural descriptions that are evaluated at runtime. Simple deformations such as random jittering and shock waves can easily be described procedurally, similar to the techniques presented in *The Cg Tutorial* [71].

With a little bit of effort, however, it is also possible to describe more complex and goal-directed movement by procedural deformation fields. As an example, the volumetric tripod creature displayed in Figure 12.1 can easily be animated in texture-space using a procedural fragment shader. For the animation clip displayed in Figure 13.8, the creature is walking by moving each of its three legs in sequence.

The texture-space deformation used to animate the creature is defined procedurally by the fragment program shown in Listing 13.5. The positions of the three legs in local model coordinates are controlled by the deformation vectors `leg1`, `leg2`, and `leg3`, specified as uniform parameters.

The procedural shader parameterizes points in texture-space in cylindrical coordinates. The point `P` defines the current position in the cylindrical coordinate system. Each leg corresponds to a specific sector of the cylinder with an angle of $\texttt{sectionangle} = \frac{2\pi}{3}$. The variable `whichLeg` is computed as an index that specifies by which leg the movement of that point is affected. The variable `weight` contains the amount of deformation. To create smooth transitions between the different cylindrical sectors, this animation weight is modulated by a sine function. The weight also smoothly decreases in the upper region of the body. Finally the texture-space deformation vector is determined by shifting the texture coordinate according to the corresponding leg movement.

```
#define PI (3.1415)

half modulo(half a, half b) {
    a -= floor(a/b)*b;
    if (a < 0) a+=b;
    return a;
}

half4 main( half3 uvw :   TEXCOORD,
            uniform sampler3D volumeTexture,
            uniform half3 legMove[3]) :   COLOR
{
    // move the center of the coordinate system
    half3 P = uvw - half3(0.32,0.5,0.5);

    // determine the cylindrical sector for the leg
    const half sectionangle = 2.0*PI/3.0;
    half angle = PI + atan2(P.z,P.x);
    // to which leg does this voxel belong?
    half whichLeg = floor(angle/sectionangle);

    // determine the weight for the motion
    half A = modulo(angle, sectionangle)*PI/2.0;
    half weight = sin(A);

    // movement will decrease in the upper region
    half moveY = 1.2-uvw.y;
    moveY *= moveY;
    moveY *= moveY;
    weight *= moveY;

    // move the respective leg by displacing the tex coords
    uvw -= weight * legMove[whichLeg];

    // sample the texture.
    return tex3D(volumeTexture,uvw);
}
```

Listing 13.5. Cg fragment program for texture-space animation using a procedural deformation field.

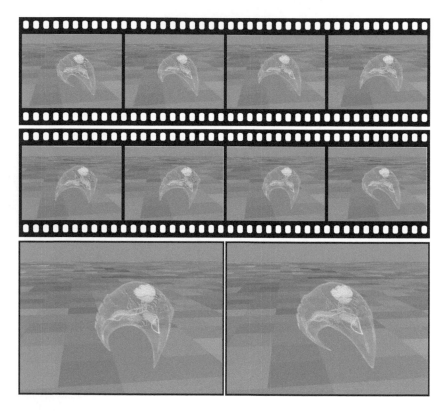

Figure 13.8. Resulting animation frames from a procedural animation of a volumetric tripod creature.

This simple deformation field demonstrates that motion of considerable complexity can be achieved by procedural animation. The example of the tripod creature is meant as an inspiration for designing your own procedural animation techniques for specific, goal-directed motion.

13.6 Further Reading

Animation and deformation techniques have a long history in computer graphics. Conventional free-form modeling techniques [8] have led to powerful commercial packages, but they are mainly restricted to polygonal surface descriptions that do not take into account the interior deformation of the object. Apart from a variety of deformable surface models, such as the ones proposed by Sederberg [236], Coquillart [32], MacCracken [177], and Chua [26], the literature on volumetric deformation is rather scarce.

For readers interested in game development, the second volume of *3D Games* [284] is a good introduction to animation concepts.

In 1995, Kurzion and Yagel [146] proposed a deformation model for both surfaces and volumes based on bending the viewing rays. They propose the use of *ray deflectors*, which attract or repel the viewing rays during ray casting. The main drawback of this original approach is its restriction to ray casting. The same authors also extended their approach to 3D texture–based volume rendering [147]. The deformation of the interior is here computed by tessellating the slice polygons into smaller triangles. A similar idea is followed by Westermann and Rezk-Salama [297], which allows for the modeling of deformation in an intuitive way by deforming arbitrary surfaces within the volume data set. Fang et al. [69] compute volumetric deformation by subdividing the volume into an octree and by slicing and texture mapping each subcube. Due to the required real-time tessellation of the slice images, these approaches only achieve moderate frame rates. The described approach to handle volumetric deformation by tessellating the proxy geometry into tetrahedra is followed in the OpenGL Volumizer API, available as a commercial product from Silicon Graphics [10, 115].

Popular models for volumetric deformation are based on the finite elements method (FEM) and mass-spring models [24]. Gibson et al. [78] have proposed an algorithm for fast propagation of deformation through the volume. Skeleton animation for volumetric objects was proposed by Gagvani et al. [76]. They also create skeleton trees for volume data automatically by a centerline extraction algorithm. Closely related to volumetric animation are the volume-morphing techniques proposed by Hughes [108] and He et al. [102].

14

Non-Photorealistic and Illustrative Techniques

A LARGE PART OF RENDERING HAS TRADITIONALLY been concerned with *photorealistic rendering*, where the goal is to mimic the appearance of reality as closely as possible. Many of these methods are based on physical models of light transport, especially global illumination methods such as ray tracing [79], radiosity [5], or photon mapping [114]. These physically based methods for generating realistic images have become more and more sophisticated over the years [55]. However, even empirical local-illumination models such as the Blinn-Phong model [12] try to emulate the appearance of real light reflection with very simple means, even though they are not completely based on actual physics.

Complementary to photorealistic rendering, the area of *non-photorealistic rendering* (or NPR) has emerged more recently. The area of NPR is usually defined exclusively and as such subsumes all rendering techniques where the goal is not photorealism. A common objective of NPR is to mimic various styles of human paintings and artistic illustrations such as pen-and-ink drawings, hatching, stippling, or painting with water colors. Although rendering works of art or supporting their creation is a worthwhile goal in itself, illustrative-rendering styles are especially important where a specific meaning has to be conveyed to viewers by deviating from an object's actual appearance in reality, such as in technical or medical illustrations. In these kinds of depictions, important parts of an object are often emphasized as the *focus*, whereas the remainder is deemphasized and only depicted as *context*. Very good introductions to the area of non-photorealistic rendering can be found in the books by Gooch and Gooch [82] and Strothotte and Schlechtweg [256].

In scientific visualization, the main goal is to communicate with the viewer and convey information and a certain meaning. Consequently, in this area, NPR styles with the look of technical or medical illustration

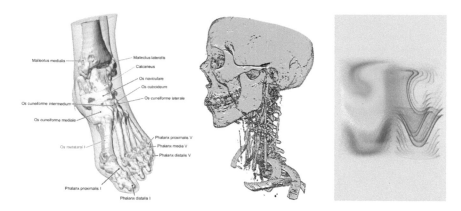

Figure 14.1. Examples of illustrative visualization. Left: labeling subobjects in VolumeShop [18]. Center: rendering a CT isosurface with deferred shading, highlighting ridge and valley lines computed from implicit curvature and contours [93]. Right: visualizing a convection flow volume [261]. (Left image courtesy of Stefan Bruckner, © 2005 IEEE. Right image courtesy of Nikolai Svakhine, Yun Jang, David Ebert, and Kelly Gaither, © 2005 IEEE.)

have had the most important influence on rendering techniques. For this reason, non-photorealistic rendering in the area of visualization and volume rendering is often called *illustrative visualization* [273]. Given these goals, human perception plays a crucial role in the design of these techniques. Examples of illustrative visualizations are depicted in Figure 14.1.

Because their origins lie in the area of general computer graphics, most NPR methods deal with surface rendering in contrast with volume rendering. The most direct way to apply these techniques to volume rendering is to adapt them for rendering isosurfaces. In addition to isosurface illustration methods, full volume illustration methods have also been developed. An especially powerful approach is to combine both volume and surface illustration methods in a single rendering.

14.1 Overview of Methods

This section gives an overview of the basic approaches to *non-photorealistic*, or *illustrative*, volume-rendering techniques. First, we discuss some basic properties such as whether methods are based on the notion of surfaces or full volumes, or whether they work in image space or object space. Then we give an overview of existing techniques. Detailed descriptions of selected methods with a focus on real-time rendering are provided in later sections.

14.1.1   Basic Properties

Surface-based versus volume-based methods. Most NPR methods in volume rendering are adaptations of surface-rendering methods. The obvious example is the rendering of isosurfaces. Even when isosurfaces are not represented by a polygonal mesh but given implicitly on a volumetric grid, the result is the image of a surface and can thus of course be shaded like a surface. The basis for this is the use of the normalized gradient of the volume as the normal vector for shading. The same is also true for standard direct volume rendering. Although in this case many samples along viewing rays are composited and no isosurface is considered explicitly, the standard method for local volume illumination uses the normalized gradient vector and a standard local surface illumination model for shading. Chapter 5 describes the adaptation of surface shading to volume shading. Therefore, modifications of local surface illumination models for non-photorealistic rendering can be used in volume rendering by substituting the shading model in the volume-rendering integral. An example is explained in Section 14.2.1.

However, there are also NPR volume-rendering approaches that do not make use of the notion of a surface at all. An example of such a style is *volume stippling* [170], which is illustrated in Figure 14.5. Still, even many "volumetric" shading models build on ideas for shading surface-like structures, even though they do not explicitly require specification of a surface (e.g., through an isovalue) and can be applied at all points in a volume simultaneously. These methods are not a direct adaptation of a surface shading model but still very often use the gradient and its magnitude. An example for rendering volumetric contours that does not require the specification of a surface but uses gradient information is described in Section 14.3.3.

Object-space versus image-space methods. A major distinction of all methods that detect surface properties, such as contours, is whether they operate in object space or in image space, i.e., whether they are computed on the actual surface in 3D space or in its 2D projection. Consider the detection of contours (or silhouettes) for which there are standard approaches in both object and image space, respectively. A simple example for object-space contour detection is the case of triangle meshes, where each edge is checked whether it connects a front-facing and a back-facing triangle with respect to the viewpoint. In this case, it is a silhouette edge. Image-space contour detection uses edge-detection filters (such as Sobel or Canny edge detectors) in order to detect discontinuities in the depth and the normal images, for instance. An example is the system by Yuan and Chen [306] for isosurface illustration in volumes, which uses image-space filtering. A discussion for both approaches on triangle meshes can be found in *Real-Time Rendering* [2]. In this chapter, we concentrate on object-space approaches.

View-independent versus view-dependent methods. Another important difference between illustrative methods is whether they depend on the relative location of the view point or not. Contours are an example for a rendering style that depends on the relative viewing direction. However, surface curvature, for example, is an intrinsic property of the surface itself, and as such is independent of the viewing direction. This property is inherited by all styles that are purely based on curvature information, such as rendering ridge and valley lines, which are described in Section 14.1.3.

In this respect, it is also an issue whether an illustrative method requires an explicit mesh, e.g., for an isosurface, or not. For example, it is easy to store view-independent information at mesh vertices in order to avoid re-computation. For methods such as ray casting that do not generate explicit geometry, however, most information has to be re-computed for every frame. In this book, we are most of all interested in methods that do not require an explicit mesh. This avoids the cost of computing this mesh which usually prevents interactive changes of the isovalue. Therefore, in this chapter all information that is required for rendering in an illustrative style must be computable in real time.

14.1.2   Modified Shading Models

A basic approach to achieving an illustrative style for surface or isosurface rendering is to modify a standard local shading model such as the Blinn-Phong model. As described in Chapter 5, this model depends on the direction to the light source, the view direction, and the surface normal, which in the case of volume rendering is the normalized gradient of the volume. In order to mimic physical behavior, it incorporates Lambert's cosine law in such a way that a surface is not lit from behind. This, however, also means that surfaces are rapidly disappearing into blackness as the normal vector turns away from the light direction. In these regions, it is impossible to discern the shape of the surface.

One of the most well-known NPR modifications to this basic model is called *tone shading* [83], which is described in Section 14.2.1. Tone shading shades the areas that would mostly be black in the Blinn-Phong model with a clearly discernible color and thus yields a better depiction of surface shape. Cartoon shading [151], described in Section 14.2.2, builds on the fact that cartoonists usually draw large areas of a surface with a constant color. In order to emulate this shading style, the dot product between the light direction and the normal vector is mapped to either one of two colors via thresholding or a 1D look-up table.

In general, many NPR modifications to the Blinn-Phong model can be mapped to programmable look-up tables for the basic dot product terms. The illustrative volume-rendering system of Bruckner and Gröller [18] is an example of this approach. The look-up tables can be specified by the user in order to obtain different surface shading models with the exact same shader code. This is described in more detail in Section 14.2.3.

14.1.3   Characteristic Lines

An important goal of illustrative rendering techniques is to illustrate *surface shape* with visual cues that would not be visible in a photorealistic image. A powerful approach to shape depiction is to draw *characteristic lines* (or *feature lines*), either by themselves or overlayed on a shaded image of the surface. The most common characteristic lines for surface shape are as follows.

- *Contours*, often also called *silhouettes*, are very important shape cues and are a basic part of almost all surface illustrations. However, contours by themselves do not provide enough information about shape and so are usually combined with other types of characteristic lines.

- *Suggestive contours* [43] add important additional "contour-like" lines to real contours, which enhance shape perception significantly. An

Figure 14.2. Left: combining ridges (white), valleys (black), and contours (gray), rendered with deferred shading and implicit surface curvature [93]. Right: even if only suggestive contours are rendered, they provide powerful shape cues. (Right image courtesy of Doug DeCarlo et al. [43], © 2003 ACM, Inc. Reprinted by permission.)

important part of their computation uses surface curvature information. See below for a discussion of curvature. Figure 14.2 (right)
shows an example of suggestive contours.

- *Ridge and valley lines* (*creases*) highlight surface locations that are
  locally shaped like a cylinder, which can be defined using surface
  curvature information. Ridges are convex cylindrical areas, whereas
  valleys are concave. Combining contours with ridge and valley lines
  produces powerful shape cues [111], as illustrated in Figure 14.2 (left).

- *Curvature isolines.* Curvature information is an important basis for
  shape depiction. There are different scalar curvature measures that
  can be computed over surfaces such as *Gaussian curvature* or *mean
  curvature.* Drawing isolines of these measures, i.e., highlighting all
  points with the same value of, e.g., Gaussian curvature, also gives
  insight into the surface's shape. Examples are shown in Figure 14.18.

Most work on extracting characteristic lines from surfaces is based on triangle meshes. For isosurfaces, this means extracting a triangle mesh from the
volume as a pre-process, e.g., using marching cubes [168]. In order to focus
on approaches that are real-time throughout, we will restrict ourselves to
methods that avoid an explicit mesh representation for isosurfaces.

A very important distinction of approaches based on characteristic lines
is whether they are based on explicit lines or not. The first option is
to determine vertices on these lines and connect them with actual line
primitives. The second approach is to perform a "point on line" test on a
per-sample basis, e.g., on equispaced samples along viewing rays that are
cast into the volume. Even when lines corresponding to surface features are
extracted explicitly, it is possible to avoid an intermediate representation
of the surface by directly generating line vertices [20].

14.1.4   Methods Based on Curvature Information

Determining surface curvature is an important part of differential geometry and a powerful tool for depicting surface shape. The determination of
characteristic lines is often based on curvature information, such as specifying ridge and valley lines according to maximum and minimum principal
curvature magnitude, as illustrated in Figure 14.2 (left). In the case of
implicitly defined isosurfaces, curvature means implicit surface curvature.
Section 14.4 describes the concept and computation of implicit isosurface
curvature in detail. Section 14.6 describes different isosurface illustration
modes building on curvature information. Figure 14.3 shows curvature
information on isosurfaces of signed distance-field volumes.

Figure 14.3. Examples of illustrative isosurface rendering depicting implicit curvature information. These are not surface meshes but signed distance fields stored on a regular volumetric grid. The left image illustrates color-encoded maximum principal curvature. The right image visualizes maximum principal curvature direction using image-space flow advection.

14.1.5 Hatching

Hatching is an illustration technique that can convey a variety of information about a surface in a single image, such as simultaneously illustrating shape, lighting, and material properties. This is illustrated in the images in Figure 14.4. Hatching strokes generally exhibit coherence in their density and direction. Very often, hatching strokes are aligned with the curvature field of the surface, e.g., drawing lines in the direction of maximum principal curvature. Cross-hatching, i.e., sets of roughly orthogonal hatching strokes, are often aligned with both the maximum and minimum curvature directions, respectively.

Most methods for hatching require polygonal meshes and make use of parameterizations of these meshes. That is, texture coordinates are precomputed and stored with the mesh vertices. Rendering can be performed in real time, for example by using *tonal art maps* that store hatching patterns of varying density in the mipmap levels of several texture maps [215]. These techniques achieve results of very high quality, as illustrated in Figure 14.4 (left). Using mipmapped textures allows the hatching-stroke density to be automatically adapted to the viewing distance. For volume rendering, hatching on isosurfaces without a parameterization allows one to avoid the construction of a triangle mesh for a given isovalue. One possibility to do this is to automatically place seed points and trace stream lines through the curvature field [194]. Hatching strokes for an isosurface can also be blended on top of a traditional volume rendering, illustrated in

Figure 14.4. Hatching for surface visualization. Left: hatching on a triangle mesh using tonal art maps requires a parameterization of a polygonal surface. Right: hatching on isosurfaces is also possible without an explicit parameterization [194]. (Left image courtesy of Emil Praun et al. [215], © 2001 ACM, Inc. Reprinted by permission. Right image courtesy of Zoltán Nagy, Jens Schneider, and Rüdiger Westermann.)

Figure 14.4 (right). A challenging problem of hatching techniques is achieving temporal coherence in animations in order to avoid excessive flickering when strokes or groups of strokes are changing too quickly or incoherently.

14.1.6   Stippling

Stippling is a common artistic technique that depicts objects with a large collection of small points of varying density and possibly different colors. Although drawing stipples is most common for surface rendering, the basic concept can be extended for full volume rendering without being constrained to individual isosurfaces. Examples of such a technique [170] are illustrated in Figure 14.5. Volumetric stippling determines the stipple density for each voxel separately according to a variety of properties, such as the density of the volume at that location, lighting, distance to the viewer, material boundary enhancement, and silhouette enhancement [170].

14.1.7   Combination with Segmented Data

Using non-photorealistic rendering modes for visualizing segmented data with per-object rendering modes is an approach to emphasizing specific object structures in volume data. Rendering of contours, for example, is a good way to provide context for focus regions rendered with more traditional volume-visualization techniques. Tone shading, for example, is

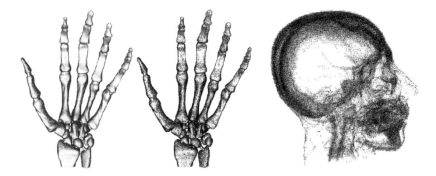

Figure 14.5. Stippling can be applied to surface and volume rendering. The density of stipples at a given voxel location is determined by characteristics such as lighting intensity, contour and boundary enhancement, and distance to the viewer [170]. Images courtesy of Lu, Morris, Ebert, Rheingans, and Hansen, © 2002 IEEE.

naturally suited as a shading mode for rendering isosurfaces or structures with high opacity, whereas objects rendered with lower opacity could be rendered with standard direct volume rendering.

Chapter 16 describes how segmented volume data can be rendered on GPUs and shows examples of combining traditional and non-photorealistic techniques in a single volume rendering in order to enhance perception of individual objects of interest and separate context from focus regions.

14.1.8   Smart Visibility and Importance-Driven Visualization

Going a step further from non-photorealistic or illustrative techniques that traditionally ask *how* an object or volume should be depicted, the question

Figure 14.6. Visibility-preserving importance compositing [274]. The visibility of a focus object is kept constant for all viewpoints. It is independent of the thickness of the occluding parts of the context that surrounds it. (Images courtesy of Ivan Viola, © 2005 IEEE.)

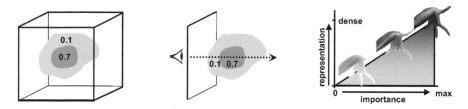

Figure 14.7. Importance-driven visualization requires *importance compositing* in order to determine view-dependent visibility of objects according to their importance [272]. (Images courtesy of Ivan Viola, © 2005 IEEE.)

of *what* part of a volume is important and should thus be visualized arises. A fundamental aspect of this problem is the *visibility* of objects or subvolumes. An example is illustrated in Figure 14.6. A volume is subdivided into focus and context objects, and the relative visibility of these objects is determined. In order to ensure that a focus object is always visible, this is usually done in a view-dependent manner.

Viola et al. [272, 274] have introduced the concept of importance-driven volume rendering, where the importance of objects determines their visibility and rendering style. Figure 14.7 illustrates the corresponding compositing of importance along viewing rays.

14.1.9   Additional Techniques for Illustrative Visualization

This section briefly summarizes additional techniques that are useful in illustrative volume rendering.

Clipping planes. Although clipping planes are a standard ingredient of most volume renderers, their usefulness cannot be overemphasized. In many approaches they are the standard way for looking into the volume, after a transfer function has been chosen. Although the transfer function also has the responsibility of making unimportant areas transparent, and interesting areas more opaque, standard transfer functions are global and do not incorporate position information. Thus, it is often necessary to clip away parts of the volume that have not been made transparent by the transfer function in order to see the desired areas of interest. Clipping is also a standard method when doing illustrations, and as such they are even more important when illustrative volume-rendering techniques are used. In this context, illustrations with parts of the object clipped away are known as *cutaway views*.

Chapter 15 contains a detailed discussion of different volume-clipping techniques, in addition to basic clipping planes.

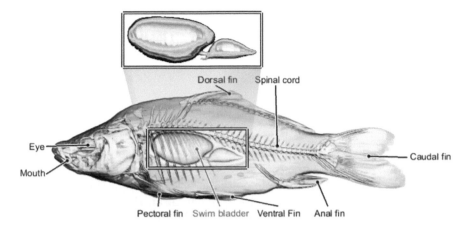

Figure 14.8. The VolumeShop illustrative-visualization system of Bruckner and Gröller [18] combines a variety of volumetric-illustration styles and additional techniques such as labeling. (Images courtesy of Stefan Bruckner, © 2005 IEEE.)

Transformations. If different parts of a volume can be moved, rotated, or scaled, it is much easier to look into the volume and avoid unwanted occlusion between objects of interest. An example is *fanning*, shown in Figure 14.8 [18], where a subvolume is rendered outside the main volume in a zoomed view. Browsing volumetric data via transformations and deformations [183] is also a powerful metaphor for volume inspection. Another approach is to warp the view with a magic lens for exploring the volume in a focus+context manner [278].

Annotations. Figure 14.8 also shows annotations in the form of labels for segmented subvolumes. In order to perform proper automatic labeling, segmentation information is usually used [18].

14.1.10   Integrated Systems

All the techniques outlined above become especially powerful when they are combined in an interactive system. The VolumeShop system of Bruckner and Gröller [18] combines a variety of illustrative volume-rendering styles with additional capabilities such as ghosting, importance-driven rendering, and labeling. The Illustration Motifs system by Svakhine et al. [260] effectively combines standard volume rendering and illustrative rendering styles. The system of Lu and Ebert [169] interactively synthesizes illustrative volume renderings from example images. Tietjen et al. [265] have presented an illustrative visualization system for surgery education and planning that effectively combines both volume and surface rendering. Krüger et al. [144] propose a similar system for neck dissection planning. Section 15.6 also contains a discussion of volume illustration systems, especially in the context of volume clipping.

14.2   Basic NPR Shading Models

This section describes extensions and variants of the standard Blinn-Phong model for non-photorealistic volume rendering. Although this model consists of an *ambient*, a *diffuse*, and a *specular* term, the term that is most commonly modified for NPR styles is just the diffuse term. Most of the time, the specular part is either left as is or removed entirely. However, it can also be useful to modify the specular term in order to gain more insight into the volume [19].

14.2.1   Tone Shading

As described in Chapter 5, the diffuse component of Blinn-Phong shading determines the intensity of diffusely reflected light with the dot product between the surface normal and the light vector: $(\mathbf{n} \cdot \mathbf{l})$. The range of this dot product is $[-1, 1]$, which encompasses the full range of angles between the two vectors. However, in order to prevent the effect that surfaces are lit from behind, the reflected light intensity has to be restricted to one "side" of the normal, i.e., $\mathbf{I} = \max(\mathbf{n} \cdot \mathbf{l}, 0)$. This restricts the range to $[0, 1]$ and has the implication that, if only one static light source is used, it is often hard to discern the actual shape of an object. The reason for this is that there is no light in areas whose normal vector points away from the light source.

Tone shading [83] (sometimes also called *Gooch shading* or *cool-warm shading*) interpolates between two user-specified colors over the full $[-1, 1]$ range of the dot product between normal and light direction. Traditionally, one of these colors is set to a warm tone, e.g., red, orange, or yellow. The other color is set to a cool tone, e.g., purple, blue, or green. Cool colors are perceived by human observers as receding into the background, whereas warm colors are seen as advancing into the foreground. Tone shading uses this observation in order to improve the depth perception of shaded images by interpolating between the warm tone and the cool tone and adding in the contribution of the object's intrinsic color.

Although originally developed for surface shading, tone shading can easily be adapted to direct volume rendering by mixing the color from the transfer function with the color obtained via tone shading. One of the possibilities to do this is the following:

$$\mathbf{I} = \left(\frac{1 + (\mathbf{n} \cdot \mathbf{l})}{2}\right) k_a + \left(1 - \frac{1 + (\mathbf{n} \cdot \mathbf{l})}{2}\right) k_b, \qquad (14.1)$$

where $\mathbf{l}$ denotes the light vector, and $\mathbf{n} = \nabla f / |\nabla f|$ is the normalized gradient of the scalar field f (the volume) that is used as the normal vector.

The two colors to interpolate, k_a and k_b, are derived from two constant colors k_{cool} and k_{warm} and the color from the transfer function k_t, using two user-specified factors α and β that determine the additive contribution of k_t:

$$
\begin{aligned}
k_a &= k_{cool} + \alpha k_t, & (14.2) \\
k_b &= k_{warm} + \beta k_t. & (14.3)
\end{aligned}
$$

The opacity of the shaded fragment is determined directly from the transfer function look-up, i.e., the alpha portion of k_t.

These tone shading equations can be evaluated on a per-fragment basis in a fragment program for high-quality results.

14.2.2 Cartoon Shading

Cartoon shading [151] tries to emulate the style of cartoonists, who usually paint large areas of an object with a constant color, e.g., one color for the part of the object that is pointing toward the light source and another color for the part that is pointing away. The diffuse part of the model consists of these two colors and the thresholding value for the dot product $(\mathbf{n} \cdot \mathbf{l})$ between the surface normal and the light direction that determines when to use which of the two colors. This can either be evaluated procedurally in the shader, or $\max(\mathbf{n} \cdot \mathbf{l}, 0)$ can be used as the texture coordinate for indexing a 1D texture map. It is also possible to use just a single color and map the dot product term to two discrete scalar light intensities, which are then multiplied by the single constant color. Figure 14.9 (c) illustrates cartoon shading with more than two colors, but still clearly discernible large areas of constant color that provide a cartoon-style look using a 2D look-up texture.

14.2.3 Lighting Look-Up Tables and Lighting Transfer Functions

Although the shading equations differ, many lighting models are similar enough that they can be computed with a single equation that is parameterized by look-up tables. Using a unified equation has the big advantage that one simple fragment program can be used for a variety of lighting models that are simply specified via different look-up tables, i.e., textures.

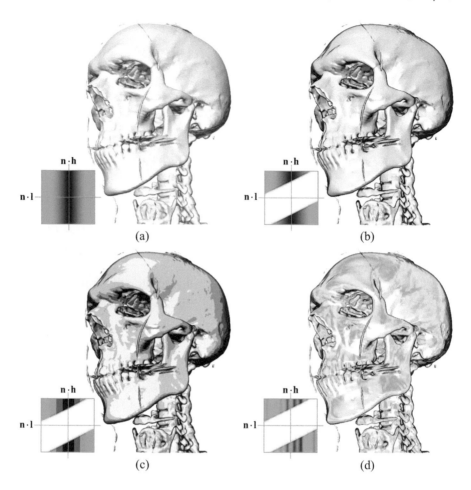

Figure 14.9. Lighting look-up tables allow a single shading equation to be used for a variety of shading models. A shading model is specified by a 2D look-up texture that is indexed with the two dot products used for computing the diffuse and specular reflection in the Blinn-Phong model: $(\mathbf{n} \cdot \mathbf{l})$ and $(\mathbf{n} \cdot \mathbf{h})$. (a) Standard shading; (b) contour enhancement; (c) cartoon shading; (d) metal shading. (Images courtesy of Stefan Bruckner [18], © 2005 IEEE.)

A well-known example from surface shading is anisotropic lighting models, where anisotropy is controlled by 2D look-up textures [105] that are indexed with dot product terms including the light direction vector, the view vector, and the tangent vector that determines the main direction of anisotropy.

In order to use standard shading and non-photorealistic shading with a single shading equation in volume rendering, the same or a similar parameterization can be used. Similar to Blinn-Phong shading, the $(\mathbf{v} \cdot \mathbf{r})$ term can be substituted by $(\mathbf{n} \cdot \mathbf{h})$, using the halfway vector $\mathbf{h}$ (see Section 5). Figure 14.9 illustrates four examples of volume shading [18], where a single 2D RGBA look-up texture parameterizes the shading model. The standard shading terms of *ambient*, *diffuse*, and *specular* illumination are stored in the RGB channels of this texture, respectively. The alpha channel can be used for additional parameterization, e.g., context-preserving shading [19], which is outlined below. Note that it is possible to include simple contour rendering in this model, as the view vector $\mathbf{v}$ is implicitly contained in the halfway vector $\mathbf{h}$. Setting the ambient, diffuse, and specular components to zero where $(\mathbf{n} \cdot \mathbf{l}) \approx 2(\mathbf{n} \cdot \mathbf{h})$ highlights contours [18].

A different goal is achieved by the related method of lighting transfer functions [172]. A lighting transfer function is used to decouple classification via assignment of opacity from lighting computations. This concept allows improved user control over the rendering of material boundaries. Similar to the 2D look-up tables described above, a lighting transfer function stores the ambient, diffuse, and specular components that parameterize the lighting model. In this case, however, the 2D table is indexed with two density values that are taken along the gradient direction in addition to the regular sample value [172]. Lighting transfer functions are also a more robust alternative to using the surface scalar that has been described in Chapter 6 for avoiding shading problems in homogeneous areas.

In the context of illustrative rendering, similar look-up tables can also be used to determine the transfer function when two volumes overlap, e.g., an object and its ghost [18]. The 2D look-up table is then indexed with the density values from the two volumes, respectively.

14.2.4   Context-Preserving Shading

Illustrative context-preserving volume rendering [19] provides an alternative to conventional clipping planes by selectively modulating opacity depending on several factors, including distance to the eye point. Other factors are a function of shading intensity, gradient magnitude, and previously accumulated opacity, whose influence on the resulting opacity is controlled by two user-defined parameters. These parameters regulate how opacity is reduced selectively in "less important" data regions. Figure 14.10 illustrates an example where opacity is successively decreased from left to right by modifying a parameter of the shading model. In contrast with clipping planes, context is preserved by smoothly deemphasizing different parts of the volume instead of entirely cutting them away.

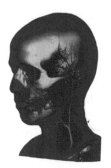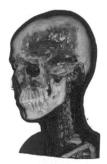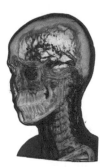

Figure 14.10. Context-preserving volume rendering [19] selectively reduces opacity with two simple user-controlled parameters and provides an interesting alternative to conventional clipping planes. (Images courtesy of Stefan Bruckner, © Eurographics Association 2005.)

14.3   Contour Rendering

Contours are one of the most important ingredients of non-photorealistic and illustrative rendering. Although most contour-rendering algorithms work on polygonal meshes, there are several established and efficient methods for computing them in volume rendering. This section summarizes contour detection in object space when there is no mesh representation available.

14.3.1   Basic Object-Space Contour Detection

The simplest way to detect a contour in volume rendering is to use a threshold for the dot product of the view direction and the normal vector used for shading, e.g., $(\mathbf{v} \cdot \mathbf{n}) < \epsilon$. The "ideal" contour would be where these two vectors are exactly orthogonal, i.e., where the dot product is zero. Using a larger threshold ϵ determines the thickness of the contour. Of course, in volume rendering the normalized gradient of the field is used instead of a surface normal vector. The following two sections illustrate how this basic method can be used for rendering contours of isosurfaces and full volumes, respectively.

14.3.2   Isosurface Contours

The simple thresholding approach just described can be used directly for rendering contours of isosurfaces. For each sample where the isosurface is rendered (e.g., because the sample value is greater than or equal to the

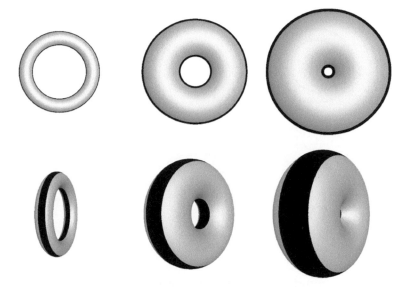

Figure 14.11.   Isosurfaces (of a single distance-field volume) with contours computed in object space. The top-row images show that contour thickness varies in screen space although the threshold for $(\mathbf{v} \cdot \mathbf{n})$ is constant. The bottom-row images show that this is due to a larger area on the surface being classified as part of the contour, which results from differing surface curvature.

isovalue), thresholding determines whether a contour color should be drawn instead of the isosurface's color.

However, a basic problem shared by all approaches using a constant threshold ϵ for contour detection is that the actual contour thickness in screen space varies according to surface curvature. This becomes especially visible when rendering isosurfaces. This problem is illustrated in Figures 14.11 and 14.12 for isosurfaces of a distance field. In Figure 14.11, the threshold is a constant. When the isovalue and thus the resulting isosurface changes, the screen-space thickness of the contours changes as well. When the same scene is viewed from the side, it becomes clear that the area on the surface that is classified as belonging to the contour varies significantly with surface curvature (the view direction used for contour detection is kept constant with respect to the volume). In contrast to this, in Figure 14.12 curvature has been used to modify the threshold ϵ accordingly, which results in contours of constant screen-space thickness. Figure 14.24 illustrates the same problem with a more complex volume. More details of using curvature for object-space detection of contours that results in constant screen-space thickness are given in Section 14.6.2.

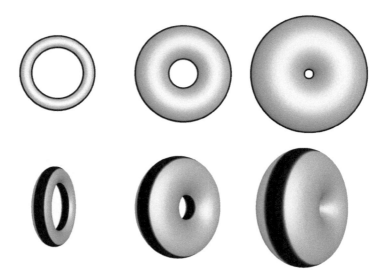

Figure 14.12.   Isosurfaces with contours computed in object space. In contrast with Figure 14.11, contour thickness has now been modulated according to surface curvature, which allows one to achieve constant screen-space thickness (top-row images). The area on the surface that is classified as being part of the contour is correspondingly smaller (bottom-row images).

14.3.3   Volumetric Contours

Even without an explicit notion of surfaces, or isosurfaces, a simple model based on the gradient magnitude and the angle between the view direction and the gradient direction can visualize the contours of material boundaries in volumes effectively [38, 57]. Two examples with different parameter settings are depicted in the left two images of Figure 14.13.

This model can be used in real-time volume rendering for obtaining a contour intensity $\mathbf{I}_{\text{contour}}$ by evaluating the following equation in a fragment program:

$$\mathbf{I}_{\text{contour}} = g\left(\|\nabla f\|\right) \cdot \left(1 - \|(\mathbf{v} \cdot \mathbf{n})\|\right)^{n}, \qquad (14.4)$$

where $\mathbf{v}$ is the viewing vector, ∇f denotes the gradient at the current position, $\mathbf{n} = \nabla f / \|\nabla f\|$ is the normalized gradient, and $g(\cdot)$ is a windowing function for the gradient magnitude. The exponent n is a constant, e.g., $n = 8$. There are two main parts in this equation. The first $\left(g\left(\|\nabla f\|\right)\right)$ is view-independent and determines if there is a material boundary and how pronounced it is. The second part is view-dependent and restricts nonzero intensities to contours as given by the relation between the view vector and the gradient direction.

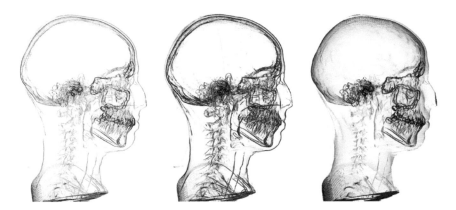

Figure 14.13. Volumetric contours using Equation 14.4. The left two images use an exponent of $n = 8$ and different gradient magnitude windows $g(\cdot)$. The right image uses an exponent of $n = 2$, which is already too low. In this case, not only the contours are visible. An exponent between $n = 4$ and $n = 16$ is usually a good choice.

Although it is view-independent, the most important parameter of this model is the windowing function $g(\cdot)$ for the gradient magnitude, which is illustrated in Figure 14.14. Instead of selecting a single isovalue and thus rendering the contours of a single isosurface, using a function of gradient magnitude allows one to depict the contours of many material boundaries simultaneously. The ramp of the windowing function determines a gradient magnitude threshold for detection of material boundaries and a smooth transition between "no material boundary" and "definite material boundary." As illustrated in the left two images of Figure 14.13, the windowing function makes it easy to control the appearance of contours. The window can be specified directly via its center and width. Alternatively, it can also be specified through a standard transfer function interface, where the alpha component specifies $g(\cdot)$, and the RGB components are simply neglected.

The exponent n in Equation 14.4 determines what is classified as a contour depending on the angle between the view vector and the gradient direction. Values between $n = 4$ and $n = 16$ usually achieve good results. The influence of the actual value for n on the overall appearance of the resulting contours is much less significant than that of the window $g(\cdot)$. An exception is the case when the exponent is too low (e.g., $n = 2$), where parts of the volume that clearly do not correspond to contours will be rendered. This is illustrated in the right image of Figure 14.13.

The fragment intensity $\mathbf{I}_{\text{contour}}$ obtained via Equation 14.4 can be multiplied by a constant contour color in order to render colored contours. If

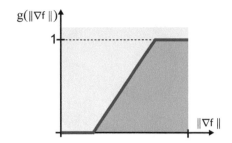

Figure 14.14. The gradient magnitude windowing function $g(\cdot)$ for volumetric contours using Equation 14.4. This function restricts the detection of contours to the interfaces, i.e., boundary surfaces, between different materials depending on local gradient magnitude.

alpha blending is used as the compositing mode, the fragment alpha can simply be set to the intensity $\mathbf{I}_{contour}$. However, a very useful compositing mode for contours obtained via this technique is maximum intensity projection (MIP), instead of using alpha blending, in order to make all contours visible equally, independent of their depth order. The images in Figure 14.13 also use MIP compositing. (Note that, since this figure shows black contours on a white background, it actually uses "minimum intensity projection.")

14.4   Surface and Isosurface Curvature

Before the subsequent sections discuss in detail how curvature information can be used for driving illustrative rendering styles, this section covers the necessary basics.

14.4.1   Surface Curvature

Figure 14.15 (left) illustrates a point on a surface with its corresponding surface normal and the surface normal of neighboring points on the surface. Intuitively, the concept of curvature at a given point on a surface describes the variation of the normal vector as we move from this point into some direction by a very small distance. The basic definition of curvature is given for curves instead of surfaces. However, the concept can easily be extended to surfaces by looking at curves on these surfaces. Observe the point in the right image of Figure 14.15, the blue normal vector at that point, and the corresponding tangent plane illustrated by the two black coordinate frame vectors. We can think of all the directions from this point in the tangent

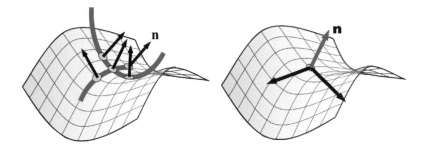

Figure 14.15. Curvature is the variation of the surface normal when moving on a surface. The tangent plane is determined by the surface normal, and maximum and minimum principal curvature directions are defined in this tangent plane (right). (Images courtesy of Gordon Kindlmann.)

plane (two of them being the two directions indicated in black) and the planes that are spanned by these directions and the normal vector. Each of these planes intersects the surface, and these intersections are curves on the surface that contain the point we are looking at. Two of these intersecting curves are illustrated in blue in the left image of Figure 14.15. The curvature at that point in a given direction is the curvature of the corresponding intersection curve at that point. This definition of curvature in a given direction on a surface is often also called *normal curvature*.

Thus, there is a whole angular range of directions and the corresponding normal curvatures at any given point on a surface. However, in the general case these curvatures have a well-defined minimum and maximum, and the corresponding directions are orthogonal to each other. These two curvatures are called the *principal curvatures*, and the corresponding curves are illustrated in blue in the left image of Figure 14.15. More specifically, the directions are called *principal curvature directions* (which we will denote below as e_1 and e_2 for maximum and minimum direction, respectively) and the scalar curvatures themselves are called *principal curvature magnitudes* (which we will denote below as κ_1 and κ_2 for maximum and minimum curvature, respectively). Note that $\kappa_1 \geq \kappa_2$ is always true, as we associate the former with maximum curvature.

Points on surfaces can be classified with respect to their principal curvatures (κ_1, κ_2) as follows (see Figure 14.16).

- *Elliptical points* are points of convex curvature, where both κ_1 and κ_2 are positive. (But they are not equal and neither of them is zero.)

- *Hyperbolic points* are points where the surface is saddle-shaped, i.e., where κ_1 is positive and κ_2 is negative. (But neither of them is zero.)

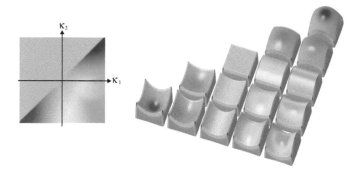

Figure 14.16. Depicting shape in the principal curvature domain (κ_1, κ_2). κ_1 is the maximum principal curvature, κ_2 the minimum principal curvature. Thus, $\kappa_1 \geq \kappa_2$. (Images courtesy of Gordon Kindlmann, © 2003 IEEE.)

- *Parabolic points* are points between the cases of elliptical and hyperbolic, i.e., where one of the two is zero. (Usually the case where both are zero is included, but these points are also umbilical points as described below.) At these points, the surface is locally shaped like a cylinder. *Ridge and valley lines* on a surface connect parabolic points where the nonzero curvature is above or below a certain threshold, respectively (see Figure 14.17).

- *Umbilical points* (or *umbilics*) are those points where both curvatures are equal. In these points, the curvature directions are not well-defined. These points are either locally sphere-shaped or locally planar. A sphere and a plane both consist entirely of umbilical points with constant curvature.

Figure 14.16 illustrates all possible shapes with respect to principal curvatures. Because $\kappa_1 \geq \kappa_2$, the valid curvature domain is a triangle, which

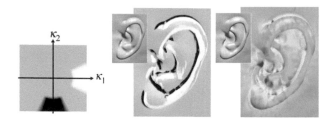

Figure 14.17. Visualizing specific shapes such as ridge and valley lines by simply painting them in the 2D curvature domain. (Images courtesy of Gordon Kindlmann, © 2003 IEEE.)

is color-coded in the left image. The corresponding surface shapes are illustrated in the right image.

The curvature in any direction on the surface can be calculated from the principal curvatures and directions.

14.4.2   Implicit Curvature

In volume rendering, we are interested in the curvature of implicitly given isosurfaces. Thus, the curvature at a point in a volume is defined as the curvature of that point on the isosurface passing through it. With this definition, the notion of curvature can be defined at any point in the volume as long as the gradient at that point is well-defined. If the gradient vanishes, i.e., its magnitude is zero, such as in a homogeneous block with a constant density, no curvature can be computed. At such a point the notion of a surface does not exist. Chapter 6 contains a discussion of the problems that occur when the gradient magnitude is very small and thus the gradient direction is unreliable.

14.4.3   Scalar Curvature Measures

Scalar curvature measures are a good way to visualize surface shape. Figure 14.18 depicts the same surface with four different curvature measures. In addition to maximum and minimum principal curvature, several measures building on them are defined. Two examples are the following.

Gaussian curvature. The Gaussian curvature is defined as the product of the two principal curvatures: $\kappa_1\kappa_2$. The *parabolic curves* on a surface are those curves where the Gaussian curvature is zero. As such, they also have the property that they separate areas with elliptical curvature from areas with hyperbolic curvature. The rightmost image of Figure 14.18 illustrates Gaussian curvature.

Mean curvature. The mean curvature is defined as $(\kappa_1 + \kappa_2)/2$. The middle-right image of Figure 14.18 illustrates mean curvature.

14.4.4   Computing Implicit Curvature via Convolution

In contrast with computing curvature on mesh representations [263, 228], implicit curvature in a volume can be computed directly via convolution on the underlying regular grid structure [124]. Assuming that the data value $f(\mathbf{x})$ increases as position $\mathbf{x}$ moves further inside objects of interest (e.g., a standard CT scan), the surface normal is $\mathbf{n} = -\mathbf{g}/|\mathbf{g}|$ where $\mathbf{g} = \nabla f$. Curvature information is contained in $\nabla \mathbf{n}^T$, which is represented as a 3×3 matrix. However, trying to evaluate the gradient of a pre-computed normalized vector field would prevent direct convolution-based

Figure 14.18.   Color-coding different curvature measures. From left to right:
maximum principal curvature κ_1, minimum principal curvature κ_2, mean curvature
$(\kappa_1 + \kappa_2)/2$, Gaussian curvature $\kappa_1\kappa_2$. Positive curvature is depicted in green and
negative curvature in magenta. Curvature isolines are drawn in black, except zero
curvature, which is highlighted in blue. (Images courtesy of Gordon Kindlmann,
©2003 IEEE.)

measurement of curvature from the original data. The expression $\nabla \mathbf{n}^T$ can
be transformed using vector calculus:

$$
\begin{aligned}
\nabla \mathbf{n}^T &= -\nabla \left(\frac{\mathbf{g}^T}{|\mathbf{g}|} \right) = -\left(\frac{\nabla \mathbf{g}^T}{|\mathbf{g}|} - \frac{\mathbf{g}\,\nabla^T |\mathbf{g}|}{|\mathbf{g}|^2} \right) \\
&= -\frac{1}{|\mathbf{g}|} \left(\mathbf{H} - \frac{\mathbf{g}\,\nabla^T (\mathbf{g}^T \mathbf{g})^{1/2}}{|\mathbf{g}|} \right) = -\frac{1}{|\mathbf{g}|} \left(\mathbf{H} - \frac{\mathbf{g}\,(2\mathbf{g}^T\mathbf{H})}{2\,|\mathbf{g}|^2} \right) \\
&= -\frac{1}{|\mathbf{g}|} \left(\mathbf{I} - \frac{\mathbf{g}\mathbf{g}^T}{|\mathbf{g}|^2} \right) \mathbf{H} = -\frac{1}{|\mathbf{g}|}(\mathbf{I} - \mathbf{n}\mathbf{n}^T)\mathbf{H} \\
&= -\frac{1}{|\mathbf{g}|}\mathbf{P}\mathbf{H}.
\end{aligned}
\tag{14.5}
$$

$\mathbf{I}$ is the identity, $\mathbf{P} = \mathbf{I} - \mathbf{n}\mathbf{n}^T$ projects vectors onto the plane tangent to
the isosurface, and the Hessian is

$$
\mathbf{H} = \begin{bmatrix}
\partial^2 f/\partial x^2 & \partial^2 f/\partial x \partial y & \partial^2 f/\partial x \partial z \\
\partial^2 f/\partial x \partial y & \partial^2 f/\partial y^2 & \partial^2 f/\partial y \partial z \\
\partial^2 f/\partial x \partial z & \partial^2 f/\partial y \partial z & \partial^2 f/\partial z^2
\end{bmatrix}.
$$

Considering the factors of Equation 14.5 from right to left helps under-
stand the structure of $\nabla \mathbf{n}^T$. The Hessian $\mathbf{H}$ represents how the gradient
$\mathbf{g}$ changes as a function of infinitesimal changes of position in $\mathbb{R}^3$. The
changes in $\mathbf{g}$ have a component along $\mathbf{g}$ (the gradient can change length),
and a component within the tangent plane (the gradient can change direction). For the purposes of describing curvature, only the latter component
matters, and it can be isolated with left-multiplication by $\mathbf{P}$. Finally, the
$-1/|\mathbf{g}|$ scaling factor converts infinitesimal changes of the (unnormalized)
gradient $\mathbf{g}$ into infinitesimal changes of the unit-length normal $\mathbf{n}$.

Though $\mathbf{P}$ and $\mathbf{H}$ are symmetric, $\nabla\mathbf{n}^T$ is not. For $\mathbf{u}$ and $\mathbf{v}$ in the tangent plane, however,

$$\mathbf{v}^T\mathbf{P}\mathbf{H}\mathbf{u} = \mathbf{v}^T\mathbf{H}\mathbf{u} = \mathbf{u}^T\mathbf{H}\mathbf{v} = \mathbf{u}^T\mathbf{P}\mathbf{H}\mathbf{v},$$

so the restriction of $\nabla\mathbf{n}^T = -\mathbf{P}\mathbf{H}/|\mathbf{g}|$ to the tangent plane is symmetric, and there exists an orthonormal basis $\{\mathbf{p}_1, \mathbf{p}_2\}$ for the tangent plane in which $\nabla\mathbf{n}^T$ is represented as a 2×2 diagonal matrix. This basis can be extended to an orthonormal basis for all of $\mathbb{R}^3$, $\{\mathbf{p}_1, \mathbf{p}_2, \mathbf{n}\}$, and in this basis, the derivative of the surface normal is represented by

$$\nabla\mathbf{n}^T = \begin{bmatrix} \kappa_1 & 0 & \sigma_1 \\ 0 & \kappa_2 & \sigma_2 \\ 0 & 0 & 0 \end{bmatrix}.$$

The bottom row is all zero because no change in position can make the normal $\mathbf{n}$ change in length. Motion within the tangent plane, along $\mathbf{p}_1$ and $\mathbf{p}_2$, leads to changes of $\mathbf{n}$ along the same directions, as scaled by κ_1 and κ_2 respectively. Motion along the normal, away from or into the surface, tilts the normal according to σ_1 and σ_2. There are no off-diagonal terms by the choice of $\{\mathbf{p}_1, \mathbf{p}_2\}$. The principal curvature directions are $\mathbf{p}_1$ and $\mathbf{p}_2$, while κ_1 and κ_2 are the principal curvatures.

Multiplying $\nabla\mathbf{n}^T$ by $\mathbf{P}$ helps isolate κ_1 and κ_2 in the $\{\mathbf{p}_1, \mathbf{p}_2, \mathbf{n}\}$ basis:

$$-\frac{\mathbf{P}\mathbf{H}\mathbf{P}}{|\mathbf{g}|} = \nabla\mathbf{n}^T\mathbf{P} = \nabla\mathbf{n}^T \begin{bmatrix} 1 & 0 & 0 \\ 0 & 1 & 0 \\ 0 & 0 & 0 \end{bmatrix} = \begin{bmatrix} \kappa_1 & 0 & 0 \\ 0 & \kappa_2 & 0 \\ 0 & 0 & 0 \end{bmatrix}.$$

Because $-\mathbf{P}\mathbf{H}\mathbf{P}/|\mathbf{g}|$ is measured in the usual (X, Y, Z) basis of the volume rather than the $\{\mathbf{p}_1, \mathbf{p}_2, \mathbf{n}\}$ basis used above, κ_1 and κ_2 are not simply available as the diagonal entries of $-\mathbf{P}\mathbf{H}\mathbf{P}/|\mathbf{g}|$. Instead, two matrix invariants, the trace and Frobenius norm (defined by $|\mathbf{M}|_F = \sqrt{\text{tr}(\mathbf{M}\mathbf{M}^T)}$), are used to compute the curvatures. The principal curvature directions are the eigenvectors of $-\mathbf{P}\mathbf{H}\mathbf{P}/|\mathbf{g}|$ corresponding to the κ_1, κ_2 eigenvalues.

The most important part of the curvature computation is measuring all the necessary partial derivatives (in $\mathbf{g}$ and $\mathbf{H}$) by convolution. The tricubic B-spline and its derivatives provide a very good basis for curvature estimation [124]. Chapter 9 describes how the necessary convolution filters can be implemented on GPUs for real-time rendering.

To summarize, the steps to measure the curvature of implicit surfaces in volume data are as follows.

1. Measure the first partial derivatives in the gradient $\mathbf{g}$, and compute $\mathbf{n} = -\mathbf{g}/|\mathbf{g}|$ and $\mathbf{P} = \mathbf{I} - \mathbf{n}\mathbf{n}^T$.

2. Measure the second partial derivatives in the Hessian $\mathbf{H}$, and compute $-\mathbf{PHP}/|\mathbf{g}|$.

3. Compute the trace T and Frobenius norm F of $-\mathbf{PHP}/|\mathbf{g}|$. Using the quadratic formula,

$$\begin{array}{ll} T = \kappa_1 + \kappa_2 & \kappa_1 = (T + \sqrt{2F^2 - T^2})/2 \\ F = \sqrt{\kappa_1^2 + \kappa_2^2} \quad \Rightarrow \quad & \kappa_2 = (T - \sqrt{2F^2 - T^2})/2\,. \end{array}$$

14.5   Deferred Shading of Isosurfaces

The big advantage of deferred shading [45, 155, 231] is that it decouples the determination of *visibility* from actually performing *shading* on samples or pixels that are known to be visible. For rendering isosurfaces in volume rendering, this means that traversing the volume in order to find the isosurface is decoupled from performing shading on the resulting points on the isosurface. Intersection positions of viewing rays with the isosurface are computed in a first step, and a completely separate—deferred—step subsequently computes shading at only these positions. This also allows us to combine different fragment programs for these two steps. Intersection positions can be determined either with slicing or via ray casting. Shading can then naturally be performed using a variety of different shading models.

14.5.1   Deferred Shading Pipeline

We briefly summarize a shading pipeline for deferred shading of isosurfaces with tricubic filtering and real-time computation of implicit isosurface curvature [93]. The first step is to generate a floating point image of ray/isosurface intersection positions, such as the one depicted in the right of Figure 14.19. Figure 14.19 illustrates this first step beginning with the original scalar volume data. In addition to the volume, a min-max grid of small blocks (e.g., 8^3 voxels) is used to cull away blocks that cannot contain a part of the isosurface. Then, a depth image of the bounding faces of these blocks is generated and used as start depths for a ray caster. Ray casting stops when the isosurface is intersected, and the intersection position in volume coordinates is written to the floating point output image. The precision of intersection positions is refined via an iterative root search procedure (e.g., bisection).

All following stages are performed in image space and are thus completely decoupled from the resolution of the volume. In order to provide the basis for complex shading effects, various differential surface properties are computed using tricubic B-spline convolution filters. These surface

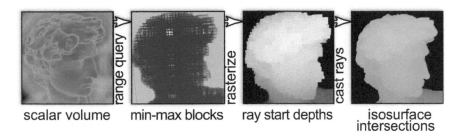

Figure 14.19. Deferred isosurface shading: from the volume to the intersection position image.

properties are likewise written to floating point images. Figure 14.20 illustrates the images that are computed at this stage. First, the first-order partial derivatives determine the gradient of the field on the isosurface. Using the gradient and the corresponding tangent plane, the maximum and minimum principal curvature magnitudes are computed. From the curvature magnitudes, the corresponding curvature directions can be computed as well.

Figure 14.20. Deferred isosurface shading: computing differential surface properties.

Finally, the differential surface properties that have been computed can be visualized and used for a variety of shading effects. Figure 14.21 illustrates examples from a simple basic shading model such as tone shading to visualizing surface curvature, drawing ridge and valley lines with 2D curvature transfer functions, and visualizing the direction field of principal curvature directions using flow advection. The following section describes the different possibilities in more detail.

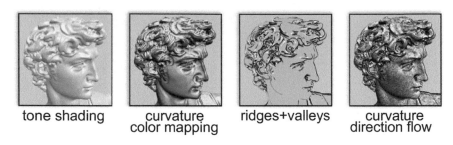

tone shading   **curvature**   **ridges+valleys**   **curvature**
                      color mapping   **direction flow**

Figure 14.21. Deferred isosurface shading: performing shading in image space.

14.6   Curvature-Based Isosurface Illustration

Computing implicit surface curvature is a powerful tool for isosurface investigation and non-photorealistic rendering of isosurfaces. This section assumes that an isosurface is shaded using *deferred shading* in image space, as described above.

When differential isosurface properties have been computed in preceding deferred shading passes, this information can be used for performing a variety of mappings to shaded images in a final shading pass.

14.6.1   Curvature-Based Transfer Functions

Principal curvature magnitudes can be visualized on an isosurface by mapping them to colors via 1D or 2D transfer function look-up textures.

One-dimensional curvature transfer functions. Color mappings of first or second principal curvature magnitude via 1D transfer function look-up tables can be computed during shading. The same approach can be used to depict additional curvature measures directly derived from the principal magnitudes, such as mean curvature $(\kappa_1 + \kappa_2)/2$ or Gaussian curvature $\kappa_1\kappa_2$. Figure 14.22 depicts a 1D curvature transfer function for a signed curvature measure. In Figure 14.23 (left), this transfer function has been used for visualization of maximum principal curvature. Note the fine detail, which is due to tricubic filtering at sub-voxel precision instead of interpolating curvature from grid points.

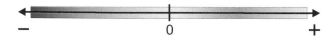

$$-\qquad\qquad 0 \qquad\qquad +$$

Figure 14.22. A 1D curvature transfer function.

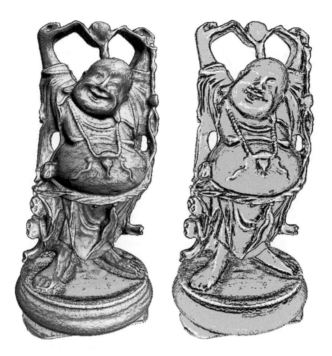

Figure 14.23. Happy buddhas. The left image uses the 1D curvature transfer function depicted in Figure 14.22 to visualize maximum principal curvature. The right image uses the 2D curvature transfer function depicted in Figure 14.17 to highlight ridge and valley lines in white and black, respectively. Note that no actual lines are drawn. These images were generated using ray casting on a $256 \times 256 \times 512$ distance-field volume [93]. No geometry was used.

Two-dimensional curvature transfer functions. Transfer functions in the 2D domain of both principal curvature magnitudes (κ_1, κ_2) are especially powerful, as color specification in this domain allows one to highlight different structures on the surface [106], including ridge and valley lines [111, 124]. Figure 14.23 (right) shows the application of the 2D curvature transfer function that is depicted in Figure 14.17. By simply painting in the 2D curvature domain of (κ_1, κ_2), ridge and valley lines can be highlighted without drawing actual lines.

14.6.2 Curvature-Controlled Contours

As described in Section 14.3.2, a major problem of detecting contours in object space with a constant threshold on the dot product of viewing and

Figure 14.24. Contour thickness in screen space changes with local curvature (left). When this curvature is computed and used to change the threshold for contour detection accordingly, constant screen-space thickness can be achieved (right). (Images courtesy of Gordon Kindlmann, © 2003 IEEE.)

normal vector $(\mathbf{v} \cdot \mathbf{n})$ is that the screen-space thickness of the resulting contours depends on the local curvature of the isosurface. Figure 14.24 illustrates this for a simple cone and a more complex volume. Constant screen-space thickness of contours can be achieved by computing the curvature in the view direction, κ_v, and using a 2D function of κ_v and $(\mathbf{v} \cdot \mathbf{n})$ instead of a constant threshold [124]. Figure 14.25 shows the 2D transfer function that can be used to achieve a constant contour thickness T. This function can be implemented as a simple 2D texture, just as the 2D curvature transfer function shown in Figure 14.17. This also allows us to achieve smooth contours by simply smoothing the boundary between "contours" and "no contours" in the transfer function image.

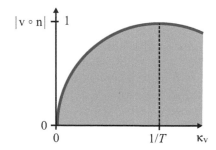

Figure 14.25. Controlling contour thickness according to surface curvature. κ_v is the curvature in view direction. T is the desired constant contour thickness in pixels. The blue area is classified as being on the contour.

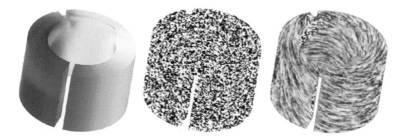

Figure 14.26. Image-space flow advection on curved surfaces. The vector field (left) is projected to image space and advects noise patterns (center) in the projected directions, which results in the illusion of flow advection on the surface in 3D (right). (Images courtesy of Bob Laramee [153], © 2003 IEEE.)

14.6.3 Visualizing Curvature Directions

Direct mappings of principal curvature directions to RGB colors are hard to interpret. However, principal curvature directions on an isosurface can be visualized using image-based flow visualization that visualizes an arbitrary 3D vector field on a curved surface [269]. In particular, flow can be advected on the surface entirely in image space [153, 154]. The basic principle is illustrated in Figure 14.26. First, a 3D vector field on a curved surface is projected to image space. Then, a noise pattern with spatial and temporal coherence is advected in image space in the directions of the projected vector field. Always blending several successive frames and periodically injecting fresh noise achieves results of very good quality [269].

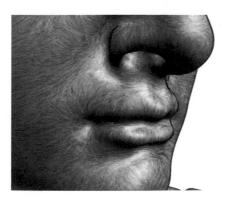

Figure 14.27. Visualizing principal curvature directions in real time using image-space flow advection. These images illustrate maximum principal curvature directions. (Right image reprinted from [93], © Eurographics Association 2005.)

These methods can be used in real time, complementing the capability of the deferred shading pipeline outlined in Section 14.5.1 to generate high-quality curvature information on-the-fly. The computation of principal curvature directions yields a potentially unsteady "flow field." In this case, it is natural to perform per-pixel advection guided by the floating point image containing principal direction vectors instead of warping mesh vertex or texture coordinates as it has been done in the original approaches [269, 153, 154]. Figure 14.27 shows two examples of using flow advection in order to visualize principal curvature directions. Note that this entire rendering process is real-time [93], from ray casting for determining the isosurface to computation of differential surface properties and curvature directions, to visualizing and shading these directions using image-based flow advection. However, a problem with advecting flow along curvature directions is that their orientation is not uniquely defined, and thus seams in the flow cannot be entirely avoided [269].

14.7   Further Reading

The area of non-photorealistic and illustrative techniques is vast, and this chapter could only touch the surface of this topic. The tutorial by Viola and others [273] provides an introduction to illustrative visualization. The book by Preim and Bartz [216] covers the use of illustrative techniques in medical visualization. The course by Ma and others [176] describes non-photorealistic approaches in the context of both art and visualization.

The paper by Ebert and Rheingans [57] describes a volume-illustration pipeline that combines several methods such as silhouette and boundary enhancement, tone shading, feature enhancement, and depth and orientation cues. Many NPR techniques that have been developed for surface illustration have been adapted to volume rendering, e.g., pen-and-ink rendering [266]. An important goal of illustrative approaches is to highlight hidden structures, e.g., using multiple layered isosurfaces [73], multiple transfer functions [171], or segmentation information [92]. Time-varying volumes can also be visualized succinctly by using techniques inspired by illustration [116], including multivariate volume data [253]. The visualization of motion can even be used to provide effective shape cues for static objects [174]. Illustration techniques are also an effective means for visualizing flow [261].

Distance fields are a powerful volumetric representation of surface- or point-based objects [205]. They can be generated with GPUs [242, 258] or software approaches, e.g., using radial hermite operators [197]. This chapter has shown how objects represented by distance-field volumes can be illustrated using implicit curvature information.

15

Volume Clipping

VOLUME VISUALIZATION TARGETS THE PROBLEM of extracting and displaying the important and relevant parts of a volumetric data set. This goal can be separated into two subgoals: first, emphasizing important regions, for example, by using bright colors and high opacities; second, deemphasizing or hiding unimportant regions. *Volume clipping* specifically addresses the second subgoal by completely cutting away unimportant areas. It can be regarded as the 3D analogue of image cropping or extraction, known from image processing and editing.

Figure 15.1 shows a traditional and common example of volume clipping: a clipping plane is applied to cut away a part of the volume rendering

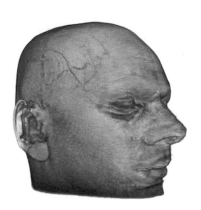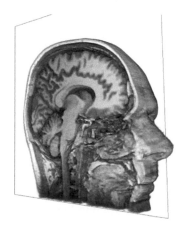

Figure 15.1. Volume clipping with a single clipping plane. The left image shows the original volume rendering of an MR (magnetic resonance) scan of a human head. In the right image, a clipping plane is applied to the same data set.

of a medical MR (magnetic resonance) scan. This image demonstrates that clipping is especially appropriate when the volume is rendered (almost) opaque. The underlying metaphor is known from cutaway illustrations and therefore very intuitive. Volume clipping cuts away selected parts of the volume based on the position of voxels in the data set. By removing these occluding parts, the user can explore otherwise hidden regions of the volume. This geometric approach can be considered as complementary to a classification via traditional transfer functions that only consider scalar data values and their derivatives (see Chapters 4 and 10).

Clipping planes are a standard tool in most volume-rendering systems; their importance and usefulness in practical volume exploration cannot be overemphasized. Clipping planes are easy to understand, very efficient, simple to implement, and widely available. This chapter briefly describes how to implement clipping planes and goes well beyond this type of clipping method. Based on a generic and flexible concept of clipping, two main issues are discussed. First, how can we define a clipping geometry that might be more complex than just a plane? Second, how can a clipped volume be rendered efficiently?

The efficiency issue is the reason several clipping methods are presented in this chapter. For example, there exist highly specialized rendering techniques that are extremely fast but support only a restricted class of clipping objects. On the other hand, more flexible clipping methods are typically associated with higher rendering costs. Therefore, the choice of method depends on the application area and user requirements. Throughout this chapter, we assume that texture slicing (see Chapter 3) is used as the basic technique for GPU-based volume rendering, unless otherwise noted.

15.1 Conceptual Description of Volume Clipping

Volume clipping can be considered as a way to modify the visibility of regions of a 3D data set. Figure 15.2 illustrates the conceptual design of volume clipping. The basic idea is that the actual scalar data volume is enriched by an additional selection volume [18]. The selection volume controls the visibility by modifying the original transfer function associated with the data volume.

We assume that the selection volume permits only a binary decision: either the data is visible at the respective position, or it is not. Therefore, the selection volume has to be given as a volume that yields the Boolean values true or false. A visible region is rendered according to the original transfer function. An invisible region is either not rendered at all or rendered completely transparent. The conceptual design is independent of how the data and selection volumes are represented internally—it works

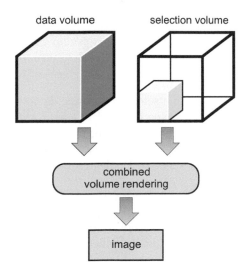

Figure 15.2. Conceptual design of volume clipping. The selection volume is used to modify the visibility of the data volume.

for a procedural representation and a discretized representation (e.g., on a uniform grid) alike.

There are two main questions. First, how can the selection volume be constructed? Second, how are the data and selection volumes rendered? With respect to the first question, the following sources are typically used to build a selection volume.

- The boundary of a selection volume can be represented by an explicitly defined clipping geometry. A clipping plane, as used in Figure 15.1, is a simple example of such a clipping geometry. The clipping plane defines a half space that is converted into the selection volume determining the visible part of the data volume. In general, the selection volume (a volumetric object) is described by a boundary representation (BRep), given by the clipping geometry.

- Segmentation provides a classification of a data volume in the form of object IDs associated with voxels. By selecting a subset of all object IDs (very often only a single ID is chosen), a volumetric region can be selected for clipping. Chapter 16 gives details on volume segmentation.

- Additional attributes of a 3D data set can be used. In general, multi-field visualization addresses the problem of displaying several data sets or several attributes of a single data set in one image. The selection volume can be defined if attributes can be mapped to Boolean values. The main challenge is to develop a useful mapping. Figure 15.5 shows an example from 3D flow visualization in which the velocity magnitude of the flow is used to select a visible region.

These three ways of defining a selection volume demonstrate that intermediate transformation steps are common. In general, the selection volume is derived from an input source by applying one operation or even a collection of several operations. Using mathematical terminology, the selection volume is a map from 3D space to Boolean values:

$$\phi_S : \ \mathbb{R}^3 \longrightarrow \{\text{true, false}\} .$$

The volumetric attributes are another map from 3D space to the respective attribute space S_A (which could be a collection of attributes such as scalar or vector values):

$$\phi_A : \ \mathbb{R}^3 \longrightarrow S_A .$$

By applying a transformation T from attribute space to Boolean values,

$$T : \ S_A \longrightarrow \{\text{true, false}\} ,$$

we can indirectly define the selection volume as

$$\phi_S = T \circ \phi_A : \ \mathbb{R}^3 \longrightarrow \{\text{true, false}\} . \tag{15.1}$$

Because the selection volume contains Boolean values true and false, a simple transformation can always be applied: negating the Boolean value results in an inversion of the visibility. We use the term *volume probing* when the volume is clipped away outside the original selection volume. Conversely, a *volume cutting* approach inverts the role of the visibility property—only the volume outside the selection volume remains visible.

The second major question concerns an efficient rendering of the data and selection volumes. The rendering method depends on the way the selection volume is represented. There exists a large variety of rendering techniques and they will be discussed in the remainder of this chapter.

15.2   Clipping via Voxelized Selection Volumes

The concept of a selection volume can be directly mapped to volume rendering by means of a voxel-based representation of the selection volume. In addition to the scalar data set, this approach stores the visibility information in a second volume texture whose voxels provide the clipping information. During rendering, the selection volume and the data volume are combined on-the-fly to compute the visibility. Therefore, this approach can be considered as a special case of multifield volume rendering, with the selection volume and the data volume being the two input fields.

15.2.1 Binary Selection Volume

The selection volume is represented by a texture similar to that for the data volume. For example, a stack of 2D textures is used for 2D texture–based volume rendering (see Section 3.2) and a 3D texture for 3D texture–based volume rendering (see Section 3.3). The selection volume is stored in a binary texture: an entry is set to true if the corresponding voxel is visible or it is set to false if the voxel should be cropped. For an implementation on graphics hardware, false is typically identified with zero and true is identified with one. In order to save texture memory, the smallest possible texture format should be used to represent these values of zero and one. A single-channel texture format is sufficient for the selection volume; an 8-bit single-channel texture format (LUMINANCE8) is typically used.

As mentioned in Section 15.1, a selection volume may originate from different sources. A voxelized version of the selection volume is quite easily generated if the selection source is already described in a volumetric form. Then, just a resampling to the target resolution of the selection volume is required, possibly combined with an evaluation of the mapping equation (Equation 15.1). This resampling may be performed on the CPU as a preprocessing step or, if possible, on the GPU. Often, however, clipping is based on a surface representation of the selection volume. Here, a voxelization of the boundary representation (BRep) is needed to fill the interior of the object. Section 12.2 provides detailed information on voxelization methods.

The other important part of the implementation concerns the actual volume rendering of a clipped data set. Fortunately, volumetric clipping can be directly mapped to graphics hardware and needs only very little hardware functionality. The key requirement is support for multitextures for the data volume and the selection volume. The set-up of texture slicing or GPU ray casting is identical to that of standard volume rendering. During rendering, both textures are accessed from the fragment-processing stage. The result of standard volume rendering (e.g., after access to the data volume and a look-up in the transfer function table) is modified by multiplying it with the value from the selection volume. This multiplication can be specified either in a fragment shader or by setting up a multitexture environment (which implements a multiplication by means of a MODULATE texture function for COMBINE_ALPHA and COMBINE_RGB). After all voxels that need to be clipped have been multiplied by zero, the fragments

```
// Cg fragment shader code for volume clipping
// via a voxelized selection volume

// Texture coords as input from the vertex stage
struct VS_OUTPUT {
    float3 TexData      :   TEXCOORD0;
    float3 TexSelection :   TEXCOORD1;
};

// Actual fragment shader
float4 main(VS_OUTPUT IN,
            uniform sampler3D SamplerDataVolume,
            uniform sampler3D SamplerSelectionVolume,
            uniform sampler1D SamplerTransferFunction)
    :  COLOR
{
    // Accesses scalar value from the data volume
    float dataValue = tex3D(SamplerDataVolume, IN.TexData);
    // Standard post-interpolative transfer function
    float4 classifiedValue = tex1D(SamplerTransferFunction,
                                    dataValue);
    // Accesses selection volume
    float selectionValue = tex3D(SamplerSelectionVolume,
                                  IN.TexSelection)-0.5;
    // Removes fragment if selectionValue < 0
    clip(selectionValue);

    return classifiedValue;
}
```

Listing 15.1. Cg fragment shader for volume clipping via a voxelized selection volume.

can be removed by the alpha test. These fragments may even be sent to the compositing stage (i.e., to alpha blending) because they are completely transparent and will not affect the final image [292].

Alternatively, a conditional fragment removal can be included in a fragment program (texkill in assembler-level language or clip in high-level Cg language). Listing 15.1 shows an example of a Cg fragment shader designed for 3D texture slicing. The data volume is held in the 3D texture SamplerDataVolume, the selection volume is stored in the 3D texture SamplerSelectionVolume. A post-interpolative transfer function is implemented by a dependent look-up in the 1D transfer function table SamplerTransferFunction. After a bias with -0.5, the selectionValue contains a value 0.5 (i.e., true) or −0.5 (i.e., false). The subsequent fragment kill operation (`clip`) removes the fragment when the biased selection value is negative. While trilinear interpolation is used as a reconstruction filter for the data volume (filter format `LINEAR`), the access to the selection volume is based on nearest-neighbor sampling (filter format `NEAREST`). Nearest-neighbor sampling is crucial for maintaining texture values that are either zero or one. If trilinear interpolation were applied, values between zero and one could be obtained, which would have no direct interpretation as Boolean values.

It is beneficial to address the data and selection volumes by two different sets of texture coordinates. When a 3D texture is used for the selection volume, any affine transformation of the clipping geometry can be achieved by a transformation of texture coordinates. Such a transformation can be implemented by computing the `TexSelection` coordinates from the original `TexData` coordinates by a matrix–vector multiplication in a vertex program, where the matrix describes the affine transformation between the selection volume and the data volume. Alternatively, the transformed texture coordinates can be computed by the CPU and attached to the vertex data. Only if the shape of the clipping geometry is completely changed, the selection texture has to be re-voxelized.

Volume clipping is similarly included in GPU-based ray casting and 2D slicing. Ray casting is typically based on 3D textures and, thus, the same texture addressing scheme can be used as before. Samples along a ray that have to be clipped are removed from the volume-rendering integral by setting their color contribution and opacity to zero. For 2D texture slicing, two sets of 2D texture stacks have to be managed. Although the resolution of the selection volume and the resolution of the data volume are independent, their slicing directions should be aligned to facilitate a simultaneous 2D texture access on a slice-by-slice basis. If both volumes have different orientations, an on-the-fly resampling on small stripes has to be employed, as described by Rezk-Salama et al. [224] in another context.

The aforementioned method for clipping with selection volumes requires multiple texture accesses to attach the selection texture to the data texture. However, volume clipping is feasible even with older graphics hardware that does not support multitexturing: multiple passes are executed to render the selection volume and the data volume on each slice; the stencil buffer and stencil test are then used to cut away clipped fragments [10].

15.2.2   Clipping Based on a Distance Field

The above techniques use a direct representation of the binary selection volume and require nearest-neighbor sampling of the respective texture. If a trilinear interpolation (for a 3D texture) is applied, intermediate values between zero and one can be obtained from the selection texture and an interpretation as Boolean values would break down. If clipping is implemented by a multiplication of selection and data values, a clearly defined surface of the clipping geometry would be replaced by a gradual transition between visible and clipped parts of the volume.

Unfortunately, a missing interpolation within the selection texture may introduce aliasing artifacts in the form of jaggy boundary surfaces. This problem can be addressed by replacing the pre-computed binary selection volume by an on-the-fly computation based on a signed distance field. The distance texture stores the signed Euclidean distance to the closest point on the clipping object. The surface of the clipping object corresponds to the isosurface for the isovalue zero. Trilinear interpolation is applied to reconstruct a continuous distance field. The rendering process is almost identical to that of the previous section. The only difference is that a comparison with the isovalue zero has to be included to determine the visibility of a fragment.

The previously described implementation (see Listing 15.1) is already prepared to handle clipping via a distance field. The only modification concerns texture sampling, which is changed from nearest-neighbor sampling of the binary selection volume to trilinear interpolation in the distance volume. The bias by -0.5 in the fragment program results in an isovalue of 0.5 for the clipping surface. In this way, an unsigned single-channel texture format such as LUMINANCE8 is appropriate for the distance field if the texture is constructed with a bias of $+0.5$. If an 8-bit texture format is employed, quantization problems could reduce the quality of the distance field representation. This quality issue is addressed by choosing an appropriate overall scaling factor that relates the coordinate spacing in world space to the spacing in the distance texture. This scaling in combination with a final clamping to the range $[0, 1]$ essentially leads to a restricted distance field that is only valid in a boundary region around the clipping surface. The thickness of the boundary zone is controlled by the scaling factor and should be chosen only a few texels wide in order to avoid quantization inaccuracies. Various methods exist for constructing signed distance fields. Osher and Fedkiw [205], for example, give a comprehensive introduction to level set techniques and fast marching methods that can be used to generate distance fields.

An alternative implementation is also feasible using the alpha test. The respective fragment shader for a binary selection volume (see Section 15.2.1) is extended by an additional conditional assignment operation that yields a value of zero when the distance is below the isovalue and a value of one for a distance above the isovalue. The other parts of the fragment program and the alpha test remain unaltered.

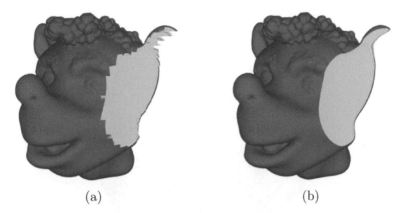

Figure 15.3. Comparison of different reconstruction filters for a voxelized clipping geometry: nearest-neighbor sampling in (a) and trilinear interpolation in (b).

One advantage of using two different textures for the data and selection (or distance) volumes is that the respective sampling resolutions can be chosen independently. Texture memory is a limited resource and, therefore, the selection or distance volumes are often represented at a lower resolution than the data volume. The effect of a low resolution for the selection and distance volumes is illustrated in Figure 15.3 for a curved clipping geometry. Nearest-neighbor sampling is used for the selection volume in Figure 15.3 (a), trilinear interpolation is used for the distance field in Figure 15.3 (b). Both the selection and distance volumes are sampled at only one-eighth of the resolution of the data volume. Aliasing artifacts occur for nearest-neighbor sampling: for example, the transition between clipped and nonclipped parts of the face look very jaggy. In contrast, trilinear interpolation avoids these problems and results in a smooth boundary between clipped and nonclipped areas.

15.2.3 Examples and Summary

A major advantage of the voxelized clipping approach is the support for arbitrary clipping objects with an unrestricted choice of topology and geometry. Figure 15.4 demonstrates that complicated clipping objects can be represented—complex with respect to geometry and topology. Here, the underlying data set is a medical CT scan.

Another advantage is that the conceptual clipping process (Section 15.1) is directly implemented and that both surface-oriented and volumetric clipping are supported. A typical example of a volumetric description is a 3D interest function, which is mapped to a selection volume to highlight important features of a data set. Figure 15.5 shows an example from 3D

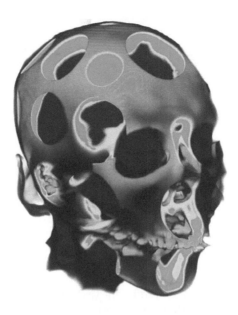

Figure 15.4. Clipping for a CT data set with a complex voxelized selection volume.

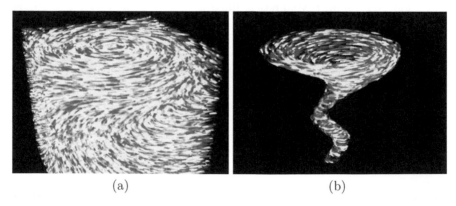

Figure 15.5. Volume clipping for 3D texture–based flow visualization. The left image shows the original volume rendering of the vector field, the right image illustrates volume clipping based on velocity magnitude. (Data set courtesy of R. Crawfis, Ohio State University.)

texture–based flow visualization [295]. The data set contains the wind velocities in a tornado. Figure 15.5 (a) depicts the original volume rendering of the vector field—important internal parts are invisible due to occlusion. In contrast, Figure 15.5 (b) removes regions with low velocity magnitude and, thus, reveals the structure of the tornado. In this example, the selection volume is constructed from the data set by computing velocity magnitudes, i.e., the selection volume is indirectly defined through Equation 15.1 by using a comparison with a threshold of velocity magnitude for the mapping from the original vector field to binary values.

A related advantage is the extensibility of voxelized clipping toward generic tagged volumes that allow for a space-variant modification of the visual representation. For example, different transfer functions can be applied to different regions of a segmented data set, where the tagged information controls which transfer function is used [99, 264]. This approach can be extended to two-level volume rendering, which even permits us to choose between different volume-rendering techniques according to the tagged information. For example, maximum intensity projection (MIP) in one region may be combined with direct volume rendering in other regions [101, 92].

Important disadvantages are a potentially large memory footprint for the voxelized selection volume and additional texture-access operations to read the selection volume during volume rendering. A related issue is the accuracy of the voxelized representation. The typical resolution is much less than 1024^3 voxels, i.e., the accuracy after projection onto the image plane is much less than the typical screen resolution. Finally and most importantly, dynamic clipping objects need a re-voxelization with a subsequent download of the modified selection volume to a texture on the GPU, which can be very time-consuming.

15.3   Surface-Based Clipping

Surface-based volume clipping uses a boundary representation (BRep) of the clipping object. The goal is to avoid an explicit voxelization of the BRep (otherwise, the techniques from the previous section could be immediately applied). In fact, the visibility of volume elements is directly obtained from the surface description by an on-the-fly computation. Triangle meshes are the most prominent example of a BRep in computer graphics. We also assume a triangle-based BRep for the clipping geometry, but any other surface representation that can be rasterized on the image plane may be used as well.

The concept of surface-based volume clipping relies on the depth structure of the clipping geometry, as illustrated in Figure 15.6. The clipping process is reduced from a geometric operation in 3D space to a 1D oper-

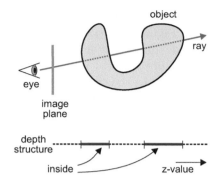

Figure 15.6. Depth structure of a clipping object.

ation along a single light ray that originates from the eye point. Due to the correspondence between light rays and pixels on the image plane, the clipping operations can be mapped to operations working in image space. During volume rendering, a fragment program accesses the depth structure to decide whether the fragment should be rendered or clipped.

Surface-based clipping consists of two essential steps: first, the construction of the depth structure and, second, depth-based clipping during volume rendering [292, 293]. The depth structure can be represented by a collection of depth images that hold the depth values for all intersections between eye rays and the clipping geometry. These depth images can be stored in image-aligned 2D textures that exhibit a one-to-one correspondence between texels and pixels. A high-resolution format (e.g., 32-bit or, at least, 16-bit) should be used for a depth texture to guarantee a high-quality depth representation. Different methods to fill the depth images are discussed in the remainder of this section. The second step—depth-oriented volume clipping—requires a comparison with the values in the depth images and a conditional fragment removal. Unless otherwise noted, we assume that texture slicing is employed for this step.

15.3.1 Clipping Against a Single Depth Layer

A simple approach uses only standard graphics functionality to model a single depth layer, as provided by the fixed-function OpenGL pipeline. Here, the depth buffer can be used to represent the depth image and the depth test provides a means for a conditional removal of fragments.

The depth structure is constructed by rendering the clipping geometry to the depth buffer. For the subsequent volume-rendering step, writing to the depth buffer is disabled and depth testing is enabled. The depth test implements the comparison with the depth image when the slices through

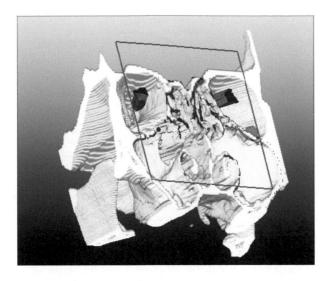

Figure 15.7. Volume and surface rendering with a clipping plane for the exploration of the spatial relations in a CT head data set. The image was created for sinus surgery planning. (Image courtesy of D. Apelt, MeVis Bremen, CT data provided by Prof. Kahn, University of Leipzig.)

the volume data set are drawn. Depending on the logical operator for the depth test (GREATER or LESS), the volume either in front or behind the clipping geometry is removed.

The major problem with the depth-buffer method is the restriction to a single depth image. A related problem is that BReps cannot be completely supported because a BRrep requires a surface that surrounds the object completely, i.e., a surface that has at least one front-facing part and one back-facing part. Advantages of this approach are its simplicity and its support by virtually any graphics hardware. For some applications, a single clipping surface might be sufficient, and here the depth buffer approach can be useful. Another advantage is that some GPUs can accelerate this type of volume clipping by means of the early z-test as the depth test is the basis for fragment removal. The early z-test is particularly helpful when a large portion of the volume is cut away.

A clipping plane is a special case of a single clipping surface. Here, the depth buffer might be used for clipping. In most applications, however, an OpenGL clip plane is applied, which avoids the first rendering phase that would fill the depth buffer. The OpenGL command `glClipPlane` specifies a clip plane through a four-component plane equation. Similar to the early z-test, the clipping-plane approach can lead to a significant acceleration of volume rendering when a large part of the data set is removed. Figure 15.7

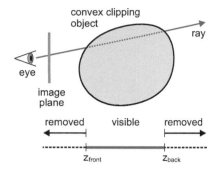

Figure 15.8. Illustration of depth-based volume probing for a convex clipping geometry.

shows an example with an OpenGL clip plane used in a medical application. This kind of visualization can be employed during sinus surgery planning and it shows the spatial relations in a CT head data set.

15.3.2   Convex Volume Clipping

The next step toward a support for arbitrary clipping geometries involves the implementation of a convex clipping object. For a convex geometry, the number of intersections between an eye ray and the object is not larger than two. Therefore, the depth structure can be represented by a collection of two depth images. Figure 15.8 illustrates the scenario for convex volume clipping.

The two depth images can be stored in two 2D textures with a high-resolution texture format (typically 16-bit floating-point or 32-bit floating-point numbers). They are filled by directly writing the depth values into the respective textures via render-to-texture functionality (e.g., by means of a frame-buffer object). In the first render pass, front-facing parts of the clipping object are rendered into the first depth image. The front faces are selectively drawn by using back-face culling (with `glCullFace(GL_BACK)`). Similarly, the second render pass uses the back-facing geometry to fill the second depth image (culling with `glCullFace(GL_FRONT)`). In the third render pass—the actual volume rendering via texture slicing—a fragment program accesses both depth textures and compares the depth of a fragment with the depth structure. This comparison leads to a conditional fragment removal when the fragment lies outside the visible region. Listing 15.2 shows a Cg fragment shader for convex volume clipping. In this example, volume probing is applied, i.e., the volume inside the clipping object remains visible. Volume cutting is easily obtained by negating the distance variable `dist`.

```
// Texture coords and homogeneous position as input from the
// vertex stage
struct VS_OUTPUT {
    float3 TexData  : TEXCOORD0;
    float4 Position : TEXCOORD1;
};

// Actual fragment shader
float4 main(VS_OUTPUT IN,
            uniform sampler3D SamplerDataVolume,
            uniform sampler2D SamplerDepthFront,
            uniform sampler2D SamplerDepthBack,
            uniform sampler1D SamplerTransferFunction)
: COLOR {
    // Accesses scalar value from the data volume
    float  dataValue = tex3D(SamplerDataVolume, IN.TexData);
    // Standard post-interpolative transfer function
    float4 classifiedValue = tex1D(SamplerTransferFunction,
                                    dataValue);

    // Homogeneous division to compute (x,y) tex coords (in
    // image space) and depth value z.  A corresponding
    // matrix multiplication is used in a vertex program
    // to determine the correct IN.Position
    float4 position = IN.Position / IN.Position.w;

    // Accesses first depth layer from 2D texture
    float  depthFront = tex2D(SamplerDepthFront,
                              position.xy);
    // Accesses second depth layer from 2D texture
    float  depthBack = tex2D(SamplerDepthBack, position.xy);

    // Z distance to front and back clipping surfaces
    float2 dist = float2(position.z - depthFront,
                         depthBack - position.z);
    // Conditional removal of fragment if any of the (two)
    // components of distance "dist" is less than zero
    clip(dist);

    return classifiedValue;
}
```

Listing 15.2. Cg fragment shader for surface-based volume clipping with a convex clipping object.

Variations of this basic clipping method are possible by slightly modifying the way in which the depth structure is represented. One alternative uses the z-buffer to store one of the depth layers (e.g., for the front-facing clipping geometry). The other depth layer (e.g., for the back-facing geometry) is still held in a high-resolution 2D texture. Conditional fragment removal relies on a combination of a fragment program that tests against the back-facing geometry and the depth test that takes into account the front-facing geometry. Therefore, this implementation is a mix between a purely texture-based approach and the depth-buffer method from Section 15.3.1. On some GPUs, this hybrid method may exhibit an improved performance because the early z-test accelerates the test against one of the depth layers.

Another variation replaces the high-resolution single-channel texture format by a specialized depth-texture format usually employed in shadow mapping [301], as provided by the OpenGL texture functionality `ARB_depth_texture` or `SGIX_depth_texture` within the `ARB_shadow` or `SGIX_shadow` extensions, respectively. Shadow mapping facilitates an implementation that does not need programmable fragment shaders and floating-point textures and thus can be useful for older GPUs.

Another alternative utilizes view-frustum clipping and depth shifting to replace shadow mapping. Once again, the depth values z_{front} for the front-facing geometry are rendered into a 2D high-resolution texture. During the following rendering passes, a fragment program shifts the depth values of all fragments by $-z_{\text{front}}$. The depth buffer is cleared and the back faces are rendered into the depth buffer (with depth shift enabled) to construct the second depth image. In this way, the depth buffer is set to $z_{\text{back}} - z_{\text{front}}$, where z_{back} is the unmodified depth of the back face. During the following pass, slices through the volume data set are rendered, without modifying the depth buffer, but with depth shift and depth testing being enabled. Therefore, fragments that are behind the back face of the clipping geometry are removed by the depth test, whereas fragments that are in front of the clipping geometry are removed by clipping against the near plane of the view frustum.

Listing 15.3 shows the Cg fragment program for the final volume-rendering pass, including the shift of depth values by $-z_{\text{front}}$. The texture that holds the depth structure (here texture sampler `SamplerDepthFront`) should be a high-resolution texture, e.g., with 32-bit floating-point resolution. The depth shift approach can also be implemented on older GPUs that only support a `HILO` texture format but no floating-point textures or flexible fragment programs. A corresponding configuration of texture shaders for NVIDIA GeForce 3 GPUs is described in detail by Weiskopf et al. [292]. This paper also explains how the depth shift approach for volume probing can be extended to volume cutting.

```
// Texture coords and homogeneous position as input from the
// vertex stage
struct VS_OUTPUT {
    float3 TexData  :  TEXCOORD0;
    float4 Position :  TEXCOORD1;
};

struct PS_OUTPUT {
    float4 Color  :  COLOR;
    float  Depth  :  DEPTH;
};

// Actual fragment shader
PS_OUTPUT main(VS_OUTPUT IN,
               uniform sampler3D SamplerDataVolume,
               uniform sampler2D SamplerDepthFront,
               uniform sampler1D SamplerTransferFunction)
{
    PS_OUTPUT OUT;

    // Accesses scalar value from the data volume
    float  dataValue = tex3D(SamplerDataVolume, IN.TexData);
    // Standard post-interpolative transfer function
    float4 classifiedValue = tex1D(SamplerTransferFunction,
                                   dataValue);
    // Homogeneous division to compute (x,y) tex coords (in
    // image space) and depth value z.  A corresponding
    // matrix multiplication is used in a vertex program
    // to determine the correct IN.Position
    float4 position = IN.Position / IN.Position.w;

    // Accesses front depth layer from 2D texture
    float  depthFront = tex2D(SamplerDepthFront,
                             position.xy);
    // Shifts current z value by negative "depthFront"
    OUT.Depth = position.z - depthFront;
    OUT.Color = classifiedValue;
    return OUT;
}
```

Listing 15.3. Cg fragment shader for surface-based volume clipping by means of depth shift.

15.3.3   Concave Clipping Geometry

For the general case of a concave clipping object, the depth structure has to be extended to represent a larger number of depth images that correspond to a larger number of possible intersections between the clipping geometry and an eye ray. Concave objects are facilitated by extending convex volume clipping to multiple render passes. The basic idea is to organize the depth structure in pairs of neighboring depth images. Each pair represents one visible segment of the viewing ray—the volume remains visible within the interval defined by such a pair of depth values. Then, concave volume clipping is reduced to a collection of convex clipping regions each of which is handled in a separate rendering pass according to convex clipping.

Let us consider the first stage—the construction of the depth structure—in more detail. The depth-peeling algorithm [67] can be adopted to "peel off" the geometry in a depth-layer by depth-layer fashion. Assuming a back-to-front scheme, the first depth image (corresponding to the most distant part of the clipping object) is extracted by rendering the clipping geometry with the depth test set to GREATER. Subsequent and increasingly closer depth images are extracted by rendering only those objects that are closer than previously generated depth images. To this end, a fragment program is used to remove fragments that are located at or behind the depth value of the current depth image. The depth values of the rendered fragments are stored in a high-resolution texture via render-to-texture functionality. Each render pass results in one depth image. The process is continued for the next closer depth layers and stops when no fragments pass the fragment program any more, i.e., when the foremost depth image is reached. The occlusion query functionality can be used to check the number of rendered fragments, in particular, it can be used to test whether fragments are rendered at all.

The second stage employs multipass rendering of the actual volume. For each pair of depth images, the respective region of the volume is rendered. Each depth pair corresponds to local volume probing against two boundaries, as discussed previously for convex volume clipping. The complete volume is reconstructed in a layer-by-layer fashion by processing the depth structure pair-by-pair with multiple render passes. In the case of volume cutting, single, unpaired depth images are produced at the front and back parts of the depth structure. This case can be handled by clipping only against a single boundary, as discussed in Section 15.3.1.

Although the two stages (construction of the depth layers and volume rendering) are conceptually separated, they can be intermingled within a combined rendering algorithm. When depth peeling has constructed one pair of neighboring depth images, two-layer volume clipping is immediately applied to construct a partial image for this depth pair. Afterwards, subsequent depth image pairs are processed. The advantage of this implementation is that only two depth textures need to be held in GPU memory—instead of the full depth structure. The only additional memory requirement is a buffer for intermediate volume-rendering results.

15.3.4 Summary

Surface-based volume clipping employs an image-space method with a one-to-one mapping between pixels on the image plane and texels in the 2D depth images. Therefore, this approach is intrinsically view-dependent and needs a re-generation of the depth structure when the viewpoint is changed. The alternative method of voxelized selection volumes (Section 15.2), in contrast, works in object space and thus avoids a continuing construction of the selection volumes.

A major advantage of surface-based clipping is its per-pixel accurate clipping that leads to high-quality images. Another advantage is the built-in support for dynamic clipping objects because the depth structure is re-built from the clipping geometry for each frame. The main disadvantage is complex and time-consuming multipass rendering for nonconvex clipping objects. The rendering costs increase with increasing depth complexity of the geometry and may lead to an inadequate performance for complex clipping objects.

15.4 Volume Clipping and Illumination

Volume illumination extends volume rendering by adding lighting terms. Local illumination is based on gradients of the scalar field and supports the user in recognizing the spatial structure and orientation of volumetric features. Chapter 5 discusses local volume illumination in detail. Unfortunately, the combination of volume illumination and volume clipping introduces the additional issue of how illumination should be computed in the vicinity of the clipping object. Two different, possibly interfering goals need to be achieved. First, illumination should represent the orientation of the clipping surface itself. Second, the scalar data volume should affect the illumination and appearance of the clipping surface (e.g., its color and transparency).

Figure 15.9 illustrates the effect of different illumination methods. Figure 15.9 (a) shows illuminated volume rendering, but without specific lighting on the clipping surface. The shape of the spherical cutting geometry is difficult to recognize due to the lack of shading cues. Figure 15.9 (b) demonstrates how the perception of the clipping object is improved by including illumination. The remaining parts of this section discuss how

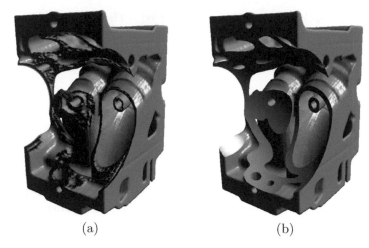

(a)   (b)

Figure 15.9.   Combining volume clipping and volume illumination. Surface-based volume cutting with a spherical clip object is applied to a technical engine data set. No specific lighting is applied at the cutting surface in (a). (b) reveals lighting on the cutting surface by combining surface-based and volumetric illumination. For example, the highlight in the lower left part of the engine appears only in (b).

volume illumination and surface shading can be combined. Starting with a modified optical model for volume clipping, extended versions of clipping algorithms with voxelized selection volumes (see Section 15.2) and depth layers (see Section 15.3) are described.

15.4.1   An Optical Model for Clipping in Illuminated Volumes

The following requirements should be met by a consistent combination of volume illumination and clipping. First, the clipping surface should be illuminated in a way that promotes the perception of its shape and orientation. Second, the optical properties (i.e., the material properties with respect to lighting) should be consistent between the clipping surface and the neighboring data volume. Third, the optical model should not modify volume illumination in parts that are distant from the clipping surface. Fourth, the results should be conceptually independent of the sampling rate along viewing rays (e.g., the slice distance), up to a change in numerical accuracy from approximating the volume-rendering integral with different sampling distances. These requirements and respective optical models are discussed in detail by Weiskopf et al. [293].

In a first approach, unmodified clipping techniques from Sections 15.2 and 15.3 are directly applied to the shaded volume. In the parts that remain visible after clipping, volume lighting is based on the gradient of

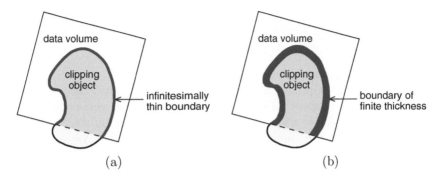

Figure 15.10. Combining volume illumination with surface-based shading on the boundary of the clipping geometry. (a) shows an infinitesimally thin "skin" around the clipping object; (b) illustrates the extension of the surrounding layer to finite thickness.

the data volume and the optical transfer function. To add perceptual shape cues for the clipping object, the shaded clipping surface is rendered on top of the data volume. Here, illumination is determined by the normal vectors of the surface and by the same transfer function that is used for volume rendering. Figure 15.10 (a) illustrates this approach, which essentially adds the surface of the clipping object as a "skin" around the data volume.

This method meets the first three requirements. First, the perception of the orientation and shape of the clipping object is supported by illuminating the "skin" based on the normal vector on the clipping surface. Second, the optical material properties for the "skin" and the neighboring data volume are consistent because the same transfer function is applied. Third, volume shading is not affected in internal regions of the volume.

Unfortunately, this approach does not meet the fourth requirement. The volume-rendering integral (see Section 1.3, Equation 1.7),

$$I(D) = I_0\, e^{-\int_{s_0}^{D} \kappa(t)\, \mathrm{d}t} + \int_{s_0}^{D} q(s)\, e^{-\int_{s}^{D} \kappa(t)\, \mathrm{d}t}\, \mathrm{d}s\,, \qquad (15.2)$$

is typically approximated by

$$I(D) = \sum_{i=0}^{n} c_i \prod_{j=i+1}^{n} T_j\,, \quad \text{with } c_0 = I(s_0)\,, \qquad (15.3)$$

according to Equation 1.11.

In a Riemann sum approximation with sampling rate Δx (i.e., slicing distance), the transparency of the ith segment is

$$T_i \approx e^{-\kappa(s_i)\Delta x} \qquad (15.4)$$

according to Equation 1.12, and the color contribution for the ith segment is

$$c_i \approx q(s_i)\Delta x \,, \tag{15.5}$$

according to Equation 1.13.

For changing sampling rate, the color source term and the absorption term have to be adapted. The discretized source term converges to zero for $\Delta x \to 0$: there is no color contribution from an infinitely thin 2D surface. Similarly, the transparency converges to one for $\Delta x \to 0$ unless κ is infinite. (Zero transparency is a special case of volume rendering that leads to surface-like regions. This case is correctly handled by both the "skin" and the following approach.) Therefore, the contribution of the "skin" vanishes for very high sampling rates. The basic issue is an inappropriate combination of a continuous volumetric description with an infinitely thin 2D surface. In the continuous volume-rendering integral from Equation 15.2, the terms q and κ have no contribution if their support is of zero length.

This issue is overcome by extending the original approach to a "skin" that is broadened to finite thickness: the data volume is surrounded by a thick layer. Illumination is based on the normal vectors of the clipping surface and the surface orientation influences the illumination of the volume for some distance—virtually "impregnating" the volume with lighting information from the clipping surface. Figure 15.10 illustrates the "skin" approach and the modified "impregnation" approach. The "impregnation" affects only the part of the volume that is visible after clipping and it does not change the visibility of voxels.

The optical model for volume rendering is modified by extending the source term to

$$q(\mathbf{x},\omega) = q_{\mathrm{emission}}(\mathbf{x}) + w(\mathbf{x})S_{\mathrm{srf}}(\mathbf{x},\omega) + (1 - w(\mathbf{x}))\,S_{\mathrm{vol}}(\mathbf{x},\omega)\,, \tag{15.6}$$

with the weight function $w(\mathbf{x})$ (with values from $[0,1]$), the surface-based illumination term $S_{\mathrm{srf}}(\mathbf{x},\omega)$, and the volumetric illumination term $S_{\mathrm{vol}}(\mathbf{x},\omega)$. The "impregnation" layer has finite thickness, often even a uniform thickness that is specified by the user. The layer thickness corresponds to the support of the weight function. The smoothness of the weight function directly affects the smoothness of the transition between the "impregnation" layer and the remaining parts of the volume.

The only remaining question is: how is the surface-related illumination term $S_{\mathrm{srf}}(\mathbf{x},\omega)$ evaluated at locations inside the layer? In particular, what is the normal vector? A normal vector field is defined inside the layer by means of parallel vector transport: for a point inside the layer, the closest point on the clipping surface is determined; the normal vector is computed at the corresponding surface location and transported to the point within the layer. The optical material properties are based on the data volume and the transfer function at this point.

The "impregnation" approach meets the fourth requirement by introducing a finite boundary layer that leads to a finite contribution to the volume-rendering integral (Equation 15.2). Therefore, the discrete approximation (Equation 15.3) converges to this contribution for increasing sampling rates. The other requirements are met because of identical arguments as for the "skin" approach.

15.4.2 Volumetric Clipping and Selection Volumes

The "impregnation" approach can be used in combination with voxelized selection volumes (Section 15.2). The clipping geometry is assumed to be represented by an isosurface in a signed-distance volume, as described in Section 15.2.2. Distances are defined by the Euclidean norm in 3D space. Furthermore, the clipping surface should be non–self-intersecting and smooth.

With these assumptions, the "impregnation" model can be directly mapped to a rendering algorithm. The weight function $w(\mathbf{x})$ is expressed in terms of the distance volume $v_{\text{distance}}(\mathbf{x})$ and another weight function $\tilde{w}(d)$ according to

$$w(\mathbf{x}) = \tilde{w}\left(v_{\text{distance}}(\mathbf{x})\right) . \tag{15.7}$$

The function $\tilde{w}(d)$ describes relative weights for surface-based and volume-based illumination in terms of the scalar distance to the clipping surface.

Surface-oriented illumination relies on the gradients of the distance volume. The gradient represents the normal vector on the clipping surface because, in general, the gradient of a scalar field is identical with the corresponding isosurface. However, even in a neighborhood of the clipping surface, the gradient is identical with the normal vector obtained by parallel transport from the isosurface. Figure 15.11 illustrates that, in a signed distance volume, the gradient represents the direction to or from the clos-

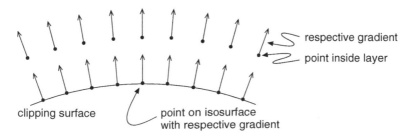

Figure 15.11. Gradients in distance field.

est point on the isosurface. The size of the neighborhood depends on the curvature of the clipping surface—the valid region typically decreases with increasing curvature.

The original clipping algorithm for signed distance fields (Section 15.2.2) and volume slicing needs only minor changes to incorporate illumination. First, the 3D textures for the data volume and the distance field are extended to include gradients. Typically, an RGBA texture format is used to store the scalar value in the alpha channel and the gradients in RGB. Second, a fragment program is used to evaluate local illumination for the data volume and the distance field during actual volume rendering. The optical properties for both illumination terms are derived from the same transfer function working on the data volume. Third, the fragment program also computes the weight according to Equation 15.7. The distance d is accessed from the distance field. The weight function $\tilde{w}(d)$ can either be evaluated by numerical operations (if $\tilde{w}(d)$ is simple) or by a dependent texture look-up in a pre-computed table. Fourth, Equation 15.6 is used to compute the weighted combination of surface-based and volume-based illumination. The other elements of the clipping algorithm are not changed by the "impregnation" approach.

15.4.3 Surface-Based Clipping and Volume Illumination

The extended optical model for volume clipping can also be combined with surface-based clipping. The main issue is that the 2D depth images that represent the depth structure of the clipping object do not provide any information on the distance to the closest point on the clipping surface. An approximation of the optical clipping model can be used to overcome this issue. This approximation does not need any distance information.

The problem with the original "skin" approach is that an infinitely thin layer will have no effect for a high sampling rate. A modified method is used to avoid this issue: the clipping boundary is not modeled as a thick layer but as a 2D hypersurface. Surface-based illumination, however, provides modified contributions to the transparency term

$$T_{\mathrm{srf}} = e^{-\kappa(s_{\mathrm{srf}})\Delta_{\mathrm{srf}}}$$

and the color values from the source term

$$c_{\mathrm{srf}} = q(s_{\mathrm{srf}})\Delta_{\mathrm{srf}}\,,$$

where s_{srf} describes the location of the clipping surface and Δ_{srf} is the thickness of the original "impregnation" layer. Therefore, the clipping boundary is treated as a 2D surface geometrically, whereas the contribution to the rendering integral comes from a thick virtual layer. Standard illumination

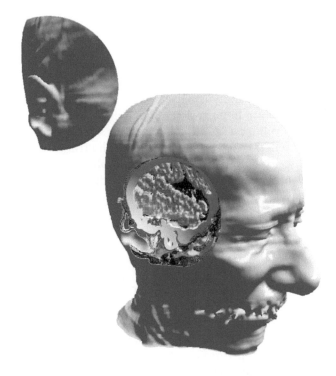

Figure 15.12. Depth-based clipping in an illuminated CT data set.

(a)   (b)

Figure 15.13. Clipping in an illuminated orbital data set. (a) is without clipping; (b) is with depth-based clipping.

is used inside the volume, with transparency values and source terms that depend on the slicing distance Δx. For typical applications, the "impregnation" layer is rather thin and, thus, the errors introduced by the surface-based approximations can be neglected. Weiskopf et al. [293] discuss in more detail what types of errors may occur.

The original implementation of surface-based clipping has to be slightly modified to incorporate illumination. Slice-based volume rendering is extended to hybrid volume and surface rendering: the volume and the surface parts are interleaved according to the depth structure of the clipping geometry, and so is the order of surface and volume rendering. The following discussion assumes back-to-front compositing, but the order could be easily reversed if needed. Surface-based clipping already partitions the depth structure into pairs of depth layers that enclose a visible part of the volume. For a convex object, only one pair is sufficient, while a concave object is represented by several pairs. A single depth pair is rendered in three passes. First, the back face of the clipping object is rendered. Here, material properties are obtained from the data volume and the transfer function; the normal vector is computed from the surface model. For a concave geometry, it is useful to compute the surface illumination already during the construction of the depth structure via depth peeling (see Section 15.3.3) and to access this information later during clipping. Second, the illuminated and clipped region of the data volume is rendered. Third, the front face of the clipping object is drawn. All three rendering steps are blended to accumulate colors (and opacities if needed). The complete volume is drawn by successively rendering all pairs of depth layers.

Figures 15.12 and 15.13 demonstrate the consistent combination of clipping and volume shading. Depth-based clipping is applied to a medical CT (computerized tomography) data set in Figure 15.12. The transfer function is chosen in a way to achieve opaque material boundaries. The visualization of an orbital data set in Figure 15.13 reveals both transparent and opaque structures. Figure 15.13 (a) shows the original data set; Figure 15.13 (b) demonstrates depth-based clipping.

15.5   Clipping and Pre-Integration

The aforementioned clipping approaches are based on a point-sampling of the volume integral, typically implemented by texture slicing. In this case, the visibility computation can be reduced to checking whether a point on the viewing ray (i.e., a fragment on a slice) is visible. Pre-integrated volume rendering (see Section 4.5) extends slice-by-slice rendering to slab-based rendering. Slabs are defined by two neighboring slices and, thus, have finite thickness.

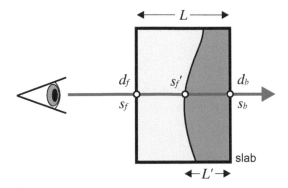

Figure 15.14. Using slabs instead of slices for pre-integrated volume clipping. The scalar data values at the entry and the exit points of the slab are s_f and s_b, respectively. The corresponding values from the signed distance field are d_f and d_b. The thickness of the slab is given by L; L' is the length of the visible part of the slab. The blue region remains visible after clipping.

Clipping may affect a slab by intersecting the slab somewhere in between, as shown in Figure 15.14. Therefore, a simple binary visibility decision is not adequate, and two modifications have to be included [227]:

- The scalar data values for pre-integration should reflect the values at the endpoints of the visible part of the slab.

- The length of a ray segment should be adapted to the length of the clipped slab.

The following discussion assumes that clipping is based on a voxelized selection volume in the form of a signed distance field (see Section 15.2.2). By shifting the distance values by +0.5, the clipping surface is located at isovalue 0.5. Let d_f and d_b denote the values of the distance volume at the entry and exit points of the original slab. If both values are either below or above 0.5, the slab is either completely invisible or visible. In both cases, the complete slab can be handled through a single binary decision on its visibility, i.e., as if point-sampling along rays were applied.

An interesting situation occurs when the clipping surface cuts through the slab. Considering the case $d_f < 0.5$ and $d_b > 0.5$ (as in Figure 15.14), only the blue part of the slab is visible. Here, the front scalar data value s_f has to be modified to the data value s'_f at entry point into the clipped region. Pre-integration is now based on a look-up in the pre-integration table according to the parameters (s'_f, s_b) instead of (s_f, s_b). In general, the modified scalar value s'_f is obtained by

$$r = \left[\frac{[0.5 - d_f]}{d_b - d_f}\right], \quad s'_f = (1 - r)s_f + r\,s_b,$$

where squared brackets denote clamping to the interval $[0, 1]$. Similarly, the scalar value s_b is replaced by s'_b:

$$g = 1 - \left[\frac{[0.5 - d_b]}{d_f - d_b}\right], \quad s'_b = (1 - g)s_f + r\,s_b.$$

If both distance values are less than 0.5, the slab is completely invisible and the scalar values can be neglected.

The second extension concerns a modification of the length L of the clipped ray segment. The numerical integration of the volume integral depends on the parameters s_f, s_b, and L. The volume-rendering integral (see Equation 15.2, Section 1.3, and Section 4.5) can be used to compute the contribution of a ray segment:

$$s_L(x) = s_b + \frac{x}{L}(s_f - s_b),$$

$$c(s_f, s_b, L) = \int_0^L q(s_L(t))\, e^{-\int_t^L \kappa(s_L(\tilde{t}))\, d\tilde{t}}\, dt,$$

$$T(s_f, s_b, L) = e^{-\int_0^L \kappa(s_L(t))\, dt},$$

$$\alpha = 1 - T.$$

Ideally, a 3D pre-integration table that depends on s_f, s_b, and L should be used. However, a modification of the ray segment length can also be taken into account by the following approximation that leads to a 2D pre-integration table for varying parameters s_f and s_b and for a fixed, original length L. Denoting the visible fraction of the slab by $b = L'/L$, the transparency T' of the clipped ray segment is the pre-integrated transparency T (associated with the original segment length L) raised to the bth power because

$$\int_0^{L'} \kappa(s_{L'}(t'))\, dt' = b \int_0^L \kappa(s_L(t))\, dt,$$

$$T' = e^{-b\int_0^L \kappa(s_L(t))\, dt} = \left(e^{-\int_0^L \kappa(s_L(t))\, dt}\right)^b = T^b.$$

A first-order approximation is sufficient if the thickness of the slabs is reasonably small. In addition, the emissive contribution of a clipped segment can be computed by $c' = bc$ if self-attenuation is neglected. Section 1.4.3 derives analogous transformations for opacity correction.

The factors for the adjustment of the scalar values, the emission, and the opacity can be computed on the fly in the fragment program. However, it is more efficient to pre-compute these factors for all combinations of the distance values d_f and d_b and to store them in a 2D texture. During actual volume rendering, a dependent texture look-up is performed to obtain the modified values.

15.6   Clipping and Volume Illustration

An illustration is an image with a communicative intent. According to the Collins English Dictionary [31], "to illustrate" means to "to explain or decorate (a book, text, etc.)." In the context of volume graphics, illustrative techniques are designed to convey complex data or structures in an intuitive and understandable way. Different kinds of abstraction are employed to achieve this goal. In general, abstraction is used to emphasize important elements, to depict these elements in a way that is easy to perceive, and to reduce visual complexity by deemphasizing or removing unimportant elements.

From a technical point of view, abstraction can be separated into two components: first, what should be rendered, and, second, how should it be rendered? Volume illustrations are typically influenced by artistic drawing styles, leading to non-photorealistic rendering (NPR) methods. The way that volume illustrations are drawn is described in detail in Chapter 14.

The first component, however, is directly related to volume clipping and the contents of this chapter. In fact, clipping is an important approach to defining selective visibility and can be immediately used for illustrations. For some applications, illustrative rendering needs to be more flexible than the clipping methods discussed so far. One extension is to add a view-dependent description of clipping and visibility, adopting the concept of view-dependent transparency for surface graphics [48].

Context-preserving volume rendering [19] is an example of an approach to view-dependent transparency. Regions that receive little volume illumination, for example contours, are emphasized, i.e., the volume illumination term is used to modulate opacity. In addition, the distance to the eye point is taken into account to mimic the properties of a clipping plane. Furthermore, gradient magnitude of the data volume and the amount of accumulated opacity (along the viewing ray) affect this transparency model. The overall effect is that the inner parts of a volume become visible, while

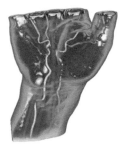 

Figure 15.15. View-dependent transparency in volume illustrations. The left image demonstrates context-preserving volume rendering. The right image shows an example of importance-driven volume rendering that allows us to view the inner parts of the gecko. Left image courtesy of S. Bruckner, S. Grimm, A. Kanitsar, and M. E. Gröller [19], © Eurographics Association, 2005. Right image courtesy of I. Viola, A. Kanitsar, and M. E. Gröller [272], © 2004 IEEE.

the outer context is still preserved (see Figure 15.15 (left)). An advantage of context-preserving volume rendering is that it just requires a slightly extended definition of a transfer function and, thus, can easily be included in existing volume-rendering software. Context-preserving volume rendering is related to silhouette enhancement (see Chapter 14), showing that a completely clear distinction between NPR styles and models for selective visibility does not exist.

Importance-driven volume rendering [272, 274] is another example of view-dependent and selective visibility. It generalizes view-dependent cutaway illustrations [49] to volumetric data. Similar to a selection volume, a 3D importance function is applied to assign visibility priorities. The most important regions are always visible—independently of the viewing parameters—because the importance values are taken into account along a viewing ray to control the sparseness of the display: where an object would occlude more important structures, it is displayed more sparsely than in areas where no occlusion occurs. Figure 15.15 (right) demonstrates importance-driven volume rendering. In this example image, inner parts of the gecko are assigned high importance values. Therefore, these interior regions are visible, while the outer skin of the gecko is almost transparent in this part of the image.

Context-preserving volume rendering and importance-driven volume rendering also use another extension of the original clipping concept. Both techniques allow for a fuzzy, gradually and smoothly varying visibility parameter—in contrast with the binary visibility definition for volume clipping. Therefore, more flexibility is provided in modeling the transition from emphasized regions to unimportant areas.

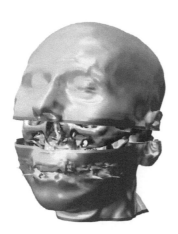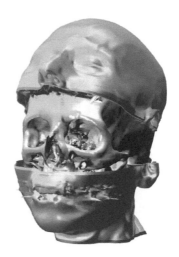

Figure 15.16.   Volume splitting applied to a CT head data set. Here, splitting is based on two semantic layers, namely bones and soft tissues. (Image courtesy of S. Islam, S. Dipankar, D. Silver, and M. Chen, based on their implementation of volume splitting [112].)

The third major extension, as compared with pure clipping, is the support for interactive volume sculpting and deformation (see Chapter 13 for details). Adopting the idea of explosion illustrations, exterior parts of a volume can be moved to another region to allow the user to view both the interior area and the shifted parts. Figure 15.12 shows a simple example of an explosion view. Figure 15.16 illustrates another example of illustrative rendering by means of volume deformations.

In general, two questions have to be addressed. First, what region is to be deformed? Second, how is it deformed? Chapter 13 discusses deformation techniques in detail. Specifically for volume illustrations, spatial transfer functions [25] can be extended to volume splitting. The idea is to apply a series of transformations to a volumetric object. Transformations may cover a large class of operations, such as rotation, scaling, deformation, or changes of color and opacity. Figure 15.16 shows an example of volume splitting. This image is based on a visualization technique by Islam et al. [112]. Here, two semantically different regions of the volume, namely bones and soft tissues, undergo different deformations. Therefore, segmentation often plays an important role in classifying regions for deformations. It should be noted that the approach by Islam et al. is implemented by CPU volume rendering and does not allow for real-time rendering at this moment. Another, related approach uses deformations to browse volumetric data [183].

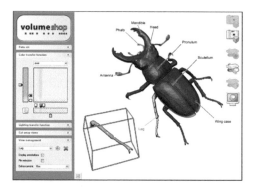

Figure 15.17. Interactive design of volume illustrations in VolumeShop. (Image courtesy of S. Bruckner and M. E. Gröller [18], © 2005 IEEE.)

Finally, interactivity is the key element in designing compelling illustrations. The aforementioned methods are especially powerful when they are combined in an interactive system that allows the user to choose from a variety of rendering styles and deformation parameters. VolumeShop by Bruckner and Gröller [18] is one example of such an integrated system. Figure 15.17 shows a snapshot of an example session with VolumeShop. Typical interactions include the selection of parts of the volume, the modification of rendering styles, and the specification of annotations. Another, related illustration approach is based on illustration motifs by Svakhine et al. [260]. Their system provides a high-level interface that allows the user to specify the type of illustration and visualization goals. Figure 15.18 shows a snapshot of their implementation. Illustration motifs particularly target scientific and biomedical visualizations.

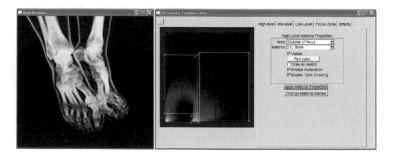

Figure 15.18. A volume-illustration system based on illustration motifs. This image shows a snapshot of the IVIS system by Svakhine et al. [260]. A demo version of their system can be downloaded from http://ivis.purpl.net. (Image courtesy of Nikolai A. Svakhine.)

15.7   Further Reading

Large portions of this chapter are related to the work of Weiskopf et al. [293] on surface-oriented clipping, clipping via voxelized selection volumes, and clipping of illuminated volumes. This paper contains technical background and additional descriptions of implementations on older graphics hardware. An alternative way of dealing with volume cutting for convex geometries is presented in another, related paper [292]. Here, details of an implementation on NVIDIA GeForce 3/4 GPUs are given. The combination of pre-integration and clipping is discussed by Röttger et al. [227].

The methods for surface-based clipping in this chapter need a texture representation of the depth structure. On graphics hardware with a fixed-function pipeline and no support for high-resolution textures, an alternative technique can be used: Westermann and Ertl [296] apply the stencil test to determine the visibility of fragments. The geometry of the clipping object is rendered for each slice to set the stencil buffer at positions that are inside of the clipping geometry. To this end, a clip plane that is co-planar with the current slice is used to remove the clipping geometry in front of the slice. Finally, the slice with the actual data is rendered, with the stencil test being enabled. This approach provides the same quality as the surface-based techniques of this chapter but has to re-render the complete clipping geometry for each volume slice. Therefore, this technique is less suitable for complex clipping objects. Rezk-Salama et al. [223] describe how stencil-based clipping can be used for 3D flow visualization.

Medical imaging is an important field of application for volume clipping. The book by Preim and Bartz [216] focuses on medical volume rendering and contains an in-depth discussion of clipping for medical applications, including further references. Tiede et al. [264] describe a CPU ray-casting system to visualize attributed data with high quality. Their system mainly targets medical visualization. Similarly, the approach by Pflesser et al. [209] discusses a clipping method for arbitrary cut surfaces in the context of medical imaging. Konrad-Verse et al. [131] describe methods for the specification and modification of virtual resections in medical volume data, employing a deformable cutting plane. Another medical application is presented by Hastreiter et al. [99], who use tagged volumes to apply different transfer functions to different regions of a 3D medical scan.

Seismic 3D data from the oil and gas industry is another prominent field of application. A major challenge is the size of these data sets, which typically comprise several gigabytes of data. Therefore, seismic data is often visualized by using only a few slice planes that can be interactively controlled by the user to explore the whole data set [75]. Volz [276] describes a method for very large data sets that relies on level-of-detail volumes, data caches, BSP trees (all processed by the CPU), and a hybrid CPU/GPU approach for trilinear interpolation on slices.

16

Segmented Volume Data

A N IMPORTANT GOAL IN VOLUME RENDERING, especially when we are dealing with medical data, is to be able to visually separate and selectively enable or disable specific objects of interest contained in a single volumetric data set. As we have seen in Chapter 15, cutaway views and general volumetric clipping very effectively allow parts of the volume to be removed during rendering that would otherwise occlude interesting areas. Rendering segmented volume data can be seen as an extension of volume clipping with a voxelized selection volume as described in Chapter 15.

Segmentation is the process of identifying or *tagging* individual voxels as belonging to one of several objects contained in a volume. Figure 16.1 shows example images of a medical data set, a CT scan of a human hand, where

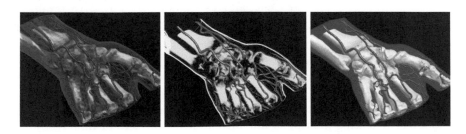

Figure 16.1. Segmented CT volume of a human hand with different rendering modes and transfer functions for different objects. Left: all objects rendered with shaded DVR (direct volume rendering); the skin partially obscures the bone. Center: skin rendered with non-photorealistic contour rendering and MIP compositing, bones rendered with DVR, vessels with tone shading. Right: skin rendered with MIP, bones with tone shading, and vessels with shaded isosurfacing; the skin merely provides context. (Images reprinted from [92], © 2003 IEEE.)

four objects have been identified via segmentation: the bone structure, the blood vessels, the skin, and the air surrounding the hand. The first three objects are rendered using different optical properties, and the voxels corresponding to air have been disabled entirely, i.e., they are clipped. Segmentation is a huge topic, and performing the actual segmentation is beyond the scope of this book. This chapter covers how to use already existing segmentation information during rendering. An introduction to the topic of segmentation can be found in other texts, e.g., in the area of medical visualization [216] or medical imaging [268]. In the context of rendering, segmentation is a very powerful approach to facilitate the perception of individual objects, especially when these objects are rendered with different optical properties such as their own transfer functions. The set of voxels that belong to a given object of interest is usually represented in the form of a *segmentation mask*.

There are two major ways of representing segmentation information in masks. First, each object can be represented by a single binary segmentation mask, which determines for each voxel whether it belongs to the given object or not. Second, an object ID volume can specify segmentation information for all objects in a single volume, where each voxel contains the ID of the object it belongs to. The second approach is well-suited to volume rendering on GPUs because it uses only one additional volume, and object IDs can easily be stored in an 8-bit texture. This object ID texture can then be used to selectively render only some of the objects contained in a single data set or render different objects with different rendering modes and transfer functions. Volumes with object ID tags are often also called *tagged volumes* [99]. As mentioned above, rendering segmented volume data is related to volume clipping in many respects. The voxelized selection volumes described in Chapter 15 could be used directly as binary object ID or tag volumes or segmentation masks. However, the goal of rendering segmented data is to display multiple objects at the same time and still be able to clearly distinguish these objects visually. Of course, some objects are often disabled during rendering, i.e., clipped away, such as the air in Figure 16.1.

Other approaches for achieving visual distinction of objects are, for example, rendering multiple semitransparent isosurfaces or direct volume rendering with an appropriate transfer function. In the latter approach, multidimensional transfer functions [123, 128] have proved to be especially powerful in facilitating the perception of different objects. These approaches are described in Chapters 4 and 10. However, it is often the case that a single rendering method or transfer function does not suffice to distinguish multiple objects of interest according to a user's specific needs, especially when spatial information needs to be taken into account.

Non-photorealistic volume rendering and illustrative visualization, which are described in Chapter 14, have also proved to be very effective approaches for achieving better perception of individual objects. An especially powerful technique is to combine different non-photorealistic and traditional volume-rendering methods in a single volume rendering. An example of this is shown in the center image of Figure 16.1. Only the contours of the skin are rendered in order to avoid occluding the bones or the blood vessels. When segmentation information is available, different objects can be rendered with individual per-object rendering modes such as standard direct volume rendering or non-photorealistic contour rendering. This allows specific modes to be used for structures they are well suited for, as well as separating *focus* from *context* objects. Even further, different objects can be rendered with their own individual compositing mode, combining the contributions of all objects with a single global compositing mode. This two-level approach to object compositing can further facilitate object perception and is known as *two-level volume rendering* [100, 101], which is described in Section 16.6.

16.1   Overview

Integrating segmentation information and multiple rendering modes with different sets of parameters into a fast high-quality volume renderer is in general not a trivial problem. GPUs are much faster if all or most fragments can be treated identically. Also, for GPU volume rendering, it is crucial to use only a single object ID volume instead of multiple segmentation masks in order to use a minimal amount of texture memory. GPUs cannot easily interpolate between voxels belonging to different objects, however, and using the object ID volume without filtering gives rise to visual artifacts. Thus, one of the major obstacles in such a scenario is filtering object boundaries in order to attain high quality in conjunction with consistent fragment assignment and without introducing nonexistent object IDs due to interpolation.

In this chapter, we show how segmented volumetric data sets can be rendered efficiently and with high quality on GPUs. The segmentation information for object distinction can be used at multiple levels of sophistication, and we describe how these different possibilities can be integrated into a single coherent hardware volume-rendering framework using slicing. We focus on algorithms that do not require data-dependent branching and looping in fragment programs. Instead of branching and looping, we are potentially using multiple rendering passes. When a single fragment program includes a variety of different shading models, performance is often reduced significantly. On current GPUs, this is a common problem even if all shading instructions that are not needed are skipped using conditional execution. However, keep in mind that building on the latest fragment program features simplifies the implementation and allows sophisticated effects with single-pass rendering, e.g., using ray casting.

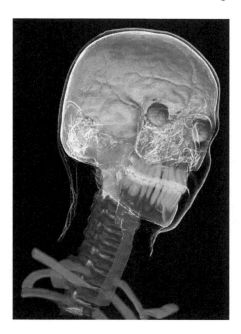

Figure 16.2. Segmented head and neck data set with eight different enabled objects. Brain: tone shading; skin: contour enhancement with clipping plane; eyes and spine: shaded DVR; skull, teeth, and vertebrae: unshaded DVR; trachea: MIP. (Image reprinted from [92], © 2003 IEEE.)

We illustrate how different objects can be rendered with the same rendering technique (e.g., DVR) but with different transfer functions. Separate per-object transfer functions can be applied in a single rendering pass even when object boundaries are filtered during rendering. Different objects can also be rendered using different fragment programs. This allows easy integration of methods as diverse as non-photorealistic and direct volume rendering, for instance. Although each distinct fragment program requires a separate rendering pass, multiple objects using the same fragment program with different rendering parameters can effectively be combined into a single pass. With certain restrictions it is also possible to evaluate different shading models with a single equation. An example is the use of lighting look-up tables [18], which are described in Section 14.2.3. This technique employs a fragment program with a single shading equation that is parameterized by a look-up table. When multiple passes cannot be avoided, the cost of individual passes can be reduced drastically by executing expensive fragment programs only for those fragments that are active in a given pass (Section 16.4.1).

Finally, different objects can also be rendered with different compositing modes, e.g., alpha blending and maximum intensity projection (MIP), for their contribution to a given pixel. These per-object compositing modes are object-local and can be specified independently for each object. The individual contributions of different objects to a single pixel can be combined via a separate global compositing mode. This two-level approach to object compositing [100, 101] has proved to be very useful in order to improve perception of individual objects. Examples are combining non-photorealistic contour enhancement using MIP (Figure 16.1 (center); Figure 16.3 (skull)) [38] with tone shading (Figure 16.1 (right)) [57, 83], which improves depth perception in contrast with standard shading.

To summarize, the major points of this chapter are the following.

- How to minimize both the number of rendering passes and the performance cost of individual passes when rendering segmented volume data with high quality on GPUs without data-dependent branching

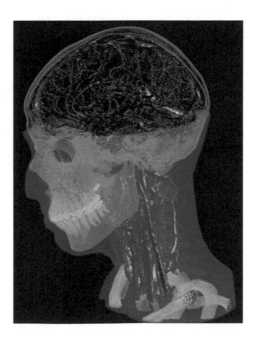

Figure 16.3. Segmented head and neck data set with six different enabled objects. The skin and teeth are rendered as MIP with different windowing functions, vessels and eyes are rendered as shaded DVR, the skull uses contour rendering, and the vertebrae use a gradient magnitude-weighted transfer function with shaded DVR. A clipping plane has been applied to the skin object. (Image reprinted from [92], © 2003 IEEE.)

and looping. Both filtering of object boundaries and the use of different rendering parameters such as transfer functions do not prevent using a single rendering pass for multiple objects. Even so, each pass can avoid execution of the corresponding potentially expensive fragment program for irrelevant fragments by exploiting the early z-test.

- How to efficiently map a single object ID volume to and from a domain where filtering produces correct results in the fragment program even when three or more objects are present in the volume.

- How to achieve correct compositing of objects with different per-object compositing modes and an additional global compositing mode (i.e., two-level volume rendering). Even when branching in the fragment program should be avoided, this can be done with an efficient object-order algorithm based on simple depth and stencil buffer operations. The result is conceptually identical to being able to switch compositing modes for any given group of samples along the ray for any given pixel.

16.2   Segmented Data Representation

For rendering purposes, we assume that in addition to the usual data such as a density and an optional gradient volume, an *object ID volume* is also available. If segmented objects are represented as separate masks, they have to be combined into a single volume that contains a single object ID for

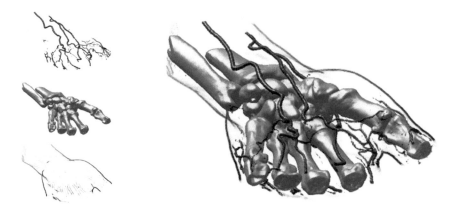

Figure 16.4. CT scan of a human hand. When individual objects are using their own rendering mode and parameters (left column), combining them into a single volume rendering without losing too much performance is crucial (right).

each voxel in a pre-process. Object IDs are often enumerated consecutively starting with one, i.e., individual bits are not assigned to specific objects. Usually, ID zero is reserved to mean "not assigned to any object."

The easiest way for a GPU implementation is to store this object ID volume as a monochrome texture with 8 bits per voxel, e.g., a texture with internal format GL_INTENSITY8. In the case of view-aligned slicing or ray casting, a single 3D texture can be used, whereas for object-aligned slicing additional 2D object ID slice textures are required. With respect to resolution, the object ID volume usually has the same resolution as the original volume data because segmentation masks commonly also have the same resolution. However, object ID volumes of differing resolutions can also be used.

See Figure 16.4 for an example of three segmented objects rendered with per-object rendering modes and transfer functions.

16.3   Rendering Segmented Data

The most important operation when rendering a segmented data set is to determine *object membership* for each rendered fragment, i.e., determining the object ID of the fragment, which is not necessarily the object ID of a voxel (due to filtering). Object membership then determines which transfer function, rendering mode, and compositing mode should be used for any given fragment.

In the simplest case, object membership can simply be determined from the object ID texture when nearest-neighbor interpolation is used. However, similar to volume clipping with nearest-neighbor selection volumes (Chapter 15), the resulting voxel-resolution artifacts are often clearly visible. In order to avoid this, object membership has to be determined after filtering object boundaries, e.g., using trilinear interpolation. As we will see in Section 16.5, however, linear filtering of object ID textures must be performed in the fragment program instead of simply using the hardware-native linear texture filter.

Even when data-dependent branching and looping are not used, the volume can be rendered in a number of rendering passes that is independent of the number of contained objects. The number of passes then depends on the required number of different hardware configurations that cannot be changed during a single pass, i.e., the fragment program and the compositing mode. Objects that share a given configuration can be rendered in a single pass. This also extends to the application of multiple per-object transfer functions (Section 16.5.3), and thus the actual number of rendering passes is usually much lower than the number of objects or transfer functions. In general, it depends on several major factors:

Enabled Objects. If all the objects rendered in a given pass have been disabled by the user, the entire rendering pass can be skipped. If only some of the objects are disabled, the number of passes stays the same, independent of the order of object IDs. Objects can be disabled by changing a single entry of a 1D look-up texture. Additionally, per-object clipping planes can be enabled. In this case, all objects rendered in the same pass usually have to be clipped identically, however.

Rendering Modes. The rendering mode, implemented as an actual GPU fragment program, determines what and how volume data is resampled and shaded. Because it cannot be changed during a single rendering pass, another pass must be used if a different fragment program is required. However, many objects often use the same basic rendering mode and thus fragment program, e.g., direct volume rendering (DVR) and isosurfacing are usually used for a large number of objects. Moreover, different shading models can sometimes be used with a single fragment program by using look-up tables such as lighting transfer functions [18].

Transfer Functions. Much more often than the basic rendering mode, a change of the transfer function is required. For instance, all objects rendered with DVR usually have their own individual transfer functions. In order to avoid an excessive number of rendering passes due to simple transfer-function changes, we describe how to apply multiple transfer functions to different objects in a single rendering pass while still retaining adequate filtering quality (Section 16.5.3).

Compositing Modes. Although usually considered a part of the rendering mode, compositing is a totally separate operation on GPUs (see Chapter 2). Where the basic rendering mode is determined by the fragment program, the compositing mode is specified as blend function and equation in OpenGL, for instance. It determines how already shaded fragments are combined with pixels stored in the frame buffer. Changing the compositing mode happens even more infrequently than changing the basic rendering mode, e.g., alpha blending is used in conjunction with both DVR and tone shading.

Different compositing modes per object also imply that the (conceptual) ray corresponding to a single pixel must be able to combine the contribution of these different modes (Figure 16.11). Combining compositing modes is very easy with ray casting. In an object-order approach such as slicing, however, special care has to be taken. The contributions of individual objects to a given pixel should not interfere with each other and are combined with a single global compositing mode (Section 16.6).

In order to ensure correct compositing when slicing is used, a good approach is to use two render buffers and track the current compositing mode for each pixel. Whenever the compositing mode changes for a given pixel, the already composited part is transferred from the *local compositing buffer* into the *global compositing buffer*. Section 16.6 shows that this can actually be done very efficiently without explicitly considering individual pixels. It is possible to achieve the same compositing behavior as a ray-oriented image-order approach, which is crucial for achieving high quality.

16.4   The Basic Rendering Loop

This section describes the basic procedure for rendering segmented data using slicing. Listing 16.1 gives a high-level overview.

Although the user is dealing with individual objects, we automatically collect all objects that can be processed in the same rendering pass into an *object set* at the beginning of each frame. For each object set, we generate an *object set membership texture*, which is a 1D look-up table that determines the objects belonging to the set. In order to further distinguish different transfer functions in a single object set, we also generate 1D *transfer-function assignment textures*. Both of these types of textures are illustrated in Figure 16.5 and described in Sections 16.4.2 and 16.5.

After this set-up, the entire slice stack is rendered. Each slice must be rendered for every object set that intersects the slice. When 2D texture–based slicing is used, this can be determined in a pre-process. In the case

```
DetermineObjectSets();
CreateObjectSetMembershipTextures();
CreateTFAssignmentTextures();
FOR each slice DO
   TransferLocalBufferIntoGlobalBuffer();
   ClearTransferredPixelsInLocalBuffer();
   RenderObjectIdDepthImageForEarlyZTest();
   FOR each object set with an object in slice DO
      SetupObjectSetFragmentRejection();
      SetupObjectSetTFAssignment();
      ActivateObjectSetFragmentProgram();
      ActivateObjectSetCompositingMode();
      RenderSliceIntoLocalBuffer();
```

Listing 16.1. The basic rendering loop. Object set membership can change every time an object's rendering or compositing mode is changed or an object is enabled or disabled.

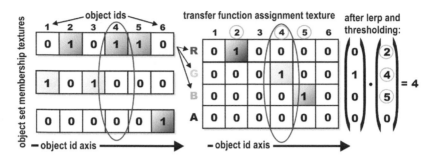

Figure 16.5. Object set membership textures (left; three ID intensity textures for three sets containing three, two, and one object, respectively) contain a binary membership status for each object in a set that can be used for filtering object IDs and culling fragments. Transfer-function assignment textures (right; one ID RGBA texture for distinction of four transfer functions) are used to filter four object boundaries simultaneously and determine the corresponding transfer function via a simple dot product. (Images reprinted from [92], © 2003 IEEE.)

of 3D volume textures, all slices are always assumed to be intersected by all objects, because they are allowed to cut through the volume at arbitrary angles. An exception is when the volume is rendered using bricking, which is described in Chapter 17. Bricked volumes allow a variety of optimizations when rendering segmented data. For each brick, the objects that are actually contained in it can be considered, and using different fragment programs for rendering different bricks is usually possible. If there is more than one object set for the current slice, we optionally render all object set IDs of the slice into the depth buffer before rendering any actual slice data. This per-slice depth pass is the basis for exploiting the early z-test during all subsequent passes for each object set intersecting a slice (Section 16.4.1).

Before a slice can be rendered for an object set, the fragment program and compositing mode corresponding to this set must be activated. Using the two types of textures mentioned above, the fragment program filters boundaries, rejects fragments not corresponding to the current pass, and applies the correct transfer function.

In order to attain two compositing levels, slices are rendered into a local compositing buffer. Before rendering the current slice, those pixels where the local compositing mode differs from the previous slice are transferred from the local into the global buffer using the global compositing mode. This is done using depth comparisons and the stencil buffer (Section 16.6). After this transfer, the transferred pixels are cleared in the local buffer to ensure correct local compositing for subsequent pixels. In the case when only one compositing mode is used, only a single compositing buffer is used, and the local to global buffer transfer and clear are not executed.

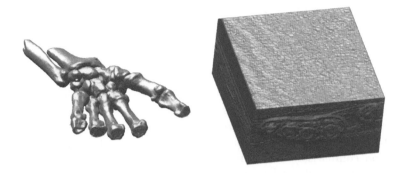

Figure 16.6. In order to render the bone structure shown on the left, many voxels need to be culled. The early z-test allows the evaluation of shading equations to be avoided for culled voxels. If it is not employed, performance will correspond to shading all voxels as shown on the right.

16.4.1 Early Fragment Culling

GPUs often avoid execution of a fragment program for fragments where the depth test fails as long as the fragment program does not modify the depth value of the fragment and certain other conditions are met. More details are given in Section 8.6.2. In the context of rendering segmented data, this early z-test is crucial to improving performance when multiple rendering passes have to be performed for each slice.

If the current slice's object set IDs have been written into the depth buffer before rendering and shading the slice, fragments not belonging to the current object set can be rejected even before the corresponding fragment program is started. In order to do this, a depth test of GL_EQUAL must be used. The vertex program generates a constant depth value for each fragment that exactly matches the current object set ID. Figure 16.6 illustrates the performance difference of using the early z-test as opposed to also shading voxels that will be culled.

Excluding individual fragments from processing by an expensive fragment program via the early z-test is also crucial in the context of GPU-based ray casting in order to be able to terminate rays individually when multiple rendering passes have to be used [139].

16.4.2 Fragment Program Operations

Most of the work in GPU volume renderers is done in the fragment program, i.e., at the granularity of individual fragments and, ultimately, pixels. In contrast with earlier approaches using look-up tables, e.g., palettized textures, nowadays most shading operations are performed procedurally in the fragment program. In this section, we focus on the operations that are required specifically for rendering segmented data. The two basic operations in the fragment program that involve the object ID volume are *fragment rejection* and *per-fragment application of transfer functions*.

Fragment rejection. Fragments corresponding to object IDs that cannot be rendered in the current rendering pass, e.g., because they need a different fragment program or compositing mode, have to be rejected. They, in turn, will be rendered in another pass, which uses an appropriately adjusted rejection comparison. Of course, if the corresponding object is disabled (clipped), they will not be rendered at all.

For fragment rejection, we do not compare object IDs individually but use 1D look-up textures that contain a binary membership status for each object (Figure 16.5 (left)). Enabled objects that can be rendered in the same pass belong to the same object set, and the corresponding object set membership texture contains ones at exactly those texture coordinates corresponding to the IDs of these objects, and zeros everywhere else. The regeneration of these textures at the beginning of each frame, which is

```
float4 main (float3 vol_coord:  TEXCOORD0,
            uniform sampler3D volume_texture,
            uniform sampler3D objectID_texture,
            uniform sampler2D transfer_functions,
            uniform sampler1D membership_texture) :  COLOR
{
    // fetch object ID from texture
    float objectID = tex3D(objectID_texture, vol_coord);
    // determine whether fragment must be discarded in this pass
    float membership = tex1D(membership_texture, objectID);
    if ( membership < 1.0 )
        discard;
    // compute coordinates for transfer function lookup
    float2 tfcoords;
    tfcoords.x = tex3D(volume_texture, vol_coord);
    tfcoords.y = objectID;
    // return color and opacity from transfer function
    float4 result = tex2D(transfer_functions, tfcoords);
    return result;
}
```

Listing 16.2. Cg function implementing fragment rejection with an object membership texture. The object ID volume uses nearest-neighbor interpolation. The transfer function is applied using both the volume density and the object ID.

negligible in terms of performance, also makes turning individual objects on and off trivial. Exactly one object set membership texture is active for a given rendering pass and makes the task of fragment rejection very easy if the object ID volume uses nearest-neighbor interpolation. Listing 16.2 shows an example fragment program that discards fragments using a 1D object set membership texture.

Handling object ID filtering. When object IDs are filtered, it is crucial to map individual IDs to zero or one in a defined way before actually filtering them. Details are given in Section 16.5, but basically object set membership textures can be used to do a binary classification of input IDs to the filter, and interpolate after this mapping. The result can then be mapped back to zero or one for fragment rejection.

Per-fragment transfer-function application.

Because we want to apply different transfer functions to multiple objects in a single rendering pass, the transfer function must be applied to individual fragments based on both their density value and the object ID of the fragment. Instead of using multiple transfer-function textures, all transfer functions are stored in a single texture of one dimension higher. That is, if the transfer functions are 1D, they are stored in a single 2D texture, which is illustrated in Figure 16.7. (If they are 2D, they are stored in a 3D texture with just a few layers in depth and everything else is analogous.) In the fragment program, this single global 2D transfer-function texture is then sampled using (`density`, `objectID`) as 2D texture coordinates instead of only `density` as a 1D coordinate. Listing 16.2 illustrates this for the simplest case when the object ID texture uses nearest-neighbor interpolation.

Sampling the combined transfer-function texture. When this combined transfer-function texture is sampled, care must be taken that the transfer functions of different objects are not mixed due to linear texture filtering. It is usually desired that the transfer function itself is filtered using

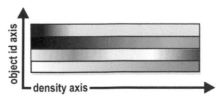

Figure 16.7. Instead of multiple ID transfer functions for different objects, a single global 2D transfer-function texture is used. After determining the object ID for the current fragment via filtering, the fragment program appropriately samples this texture with 2D texture coordinates (`density`, `objectID`). (Image reprinted from [92], © 2003 IEEE.)

linear interpolation. However, along the object ID axis, nearest-neighbor interpolation would be ideal in order to avoid erroneous interpolation between two different transfer functions. Quite understandably, it is not possible on GPUs to use different filtering modes for individual axes of a texture. There are two easy solutions to this problem. The first is to leave the fragment program unchanged and simply store each transfer function twice, in adjacent locations. (This is assumed in Listing 16.2.) Because linear interpolation between the same values results in the same value, this naturally solves the problem. Note that object IDs must then either be adapted in the fragment program or assigned accordingly right from the start, e.g., using $\texttt{objectID} \in \{1, 3, 5, ...\}$ instead of $\texttt{objectID} \in \{1, 2, 3, ...\}$. The transfer function for $\texttt{objectID} = i$ would then be stored at locations $i - 1$ and i, with $i \in \{1, 3, 5, ...\}$. The second method is to make sure that along the object ID axis each sample is taken at the exact center of a texel. In both OpenGL and Direct3D, the center of a texel is at coordinate 0.5, given that a single texel is in $[0, 1]$. In order to achieve the desired filtering behavior, the fragment program can simply add this offset to the second texture coordinate ($\texttt{tfcoords.y}$ in Listing 16.2). Note that texture coordinates are usually given in $[0, 1]$ for the entire texture and thus the actual offset would be $0.5/$ $\texttt{texture\_size}$. Therefore, this requires an additional uniform fragment program parameter $\texttt{texture\_size}$.

Handling object ID filtering. An extended version of the pixel-resolution filter that is employed for fragment rejection can be used in order to determine which of multiple transfer functions in the same rendering pass a fragment should actually use. Basically, the fragment program uses multiple RGBA transfer-function assignment textures (Figure 16.5, right) for both determining the transfer function and rejecting fragments, instead of a single object set membership texture with only a single color channel. Each one of these textures allows filtering the object ID volume with respect to four object boundaries simultaneously. If there are more objects in a single rendering pass, more transfer-function assignment textures can easily be used. A single look-up yields binary membership classification of a fragment with respect to four objects. The resulting RGBA membership vectors can then be interpolated directly. The main operation for mapping back the result to an object ID is a simple dot product with a constant vector of object IDs. If the result is the nonexistent object ID of zero, the fragment needs to be rejected. The details are described in Section 16.5.3.

16.5   Boundary Filtering

An important part of rendering segmented volumes with high quality is that the object boundaries must be determined during rendering at the pixel resolution of the output image instead of the voxel resolution of the

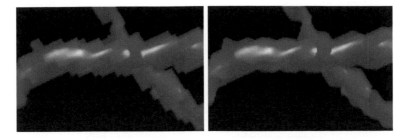

Figure 16.8. Object boundaries with voxel resolution (left) versus object boundaries determined per-fragment with linear filtering (right). (Images reprinted from [92], © 2003 IEEE.)

object ID volume. In order to do this, object IDs must be filtered instead of using them with nearest-neighbor interpolation. Simply retrieving the object ID for a given fragment from the segmentation volume is trivial, but causes artifacts. Figure 16.8 (left) shows that using nearest-neighbor interpolation for the object ID texture leads to object boundaries that are easily discernible as individual voxels. Instead, the object ID can be determined via filtering for each fragment individually, thus achieving pixel-resolution boundaries.

Unfortunately, filtering of object boundaries cannot be done directly using the hardware-native linear interpolation, because direct interpolation of numerical object IDs leads to incorrectly interpolated intermediate values when more than two different objects are present. When filtering object IDs, a threshold value s_t (see Figure 16.9) must be chosen that determines which object a given fragment belongs to, which is essentially an isosurfacing problem.

However, this cannot be done if three or more objects are contained in the volume, which is illustrated in the top row of Figure 16.9. In that case, it is not possible to choose a single s_t for the entire volume. The crucial observation to make in order to solve this problem is that the segmentation volume must be filtered as a successive series of binary volumes in order to achieve proper filtering [264], which is shown in the second row of Figure 16.9. Mapping all object IDs of the current object set to 1.0 and all other IDs to 0.0 allows use of a global threshold value s_t of 0.5. Of course, we do not want to store these binary volumes explicitly but to perform this mapping on-the-fly in the fragment program by indexing the *object set membership texture* that is active in the current rendering pass. Filtering in the other passes simply uses an alternate binary mapping, i.e., other object set membership textures.

One problem with respect to a hardware implementation of this approach is that texture filtering happens before the sampled values can be altered in the fragment program. Therefore, filtering of object IDs is per-

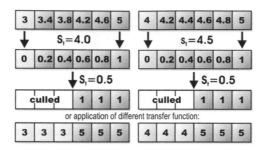

Figure 16.9. Each fragment must be assigned an exactly defined object ID after filtering. Here, IDs 3, 4, and 5 are interpolated, yielding the values shown in blue. Top row: choosing a single threshold value s_t that works everywhere is not possible for three or more objects. Second row: object IDs must be converted to 0.0 or 1.0 in the fragment program before interpolation, which allows use of a global s_t of 0.5. After thresholding, fragments can be culled accordingly (third row) or mapped back to an object ID in order to apply the corresponding transfer function (fourth row). (Image reprinted from [92], © 2003 IEEE.)

formed directly in the fragment program. Note that this approach could in part also be implemented using texture palettes and hardware-native linear interpolation, with the restriction that not more than four transfer functions can be applied in a single rendering pass. However, performing all filtering in the fragment program ensures a coherent framework with a potentially unlimited number of transfer functions in a single rendering pass. Furthermore, paletted textures are not supported anymore on most current GPU architectures.

After filtering yields values in the range $[0.0, 1.0]$, we once again come to a binary decision whether a given fragment belongs to the current object set by comparing with a threshold value of 0.5 and rejecting fragments with an interpolated value below this threshold (Figure 16.9 (third row)). Actual rejection of fragments can be done using Cg's `discard` instruction (Listings 16.3 and 16.5). It can also be done by mapping the fragment to RGBA values constituting the identity with respect to the current compositing mode (e.g., an alpha of zero for alpha blending), in order to not alter the frame buffer pixel corresponding to this fragment. Note that, on NVIDIA architectures, the `discard` instruction usually disables the early z-test and thus needs to be avoided.

16.5.1 Linear Boundary Filtering

For object-aligned volume slices, bilinear interpolation is done by setting the hardware filtering mode for the object ID texture to nearest-neighbor and sampling it four times with offsets of whole texel increments in order

```
float4 main (float2 vol_coord:  TEXCOORD0,
             uniform float transfer_function_ID,
             uniform float4 filter_offset,
             uniform float2 vol_size,
             uniform sampler2D volume_texture,
             uniform sampler2D objectID_texture,
             uniform sampler2D transfer_functions,
             uniform sampler1D membership_texture) :  COLOR
{
    // determine coordinates of four nearest neighbors
    float2 vol_coord00 = vol_coord - filter_offset.xy;
    float2 vol_coord01 = vol_coord - filter_offset.zw;
    float2 vol_coord10 = vol_coord + filter_offset.zw;
    float2 vol_coord11 = vol_coord + filter_offset.xy;
    // fetch object IDs of the four nearest neighbors
    float4 objectIDs;
    objectIDs.x = tex2D(objectID_texture, vol_coord00);
    objectIDs.y = tex2D(objectID_texture, vol_coord01);
    objectIDs.z = tex2D(objectID_texture, vol_coord10);
    objectIDs.w = tex2D(objectID_texture, vol_coord11);
    // map all object IDs to binary IDs {0,1}
    float4 binIDs;
    binIDs.x = tex1D(membership_texture, objectIDs.x);
    binIDs.y = tex1D(membership_texture, objectIDs.y);
    binIDs.z = tex1D(membership_texture, objectIDs.z);
    binIDs.w = tex1D(membership_texture, objectIDs.w);
    // perform bilinear interpolation on binary IDs
    float4 weights = GetBilinearWeights(vol_coord, vol_size);
    float binID = dot(binIDs, weights);
    if ( binID < 0.5 )
        discard;
    // compute coordinates for transfer function lookup
    float2 tfcoords;
    tfcoords.x = tex2D(volume_texture, vol_coord);
    tfcoords.y = transfer_function_ID;
    // return color and opacity from transfer function
    float4 result = tex2D(transfer_functions, tfcoords);
    return result;
}
```

Listing 16.3.   Cg function implementing bilinear filtering of segmented object boundaries using an object set membership texture. Boundary filtering is used to reject the current fragment if it is outside the current boundary. Only one transfer function is applied, which is specified via the uniform program parameter transfer_function_ID.

```
float4 GetBilinearWeights(float2 vol_coord, float2 vol_size) {
    float4 weights;
    // compute fractional weights for s and t axes
    weights.y = frac(vol_coord.x * vol_size.x - 0.5);
    weights.w = frac(vol_coord.y * vol_size.y - 0.5);
    // compute complementary weights
    weights.xz = float2(1.0, 1.0) - weights.yw;
    // return all four weights in one vector
    return ( weights.xyxy * weights.zzww );
}
```

Listing 16.4. Cg function that returns four weights for bilinear interpolation. The offset of -0.5 is needed in order to adjust for the texel center at $(0.5, 0.5)$.

to get access to the four ID values needed for interpolation. Before actual interpolation takes place, the four object IDs are individually mapped to 0.0 or 1.0, respectively, using the current object set membership texture.

Listing 16.3 shows a fragment program for bilinear filtering of an object ID volume stored in 2D texture slices. First, the coordinates of all four neighbors that are needed for interpolation must be computed. Note that this can be performed in a vertex program instead, but for simplicity we have included it in the fragment program. Next, the object IDs at these coordinates must be fetched. Then, the IDs must be mapped to a binary $\{0, 1\}$ domain using the object set membership texture of the current rendering pass (membership_texture). Interpolation is then performed in this binary domain. The resulting fractional value in $[0, 1]$ is conceptually mapped back again to 0.0 or 1.0 by thresholding with 0.5. However, because we use this classification only for discarding or not discarding the fragment, we can combine thresholding with this decision without doing the actual mapping. Because this fragment program supports only a single transfer function, its ID is supplied as a uniform program parameter transfer_function_ID. Note, however, that supporting more transfer functions requires only minimal changes, which can be seen in Listing 16.5 (see Section 16.5.3). When intermediate slices are interpolated on-the-fly [224], or view-aligned slices are used, eight instead of four input IDs have to be used in order to perform trilinear interpolation.

16.5.2 Combination with Pre-Integration

The combination of pre-integration [64] and clipping is described in Section 15.5. Because filtering of object IDs effectively reduces the problem to a binary clipping problem on-the-fly, the same approach as for clipping can be used when rendering segmented data after object IDs have been mapped to 0.0 or 1.0, respectively. In this case, the interpolated binary values must be used for adjusting the pre-integration look-up.

16.5.3 Multiple Per-Object Transfer Functions in a Single Rendering Pass

In addition to simply determining whether a given fragment belongs to a currently active object (object set) or not, which has been described in Section 16.5.1 above, this filtering approach can be extended to the application of multiple transfer functions in a single rendering pass without sacrificing filtering quality. Figure 16.10 shows the difference in quality for two objects with different transfer functions (one entirely red, the other entirely yellow for illustration purposes).

The easiest way to apply multiple transfer functions in a single rendering pass is to use the original volume texture with linear interpolation and an additional separate object ID texture with nearest-neighbor interpolation. However, it is also possible to apply linear interpolation to the object ID volume in a fragment program in almost the same way as it has been described for just a single transfer function in Section 16.5.1. Although actual volume and ID textures could be combined into a single texture, the use of a separate texture to store the IDs is mandatory in order to prevent filtering of the actual volume data to also revert back to nearest-neighbor interpolation. A single texture cannot use different filtering modes for different channels, and nearest-neighbor interpolation is mandatory for the ID texture. The hardware-native linear interpolation cannot be turned on

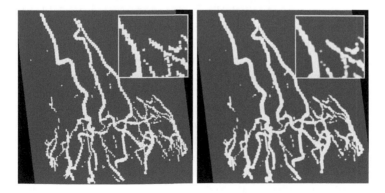

Figure 16.10. Selecting the transfer function on a per-fragment basis. In the left image, point-sampling of the object ID volume has been used, whereas in the right image procedural linear interpolation in the fragment program achieves results of much better quality. (Images reprinted from [92], © 2003 IEEE.)

in order to filter object IDs, and thus the resolution of the ID volume is easily discernible if the transfer functions are sufficiently different.

In order to avoid the artifacts related to nearest-neighbor interpolation of the ID texture, we perform several almost identical filtering steps in the fragment program, where each of these steps simultaneously filters the object boundaries of four different objects. After the fragment's object ID has been determined via filtering, it can be used to access the global transfer-function table as described in Section 16.4.2 and illustrated in Figure 16.7. For multiple simultaneous transfer functions, we do not use object set membership textures but the similar extended concept of *transfer-function assignment textures*, which is illustrated in the right image of Figure 16.5.

Each of these textures can be used for filtering the object ID volume with respect to four different object IDs at the same time by using the four channels of an RGBA texture in order to perform four simultaneous binary classification operations. In order to create these textures, each object set membership texture is converted into $\lceil \#objects/4 \rceil$ transfer-function assignment textures, where $\#objects$ denotes the number of objects with different transfer functions in a given object set. All values of 1.0 corresponding to the first transfer function are stored into the red channel of this texture, those corresponding to the second transfer function into the green channel, and so on (see Figure 16.5 (right)).

The filtering algorithm is illustrated in the fragment program in Listing 16.5. Similar to Listing 16.3, we must index the transfer-function assignment texture at four different locations that are determined by the object IDs of the four input values to interpolate. This classifies the four input object IDs with respect to four objects with just four 1D texture sampling operations. A single linear interpolation step yields the linear interpolation of these four object classifications, which can then be compared against a threshold of $(0.5, 0.5, 0.5, 0.5)$, also requiring only a single operation for four objects. Interpolation and thresholding yields a vector with at most one component of 1.0, the other components set to 0.0. In order for this to be true, it is mandatory that interpolated and thresholded repeated binary classifications never overlap, which is not guaranteed for all types of filter kernels. In the case of bilinear or trilinear interpolation, however, overlaps can never occur [264].

The final step that has to be performed is mapping the binary classification to the desired object ID. This is done with a single dot product with a vector that contains the four object IDs corresponding to the four channels of the transfer-function assignment texture (transfer_function_ID_vector). See Figure 16.5 (right). By calculating this dot product, we multiply exactly the object ID that should be assigned to the final fragment by 1.0. The other object IDs are multiplied

```
float4 main (float2 vol_coord:  TEXCOORD0,
             uniform float4 transfer_function_ID_vector,
             uniform float4 filter_offset,
             uniform float2 vol_size,
             uniform sampler2D volume_texture,
             uniform sampler2D objectID_texture,
             uniform sampler2D transfer_functions,
             uniform sampler1D tf_assignment_texture) :  COLOR
{
    // determine coordinates of four nearest neighbors
    float2 vol_coord00 = vol_coord - filter_offset.xy;
    float2 vol_coord01 = vol_coord - filter_offset.zw;
    float2 vol_coord10 = vol_coord + filter_offset.zw;
    float2 vol_coord11 = vol_coord + filter_offset.xy;
    // fetch object IDs of the four nearest neighbors
    float4 objectIDs;
    objectIDs.x = tex2D(objectID_texture, vol_coord00);
    objectIDs.y = tex2D(objectID_texture, vol_coord01);
    objectIDs.z = tex2D(objectID_texture, vol_coord10);
    objectIDs.w = tex2D(objectID_texture, vol_coord11);
    // map all object IDs to binary ID vectors {0,1}^4
    float4 tfa00 = tex1D(tf_assignment_texture, objectIDs.x);
    float4 tfa01 = tex1D(tf_assignment_texture, objectIDs.y);
    float4 tfa10 = tex1D(tf_assignment_texture, objectIDs.z);
    float4 tfa11 = tex1D(tf_assignment_texture, objectIDs.w);
    // perform bilinear interpolation on mapped vectors
    float4 weights = GetBilinearWeights(vol_coord, vol_size);
    float4 tfavec  = weights.x * tfa00 + weights.y * tfa01;
           tfavec += weights.z * tfa10 + weights.w * tfa11;
    // map back to binary domain via thresholding
    tfavec = ( tfavec > 0.5 ) ?  float4(1.0) :  float4(0.0);
    // determine post-filtering transfer function ID
    float tfID = dot(tfavec, transfer_function_ID_vector);
    if ( tfID == 0.0 )
        discard;
    // compute coordinates for transfer function lookup
    float2 tfcoords;
    tfcoords.x = tex2D(volume_texture, vol_coord);
    tfcoords.y = tfID;
    // return color and opacity from transfer function
    float4 result = tex2D(transfer_functions, tfcoords);
    return result;
}
```

Listing 16.5. Cg function implementing bilinearly filtered application of four transfer functions in a single rendering pass using a transfer-function assignment texture. Note that this is very similar to Listing 16.3.

by 0.0 and thus do not change the result. If the result of the dot product is 0.0, the fragment does not belong to any of the objects under consideration and can be culled. Note that this is a major reason why object ID zero is reserved and not assigned to any object.

For the application of more than four transfer functions in a single rendering pass, the steps outlined above can be executed multiple times in the fragment program. The results of the individual dot products are simply summed up, once again yielding the ID of the object that the current fragment belongs to or zero if it needs to be culled.

16.6   Two-Level Volume Rendering

The final possibility presented in this chapter with respect to the visual separation of different objects is the use of individual object-local compositing modes, as well as a single global compositing mode, i.e., *two-level volume rendering* [100, 101, 92]. The most common local compositing modes are alpha blending (e.g., for standard direct volume rendering, or semitransparent tone shading), maximum intensity projection (e.g., for MIP or contour rendering), and alpha testing for isosurface rendering. Global compositing can, for example, be done with alpha blending, MIP, or a simple summation of all contributions.

Although the basic concept of two-level volume rendering is best explained using an image-order approach, i.e., individual rays (Figure 16.11),

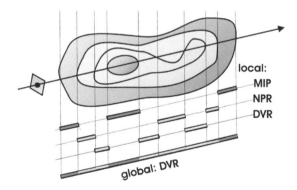

Figure 16.11. A single ray corresponding to a given image pixel is allowed to pierce objects that use their own object-local compositing mode. The contributions of different objects along a ray are combined with a single global compositing mode. Rendering a segmented data set with these two conceptual levels of compositing (local and global) is known as *two-level volume rendering* [100, 101, 92]. (Image reprinted from [92], © 2003 IEEE.)

in the context of texture-based volume rendering with slicing it has to be implemented with an object-order approach. As described in Section 16.3, there are two separate rendering buffers, a local and a global compositing buffer, respectively. Actual volume slices are only rendered into the local buffer, using the appropriate local compositing mode. When a new fragment has a different local compositing mode than the pixel that is currently stored in the local buffer, that pixel has to be transferred into the global buffer using the global compositing mode. Afterward, these transferred pixels have to be cleared in the local buffer before the corresponding new fragment is rendered. Naturally, it is important that both the detection of a change in compositing mode and the transfer and clear of pixels is done for all pixels simultaneously.

In order to do this, we use the depth buffer to track the current local compositing mode of each pixel and the stencil buffer to selectively enable pixels where the mode changes from one slice to the next. The depth buffer is shared between the local and global compositing buffer, either by using OpenGL frame-buffer objects (Section 2.4.2), or using auxiliary buffers of a single OpenGL context. Before actually rendering a slice (see Listing 16.1), IDs that correspond to the local compositing mode are rendered into the depth buffer. During these passes, the stencil buffer is set to one where the ID already stored in the depth buffer (from previous passes) differs from the ID that is currently being rendered. This creates both an updated ID image in the depth buffer and a stencil buffer that identifies exactly those pixels where a change in compositing mode has been detected.

We then render the image of the local buffer into the global buffer. Due to the stencil test, pixels will only be rendered where the compositing mode has actually changed. Listing 16.6 gives pseudocode for what is happening in the global buffer. Clearing the pixels in the local buffer that have just

```
void TransferLocalBufferIntoGlobalBuffer() {
    ActivateGlobalBuffer();
    DepthTest( NOT_EQUAL );
    StencilTest( RENDER_ALWAYS, SET_ONE );
    RenderSliceCompositingIds( DEPTH_BUFFER );
    DepthTest( DISABLE );
    StencilTest( RENDER_WHERE_ONE, SET_ZERO );
    RenderLocalBufferImage( COLOR_BUFFER );
}
```

Listing 16.6. Detecting for all pixels simultaneously where the compositing mode changes from one slice to the next and transferring those pixels from the local into the global compositing buffer.

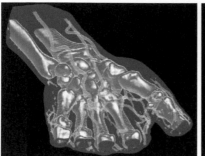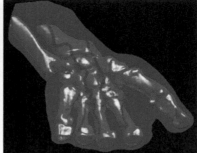

Figure 16.12. Detecting changes in compositing mode for each individual sample along a ray can be done exactly using two rendering buffers (left) or approximately using only a single buffer (right).

been transferred to the global buffer works almost identically. The only difference is that in this case we do not render the image of another buffer but simply a quad with all pixels set to zero. Due to the stencil test, pixels will only be cleared where the compositing mode has actually changed.

Note that all these additional rendering passes are much faster than the passes actually rendering and shading volume slices. They are independent of the number of objects and use extremely simple fragment programs. Figure 16.12 shows a comparison between a correct separation of compositing modes along all rays with two compositing buffers and the stencil buffer algorithm just described (left image), and simply compositing with a single buffer (right image). When only a single buffer is used, the compositing mode is simply switched according to each new fragment without avoiding interference with the previous contents of the frame buffer.

The visual difference depends highly on the combination of compositing modes and spatial locations of objects. The example in Figure 16.12 uses MIP and DVR compositing in order to highlight the potential differences. It illustrates a major advantage of two-level volume rendering, which is that it makes it very easy to highlight specific objects by simply using different compositing modes without tedious transfer-function tweaking. Where the vessels are clearly visible in the left image in Figure 16.12, they are only clearly discernible in the right image where they overlap the bones behind them.

16.7   Further Reading

Tiede et al. [264] emphasize the importance of determining the boundaries of segmented objects with subvoxel precision. They employ software ray casting and determine the object membership of a sample by classifying the grid points in its neighborhood. Combining this approach with interpolation of surface intersection and attributes yields results of very high quality. Naturally, when object boundaries are filtered from binary masks, the quality of the filter that is used is important. Kadosh et al. [117] employ a tricubic filter in order to obtain smooth surfaces from binary volumes.

Although most early approaches have focused on software rendering, tagged volumes have been a topic for texture-based volume renderers for a long time [99]. A recent paper by Vega-Higuera et al. [271] shows that segmented data can also be rendered efficiently and with high quality using splatting and 2D transfer functions. Their system is optimized for rendering neurovascular structures.

17

Large Volume Data

BECAUSE IMPROVED DATA-ACQUISITION METHODS and more accurate simulations have continued to produce ever more detailed results, the size of volumetric data generated in many application areas has risen tremendously in recent years. This trend is likely to continue in the foreseeable future.

In medical visualization long-leg studies with approximately 2000 slices are now routinely acquired for leg artery bypass surgeries (see Figure 17.1). At a resolution of 512×512 pixels for each slice and with 12-bit precision for

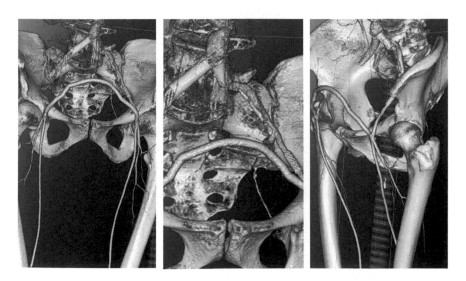

Figure 17.1. Long-leg study of a bypass operation ($512 \times 512 \times 1747$ @ 12-bit).

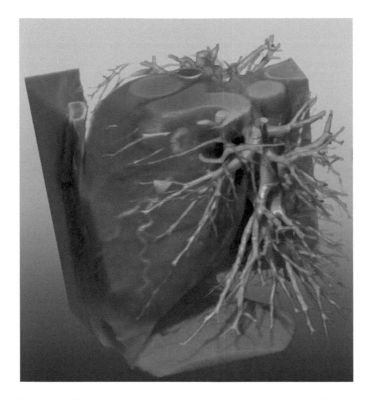

Figure 17.2. Single frame from a 4D sequence of a beating heart (512 × 512 × 240 @ 12-bit, 20 time steps).

each voxel, such CT (computerized tomography) studies result in roughly a gigabyte of data. Four-dimensional sequences from cardiology, which allow visualization of a beating heart (see Figure 17.2), quickly approach or even surpass the virtual address limit of current 32-bit PC computers. Full-body scans provide even larger data sets, but due to the high radiation dose and the resulting radiation risks, such data sets are currently not acquired in the clinical routine. Nevertheless, with the constantly reduced radiation dose of newer scanner technology, the resolution and quality of CT scans will further increase in the future.

In contrast with medical imaging, the radiation dose is not an obstacle in archaeology. As part of a project being conducted by Egypt's Supreme Council of Antiquities, 1700 slices reconstructed by a portable Siemens Somatom Emotion 6 CT system revealed that Pharaoh Tutankhamen died from an infected leg wound some 3,000 years ago. Before, a bone splinter embedded in the pharaoh's skull in combination with the hasty mummi-

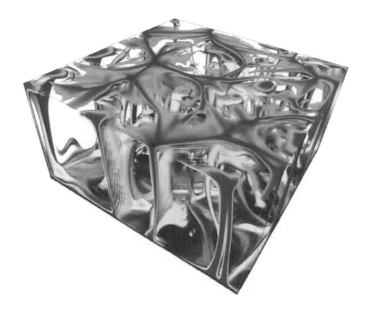

Figure 17.3. Single frame from a 4D simulation of convection flow in Earth's mantle. (Image from [63], © Eurographics Association 2002.)

fication and burial had led to speculations that the pharaoh had been murdered. Just recently, researchers from the Rosicrucian Museum and Stanford University created a 3D model of a child mummy consisting of 60,000 slices. A Siemens Axiom scanner produced 2D slices as thin as 200 microns, resulting in a 92-gigabyte database of image data.

With voxel sizes of a few micro- or a few hundred nanometers, micro CT and nanotomography scans from material sciences, biology, or molecular imaging can also deliver several gigabytes of data. In cryoelectron microscopy, even image data of structures as small as a molecule or a cell can be visualized. To protect the structure being scanned from the effects of electron beams, it is frozen to liquid-nitrogen temperatures during the scan. The image data resulting from such scans has a voxel resolution of just a few ångstroms ($1 \text{ Å} = 10^{-1} \text{ nm} = 10^{-4} \ \mu\text{m} = 10^{-7} \text{ mm} = 10^{-10} \text{ m}$).

On the other side of the scale, application areas like geosciences produce data sets exceeding a terabyte of data. Here, a single voxel can have a size of several hundred meters or a few kilometers, however covering a large area such as a continent or the entire earth crust. Geophysical phenomena, such as 3D mantle convection (see Figure 17.3), are typically computed on grids with a resolution of 1024^3 voxels with several output variables and 1000 time steps.

Considering the limited amount of GPU memory, rendering large data sets at interactive rates on a single GPU is a challenging task. Therefore, either more efficient compressed or packed representations of the data are required or memory other than the on-board GPU memory has to be utilized. In either case, the rate in which data can be provided to the rendering engine plays a key role in volumetric rendering. Indirect and nonlinear memory access as well as on-the-fly decoding of data further reduce the theoretical bandwidth of available memory systems.

17.1 Memory Performance Considerations

On standard PCs, the following types of memory are involved in the process of volume rendering (see Figure 17.4). Volume data is first loaded into main memory from a storage device such as a hard disk. Theoretically, current

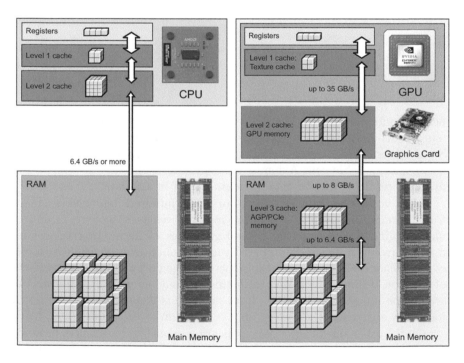

Figure 17.4. Similar to cache hierarchies in modern CPUs (left), we can interpret the different types of memory involved in GPU-based rendering as a cache hierarchy (right). The memory bandwidth increases the closer the memory is to the CPU/GPU while latency decreases at the same time. © 2005 IEEE.

32-bit CPUs address up to 4 gigabytes of memory, while 64-bit CPUs have the ability to address a much larger amount of memory. However, usually the maximum size of memory available on 64-bit systems is still limited due to the limitations of current memory modules. A segment of system memory is reserved for the graphics controller, the so-called AGP/PCIe[1] memory or nonlocal video memory. Before texture data is transferred to the local video memory of the GPU, the data has to be copied to AGP memory.

17.1.1 Memory Bandwidth

The current peak transfer bandwidth of dual channel DDR400 memory is approximately 6.4 GB/s. From AGP memory, volume data is transferred to video memory using AGP or PCI Express (PCIe). If the CPU does not need to change the data being uploaded (for example for conversion into a native GPU data format), the data can be uploaded asynchronously without involvement of the CPU using DMA (direct memory access).

AGP8x provides a maximum of 2.1 GB/s bandwidth for uploading to the local video memory, while a PCI Express slot with 16 lanes delivers twice the bandwidth of AGP8x. However, sustained throughput in many applications is usually less than 1 GB, far away from the theoretical limit. Note that 3D texture data is often rearranged by the CPU before it is transferred into GPU memory to allow for more uniform memory access patterns along all viewing directions (see Section 8.1), reducing the effective transfer rate even further. Moreover, it should also be noted that the read-back performance from GPU memory to main memory using AGP is much smaller than the transfer rate in the other direction. PCI Express interface currently provides for up to 4 GB/s transfer rate in both directions.

Local GPU memory provides very high memory bandwidth compared with main memory—more than 30 GB on a typical 256-bit wide memory interface. Data is transferred with this bandwidth to an internal texture cache on the GPU chip. Unfortunately, GPU manufacturers do not provide any details about the amount and bandwidth of the GPU internal texture caches, however one can assume that the memory bandwidth of the texture cache is several times higher than that of the GPU memory. More importantly, texture cache latency is probably much smaller compared with GPU memory latency.

Similar to the situation with cache hierarchies found in modern CPUs, we should interpret all previously described types of memory as different levels of texture cache in a cache hierarchy. The local texture cache on the GPU chip can be considered as level 1 cache, local video memory as level 2 cache, and AGP memory as level 3 cache. It is desirable to keep

---

[1] AGP: accelerated graphics port.

texture data as close to the chip as possible, i.e., in level 1 or level 2 of the cache hierarchy. OpenGL extensions like VBO (vertex buffer objects, see ARB_vertex_buffer_object extension) and PBO (pixel buffer objects, see ARB_pixel_buffer_object extension) address this problem by allowing flexible mechanisms to keep vertex or pixel data as close to the GPU as possible. The closer data is kept to the GPU, the harder it is to access the data with the CPU. Thus, if data needs to be updated frequently by the CPU, it is better to keep the data in level 3 cache (AGP memory). On the other hand, if the data is mostly static, it is better to keep the data in the level 2 cache (local video memory). GPU internal texture caches are managed automatically by the GPU, i.e., an API for controlling which data is kept in the level 1 cache does not exist. However, there are mechanisms to ensure that texture caches are utilized efficiently (see Section 8.1).

17.1.2   Memory Latency

The same way the bandwidth is increasing with memory closer to the actual processor, the memory latency is decreasing. Memory latency is the time between a memory read request and the data delivery. It is often even more critical to high-performance volume rendering than memory bandwidth, because high-performance ALUs (arithmetic logic units) waste most of their processing power nowadays by waiting for data-value delivery from the memory subsystem. The performance penalty of indirect memory access using dependent texture fetches is mostly due to memory latency issues. Dependent texture fetches use the result of a previous texture fetch as the texture coordinate for a subsequent texture fetch. GPUs do their best to hide memory latency by utilizing strategies such as pre-fetching of data values and pairing ALU with texture fetch operations. However, random memory access patterns that result from dependent texture fetch operations make it hard for the GPU to apply those optimizations.

In this chapter, we present different techniques that try to utilize the available amount of memory to render large volumetric data sets. Those techniques differ in how efficiently they utilize the individual levels of the texture cache hierarchy.

17.2   Bricking

The most straightforward method to deal with a large volume is the divide-and-conquer approach, which is called bricking in the context of volume rendering (also see Section 3.3.1). The volume is subdivided into several blocks in such a way that a single sub-block (brick) fits into video memory

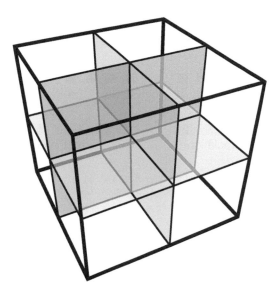

Figure 17.5. Subdivision of a large volume into several smaller bricks.

(see Figure 17.5). Bricks are stored in main memory and rendered in a front-to-back or back-to-front manner, dependent on the blending sequence.

We load bricks into the local memory of the GPU board one at a time. To achieve the best performance when uploading a brick into GPU memory, each brick should be stored as a continuous block of data in main memory. In theory, we could create a 3D texture for each brick and let the texture memory management of the driver handle the loading of the currently rendered brick into GPU memory. However, the memory occupied by 3D textures is restricted by some GPU drivers. NVIDIA OpenGL drivers for example only allow as many 3D textures to be created as fit into GPU and AGP/PCIe memory. Thus, it is instead advantageous to create a single 3D texture and reuse this single texture for rendering of all subvolumes. In OpenGL, data is copied from main memory into this 3D texture using a `glTexSubImage3D` command.

Note that some graphics cards (for example from NVIDIA) use a rearranged format for 3D texture data in GPU memory to increase the locality of neighboring data values (see Section 8.1). This increases the cache-hit ratio in the GPU-internal textures cache and allows for view-independent rendering performance. However, this has the consequence that the driver will rearrange the data in main memory before uploading the brick to GPU memory. Hence, the data cannot be uploaded asynchronously using DMA transfers and the resulting upload performance for 3D texture data is of-

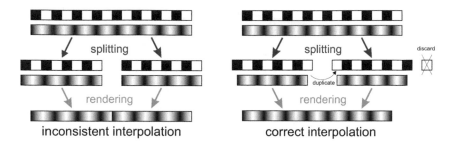

Figure 17.6. Bricking illustrated for the 1D case. Simply splitting the texture leads to inconsistent interpolation at the transition (left). Duplicating a voxel at the boundary between bricks (a plane of voxels in 3D) leads to correct interpolation results (right).

ten far from the theoretical limit. A solution employing non-power-of-two textures to circumvent this problem is discussed in Section 8.2.

Each brick is rendered using standard volume rendering techniques, i.e., by slicing (see Sections 3.2 and 3.3) or ray casting (see Chapter 7). Note that bricking also permits the rendering of large volumes on multiple GPU boards. Each GPU renders a different brick. An additional compositing step is required to assemble the partial RGBA images generated by the individual GPUs into the final image [178, 254, 255].

Section 3.3.1 showed that bricks must overlap by at least one voxel size to avoid discontinuities on brick boundaries when using trilinear filtering. The same is true for bricking large volumes. Figure 17.6 (left) demonstrates the result of rendering two bricks with linear filtering and no overlap. By repeating one voxel of brick 1 at the brick boundary in brick 2 as shown in Figure 17.6 (right), we can ensure a smooth transition between bricks. For best upload performance (see Chapter 8), the bricks should already be stored in main memory with at least one voxel overlap.

Note that, in the case of high-quality filtering as presented in Chapter 9.2 or on-the-fly gradient computation as presented in Sections 5.3.1 and 9.4, the overlap has to be increased. For example, when fetching neighboring voxel values for a central differences during on-the-fly gradient computation, the bricks actually have to overlap by two voxels to ensure continuous interpolation of neighboring gradients as well.

Bricking does not reduce the amount of memory required to represent the original volume data. Each brick has to be transferred to the local memory on the GPU board before it can be rendered. Thus, the performance of bricking is mainly limited by the AGP or PCI Express transfer rate. In order to circumvent this problem, a common technique is to use a subsampled version of the volume data that is entirely stored in the GPU memory during interaction. The full-resolution volume is only rendered for the final image quality using bricking.

Another optimization to prevent transfer of texture data over AGP or PCIe is to cache frequently used bricks in GPU memory. The following techniques try to prevent transfer over AGP/PCIe by better utilizing the available high-bandwidth texture memory on the GPU.

17.3   Multiresolution Volume Rendering

In comparison with a static subdivision as previously presented, a subdivision of the volume that adapts to the local properties of the scalar field or some user-defined criteria has many advantages. One option is to render the volume in a region-of-interest at a high resolution and away from that region with progressively lower resolution. The algorithm presented in [152] is based on an octree hierarchy (see Figure 17.7) where the leaves of the tree represent the original data and the internal nodes define lower-resolution versions. An octree representation of volumetric data can be obtained by either a top-down subdivision or a bottom-up merging strategy. The top-down subdivision strategy divides the volume data into eight blocks of equal size. Each block is further subdivided recursively into smaller blocks until the block size reaches a minimum size or the voxel dimension. The bottom-up strategy merges eight neighboring voxels (or atom-blocks) into a larger block. Each block is again merged with its neighboring blocks into a larger block until the complete volume remains as a block. Each block is a down-sampled version of the volume data represented by its child nodes.

Given such an octree representation of the volume data, one can traverse the tree in a top-down manner, starting from the coarsest version of the

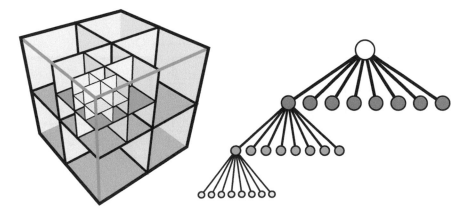

Figure 17.7. Octree decomposition of a volume.

data at the root node. At each node, one can decide whether the child nodes of the specific node need to be traversed further based on some criteria. Possible criteria are the distance of the node to the viewer position, detail contained within the subtree, or the desired rendering resolution based on a global or local parameter such as a focus point. It is also possible to adapt the sampling rate in the levels of the hierarchy to the detail level. Due to the abrupt change in resolution and sampling rate at the boundaries of different levels of multiresolution representations, some authors have introduced special algorithms to ensure a smooth transition from one block to another [288].

This multirepresentation allows memory to be saved for empty or uniform portions of the volume data by omitting subtrees of the hierarchy. Furthermore, rendering performance may increase due to lower sampling rates for certain blocks or omitting of empty blocks.

17.4   Built-In Texture Compression

The multiresolution techniques introduced in Section 17.3 already introduce compression of volume data if the octree is not refined to the maximum level in all branches. In this section, we will examine compression techniques for volumetric data sets that try to utilize the available high-performance memory as efficiently as possible.

In fact, GPUs already have built-in texture compression schemes. In OpenGL, texture compression is available using the S3 texture compression standard, which is accessible using the EXT_texture_compression_s3tc extension. In this compression method, 4×4 RGBA texels are grouped together. For each 4×4 pixel group, two colors are stored; two additional colors

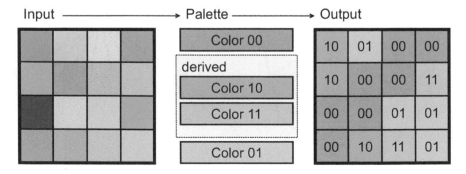

Figure 17.8. S3 texture compression stores two colors for each 4×4 texel block; two additional colors are derived by linear interpolation. The total of four colors are accessed with two bits per texel.

are obtained by linear interpolation of the stored colors. For each pixel of the 4 × 4 block, two bits are used as look-up values to access these four colors (see Figure 17.8). The NV_texture_compression_vtc OpenGL extension provides a similar kind of compression to the 3D texture domain.

Several graphics chips support S3 texture compression in hardware, e.g., the NVIDIA GeForce and ATI Radeon series. S3 texture compression provides a fixed compression ratio of 4:1 or 8:1. However, for compression of volumetric data it has some severe disadvantages. First, block artifacts can easily be observed for nonsmooth data due to the block compression scheme. Second, this compression technique is only available for RGB(A) data. As we are mainly interested in scalar volume data, S3 texture compression cannot be used. For compression of RGB textures that store precomputed gradients, S3 texture compression provides unsatisfactory quality because illumination is very sensitive to block-compression artifacts in pre-computed gradients.

17.5   Wavelet Compression

Wavelet transforms [81, 252] provide an invaluable tool in computer graphics. This is due to the fact that, in computer graphics, we often encounter signals that are mostly smooth but contain important regions with high-frequency content. The same applies to volumetric data sets, which (in most cases) contain some areas with rich detail while at the same time they have other regions that are very homogeneous. A typical data set from CT, for example, has very fine detail for bone structures while surrounding air and tissue is given as very smooth and uniform areas. Figure 17.9 shows gradient-magnitude modulation of a CT data set; i.e., areas where the data values change rapidly are enhanced while homogeneous regions are suppressed. Note that most of the data is smooth while high-frequency detail is most apparent at certain material boundaries.

The wavelet transform is the projection of a signal onto a series of basis functions called wavelets. Wavelets form a hierarchy of signals that allow the analysis and reconstruction of an input signal at different resolutions and frequency ranges, providing a basis for multiresolution volume rendering. As wavelet-transformed signals often contain many coefficients that are nearly zero, wavelets form a natural technique for building a compressed representation of a signal by omitting coefficients that are smaller than a specified threshold.

In fact, many wavelet compression schemes have been proposed for 3D volume data [110, 122, 191, 195, 225, 298] as well as for 4D volume data [50, 89]. Methods for 3D volume data often use a block-based wavelet compression scheme to allow for fast random access to data values without requiring decompression of the whole data set.

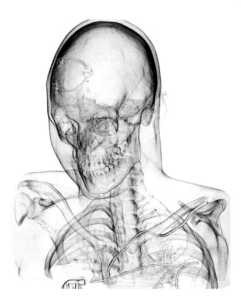

Figure 17.9. Gradient-magnitude modulation volume rendering of a large CT data set.

GPU-accelerated visualization of wavelet-compressed 4D volume data sequences using motion compensation techniques have been proposed [89]. However, each time step of the sequence must be fully decompressed on the CPU before it can be rendered. Thus, no bandwidth is saved when transferring a single time step of the sequence over AGP/PCIe, therefore limiting the rendering performance to the AGP or PCIe bandwidth.

For large 3D volumes, it is possible to avoid the problem of transferring a decompressed full-resolution volume from main memory to the GPU by introducing a multiresolution hierarchy that provides fast access to each node of the hierarchy [90]. Consequently, it is possible to store very large data sets in main memory and to reconstruct the levels of detail that are necessary for an interactive exploration on the fly.

A pre-processing step is required to transform the volume data into the hierarchical wavelet representation. For that purpose, the data is divided into cubic blocks of $(2k)^3$ voxels, where $k = 16$ is a good choice. The wavelet filters are applied to each of the blocks, resulting in a low-pass–filtered block of size k^3 voxels and $(2k)^3 - k^3$ wavelet coefficients representing high frequencies that are lost in the low-pass filtered signal. This scheme is applied hierarchically by grouping eight neighboring low-pass-filtered blocks together with new blocks with $(2k)^3$ voxels. This process is repeated until only a single block remains (see Figure 17.10).

The data is now given as a multiresolution tree, with a very coarse representation of the data in the root-node (see Figure 17.11). Each descent in the octree increases the resolution by a factor of two. To decide at which resolution a block should be decompressed by the CPU during rendering, a projective classification and a view-dependent priority schedule is applied. Projective classification projects the voxel spacing of a node of the hierarchy to screen space. If the voxel spacing is above the screen resolution, then the node must be refined, else it is passed to the renderer. The view-dependent classification scheme prioritizes nodes that are closer to the camera position. The error introduced by rendering a node can also be used to determine if a node needs to be refined. To reduce the amount of data transferred over AGP/PCIe, an optional caching strategy caches blocks that are frequently used in GPU memory.

Wavelet coefficients of low importance are discarded using a threshold approach. For typical data sets, a 4:1 compression can already be achieved with lossless compression using a threshold of zero. In the paper several encoding schemes for the wavelet coefficients are discussed, which achieve compression rates of up to 40:1 for the visible female and up to 30:1 for the visible male data sets. Interactive exploration is possible with 3 to 10 frames per second depending on quality settings.

The multiresolution representation of the volumetric data in conjunction with the wavelet transform enables rendering of data sets far beyond the virtual address limit of today's PCs. However, in all presented techniques compressed data is stored in main memory and decompressed by the CPU before it can be rendered on the GPU. An ideal solution would store the compressed data in local memory of the GPU and decompress it using the GPU before rendering. However, no work has yet been published to do this, and it is unclear so far if a decompression of wavelet-transformed data can be efficiently implemented using a GPU in the near future.

In contrast with the CPU-based decoding of the volume data, the techniques presented in the following sections can easily be realized on GPUs by utilizing dependent texture fetch operations. That is, the result of a previous texture-fetch operation is used as a texture coordinate for a subsequent texture fetch. This provides the basis for indexed or indirect memory access required for certain packing or compression techniques.

17.6 Packing Techniques

Packing techniques try to make efficient use of GPU memory by packing equal or similar blocks of an input volume into a smaller volume as compactly as possible. The original volume can then be represented by an index volume referencing those packed blocks (see Figure 17.12).

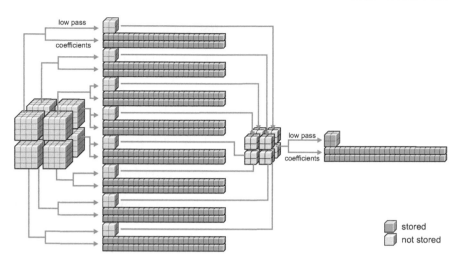

Figure 17.10. Construction of the wavelet coefficient tree for $k = 2$.

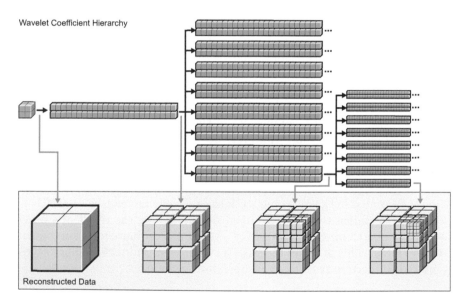

Figure 17.11. The compressed wavelet coefficient tree for $k = 2$. The lower part of the image shows the reconstruction of data from the wavelet coefficient tree.

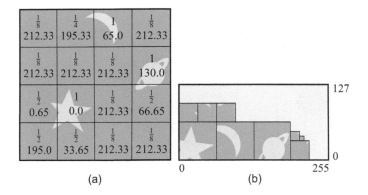

Figure 17.12. (a) Index data: scale factors and coordinates of packed data blocks are stored for each cell of a 4 x 4 grid representing the whole texture map. (b) Packed data: the data blocks packed into a uniform grid of 256 x 128 texels. (Images courtesy of M. Kraus and T. Ertl [133], © Eurographics Association 2002.)

One idea is to pack nonempty blocks of the input data into a smaller packed volume representation [133]. This packed representation is then referenced using an index volume that stores the position of the origin of the indexed block in the compact representation and a scaling factor. The scaling factor accommodates nonuniform block sizes (see Figure 17.13). During rendering, the decompression is performed in a fragment program. A relative coordinate to the origin of the index cell is computed first. Then the coordinate and the scaling factor of the packed data block are looked up from the texture. From the relative coordinate, the position of the packed block, and the scaling factor, a position in the packed data is computed, which is used to look up the decoded voxel value. In order to support linear interpolation provided by the graphics hardware, texels on the boundaries of data blocks are replicated. As the texture coordinate to look up the data value in the packed texture is computed based on the result of another texture look-up, the complete decoding algorithm is implemented in the fragment stage. The disadvantage is that dependent texture look-up introduces a big performance penalty, as it results in nonpredictable memory-access patterns.

In contrast with decoding the packed representation in the fragment stage, it can alternatively be decoded in the vertex stage [162]. The idea is to allow arbitrarily sized subtextures that are generated by a box-growing algorithm to determine boxes with similar densities and gradient magnitudes. The main purpose is to accelerate volume rendering by skipping blocks that are empty after the transfer functions are applied. The approach also allows the packing of pre-computed gradients data into a com-

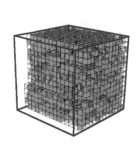

Figure 17.13. Volume rendering of a $512 \times 512 \times 360$ CT scan with adaptive texture mapping. Left: nonempty cells of the 32^3 index data grid. Middle: data blocks packed into a 256^3 texture. Right: resulting volume rendering. (Images courtesy of M. Kraus and T. Ertl [133], © Eurographics Association 2002.)

pact representation (see Figure 17.14). Boxes with similar density and nonzero gradient magnitude are packed into a single texture as subtextures. During rendering of a box, a subtexture can be selected from the packed representation by applying appropriate texture coordinates in the vertex stage.

The main advantage to the previously described technique is that the decoding of the packed volume representation is done in the vertex stage instead of the fragment stage. As the dependent texture operations required for decoding in the fragment stage are quite "expensive" due to inefficient memory access patterns, vertex stage decoding has a significant performance advantage over fragment-stage decoding.

All packing techniques discussed in this section support blocks of different sizes. Using uniformly sized blocks brings us to the concept of vector quantization.

Figure 17.14. Gradient subtextures defined by the boxes enclose all the voxels of similar densities and nonzero gradient magnitude (left two images). The gradient subtextures are packed into a single texture (middle). Resulting rendering of the foot with mixed boxes and textures (right two images). (Images courtesy of Wei Li and Arie Kaufman [162], © 2003 Canadian Information Processing Society.)

17.7 Vector Quantization

Due to the availability of indirect memory access provided on GPUs by means of dependent texture-fetch operations, vector quantization [198] is an obvious choice for a compression scheme to make more efficient use of available GPU memory resources. In general, a vector-quantization algorithm takes an n-dimensional input vector and maps it to a single index that references a closely matching vector inside a codebook containing vectors of equal length as the input vector. As the codebook should have a significantly smaller size than the set of input vectors, a codebook should be capable of reproducing an original input vector as closely as possible. Hence, a codebook must be generated from the set of input vectors.

For GPU-based vector quantization [234], the encoding of the data is performed using the CPU. Vector quantization is applied on two different frequency bands of the input volume data. For that purpose, the data is partitioned into blocks with 4^3 voxels dimension. Each block is down-sampled to a 2^3 block and a difference vector with 64 components is obtained by computing the difference between the original and the down-sampled block. This process is repeated for the 2^3 blocks resulting in a single mean value for the block and a second 8-component difference vector. Vector quantization is applied to two difference vectors, and the two resulting indices are stored together with the mean value into an RGB 3D texture (see Figure 17.15). The indices and the mean value are fetched during rendering and used to reconstruct the input value. For decoding using the GPU, two dependent texture-fetch operations look up the 8- and 64-component difference vectors from two codebooks stored as 2D textures.

For a codebook with 256 entries, it is possible to achieve a compression factor of 64 : 3 neglecting the size of the codebooks; i.e., a 1024^3 volume is compressed to 3×256^3 bytes = 48 MB. Thus, it fits easily into the GPU memory, and no AGP/PCIe transfer is required to swap in data during rendering. It should be noted that, despite the fact that the decoding stage for vector-quantized data is very simple, frame rates considerably drop compared with uncompressed data due to texture cache misses produced by dependent texture-fetch operations. To improve performance, a deferred decompression based on early z-tests available on modern GPUs is employed. That is, every slice polygon is rendered twice, first with a simple (and thus fast) shader and then with the full (and thus slow) decoding shader. To prevent decoding of empty regions of the data, the first pass evaluates the median value stored in the 3D texture. If the median value is zero, the execution of the complex shader for this fragment is prevented by masking the fragment with a z-value (see Section 8.6.2).

For the generation of the codebooks, a modified LBG algorithm [166] based on an initial codebook generated by principal component anal-

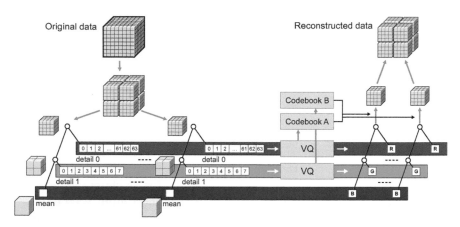

Figure 17.15. Hierarchical decompression and quantization of volumetric data sets. Blocks are first split into multiple frequency bands, which are quantized separately. This generates three index values per block, which are used to reference the computed codebook.

ysis (PCA) is performed by the CPU. For details, we refer the reader to [234].

Due to the close coupling of the decoding and the rendering of data in the implementation, linear filtering capabilities of GPUs cannot be used. This problem can be solved by separating decoding and rendering, i.e., the data is first decoded into a temporary texture before the decoded data is rendered. This also solves the problem of high decoding costs when using high zoom factors. In this case, the number of fragments rendered is large compared with the number of voxels in the data set.

This GPU-accelerated vector quantization approach is also applicable to 4D volume data. A shock wave simulation sequence with 89 time steps can be compressed from 1.4 GB to 70 MB. Thus, it can be stored entirely in the local GPU memory. Rendering from the compressed data is then possible directly from GPU memory. The additional decoding overhead is usually far compensated by the avoided AGP/PCIe data transfer bottlenecks.

17.8   Discussion

GPUs provide sufficient computational power to render large volume data sets with high quality at interactive frame rates. As many traditional techniques, like pre-computed gradients, are not feasible for large volumes, certain properties of the scalar field must be computed on-the-fly. This, however, introduces additional computational costs that require optimization techniques to prevent unnecessary memory access and calculations.

Rendering techniques for large volume data try to reduce the transfer of texture data over AGP/PCIe and try to make more efficient use of the available high-speed GPU memory. If possible, data should always be kept in GPU memory. However, this cannot always be achieved, even by using packed or compressed representations of the data. In this case, optimized caching strategies and asynchronous data transfers are essential to maintain a constant flow of data.

17.9   Further Reading

For further work on the visualization of large 4D volume data using a single PC equipped with a modest amount of memory, a texture-capable graphics card, and an inexpensive disk array, we refer the reader to [173]. The algorithm employs a palette-based decoding technique and an adaptive bit allocation scheme to utilize the capabilities of a GPU. The use of fragment shaders to visualize time-varying data has also been investigated by other authors [11]. Although we mainly focused on rendering large volume data using a single PC equipped with a single GPU, there is also work on rendering large volume data on multiple GPUs and GPU clusters [178, 254, 255].

Procedural techniques often circumvent the need for an explicit representation of volumetric phenomena using high-resolution volumes (see Section 12.3). This is especially useful for application areas in the entertainment industry like computer games or movies, where often a high level of detail is required when rendering volumetric effects such as clouds, smoke, or explosions. However, to achieve these effects, no explicit representation of the high-level detail is required.

Bibliography

[1] M. Abidi and R. Gonzales. *Data Fusion in Robotics and Machine Intelligence.* Boston: Academic Press, 1992.

[2] Tomas Akenine-Möller and Eric Haines. *Real-Time Rendering,* Second edition. Natick, MA: A K Peters, Ltd., 2002.

[3] Martin Artner, Torsten Möller, Ivan Viola, and Eduard Gröller. "High-Quality Volume Rendering with Resampling in the Frequency Domain." In *Proceedings of Eurographics/IEEE-VGTC Symposium on Visualization (EuroVis),* pp. 85–92. Aire-la-Ville, Switzerland: Eurographics Association, 2005.

[4] James Arvo and David Kirk. "Particle Transport and Image Synthesis." *Proc. SIGGRAPH '90, Computer Graphics* 24:4 (1990), 63–66.

[5] Ian Ashdown. *Radiosity: A Programmer's Perspective.* New York: Wiley Professional, 1994.

[6] Ulf Assarsson and Tomas Akenine-Möller. "A Geometry-based Soft Shadow Volume Algorithm using Graphics Hardware." *Proc. SIGGRAPH '03, Transactions on Graphics* 22:3 (2003), 511–520.

[7] Ulf Assarsson, Michael Dougherty, Michael Mounier, and Tomas Akenine-Möller. "An Optimized Soft Shadow Volume Algorithm with Real-Time Performance." In *Proceedings of Graphics Hardware 2003,* pp. 33–40. Aire-la-Ville, Switzerland: Eurographics Association, 2003.

[8] D. Bechmann. "Space Deformation Models Survey." *Computers & Graphics* 18:4 (1994), 571–586.

[9] Stephan Behrendt, Carsten Colditz, Oliver Franzke, Johannes Kopf, and Oliver Deussen. "Realistic Real-Time Rendering of Landscapes

Using Billboard Clouds." In *Proceedings of Eurographics*, pp. 507–516. Aire-la-Ville, Switzerland: Eurographics Association, 2005.

[10] Praveen Bhaniramka and Yves Demange. "OpenGL Volumizer: A Toolkit for High Quality Volume Rendering of Large Data Sets." In *Symposium on Volume Visualization and Graphics*, pp. 45–53, 2002.

[11] Binotto Binotto, Joao L. D. Comba, and Carla M. D. Freitas. "Real-Time Volume Rendering of Time-Varying Data Using a Fragment-Shader Compression Approach." In *Proceedings of the 2003 IEEE Symposium on Parallel and Large-Data Visualization and Graphics (PVG '03)*, p. 10. Los Alamitos, CA: IEEE Press, 2003.

[12] J. F. Blinn. "Models of Light Reflection for Computer Synthesized Pictures ." *Computer Graphics* 11:2 (1977), 192–198.

[13] J. F. Blinn. "Light Reflection Functions for Simulation of Clouds and Dusty Surfaces." *Proc. SIGGRAPH '82, Computer Graphics* 16, (1982), 21–29.

[14] J. F. Blinn. "Jim Blinn's Corner: Image Compositing – Theory." *IEEE Computer Graphics and Applications* 14:5 (1994), 83–87.

[15] I. Bloch. "Information Combination Operators for Data Fusion: A Review with Classification." *IEEE Transactions on Systems, Man and Cybernetics. Part A: Systems and Humans* 26:1 (1996), 52–67.

[16] Craig F. Bohren. "Multiple Scattering of Light and Some of Its Observable Consequences." *American Journal of Physics* 55:6 (1987), 524–533.

[17] M. Brady, K. Jung, H. Nguyen, and T. Nguyen. "Two-Phase Perspective Ray Casting for Interactive Volume Navigation." In *Proceedings of IEEE Visualization*, pp. 183–190. Los Alamitos, CA: IEEE Press, 1997.

[18] Stefan Bruckner and Eduard Gröller. "VolumeShop: An Interactive System for Direct Volume Illustration." In *Proceedings of IEEE Visualization*, pp. 671–678. Los Alamitos, CA: IEEE Press, 2005.

[19] Stefan Bruckner, Sören Grimm, Armin Kanitsar, and Eduard Gröller. "Illustrative Context-Preserving Volume Rendering." In *Proceedings of EuroVis 2005*, pp. 69–76. Aire-la-Ville, Switzerland: Eurographics Association, 2005.

[20] Michael Burns, Janek Klawe, Szymon Rusinkiewicz, Adam Finkelstein, and Doug DeCarlo. "Line Drawings from Volume Data." *Proc. SIGGRAPH '05, Transactions on Graphics* 24:3 (2005), 512–518.

[21] Kenneth M. Case and Paul F. Zweifel. *Linear Transport Theory*. Reading, MA: Addison-Wesley, 1967.

[22] Eric Chan and Frédo Durand. "Rendering Fake Soft Shadows with Smoothies." In *Proceedings of Eurographics Workshop on Rendering 2003*, pp. 208–218. Aire-la-Ville, Switzerland: Eurographics Association, 2003.

[23] Subrahmanyan Chandrasekhar. *Radiative Transfer*. Oxford: Clarendon Press, 1950.

[24] Y. Chen, Q. Zhu, and A. Kaufman. "Physically-based Animation of Volumetric Objects." Technical Report TR-CVC-980209, State University of New York, Stony Brook, 1998.

[25] M. Chen, D. Silver, A. S. Winter, V. Singh, and N. Cornea. "Spatial Transfer Functions – A Unified Approach to Specifying Deformation in Volume Modeling and Animation." In *Proceedings of the 2003 Eurographics/IEEE TVCG Workshop on Volume Graphics*, pp. 35–44. Aire-la-Ville, Switzerland: Eurographics Association, 2003.

[26] C. Chua and U. Neumann. "Hardware-Accelerated Free-Form Deformations." In *Proceedings of ACM SIGGRAPH/Eurographics Workshop on Graphics Hardware*. Aire-la-Ville, Switzerland: Eurographics Association, 2000.

[27] P. Cignino, C. Montani, D. Sarti, and R. Scopigno. "On the Optimization of Projective Volume Rendering." In *Visualization in Scientific Computing*, edited by R. Scateni, J. van Wijk, and P. Zanarini, pp. 58–71. New York: Springer, 1995.

[28] J. Clark and A. Yuille. *Data Fusion for Sensory Information Processing Systems*. Boston: Kluwer Academic Publishers, 1990.

[29] M. Cohen, J. Shade, S. Hiller, and O. Deussen. "Wang Tiles for Image and Texture Generation." *Proc. SIGGRAPH '03, Transactions on Graphics* 22:3 (2003), 287–294.

[30] D. Cohen-Or and A. Kaufman. "Fundamentals of Surface Voxelization." *CVGIP: Graphics Models and Image Processing* 56:6 (1995), 453–461.

[31] *Collins English Dictionary: Complete and Unabridged*, sixth edition. Glasgow: HarperCollins Publishers, 2004.

[32] S. Coquillart. "Extended Free-Form Deformations." In *Proc. SIGGRAPH '90, Computer Graphics*, 24, 24, pp. 187–196, 1990.

[33] NVIDIA Corporation.

[34] NVIDIA Corporation. "NVIDIA Developer Website." Available online (http://developer.nvidia.com/).

[35] NVIDIA Corporation. "NVIDIA OpenGL Extension Specifications." Available online (http://developer.nvidia.com/object/nvidia_opengl_specs.html).

[36] R. Crawfis, D. Xue, and C. Zhang. "Volume Rendering Using Splatting." In *The Visualization Handbook*, edited by Charles. D. Hansen and Christopher R. Johnson, pp. 175–188. Amsterdam: Elsevier, 2005.

[37] Franklin C. Crow. "Shadow Algorithms for Computer Graphics." *Proc. SIGGRAPH '77, Computer Graphics* 11:3 (1977), 242–248.

[38] B. Csébfalvi, L. Mroz, H. Hauser, A. König, and E. Gröller. "Fast Visualization of Object Contours by Non-Photorealistic Volume Rendering." In *Proceedings of Eurographics*, pp. 452–460. Aire-la-Ville, Switzerland: Eurographics Association, 2001.

[39] M. de Boer, A. Gröpl, J. Hesser, and R. Männer. "Reducing Artifacts in Volume Rendering by Higher Order Integration." In *Proceedings of IEEE Visualization, Late Breaking Hot Topics*, pp. 1–4. Los Alamitos, CA: IEEE Press, 1997.

[40] Paul Debevec and Jitendra Malik. "Recovering High Dynamic Range Radiance Maps from Photographs." In *Proceedings of SIGGRAPH 97, Computer Graphics Proceedings, Annual Conference Series*, edited by Turner Whitted, pp. 369–378. Reading, MA: Addison Wesley, 1997.

[41] Paul Debevec. "Rendering Synthetic Objects Into Real Scenes: Bridging Traditional and Image-Based Graphics with Global Illumination and High Dynamic Range Photography." In *Proceedings of SIGGRAPH 98, Computer Graphics Proceedings, Annual Conference Series*, edited by Michael Cohen, pp. 189–198. Reading, MA: Addison Wesley, 1998.

[42] J.S. DeBonet. "Multiresolution Sampling Procedure for Analysis and Synthesis of Texture Images." In *Proceedings of SIGGRAPH 97, Computer Graphics Proceedings, Annual Conference Series*, edited by Turner Whitted, pp. 361–368. Reading, MA: Addison Wesley, 1997.

[43] Doug DeCarlo, Adam Finkelstein, Szymon Rusinkiewicz, and Anthony Santella. "Suggestive Contours for Conveying Shape." *Proc. SIGGRAPH '03, Transactions on Graphics* 22:3 (2003), 848–855.

[44] Xavier Décoret, Frédo Durand, François Sillion, and Julie Dorsey. "Billboard Clouds for Extreme Model Simplification." *Proc. SIG-GRAPH '03, Transactions on Graphics* 22:3 (2003), 689–696.

[45] M. Deering, S. Winner, B. Schediwy, C. Duffy, and N. Hunt. "The Triangle Processor and Normal Vector Shader: A VLSI System for High Performance Graphics." *Proc. SIGGRAPH '88, Computer Graphics* 22:4 (1988), 21–30.

[46] P. Desgranges, K. Engel, and G. Paladini. "Gradient-Free Shading: A New Method for Realistic Interactive Volume Rendering." In *Proceedings of Vision, Modeling, and Visualization.* Berlin: Akademische Verlagsgesellschaft Aka GmbH, 2005.

[47] Kate Devlin, Alan Chalmers, Alexander Wilkie, and Werner Purgathofer. "Tone Reproduction and Physically Based Spectral Rendering." In *Proceedings of Eurographics*, pp. 101–123. Aire-la-Ville, Switzerland: Eurographics Association, 2002. State-of-the-art report.

[48] J. Diepstraten, D. Weiskopf, and T. Ertl. "Transparency in Interactive Technical Illustrations." *Computer Graphics Forum (Proceedings of Eurographics 2002)* 21:3 (2002), 317–317.

[49] J. Diepstraten, D. Weiskopf, and T. Ertl. "Interactive Cutaway Illustrations." *Computer Graphics Forum (Proceedings of Eurographics 2003)* 22:3 (2003), 523–523.

[50] Y. Dobashi, V. Cingoski, K. Kaneda, and H. Yamashita. "A Fast Volume Rendering Method for Time-Varying 3D Scalar Field Visualization Using Orthonormal Wavelets." *IEEE Transactions on Magnetics* 34:5 (1998), 3431–3434.

[51] Y. Dobashi, T. Yamamoto, and T. Nishita. "Interactive Rendering Method for Displaying Shafts of Light." In *Proceedings of Pacific Graphics*, pp. 31–37. Los Alamitos, CA: IEEE Press, 2000.

[52] R. A. Drebin, L. Carpenter, and P. Hanrahan. "Volume Rendering." In *Proc. SIGGRAPH '88, Computer Graphics*, 22, 22, pp. 65–74, 1988.

[53] Richard O. Duda, Peter E. Hart, and David G. Stork. *Pattern Classification*, Second edition. New York: Wiley-Interscience, 2001.

[54] James J. Duderstadt and William R. Martin. *Transport Theory.* New York: Wiley, 1979.

[55] Philip Dutré, Philippe Bekaert, and Kavita Bala. *Advanced Global Illumination.* Natick, MA: A K Peters, 2003.

[56] David H. Eberly. *3D Game Engine Design: A Practical Approach to Real-Time Computer Graphics.* San Francisco: Morgan Kaufmann, 2001.

[57] D. Ebert and P. Rheingans. "Volume Illustration: Non-Photorealistic Rendering of Volume Models." In *Proceedings of IEEE Visualization*, pp. 195–202. Los Alamitos, CA: IEEE Press, 2000.

[58] D. Ebert, F. K. Musgrave, D. Peachey, K. Perlin, and S. Worley. *Texturing and Modeling: A Procedural Approach*, Third edition. San Francisco: Morgan Kaufmann, 2003.

[59] Mark DeLoura (ed.). *Game Programming Gems.* Hingham, MA: Charles River Media, 2000.

[60] Wolfgang Engel (ed.). *ShaderX 3: Advanced Rendering with DirectX and OpenGL.* Boston: Charles River Media, 2005.

[61] A. Efros and W. Freeman. "Image Quilting for Texture Synthesis." In *Proceedings of SIGGRAPH 2001, Computer Graphics Proceedings, Annual Conference Series*, edited by E. Fiume, pp. 341–346. Reading, MA: Addison-Wesley, 2001.

[62] A. Efros and T. Leung. "Texture Synthesis by Non-Parametric Sampling." In *Proceedings of Int. Conf on Computer Vision*, pp. 1033–1038. Los Alamitos, CA: IEEE Press, 1999.

[63] K. Engel and T. Ertl. "Interactive High-Quality Volume Rendering with Flexible Consumer Graphics Hardware." In *Eurographics '02 State-of-the-Art (STAR) Report*. Aire-la-Ville, Switzerland: Eurographics Association, 2002.

[64] K. Engel, M. Kraus, and T. Ertl. "High-Quality Pre-Integrated Volume Rendering Using Hardware-Accelerated Pixel Shading." In *Proceedings of ACM SIGGRAPH/Eurographics Workshop on Graphics Hardware*, pp. 9–16. Aire-la-Ville, Switzerland: Eurographics Association, 2001.

[65] Douglas Enright, Stephen Marschner, and Ronald Fedkiw. "Animation and Rendering of Complex Water Surfaces." *Proc. SIGGRAPH '02, Transactions on Graphics* :3 (2002), 736–744.

[66] Cass Everitt and Mark Kilgard. "Practical and Robust Stenciled Shadow Volumes for Hardware-Accelerated Rendering." White paper, NVIDIA, 2002.

[67] Cass Everitt. "Interactive Order-Independent Transparency." White paper, NVIDIA, 2001.

[68] S. Fang and D. Liao. "Fast CSG Voxelization by Frame Buffer Pixel Mapping." In *Proceedings of IEEE Symposium on Volume Visualization*, pp. 43–48. New York: ACM Press, 2000.

[69] S. Fang, S. Rajagopalan, S. Huang, and R. Raghavan. "Deformable Volume Rendering by 3D-Texture Mapping and Octree Encoding." In *Proceedings of IEEE Visualization*. Los Alamitos, CA: IEEE Press, 1996.

[70] T. J. Farrell, M. S. Patterson, and B. C. Wilson. "A Diffusion Theory Model of Spatially Resolved, Steady-State Diffuse Reflectance for the Non-Invasive Determination of Tissue Optical Properties in Vivo." *Medical Physics* 19 (1992), 879–888.

[71] R. Fernando and M. Kilgard. *The Cg Tutorial: The Definitive Guide to Programmable Real-Time Graphics*. Reading, MA: Addison-Wesley, 2003.

[72] Randima Fernando, editor. *GPU Gems: Programming Techniques, Tips, and Tricks for Real-Time Graphics*. Reading, MA: Addison-Wesley, 2004.

[73] Jan Fischer, Dirk Bartz, and Wolfgang Straßer. "Illustrative Display of Hidden Iso-Surface Structures." In *Proceedings of IEEE Visualization*, pp. 663–670. Los Alamitos, CA: IEEE Press, 2005.

[74] J. Foley, A. van Dam, S. Feiner, and J. Hughes. *Computer Graphics, Principle And Practice*. Reading, MA: Addison-Wesley, 1993.

[75] Bernd Fröhlich, Stephen Barrass, Björn Zehner, John Plate, and Martin Göbel. "Exploring Geo-Scientific Data in Virtual Environments." In *Proceedings of IEEE Visualization*, pp. 169–174. Los Alamitos, CA: IEEE Press, 1999.

[76] Nikhil Gagvani, D. Kenchammana-Hosekote, and D. Silver. "Volume Animation using the Skeleton Tree." In *IEEE Symposium on Volume Visualization*, pp. 47–53. New York: ACM Press, 1998.

[77] Michael P. Garrity. "Raytracing Irregular Volume Data." In *Proceedings of the 1990 Workshop on Volume Visualization*, pp. 35–40, 1990.

[78] S.F. Gibson. "3D ChainMail: A Fast Algorithm for Deforming Volumetric Objects." In *Symposium on Interactive 3D Graphics (I3D)*, pp. 149–154. New York: ACM Press, 1997.

[79] Andrew Glassner. *An Introduction to Ray Tracing.* San Francisco: Morgan Kaufmann, 1989.

[80] Andrew S. Glassner. *Principles of Digital Image Synthesis.* San Francisco: Morgan Kaufmann, 1995.

[81] Andrew S. Glassner. "Wavelet Transforms." In *Principles of Digital Image Synthesis,* edited by A. Glassner, pp. 243–298. San Francisco: Morgan Kaufmann, 1995.

[82] B. Gooch and A. Gooch. *Non-Photorealistic Rendering.* Natick, MA: A.K. Peters Ltd., 2001.

[83] A. Gooch, B. Gooch, P. Shirley, and E. Cohen. "A Non-Photorealistic Lighting Model for Automatic Technical Illustration." In *Proceedings of SIGGRAPH 99, Computer Graphics Proceedings, Annual Conference Series,* edited by Michael Cohen, pp. 447–452. Reading, MA: Addison Wesley, 1998.

[84] Naga K. Govindaraju, Michael Henson, Ming C. Lin, and Dinesh Manocha. "Interactive Visibility Ordering and Transparency Computations among Geometric Primitives in Complex Environments." In *Proceedings of I3D,* pp. 49–56. New York: ACM Press, 2005.

[85] "GPGPU." Available online (http://www.gpgpu.org/).

[86] Simon Green. "Volume Rendering in Games." Talk at Game Developers Conference (GDC), 2005.

[87] N. Greene. "Environment Mapping and Other Applications of World Projections." *IEEE Computer Graphics and Applications* 6:11 (1986), 21–29.

[88] Gene Greger, Peter Shirley, Philip M. Hubbard, and Donald P. Greenberg. "The Irradiance Volume." *IEEE Computer Graphics and Applications* 18:2 (1998), 32–43.

[89] Stefan Guthe and Wolfgang Straßer. "Real-time Decompression and Visualization of Animated Volume Data." In *Proceedings of IEEE Visualization,* pp. 349–356. Los Alamitos, CA: IEEE Press, 2001.

[90] Stefan Guthe, Michael Wand, Julius Gonser, and Wolfgang Straßer. "Interactive Rendering of Large Volume Data Sets." In *Proceedings of IEEE Visualization,* pp. 53–60. Los Alamitos, CA: IEEE Press, 2002.

[91] M. Hadwiger, T. Theußl, H. Hauser, and E. Gröller. "Hardware-Accelerated High-Quality Filtering on PC Hardware." In *Proceedings of Vision, Modeling, and Visualization*, pp. 105–112. Berlin: Akademische Verlagsgesellschaft, 2001.

[92] M. Hadwiger, C. Berger, and H. Hauser. "High-Quality Two-Level Volume Rendering of Segmented Data Sets on Consumer Graphics Hardware." In *Proceedings of IEEE Visualization 2003*, pp. 301–308. Los Alamitos, CA: IEEE Press, 2003.

[93] M. Hadwiger, C. Sigg, H. Scharsach, K. Bühler, and M. Gross. "Real-Time Ray-Casting and Advanced Shading of Discrete Isosurfaces." In *Proceedings of Eurographics*, pp. 303–312. Aire-la-Ville, Switzerland: Eurographics Association, 2005.

[94] Mark Harris and Anselmo Lastra. "Real-Time Cloud Rendering." In *Proceedings of Eurographics*, pp. 76–84. Aire-la-Ville, Switzerland: Eurographics Association, 2001.

[95] Mark Harris, William Baxter, Thorsten Scheuermann, and Anselmo Lastra. "Simulation of Cloud Dynamics on Graphics Hardware." In *Proceedings of Graphics Hardware 2003*, pp. 92–101. New York: ACM Press, 2003.

[96] Mark Harris, David Luebke, Ian Buck, Naga Govindaraju, Jens Krüger, Aaron Lefohn, Tim Purcell, and Cliff Woolley. "A Survey of General-Purpose Computation on Graphics Hardware." ACM SIGGRAPH 2005 Course Notes, 2005.

[97] Mark J. Harris. "Real-Time Cloud Simulation and Rendering." PhD Thesis TR03-040, University of North Carolina, 2003.

[98] John C. Hart. "Perlin Noise Pixel Shaders." In *Proceedings of the ACM SIGGRAPH/Eurographics Workshop on Graphics Hardware*, pp. 87–94. New York: ACM Press, 2001.

[99] P. Hastreiter, H.K. Çakmak, and T. Ertl. "Intuitive and Interactive Manipulation of 3D Datasets by Integrating Texture Mapping Based Volume Rendering into the OpenInventor Class Hierarchy." In *Bildverarbeitung für die Medizin – Algorithmen, Systeme, Anwendungen*, edited by T. Lehman, I. Scholl, and K. Spitzer, pp. 149–154. Universität Aachen: Verl. d. Augustinus Buchhandlung, 1996.

[100] Helwig Hauser, Lukas Mroz, Gian-Italo Bischi, and Eduard Gröller. "Two-level volume rendering - fusing MIP and DVR." In *Proceedings of IEEE Visualization*, pp. 211–218. Los Alamitos, CA: IEEE Press, 2000.

[101] Helwig Hauser, Lukas Mroz, Gian Italo Bischi, and Eduard Gröller. "Two-Level Volume Rendering." *IEEE Transactions on Visualization and Computer Graphics* 7:3 (2001), 242–252.

[102] T. He, S. Wang, and A. Kaufman. "Wavelet-based Volume Morphing." In *Proceedings of IEEE Visualization*, pp. 85–92. Los Alamitos, CA: IEEE Press, 1994.

[103] H.C. Hege, T. Höllerer, and D. Stalling. "Volume Rendering – Mathematical Models and Algorithmic Aspects." Report TR 93-7, ZIB (Konrad-Zuse-Zentrum), Berlin, 1993.

[104] Tim Heidmann. "Real Shadows, Real Time." *Iris Universe* 18 (1991), 23–31.

[105] Wolfgang Heidrich and Hans-Peter Seidel. "Efficient Rendering of Anisotropic Surfaces Using Computer Graphics Hardware." In *Proceedings of Image and Multi-dimensional Digital Signal Processing Workshop*. Berlin: Akademische Verlagsgesellschaft, 1998.

[106] J. Hladůvka, A. König, and E. Gröller. "Curvature-Based Transfer Functions for Direct Volume Rendering." In *Proceedings of Spring Conference on Computer Graphics 2000*, pp. 58–65, 2000.

[107] Samuel Hornus, Jared Hoberock, Sylvain Lefebvre, and John C. Hart. "ZP+: Correct Z-pass Stencil Shadows." In *Symposium on Interactive 3D Graphics and Games 2005*. New York: ACM Press, 2005.

[108] J. F. Hughes. "Scheduled Fourier Volume Morphing." *Computer Graphics* 26:2 (1992), 43–46.

[109] M. Hurn, K. Mardia, T. Hainsworth, J. Kirkbridge, and E. Berry. "Bayesian Fused Classification of Medical Images." Technical Report STAT/95/20/C, Department of Statistics, University of Leeds, 1995.

[110] Insung Ihm and Sanghun Park. "Wavelet-Based 3D Compression Scheme for Very Large Volume Data." In *Graphics Interface*, pp. 107–116, 1998.

[111] V. Interrante, H. Fuchs, and S. Pizer. "Enhancing Transparent Skin Surfaces with Ridge and Valley Lines." In *Proceedings of IEEE Visualization*, pp. 52–59. Los Alamitos, CA: IEEE Press, 1995.

[112] Shoukat Islam, Swapnil Dipankar, Deborah Silver, and Min Chen. "Spatial and Temporal Splitting of Scalar Fields in Volume Graphics." In *Proceedings of IEEE Symposium on Volume Visualization and Graphics (VolVis)*, pp. 87–94. New York: ACM Press, 2004.

[113] Henrik Wann Jensen, Stephen R. Marschner, Marc Levoy, and Pat Hanrahan. "A Practical Model for Subsurface Light Transport." In *Proceedings of SIGGRAPH 2001, Computer Graphics Proceedings, Annual Conference Series*, edited by E. Fiume, pp. 511–518. Reading, MA: Addison-Wesley, 2001.

[114] Henrik Wann Jensen. *Realistic Image Synthesis Using Photon Mapping*. Natick, MA: A K Peters, 2001.

[115] Ken Jones and Jenn McGee. "OpenGL Volumizer Programmer's Guide.", 2005. Available online (http://www.sgi.com/products/software/volumizer/documents.html).

[116] Alark Joshi and Penny Rheingans. "Illustration-inspired Techniques for Visualizing Time-varying Data." In *Proceedings of IEEE Visualization*, pp. 679–686. Los Alamitos, CA: IEEE Press, 2005.

[117] Arie Kadosh, Daniel Cohen-Or, and Roni Yagel. "Tricubic Interpolation of Discrete Surfaces for Binary Volumes." *IEEE Transactions on Visualization and Computer Graphics* 9:4 (2003), 580–586.

[118] James T. Kajiya and Brian P. Von Herzen. "Ray Tracing Volume Densities." *Proc. SIGGRAPH '84, Computer Graphics* 18:3 (1984), 165–174.

[119] James Kajiya and Timothy Kay. "Rendering Fur with Three-dimensional Textures." *Proc. SIGGRAPH '89, Computer Graphics* 23:3 (1989), 271–280.

[120] M. Karasick, D. Lieber, L. Nackmann, and V. Rajan. "Visualization of Three-Dimensional Delaunay Meshes." *Algorithmica* 19:1–2 (1997), 114–128.

[121] A. Kaufman and K. Mueller. "Overview of Volume Rendering." In *The Visualization Handbook*, edited by Charles. D. Hansen and Christopher R. Johnson, pp. 127–174. Amsterdam: Elsevier, 2005.

[122] Tae-Young Kim and Yeong Gil Shin. "An Efficient Wavelet-Based Compression Method for Volume Rendering." In *Proceedings of Pacific Graphics*, p. 147. Los Alamitos, CA: IEEE Press, 1999.

[123] Gordon Kindlmann and James Durkin. "Semi-automatic Generation of Transfer Functions for Direct Volume Rendering." In *Proceedings of IEEE Symposium on Volume Visualization*, pp. 79–86. New York: ACM Press, 1998.

[124] G. Kindlmann, R. Whitaker, T. Tasdizen, and T. Möller. "Curvature-Based Transfer Functions for Direct Volume Rendering: Methods and Applications." In *Proceedings of IEEE Visualization*, pp. 513–520. Los Alamitos, CA: IEEE Press, 2003.

[125] Davis King, Craig M. Wittenbrink, and Hans J. Wolters. "An Architecture for Interactive Tetrahedral Volume Rendering." In *Volume Graphics 2001, Proceedings of the International Workshop on Volume Graphics 2001*, pp. 163–180. New York: Springer, 2001.

[126] P. Kipfer, M. Segal, and R. Westermann. "UberFlow: A GPU-Based Particle Engine." In *Proceedings of Graphics Hardware*, pp. 115–122, 2004.

[127] T. Klein, M. Strengert, S. Stegmaier, and T. Ertl. "Exploiting Frame-to-Frame Coherence for Accelerating High-Quality Volume Raycasting on Graphics Hardware." In *Proceedings of IEEE Visualization '05*, pp. 223–230. Los Alamitos, CA: IEEE Press, 2005.

[128] Joe Kniss, Gordon Kindlmann, and Chuck Hansen. "Interactive Volume Rendering using Multi-dimensional Transfer Functions and Direct Manipulation Widgets." In *Proceedings of IEEE Visualization*, pp. 255–262. Los Alamitos, CA: IEEE Press, 2001.

[129] Joe Kniss, Simon Premoze, Charles Hansen, Peter Shirley, and Allen McPherson. "A Model for Volume Lighting and Modeling." 9:2 (2003), 150–162.

[130] A. Kolb, L. Latta, and C. Rezk-Salama. "Hardware-based Simulation and Collision Detection for Large Particle Systems." In *Proceedings of Graphics Hardware*, pp. 223–231, 2004.

[131] Olaf Konrad-Verse, Bernhard Preim, and Arne Littmann. "Virtual Resection with a Deformable Cutting Plane." In *Proceedings of Simulation und Visualisierung*, pp. 203–214. Erlangen, Germany: SCS Publishing House e.V., 2004.

[132] M. Kraus and T. Ertl. "Cell-Projection of Cyclic Meshes." In *Proceedings of IEEE Visualization*, pp. 215–222, 2001.

[133] Martin Kraus and Thomas Ertl. "Adaptive Texture Maps." In *Proceedings of ACM SIGGRAPH/Eurographics Workshop on Graphics Hardware*, 2002.

[134] Martin Kraus and Thomas Ertl. "Simplification of Nonconvex Tetrahedral Meshes." In *Hierarchical and Geometrical Methods in Scientific*

Visualization, edited by G. Farin, H. Hagen, and B. Hamann, pp. 185–196. New York: Springer, 2003.

[135] M. Kraus. "Direct Volume Visualization of Geometrically Unpleasant Meshes." Ph.D. thesis, University of Stuttgart, 2003.

[136] Anders Wang Kristensen, Tomas Akenine-Möller, and Henrik Wann Jensen. "Precomputed Local Radiance Transfer for Real-Time Lighting Design." *Proc. SIGGRAPH '05, Transactions on Graphics* 24:3 (2005), 1208–1215.

[137] W. Krueger. "The Application of Transport Theory to Visualization of 3D Scalar Data Fields." In *Proceedings of IEEE Visualization*, pp. 273–280. Los Alamitos, CA: IEEE Press, 1990.

[138] W. Krueger. "Volume Rendering and Data Feature Enhancement." *Computer Graphics* 24:5 (1990), 21–26.

[139] Jens Krüger and Rüdiger Westermann. "Acceleration Techniques for GPU-based Volume Rendering." In *Proceedings of IEEE Visualization 2003*, pp. 287–292. Los Alamitos, CA: IEEE Press, 2003.

[140] Jens Krüger and Rüdiger Westermann. "Acceleration Techniques for GPU-based Volume Rendering." In *Proceedings of IEEE Visualization*, 2003.

[141] Jens Krüger and Rüdiger Westermann. "Linear Algebra Operators for GPU Implementation of Numerical Algorithms." *Proc. SIGGRAPH '03, Transactions on Graphics* 22:3 (2003), 908–916.

[142] Jens Krüger and Rüdiger Westermann. "A GPU Framework for Solving Systems of Linear Equations." In *GPU Gems 2*, edited by Matt Pharr and Randima Fernando, pp. 703–718. Reading, MA: Addison-Wesley, 2005.

[143] Jens Krüger and Rüdiger Westermann. "GPU Simulation and Rendering of Volumetric Effects for Computer Games and Virtual Environments." In *Proceedings of Eurographics 2005*, pp. 685–693. Aire-la-Ville, Switzerland: Eurographics Association, 2005.

[144] Arno Krüger, Christian Tietjen, Jana Hintze, Bernhard Preim, Ilka Hertel, and Gero Strauß. "Interactive Visualization for Neck Dissection Planning." In *Proceedings of Eurovis*, pp. 295–302. Aire-la-Ville, Switzerland: Eurographics Association, 2005.

[145] Jens Krüger, Peter Kipfer, Polina Kondratieva, and Rüdiger Westermann. "A Particle System for Interactive Visualization of 3D Flows."
IEEE Transactions on Visualization and Computer Graphics 11:6
(2005), 744–756.

[146] Yair Kurzion and Roni Yagel. "Space Deformation using Ray Deflectors." In *Rendering Techniques '95 (Proceedings of the Sixth Eurographics Workshop on Rendering)*, pp. 21–30. Aire-la-Ville, Switzerland: Eurographics Association, 1995.

[147] Yair Kurzion and Roni Yagel. "Interactive Space Deformation with
Hardware-Assisted Rendering." *IEEE Computer Graphics & Applications* 17:5 (1997), 66–77.

[148] V. Kwatra, A. Schödl, I. Essa, G. Turk, and A. Bobick. "Graph-
cut Textures: Image and Video Synthesis Using Graph Cuts." *Proc.
SIGGRAPH '03, Transactions on Graphics* 22:3 (2003), 277–286.

[149] P. Lacroute and M. Levoy. "Fast Volume Rendering Using a Shear-
Warp Factorization of the Viewing Transformation." In *Proc. SIG-
GRAPH '94, Computer Graphics Proceedings, Annual Conference Se-
ries*, pp. 451–458, 1994.

[150] Samuli Laine. "Split-Plane Shadow Volumes." In *Graphics Hardware
2005*, pp. 23–32, 2005.

[151] A. Lake, C. Marshall, M. Harris, and M. Blackstein. "Stylized Rendering Techniques for Scalable Real-Time 3D Animation." In *Proceedings of NPAR 2000*, pp. 13–20. New York: ACM Press, 2000.

[152] E. LaMar, B. Hamann, and K. Joy. "Multiresolution Techniques
for Interactive Texture-based Volume Visualization." In *Proceedings
of IEEE Visualization*, pp. 355–362. Los Alamitos, CA: IEEE Press,
1999.

[153] B. Laramee, B. Jobard, and H. Hauser. "Image Space Based Visualization of Unsteady Flow on Surfaces." In *Proceedings of IEEE
Visualization*, pp. 131–138. Los Alamitos, CA: IEEE Press, 2003.

[154] B. Laramee, J. van Wijk, B. Jobard, and H. Hauser. "ISA and IBFVS:
Image Space Based Visualization of Flow on Surfaces." *IEEE Transactions on Visualization and Computer Graphics* 10:6 (2004), 637–648.

[155] A. Lastra, S. Molnar, M. Olano, and Y. Wang. "Real-time Programmable Shading." In *ACM Symposium on Interactive 3D Graphics*, pp. 59–66. New York: ACM Press, 1995.

[156] Lutz Latta and Andreas Kolb. "Homomorphic factorization of BRDF-based lighting computation." *Proc. SIGGRAPH '02, Transactions on Graphics* 21:3 (2002), 509–516.

[157] Sylvain Lefebvre, Jerome Darbon, and Fabrice Neyret. "Unified Texture Management for Arbitrary Meshes." Technical Report 5210, Institut National de Recherche en Informatique et en Automatique (INRIA), 2004.

[158] Aaron Lefohn, Joe Kniss, Chuck Hansen, and Ross Whitaker. "Interactive Deformation and Visualization of Level Set Surfaces Using Graphics Hardware." In *Proceedings of IEEE Visualization*, pp. 75–82. Los Alamitos, CA: IEEE Press, 2003.

[159] Jed Lengyel, Emil Praun, Adam Finkelstein, and Hugues Hoppe. "Real-Time Fur Over Arbitrary Surfaces." In *Proceedings of Symposium on Interactive 3D Graphics*, pp. 227–232. New York: ACM Press, 2001.

[160] H. Lensch, K. Daubert, and H.-P. Seidel. "Interactive Semi-Transparent Volumetric Textures." In *Proceedings of Vision Modeling and Visualization*, pp. 505–512. Berlin: Akademische Verlagsgesellschaft, 2002.

[161] Marc Levoy. "Display of Surfaces From Volume Data." *IEEE Computer Graphics and Applications* 8:3 (1988), 29–37.

[162] Wei Li and Arie Kaufman. "Texture Partitioning and Packing for Accelerating Texture-based Volume Rendering." *Graphics Interface*, pp. 81–88.

[163] H. Li, B. Manjunath, and S. Mitra. "Multi-sensor Image Fusion Using the Wavelet Transform." *GMIP: Graphical Model Image Process* 57:3 (1995), 235–245.

[164] Wei Li, Klaus Mueller, and Arie Kaufman. "Empty Space Skipping and Occlusion Clipping for Texture-based Volume Rendering." In *Proceedings of IEEE Visualization*, pp. 317–324. Los Alamitos, CA: IEEE Press, 2003.

[165] Barthold Lichtenbelt, Randy Crane, and Shaz Naqvi. *Introduction to Volume Rendering.* Upper Saddle River, NJ: Prentice Hall PTR, 1998.

[166] Y. Linde, A. Buzo, and R. Gray. "An Algorithm for Vector Quantizer Design." *IEEE Transactions on Communications* 28 (1980), 84–95.

[167] Tom Lokovic and Eric Veach. "Deep Shadow Maps." In *Proceedings of SIGGRAPH 2000, Computer Graphics Proceedings, Annual Conference Series*, edited by Kurt Akeley, pp. 385–392. Reading, MA: Addison-Wesley, 2000.

[168] W. E. Lorensen and H. E. Cline. "Marching Cubes: A High Resolution 3D Surface Construction Algorithm." *Proc. SIGGRAPH '87, Computer Graphics*, pp. 163–169.

[169] A. Lu and D. Ebert. "Example-Based Volume Illustrations." In *Proceedings of IEEE Visualization*, pp. 655–662. Los Alamitos, CA: IEEE Press, 2005.

[170] A. Lu, C. Morris, D. Ebert, P. Rheingans, and C. Hansen. "Non-Photorealistic Volume Rendering Using Stippling Techniques." In *Proceedings of IEEE Visualization*, pp. 211–218. Los Alamitos, CA: IEEE Press, 2002.

[171] Eric Lum and Kwan-Liu Ma. "Hardware-Accelerated Parallel Non-Photorealistic Volume Rendering." In *Proceedings of the International Symposium on Nonphotorealistic Animation and Rendering (NPAR)*. New York: ACM Press, 2002.

[172] Eric Lum and Kwan-Liu Ma. "Lighting Transfer Functions using Gradient Aligned Sampling." In *Proceedings of IEEE Visualization*, pp. 289–296. Los Alamitos, CA: IEEE Press, 2004.

[173] Eric B. Lum, Kwan Liu Ma, and John Clyne. "Texture Hardware Assisted Rendering of Time-Varying Volume Data." In *Proceedings of IEEE Visualization*, pp. 263–270. Los Alamitos, CA: IEEE Press, 2001.

[174] Eric B. Lum, Aleksander Stompel, and Kwan-Liu Ma. "Kinetic Visualization: A Technique for Illustrating 3D Shape and Structure." In *Proceedings of IEEE Visualization*, pp. 435–442. Los Alamitos, CA: IEEE Press, 2002.

[175] R. Luo, M. Lin, and R. Scherp. "Multi-Sensor Integration and Fusion in Intelligent Systems." In *IEEE Transactions on Systems, Man and Cybernetics*, 19, 19, pp. 901–931, 1989.

[176] Kwan-Liu Ma, Aaron Hertzmann, Victoria Interrante, and Eric B. Lum. "Recent Advances in Non-Photorealistic Rendering for Art and Visualization." SIGGRAPH 2002 Course Notes, 2002.

[177] R. MacCracken and K. Roy. "Free-Form Deformations with Lattices of Arbitrary Topology." In *Proceedings of SIGGRAPH 96, Computer Graphics Proceedings, Annual Conference Series*, edited by Holly Rushmeier, pp. 181–188. Reading, MA: Addison Wesley, 1996.

[178] M. Magallon, M. Hopf, and T. Ertl. "Parallel Volume Rendering using PC Graphics Hardware." In *Pacific Graphics*, 2001.

[179] G. Matsopoulos, S. Marshall, and J. Brunt. "Multi-Resolution Morphological Fusion of MR and CT Images of the Human Brain." In *Proceedings of IEE Visual, Image and Signal Processing*, p. 137.

[180] N. Max, P. Hanrahan, and R. Crawfis. "Area and Volume Coherence for Efficient Visualization of 3D Scalar Functions." *Proc. SIGGRAPH '92, Computer Graphics* 24:5 (1990), 27–33.

[181] N. Max. "Optical Models for Direct Volume Rendering." *IEEE Transactions on Visualization and Computer Graphics* 1:2 (1995), 99–108.

[182] Michael D. McCool, Jason Ang, and Anis Ahmad. "Homomorphic Factorization of BRDFs for High-Performance Rendering." In *Proceedings of SIGGRAPH 2001, Computer Graphics Proceedings, Annual Conference Series*, edited by E. Fiume, pp. 171–178. Reading, MA: Addison-Wesley, 2001.

[183] Michael J. McGuffin, Liviu Tancau, and Ravin Balakrishnan. "Using Deformations for Browsing Volumetric Data." In *Proceedings of IEEE Visualization*, pp. 401–408. Los Alamitos, CA: IEEE Press, 2003.

[184] Tom McReynolds and David Blythe. *Advanced Graphics Programming Using OpenGL*. San Francisco: Morgan Kaufmann, 2005.

[185] D. P. Mitchell and A. N. Netravali. "Reconstruction Filters in Computer Graphics." In *Proc. SIGGRAPH '88, Computer Graphics*, 22, 22, pp. 221–228, 1988.

[186] Jason Mitchell. "Light Shafts: Rendering Shadows in Participating Media." Talk at Game Developers Conference (GDC), 2004.

[187] B. Mora and D. S. Ebert. "Instant Volumetric Understanding with Order-Independent Volume Rendering." *Computer Graphics Forum (Eurographics 2004)* 23:3 (2004), 489–497.

[188] K. Mueller and R. Crawfis. "Eliminating Poping Artifacts in Sheet Buffer-Based Splatting." In *Proceedings of IEEE Visualization*, pp. 239–245. Los Alamitos, CA: IEEE Press, 1998.

[189] D. Mukherjee, P. Dutta, and D. Dutta Majumdar. "Entropy Theoretic Fusion of Multimodal Medical Images." Technical Report ECSU/2/98, Electronics and Communication Science Unit, Indian Statistical Institute, 1998.

[190] S. Mukhopadhyuy and B. Chanda. "Fusion of 2D Grayscale Images using Multiscale Morphology." *Pattern Recognition* 34:10 (2001), 1939–1949.

[191] Shigeru Muraki. "Volume Data and Wavelet Transforms." *IEEE Computer Graphics and Application* 13:4 (1993), 50–56.

[192] Ken Museth, David Breen, Ross Whitaker, and Alan Barr. "Level Set Surface Editing Operators." In *Proc. SIGGRAPH 2002, Transactions on Graphics*, 21, 21, pp. 330–338, 2002.

[193] Zoltán Nagy and Reinhard Klein. "Depth-Peeling for Texture-Based Volume Rendering." In *Proceedings of Pacific Graphics*, pp. 429–433. Los Alamitos, CA: IEEE Press, 2003.

[194] Zoltán Nagy, Jens Schneider, and Rüdiger Westermann. "Interactive Volume Illustration." In *Proceedings of Vision, Modeling, and Visualization*, pp. 497–504. Berlin: Akademische Verlagsgesellschaft, 2002.

[195] Ky Giang Nguyen and Dietmar Saupe. "Rapid High Quality Compression of Volume Data for Visualization." *Computer Graphics Forum* 20:3 (2001), 49–56.

[196] Duc Quang Nguyen, Ronald Fedkiw, and Henrik Wann Jensen. "Physically Based Modeling and Animation of Fire." In *Proc. SIGGRAPH '02, Transactions on Graphics*, 21, 21, pp. 721–728, 2002.

[197] Gregory Nielson. "Radial Hermite Operators for Scattered Point Cloud Data with Normal Vectors and Applications to Implicitizing Polygon Mesh Surfaces for Generalized CSG Operations and Smoothing." In *Proceedings of IEEE Visualization*, pp. 203–210. Los Alamitos, CA: IEEE Press, 2004.

[198] Paul Ning and Lambertus Hesselink. "Vector Quantization for Volume Rendering." In *Proceedings of the Workshop on Volume Visualization*, pp. 69–74. New York: ACM Press, 1992.

[199] Kevin Novins and James Arvo. "Controlled Precision Volume Integration." In *Proceedings of the 1992 Workshop on Volume Visualization*, pp. 83–89. New York: ACM Press, 1992.

[200] NVIDIA Corporation. "NVIDIA Software Development Kit (SDK).", 2004. Available online (http://developer.nvidia.com/object/sdk_home. html).

[201] H. Nyquist. "Certain Topics in Telegraph Transmission Theory." *Transactions of the AIEE* 47 (1928), 617–644.

[202] Marc Olano, John C. Hart, Wolfgang Heidrich, and Michael McCool. *Real-Time Shading.* Natick, MA: AK Peters Ltd., 2002.

[203] Manuel Oliveira, Gary Bishop, and David McAllister. "Relief Texture Mapping." In *Proceedings of SIGGRAPH 2000, Computer Graphics Proceedings, Annual Conference Series*, edited by Kurt Akeley, pp. 359–368. Reading, MA: Addison-Wesley, 2000.

[204] A. V. Oppenheim and R. W. Schafer. *Digital Signal Processing.* Englewood Cliffs, NJ: Prentice Hall, 1975.

[205] Stanley Osher and Ronald Fedkiw. *Level Set Methods and Dynamic Implicit Surfaces.* New York: Springer, 2003.

[206] J. Owens, D. Luebke, N. Govindaraju, M. Harris, J. Krüger, A. Lefohn, and T. Purcell. "A Survey of General-Purpose Computation on Graphics Hardware." Eurographics 2005 State of the Art Report, 2005.

[207] K. Perlin and E. M. Hoffert. "Hypertexture." *Proc. SIGGRAPH '89, Computer Graphics* 23:3 (1989), 253–262.

[208] H. Pfister. "Hardware-Accelerated Volume Rendering." In *The Visualization Handbook*, edited by Charles. D. Hansen and Christopher R. Johnson, pp. 229–258. Amsterdam: Elsevier, 2005.

[209] Bernhard Pflesser, Ulf Tiede, and Karl Heinz Höhne. "Specification, Modelling and Visualization of Arbitrarily Shaped Cut Surfaces in the Volume Model." In *Medical Image Computing and Computer-Assisted Intervention, Proceedings of MICCAI '98*, 1496, 1496, pp. 853–860. Berlin: Springer, 1998.

[210] Matt Pharr and Randima Fernando, editors. *GPU Gems 2: Programming Techniques for High-Performance Graphics and General-Purpose Computation.* Reading, MA: Addison-Wesley, 2005.

[211] Matt Pharr and Greg Humphries. *Physically Based Rendering.* San Francisco: Morgan Kaufmann, 2004.

[212] Matt Pharr. "Ambient Occlusion." In *GPU Gems*, edited by Randima Fernando, pp. 279–292. Reading, MA: Addison-Wesley, 2004.

[213] Fabio Policarpo, Manuel Oliveira, and João Comba. "Real-Time Relief Mapping on Arbitrary Polygonal Surfaces." In *Proceedings of Symposium on Interactive 3D Graphics*, pp. 155–162. New York: ACM Press, 2005.

[214] J. Portilla and E. Simoncelli. "A Parametric Texture Model Based on Joint Statistics of Complex Wavelet Coefficients." *Int. Journal of Computer Vision* 40:1 (2000), 49–70.

[215] Emil Praun, Hugues Hoppe, Matthew Webb, and Adam Finkelstein. "Real-Time Hatching." In *Proceedings of SIGGRAPH 2001, computer Graphics Proceedings, Annual Conference Series*, edited by E. Fiume, pp. 581–586. Reading, MA: Addison-Wesley, 2001.

[216] Bernhard Preim and Dirk Bartz. *Visualization in Medicine: Theory, Algorithms, and Applications*. San Francisco: Morgan Kaufmann, 2006.

[217] W. H. Press, S. A. Teukolsky, W. T. Vetterling, and B. P. Flannery. *Numerical Recipes in C: The Art of Scientific Computing*, Second edition. Cambridge, UK: Cambridge University Press, 1992.

[218] M. Prokop, H. O. Shin, A. Schanz, and C. M. Andschaefer-Prokop. "Use of Maximum Intensity Projections in CT Angiography." *Radiographics* 17 (1997), 433–451.

[219] F. Reck, C. Dachsbacher, R. Grosso, G. Greiner, and M. Stamminger. "Realtime Isosurface Extraction with Graphics Hardware." In *Proceedings of Eurographics*. Aire-la-Ville, Switzerland: Eurographics Association, 2004.

[220] W. Reeves. "Particle Systems – Technique for Modeling a Class of Fuzzy Objects." In *ACM Transactions on Graphics*, 2, 2, pp. 91–108, 1983.

[221] Erik Reinhard, Greg Ward, Sumanta Pattanaik, and Paul Debevec. *High Dynamic Range Imaging*. San Francisco: Morgan Kaufmann, 2005.

[222] Craig W. Reynolds. "Flocks, Herds and Schools: A Distributed Behavior Model." *Proc. SIGGRAPH '87, Computer Graphics* 21:4 (1987), 25–34.

[223] C. Rezk-Salama, P. Hastreiter, C. Teitzel, and T. Ertl. "Interactive Exploration of Volume Line Integral Convolution Based on 3D-Texture Mapping." In *Proceedings of IEEE Visualization*, pp. 233–240. Los Alamitos, CA: IEEE Press, 1999.

[224] C. Rezk-Salama, K. Engel, M. Bauer, G. Greiner, and T. Ertl. "Interactive Volume Rendering on Standard PC Graphics Hardware Using Multi-Textures and Multi-Stage Rasterization." In *Proceedings of ACM SIGGRAPH/Eurographics Workshop on Graphics Hardware*, 2000.

[225] Flemming Friche Rodler. "Wavelet Based 3D Compression with Fast Random Access for Very Large Volume Data." In *Proceedings of Pacific Graphics*, p. 108. Los Alamitos, CA: IEEE Press, 1999.

[226] S. Röttger, M. Kraus, and T. Ertl. "Hardware-Accelerated Volume and Isosurface Rendering Based On Cell-Projection." In *Proceedings of IEEE Visualization*, pp. 109–116. Los Alamitos, CA: IEEE Press, 2000.

[227] S. Röttger, S. Guthe, D. Weiskopf, and T. Ertl. "Smart Hardware-Accelerated Volume Rendering." In *Procceedings of EG/IEEE TCVG Symposium on Visualization VisSym '03*, pp. 231–238, 2003.

[228] Szymon Rusinkiewicz. "Estimating Curvatures and Their Derivatives on Triangle Meshes." In *Proceedings of Symposium on 3D Data Processing, Visualization, and Transmission*, pp. 486–493. Los Alamitos, CA: IEEE Press, 2004.

[229] John C. Russ. *The Image Processing Handbook*, Fourth edition. Boca Raton, FL: CRC Press, 2002.

[230] Paolo Sabella. "A Rendering Algorithm for Visualizing 3D Scalar Fields." In *Proc. SIGGRAPH '88, Computer Graphics*, 22, 22, pp. 51–58, 1988.

[231] T. Saito and T. Takahashi. "Comprehensible Rendering of 3D Shapes." In *Proc. SIGGRAPH '90, Computer Graphics*, 24, 24, pp. 197–206, 1990.

[232] Henning Scharsach, Markus Hadwiger, André Neubauer, Stefan Wolfsberger, and Katja Bühler. "Perspective Isosurface and Direct Volume Rendering for Virtual Endoscopy Applications."

[233] Gernot Schaufler and Wolfgang Stürzlinger. "A Three Dimensional Image Cache for Virtual Reality." In *Proceedings of Eurographics*, pp. 227–235. Aire-la-Ville, Switzerland: Eurographics Association, 1996.

[234] J. Schneider and R. Westermann. "Compression Domain Volume Rendering." In *Proceedings of IEEE Visualization*, pp. 168–175. Los Alamitos, CA: IEEE Press, 2003.

[235] J. P. Schulze, Roland Niemeier, and Ulrich Lang. "The Perspective Shear-Warp Algorithm in a Virtual Environment." In *Proceedings of IEEE Visualization*, pp. 207–214. Los Alamitos, CA: IEEE Press, 2001.

[236] T. Sederberg and S. Parry. "Free-Form Deformation of Solid Geometric Models." In *Proc. SIGGRAPH '86, Computer Graphics*, 20, 20, 1986.

[237] J. Shade, D. Lischinski, D. Salesin, T. DeRose, and J. Snyder. "Hierarchical Image Caching for Accelerated Walkthroughs of Complex Environments." In *Proceedings of SIGGRAPH 96, Computer Graphics Proceedings, Annual Conference Series*, edited by Holly Rushmeier, pp. 75–82. Reading, MA: Addison Wesley, 1996.

[238] C. E. Shannon. "Communication in the Presence of Noise." In *Proceedings of Institute of Radio Engineers, vol. 37, no.1*, pp. 10–21, 1949.

[239] Peter Shirley and Allan Tuchman. "A Polygonal Approximation to Direct Scalar Volume Rendering." *Computer Graphics (San Diego Workshop on Volume Visualization)* 24:5 (1990), 63–70.

[240] D. Shreiner, J. Neider, M. Woo, and T. Davis. *OpenGL Programming Guide*, Fourth edition. Reading, MA: Addison-Wesley, 2003.

[241] Christian Sigg and Markus Hadwiger. "Fast Third-Order Texture Filtering." In *GPU Gems 2: Programming Techniques for High-Performance Graphics and General-Purpose Computation*, edited by Matt Pharr and Randima Fernando, pp. 313–329. Reading, MA: Addison-Wesley, 2005.

[242] Christian Sigg, Ronald Peikert, and Markus Gross. "Signed Distance Transform Using Graphics Hardware." In *Proceedings of Visualization 2003*, pp. 83–90. Los Alamitos, CA: IEEE Press, 2003.

[243] Silicon Graphics, Inc. "OpenGL Extension Registry." Available online (http://oss.sgi.com/projects/ogl-sample/registry/).

[244] C. Silva, J. Comba, S. Callahan, and F. Bernardon. "A Survey of GPU-Based Volume Rendering of Unstructured Grids." *Brazilian Journal of Theoretic and Applied Computing (RITA)* 12:2 (2005), 9–29.

[245] Peter-Pike Sloan, Jan Kautz, and Jon Snyder. "Precomputed Radiance Transfer for Real-Time Rendering in Dynamic, Low-Frequency Lighting Environments." *Proc. SIGGRAPH '02, Transactions on Graphics* 21:3 (2002), 527–536.

[246] Miloš Srámek and Arie Kaufman. "Object Voxelization by Filtering." In *Proceedings of IEEE Symposium on Volume Visualization*, pp. 111–118. New York: ACM Press, 1998.

[247] Jos Stam and Eugene Fiume. "Depiction of Fire and Other Gaseous Phenomena Using Diffusion Processes." In *Proceedings of SIGGRAPH 95, Computer Graphics Proceedings, Annual Conference Series*, edited by Robert Cook, pp. 129–136. Reading, MA: Addison Wesley, 1995.

[248] Jos Stam. "Aperiodic Texture Mapping." Techical report, European Research Consortium for Informatics and Mathematics (ERCIM), 1998.

[249] Jos Stam. "Stable Fluids." In *Proceedings of SIGGRAPH 99, Computer Graphics Proceedings, Annual Conference Series*, edited by Alyn Rockwood, pp. 121–128. Reading, MA: Addison Wesley Longman, 1999.

[250] Oliver Staubli, Christian Sigg, Ronald Peikert, Daniel Grubler, and Markus Gross. "Volume Rendering of Smoke Propagation CFD Data." In *Proceedings of IEEE Visualization*, pp. 335–342. Los Alamitos, CA: IEEE Press, 2005.

[251] S. Stegmaier, M. Strengert, T. Klein, and T. Ertl. "A Simple and Flexible Volume Rendering Framework for Graphics-Hardware-based Raycasting." In *Proceedings of the International Workshop on Volume Graphics '05*, pp. 187–195. Aire-la-Ville, Switzerland: Eurographics Association, 2005.

[252] Eric J. Stollnitz, Tony D. Derose, and David H. Salesin. *Wavelets for Computer Graphics: Theory and Applications*. San Francisco: Morgan Kaufmann, 1996.

[253] Aleksander Stompel, Eric B. Lum, and Kwan-Liu Ma. "Feature-Enhanced Visualization of Multidimensional, Multivariate Volume Data Using Non-Photorealistic Rendering Techniques." In *Proceedings of Pacific Graphics*, pp. 1–8. Los Alamitos, CA: IEEE Press, 2002.

[254] M. Strengert, M. Magallon, D. Weiskopf, S. Guthe, and T. Ertl. "Hierarchical Visualization and Compression of Large Volume Datasets Using GPU Clusters." In *Eurographics Symposium on Parallel Graphics and Visualization (EGPGV04)*, pp. 41–48. Aire-la-Ville, Switzerland: Eurographics Association, 2004.

[255] M. Strengert, M. Magallon, D. Weiskopf, S. Guthe, and T. Ertl. "Large Volume Visualization of Compressed Time-Dependent Datasets on GPU Clusters." *Parallel Computing* 31:2 (2005), 205–219.

[256] T. Strothotte and S. Schlechtweg. *Non-Photorealistic Computer Graphics: Modeling, Rendering and Animation.* San Francisco: Morgan Kaufmann, 2002.

[257] B. Stroustrup. *The C++ Programming Language,* Third edition. Reading, MA: Addison-Wesley, 1997.

[258] Avneesh Sud, Miguel Otaduy, and Dinesh Manocha. "DiFi: Fast 3D Distance Field Computation Using Graphics Hardware." In *Proceedings of Eurographics 2004,* pp. 557–566. Aire-la-Ville, Switzerland: Eurographics Association, 2004.

[259] Bo Sun, Ravi Ramamoorthi, Srinivasa G. Narasimhan, and Shree K. Nayar. "A Practical Analytic Single Scattering Model for Real Time Rendering." *Proc. SIGGRAPH '05, Transactions on Graphics* 24:3 (2005), 1040–1049.

[260] N. Svakhine, D. S. Ebert, and D. Stredney. "Illustration Motifs for Effective Medical Volume Illustration." *IEEE Computer Graphics and Applications* 25:3 (2005), 31–39.

[261] N. Svakhine, Y. Jang, D. Ebert, and K. Gaither. "Illustration and Photography Inspired Visualization of Flows and Volumes." In *Proceedings of IEEE Visualization,* pp. 687–694. Los Alamitos, CA: IEEE Press, 2005.

[262] Natalya Tatarchuk. "Irradiance Volumes for Games." Talk at Game Developers Conference Europe (GDCE), 2005.

[263] Gabriel Taubin. "Estimating the Tensor of Curvature of a Surface from a Polyhedral Approximation." In *Proceedings of ICCV '95,* pp. 902–908. Los Alamitos, CA: IEEE Press, 1995.

[264] Ulf Tiede, Thomas Schiemann, and Karl Heinz Höhne. "High Quality Rendering of Attributed Volume Data." In *Proceedings of IEEE Visualization,* pp. 255–262, 1998.

[265] Christian Tietjen, Tobias Isenberg, and Bernhard Preim. "Combining Silhouettes, Surface, and Volume Rendering for Surgery Education and Planning." In *Proceedings of Eurovis,* pp. 303–310. Aire-la-Ville, Switzerland: Eurographics Association, 2005.

[266] Sean Treavett and Min Chen. "Pen-and-ink rendering in volume visualisation." In *Proceedings of IEEE Visualization,* pp. 203–210. Los Alamitos, CA: IEEE Press, 2000.

[267] Greg Turk and James O'Brien. "Shape Transformation Using Variational Implicit Functions." In *Proceedings of SIGGRAPH 99, Computer Graphics Proceedings, Annual Conference Series*, edited by Alyn Rockwood, pp. 335–342. Reading, MA: Addison Wesley Longman, 1999.

[268] K. Udupa and G. Herman. *3D Imaging in Medicine*. Boca Raton, FL: CRC Press, 1999.

[269] J. van Wijk. "Image Based Flow Visualization for Curved Surfaces." In *Proceedings of IEEE Visualization*, pp. 745–754. Los Alamitos, CA: IEEE Press, 2003.

[270] T. Vassilev, B. Spanlang, and Y. Chrysanthou. "Fast Cloth Animation on Walking Avatars." In *Proceedings of Eurographics*, pp. 260–267. Aire-la-Ville, Switzerland: Eurographics Association, 2001.

[271] Fernando Vega-Higuera, Peter Hastreiter, Rudolf Fahlbusch, and Günther Greiner. "High Performance Volume Splatting for Visualization of Neurovascular Data." In *Proceedings of IEEE Visualization*, pp. 271–278. Los Alamitos, CA: IEEE Press, 2005.

[272] Ivan Viola, Armin Kanitsar, and Eduard Gröller. "Importance-Driven Volume Rendering." In *Proceedings of IEEE Visualization*, pp. 139–145. Los Alamitos, CA: IEEE Press, 2004.

[273] Ivan Viola, Eduard Gröller, Katja Bühler, Markus Hadwiger, David Ebert, Bernhard Preim, Mario Costa Sousa, and Don Stredney. "Illustrative Visualization." IEEE Visualization 2005 Tutorial Notes, 2005.

[274] Ivan Viola, Armin Kanitsar, and Eduard Gröller. "Importance-Driven Feature Enhancement in Volume Visualization." *IEEE Transactions on Visualization and Computer Graphics* 11:4 (2005), 408–418.

[275] J.E. Vollrath, D. Weiskopf, and T. Ertl. "A Generic Software Framework for the GPU Volume Rendering Pipeline." In *Proceedings of Vision, Modeling, and Visualization*. Berlin: Akademische Verlagsgesellschaft, 2005.

[276] William R. Volz. "Gigabyte Volume Viewing Using Split Software/Hardware Interpolation." In *Proceedings of IEEE Symposium on Volume Visualization*, pp. 15–22, 2000.

[277] S. Wang and A. Kaufman. "Antialiased Voxelization." In *Proceedings of IEEE Visualization*, 1993.

[278] Lujin Wang, Ye Zhao, Klaus Mueller, and Arie Kaufman. "The Magic Volume Lens: An Interactive Focus+Context Technique for Volume Rendering." In *Proceedings of IEEE Visualization*, pp. 367–374. Los Alamitos, CA: IEEE Press, 2005.

[279] Rui Wang, John Tran, and David Luebke. "All-Frequency Interactive Relighting of Translucent Objects with Single and Multiple Scattering." *Proc. SIGGRAPH '05, Transactions on Graphics* 24:3.

[280] Lihong V. Wang. "Rapid Modelling of Diffuse Reflectance of Light in Turbid Slabs." *Journal of the Optical Society of America. A, Optics, Image Science and Vision* 15:4 (1998), 936–944.

[281] Greg Ward, Paul Debevec, Rod Bogart, Dan Lemmon, and Frank Vitz. "HDRI and Image-Based Lighting." In *ACM SIGGRAPH Course Notes*, 2003.

[282] Greg Ward. "High Dynamic Range Imaging." In *Proceedings of the Ninth Color Imaging Conference*, pp. 9–16. Springfield, VA: IS&T - The Society for Imaging Science and Technology, 2001.

[283] Alan Watt and Fabio Policarpo. *3D Games: Real-time Rendering and Software Technology*, 1. Reading, MA: Addison-Wesley, 2001.

[284] Alan Watt and Fabio Policarpo. *3D Games: Animation and Advanced Real-time Rendering*, 2. Reading, MA: Addison-Wesley, 2003.

[285] Alan Watt and Fabio Policarpo. *Advanced Game Development with Programmable Graphics Hardware*. A K Peters, 2005.

[286] L.-Y. Wei and M. Levoy. "Fast Texture Synthesis Using Tree-Structured Vector Quantization." In *Proceedings of SIGGRAPH 2000, Computer Graphics Proceedings, Annual Conference Series*, edited by Kurt Akeley, pp. 479–488. Reading, MA: Addison-Wesley, 2000.

[287] Xiaoming Wei, Wei Li, Klaus Mueller, and Arie Kaufman. "The Lattice-Boltzmann Method for Simulating Gaseous Phenomena." *IEEE Transactions on Visualization and Computer Graphics* 10:2 (2004), 164–176.

[288] Manfred Weiler, Rüdiger Westermann, Charles Hansen, K. Zimmerman, and Thomas Ertl. "Level-Of-Detail Volume Rendering via 3D Textures." In *Proceedings of IEEE Symposium on Volume Visualization*, pp. 7–13. New York: ACM Press, 2000.

[289] Manfred Weiler, Martin Kraus, Markus Merz, and Thomas Ertl. "Hardware-Based Ray Casting for Tetrahedral Meshes." In *Proceedings of IEEE Visualization 2003*, pp. 333–340, 2003.

[290] Manfred Weiler, Martin Kraus, Markus Merz, and Thomas Ertl. "Hardware-Based View-Independent Cell Projection." *IEEE Transactions on Visualization and Computer Graphics* 9:2 (2003), 163–175.

[291] Manfred Weiler, Paula N. Mallón, Martin Kraus, and Thomas Ertl. "Texture-Encoded Tetrahedral Strips." In *Proceedings of IEEE Symposium on Volume Visualization*, pp. 71–78, 2004.

[292] D. Weiskopf, K. Engel, and T. Ertl. "Volume Clipping via Per-Fragment Operations in Texture-Based Volume Visualization." In *Proceedings of IEEE Visualization*, pp. 93–100. Los Alamitos, CA: IEEE Press, 2002.

[293] D. Weiskopf, K. Engel, and T. Ertl. "Interactive Clipping Techniques for Texture-Based Volume Visualization and Volume Shading." *IEEE Transactions on Visualization and Computer Graphics* 9:3 (2003), 298–312.

[294] D. Weiskopf, M. Weiler, and T. Ertl. "Maintaining Constant Frame Rates in 3D Texture-Based Volume Rendering." In *Procceedings of Computer Graphics International (CGI) 2004*, pp. 604–607. Los Alamitos, CA: IEEE Press, 2004.

[295] D. Weiskopf, T. Schafhitzel, and T. Ertl. "Real-Time Advection and Volumetric Illumination for the Visualization of 3D Unsteady Flow." In *Proceedings of Eurovis (EG/IEEE TCVG Symposium on Visualization)*, pp. 13–20. Aire-la-Ville, Switzerland: Eurographics Association, 2005.

[296] R. Westermann and T. Ertl. "Efficiently Using Graphics Hardware in Volume Rendering Applications." In *Proceedings of SIGGRAPH 98, Computer Graphics Proceedings, Annual Conference Series*, edited by Michael Cohen, pp. 169–178. Reading, MA: Addison Wesley, 1998.

[297] R. Westermann and C. Rezk-Salama. "Real-Time Volume Deformation." In *Proceedings of Eurographics*. Aire-la-Ville, Switzerland: Eurographics Association, 2001.

[298] R. Westermann. "A Multiresolution Framework for Volume Rendering." In *Proceedings of the IEEE Symposium on Volume Visualization*, pp. 51–58. New York: ACM Press, 1994.

[299] L. Westover. "Footprint Evaluation for Volume Rendering." *Proc. SIGGRAPH '90, Computer Graphics* 24:4 (1990), 367–376.

[300] Peter L. Williams and Nelson Max. "A Volume Density Optical Model." In *Proceedings of Workshop on Volume Visualization*, pp. 61–68. New York: ACM Press, 1992.

[301] Lance Williams. "Casting Curved Shadows on Curved Surfaces." *Proc. SIGGRAPH '78, Computer Graphics* 12:3 (1978), 270–274.

[302] Peter L. Williams. "Visibility Ordering Meshed Polyhedra." *ACM Transactions on Graphics* 11:2 (1992), 103–126.

[303] Craig M. Wittenbrink, T. Malzbender, and M. E. Goss. "Opacity-Weighted Color Interpolation for Volume Sampling." In *Proceedings of IEEE Symposium on Volume Visualization*, pp. 135–142, 1998.

[304] Craig M. Wittenbrink. "CellFast: Interactive Unstructured Volume Rendering." In *Proceedings of IEEE Visualization, Late Breaking Hot Topics*, pp. 21–24. Los Alamitos, CA: IEEE Press, 1999.

[305] Craig M. Wittenbrink. "R-Buffer: A Pointerless A-Buffer Hardware Architecture." In *Proceedings ACM SIGGRAPH/Eurographics Workshop on Graphics Hardware 2001*, pp. 73–80, 2001.

[306] Xiaoru Yuan and Baoquan Chen. "Illustrating Surfaces in Volume." In *Procceedings of EG/IEEE TCVG Symposium on Visualization (VisSym)*, pp. 9–16, 2004.

[307] Xiaoru Yuan, Minh X. Nguyen, Baoquan Chen, and David H. Porter. "High Dynamic Range Volume Visualization." In *Proceedings of IEEE Visualization*, pp. 327–334, 2005.

Index

T - #0316 - 071024 - C516 - 229/152/23 - PB - 9780367659424 - Gloss Lamination